The Message of Acts in Codex Bezae

A Comparison with the Alexandrian Tradition

VOLUME 3
Acts 13.1–18.23:
The Ends of the Earth
First and Second Phases of the Mission to the Gentiles

Josep Rius-Camps and
Jenny Read-Heimerdinger

t & t clark

Published by T&T Clark
A Continuum imprint
The Tower Building, 11 York Road, London SE1 7NX
80 Maiden Lane, Suite 704, New York, NY 10038

www.tandtclark.com

ISBN 0567032485 (hardback)
ISBN-13 9780567032485

British Library Cataloguing-in-Publication Data
A catalogue record for this book is available from the British Library

Printed and bound in Great Britain by Biddles Ltd, King's Lynn, Norfolk

CONTENTS

This is the third volume out of four in a commentary that compares the message of Acts as it has been transmitted by Codex Bezae with that of the Alexandrian manuscripts, principally Codex Vaticanus. It covers the chapters relating to the first two phases of Paul's mission – the reasons for taking 18.23 as the closing verse are explained in the *General Introduction*. In the same pages, we explain various aspects of our approach, including key issues that profoundly affect the interpretation of Luke's work.

As in the previous volumes, we treat the MSS as documents standing in their own right, and examine every variant reading between them. By presenting the readings in their textual context, our aim is to illustrate our conclusion that the variation has arisen less through uninformed scribal activity than through a sustained and deliberate attempt to modify the message of the book; the purpose of the alteration, from the Bezan form to the Alexandrian, would be to render the account of the Church's beginnings more comprehensible and more acceptable to later generations of Christians.

To facilitate the reading of Codex Bezae, we are preparing a separate edition of Acts that sets out in parallel columns the Greek texts of Codex Vaticanus and Codex Bezae, alongside the Latin text of Codex Bezae and an English translation. The intention is to publish this at the same time as the fourth and final volume of the series. Meanwhile, F.H. Scrivener's edition of Codex Bezae may be consulted for the Greek and Latin texts.

During the period of preparation for this third volume we have been conscious of generous support from our colleagues, families and communities. We would especially like to thank the *Bibliotheca Biblica* of the State University of St Petersburg, Russia, for the use of their facilities during the autumn of 2006; and the Oxford Centre for Hebrew and Jewish Studies for a Visiting Scholarship to Jenny Read-Heimerdinger during the first half of 2007. A Small Research Grant was also made available by the British Academy to Jenny Read-Heimerdinger, specifically for the investigation of the Jewish context of the Bezan readings concerning Paul's mission, which is acknowledged with gratitude. As always, we are deeply indebted to the cheerful encouragement and technical expertise of Enric Muñarch in preparing our work for publication.

Josep Rius-Camps and Jenny Read-Heimerdinger

ABBREVIATIONS OF JOURNALS

Bib	*Biblica*
CBQ	*Catholic Biblical Quarterly*
ExpT	*Expository Times*
FN	*Filología Neotestamentaria*
JBL	*Journal of Biblical Studies*
JSNT	*Journal for the Study of the New Testament*
JSNTSup	*Journal for the Study of the New Testament: Supplement Series*
JSOTSup	*Journal for the Study of the Old Testament: Supplement Series*
JTS	*Journal of Theological Studies*
NTS	*New Testament Studies*
RB	*Revue Biblique*
RCatT	*Revista Catalana de Teologia*
REG	*Revue d'Études Grecques*
Rev. Sc. ph. th.	*Revue des Sciences philosophiques et théologiques*
SBL	*Society of Biblical Literature*
SE	*Studia Evangelica*
SNTS Bulletin	*Studiorum Novi Testamenti Societas Bulletin*
ZNW	*Zeitschrift für die neutestamentliche Wissenschaft*

ABBREVIATIONS OF REFERENCE WORKS

ABD	D.N. Freedman (ed.), *Anchor Bible Dictionary* (6 vols; New York: Doubleday, 1992).
Atlas of the Bible	J. Pritchard (ed.), *Atlas of the Bible* (London: HarperCollins, 2nd edn, 1989).
B-A-G	W. Bauer, *A Greek English Lexicon of the New Testament and Other Early Christian Literature* (ed. and trans. W.F. Arndt and F.W. Gingrich; Chicago: Chicago University Press, 1957).
B-D-B	F. Brown, S. Driver and C. Briggs, *Hebrew and English Lexicon* (Peabody, MA: Hendrickson Publishers Inc., repr. 2003).
B-D-R	F. Blass, A. Debrunner and F. Rehkopf, *Grammatik des neutestamentlichen Griechisch* (Göttingen: Vandenhoeck & Ruprecht, 15th edn, 1979).

Dictionary of Judaism

    J. Neusner and W.S. Green (eds), *Dictionary of Judaism in the Biblical Period 450 BCE to 600 CE* (New York: Macmillan Reference Library, 1996).

Enc. Jud.   C. Roth (ed.), *Encyclopaedia Judaica* (16 vols; Jerusalem: Ketev Publishing House, 3rd edn, 1974).

EWNT   H. Balz and G. Schneider (eds), *Exegetisches Wörterbuch zum Neuen Testament* (Stuttgart: Verlag W. Kohlhammer GmbH, 1980–83).

IGNTP   The American and British Committees of the International Greek New Testament Project (eds), *The Gospel According to St. Luke.* Part I, Chapters 1–12; Part II, Chapters 13–24 (Oxford: Clarendon Press, 1984, 1987).

Interpreter's Dictionary

    G.A. Buttrick (ed.), *The Interpreter's Dictionary of the Bible: An Illustrated Encyclopaedia* (4 vols; New York: Abingdon Press, 1962).

Jew. Enc.   I. Singer (ed.), *The Jewish Encyclopaedia* (12 vols; New York: KTAV Publishing House, 1901).

Jewish Study Bible

    A. Berlin and M.Z. Brettler (eds), *The Jewish Study Bible* (Jewish Publication Society; TANAKH Translation; Oxford: Oxford University Press, 2004).

Jewish Symbols

    E.R. Goodenough, *Jewish Symbols in the Greco-Roman Period* (13 vols; New York: Pantheon Books, 1953–65).

L-S-J   H.G. Liddell, R.J. Scott and H.S. Jones, *A Greek-English Lexicon: A New Edition* (Oxford: Clarendon Press, 1940).

N-A^{27} B. Aland, K. Aland *et al.* (eds), *Novum Testamentum Graece* (Stuttgart: Deutsche Bibelgesellschaft, 27th edn, 1993).

Rahlfs   A. Rahlfs (ed.), *Septuaginta* (Stuttgart: Deutsche Bibelstiftung, 1985).

UBS^4 B. Aland, K. Aland *et al.* (eds), *The Greek New Testament* (Stuttgart: Deutsche Bibelgesellschaft/United Bible Societies, 4th edn, 1993).

TEXT-CRITICAL SIGNS AND ABBREVIATIONS

In addition to the conventional signs and abbreviations adopted by N-A^{27}, the following are used:

cj.   conjectured reading
lac.   lacuna
MS, MSS   manuscript, manuscripts
vl, vll   variant reading, variant readings

After a manuscript letter or number, in superscript:

*	original hand
p.m.	first hand
s.m.	second hand
2, c	second hand
B, C, D…	capital letter assigned to successive correctors of D05, or to manuscripts of vg or sy
ms, mss	one or several manuscripts only

Principal manuscripts cited

ℵ01	Codex Sinaiticus
B03	Codex Vaticanus
D05	Codex Bezae: Greek pages
d5	Codex Bezae: Latin pages

GENERAL INTRODUCTION

The approach adopted in this work for comparing the message of Acts in two distinct textual traditions is based on a number of fundamental principles. They were presented in some detail in the *General Introduction* of the first volume, and summarized with additional observations in the *General Introduction* to the second volume.[1] Further comments are added here in this third volume, taking into account new issues that arise in the course of Acts 13.1–18.23, as well as the development of ideas.

I. *Codex Bezae*

It is important to note that in this study of Acts it is the text of Codex Bezae and not the 'Western' text in general that is compared with the Alexandrian text (which is essentially the one represented in the current editions of the Greek New Testament). There are three essential reasons for this choice: 1) the 'Western' text does not exist as a single text but only as a series of readings that differ from the readings of the Alexandrian text (which can, on the contrary, be so identified) and that are scattered throughout many witnesses; 2) Codex Bezae is the only Greek witness to consistently differ from the Alexandrian text; 3) the text of Codex Bezae has its own inner consistency and coherence, both from a linguistic and a theological point of view.

The first step in examining the text of Acts in Codex Bezae was thus to study it synchronically, as a narrative standing in its own right and not as a series of variant readings. Furthermore, it was approached without any presuppositions about the date of its text (which is, of course, distinct from the date of the actual manuscript) or about its relationship to the Alexandrian text or any other text-form of the book. Only at a second stage, once analysis had been made of the Bezan form of the narrative, was comparison made with the Alexandrian text, examining the variants one by one. Having built up a picture of the distinct texts, the next step was to compare the message transmitted in each case, before finally forming conclusions about the relationship of the two texts.[2] The current work draws extensively on our earlier, independent studies

1. *The Message of Acts in Codex Bezae: A Comparison with the Alexandrian Tradition*. I. *Acts 1.1–5.42: Jerusalem* (JSNTSup, 257; London: T&T Clark, 2004), pp. 1–44; II. *Acts 6.1–12.25: From Judaea and Samaria to the Church in Antioch* (LNTS, 302; London: T&T Clark, 2006), pp. 1–10.
2. The justification for taking the text of Acts in Codex Bezae as a narrative in its own right is the evident inner coherence of purpose and high level of consistency that emerges from such an

of the characteristic features of Codex Bezae,[3] making modifications or additional observations as necessary.

II. *Luke's Two-Volume Work*

The unity of Luke's two volumes is an interpretative key for understanding the text of Acts in Codex Bezae, not only because they are addressed to the same person but because the first volume prepares for the second and also because neither is complete without the other. The same overall purpose is evident throughout both volumes, namely to set out for Theophilus the theological meaning of what hads happened, from the time of the events surrounding the birth of Jesus to the arrival of Paul in Rome. The theological context is a Jewish one, in which Luke seeks to place the incidents and characters in such a way that his addressee might understand their significance from a Jewish perspective.

Both books thus share the same genre, which is neither gospel nor historical chronicle or biography. Their aim is not to proclaim a kerygma, but to demonstrate theological truth, to provide reliable information following careful investigation and in response to questions raised by the addressee. The demonstration is made in the context of contemporary Jewish preoccupations and expectations, while being grounded in the historical context of Israel and the Jewish Scriptures. It is carried out by means of taking specific characters in order either to acknowledge their worth or to indicate their weaknesses; evaluation is thereby an integral device the author employs to communicate his message. Such a genre might be termed 'epideixis' as long as the label is not used to mean an empty show of rhetoric but rather in the sense Irenaeus and Eusebius use it.[4]

The conceptual unity between the two volumes is derived from the relationship between Jesus as the master and the disciples as his followers. The first book presents Jesus as the model, with whom the disciples are compared in the second book as they strive to put into practice his teachings while he was with them on the earth, and to learn from his subsequent inter-

---

analysis. The usual presuppositions about the date of the Bezan text and its secondary nature generally prevent this picture from being seen (cf. C. Tuckett, 'How Early is the "Western" Text of Acts?', in T. Nicklas, and M. Tilly (eds), *Apostelgeschichte als Kirchengeschichte. Text, Traditionen und antike Auslegungen* [BZNW, 122; Berlin-New York: Walter de Gruyter, 2003], pp. 69–86).

3.   For the theological coherence and consistency of the Bezan text of Acts, this work is based on J. Rius-Camps, *Comentari als Fets dels Apòstols* (4 vols; Barcelona: Facultat de Teologia de Catalunya-Herder, 1991–2000). On the linguistic coherence and consistency, see J. Read-Heimerdinger, *The Bezan Text of Acts. A Contribution of Discourse Analysis to Textual Criticism* (JSNTSup, 236; Sheffield: Sheffield Academic Press, 2002). Further works cited in the *Bibliography* deal with specific features or passages.

4.   For a thorough and insightful examination of epideixis, see L.W. Rosenfield, 'A Practical Celebration of Epidexis' (www.natcom.org/convention/2002/keynote%20materials/rosenfield.htm; accessed 10/4/2007). The study highlights a number of features that are characteristic of the Bezan text of Luke's writings, though they are not described as such.

ventions and communication after his ascension. The many parallels that are adduced between the disciples and Jesus are not always positive – their point is often to show how, on the one hand, the various characters fall short of the model but, on the other, how they will progress.

The interdependence of Luke and Acts in Codex Bezae makes it most probable that the text of Acts dates from a time before the two volumes were separated, that is the early part of the second century.

III. *Luke as Narrator*

Because of the difference in purpose and ideology of the Bezan narrator compared with that of the narrator of the , it is unlikely that they were the same person. The narrator of the Bezan text was thoroughly immersed in Jewish ways of thinking, as well as being quite at home in a Hellenistic setting. He interpreted the events concerning Jesus and the early Church as re-enactments of scriptural paradigms, using intricate play on Hebrew or Aramaic terms and other sophisticated techniques of Jewish exegesis. Now, because Gentiles who became believers in Jesus were integrated into Judaism, it is difficult to distinguish between Jewish and Gentile believers in the first century, in fact as long as the Church was part of Judaism or, indeed, was a form of Judaism. However, various considerations point to a Jewish, and not a Gentile, author of the Bezan text: 1) he speaks of 'our synagogue', Acts 13.16 D05; 2) in comparison with the Alexandrian text, there is considerably more by way of Jewish allusions and evidence of Jewish ways of thinking in Codex Bezae, even though the Alexandrian text is also an early text; 3) the author is able to reproduce with a high degree of authenticity and accuracy complex Jewish exegetical methods, notably in Paul's speeches; 4) despite an increased concern with Gentiles compared with the Alexandrian text, no sustained interest is displayed in Gentile converts except for the God-fearers – concerning the only two Gentiles mentioned by name in Codex Bezae (the proconsul Sergius Paulus, 13.7-12; and Dionysius the Areopagite, 17.34), nothing is said about their belief in Jesus or their baptism.

IV. *Theophilus his Addressee*

The factors described above, which point to the Bezan narrator's Jewish perspective, are an indication that the story of Luke-Acts is not being told to a Gentile audience but a Jewish one; in writing about issues from a Jewish point of view, the narrator seems to have assumed that his addressee was capable of understanding the message he communicated since much of his expression of it is implicit. While Theophilus was a common enough name in the hellenistic period, the only Jewish person with the name in the first century CE according to extant records[5] was Theophilus the third son of the High Priest Annas, who himself served as High Priest from 37–41 CE. Appointed

---

5. The evidence for Jewish names is collected in T. Ilan, *A Lexicon of Jewish Names. I. Palestine 330 BCE –200 CE* (Tübingen: Mohr-Siebeck, 2003).

by Vitellius as Governor of Syria, he was removed from office by Agrippa I as soon as he became king of Judaea. It may be thought that Agrippa's strong opposition to the Jesus-believers and his desire to please the Jews on this count (cf. Acts 12.1-3, esp. D05) had something to do with his replacing Theophilus with a member of another family,[6] as if Theophilus was not in favour of Agrippa's attacks on the church in Judaea because he had a certain sympathy with them.

It may be objected that the addressee of the Alexandrian text cannot plausibly be regarded as a Jew, especifically one of high standing. That very difficulty is further evidence that the two texts correspond to different authors writing to different audiences in quite distinct circumstances. As far as the Bezan text is concerned, it has been adopted as a working hypothesis in this work that the addressee was Theophilus the High Priest, and that Luke wrote to him in order to answer his many questions about what he had seen and heard (cf. Lk. 1.1-4) but had not understood from the point of view of Jewish teachings and expectations as discussed and debated at the highest level. Theophilus would have sought out someone who could answer his questions, at a time when he had observed the many apparent contradictions with traditional teachings as well as the opposing views among the Jesus-believers, maybe after the fall of Jerusalem. His motivation would have been far from mere curiosity for he had witnessed, on the one hand, some atrocious acts carried out by his own family (starting with his father and his brother-in-law Caiaphas and culminating with his younger brother, also Annas, who was responsible for killing James, the leader of the Jerusalem church, in the Temple in 62 CE); and on the other, the actions of the Jewish followers of Jesus who proclaimed radical (and sometimes contradictory) teachings and acted in profoundly disturbing (and sometimes conflicting) ways.[7]

Luke's explanations about the early Church take on a special importance if the addressee was Theophilus the High Priest, especially with regard to the authority of either his own interpretations or those he places in the mouth of his characters. This is notably true of the authority assumed by James when he pronounced his judgement concerning the Gentiles, appealing to the interpretation of the Law given by a former High Priest, Simeon II (Acts 15.14-18 D05).

---

6.   On the remarkable succession of High Priests during Agrippa's short reign, see E.M. Smallwood, *The Jews under Roman Rule: From Pompey to Diocletian. Recovering the True History of Early Christianity* (Leiden: E.J. Brill, 1976), pp. 173–74.

7.   Similarities between the work of Josephus and the book of Acts suggest to R.H. Eisenman (*James, the Brother of Jesus. Recovering the True History of Early Christianity* [London: Faber and Faber, 1997]) that Luke re-worked Josephus' writings. It may be pointed out that if Luke knew the work of Josephus (or even the person), then Theophilus the High Priest would most probably have done so, too. In so far as Eisenman's claim may be substantiated (the dating is problematic), it may be surmised that Luke could in part have been responding to queries Theophilus had about Josephus by explaining, from another point of view, his references to characters who belonged to the Church.

V. *Character Development*

In the earlier chapters of Acts, it was seen that the narrator was interested in the spiritual development of his characters, especially Peter. He does not present the apostles as perfect disciples, invested with the authority of the founding fathers of the Church who unerringly acted out God's plan but, on the contrary, as fallible human beings who struggled to comprehend, and then to accept, the radical nature of the teaching of Jesus. The problem they were faced with was that the familiar Jewish interpretations of Scripture and the eschatological hopes concerning the Messianic age that they had been taught did not correspond to what they witnessed after the death and resurrection of Jesus. Little by little, Peter is seen progressing in his understanding until he achieves freedom from his Jewish understanding by means of the miraculous release from prison in chapter 12.

From chapter 13, it is the turn of Paul to come under scrutiny, and he will be seen to have even more difficulty than Peter in revising and re-forming his understanding of the Messiah. Throughout his missionary journey, he will be portrayed as only partially comprehending the message of Jesus and as frequently following his own plan instead of that shown to him by God. The struggle of Paul to free himself from his traditional understanding and expectations will provide the framework of the narrative.

The main aspect of Paul's theology that Luke portrays as defective in odex Bezae is his belief that with the coming of Jesus as the Messiah, Israel continues to retain her status as the Chosen People, into which the Gentiles are to be grafted by their belief in Jesus as the Messiah. Paul is, nonetheless, well aware that the continuity of Israel's privilege is dependent on the acceptance of him by the Jews and that the consequence of their rejection of the Messiah is that Israel will be overrun by Gentiles. It is for that reason that he is so urgent and so insistent in going to the synagogue in place after place, trying to persuade his own people to accept his arguments and demonstrations from the Scriptures, for he sees his role as being to persuade the Jews to believe that the Lord (YHWH) is Jesus, and that Jesus is the Messiah (Christ). With respect to the Gentiles, he takes upon himself the responsibility to fulfil the scriptural prophecies that portray their gifts being brought to Jerusalem, as an attestation of their freedom to enter Israel.

Luke's interest, according to Codex Bezae, in the spiritual development of his characters accounts for the way they are each apparently abandoned midway without their stories being brought to a full conclusion. He follows the path of a character until, as it were, it is safe to leave them because they have progressed to the point of being in line with Jesus' teaching. As far as Paul is concerned, Luke gradually reveals, chiefly in the fourth and final part of Acts, that Jesus intended Paul to go directly to the Gentiles, a mission that he will only fully accept when he reaches Rome, when the book is brought to an end.

VI. *Speeches*

Far from expressing his own opinions through the speeches of his characters, Luke composes them in accordance with their individual ways of speaking and also with the development of their understanding of the teaching of Jesus. As a result, what they say on different occasions may vary; and it may also vary from what another character says. These features are commonly recognized with regard to the speeches of the non-Christian characters but they also characterize the speeches of the apostles and other leading disciples, who not only sometimes disagree among themselves but also modify their own message as they progress in their grasp of Jesus' teaching.

This understanding of Luke's role in the creation of the speeches is a critical exegetical key to interpreting them as he intended. It accounts for the various difficulties in attempting to reconstruct a Lukan theology from the speeches and, indeed, renders such attempts futile. Luke's theology is found by identifying those characters of whom he expresses his approval, and with whose words he indicates his agreement. The principal means he uses to signal his endorsement of a speech is by prefacing it with the indication that the speaker spoke through the Holy Spirit (e.g. Peter, Acts 15.7-11 D05).

Such an interpretation of Luke's role as narrator does not mean that he reproduces the speeches exactly as they were spoken, but it does mean that he knew how to alter speeches according to the speaker and their objectives, and that in the case of Paul in particular, he was perfectly at home with his Jewish methods of exegesis.[8]

VII. *Dual terms*

The narrator of Codex Bezae employs a system of parallel terms, which serve to support and interpret each other; it is a deliberate coding device that creates a dense and intricate narrative texture. It is important to recognize that the binary pattern of Codex Bezae is not one that is derived from the narrative by the hearer but is, on the contrary, given to the discourse by the speaker.[9] Examples that appear with some frequency in the chapters covered in the present volume are: πᾶς/ἅπας; οἶκος/οἰκία; θεός/κύριος; Ἰερουσαλήμ/ Ἰεροσόλυμα. The last two terms are of especial importance for Luke as a means to convey accurately and precisely his theological message. The phrases ὁ λόγος τοῦ θεοῦ and ὁ λόγος τοῦ κυρίου are examined in detail in *Excursus* 1. The distinction between Ἰερουσαλήμ (Ierousalem) representing the spiritual centre for the worship of the God of Israel[10] and Ἰεροσόλυμα (Hierosoluma) as the

---

8. As Doeve observed (*Jewish Hermeneutics*, p. 175), 'If the author of Acts composed the discourse in Chap. XIII himself, then he must have had an excellent command of hermeneutics as practised in rabbinic Judaism. If we assume that he also composed the discourse in Acts II, this implies that he was capable of imitating different styles of exegesis'.

9. As well as being a typically Semitic device of word-play, the use of parallel expressions with distinct meanings is a device also found in secular Hellenistic writings; see D. Sylva, 'Ierousalem and Hierosoluma in Luke-Acts', *ZNW* 74 (1983), pp. 207–19.

10. See M. Goodman, *Rome and Jerusalem: The Clash of Ancient Civilisations* (London: Allen Lane, 2007), esp. pp. 18, 175–76, on the pre-eminence of Jerusalem for a Jew.

neutral, geographical location, has been observed ever since the opening chapter of Acts; it continues throughout Acts 13–18 to be a crucial tool Luke uses to evaluate the spiritual progress of his characters. The two spellings in English will be maintained to reflect Luke's meaning.

VIII. *We-group*

The identity and role of the 'we'-group are much-debated topics in studies of Acts. In Codex Bezae, there are three references that are not present in other manuscripts (11.28 D05; 13.14 D05; 21.29 D05), and at two other places, their importance is enhanced (16.10 D05; 21.14 D05).

The reference to 'our synagogue' at 13.14 D05 is a clue in Codex Bezae as to the real-life identity of 'we', as it identifies the narrator as a Jew from Antioch of Pisidia. The first introduction of the 'we'-group into the narrative at 11.28 D05 establishes them as disciples of Jesus who are in tune with the Holy Spirit, as shown by their joy in association with the prophets from Hierosoluma. The enhanced reference at 16.10 D05 illustrates their significance as they guide Paul and help him follow the divine plan. They act as a standard against whom Paul is measured, on several occasions showing him to be out of step with the Spirit. Their pastoral function will be later confirmed by the reading of 21.12-14 D05.

IX. *Structure*

The narrative of Acts 13.1–18.23 forms a cohesive unit, just like the two parts of Acts examined in the earlier volumes. Its own internal structure binds the narrative together as well as distinguishing between separate units within it.

Three major *sections* are identified, numbered as I, II and III (see §XII below). They correspond to the broad themes of the narrative as it moves through successive events. Each section is composed of a number of *sequences* (labelled with capital letters A, B, etc.), each of which in turn can be broken down into smaller units or *episodes* (one large sequence in Section III first sub-divides into *sub-sequences*). The episodes are labelled with italic capitals (*A, B*, etc.), attached to their relevant sequence letter. Finally, these episodes are made up of units at the smallest level, referred to as *elements* which, viewed from a grammatical point of view, correspond to single and entire sentences and are identified with lower case letters (e.g. a, b, c).

From the level of the book overall down to the level of individual elements, the book of Acts is constructed to form a hierarchy of finely balanced patterns. At each level, a carefully planned framework organizes the narrative in arrangements that are frequently concentric (e.g. A B C B' A') or symmetrical (e.g. A B B' A'), with the centre of the structure being the point that the narrator wants to highlight as the focus of that part of the story.[11]

---

11. Two works of particular interest for an analysis of the structure are S. Bar-Efrat, *Narrative Art in the Bible* (Sheffield: Sheffield Academic Press, 1989; repr. T&T Clark, 2004); J.W. Welch, *Chiasmus in Antiquity* (Hildesheim: Gerstenberg, 1981).

The boundaries between divisions are identified by a number of markers. Changes in place, time or participant indicate a new division, so that within Sections I and III, the route taken by Paul and Barnabas, or Paul and Silas, as the protagonists of the mission provides a structural framework for the section, each location giving rise to an independent sequence. It will be noticed several times that the opening or concluding episodes of sequences overlap with the beginning or end of the adjacent sequence, because they serve as transitions to move the narrative on to the next stage of the action.

Formal linguistic linking devices are important for determining boundaries and also the connections between narrative units. Including conjunctions and also linking without any kind of connecting word (asyndeton), they are linguistic features that have been examined in some detail by linguists working within the field of Discourse Analysis.[12] They are critical for determining the structure of a unit, serving as signs of punctuation in place of capital letters, commas, semi-colons, full-stops, paragraph breaks and so on. Most importantly, they are often affected by variant readings in the manuscripts of Acts. Their use may be summarized as follows:

1. δέ is the most common conjunction used by Luke to open a new unit and is found at all levels of the structural hierarchy. It is also used within units, and not infrequently introduces the conclusion to a unit;[13]

2. μὲν οὖν builds on the previous unit by presenting an event or action that resulted from it, or was in accordance with it (the function of οὖν, see below). μεν anticipates a second clause introduced with δέ, which contains a second event or action that is linked to the previous unit in a similar way to the first. Sometimes the second clause is omitted or is implied. Because of this special anticipatory function of μὲν οὖν, and because the two clauses that belong together are so closely associated, it never concludes a unit. It is found at the opening of a new unit at various levels in the hierarchical structure;

3. asyndeton in the narrative text of Acts is not common. The absence of a connecting word has the special function of marking a clear break, or of anticipating a dramatic action or event. At 17.33, asyndeton occurs at the juncture of speech and narrative to signal an abrupt development. In addition, B03 has no connective at 18.1 (at the start of a new sequence); D05 has no connective at 17.2b (to expand on a previous statement); or at 14.19; 18.7 (to prepare for a critical development in the story);

4. οὖν is rare within the narrative of Acts (though it is more common in the speeches). When it does occur, it is always at the juncture of speech and narrative;

5. καί in Luke never introduces a new unit because it links together elements that are on the same level. It arises frequently within a structural unit. Some sentences linked by καί are so closely linked that they form part of the same element, because the two verbs refer to different aspects of the same action and in this case καί is not considered to introduce a new element;

6. γάρ introduces a narrator's comment that looks back to the previous element. Occasionally, such comments are so closely related to the previous main verb that they can be considered to belong to the same element;

12. See in particular Levinsohn, *Textual Connections*, pp. 83–161.
13. It should be noted, however, that occasionally δέ can signal a parenthetical comment constituting a narrative aside that does not belong to the story line but looks forward to prepare for the narrative that follows (cf. γάρ which looks back at the preceding narrative).

7. τότε (when not an adverb) introduces an action or event that results from the previous one, or draws a scene to a close. It operates at a local level, that is, it conjoins elements within the same structural unit;

8. *a relative pronoun* sometimes presents a verb that is a separate action, that is, a new sentence, though never at the start of a new unit;

9. *a demonstrative pronoun* is not often used without another connecting word, but it is used occasionally on its own to introduce a separate clause that expands on a previous reference to a character (14.9; 16.3, 17).

It may be observed from the above list that only δέ and μὲν οὖν are found at the beginning of a unit.

Certain types of main clauses are not considered to constitute an independent element because they refer to aspects of the same action or situation as the previous one. This point has already been noted with καί and γάρ. Likewise, when the particle τε introduces a new clause (τε *solitarium*) it is regarded as intrinsically linked to the previous clause (usually a καί clause) and therefore is never considered to mark off an element. Since τε frequently has variant readings, most commonly δέ though also καί,[14] it gives rise to some variation in structure between the Bezan and the Alexandrian texts.

The structural analysis suggested in these volumes goes further than other studies in systematically proposing a structural pattern for each pericope, but to some extent remains experimental and provisional, so that the exact pattern in places, especially on the level of the elements, is open to discussion.

X. *English Translation*
A deliberate effort has been made to reflect the differences between the Greek of Codex Bezae and that of Codex Vaticanus, taken as a representative of the Alexandrian text. The concern with conveying the force of the original language as closely as possible has taken precedence over the search for an idiomatic or natural English translation where the Greek can be better reflected in a more literal rendering.

XI. *Critical Apparatus*
The comparison of Codex Bezae with the Alexandrian text follows the readings of its two chief representatives, Codex Sinaiticus (‎01) and Codex Vaticanus (B03). The latter is selected for the practical purposes of the translation and the presentation of the variant readings in the *Critical Apparatus*.

In the *Critical Apparatus* sections, all the variant readings between B03 and D05 are presented, in that order and together with their respective support. Where ‎01 differs from B03, those readings are also listed. Discussion of technical points concerning the Greek text is kept as far as possible to the *Critical Apparatus*, so that the *Commentary* can be read on the whole without a knowledge of Greek.

---

14. The variant readings of ‎01, B03 and D05 involving τε have been quantified in Read-Heimerdinger, *The Bezan Text*, pp. 205–206; 210–11.

Manuscripts are generally referred to by the letter or number they are assigned in N-A[27]. All uncial MSS are cited with their number as well as their letter if they have one (e.g. ℵ01, B03, D05), except in the list of support for the variant readings given in the *Critical Apparatus* to avoid making the apparatus too cumbersome. The Latin page of Codex Bezae, in common with other Old Latin manuscripts, is referred to with a small letter and a Roman number, thus d5. The occasional manuscript that is not cited by N-A[27] but is listed among the witnesses of UBS[4] is cited with the designation given it in that edition (e.g. sin = a Latin MS of the tenth century [UBS[4], p. 25*], listed as z by Boismard and Lamouille, pp. 40–41).

There is a noticeable increase in the quantity of variation between Codex Bezae and the Alexandrian text in Acts 16 and 18. Thereafter, the amount of material present in Codex Bezae and absent in the Alexandrian manuscripts decreases significantly, while the amount of different material increases in inverse proportion. These features are discussed at the appropriate places of the *Critical Apparatus*.

XII. *General Overview of the Third Part of Acts*

There are three Sections in this third part of Acts, with the first and the last relating to two distinct phases of the mission, and the meeting to discuss the entry of the Gentiles into the Church in the centre:

I   13.1–14.27   The first phase of the mission to the Gentiles (Paul and Barnabas)
II   14.28–15-41   The judicial review in Ierousalem
III   16.1–18.23   The second phase of the mission to the Gentiles (Macedonia and Greece)

The end point of the third part of Acts has been identified as 18.23 because it corresponds to the conclusion of the second phase of Paul's missionary journeys, according to Codex Bezae. In that text, a new narrative section begins at 18.24, preparing for the subsequent sections through to the end of the book whose overall theme is Paul's mission to Rome.[15] Thus, there is a major section division in Codex Bezae, equivalent to that at 6.1 and 13.1, between the end of the second phase of Paul's missionary activity in the nations beyond Israel (13.1–18.23) and the start of his journey to Rome via Ephesus and Jerusalem (18.24–28.31).

Although it is customary to speak of Paul's three missionary journeys, there are not, in fact, separate and distinct voyages but rather successive phases of the one journey.[16] The final goal is Rome, which will only be reached after a fourth 'phase' of the journey at which point Luke brings his narrative to an end. Meanwhile, the starting point of the first phase at 13.1 is Antioch in Syria

---

15. The unity of this final part of Acts will be discussed in the forthcoming volume, *The Message of Acts*, IV.

16. As Marshall points out, following the first so-called 'journey', 'the later periods were much more devoted to extended activity in significant key cities in the ancient world' (*Acts*, p. 214). The itinerary Paul followed was not according to a plan that he worked out, but rather the move from place to place was prompted by the response of his audience or the direct intervention of God.

and also the end point at 14.27. The second phase begins likewise in Antioch (16.1) and terminates there (18.22), with a concluding summary statement preparing for the third phase (18.23).

The mission should have been the mission of Barnabas and Paul in that order (13.2). That is, indeed, how it starts off at 13.3, but by 13.13 Paul has taken over the leadership. Barnabas continues with him throughout the first phase, working with him in unity. However, after the meeting in Ierousalem, Barnabas separates from Paul (15.39), a split that Codex Bezae portrays as arising because of Paul's weakness, not that of Barnabas. The second phase of the mission is therefore led by Paul alone, accompanied by Silas (15.40) and also Timothy (16.3).

The meeting in Ierousalem in Acts 15, where a decision is taken concerning the Gentiles, is more of a trial than a council in Codex Bezae, held for the purpose of judging Paul and Barnabas concerning their acceptance of Gentiles into the Church without circumcision. According to the Bezan narrator, the view of Peter, insisting on the uselessness of the Law for salvation and the sole value of the grace of the Lord Jesus Christ for Jew and Gentile alike, is inspired by the Holy Spirit; the practical experience described by Barnabas and Paul endorses his view; but James, as leader of the Jerusalem church and mentioned by name only for the second time in Acts (cf. 12.17), pronounces a decisive judgement that upholds instead the value of the Law, despite making significant concessions for the Gentiles. James' judgement is the view transmitted by the letter to the Gentile brethren of Antioch, Syria and Cilicia (15.23-29). The conflict between the different opinions is of major interest to the Bezan narrator and provides the theological impetus for continuing the story.

I. THE FIRST PHASE OF THE MISSION TO THE GENTILES
(PAUL AND BARNABAS)
13.1–14.27

General Overview

The third part of Acts opens with an account of Paul's initial journeys as, together with Barnabas, he takes the gospel beyond the boundaries of the countries hitherto evangelized into the countries of the Gentiles. According to the original intention stated by the Holy Spirit at the outset of the mission, the pair was to be Barnabas and Saul in that order and as a unit (with one article, τὸν Βαρναβᾶν καὶ Σαῦλον, 13.2; cf. 12.25), but at 13.9 it is recorded that Saul had changed his name to Paul and he then emerges as the leader, 'Paul and his circle' (οἱ περὶ Παῦλον), in 13.13. When he is next mentioned together with Barnabas at 13.43, the pair had become 'Paul and Barnabas' (with one article in D05, τῷ Παύλῳ καὶ Βαρναβᾷ [with separate articles in B03, τῷ Π. καὶ τῷ B.]). Thereafter, Paul dominates the partnership as the first named, except for three occasions (14.14; 15.12, 25) where the order Barnabas and Paul is all the more telling for its unusual occurrence.

The focus of the narrative in Section I is on the way Paul undertakes the evangelization of the Gentiles as he continues, despite the order of Jesus that Paul will reveal at his trial in Jerusalem (cf. 22.6-21), to believe that his task is to take the gospel first to the Jews. Notwithstanding the formal declaration he will make in Antioch of Pisidia towards the end of chapter 13, to the effect that he is turning from the Jews to the Gentiles (which constitutes an overall change in policy rather than a localized decision according to Codex Bezae), he continues in the next towns he visits to go first to the synagogues. The way Luke presents Paul's inconsistent behaviour, and his persistence in trying to convert his fellow Jews to believe in Jesus, is part of his narrative plan to demonstrate the struggle Paul had in coming to terms with accepting Jesus' command to go to the Gentiles. The struggle will continue in the subsequent sections, and will culminate in Paul's journey to Jerusalem in chapters 19–21, which he undertakes despite warnings against it from the Holy Spirit.[1]

---

1. On Paul's growing realization that the attempt to persuade his own people to accept the gospel was not part of his mission, see J. Rius-Camps, 'The Gradual Awakening of Paul's Awareness of his Mission to the Gentiles', in T. Nicklas and M. Tilly (eds), *Apostelgeschichte als Kirchengeschichte. Text, Traditionen und antike Auslegungen* (BZNW, 122; Berlin: Walter de Gruyter, 2003), pp. 281-96.

Structure and Themes

The new overall theme introduced in Section I of this part of Acts is the expansion of the gospel outside Israel and beyond the immediately surrounding areas previously mentioned (Syria, Cilicia, Phoenicia and Cyprus, cf. 9.2, 30, 31; 11.19), in a mission that will be directed towards Gentiles, and also by Paul to Jews. The route taken by Barnabas and Paul as the protagonists of the mission provides a structural framework for the section, each location giving rise to an independent sequence [A B C // D \\ C′ B′ A′] (see *General Introduction* §IX, for an explanation of the structural analysis adopted in this work). The section begins and ends in Antioch [A // \\ A′]; the central sequence [D] is located in Antioch in Pisidia, where there are two sub-sequences corresponding to two distinct locations [DA ‖ DA′] and within each of them two separate episodes [DA-*A* | DA-*B* ‖ DA′-*A* | DA′-*B*]. Both before and after the central sequence, two places are mentioned: first, Cyprus where there are two episodes [B-*A* | B-*B*] and Pamphylia [C], and then Iconium [C′-*A* ‖ C′-*A*′] and Lystra [B′-*A* ‖ B′-*A*′], again with two episodes in each:

[A] 13.1-3	The commissioning by the Holy Spirit	
[B] 13.4-12	Cyprus	
[B-*A*]	13.4-5	Salamina
[B-*B*]	13.6-12	Paphos
[C] 13.13	Pamphylia: Perga	
[D] 13.14-52	Pisidia: Antioch	
[DA]	13.14-43	The Jews in Antioch
[DA-*A*]	13.14-41	In the synagogue
[DA-*B*]	13.42-43	Synagogue response
[DA′]	13.44-52	The Gentiles in Antioch
[DA′-*A*]	13.44-49	In the city
[DA′-*B*]	13.50-52	Jewish response
[C′] 14.1-7b	Phrygia: Iconium	
[C′-*A*]	14.1-2	In the synagogue
[C′-*A*′]	14.3-7b	In the city
[B′] 14.7c-20	Lycaonia: Lystra	
[B′-*A*]	14.7c-18	The healing of the lame man
[B′-*A*′]	14.19-20	Jewish attack on Paul
[A′] 14.21-27	Return to Antioch in Syria	

In each of these places until they reach Lycaonia, it is noted that Paul and Barnabas preach in the synagogues where the reception by the Jews is sharply divided between enthusiastic welcome and hostile rejection. Increasingly, Gentiles, too, are won over but Jewish opponents to the gospel repeatedly encourage them to turn against the apostles. At the end of some of the sequences, one or more concluding elements provide details of the itinerary between towns, and so serve as transitional statements.

[A] 13.1-3 *The Commissioning by the Holy Spirit*

Overview

The opening sequence of Section I brings back into focus the church in Antioch, which had been introduced in Acts 11.19-30 where it was presented in a positive light as the first community to which Greeks as well as Jews belonged on an equal footing. Barnabas and Saul, who played a leading role in establishing the church (11.22-26), had recently returned from Jerusalem, having been sent there with gifts from the Antioch church (11.29-30; cf. 12.25). They are now brought to the fore in preparation for the subsequent action of the narrative.

Structure and Themes

The brief sequence serves as an introduction to Section I overall, preparing for the taking of the gospel to new countries by describing succinctly the appointment of the two men responsible for the mission. It begins by presenting the prophets and teachers of the church, before describing the command of the Holy Spirit concerning Barnabas and Saul, the first and the last named among them, which was promptly obeyed:

> [a] 13.1   The prophets and teachers of the Antioch church
> [b] 13.2   The Holy Spirit's call to Barnabas and Saul
> [b'] 13.3   The commissioning of Barnabas and Saul by the church

The brevity and simplicity of the description of such an important event confer solemnity on the selection and sending out of Barnabas and Saul. As has been noted in commenting on earlier chapters of Acts,[2] Luke typically underscores the significance of key moments in the life both of Jesus and of the Church by providing a straightforward and unelaborated description, which is all the more powerful for its succinctness.

Parallels can be observed between the first phase of Jesus' mission as the Messiah of Israel and that of Barnabas and Saul in Gentile territory. As these extend to Acts 13.14, they will be discussed in *Excursus* 7.

Translation

Codex Bezae D05

[a]   **13.1** There were in Antioch, according to the custom of the church there, prophets and teachers, among whom were Barnabas and Simeon known as the Black and Lucius a Cyrenian, as well as Manaen, who had been brought up with Herod, that is the Tetrarch, and Saul.

[b]   **2** While they were performing an act of worship to the Lord and fasting, the Holy Spirit said, 'Come now, set apart

Codex Vaticanus B03

13.1 There were in Antioch, according to the custom of the church there, prophets and teachers: Barnabas and Simeon called the Black, Lucius the Cyrenian as well as Manaen, who had been brought up with Herod the Tetrarch, and Saul.

2 While they were performing an act of worship to the Lord and fasting, the Holy Spirit said, 'Come now, set apart for me

---

2.   See, e.g., *The Message of Acts*, I, pp. 298–300 on the presentation of Barnabas in 4.36.

	for me Barnabas and Saul for the work to which I have called them'.	Barnabas and Saul for the work to which I have called them'.
[b']	3 So, when they had finished fasting and after they had all prayed and laid hands on them, they let them go.	3 So, when they had finished fasting and after they had prayed and laid hands on them, they let them go.

Critical Apparatus

13.1 ὅ τε (Βαρναβᾶς) B 𝔓⁷⁴ ℵ *rell* ‖ ἐν οἷς D* (+ ἦν καί Dᶜ, *in quo* d) p vg aeth.

The various members of the Antioch church are presented differently according to the MSS (see the following *vll* in this verse). First, in B03 Barnabas is brought back into the narrative as a character who has recently played an active part (cf. 12.25), as signalled by the presence of the article before his name; with the connective τε, he is viewed as the first of a series of named characters who represent the prophets and teachers just mentioned as a general group of people. D05, in contrast, views him and the other named characters as examples of the prophets and teachers ('among whom'); by omitting the article before his name, D05 further places him on a par with the others, none of whom have the article before their names. Even though Barnabas has already played a prominent role in the narrative so far, this is the first time that he has been presented from a viewpoint within the Antioch church, which justifies the absence of the article. The same can be said of Saul who is named last in the list.

(Συμεὼν ὁ) καλούμενος B 𝔓⁷⁴ ℵ *rell, qui vocatur* d ‖ ἐπικ- D 424. 431. 440. 453. 2147 *pc*.

There are a number of *vll* in Luke–Acts involving the form of the participle that is used to introduce a character's given or acquired name. The simple form of the verb καλέω is used to designate a name given to someone (cf. John: Lk. 1.59, 60; Mary: 10.39; Cephas: Jn 1.42; Saul: Acts 7.58b). The compound ἐπικαλέω implies that the name given is a secondary name, usually one in addition to the other name mentioned rather than a replacement (cf. Beelzebul: Mt. 10.25 [not D05 *et al*]; Thomas Didymus: Lk. 6.15 D05; Joseph the Just: Acts 1.23; Joseph Barnabas: 4.36; Simon Peter: 10.5, 18, 32; 11.13; John Mark: 12.12, 25; 15.37 D05).

ὁ (Κυρηναῖος) B P⁷⁴ *rell* ‖ *om.* D 2147.

The article in B03 presupposes that Lucius was identified by his place of origin, possibly to distinguish him from another Lucius. The absence of the article in D05 is to be expected as the adjective is in apposition to an anarthrous noun; it identifies Lucius as a Cyrenian but not as a distinguishing feature.

τοῦ (τετρά[-αά- ℵ]ρχου) B 𝔓⁷⁴ ℵ Dᴴ *rell* ‖ καί D*, *et* d.

The text of B03 clarifies the identity of Herod as the Tetrarch, whose name was Antipas and who was one of the many sons of Herod the Great. The wording of D05 can be understood in the same way, where καί is epexegetic (Manaen was 'the intimate friend [or foster-brother – see *Commentary*] of Herod, that is the Tetrarch'). An alternative interpretation is also possible, by taking the genitive Ἡρῴδου in the sense of 'the son of Herod (the Great)' and the genitive τετράρχου as dependent on σύντροφος, to give: the son of Herod [the Great] and the foster-brother of the Tetrarch' (cf. Haenchen, pp. 336–37, n. 5: 'Manaen, der "Milchbruder" des Tetrarchen, zum Sohn Herodes' der Großen erhöht').

13.3 (προσευξάμενοι) πάντες D, *omnes* d ‖ *om.* B 𝔓[74] ℵ *rell.*

D05 portrays the whole church of Antioch as praying in response to the order of the Holy Spirit, whereas in B03 the response does not involve anyone outside the five prophets and teachers.

ἀπέλυσαν B 𝔓[74] ℵ A *rell* | ἀπ. αὐτούς E lat sy sa bo; Lcf ‖ *om.* D d.

The main verb is left out of D05. If ἀπέλυσαν αὐτούς was read by D05, as it is by E08 and the versions, it could be that there was confusion with the end of the previous line and that the error was caused by homoioteleuton: ΑΥΤΟΙΣ … ΑΥΤΟΥΣ. The omission of the accusative pronoun after ἀπέλυσαν in B03 is to be noted: in most cases where the pronoun is omitted after the second of two verbs that have the same object, both verbs take the direct object. Here in B03, as at 4.3 B03 and 21.33, the object of the first verb is indirect and is included, but the object of the second verb (omitted) is direct (see the analysis by J. Read-Heimerdinger, 'The Tracking of Participants with the Third Person Pronoun: A Study of the Text of Acts', *RCatT* 31 (2006), pp. 439–55).

Commentary

[a] 13.1 *The Prophets and Teachers of the Antioch Church*
13.1 The chapter opens with an account of the roles played by members of the Antioch church. The preposition κατά could be distributive meaning 'throughout',[3] but it could equally well have the sense of 'according to' and refer to the customary practice of the local church of Antioch (the participle of the verb 'to be', οὔσης, is used in this sense elsewhere in Acts),[4] which distinguished it from the church in Jerusalem (cf. 11.22).[5] There, in contrast, the church was governed by a group of elders (cf. 11.30) under the leadership of the apostles and, ultimately, of James the brother of Jesus.[6] In Codex Bezae, all five people listed can be assumed to be known to the addressee of Acts since they are singled out from 'among' the prophets and teachers. In B03, they represent all the prophets and teachers and their names may be given for completeness of information rather than because they were all known people.

---

3.   This is the interpretation of Zerwick and Grosvenor, *Analysis*, p. 391.
4.   See *The Message of Acts*, II, p. 310.
5.   Delebecque, *Les deux Actes*, describes the use of κατά in this way as 'cet héllenisme caractérisé, qui semble particulier à Luc' (p. 198).
6.   See *The Message of Acts*, II, p. 329 on 11.30; p. 364 on 12.17b.

The list Luke provides recalls earlier lists of names or references to a certain number of disciples in his two-volume work, all of which are of critical importance: the Twelve (Lk. 6.14-16) who represent the twelve tribes of Israel; the three women representatives of the circle who supported the community of Jesus (8.2-3); the Seventy (-Two)[7] disciples who prepared for the arrival of Jesus in Samaritan villages (10.1, 17) in anticipation of the mission to the (seventy) nations; the Eleven apostles who are re-listed after the death of Judas (Acts 1.13) and are themselves part of the 120 disciples who represent Israel (1.15b);[8] finally, the list of the Seven Hellenists by name who, like the Seventy (-Two) before them, are instrumental in the announcement of Jesus outside Israel (8.1b, 5, 14; 11.19) and are set in contrast to the apostles (6.3, 5; cf. 21.8). In each case, the number has a symbolic value, as is typical in Jewish writings, as a means to convey a spiritual reality. Here, the number is 'five', a number that has previously been observed to be specially associated with the Holy Spirit. This is true of Pentecost (50 days after Passover, cf. Acts 1.5 D05; 2.1; 20.16) as it was also true of the 50 prophets in the time of Elijah (3 Kgdms 18.4, 13; 4 Kgdms 2.7). As a multiple of five, Luke has mentioned 5,000 men in the story of the multiplication of the two loaves and five (again!) fishes, and later 5,000 people who were mature believers in Jerusalem when the Spirit was manifested for a second time (Acts 4.31).[9] The association of the number five with the abundance of the Spirit or divine gifts more generally is particularly appropriate in relation to the list of the five prophets and teachers in Antioch, for they have each acquired their function through the gift of the Holy Spirit with whom they have a special relationship.

The gifts of prophecy and of teaching are not to be confused. They are discrete ministries and in the list of 13.1 they are represented by two separate lists of people, the first three being prophets and the last two teachers. The distinction is made in Greek with the particle τε between the two groups, translated here by 'as well as'. In consequence, the first and last named, Barnabas and Saul, exercise distinct charismatic gifts, their place at the front and the end of the list giving them special prominence in view of the task that is about to be assigned to them.

Barnabas is not presented by his real name, Joseph, but with the name that was given to him by the apostles meaning 'son of encouragement' (cf. 1.23 D05; υἰὸς παρακλήσεως, 4.36), which has always been used after the initial explanation of his acquired name (cf. 9.27; 11.22, 30; 12.25). He is a Hellenist, originally from Cyprus which stands as a place of Jewish openness to the Gentiles in contrast to the religious centre of Ierousalem where disciples (including the apostles!) with a Jewish exclusive mentality were much more

---

7.   'Seventy' is read by ℵ A C K L U W Γ Δ Θ Λ Ξ Π Ψ *f*[1.13] 565. 1071 𝔐 f q sy[p. h] bo; Ir[lat] Cl Or; 'Seventy-two' by 𝔓[75] B D 0181 *pc* lat sy[s.c] sa bo[ms]; Ad.

8.   See *The Message of Acts*, I, pp. 100–103; 116–18.

9.   See *The Message of Acts*, I, p. 244 for a discussion of the number five in association with ἄνδρες to refer to mature adults.

resistant to the universal nature of Jesus' message.[10] It is therefore no coincidence that the mission he is chosen to lead together with Saul (only later to become known as Paul) begins in Cyprus. His role so far has truly been one of 'encouragement', or 'exhortation' as the term παράκλησις/παρακαλέω may also be rendered (cf. 4.36; 9.27; 11.25-26),[11] which sits well with the ministry of a prophet. For what was implied by the gift of prophecy in Jewish and early Christian tradition was to speak or act on behalf of God, not just to foretell the future but more broadly to communicate to the people, in God's name, the divine view of reality.[12]

Saul is likewise a Hellenist, being from Tarsus (cf. 9.11; 22.3; see *Excursus* 3). He had been introduced to the church in Antioch by Barnabas who, having been acquainted with him in Jerusalem, later sought him out in his home town (11.25-26).[13] His place at the end of the list, rather than relegating him to an inferior position, in fact sets him in balance with Barnabas at the head of the list and confers on him a prominence. His particular gift is that of a teacher, one for which his earlier training in the interpretation of the Jewish Law prepared him especially well (cf. 22.3). From his speeches as well as from his letters, it is apparent that his teaching specifically related to the interpretation of the Jewish Scriptures in the light of the coming of Jesus Christ and the application of his interpretation to the lives of the people he taught. The ministry of teaching has already been mentioned in relation to Antioch in the Alexandrian text of 11.26, where Barnabas and Saul are said to have taught the church – either this activity is seen as preceding the distinction between their gifts or the Alexandrian text does not recognize the distinction. The mention of teaching at 11.26 is omitted in Codex Bezae.[14]

Two other prophets are named apart from Barnabas. Simeon has the Hebrew form of the name (cf. Lk. 2.25, 34; 3.30; Acts 15.14) as opposed to the Greek form 'Simon' (cf. Acts 9.43; 10.5, 6, 17, 32). He is either known as 'the Black' (D05), or called 'Simeon the Black' (AT). He is, therefore, in all probability a Jew from Africa, and from a Roman city there since his new name is given in Latin (cf. 1.23, Joseph the Just, Ἰοῦστος). The fact that members of the

---

10. Luke makes use of the dual spelling of Jerusalem to distinguish between Ἰερουσαλήμ, the holy city of the Jews, and Ἰεροσόλυμα, the geographical location (see *General Introduction*, §VII).

11. Barnabas' overall function of exhorter or encourager in Acts is examined in J. Read-Heimerdinger, 'Barnabas in Acts: A Study of his Role in the Text of Codex Bezae', *JSNT* 72 (1998), pp. 23–66.

12. B. Chilton, *The Glory of Israel: The Theology and Provenience of the Isaiah Targum* (JSOT Sup. 23; Sheffield: JSOT Press, 1982), pp. 48–56, discusses the nature of prophecy in the targumic tradition of Isaiah, which closely resembles the picture in the narrative of Acts. Thus, '"Holy Spirit" is the normal means of God's address to his people, accomplished through prophets' (p. 50).

13. There are some significant textual differences in these verses, on which see *The Message of Acts*, II, pp. 316–18.

14. The *vll* of 11.26 are discussed in *The Message of Acts*, II, pp. 315–16, 318.

Antioch church were using the Latin name may indicate that there were people who spoke Latin among them. The third prophet also has a Latin name, Lucius, although in the Hellenized form Λούκιος; he comes from Cyrene (cf. 2.10) at the far south-west fringe of the Roman Empire. Cyrenians have already been mentioned several times by Luke: Simon the Cyrenian (Lk. 23.26), the Cyrenians who opposed Stephen (Acts 6.9) and those who, together with people from Cyprus, announced the message of Jesus to the Greeks in Antioch (11.20). Lucius may well have been one of the latter group. Together, the three prophets, all Hellenists, represent a wide geographical span of regions far removed from the centre of the Jewish institution and as such are well placed to speak out against it since they share a natural advantage of being less attached to Ierousalem than if they were Hebrew Jews.

The first of the teachers has a Hebrew name, Manaen (Menachem, cf. 4 Kgdms 15.14 LXX) who is closely associated with the court of Herod, for Luke specifies that he was brought up with Herod the tetrarch as σύντροφος. The 'tetrarch' was one of the sons of Herod the Great who had ten wives and many children.[15] On his death in 4 BCE, Herod the Great's kingdom had been divided among three of his children: the oldest son, Archelaus, was made the ruler of Judaea together with Idumaea and Samaria, but was deposed in 6 CE; Antipas, who was the son of the Samaritan Malthrace and was also known as Herod, was made tetrarch of Galilee and Peraea which he ruled until he was banished to Gaul in 39 CE; finally, their half-brother Philip, whose mother was Jewish, was also made tetrarch, and ruled the territories to the north and east of Galilee until his death in 34 CE. It is to Antipas that Luke refers in his Gospel as 'Herod the tetrarch of Galilee' (Lk. 3.1, 19; 9.7). This is the Herod who was responsible for beheading John the Baptist (9.9) and who was implicated in the death of Jesus (23.7-12). Agrippa I, a grandson of Herod the Great, inherited most of the territory of his three uncles between 37 and 41 CE, and ruled as king until his death in 44 CE, some time shortly before the current incidents (cf. Acts 12.1, 20-23).[16]

The term σύντροφος is used of a child who was reared with another (from σύν + τροφή, 'nourishment') but also with the weaker sense of a companion or close friend, either in childhood or later in life.[17] On the first meaning, Menaen may have actually been a son of Herod the Great by another woman and therefore a half-brother of the tetrarch, both being brought up at court by the same nurse. The wording of Codex Bezae could indeed be interpreted in this way (see *Critical Apparatus*). The wording of the Alexandrian text does not exclude such an interpretation, though most commentators take it to mean no more than that Menaen was brought up with the tetrarch as a close companion.[18]

15. M. Grant, *The Jews in the Roman World* (London: Weidenfeld and Nicolson, 1973), p. 83.

16. Safrai and Stern, *Jewish People,* I, p. 94.

17. B-A-G, σύντροφος.

18. E.g. Barrett, I, pp. 603–604; Bruce, *Text,* p. 253; Witherington, *Acts,* p. 392.

[b] 13.2 *The Holy Spirit's Call to Barnabas and Saul*
13.2 The prophets and teachers are immediately presented in action in the church of Antioch, engaged in two concurrent activities: performing an act of worship and fasting. The term used for the act of worship, λειτουργέω, is used by Luke only here and as the cognate noun, λειτουργία, with reference to the worship of YHWH in the Temple by Zechariah (Lk. 1.23). Although both noun and verb were used of any kind of public service, which was not necessarily one of worship (cf. Phil. 2.30),[19] Luke's use of the noun follows the way it was used in the LXX to refer to the service of the priests and Levites (cf. Exod. 37.19 [not MT]; Num. 8.22; 16.9; 18.4; 2 Chr. 31.2). His general custom of using vocabulary to create deliberate links between the two volumes of his work[20] suggests that his choice of a related verb to describe the activity of the prophets and teachers in Antioch is intentional, expressing the idea that they were celebrating a solemn and formal rite. The link is reinforced by the detail that the worship was addressed to 'the Lord', κύριος, a term referring to YHWH in the LXX but applied increasingly to Jesus in the book of Acts.[21] Here in Antioch then, the prophets and the teachers have taken over the function of the priests and Levites and the worship is addressed to Jesus, but their celebration echoes the official Jewish liturgical rites that were carried out in the Temple on a twice-daily basis to seek the favour of God. That picture is further completed by the indication that their worship was accompanied by fasting. This Jewish practice, though apparently not carried out by Jesus, was not forbidden by him but was associated by him with the time after his death (Lk. 5.33-35) as an expression of grief. Elsewhere in Luke's Gospel, it is used of Anna who devoted her life to prayer and fasting in the Temple (2.37), and of a Pharisee who fasts twice weekly; in Acts, the churches are seen fasting as they pray for the elders they have appointed (Acts 14.23), and otherwise the Jewish fast of Yom Kippur (Day of Atonement) is mentioned at 27.9.

The combination of solemn ritual worship and fasting in Antioch is an indication of a particularly intense time of seeking divine favour or help. This might seem to anticipate the Spirit's call of Barnabas and Saul, as if the leaders were seeking the Lord's will for the Church and its future. Such an interpretation tends to read back into the text of Acts a later Christian practice. It may not need to be altogether excluded from the present context but there was, in fact, a situation facing the Antioch church that was particularly critical and that would demand their urgent attention. For all that chapter 13 opens a new section in the narrative of Acts without any overt link to the preceding narrative, the church in Antioch was intimately involved in the events of chapter 12, since the persecution of the church in Judaea by Herod Agrippa, which led

---

19. B-A-G, λειτουργέω, 3; λειτουργία, 2.

20. See *The Message of Acts*, I, *General Introduction*, pp. 26–32.

21. An analysis of the term in Luke–Acts can be found in Read-Heimerdinger, *The Bezan Text*, pp. 275–93.

to the killing of James and the imprisonment of Peter (12.2-3), was prompted by the sending of their gifts to the Jewish brethren in Jerusalem (11.29-30; cf. 12.25).[22] As a result of his imprisonment, Peter saw clearly and for the first time that Ierousalem was no longer the dwelling place of God nor the spiritual centre for the church. He left Ierousalem and 'went to another place', just like Ezekiel (Ezek. 12.3) who had been instructed by God to do likewise as a gesture symbolic of the exile into which the people of God were going to be led.[23] In such a situation of crisis, it is to be expected that the church leaders in Antioch should be interceding on behalf of the Church in general and of the Ierousalem church in particular.

Their service is interrupted by the intervention of the Holy Spirit[24] with an urgent call that occurs not in accordance with the praying and fasting but rather in contra-expectation to it.[25] The form of the expression found here to refer to the Holy Spirit (τὸ πνεῦμα τὸ ἅγιον – with the article and the adjective in post-position) is the one Luke typically uses when he describes the Holy Spirit as intervening in a situation, as the subject of the verb. The Spirit's action in this instance is to give instructions concerning the broad plan of the Church's mission. Three other forms of the expression of the Holy Spirit, in which the presence of the article/adjective or the place of the adjective vary, are used in Luke–Acts, each form belonging to a distinct context as will be observed with the subsequent mention of the Spirit at 13.4 (see also *Critical Apparatus*).

The words of the Spirit were doubtless conveyed by one of the prophets (not necessarily one of the three named according to Codex Bezae [see *Commentary*, 13.1] since there were other prophets in the church) and addressed to the church of Antioch as a whole, again according to Codex Bezae (see *Commentary*, 13.3). The action advised by the Spirit is not to respond to the seriousness of the situation by continuing with worshipping and fasting but to engage in an activity that would turn their attention outwards to new horizons.

The terms used by the Spirit are succinct but dense in implications. First, the church is to set apart (ἀφορίσατε) the first and last of the list of five, Barnabas the first of the prophets and Saul the last of the teachers. These two, who between them had been responsible for the emergence of the first Christian church, will no longer play a part in the leadership of the community in Antioch.[26] Secondly, as if it were a matter of the tithing of the first fruits, the two are to be set apart for the Holy Spirit (μοι, strongly emphatic),[27] so that

22. The idea that it was the gift from Antioch that sparked the persecution in Judaea is discussed in *The Message of Acts*, II, pp. 332, 335–37.

23. *The Message of Acts*, II, pp. 331–73, esp. 364–65, 381–83.

24. The continuous tense of the present participles λειτουργούντων – νηστευόντων is interrupted by the aorist εἶπεν.

25. The particle δή has a note of urgency in the invitation it expresses (B-D-R, §451.4).

26. See *The Message of Acts*, II, pp. 318–20 on 11.26c.

27. The Spirit could have simply said Ἀφορίσατε ... εἰς τὸ ἔργον, along the lines of Rom. 1.1 (cf. Gal. 1.15). Cf. in contrast Ezek. 45.1, 4 LXX: ἀφοριεῖτε ἀπαρχὴν τῷ κυρίῳ ἅγιον ἀπὸ

once they are no longer part of the team of leaders they are under the guidance of the Holy Spirit. Thirdly, the two men who are to be set apart are to operate under the leadership of Barnabas (the first-named) as a single unit (with the article preceding his name alone as an indication of their unity: τὸν Βαρναβᾶν καὶ Σαῦλον).[28] Finally, the work (τὸ ἔργον) to which the Spirit has called them is not described here; it will not be made explicit until 14.26-27 when it becomes clear that the work in which God has used them is 'the opening to the Gentiles a door of faith'. It should be noted that there is something permanent about the call of the Spirit, with the perfect προσκέκλημαι denoting a fixed state of affairs.[29] This is not a casual or temporary call but a definitive decision that has already been taken.

[b'] 13.3 *The Commissioning of Barnabas and Saul by the Church*
13.3 The response of the church to the instruction of the Holy Spirit is immediate, as expressed by the conjunction τότε. The repeated mention of fasting is, however, ambiguous – the aorist participle (νηστεύσαντες, 'having fasted') could mean either that the interruption by the Spirit was considered to have brought the fasting to an end, or that the fast was first of all finished before the next actions were taken. The very repetition of the fast suggests that it was still viewed as important even after the intervention of the Spirit and so the latter option has been selected for the translation here.

A further ambiguity concerns the people involved in the actions. Codex Bezae specifies 'all' after the second aorist participle προσευξάμενοι, 'having prayed', implying that if only the leaders were engaged in the worship and fasting, all the church now participate in the commissioning of Barnabas and Saul, following a pattern similar to that already described with the election of the Seven Hellenists (6.5). If that is what is meant, it tends to confirm that the fast was continued and brought to an end before further action was taken by the community as a whole. In the Alexandrian text, it appears that only the leaders took part in the commissioning activity.

Three further steps were carried out in order to put into practice the Spirit's instruction – prayer, laying on of hands and letting the two men go. The accumulation of participles has the effect of presenting the scene as a progressive realization of what was entailed rather than a prompt and rapid execution of the Spirit's command. Such a process is not surprising since nothing like this has been recorded in the experience of the Church hitherto. The difficulty for the Antioch church to let go the two key people in the set-

τῆς γῆς ... ἔσται τοῖς ἐγγίζουσι λειτουργεῖν τῷ κυρίῳ, of which the terms are now inverted: λειτουργούντων δὲ αὐτῶν τῷ κυρίῳ ... εἶπεν ...’ Ἀφορίσατε δή μοι...

28. The function of the article before the names of persons is analysed in J. (Read-)Heimerdinger and S.H. Levinsohn, 'The Use of the Definite Article before Names of People in the Greek Text of Acts with Particular Reference to Codex Bezae', *FN* 5 (1992), pp. 15–44.

29. The function of the perfect aspect to denote a state of affairs is explained in R.A. Young, *Intermediate New Testament Greek* (Nashville, TN: Broadman & Holman, 1994), pp. 126–29.

ting up of the Christian community must also be taken into account. The outcome is that they 'release' them (ἀπέλυσαν), a verb that expresses the sense of leaving a place or person to whom there has been previous attachment rather than the more positive idea of being 'sent out', which may have been expected.[30]

[B] 13.4-12 *Cyprus*

Overview

The second sequence of Section I describes the beginning of the mission undertaken by Barnabas and Saul who, at the leading of the Holy Spirit, embark on the first phase of their journey.[31] Early on in the narrative, Saul will become known as Paul and he will effectively become the leader of the mission from there on. The location is Cyprus, the first country reached across the sea from Israel. The island has already been introduced into the story of Acts, first as the place of origin of Barnabas (cf. 4.36).[32] It was mentioned for a second time as a place visited by those Hellenist disciples who were forced to flee because of the persecution following the death of Stephen (11.19) and, indeed, from where disciples went to Antioch to preach the good news to Greeks (11.20). It is, in consequence, a place of positive connotations where the gospel has already been announced and which is characterized by an openness to the teaching of Jesus concerning the Gentiles. This view will be confirmed by the events related in the present sequence.

In the background throughout this sequence is John-Mark who had come with Barnabas and Saul when they left Jerusalem after delivering the famine aid they had brought from Antioch. His will be a silent presence, mentioned only briefly but used by the narrator to make implicit comment on the work carried out by Barnabas and Saul. His role will be developed in the next sequence [C].

A key incident in Cyprus will be the confrontation by Paul of the Jewish false prophet, Bar-Iesoua. This character personifies the way of thinking that Paul is constantly tempted by, namely to view the conversion of the Jews, his own people, as of primary importance, as a preparation for the entry of the Gentiles into Israel. The parallels between this scene and the temptation of Jesus by the devil in Luke's Gospel (see *Excursus* 7), make clear how Bar-

---

30. The verb ἀπολύω is used in the sense of 'release from arrest' at 3.13; 4.21, 23; 5.40; 16.35, 36; 17.9; 26.32; 28.18. Elsewhere, it has a weaker sense of 'dismiss', or simply 'depart' in the middle, but there is always the notion of attachment to the person or group which is left behind: 13.3; 15.30, 33; 19.40; 23.22; 28.25, cf. Lk. 8.38.

31. For the view that there is but one journey divided into several phases rather than three separate journeys, see *General Introduction*, §XII.

32. The first mention was by means of an adjective (Κύπριος), a way of introducing a key feature into the narrative that is typical of Luke (cf. Roman ['Ρωμαίους, 16.37] and Rome ['Ρώμη, 18.2]).

Iesoua represents the Tempter and underline Paul's success in overcoming him, though only temporarily, as will be seen.

Structure and Themes

The visit to Cyprus falls into two episodes, which will be dealt with together since they are intimately connected:

[B-*A*] 13.4-5   Cyprus I: Salamis
    [a]   13.4   Departure for Cyprus
    [b]   13.5a   Proclamation of the gospel in Salamis
    [b'] 13.5b   John as an assistant
[B-*A'*]13.6-12 Cyprus II: Paphos
    [a]   13.6-7a   Bar-Iesoua, the magician and Sergius Paulus, the proconsul
    [b]   13.7b   The proconsul's invitation to Barnabas and Saul
    [c]   13.8   The opposition of the magician
    [c'] 13.9-11a   Paul's rebuke
    [b'] 13.11b   The magician's blindness
    [a'] 13.12   The proconsul's belief in God

The first episode [B-*A*] appears to serve simply as an introduction to move the narrative to Cyprus via the port of Salamis but, in fact, it contains several pieces of vital information and implicit comment on the part of the narrator that are critical for the understanding of the following events of the story. First, it shows Barnabas and Saul going to the synagogue as soon as they arrive in Cyprus and preaching to the Jews, which was not part of their mission. This anomaly is highlighted by the presence of John, who is John-Mark from the forward-looking church in Jerusalem (cf. 12.12, 25) and to be understood as the author of the second Gospel from which Luke draws much of his Gospel material.[33] His disagreement with Barnabas' and Saul's practice of visiting the synagogues will result in his leaving them as they move on from Cyprus back to the mainland (13.13b), though eventually he and Barnabas will return to Cyprus (15.39), with Codex Bezae endorsing their activity and criticizing the attitude of Paul (see *Commentary, ad loc.*).

The second episode [B-*A'*] moves to a setting across the island in Paphos where two important and opposing characters are introduced, the Jewish false prophet Bar-Iesoua as he is known in Codex Bezae (Bar-Jesus in the AT) and the Roman proconsul Sergius Paulus. As the gospel is now proclaimed to a Gentile in accordance with their calling, Saul will be seen to emerge as the spokesperson of the pair (cf. *Commentary*, 13.1). The change of name to Paul which is noted at this point will establish his role as the opponent of Jewish exclusivism on behalf of the Gentiles. The structure of the narrative reflects the main point of the story by placing at the centre not the proclamation of the gospel as such but rather the confrontation between the Jewish magician and

---

33. On the identification of John-Mark as Mark the evangelist, see *The Message of Acts*, II, p. 360 on 12.12.

Paul, in which the hindrance of the Jewish erroneous teachings to the Gentiles' belief in God is dealt with, at least 'for a time' (13.11).

In order to discern and understand the theological significance of the presence of Bar-Iesoua in Paphos, it is essential to bear in the mind the paradigm of Jeremiah 5–6 on which Luke models the story. The parallels are discussed in detail in *Excursus* 4.

Translation

Codex Bezae D05	Codex Vaticanus B03
[Aa] **13.4** So the ones who had been sent out by the Holy Spirit, having gone down to Seleucia from there they sailed away to Cyprus.	**13.4** So they who had been sent out by the Holy Spirit went down to Seleucia, and sailed away from there to Cyprus;
[b] **5a** Once they were in Salamis, they announced the word of the Lord in the synagogues of the Jews;	**5a** and when they were in Salamis, they began to announce the word of God in the synagogues of the Jews;
[b′] **5b** yet they had John assisting them.	**5b** yet they had John as an assistant.
[A′a] **6** When they had gone round the whole of the island as far as Paphos, they found a certain magician, a Jewish false prophet called by the name of Bar-Iesoua **7a** who was with the proconsul, Sergius Paulus, an intelligent man.	**6** When they had gone across the whole of the island as far as Paphos, they found a certain magician, a Jewish false prophet who had the name of Bar-Jesus **7a** and who was with the proconsul, Sergius Paulus, an intelligent man.
[b] **7b** He, having invited Barnabas and Saul, was intent on hearing the word of God.	**7b** He, having called Barnabas and Saul, sought to hear the word of God.
[c] **8** But Etoimas the magician – for that is how his name is translated – opposed them, intent on diverting the proconsul from the faith since he was listening to them with great pleasure.	**8** But Elymas the magician – for that is how his name is translated – opposed them, intent on diverting the proconsul from the faith.
[c′] **9** So Saul, that is Paul, filled with the Holy Spirit **10** and looking intently at him, said, 'O you son of the devil, full of all deceit and fraud, the enemy of all righteousness, will you not stop making crooked the ways of the Lord those that are straight? **11a** Now see, the hand of the Lord is upon you and you will be blind, not able to see the sun, for a time.'	**9** So Saul, that is Paul, filled with the Holy Spirit, **10** looking intently at him, said, 'O you son of the devil, full of all deceit and all fraud, the enemy of all righteousness, will you not stop making crooked the straight ways of the Lord? **11a** Now see, the hand of the Lord is upon you and you will be blind, not able to see the sun, for a time.'
[b′] **11b** And immediately mist and darkness fell on him, and as he wandered about he tried to find people to lead him by the hand.	**11b** And at once mist and darkness fell on him, and as he wandered about he tried to find people to lead him by the hand.
[a′] **12** When the proconsul saw what had happened, he marvelled and believed in God, being astounded at the teaching about the Lord.	**12** Then the proconsul, seeing what had happened, believed, being astounded at the teaching about the Lord.

Critical Apparatus

13.4 Αὐτοὶ (μὲν οὖν) B 𝔓⁷⁴ ℵ A C(*) 36. 81. 453. 945. 1175. 1739 *al, ipsi* d |
Οὗτοι E H L P Ψ 049. 056. 614 ℵ gig; Lcf ‖ Οἱ D p; Ps-Chr.

Αὐτοὶ μὲν οὖν of B03 is deemed by Delebecque to be a construction 'peu
conforme à l'usage grec' (*Les deux Actes*, p. 185); αὐτοί nevertheless occurs
elsewhere in Luke as the resumed subject (Lk. 24.14 [not D05], 34 D05), and
has the effect here of underlining the subject of the three aorist verbs (passive
participle followed by an active participle, then a finite verb), so that, even
though the Holy Spirit is the agent of the passive participle, it is Barnabas and
Saul who take the initiative in determining their own movements. Οἱ μὲν οὖν
of D05 is the more usual construction found elsewhere in Acts: 1.6; 2.41;
5.41; 8.4, 25; 9.31 (fem.); 11.19; 15.3, 30; 16.5 (fem.); 23.31.

(ὑπὸ τοῦ) ἁγίου πνεύματος B 𝔓⁷⁴ ℵ A C Dˢ·ᵐ· 81. 945. 1175. 1739. 1891. 2344
‖ πν. ἁγ. D*, (ab) spiritu sancto d | πν. τοῦ ἁγ. E H L P Ψ 049. 056. 614 𝔐
(aeth; Chr BarSal).

The form of the phrase used for the Holy Spirit changes according to the
context, the variables being the presence of the article and/or the presence and
place of the adjective (Read-Heimerdinger, *The Bezan Text*, pp. 145–72). The
form τὸ ἅγιον πνεῦμα used by B03 is characteristically found in situations
where the Spirit acts in direct relation to Christians in a local church setting,
as is the case here. The reading of D05, τὸ πνεῦμα ἅγιον, is unusual in that the
adjective in post-noun position does not have an article; although the same
pattern is found once more in the Bezan text of 10.45 (τοῦ ἁγίου πνεύματος
ℵ01, τοῦ πνεύματος τοῦ ἁγίου B03), it occurs nowhere else in Luke's writings, neither with the expression for the Holy Spirit nor any other noun-
adjective for that matter (*The Bezan Text*, p. 171). The usual arthrous form with
the adjective in post-position is τὸ πνεῦμα τὸ ἅγιον. In contrast, the anarthrous
form πνεῦμα ἅγιον is common throughout Acts as a fixed expression in repeated
situations such as baptism in the Holy Spirit or God speaking through the
Holy Spirit in a public rather than an intimate situation, where the position of
the adjective after the noun causes the Spirit to be prominent and the focus to
be on the presence of the Spirit rather than on the quality of holiness (*The
Bezan Text*, pp. 160–61). It may be that the idea of God acting through the
Spirit for a public purpose at the outset of the mission to the Gentiles causes
the stereotyped expression to be chosen here in D05, and that it is prefaced
with the article because it is an anaphoric reference within the immediate
context of the Antioch church (cf. 13.2, and see *Commentary* on the form of
the expression there; at 10.45, the reference to τὸ πνεῦμα ἅγιον is also anaphoric).

κατῆλθον B 𝔓⁷⁴ ℵ *rell descenderunt* d ‖ καταβάντες δέ D (gig; Lcf).— ἐκεῖθέν
τε B 𝔓⁷⁴ ℵ A C E Ψ 36. 81. 226ᶜ. 323. 547. 927. 945. 1175. 1270. 1646. 1739.

1837. 1891 al lat sy^h | ἐκεῖθεν δέ H L P 049. 056. 614 𝔐, inde vero d sy^hmg | κἀκεῖθεν 431. 453. 1108. 1518. 2138. 2412. 2495; Chr ‖ ἐκεῖθεν D 614.

The first difference concerns the choice of the verb. κατέρχομαι of B03 has a neutral sense and simply describes the movement of going down to the sea. In contrast, καταβαίνω of D05 is a synonym chosen by Luke when the movement has a metaphorical connotation, often implying a distancing from a place of sanctuary or safety: Jerusalem (Lk. 2.51; 10.30, 31; Acts 8.15, 26; 18.22; 24.1, 22; 25.6, 7); the temple (Lk. 18.14); Israel (Acts 7.15); heaven (Lk. 3.22; 8.23; 9.54; Acts 7.34; 10.11; 11.5; 14.11); mountain of prayer (Lk. 6.17); rooftop/upper room (Lk. 17.31; Acts 10.20, 21; 20.10); treetop (Lk. 19.5, 6). These references may be compared with others that imply descent into places of death (even symbolical) or danger: Hades (Lk. 10.15); water of baptism (Acts 8.38); the sweat of Jesus falling to the ground (Lk. 22.44 א01* D05); the tumultuous Sanhedrin (Acts 23.10). Variant readings with the same strong sense are found in D05 at Acts 12.10 (the Temple figuratively, see *The Message of Acts*, II, p. 357), 23 (the king's throne). A further occurrence of καταβαίνω is found at Acts 16.8 AT but without metaphorical connotations. The correlative, ἀναβαίνω, expresses the opposite notion of movement towards a sacred place (e.g. Lk. 18.10; Acts 18.22; 25.1).

The occurrence of καταβαίνω here in D05 can be compared with that of 14.25 (no *vll*) where Paul and Barnabas go down to Attalia. Both Seleucia and Attalia were ports from which the pair set sail (ἀπέπλευσαν), so that their 'going down' was to the sea, a place of potential danger in contrast to the safety and security of the land.

In B03, the verb is finite, resulting in two finite verbs following the passive participle ἐκπεμφθέντες (κατῆλθον ... τε ἀπέπλευσαν), with the conjunction τε conferring greater importance on the second action of sailing away (Levinsohn, *Textual Connections*, pp. 129–35). In D05, the first verb is rendered as an active participle καταβάντες, which is set in contrast with the first, ἐκπεμφθέντες, by means of δέ. Since ἀπέπλευσαν is then the only conjugated verb, no conjoining τε is necessary.

δέ in D05 does not introduce a new clause and so is not to be taken as the correlative of μὲν οὖν (see 13.5 below). Rather, the particle marks a certain disjunction between the two participles it links (ἐκπεμφθέντες ... καταβάντες δέ) – the first is passive with the Holy Spirit as the agent whereas the second is active showing that Barnabas and Saul, once sent out by the Spirit, take the initiative themselves.

13.5 καὶ γενόμενοι B 𝔓^74 א *rell, et* d ‖ γεν. δέ D.— ἐν Σαλαμῖνι B 𝔓^74 א^2 *rell* ‖ ἐν τῇ Σαλ. D | εἰς Σαλαμίνη א* (1243).

With δέ, D05 signals that this clause is the correlative of the μὲν οὖν clause of v. 4. An analysis of μὲν οὖν ... δέ clause sequences in Acts indicates that the two clauses present events that result (οὖν) from the previous incident, with the first (μέν) being a preliminary to the second (δέ; see Levinsohn, *Textual*

Connections, pp. 138–50; Read-Heimerdinger, *The Bezan Text*, pp. 237–40). The δέ clause in B03, on the other hand, is held over to v. 6 (see below).

Salamis is the port where the disciples would have disembarked when they arrived in Cyprus (cf. 13.4). This accounts for the article prefacing the name of the town in D05, for an audience familiar with the geography of the area would know that it was the place at which the disciples were expected to land; there is no need to suppose that the article indicates that either the addressee or Luke knew the place personally. The reading of ℵ01 (εἰς + acc. [not dat. Σαλαμίνῃ]) is equivalent of the B03 reading, with εἰς expressing the movement of the journey.

κατήγγελλον B 𝔓⁷⁴ ℵ *rell, adnuntiabant* d ‖ -ήγγειλαν D 618. 1245. 1522. 1838 pc vg^W; Chr^pt.— (τὸν λόγον) τοῦ θεοῦ B 𝔓⁷⁴ ℵ *rell, dei* d ‖ τ. κυρίου D 623. 1270 gig sy^p sa^ms; Lcf.

The text of B03 presents the missionary group as undertaking the proclamation of the word of God in the synagogues over a certain duration (imperf.) – the statement is a simple description of events. D05 views the matter differently for it presents, first, the proclamation as a global event, as an action taken (aor.), and secondly it describes the word as 'of the Lord'. Within the Bezan text, there is a clear distinction between the 'word of God' and the 'word of the Lord' (see *Excursus* 6).

ὑπηρέτην B 𝔓⁷⁴ ℵ A C H L P Ψ 049. 056. 33. 1739 𝔐 ‖ ὑπηρετοῦντα αὐτοῖς D, *ministrantem eis* d 614. 2412 p sy^hmg sa mae aeth ‖ εἰς διακονίαν E (in *ministerio* vg).

The present participle of D05 indicates that John was actively engaged in exercising his role of 'assistant' for the benefit of Barnabas and Saul, in contrast to the noun of B03 which rather presents a static state of affairs. The significance of the terms ὑπηρέτης/ὑπηρετέω is discussed in the *Commentary*.

13.6 Διελθόντες δέ B 𝔓⁷⁴ ℵ (Διελθόντων D^H) *rell, cum pergressi fuissent* d ‖ Καὶ περιελθόντων δὲ αὐτῶν D* gig vg; Lcf.

The verb of B03 suggests that the island was crossed by an interior route, unlike the implication of the D05 verb that a coastal route round the island was followed. The prefix does not necessarily imply that the island was completely circled (Delebecque, *Les deux Actes*, p. 278).

The genitive absolute in D05 looks, at first sight, incorrect since the subject appears to be the same as that of the main verb (though Delebecque, *Les deux Actes*, p. 202, comments: 'l'accord du génitif du participe avec le sujet au nominatif est très grec'). A closer reading, however, shows that there is a contrast, signalled by δέ, between Barnabas and Saul as the subject of the previous clauses (κατήγγειλαν ... εἶχον ... αὐτοῖς) and the inclusion of John in the action of the new clause where the subject αὐτῶν refers to all three members of the party. The sentence connective is καί, linking John's role directly with the progression from the synagogue to other parts of the island. The importance of John's ministry and its incongruity in the synagogue context is discussed in the *Commentary*.

For other instances of καὶ ... δέ in Acts, see 6.15 D05; 12.14b D05; 18.4b D05; 21.40 D05; 22.29b (D05 lac.).

ᾧ ὄνομα B 𝔓⁷⁴ ℵ² *rell* ‖ ὀνόματι D, *nomine* d 𝔓⁴⁵ 36. 181. 431. 453. (1837) p.— Βαριησοῦς B C E 056. 33. 323. 440. 547. 945. 1175. 1245. 1270. 1739. 1891. 2147 I B-οῦ 𝔓⁷⁴ ℵ 81. 242. 257. 460. gig p^vid vg sy^htxt bo I B-οῦμ Ψ I B-οῦν A D^H H L P 049. 81 𝔐 ‖ καλούμενον B-οῦα D* sy^h aeth (ΒΑΡΙΕΣΟΥΑΝ/-ΑΜ D^p.m.?, *Bariesuam* d mae) I Βαρσουμα sy^p; Ephr I *bariesuban* Lcf.

The reading of D* is given by Scrivener, with a note on the correction apparently made by the first hand: '*Forsan* βαρίησουαν *vel cum Wetst.* -σουαμ (cf. 467 b. l. 32 et vers. Lat.) *p. m.: v pro α in fine* H, *v vel* μ *sequente deperdito*' (p. 443).

Luke uses a complex system of terminology to identify the name of a person or place: ὀνόματι indicates the real name, and ᾧ ὄνομα to indicate a pseudonym or fictitious name (see J. Read-Heimerdinger and J. Rius-Camps, 'Emmaous or Oulammaous? Luke's Use of the Jewish Scriptures in the Text of Luke 24 in Codex Bezae', *RCatT* 27 [2002], pp. 23–42). The reasons for presenting a name as not the real one need to be analysed according to the context of each occurrence (see *Excursus* 2).

According to the system Luke adopts, ᾧ ὄνομα Βαριησοῦς in B03 indicates that Bar-Jesus was a name that was given to the man, but that it was a pseudonym. The real name is seemingly to be understood as Elymas (13.8, again according to B03), though the text actually says that 'Elymas' was 'how his name is translated'.

The construction of D05, ὀνόματι καλούμενος, is unique in the Bezan text of Luke–Acts but is read by B03 at Lk. 19.2 (Zaccheus; D05 reads simply ὀνόματι). καλούμενος is a third formula Luke employs to indicate the name by which a person was known (cf. Paul; see *Excursus* 2): it presents a name that is not the real name, without going so far as to say it was a pseudonym. With respect to the Jewish false prophet, then, Luke says in the Bezan text that his real name (ὀνόματι) was, at the same time, the name given to him, the one by which he was known (καλούμενος).

The redundancy apparent in the Bezan text reflects perfectly the double meaning of the name of the magician in that text: Βαριησοῦα. As Metzger points out (*Commentary*, p. 402), the spelling of 'Bar-Jesus' in D05 'presupposes a more exact transliteration of the Semitic Bar Jeshua'. At the same time, however, the Greek transliterates even more exactly the Hebrew verb, שׁוה ('*savah*') of which the imperfect form is ישׁוה ('*yisvah*'), and which means in the Piel 'make ready' (see Zahn, p. 418: 'Da שׁוה einer der zahlreichen aus der 3. Person des Imperfekts gebildeten Eigennamen, den Begriff von שׁוה wiedergibt, was in Hebr. [wie auch syr. שׁוא] "eben, glatt, würdig sein" bedeutet, im Piel "ebnen, zurechtmachen, fertigstellen", so konnte בר־ישׁוּה sehr wohl durch ἕτοιμος wiedergegeben werden'). The correspondence between this name and the translation of it given by 13.8 D05 as Ἐτοιμᾶς ('ready'; see below) then becomes clear. Bar-Iesoua thus has two functions: it is the name that conveys the reality of the man being a disciple of Jesus, and at the same time signals that he was known as one who 'makes ready'. The reason for which the Jewish false prophet would have been called 'he makes ready' is discussed in the *Commentary*.

13.7 (οὗτος) προσκαλεσάμενος B 𝔓⁴⁵·⁷⁴ ℵ *rell* ‖ συγκ- D (*cum vocasset* d).

B03 uses the same verb as that used of the divine call of Barnabas and Saul (cf. 13.2; 16.10), although here, it has the weaker meaning of 'summoned' or simply 'invited' (B-A-G, προσκαλέω 1a). συγκαλέομαι in the middle voice has a similar sense of 'invite' (B-A-G, συγκαλέω 2; cf. 5.21b D05), and echoes the invitation of Cornelius to his friends and family to hear Peter (10.24).

ἐπεζήτησεν B 𝔓⁴⁵·⁷⁴ ℵ *rell* ‖ καὶ (– Dˢ·ᵐ·) ἐζήτησεν D*, *et quaesire voluit* d.

In B03, the prefix ἐπι- of the verb has a *directive* sense, 'indicating the concentration of the verb's action upon some subject' (Moulton and Howard, II, p. 312). It has the effect of directing attention to Barnabas and Saul. This is achieved in D05 by use of the adverbial καί. καί between the participle συγκαλεσάμενος and the finite verb ἐζήτησεν is a construction characteristic of D05 which the AT regularly avoids. The force of καί is to draw attention to the action of the finite verb (Read-Heimerdinger, *The Bezan Text*, pp. 208–210). The purpose of highlighting the action in this instance appears to be to underline the active part played by the proconsul, the first Gentile to deliberately seek out Barnabas and Saul to hear their message.

13.8 Ἐλύμας (ὁ μάγος) B 𝔓⁴⁵·⁷⁴ ℵ Dᴰ *rell* ‖ Ἐτοιμᾶς D* (ΕΤ.ΙΜΑΣ), *etoemas* d; *etoemus* Lcf, *etimas* Ambst, *hetymam* Pac.

At 13.6, gig w vgᵐˢˢ Lcf read *paratus* (i.e. ἕτοιμος). The reading ΕΤΟΙΜΑΣ in D05 is affirmed by Scrivener, p. 443 (fol. 466b, l. 19).

The two names and their interpretation have been the subject of some debate, for a recent discussion of which see R. Strelan, 'Who Was Bar Jesus (Acts 13.6-12)?', *Bib.* 85 (2004), pp. 65–81 (esp. 74–78).

The meaning of Ἐλύμας in B03 has been examined in a number of articles (summarized by Strelan, 'Who Was Bar Jesus?'), of which the conclusions are discussed in the *Commentary*. The D05 reading Ἐτοιμᾶς, from the adjective ἕτοιμος, 'ready', is confirmed by the Latin text and those witnesses that read *paratus* at 13.6. Following the analysis of the name given at 13.6 above, the translation of Βαριησοῦα as Ἐτοιμᾶς is appropriate. As Zahn points out (p. 418), the prefix 'bar-' is common in Semitic languages to express the nature of a person, but it is not necessary to translate it to render the sense in Greek.

The adjective ἕτοιμος is used of Peter, Lk. 22.33; and adverbially (ἑτοίμως) of Paul, Acts 21.13. In both cases, the word expresses their readiness to die for the sake of the Messiah, but in a context that involves their failure to grasp the universal scope of the Messiahship of Jesus.

(πίστεως) ἐπειδὴ ἥδιστα ἤκουεν αὐτῶν D*, *quoniam libenter audiebat eos* d (E) sy^h** mae ‖ *om.* B 𝔓^45.74 ℵ D^s.m. *rell.*

D05 makes the explicit observation that the proconsul was particularly interested by what he was hearing. Cf. Mk 6.20: καὶ ἡδέως αὐτοῦ (John the Baptist) ἤκουεν (Herod).

13.9 καὶ (ἀτενίσας) D, *et* d 𝔓^45 E H P Ψ 049. 056. 614 𝔐 e gig ‖ *om.* B 𝔓^74 ℵ A C D^D L 33. 81. 88. 104. 945. 1175. 1739. 1837. 1891. 2344.

It was observed with reference to 3.3-5 (*The Message of Acts*, I, pp. 206; 212–13) that the verb ἀτενίζω is restricted in the Bezan text to a gaze directed towards divine power or a gaze of someone exercising divine power. It is the latter that is the case here, with καί in the Bezan text separating it from the previous participle πλησθείς and thus highlighting its presence (cf. on 13.7 above).

13.10 πάσης (ῥᾳδιουργίας) B 𝔓^45.74 ℵ D^B *rell* ‖ *om.* D* d P 383*. 2147 *pc* gig aeth; Lcf Vig Or^lat Ephr.

D05 omits the second occurrence of the adjective πᾶς in this clause.

(τὰς ὁδοὺς) τοῦ κυρίου B ℵ* *pc* ‖ κυρίου D 𝔓^74 ℵ^2 A C E H L P Ψ 049. 056. 33. 1739 𝔐; Did Tit.— τὰς εὐθείας B 𝔓^74 ℵ D^s.m. *rell* ‖ τ. οὔσας εὐθ. D*, *quas sunt rectas* d sa mae; Vig.

D05 omits the article in this fixed expression which, like other familiar phrases from the Jewish Scriptures, is similarly anarthrous in the LXX (cf., e.g., Isa. 40.3; Ezek. 18.25, 29, and see next variant).

The presence of the present participle underlines the force of the adjective εὐθείας, thus signalling the parallels with two previous references in Luke's work to the 'straight paths' of the Lord at Lk. 3.4-5 and Acts 9.11, as well as the indirect allusion to Scriptures such as Isa. 40.3-4 or Hos. 14.9.

13.11 ἡ (χείρ) D* 1243 ‖ *om.* B 𝔓^45.74 ℵ D^p.m.? *rell.*

The phrase without the article before χείρ is another fixed expression that frequently recurs in the LXX. The presence of the article reactivates the phrase as a live expression, as it were. Usually, the expression has a positive connotation referring to the blessing of the Lord but, in this case, Paul's reference to 'the hand of the Lord' has a negative force for which the stereotyped phrase may be considered inappropriate. (In the MS of D05 there is a dot above the article to indicate that the letter η is an error but this would seem to have been inserted by a corrector rather than the first hand.)

ἄχρι καιροῦ B 𝔓⁴⁵·⁷⁴ ℵ *rell* ‖ ἕως κ. D.

Wilcox (*The Semitisms of Acts* [Oxford: Clarendon Press, 1965], p. 24) refers to an unpublished note of Torrey and Wensinck claiming that ἄχρι καιροῦ is a Semitism. It occurs already at Lk. 4.13 (ἄχρι χρόνου D05). The alternative reading of ἕως καιροῦ in D05 is not found elsewhere.

παραχρῆμα δέ B 𝔓⁷⁴ A E H L P 049. 056. 33. 614. 1739 𝔐 syʰ sa arm ‖ π. τε 𝔓⁴⁵ ℵ C Ψ 81. 623. 1175 *pc* vg syᵖ aeth I καὶ π. 1270, *et confestim* d ‖ καὶ εὐθέως D bo.

εὐθέως is read four times in Acts D05 but is omitted by ℵ01/B03, each time in the context of a supernatural event: here at 13.11, when the magician became blind; 14.10, in combination with παραχρῆμα, when the lame man got up; 16.18, as the spirit of divination left the girl in Philipi; 19.6, when the Holy Spirit fell on the Ephesians.

All the other occurrences in Acts of the adverb εὐθέως, including two omitted by D05 (16.10; 17.14), arise in the context of a human action, with the sole exception of 9.18 (D05 lac.) when Paul's sight was restored.

παραχρῆμα is also used in a supernatural context, though not exclusively: 3.7, the lame man's feet were made strong (the lame man stood D05); 5.5 D05 (*om.* παραχρῆμα AT), Ananias died; 5.10, Sapphira fell and died at Peter's feet; 12.23, the angel of the Lord struck Herod; 16.26 (*om.* παραχρῆμα B03), the doors of the prison were opened; 16.33, the Philippian jailor was baptized.

The connective δέ in B03 views the fulfilment of Paul's words as a new development; καί in D05, especially combined with εὐθέως, presents it more as an expected counterpart.

(ἔπεσεν) ἐπ' αὐτόν D 𝔓⁷⁴ ℵ *rell* ‖ *om.* B 𝔓⁴⁵ᵛⁱᵈ.

The omission of ἐπ' αὐτόν by B03 is probably due to homoioteleuton, for the idea that the mist and darkness was a general phenomenon contradicts the following statement, namely that the magician looked for someone to guide him.

13.12 τότε ἰδών B 𝔓⁴⁵·⁷⁴ ℵ *rell*, *tunc cum vidisset* d ‖ ἰδὼν δέ D gig (syᵖ aeth); Lcf.— ἐθαύμασεν καὶ (ἐπίστευσεν) D, *miratus est et credidit* d E (gig) syᵖ aeth; Lcf Ephr Vig ‖ *om.* B 𝔓⁴⁵·⁷⁴ ℵ *rell*.

The observation that 'τότε ἰδών ne se lit nulle part ailleurs' (Boismard and Lamouille, II, p. 89) is not especially significant since τότε commonly introduces a prompt and conclusive response in the narrative of Acts, such as the proconsul's belief, which is presented here by B03 as the outcome of the present incident (Read-Heimerdinger, *The Bezan Text*, pp. 211–25). D05, on the other hand, first makes the comment that the proconsul marvelled, which does not need to be underlined as prompt nor was it in itself the conclusive response, and so τότε is not appropriate. This is a clear example of the articulation of the text being adjusted to the story being told; it is not a simple matter of scribal habit or liking for certain words.

(ἐπίστευσεν) τῷ θεῷ D, *in deo* d (aeth) ‖ *om.* B 𝔓⁴⁵·⁷⁴ ℵ *rell.*

The detail that the proconsul believed in God is important for D05 since, from a Jewish point of view, it is an essential first step in the conversion of a Gentile to acknowledge the reality of God before believing in Jesus. It should be noted that it was the word of God he wanted to hear (cf. 13.7) – having never heard it (being a Gentile), he could not yet take the step of hearing the word of the Lord (see on 13.5 above, and *Commentary, 13.7*; see *Excursus 1*).

Commentary

[B-A] 13.4-5 *Cyprus I: Salamis*

[a] 13.4 *Departure for Cyprus*

13.4 The new sequence is marked with a resuming formula in Greek (μὲν οὖν) typical of Luke, indicating that the action taken is in accordance with the immediately preceding narrative in which the Holy Spirit designated Barnabas and Saul to undertake the 'work to which I have called them' (13.1-3). This action, however, is marked by μέν and as such is preliminary to a second, and principal, action marked by the connective δέ, which varies according to the MSS (see *Critical Apparatus* for further information). In Codex Bezae, it will be the arrival of Barnabas and Saul at the Cypriot port of Salamis (13.5a), whereas in the Alexandrian text it will be their discovery of the magician, Bar-Jesus (13.6).

In the previous sequence, the task to which Barnabas and Saul were called is not made explicit; indeed, it will not be so until 14.26-27 when a backwards-looking summary describes it as 'the opening to the Gentiles of a door of faith'. A first hint of this is given by the narrator as he presents their departure from Antioch as a 'sending out' by the Holy Spirit. The wording of the expression used to refer to the Holy Spirit varies according to the MSS. In both the Alexandrian text and the Bezan text, a change may be observed from the wording of 13.2 where the Spirit is mentioned in the context of a declaration. It is an example of Luke's narrative art that he typically modifies the form of the expression according to the context in which the reference to the Spirit is made. The form attested by the Alexandrian text (art. + adj. + noun) is characteristic of the way Luke refers to the Holy Spirit when the Spirit intervenes directly in a local church setting. The intimacy of the revelation to the Antioch church community accounts for its use here. In comparison, the form adopted by the Bezan text resonates more with the wider context of the mission of the Church as a whole, to which the Holy Spirit sends out Barnabas and Saul (see *Critical Apparatus* for fuller discussion).

The verb chosen to describe the departure of Barnabas and Saul from Antioch (ἐκπέμπω) is interesting, for it does not portray them being sent off on a mission but rather expresses the more negative idea of them being sent out of Antioch.[34] The notion of departing from a place of safety, even of sanctuary, is reinforced in the Bezan text by the verb καταβαίνω, as opposed to κατέρχομαι of the Alexandrian text which simply expresses their travelling down to the coast as an event in their journey (see *Critical Apparatus*). In view of these connotations in Codex Bezae – the Holy Spirit sending Barnabas and Saul out of the city and their travelling away from there as a place of security (expressed by two parallel participles in the Bezan text) – Luke insinuates that they experienced Antioch as a home-base, to which they were attached.

Their initial goal was Seleucia, the Mediterranean port at the mouth of the Orontes river that served Antioch, which was some 15 miles further inland. Seleucia, however, was not a destination in itself but the place from which they could sail to Cyprus. It is Cyprus that is the principal goal of the start of the missionary journey, the homeland of Barnabas, on the one hand, so not unknown territory for him as the leader of the venture; on the other, because of its location across the sea from Israel and by virtue of its being an island, it also has a symbolic value signifying exodus from the constraints of Judaism. The sea in Luke's work is a recurrent theme with this meaning: in the Gospel, Jesus himself never crossed the sea (except the inner sea of Galilee) to go to non-Jewish country for he himself never had direct dealings with the Gentiles and his own 'exodus' was undertaken from Ierousalem (Lk. 9.31). It was the community of his disciples who would be the first to have contact with a Gentile country, with Peter having the very first taste of it when he stayed with Simon the Tanner 'whose house was beside the sea' (Acts 10.5-6) before going to the town of Caesarea (10.23b).[35]

Cyprus has been mentioned on two occasions previously, first at 4.36 as an adjective describing Barnabas' place of origin (or his race in the AT),[36] and secondly in a double reference at 11.19-20 as one of the places to which Hellenist disciples fled from the persecution in Hierosoluma (cf. 8.1) and from where people came to Antioch and preached to non-Jews. Both mentions establish the island as a place of openness to the Gentiles, a notion that is reinforced now as the first destination on the mission to the Gentiles and will be repeated later when Barnabas and John-Mark return there (15.39). The moment has at last come for the Church to fulfil the mission entrusted to the

---

34. The verb ἐκπέμπω operates in Luke's vocabulary in contrast with the verb ἐξαποστέλλω, which has a similar meaning but different connotations. The first is found only here at Acts 13.4 and 17.10 in the whole of the New Testament, with the idea of being sent out of a place. The second is predominantly Lukan (Lk. × 4; Acts × 7; × 2 in the rest of the NT) and has positive connotations associated with being sent out on a mission (cf. Lk. 24.49 B03; Acts 12.11; 13.26; 17.14 [the idea of mission is only apparent from the Bezan text of 17.15]; 22.21 D05).

35. See *The Message of Acts*, II, pp. 247–48, 260–61.

36. See *The Message of Acts*, I, pp. 299–300.

apostles by Jesus, by departing from Judaism and going to the nations. In order to address the Gentiles with the message of Jesus, it was essential for the disciples to be free from the ancient Jewish traditions and teachings that prevented them from understanding the radically new view of the Gentiles that Jesus taught – that is, that they were not required to be integrated into Judaism and that the Church, in consequence, stood outside it. Paul, in particular, will struggle with this view throughout the various stages of his journey, as will be seen.[37] Standing in contrast to Paul, and ultimately in opposition to him, are Barnabas and John-Mark who will come to represent those believers who both understood and accepted Jesus' teaching and whose definitive journey across the sea to Cyprus as they separate from Paul (15.39) marks their complete 'exodus' from Israel (see *Commentary, ad loc.*).

[b] 13.5a *Proclamation of the Gospel in Salamis*

13.5a Codex Bezae marks the arrival of Barnabas and Saul in Cyprus as the second event (δέ) arising from (οὖν) the action of the Holy Spirit among the disciples in Antioch (the first [μέν] being the departure of Barnabas and Saul from the city for Cyprus, see *Commentary* on v. 4 above). It is thereby given special prominence in the Bezan text in comparison with the Alexandrian text, which marks the encounter with the magician Bar-Jesus as the more prominent event. They are seen arriving at the port of Salamis which lies on the western side of the island opposite Antioch, and therefore was the natural place for them to arrive at.

There, Barnabas and Saul are found in the synagogue, which Luke qualifies with the unnecessary epithet 'of the Jews' – by underlining the religious identity of the people the pair first spoke to, Luke expresses his disapproval of their strategy.[38] Significant differences are contained in this main clause. The Alexandrian text has Barnabas and Saul proclaiming (imperf.) the word of God as they embark on their mission. Within the Alexandrian text, nothing appears out of place as they begin their work by announcing the gospel to the Jews. The Bezan text uses the expression not the 'word of God' but the 'word of the Lord'. Within that text, there is a real distinction between the two, with the 'word of God' meaning the commands of God in general as expressed in the Torah, and the 'word of the Lord' meaning the message of or concerning Jesus in particular (see *Excursus* 6). So the 'word of God' is never announced in the synagogues in this text of Acts since Israel has already received the Torah – indeed it is a major distinguishing feature of the Jewish people. Furthermore, the proclamation of the 'word of the Lord' is presented here in

---

37. The theme of Paul's progressive discovery of the radical nature of the Church is explored in Rius-Camps, 'Gradual Awakening', pp. 281–96.

38. Luke does not usually qualify the word 'synagogue' with a mention of the Jews; cf. Lk. *passim*; Acts 9.2, 20; 13.14, 43; 15.21; 17.17; 18.4, 7, 19, 26; 19.8; 22.19; 24.12; 26.11. At 14.1 and 17.1, 10, however, the same qualification is made, in circumstances that are discussed in the *Commentary, ad loc.*

Codex Bezae as a global event (aor.; the AT has the imperf.) because this is what interests the narrator, the fact that they preached the gospel to Jews – for Barnabas and Saul were not sent to announce the gospel to the Jews but to the Gentiles (cf. 14.26-27). The bald comment that they preached in the synagogues in Salamis, the first place of their mission, stands therefore as a negative evaluation in so far as they had gone where they were not supposed to. It prepares for the brief statement concerning John-Mark that follows.

[b'] 13.5b *John As an Assistant*
13.5b The reference to John (-Mark) at this point may be read as a simple parenthetical aside in the Alexandrian text. Because of the comment implicit in the preceding context in Codex Bezae, in that text it is an aside full of irony. John has always been something of a silent figure in the shadows, always referred to indirectly but in a way that draws attention to him: it was at his mother's house that part of the church had gathered to pray for Peter's release from prison, the part that understood the separation the Jesus-believers had to make from the Jewish religious institution. At that point, he was said to be exercising his role as 'Mark', none other than the author of the second Gospel with which Luke was closely familiar. He was taken by Barnabas and Saul to accompany them when they left Ierousalem (12.25) because of the function he had acquired as 'Mark'.[39] Here he is simply mentioned as 'John' but it is clear from later events that it is the same John-Mark who is meant (cf. 15.37).

The term Luke uses to describe John's role alongside Barnabas and Saul is highly significant: ὑπηρέτης, as the noun in the Alexandrian text and as the corresponding verb ὑπηρετέω in Codex Bezae. The term often simply means 'a servant', with the idea of 'assisting' a superior. In official language, it has the more specific sense of a public official who has a position of responsibility, for example for the administration of the law, the authentication of documents, the safekeeping of public documents.[40] So in the synagogue, the ὑπηρέτης was in charge of looking after the scrolls and ensuring that they were not tampered with; he was a 'keeper' in the way the word is used today

---

39. On this interpretation of the church at Mary's house in 12.12 and the significance of John-Mark's departure from Ierousalem with Barnabas and Saul in 12.25, see *The Message of Acts*, II. pp. 360–61, 390–91.

40. See the excellent study by B.T. Holmes, 'Luke's Description of John Mark', *JBL* 54 (1935), pp. 63–72, on the technical use of this word in the papyri contemporary with the New Testament. He concludes that in the New Testament generally, 'the ὑπηρέτης is a public official connected with the administration of the law' (p. 67), and that at Lk. 1.2; 4.20; Acts 13.5; 26.16, Luke 'appears to use the word to describe a man who handles documents and delivers their contents' (p. 68). He connects Lk. 1.2 closely with Acts 13.5, saying 'Mark carried a written memorandum dealing with "the message of God", in other words a document similar to the gospel which now bears his name' (p. 69). In Acts 5.22, 26, the ὑπηρέται sent by the Temple authorities to the prison should probably be understood as having more specific responsibilities than mere servants (cf. Jn 18.3, 12, 18, 22, 36; 19.6). For the verb, cf. Acts 13.36 where it is used of David serving the will of God.

of a museum curator, for example. Luke uses it at least three times in this strong sense: Lk. 1.2, of the eyewitnesses of the Gospel events and keepers of their message; 4.20, of the keeper of the scrolls in the synagogue of Nazareth; Acts 26.16, of Paul designated as keeper and witness of what he had seen of Jesus. Since Mark was one of the first writers to undertake an account to which Luke referred in writing his own Gospel (Lk. 1.1), it may be supposed that Luke also views him as a 'keeper' of the true message of Jesus and that it is in that sense that he speaks of him here as a ὑπηρέτης. The verb ὑπηρετέω is likewise found in the LXX in association with the study, preservation and promulgation of the Law, including its application to all of humanity (Wis. 16.24-26; 19.6; Sir. 39.4).

Here, Barnabas and Saul are described as having John as an assistant/assisting them when they preached the gospel in the synagogues of the Jews. The very fact of going to the synagogue as the starting point of their mission is a sign that something is wrong, that they have not understood that their mission is to the Gentiles. John's presence is consequently anomalous for he, whatever the thinking of those he is assisting, is aware of the universal purpose of the mission – this much will become clear when he leaves them as they move on from Cyprus to go to other synagogues back on the mainland (13.13, see *Commentary*). The fact that he is out of place here explains why Luke simply refers to him as John – he has no means to exercise his function as Mark.

[B-A'] 13.6-12 *Cyprus II: Paphos*

[a] 13.6-7a *Bar-Iesoua, the Magician and Sergius Paulus, the Proconsul*
13.6 The action now transfers to Paphos, the capital on the other side of the island – with the Alexandrian text presenting the journey as taking place across the interior of the country but Codex Bezae suggesting a route round the coast, possibly along the southern coast road or alternatively by sea. Codex Bezae furthermore makes it quite clear that John is now included in the travelling, whereas previously the subject of the verbs ('sent out ... gone down ... sailed away ... announced ... had') was limited to Barnabas and Saul as, indeed, it will be they who are named as taking part in the action once the group arrives in Paphos (cf. 13.7b).

The principal event in this initial element is the finding of the magician who was at the court of the proconsul. By virtue of the introductory the phrase 'a certain man' (ἄνδρα τινά), this person stands as a representative of a type, not just as an individual in his own right. The name and the description of him define the community of which he is a representative, for he is a 'son of Jesus', the meaning of his name Bar-Jesus in Aramaic, which the Bezan text reproduces more exactly in Greek as Bar-Iesoua. So he is a Jewish believer in Jesus, but a 'false prophet'. In this person, there appears the type against which Jesus warned his disciples shortly before his death according to the

Gospel of Mark: 'There will arise (false Messiahs and, *om.* D05) false prophets who will give (perform, D05) signs and wonders so as to lead astray, if it were possible, the chosen ones' (Mk 13.22) – Luke did not cite this warning, along with other Markan material, in his first book, but held it over to the second volume where he took up all the material that related to the post-Easter communities of disciples. He personified Jesus' prophecy first in Simon Magus of Samaria (cf. 8.9, 11)[41] and now in the magician of Paphos, replacing the 'signs and wonders' (which is always a positive expression in Luke's choice of language) with acts of magic.[42]

Although Bar-Iesoua/Jesus was a disciple of Jesus, he was not following the true message of Jesus: he was a 'false prophet' and a 'magician'.[43] The spelling of his name in the Bezan text explains why he was a false prophet: not only does the form given there represent 'son of Jesus', but also the Hebrew verb 'he makes ready', which will be precisely the Greek translation given of his name in 13.8 (see *Critical Apparatus* for fuller explanation). It will be seen as the scene progresses that the role of Bar-Iesoua is to represent the tempter of Saul (see *Overview*). In seeking to identify, therefore, the falsehood of the man, it is essential to consider to what temptation Saul was subject at this particular point. It will be recalled that in the previous town of Salamis, which he had visited with his companions Barnabas and John, he had gone to the 'Jewish synagogues'; and that this strategy was not consistent with his call to go to the Gentiles. It reflected, on the contrary, his preoccupation with convincing the Jews of the truth of the gospel in order to prepare for the entry of the Gentiles into the people of God, as prophesied in the Scriptures (a theme that is developed extensively in the speech by Saul, as Paul, in the Antioch synagogue, see *Commentary*, 13.16-41).

This inclination of Saul accounts for the role of Bar-Iesoua as both the Jesus-believer and as 'one who makes ready', the tempter who tries to lure Saul into maintaining his concern with the Jews as a means to achieve the fulfilment of the scriptural prophecies. The falsehood of which he is guilty will be seen, indeed, to concern the question of the Gentiles, for it is when Barnabas and Saul speak the truth about Jesus to the proconsul that he interrupts to contest the faith they proclaim (13.8). The two particular issues that are at stake are the conditions on which Gentiles could become believers in Jesus, and the status of Israel within the Church, both issues that have already been dealt with in detail in the preceding chapters of Acts, especially chapter 12.[44] False prophecy based on erroneous belief concerning either or both of

41. On Simon Magus, see *The Message of Acts*, II, pp. 132–47.

42. According to Philo (*Vit. Mos.* 1.277), divination and magic are opposed to the spirit of prophecy.

43. The identification of Bar-Iesoua as a believer in Jesus makes it clear that the conflict between him and Saul was a problem within the church, not between the church and people outside it; see Strelan, 'Who Was Bar Jesus?', pp. 65–81.

44. For the underlying theological message concerning the status of the Gentiles and of Israel in Acts 12, see *The Message of Acts*, II, pp. 331–91.

these matters would constitute a serious obstacle to the entry of Gentiles into the Jesus-believing community.

What exactly is to be understood by 'magician' (μάγος) is not clear. The term is only found in Matthew's Gospel in the New Testament to describe the men who, guided by a star, came from the East at the time of Jesus' birth. Outside the New Testament, the term refers to people acknowledged as wise, skilled 'in the interpretation of dreams and various other secret arts', which could include magic.[45] In general terms, it identifies Bar-Iesoua as one who displayed an insight into the spiritual world that was out of the normal but that was not given by the Holy Spirit, and to that extent he is comparable to Simon of Samaria in Acts 8.9-24.[46]

It is quite possible in view of the fact that Bar-Iesoua represented a Jewish community, that Barnabas and Saul deliberately sought him out and that they 'found' him by design rather than accident. They would be well aware that there were Jewish believers in Jesus on the island since there had been disciples who had gone there several years earlier following the death of Stephen, and others who had gone from there to Antioch where they even spoke to non-Jews for the first time (11.19-20). They may well have expected, in view of this history, to find communities of disciples who were following the teaching of Jesus faithfully yet the only recorded encounter with disciples in Cyprus is the community represented by Bar-Iesoua, who must have been no small disappointment to them. It would have facilitated considerably their task of evangelizing the Gentiles if they had found an open and faithful group of disciples.

13.7a Before they arrived in Paphos, Bar-Iesoua was keeping company with[47] the Gentile Sergius Paulus. This is another representative character, belonging to the class of rulers on behalf of Rome. His position as proconsul meant that he governed Cyprus, a Roman province, on behalf of the senate of Rome (rather than the emperor). There is some debate over the relative significance of a number of inscriptions that attest to the presence of Sergius Paulus in Cyprus, especially with respect to the date indicated by them. Since Barnabas' and Saul's journey to Cyprus is situated by Luke after their visit to Jerusalem, which took place in or before 41 CE (the year of Herod Agrippa I's death, cf. 12.23), a date preceding that year is ruled out unless Luke had reasons to seriously disturb the chronology at this point.[48]

---

45. B-A-G lists the meaning of 'magician' as a separate meaning, see μάγος, 1, 2.

46. *The Message of Acts*, II, pp. 132–47.

47. The relative clause ὃς ἦν presupposes a state of affairs that preceded the time of the main verb εὗρον. The expression εἶναι σύν + dative is found elsewhere in Luke's work, always with the meaning of 'being or living in the company of someone': Lk. 7.12 B03; 8.38; 22.56; 24.44; Acts 4.13; 14.4 (equivalent to εἶναι κολλώμενος σύν + dat. in D05); 22.9.

48. The inscriptions and their significance are evaluated most recently in D.A. Campbell, 'Possible Inscriptional Attestation to Sergius Paul(l)us (Acts 13.6-12), and the Implications for Pauline Chronology', *JThS* 56 (2005), pp. 1–29. His conclusion that the date of Sergius Paulus must be before 37 CE is, however, not without serious difficulties.

A favourable attitude has been established towards these Roman officials in Acts by virtue of the character of Cornelius, a centurion who was a model of piety and charity (10.1-3, 22, 30-31). His positive response to the proclamation of the gospel and the demonstration of God's acceptance of him by his gift of the Spirit set the tone for the appearance of other Roman characters in subsequent sections of the book whether they be centurions,[49] tribunes,[50] proconsuls,[51] governors,[52] Caesar,[53] or the emperor.[54] The positive tone is reinforced here by the description of Sergius Paulus as 'an intelligent man'. As was common among Roman rulers, he would have kept Bar-Iesoua in his household to consult as a seer and to be advised by him. This supposes that Bar-Iesoua was well-known and exercised a position of responsibility and authority before becoming connected with Sergius Paulus.

By specifying that Cornelius was of the Italian cohort (10.1) and based in Caesarea (10.1, 24; 11.11), the chief Roman city named in honour of Augustus Caesar, Luke had already indicated at that early stage in his narrative that the goal of the mission to the Gentiles was Italy[55] and ultimately Rome.[56] Cyprus ought to have served as a bridge for the exodus out of Judaism ('Ιερουσαλήμ, cf. 12.25) towards the Gentile world ('Ρώμη) that the Antioch missionaries, under the leadership of Barnabas (himself from Cyprus) and Saul were intended to carry out. The story that now unfolds will show to what extent the plan was accomplished.

[b] 13.7b *The Proconsul's Invitation to Barnabas and Saul*
13.7b It is worthy of note that the initiative for Barnabas and Saul to talk with the proconsul was taken by himself, not by them. The same relative passivity was observed in relation to Peter and John who were intercepted on their way into the Temple by the lame man (3.1-3).[57] The action of the proconsul echoes, in the Alexandrian text, the call of Barnabas and Saul by the Holy Spirit (cf. 13.2); but in the Bezan text, there is rather a reminiscence of Cornelius who, in a detail recorded only by that text, 'invited' his family and close friends to hear Peter (10.24).[58]

---

49. Anonymous centurions, ἑκατοντάρχης: 21.32; 22.25, 26; 23.17, 23; 24.23; Publius of the Augustan cohort: 27.1, 6, 11, 31, 43. The centurions are viewed in a positive light in Lk. 7.2, 6; 23.47.

50. χιλίαρχος, Claudius Lysias of the Jerusalem cohort: 21.31, 32, 33, 37; 22.24, 26, 27, 28, 29; 23.10, 15, 17, 18, 19, 22, 26; 24.7 (*vl*), 22; anonymous: 25.23.

51. ἀνθύπατος, Sergius Paulus of Cyprus: 13.7, 8, 12; Gallio of Acachia: 18.12; anonymous: 19.38.

52. ἡγεμών, Felix: 23.24, 26, 33; 24.1, 3, 10, 22, 24, 27a, 27b; Porcius Festus: 24.27; 25.1, 4, 9, 12, 13, 14, 22, 23, 24; 26.24, 25, 30, 32.

53. Καῖσαρ: 17.7; 25.8, 10, 11, 12, 21; 26.32; 27.24; 28.19.

54. Σεβαστός: 25.21, 25; 27.1.

55. Acts 27.1, 6; cf. 18.2.

56. Acts 19.21; 23.11; 28.14, 16; cf. 18.2.

57. See *The Message of Acts*, I, p. 212.

58. The invitation of Cornelius recalls, in its turn, that of Lk. 15.6, 9. Elsewhere, the verb συγκαλέω expresses a certain solemnity in the meeting: Lk. 9.1; 23.13; Acts 5.21; 28.17.

His action expresses the strength of his desire to know the word of God. As was observed earlier in connection with the proclamation of the word in the synagogues of Salamis (see *Critical Apparatus*, 13.5a above), the phrase 'the word of God' operates alongside 'the word of the Lord' in Luke's vocabulary (according to the Bezan text at least) where the latter refers specifically to the gospel in contrast to the former which designates God's communication with humankind in a more general and fundamental sense (see *Excursus* 1). Similarly, from the perspective of a Gentile such as Sergius Paulus, 'God' is always the term used and not 'Lord' until belief in Jesus as Lord is expressed.[59] The teaching of Jesus is not the specific purpose of the quest he is pursuing, although that will not stop Barnabas and Saul explaining about Jesus (cf. v. 8).

[c] 13.8 *The Opposition of the Magician*

13.8 At the point when Barnabas and Saul speak to the proconsul, Bar-Iesoua intervenes to prevent him from accepting what they have to say about 'the faith', a term established in the narrative to refer to belief in Jesus.[60] His opposition is directed towards the visitors rather than the proconsul directly and, though the contents of it are not made explicit, they may be guessed at given the clues in the Bezan text (see on 13.6 above). According to the form of his name in Codex Bezae, Bar-Iesoua was a believer in Jesus, a Jew but a false prophet who believed that it was necessary to make preparations in order for the Gentiles to enter Israel. The focus of his arguments may well, then, have been the terms on which Gentiles could be accepted into the Jesus-believing community. Barnabas and Saul will have been announcing to the proconsul the good news that belief in Jesus was sufficient, without the need for circumcision, a message that appears to have been consistently theirs from the outset even though the open challenge to it is not recorded until their return to Antioch (14.26–15.1).

With the explanation of the meaning of his name,[61] Luke gives a clue as to the grounds on which Bar-Jesus opposed the disciples, at least he does in the Bezan text. The Alexandrian text refers to him as Elymas (pronounced *Elimas*) the magician, and opinion is divided as to whether the following phrase 'for

59. For an analysis of the parallel terms θεός and κύριος in Acts, see Read-Heimerdinger, *The Bezan Text*, pp. 286, 287, 291.

60. Cf. πίστις 3.16 × 2; 6.5, 7; 11.24; cf. πιστοί, 'the faithful', 10.45; 12.3 D05. It is grammatically possible here that the word is used in the subjective sense to refer to 'the faith of the proconsul', but in view of the summary Paul gives in v. 10 of Bar-Iesoua's interference, it is more likely to be used in an objective sense, to mean the content of the faith being expounded.

61. The translation of a Hebrew or Aramaic name into Greek occurs several times in the Gospels (cf. Mt. 1.23; 27.33; Mk 3.17; 5.41; 7.11, 34; 15.22, 34; Jn 1.38, 41, 42; 9.7), though never in Luke. In Acts, there are four comparable occurrences, all involving Aramaic rather than Hebrew, including the one at Acts 13.8: 1.19 (τοῦτ᾽ ἔστιν – Akeldaimach); 4.36 (μεθερμηνευόμενον – Barnabas) and 9.36 (ἣ διερμηνευονένη λέγεται – Tabitha); 13.8 (μεθερμηνεύεται – Bar-Iesoua).

that is the translation of his name' is an interpretation of Elymas as a) the Greek equivalent of the Hebrew Bar-Jesus or b) the equivalent in Aramaic or Arabic of the Greek word for magician. Those who defend the first position[62] are unable to justify the supposed translation of the Hebrew name, for Elymas does not mean anything in Greek. Those who argue for the second explanation,[63] on the other hand, with recourse to sometimes tortuous steps, do not account for the name Elymas being given at all – since the narrator has already provided the name Bar-Jesus together with the information that he was a magician and a false prophet, why is it necessary to now give another name that simply explains that the man was a 'magician', a fact that the audience has already been told?[64]

The variant form of the name in Codex Bezae, Etoimas, was pronounced *Etimas* in Koine Greek so only differing in one consonant in sound from Elymas.[65] This name is derived from the adjective ἕτοιμος meaning 'ready, prepared', which, as was seen at 13.6 above, is one of the meanings of his name in Hebrew, Bar-Iesoua.

Codex Bezae spells out the fact that Sergius Paulus was deeply interested in what he was hearing, a comment that is reminiscent of Mk 6.20: 'He (Herod) used to listen to him (John the Baptist) with great pleasure' (καὶ ἡδέως αὐτοῦ ἤκουεν).

[c'] 13.9-11a *Paul's Rebuke*

13.9 An important and definitive shift takes place as Saul prepares to rebuke the magician for his interference in his conversation. Three brief and incisive comments summarize the change: first, he changes his name to Paul; then, for the first time, he is said to be 'filled with the Holy Spirit'; and finally, he 'gazes intently' at the magician, where the particular verb chosen (ἀτενίζω) always carries the sense of spiritual awareness in the Bezan text of Acts. It is at this point that Paul is seen for the first time exercising his spiritual gifts, that he is accomplishing 'the work to which he was called' (13.2; cf. 14.26-27).

The name change is a literary device, the reason for which is theological. The name Saul will no longer be in the narrative, and will only reappear in Paul's speeches when he describes his encounter with Jesus retrospectively.

---

62. Cf. B-A-G, Ἐλύμας: 'Ac obviously considers the two names to be linguistically equiv. to each other; it is hardly correct to assume, w. some, that v. 8 means to say that the word Elymas = μάγος (but s. Haenchen, Acts, ad loc.)'.

63. See Haenchen, p. 341, n.1; Schneider II, p. 122, n. 35; Barrett, I, p. 615.

64. Strelan ('Who Was Bar Jesus?') proposes an original and interesting explanation of Elymas, based on the form of the name ending in μ read at 13.6 by Ψ and syr^p (see *Critical Apparatus*), which avoids the difficulties mentioned and provides a satisfying answer to the question of the correspondence between Bar-Jesus and Elymas.

65. Moulton and Howard (II, pp. 82-83) give other examples of the assimilation of οι and υ due to itacism: 'by the time our uncials were written οι and υ must have been everywhere identical except in rather artificial speech' (p. 82). Cf. Á. Urbán, 'Bezae Codex Cantabrigiensis (D): intercambios vocálicos en los textos griegos de Lucas y Hechos', *Collectanea Christiana Orientalia* 3 (2006), pp. 269–316 (308–309, 310).

Saul is a Jewish name, Σαῦλος being the Greek form of the Aramaic שָׁאוּל, which was usual in the Hellenistic world.[66] The name would have been given by his parents when he was circumcised, but his other name Παῦλος may well have been a second Latin name that was given to him as a Roman citizen (cf. 22.28b), also at birth. Luke does not say that he changed his name when he was in Paphos but simply that Saul was also Paul. Paul himself never mentions the Jewish form of his name, and it would be expected that if he had changed it on becoming a Jesus-believer, he would have done so; and furthermore, Luke would have noted it at the outset of his conversion rather than later on (see *Excursus* 2).

Whether or not the introduction of the name Paul has anything to do with the presence of the proconsul Sergius Paulus is another question. It is unlikely, since Paul himself never calls himself by any other name, that it is no more than an adopted name, borrowed from a Roman figure of high standing.[67]

The use of Saul up to this point is probably to be seen as a device Luke has chosen to show his initial strong attachment to the Jewish world and to signal, by the introduction of the name Paul, the first recorded occasion on which, in the power of the Holy Spirit, he challenged the Jewish way of thinking that prevented the Gentiles from becoming Jesus-believers on an equal footing with Jews. That is not to say that he had never been filled with the Holy Spirit previously nor, indeed, that he has abandoned his primary concern with the conversion of the Jews, for this will re-emerge at various points in the future, but the confrontation with the Jewish false prophet and magician in the course of his proclamation of the word of God to the Gentile proconsul marks a significant turning point in his ministry. It is to this confrontation with the blindness of Judaism that Luke points by the use of another name, rather than to the beginning of Paul's ministry to the Gentiles. The reason for saying this is that the act that follows under the influence of the Holy Spirit is directed to Bar-Iesoua and not to the proconsul at all.

13.10-11a The significance of the confrontation lies in the similarities between the consequence Paul pronounces on Bar-Iesoua and his own experience on the road to Damascus (9.1-19a).[68] It will be remembered that following his hearing of the voice of Jesus, who identified himself as the one Saul was persecuting, he found himself unable to see. His blindness, though it could be conceived as a punishment for his persecution of Jesus, was a meta-

---

66. Σαῦλος is found 15 times between his first introduction at 7.58 and the present reference at 13.9. The Hebrew form Σαούλ is found 8 times as a form of address in the three accounts of his conversion but only in the AT (9.4 [× 2], 17; 22.7 [× 2], 13; 26.14 [× 2]); the WT (or D05 where it is extant, cf. 22.7 D05 [× 2], 13 d5 [× 2]) reads the Greek form, the vocative Σαῦλε (see *Critical Apparatus* of the above references in *The Message of Acts*, II, pp. 170, 182).

67. See H.J. Cadbury, *The Making of Luke–Acts* (London: SPCK, 1968), p. 225: 'The transition from the Hebrew to the Roman name is scarcely to be attributed merely to the mention in this context of the proconsul Sergius Paulus'. Cf. Haenchen, p. 342, n. 1.

68. For the interpretation of Paul's encounter with Jesus followed here, see *The Message of Acts*, II, pp. 165–88.

phor for his spiritual blindness to the truth concerning Jesus, represented by those of the 'Way' (9.2). Saul was not, in fact, attacking the disciples simply because they believed in Jesus but because they were Jews who, like their leader Stephen, were not maintaining the strict exclusivism of Judaism (the apostles who stayed in Ierousalem [cf. 8.1 D05] were not persecuted). He recovers his sight while in a house in a street called 'Straight' (9.11), when Ananias conveys to him the message of Jesus (9.17-18) and it seems that right from the start he accepted Gentiles as Jesus-believers, without the need for circumcision. Saul/Paul's experience of being blind is now mirrored in what happens with Bar-Iesoua as he intervenes to stop the magician from hindering the proconsul from believing the message about Jesus: in response to his perverting the 'ways of the Lord, those that are straight', he loses his sight as a divine chastisement.

The parallels between the blinding of Paul, as Saul, and that of Bar-Iesoua are one indication of what the real problem is – it is not just that an individual is stopping another from grasping the message of Jesus, but that the grounds used by Bar-Iesoua are Jewish false doctrines, doctrines that are being perpetrated by him as a Jesus-believer and accompanied in all probability by manifestations of supernatural power since he is described as a magician. The falsehood relates not to the Messiahship of Jesus as such but to the role of the Gentiles in relation to the believing Jews. Furthermore, Bar-Jesus is not an isolated individual but represents a community of like-minded believers. Paul, recognizing the hindrance posed by these people to the freedom of the message of Jesus and to the acceptance of the gospel by Gentiles, here represented by Sergius Paulus, identifies him as a spiritual force of darkness, addressing him as 'son of the devil', a description that contrasts with his name, Bar-Iesoua, 'son of Jesus'. His opposition is based on 'deceit and fraud', of which he is 'full' (πλήρης), not like Paul who is filled (πλησθείς) with the Holy Spirit for a particular task, but as a permanent state. Far from being the faithful Jew that he believes himself to be, he is an 'enemy of all righteousness' (where the technical term δικαιοσύνη meaning God's righteousness is used), who twists the truth – the straight paths – of the Lord. There is nothing to indicate that Bar-Iesoua was deliberately falsifying the truth, knowingly deceiving people and spreading lies, but his sincerity does not negate the seriousness of the erroneous beliefs and hopes about Jesus that he was perpetuating and using as obstacles for the Gentiles to come to faith in him.

A series of markers sets up a parallel between this scene and the temptation of Jesus in the desert (Lk. 4.1-13; see *Excursus* 7). They combine to equate Jesus' temptations, with which Satan sought to get Jesus to prove his spiritual power and strength by worldly means that could be justified from the Scriptures but were contrary to God's plan, with the prophecies and acts of magic with which Bar-Iesoua, no doubt with good scriptural backing, was seeking to demonstrate the power of the God of Israel to the Gentiles. But his efforts were not in line with God's ways.[69] The parallel is critically important, for it shows the struggle Paul himself was experiencing with Jewish teachings about the Gentiles. Repeatedly, Luke will reveal how Paul, for all his clear theological thinking in places, was constantly tempted to maintain the traditional understanding of the Jews as a privileged people with whom the Gentiles were to be assimilated; only when he reaches Rome in Acts 28 will he finally accept that Israel is no longer a special nation but on a par with all the nations (see on 13.4 above).

Paul goes on to make a performative declaration by which he announces the punishment of the Lord on Bar-Iesoua, using a metaphor found in Ps. 58.9 where the psalmist prays for the punishment of the wicked[70] – he will be blind, a physical manifestation of his spiritual blindness to the truth of Jesus which Paul himself had experienced when he first encountered Jesus on the road to Damascus. The punishment will be executed by the hand of the Lord, the same 'hand' that had earlier brought blessing on the disciples from Cyprus and Cyrene who had announced the gospel to non-Jews in Antioch (cf. 11.21).

Paul's final phrase adds to the list of markers that establish a parallel between this scene where he and Barnabas are 'tempted' or 'tested' and that of the temptation of Jesus in the desert (see *Excursus* 7):[71] there, the devil left Jesus 'for a time' (ἄχρι καιροῦ [χρόνου D05], Lk. 4.13), until he had another opportunity to attack him; here, Paul does not have the boldness to silence the devil definitively but only 'for a time' (ἕως [ἄχρι, AT] καιροῦ). In the case of Jesus, an opportunity presented itself when Satan entered Judas to betray Jesus. In the case of Bar-Iesoua, that is, of the false Jewish teaching that he represents, Paul will be found once more according a privileged importance to the conversion of the Jews when he arrives in the next town, Antioch of Pisidia (13.14). He has resisted temptation 'only for a time'.

Paul's hesitation in acting in a more decisive way, permanently silencing the false doctrines about the primacy of Israel and the validity of the Jewish Law, reflects his own lack of conviction on these issues that he will continue to struggle over until he finally arrives in Rome. If he had acted otherwise in Paphos, Luke could have brought his second volume to a close at this point, for there would have been no further evidence that Paul was not totally convinced about the radical nature of Jesus' teaching that made all peoples equally favoured by God. In fact, though, he will continue to give special con-

---

69. Comparison may be made between Bar-Iesoua the false prophet and magician who made crooked the ways of the Lord (Ἐτοιμᾶς ... οὐ παύσῃ διαστρέφων τὰς ὁδοὺς τοῦ [*om.* D05] κυρίου τὰς [+ οὔσας D05] εὐθείας;) and the proclamation of John the Baptist (ἑτοιμάσατε τὴν ὁδὸν κυρίου, εὐθείας ποιεῖτε τὰς τρίβους αὐτοῦ [ὑμῶν D05], Lk. 3.4 = Isa. 40.3).

70. The form of Paul's expression is remarkably similar to that of the targum of the Psalms, as pointed out by Wilcox, *The Semitisms of Acts*, p. 24: the punishment is that the wicked should be 'Like the untimely born and the mole, who are blind and do not see the sun'.

71. D05 adds one more marker to the parallel between Jesus' temptation and that of Paul by Bar-Iesoua. In 15.26, D05 includes the comment that Barnabas and Paul had handed their souls over to every trial, the same word in Greek for 'temptation' (εἰς πάντα πειρασμόν, cf. Lk. 4.13).

sideration to his own people and seek to make the total acceptance of the Gentiles conditional on the prior conversion of the Jews. For this reason, he will be seen time and again going into the synagogue when he arrives in a place, as he will also be seen collecting money from the Gentiles for Jerusalem. Thus he does not proclaim permanent blindness on Bar-Iesoua but allows him the possibility of coming to the truth at some future date. This corresponds well to his hope in the eventual acceptance of Jesus by his own people, a hope that he finally abandons only when he is confronted with their deafness and blindness and hardness of heart in Rome (28.26-27).

[b'] 13.11b *The Magician's Blindness*
13.11b The negative effects of Paul's warning of blindness do not take long to be felt. As he loses his power of sight, he gropes for people to lead him. In the parallel case of Paul, he had companions who took him to Damascus, to the house of Judah in the street called Straight (9.8, 11; cf. 22.11); there, he recovered his sight as Ananias, sent to him by Jesus, laid hands on him (9.17). As for Bar-Iesoua, it is not even recorded whom he found to guide him; the matter is left open, as an indication that the Jewish-believing communities in Paphos would be entirely dependent on more open groups leading them in the 'straight ways of the Lord'.

[a'] 13.12 *The Proconsul's Belief in God*
13.12 The result of the magician being blinded, and therefore silenced, is that the proconsul believed. The Alexandrian text leaves it at that but Codex Bezae specifies, first, that his initial response to seeing Paul's prophetic gesture and its immediate fulfilment was that he 'marvelled' at what had happened;[72] and secondly, that his belief was 'in God'. That God should be the object of his belief is in accordance with the pattern maintained throughout Acts in Codex Bezae, where a Gentile always comes to faith in God, or seeks to know God or his word as a first step towards the faith (cf. 8.24; 10.33; 15.17a; 16.15; see *Commentary*, 13.7 above). It was, in fact, impossible for Sergius Paulus to become a disciple of Jesus in his position as Roman pro-consul, since it required him to participate in worship of the Emperor,[73] but he has acquired a belief in the God whom Barnabas and Paul were preaching.

Not only was he moved to belief by what he saw, however, but also by 'the teaching about the Lord'. His amazement at hearing this, from presumably Barnabas as well as Saul/Paul, is evidence that a distinctive message, which he had not previously heard from the Jesus-believers in Paphos, was taught. Sergius Paulus is thus the first fruit of the mission of Barnabas and Saul to the Gentiles, even though Barnabas himself is kept in the background

72. The perfect τὸ γεγονός expresses not an event in the past but a change of state that has taken place – here the blindness of the magician.
73. See B. Chilton, *Rabbi Paul. An Intellectual Biography* (New York: Doubleday, 2004), p. 117.

throughout the scene – because it is Paul on whom Luke particularly wishes to focus, not because Barnabas is a weaker character, any more than is John-Mark whose role in Paphos is not mentioned at all. This could give the impression that they leave Paul to do all the work, or that only he is capable of it, but that is to miss the point of Luke's narrative. He does not devote space to those who have grasped correctly the teaching of Jesus but mentions them with a positive evaluation in passing. His concern in these chapters of Acts is to describe the spiritual development of Paul and the maturing of his thought from the time of his encounter with Jesus on the Damascus road to the time he reaches Rome. At this stage, little is known of the precise command he had received from Jesus except that he was to 'bear [his] name before Gentiles, kings and Jews' (9.15). His specific role to take the gospel to the Gentiles will become clearer as the narrative progresses (cf. 22.15, 21; and esp. 26.17-18). For the time being, however, he will continue to reveal his concern to announce the message first to the Jews then to the Gentiles (cf. 13.46-47; Rom. 1.16).

Excursus 1

The Word of God and the Word of the Lord

Within the work of Luke, two parallel expressions are found to describe the content of the preaching and proclamation carried out by Jesus in the Gospel and by the disciples in Acts: ὁ λόγος τοῦ θεοῦ, the 'word of God', and ὁ λόγος τοῦ κυρίου, the 'word of the Lord'. Although it is often assumed that the two expressions are synonymous, and that the alternation between them is simply stylistic, a detailed analysis of their occurrences reveals that, on the contrary, Luke ascribes a distinct meaning to the separate expressions. The distinction is maintained consistently in the Bezan text but not in the Alexandrian one.

The Jewish Scriptures
When the divine word is spoken of in the Hebrew Bible, it is generally ascribed to 'YHWH'. The Hebrew term for 'word', דבר, almost always has a prophetic force in the phrase 'the word of YHWH', referring to God's plans or intentions, or to his judgement. In the targumic traditions of the writings of the Prophets, the word of YHWH takes on an increased importance and is often designated by the term 'memra', which comes to mean not only the words or actions but even the presence of God.[74]

In the LXX, the Hebrew expression is almost always translated as λόγος κυρίου (× 160) with no article; only occasionally is the phrase arthrous (× 7).[75] Rarer still are the references to λόγος θεοῦ (× 5)[76] or λόγος τοῦ θεοῦ (× 2).

---

74. Chilton, *The Glory of Israel*, pp. 59–69.
75. Figures are given according to the edition of Rahlfs.
76. According to the critical apparatus of Rahlfs, λόγος θεοῦ is also found in most MSS at Sir. 1.7, where the word of God is described as the fountain of wisdom. This is the reference probably alluded to by Paul at 13.46.

The Gospel of Luke

In Luke's Gospel, ὁ λόγος τοῦ θεοῦ is found four times (five D05): 5.1; 8.11, 15 D05, 21; 11.28.

On each of these occasions, the 'word of God' is a general term meaning the teaching or the commandments that had already been communicated through the Jewish religious system. It is not a question of a new prophecy or instruction. Even at 5.1, where Jesus is the one whom the people want to hear, his preaching is perceived as pertaining to the familiar Jewish teaching proclaimed in the synagogues (4.44), albeit with a new focus ('the kingdom of God', 4.43), and delivered with authority (4.32).

ὁ λόγος τοῦ κυρίου is found only once, at Lk. 22.61 D05 as Peter remembered the warning pronounced by Jesus about his denial before the cock had crowed three times (cf. Lk. 22.34). This is a reference to a specific word, rendered in the Alexandrian text by τὸ ῥῆμα.

Acts

ὁ λόγος τοῦ θεοῦ continues to be used in Acts, but now alongside ὁ λόγος τοῦ κυρίου. In both expressions, ὁ θεός and ὁ κύριος are regularly arthrous except at 16.32 D05. τὸ ῥῆμα τοῦ θεοῦ is found only once, when Peter recalls Jesus' words about the baptism of the Holy Spirit (11.16; cf. Lk. 22.61, not D05).[77] Taken together, ὁ λόγος τοῦ θεοῦ and ὁ λόγος τοῦ κυρίου occur at a total of 23 places, of which just over half are affected by variant readings between the Bezan and the Alexandrian texts. In Codex Bezae, a pattern of usage is clearly apparent: whereas ὁ λόγος τοῦ θεοῦ is a generic term, often the equivalent of the Jewish concept of the Torah, ὁ λόγος τοῦ κυρίου is specific and means the message about or of Jesus.[78] (More often than not, τοῦ κυρίου can be understood as an objective genitive, whereas τοῦ θεοῦ is always a subjective genitive.)

In order to clarify Luke's usage, all the occurrences of both expressions in Acts are set out here, taking the readings of D05 and indicating the variant readings of ‭01 and B03, which will be seen to be sometimes divided. In the following table, ὁ λόγος τοῦ θεοῦ is represented by λ.θ. and ὁ λόγος τοῦ κυρίου by λ.κ. A variant reading concerning θεός or κύριος in one or both of ‭01/B03 is indicated by (*vl*); a reading absent from those MSS is accompanied by (+).

---

77. When ῥῆμα is used of Paul's words to the magistrates in Philippi (16.38), it is a means to signal that Paul had failed on this occasion to speak the words of the gospel to the Gentile rulers (see *Commentary, ad loc.*). A similar observation may be made of Paul's talk in the market place (17.20 D05, see *Commentary, ad loc.*).

78. Metzger (*Commentary*, pp. 253–54) appeals to the greater frequency of ὁ λόγος τοῦ θεοῦ as proof of its earlier origin, calling ὁ λόγος τοῦ κυρίου 'the Christianization of the traditional expression'. At places of variation (e.g. 13.44), therefore, it is the relative frequency of the two expressions that serves to inform the decision taken by the committee as to the original reading. This process ignores the theological distinction that Luke as narrator applies to the two expressions.

Ref.	ὁ λόγος τοῦ θεοῦ Context	ὁ λόγος τοῦ κυρίου Context
4.31	apostles spoke λ.θ. to all wishing to believe	
6.2	apostles did not wish to leave λ.θ.	
6.7 *vl*		λ.κ. grew after election of Hellenist leaders
8.14	apostles heard that Samaria had received λ.θ.	
8.25		Peter and John spoke λ.κ. in Samaria
11.1	apostles and Judaean brethren heard that Gentiles received λ.θ.	
12.24 *vl* ℵ01	λ.θ. grew after Jewish persecution	
13.5 *vl*		Barnabas and Saul proclaimed λ.κ. in synagogues of Salamis
13.7	Sergius Paulus wanted to hear λ.θ.	
13.44a +	λ.θ. went through all of Antioch of Pisidia	
13.46	λ.θ. first given to Jews	
13.48 *vl*	Gentiles received λ.θ.	
13.49		λ.κ. was carried throughout Pisidia
14.4 +	Some in Iconium adhered to Paul and Barnabas because of λ.θ.	
15.35		Paul and Barnabas taught λ.κ. in Antioch
15.36		Paul went to visit cities where they had announced λ.κ.
16.32		Paul and Silas spoke τὸν λόγον κυρίου to Philippian jailor
17.13	Jews heard that λόγος θεοῦ is preached in Beroea (*vl*)	
18.11	Paul taught λ.θ. to Gentiles in Corinth	
18.25		Apollo(nius) was instructed in λ.κ. in his fatherland
19.10		All in Asia heard τοὺς λόγους τοῦ κυρίου (*vl*)

Certain factors that characterize the distinct expressions can be observed.

ὁ λόγος τοῦ θεοῦ

This is the first expression used and it dominates the book up to Acts 13.48. It was the only term used in Luke's Gospel (apart from ὁ λόγος τοῦ κυρίου with the sense of words spoken by Jesus at Lk. 22.61 D05).

In the first four references, it is used of the apostles or the disciples in Jerusalem (4.31; 6.2; 8.14; 11.1), the latter two references being made from their point of view with respect to the word of God being received firstly in Samaria, secondly among the Gentiles. Similarly, it is used of the first Gentile of Paul's and Barnabas' mission reported to show an interest in the word of God (13.7). Notably, ὁ λόγος τοῦ θεοῦ is the term used in Codex Bezae to express the reception of the word by Gentiles when Paul first witnesses its rejection by Jews (13.46, 48)

The different points at which ὁ λόγος τοῦ θεοῦ is found in Codex Bezae up to Acts 13.48 represent successive stages in the spread of the word from the Jews (4.31; 6.2) to people in Samaria (8.14), and then to the Gentiles in Antioch in Syria (11.1), Cyprus (13.7) and, finally, Antioch in Pisidia (13.48), where the reception of the word of God is presented as definitive in the Bezan text. The word is a generic one, without any definition of its contents. ὁ λόγος τοῦ θεοῦ in Acts can thus be seen to represent the concept of God speaking to people, a privilege that was previously reserved for Israel. It corresponds to its use in Luke's Gospel where it was seen to have a general sense of the teachings or commandments revealed by God, or at the most the interpretation of them, rather than a specifically new message.

ὁ λόγος τοῦ κυρίου

ὁ κύριος in Acts is above all the designation for Jesus as the risen Lord, and it is to him specifically that the expression ὁ λόγος τοῦ κυρίου relates: it is his own particular message (subjective genitive) or, more usually, it is about him (objective genitive). This explains why the phrase is not generally found in the Gospel, since Jesus' lordship does not become apparent, or is not recognized by the other participants, until after the resurrection. At its occurrence at Lk. 22.61 D05, it is a retrospective allusion by the narrator to a prophetic word spoken by Jesus to Peter.

When ὁ λόγος τοῦ κυρίου arises in Acts, it is not in a haphazard or casual way but rather at places where the narrator wishes to insist on the way the message about Jesus was proclaimed. At several places, there is an implied connection with a recent occurrence of ὁ λόγος τοῦ θεοῦ. Such instances demonstrate that whereas ὁ λόγος τοῦ θεοῦ is a global concept, representing the fact of God's revelation, ὁ λόγος τοῦ κυρίου is a particular communication about Jesus. Consequently, when ὁ λόγος τοῦ θεοῦ reaches a new place, it is a once-for-all event; this can be noticed of such references in D05 as 8.14; 11.1; 13.48. In contrast, ὁ λόγος τοῦ κυρίου can be, and is, preached on repeated occasions.

In places, ὁ λόγος τοῦ θεοῦ refers to the interpretation of the Scriptures, with a focus on the things pertaining to the Messiah of Israel (e.g. 4.31; 6.2). Although there is some overlap, the contents of ὁ λόγος τοῦ κυρίου goes further than this. To a certain extent, Jesus fulfilled the promises and prophecies regarding Israel that were contained in the Scriptures (ὁ λόγος τοῦ θεοῦ) and this would seem to be how his role was understood until teaching about him reached people outside Jerusalem, though Luke does not necessarily agree with this understanding. From that point on, the message of Jesus (ὁ λόγος τοῦ κυρίου) includes the good news that the Messiah is for all, beyond the confines of Judaism.

The Readings of Codex Vaticanus and Codex Sinaiticus

The reasons for the variants of ℵ01 and B03 are discussed in detail at the relevant places in the *Commentary*. Two additional references in these MSS are to be noted: 13.44 (ὁ λ. τ. θ. B03 / ὁ λ. τ. κ. ℵ01) where D05 has πολύν τε λόγον ποιησαμένου (Παύλου) περὶ τοῦ κυρίου...; and 14.25 (ὁ λ. τ. κ. ℵ01), where B03 and D05 use ὁ λόγος without qualification.

The variant forms in D05 concerning the article (16.32; 17.13) and the plural (19.10) are read in the Alexandrian text as the regular forms of either ὁ λόγος τοῦ θεοῦ or ὁ λόγος τοῦ κυρίου. The flexibility of the Bezan text suggests that the editor is happy to vary expressions that otherwise have a fixed form.

Conclusions

In the text of Codex Bezae, a pattern of alternance between the two expressions emerges, with ὁ λόγος τοῦ θεοῦ being used of communication with God in a general sense, hitherto the privilege of Israel, and ὁ λόγος τοῦ κυρίου, meaning specifically the teaching of or about Jesus. In neither of the Alexandrian MSS is a pattern evident in the choice of expressions.

This is but one example of the use of parallel expressions or forms in Luke's writings, both the Gospel and Acts and particularly in their Bezan form, which is so extensive that it is not possible for it to have occurred by accident.

Excursus 2

Saul, or Paul

The naming of Saul as Paul, recorded by Luke in the briefest of comments at 13.9, marks a striking and decisive point in the unfolding of the narrative concerning the mission to the Gentiles. The points made in the course of the *Commentary* above are restated here and further expanded.

1. The usual name of the man would seem to have been Paul, the only name that he himself uses in his letters. Nevertheless, several times he makes much of his Jewish background, and at one place makes a curious indirect reference to Saul in appealing to his family credentials. At Rom. 11.1, he asks the question, 'Has God rejected his people?' He answers his own question in the negative, 'By no means!', by describing his ancestry (as he does in other places):[79] 'I myself am an Israelite, a descendant of Abraham a member of the tribe of Benjamin', and concludes with the declaration, 'God has not rejected his people whom he foreknew'. The final statement is a modified form of the promise proclaimed by Samuel to the people of Israel on the day he anointed Saul as their king: 'For the sake of his great name, the Lord will not abandon his people, seeing that the Lord undertook to make you his people' (1 Sam. 12.22). In the Hebrew text as in the LXX, the verb is in the future (ἀπώσεται). Paul changes it to the past (ἀπώσατο), so presenting the promise as realized. By associating the fulfilment of the promise with his own identity as a Jew,

79. Cf. 2 Cor. 11.22; Phil. 3.5; Acts 23.6; 26.5.

Paul seems to justify his confidence that God still considers Israel to be his special people, on the basis that he, like Saul in the past, has been chosen to lead Israel, or at least the remnant of it (cf. Rom. 11.2b-10). And yet, despite this association of himself with Saul, he does not make any mention of Saul as his own name.

2. When Luke first introduced Paul into his narrative, it was by the name of Saul (7.58b), but in such a way as to indicate that Saul was a name by which he was called: 'The witnesses laid their cloaks aside at the feet of a (certain, D05) young man called (καλουμένου) Saul'. Whenever Luke introduces a character for the first time by his real name, he always uses the expression 'by the name of' (ὀνόματι).[80] On the other hand, when he wishes to indicate that the name is some kind of given name, which may be a pseudonym, or a nickname,[81] or a customary name, he uses other expressions.[82]

80. ὀνόματι + name (ˢ indicates the reverse order, name + ὀνόματι): Lk. 1.5 (Zachariah); 5.27 AT (Levi; *om.* ὀνόματι D05; *add.* καλούμενον C*); 10.38 (Martha); 16.20 (Lazarus); 19.2 (Zacchaeus; *add.* καλούμενος AT); 23.50 (Joseph of Arimathea); 24.13 D05 (Oulammaous; ἧ ὄνομα Ἐμμαοῦς AT), 18 AT (Cleopas; ᾧ ὄνομα D05); Acts 5.1 (Ananias [ˢ AT]), 34 (Gamaliel); 8.9 (Simon); 9.10 (Ananias; D05 lac.), 11 (Saul [ˢ]; D05 lac.), 12 (Ananias [ˢ]; D05 lac.), 33 (Aeneas; D05 lac.), 36 (Tabitha; D05 lac.); 10.1 (Cornelius; D05 lac.); 11.28 (Agabus); 12.13 (Rhoda); 13.6 D05 (Bar-Iesoua; *add.* καλούμενον D05 Ι ᾧ ὄνομα Βαριησοῦς AT); 16.1 (Timothy), 14 (Lydia); 17.34 AT (Damaris; *om.* D05); 18.2 (Aquila), 7 (Titius AT / Justos D05), 24 (Apollos AT [ˢ]/Apollonius D05); 19.24 AT (Demetrios [ˢ]; *om.* ὀνόματι D05); 20.9 (Eutychus); 21.10 (Agabus); 27.1 (Julius; D05 lac.); 28.7 (Publius; D05 lac.).

81. For a pseudonym or nickname Luke always uses the expression ᾧ/ἧ ὄνομα: Lk. 1.26 (Nazareth; *om.* D05), 27 (Joseph); 2.25 (Simeon); 8.41 (Jairus; D05 lac. [*cui nomen* d5, Dᴴ⁻ᴸ]); 24,13 AT (Emmaus; ὀνόματι Οὐλαμμαοῦς D05), 18 D05 (Cleopas; ὀνόματι AT); Acts 13.6 AT (Bar-Iesoua; ὀνόματι καλούμενον Βαριησουᾶ D05).

82. a. καλέω:

i. followed by a given or customary name: Lk. 1.32 (Son of the Most High), 35 (Son of God), 60 (John), 76 (Prophet of the Most High); 2.4 (Bethlehem), 23 (holy to the Lord), 39 D05 (Nazorene; *om.* AT); 6.13 (apostles), 46 (Lord, Lord); 15.19 (your son), 21 (your son); 20.4 (Lord); 22.25 (benefactors); Acts 1.19 (Akeldamach); 14.12 (Zeus);

ii. followed by τὸ ὄνομα / (ἐπὶ) τῷ ὀνόματι and a given name: Lk. 1.13 (John), 31 (Jesus), 59 (Zechariah), 61 ([John]); 2.21 (Jesus);

iii. the passive participle καλούμενος followed by a given name: Lk. 1.36 (the barren one); 6.15 AT (Zealot); 7.11 (Nain; *om.* ℵ*); 8.2 (Magdalene); 9.10 (Bethsaida; τὴν λεγομένην D05); 10.39 (Maria; Μαριάμ ℵ); 19.2 AT (Zacchaeus; *om.* D05), 29 (Olivet; ˢD05); 21.37 (Olivet); 22.3 (Iscariot), 47 D05 (Judas; ὁ λεγόμενος AT); 23.33 (the Skull); Acts 1.12 (Olivet), 23 (Barsabbas AT / Barnabas D05); 3.11 (Solomon's); 7.58 (Saul); 8.10 (Great); 9.11 (Straight; D05 lac.); 10.1 (the Italian [Cohort] D05 lac.); 13.1 (Niger; ὁ ἐπικαλούμενος D05), 6 D05 (Bar-Iesoua; *om.* AT); 15.22 (Barsabbas AT / Barabbas D05), 37 AT (Mark; τὸν ἐπικαλούμενον D05); 27.8 (Fair Havens; D05 lac.), 14 (the North-Easter; D05 lac.), 16 (Cauda; D05 lac.); 28.1 (Malta; D05 lac.);

iv. the force of καλέω to indicate a customary or given name can be seen with the name of places: Bethsaida, Olivet, the Skull (Golgotha), Fair Havens, the North-Easter, Cauda and Malta.

b. ἐπικαλέω (not in the sense of 'invoke', 'appeal to') is reserved for special cases to indicate the function of a person: Lk. 6.15 D05, τὸν ἐπικαλούμενον (the Twin; *om.* AT [ὁ λεγόμενος Δίδυμος: Jn. 11.16; 20.24; 21.2]); Acts 1.23, ὃς ἐπεκλήθη (Justus); 4.36, ὁ ἐπικληθείς (Barnabas); 10.5, ὃς ἐπικαλεῖται (Peter; D05 lac.); 10.18, ὁ ἐπικαλούμενος (Peter); 10.32, ὃς ἐπικαλεῖται (Peter); 11.13, τὸν ἐπικαλούμενον (Peter); 12.12, τοῦ ἐπικαλουμένου (Mark); 12.25, τὸν ἐπικληθέντα (Mark; τὸν ἐπικαλούμενον ℵ01); 13.1 D05, ὁ ἐπικαλούμενος (Niger; ὁ καλούμενος AT); 15.37 D05, τὸν ἐπικαλούμενον (Mark; τὸν καλούμενον AT).

3. That is not to say that Saul was a totally fictitious name with no connection with the name given to him by his parents. It was customary for Jewish children in the Diaspora to be given a Jewish name, Σαῦλος being the Greek form of the Aramaic שָׁאוּל;[83] but at the same time, a Greek name could be given, a practice that was known also in non-Jewish families in the Greek and Roman Empires.[84] It would seem, however, from Paul's own practice (see §1) that he referred to himself as Paul and that this was the name by which he was usually called. By saying at 7.58 that he was called by his Jewish name of Saul, Luke is alluding to his total identification with his Jewish heritage and his dedication to defending the purity of his ancestral religion. Everyone, including Jesus (9.4) and the Holy Spirit (13.2), referred to him in that way, until after 13.9 (cf. 27.24, where Jesus addresses him as Paul), as if in recognition of his zeal.

4. The name of Saul presents Paul as a person profoundly in tune with his Jewish identity, as representative as Saul the biblical king of Israel. The rhyming word-play has the effect, of which Luke takes advantage, of showing how this person moves from being thoroughly in line with the Jewish view of the exclusive rights of Israel to being the one to defend the cause of the Gentiles.

5. The moment at which Luke brings in the change of name is important. The name Saul is used from his first entry into the narrative at 7.58, in the section where he is seen persecuting the Church (8.3; 9.1), and when he is addressed by Jesus, as his persecutor (9.4; cf. 22.7; 26.14). He continues to be referred to as Saul after his encounter with Jesus (9.8, 11), even after his baptism (9.18) and his acknowledgement of Jesus as the son of God (9.20; cf. 11.25). It is not, in other words, his initial experience of Jesus that transforms him into the champion of the Gentiles for even the Holy Spirit refers to him as Saul when he is chosen along with Barnabas to go to the Gentiles' countries (13.2) – even though Barnabas, in contrast, is referred to by his new name (cf. 1.23 D05; 4.36). The turning point is later, when he confronts his tempter in the form of Bar-Iesoua, confronting and challenging his attempts to proclaim a false teaching concerning the Gentiles (13.9-11).

6. The way the two names are presented at 13.9 is striking: Saul, who was also Paul...', or 'who was, in fact, Paul...' (Σαῦλος δὲ ὁ καὶ Παῦλος...). The simple transfer from one name to the other signals the moment at which Paul, filled with the Holy Spirit (the only time this is ever said of Paul), decides to take on the reality of his Greek name and to accept his oneness with people outside Judaism.

c. The verb ὀνομάζω is used at Lk. 2.21 D05, ὠνομάσθη τὸ ὄνομα αὐτοῦ (Jesus; ἐκλήθη τ. ὄν. αὐτοῦ AT); 6.13 AT, ὠνόμασεν (apostles; ἐκάλεσεν D05); 6.14 AT, ὠνόμασεν (Peter; ἐπωνόμασεν D05).

d. The verb ἐπονομάζω is used at Lk. 6.14a D05, ἐπωνόμασεν (Peter; ὠνόμασεν AT); 6.14b D05, ἐπωνόμασεν (Boanerges; om. AT).

83. The unsavoury meaning of the adjective σαῦλος in Greek, 'effeminate', has caused some to question whether parents would have given the name to a male child in the Greek-speaking Diaspora (T.J. Leary, 'Paul's Improper Name', *NTS* 38 [1992], pp. 467–69), suggesting that he himself adopted it once in Jerusalem where the unwanted connotations would not be recognized (Chilton, *Rabbi Paul*, p. 29). The difficulty with that suggestion is that Paul himself never refers to it, except indirectly at Rom. 11.1-2 (see §1). It can be imagined, however, that the name was originally given to him by his parents in honour of the king of Israel, but that it was not used if, indeed, it would have brought ridicule on the boy in his home town.

84. Cf. M. Lambertz, 'Zur Ausbreitung des Supernomen oder Signum im römischen Reiche', I, *Glotta* 4 (1912), pp. 78–143; II, *Glotta* 5 (1913), pp. 99–170 (esp. 79).

7. The similarity between the usual name of Paul and that of Sergius Paulus, the proconsul of Cyrpus who had invited him to talk with him, is no mere coincidence (or, at least, Luke does not allow it to be so, since it is precisely during this scene that he introduces the name change). Nor, on the other hand, can it be concluded that the similarity confers on Paul a status equivalent to that of the proconsul, as the leader of the world-wide mission.[85] The change of name happens under the influence of the Holy Spirit, whereas Paul's domination of the mission from this point onwards is by no means what the Spirit intended when the Antioch church were instructed to 'set aside Barnabas and Saul', in that order and closely united as a harmonious pair.[86]

To attribute to Luke the conscious act of playing on the two names of Saul and Paul is to recognize that he does exactly this with other characters. Indeed, the procedure of conferring a name on a person to represent his character is seen elsewhere in his work: Simon becomes Peter (πέτρος, hard-headed) as a warning given to him by Jesus of the resistance he would put up against accepting his teaching (Lk. 6.14; cf. Mt. 16.18.);[87] just as Joseph becomes Barnabas (Acts 1.23 D05; cf. 4.36); and John becomes Mark (12.12, 25; 15.37, 39). In the case of these characters, however, it is the new name that expresses something about the quality of their character, whereas in the case of Paul it is his original name. It should be remembered that in the ancient world, and in the Jewish world in particular, names were not simply arbitrary labels of convenience by which to refer to a person but were invested with power and profound significance. Luke could not fail to be aware of this and make full use of the meaning of names in writing to Theophilus who, as a Jewish High Priest (see *General Introduction* §IV), would have fully appreciated the message Luke was communicating in this way.

Excursus 3

Was Paul a Hellenistic Jew?

There is some debate over the origins of Paul and whether he should be viewed as a Hellenist or not.[88] On the one hand, he himself states he is from Tarsus in Cilicia, making him a Diaspora Jew whose first language was Greek (Acts 21.39; 22.3a; 23.34; cf. 9.11); on the other, he insists on his upbringing in Jerusalem (22.3b; 26.4-5) and even declares himself to be 'a Hebrew born of Hebrew parents' (Phil. 3.5; cf. Acts 22.6), which sounds as if he were wanting to insist on the purity of his origins, uncontaminated by foreign

---

85. Cf. Leary, 'Paul's Improper Name', p. 468, n. 4.

86. The single article that prefaces the two names in Greek presents them as a united team, under the leadership of Barnabas (see *Commentary*, 13.2). This is how the church in Antioch, and in Ierousalem, continued to view them (cf. 15.12, 25, and see *Commentary, ad loc.*).

87. The meaning of the name of Peter, and its significance as a name given to him by Jesus, is discussed in *The Message of Acts*, II, pp. 248, 253, 366.

88. See *The Message of Acts*, II, *Excursus* 1 for an investigation of the Hellenists in Acts.

influences (cf. Rom. 11.1; 2 Cor. 11.22). How can the two accounts be reconciled? Was Paul a Hellenistic Jew or was he a Jew from Israel?

In his defence to the people of Jerusalem for supposedly defiling the Temple, Paul presents a summary of who he is.[89] He begins by stating that he is a Jewish man, and that he was born in Tarsus of Cilicia (Acts 22.3a). But his next statement suggests that he moved to Jerusalem when he was young: 'I was brought up in this city' (22.3b). He goes on to claim that he was 'trained at the feet of Gamaliel in the exactness of the Law of our ancestors' (22.3d). Gamaliel was a moderate teacher in Jerusalem of the school of Hillel, one of the two opposing schools of Jewish teaching that had its origins in the first century BCE, the other being the school of Shammai which was characterized by its strictness.

This account, in which Paul explains to the Jewish people that he was born in Tarsus but was brought up and educated in Jerusalem, concords with the brief explanation he had given to the chiliarch in order to get permission to speak to the people, especially in the Bezan text, which makes it clear that Tarsus was the place of his birth (21.39):[90] ἐγὼ ἄνθρωπος μέν εἰμι ᾽Ιουδαῖος ἐν Ταρσῷ δὲ τῆς Κιλικίας γεγεννημένος.

In his letters, Paul never mentions his birthplace as being outside Israel, and it is in his own writings above all that he insists instead on his Hebrew 'pedigree' (see, e.g., Rom. 11.1-2). His self-portrait concords with the fact that Paul viewed himself first and foremost as a Jew from Israel and that this was important to him because it enhanced – so it seems from the way he keeps drawing attention to it – his purity as a Jew and the authenticity of his claims to know what the Torah really was about, as well as his reliability as an interpreter of Jesus' role for Jews. That by no means implies that in Acts Luke puts wrong information into Paul's mouth (twice, according to Codex Bezae). What happened, according to the Bezan text, was that the first occasion Paul

89. The wording of Acts 22.3 D05 causes Paul's self-portrait to read somewhat differently from that of the AT: ἐγώ εἰμι ᾽Ιουδαῖος ἀνήρ, ἐν Ταρσῷ τῆς Κιλικίας γεγεννημένος, ἀνατεθραμμένος δὲ ἐν τῇ πόλει ταύτῃ, παρὰ τοὺς πόδας Γαμαλιὴλ παιδευόμενος κατὰ ἀκρίβειαν τοῦ πατρῴου νόμου, ζηλωτὴς τοῦ θεοῦ καθώς ἐστε ὑμεῖς πάντες σήμερον.

The first clause places particular emphasis on the adjective ᾽Ιουδαῖος before the noun, using the word order that highlights the adjective (see Read-Heimerdinger, *The Bezan Text*, pp. 89–94); the second clause underlines his place of birth; the present participle παιδευόμενος refers to his education during his upbringing in Jerusalem, ἀνατεθραμμένος ἐν τῇ πόλει ταύτῃ ; ζηλωτὴς τοῦ θεου is the complement of ἐγώ εἰμι, a present reality as Paul is speaking, rather than associated with his past as the AT participle ὑπάρχων tends to suggest if it refers to the time contemporary with the perfect participles ἀνατεθραμμένος and πεπαιδευμένος. It is thus possible to see in the Bezan text that for Paul, being a zealot was separate from being trained by Gamaliel, which makes sense in view of Gamaliel's moderate views.

90. Most MSS read: ἐγὼ ἄνθρωπος μέν εἰμι ᾽Ιουδαῖος, Ταρσεὺς τῆς Κιλικίας, οὐκ ἀσήμου πόλεως πολίτης, suggesting that his connections with Tarsus went beyond being born there and insisting on Tarsus as a place of worth, as if that were necessary to persuade the chiliarch of his credentials. The Bezan text assumes that being born in a city of a Roman province is sufficient to obtain the right to speak.

chose to say he was born in Tarsus (Acts 21.39 D05) arose only because it helped his cause to play on the fact that he was from a Roman province (cf. his claim to be a Roman citizen, 16.37; 23.28). When he repeated the information moments later in addressing the Jewish crowd, he was more or less obliged to do so for the sake of the chiliarch listening on, since the latter had just allowed Paul to speak on the grounds of his birthplace. But he quickly went on to situate the rest of his life firmly in Jerusalem, as he will later when defending himself before Agrippa II whom he carefully addresses as a Jew (26.1-23).

There remains the description of Saul that Jesus is reported to have given Ananias so that he could identify him when he went to look for him in Damascus: 'Look in the house of Judah for the man called Saul, from Tarsus' (9.11). It would seem, if this wording is authentic (the pages of Codex Bezae are missing for the whole incident of Saul's encounter with Jesus in Damascus and therefore its text cannot be appealed to), that in Damascus, and therefore probably elsewhere, Saul was identified by his place of birth, which certainly suggests that it was something more than a long-forgotten place of origin that had no more relevance once he moved to Jerusalem. Given the extensive and detailed knowledge Paul had of the Jewish mentality and practices in the Diaspora, it is probable that even if he did spend his childhood and years of education in Jerusalem he maintained contact with people in Tarsus (it was to there that he was sent when there were problems with the Hellenists in Jerusalem, 9.30).[91]

To go back to Paul's speech to the Jews in Jerusalem when he was first arrested, a further piece of information needs to be clarified, for he concludes his 'identity card', so to speak, by saying that he is 'a zealot for God' (22.3e), a term that sits uneasily with the name of Gamaliel but, in contrast, corresponds to the attitudes of the Shammaites who made up the greater part of the Pharisee party and who were aggressively active in their fervent pursuit of the purity of Israel.

It has been proposed, in line with Paul's claim to be 'a zealot for God' (cf. Gal. 1.13-14; Phil. 3.6), to see Paul not just as a particularly enthusiastic Jew but as a 'zealot' in the technical sense of the term. Just who the Zealots were, what kind of a group they formed and how they evolved during the years leading up to the Jewish revolt is not at all clear from the historical evidence available. Josephus refers to Zealots as apparently belonging to an organized group of revolutionaries and, while some scholars limit the application of the name specifically to the Jewish rebels in the final stage of the defence of Jerusalem against Rome,[92] others associate the title more widely with the division

---

91. Against the evidence for Tarsus as the birthplace of Saul may be adduced the evidence of Jerome (who almost certainly obtained it from Origen) that he was born 'in Gischala in Judaea' (in northern Galilee to be precise; *In Ep. ad Philem.* 23; cf. *De viris illustribus* 5).

92. Schürer, *The History of the Jewish People*, II, pp. 598–606.

of the Pharisees who were disciples of Shammai,[93] and who may, or may not, have been those Josephus meant by his reference to the 'fourth sect of philosophy'.[94] On this understanding, Saul, who presents himself as a Pharisee, son of Pharisees (*sic,* Acts 23.6), would have been a disciple of Shammai before he became a disciple of Jesus. The focus of the teachings of the Shammaites was the call to preserve Israel as a people faithfully upholding the Law, free from the domination and the contamination of the Gentiles, and ready for Israel's restoration in the end-times. When necessary, violence and killing were used as a means to achieve this end as part of their wide-scale revolutionary activity, against corrupting forces among the Jews as much as against opposing powers of the Gentiles, with goals that were at the same time religious and political.

Such a context would account for Saul's zeal in persecuting Jews who in any way compromised the ancient traditions of Israel (cf. Gal. 1.14), for example by speaking against the Torah or the Temple as Stephen and other Jesus-believers appeared to do. The aim was not just to defend Israel against foreign influences but to hasten the arrival of the kingdom of God by purifying the people in readiness for its arrival. This sense of human responsibility for enabling God to carry out his purposes was not something that disappeared from Saul's thinking as soon as he became a disciple of Jesus. It continued to be evident (more so in Codex Bezae than in the AT) in his urgent insistence, as Paul the disciple and apostle to the Gentiles, on taking the gifts of the Gentiles to Jerusalem in order to fulfil the scriptural prophecies concerning the end-times (cf. Rom. 15.16, 25-27, 31).[95] It also makes sense of his repeated obstinacy in preaching in the synagogues in practically each town he went to before he went to the Gentiles, and announcing a message of national salvation of Israel.[96]

Paul was more at ease in a Hellenistic culture than might be expected from someone who had been closeted throughout his life in the Jewish religious life of the Temple and Jerusalem. Some of his speeches in Acts, like his own writings, display apparent familiarity with Greek philosophers and literature, in their themes, their thought, their literary structure and their language (cf.

---

93. J. Taylor, 'Why did Paul Persecute the Church?', in G.N. Stanton and G.G. Strousma (eds), *Tolerance and Intolerance in Early Judaism and Christianity* (Cambridge: Cambridge University Press, 1998), pp. 99–120; cf. N.T. Wright, *What Saint Paul Really Said: Was Paul of Tarsus the Real Founder of Christianity?* (Oxford: Lion, 1997), pp. 25–38.

94. Josephus, *War* II, 117–19; *Ant.* XVIII, 1-25.

95. See B. Chilton, 'Aramaic and Targumic Antecedents of Pauline Justification', in D.R.G. Beattie and M.J. McNamara (eds), *The Aramaic Bible: Targums in their Historical Context* (JSOTSup, 166; Sheffield: Sheffield Academic Press, 1994), pp. 379–97.

96. On Luke's portrait of Paul as mistakenly continuing to view Israel as a privileged nation and the Jews as the Chosen People of God, see Rius-Camps, 'Gradual Awakening', pp. 281–96. Cf. Taylor, 'Why Did Paul Persecute the Church?', pp. 109–110, who would class Paul as a 'Jewish religious nationalist' not only before, but also in the early years following, his conversion.

Acts 17.17-31).[97] And yet it will not do to draw sharp distinctions between the Jewish and the Hellenistic worlds in the first century, when there was so much in the way of general culture and world view, family life and social customs and expectations, that was shared by people all over the Mediterranean area.[98] Moreover, Paul was speaking and writing for much of the time in Greek and it would be a normal phenomenon for secular Greek literature to give a certain shape to his expression. Jerusalem itself was a cosmopolitan city and with his roots in Tarsus, and very possibly members of his family still there (cf. 23.16-22), he would have been particularly sensitive to anything he observed that related to Jewish life in the Diaspora.

What is clear is that Paul moved around the different places and countries he visited outside Israel with ease, both during his travels and within the communities he stayed with, at least so far as the Jewish communities were concerned. What makes it especially likely that he had strong personal contact with Diaspora Judaism is his attitude towards Jesus-believers among the Hellenists. It may be noted that those who were most liable and most apt to clamp down on deviations from the restrictions imposed by the authorities of Judaism in Jerusalem were the Hellenists themselves.[99] Paul understands this mentality only too well (see Gal. 6.12-16). His zeal and violence in perse-cuting the Hellenistic Jesus-believers in Jerusalem, in the synagogues in Damascus and elsewhere are illustrative, on the one hand, of a profound concern to maintain the highest levels of purity among the Hellenist Jews because of his own association with them, and on the other, of an identifica-tion with the fanatical movements in Israel to prepare the land and the people for the restoration of the end-times.

Excursus 4

The Paradigm of Jeremiah 5–6

In the first group of oracles that Jeremiah is asked to preach against Judah, there appears a series of motifs that Luke uses in the scene set in Paphos. The key term that alerts the reader of Acts to the scriptural paradigim is ψευδο-προφήτης.[100] There is a parallel of a more general nature between Paul and Jeremiah that will only become clear later in the narrative but that justifies seeing the Jeremiah prophecies as the basis for the Paphos narrative: they are

97. See M. E. Thrall, 'Paul of Tarsus: a Hellenistic Jew', in R. Pope (ed.), *Honouring the Past and Shaping the Future: Religious and Biblical Studies in Wales* (Leominster: Gracewing, 2003), pp. 97–111, for a summary and discussion of the evidence.

98. A useful study is M. Hengel, *The 'Hellenization' of Judaea in the First Century after Christ* (London: SCM, 1989).

99. See *The Message of Acts*, II, *Excursus* 1, pp. 27–31.

100. Occurrences of ψευδοπροφήτης in the LXX are found almost wholly in the book of Jeremiah; see Strelan, 'Who Was Bar Jesus?', pp. 69–70.

both called to speak on God's behalf to the nations (cf. Jer. 1.5, 7-8, 10, 19 with Acts 9.15; 18.9-10; 26.17).

The similarity between Acts 13.6-12 and the oracles of Jeremiah 5–6 turns on the role played by Bar-Iesoua, the Jewish false prophet and magician, with respect to Paul, and that played by the people of Israel in the time of Jeremiah. They are set out in the table below following the order of the Acts narrative:

A journey: through (or around D05) the whole of the island of Cyprus: Διελθόντες δὲ (B03) / Καὶ περιελθόντων δὲ αὐτῶν (D05) ὅλην τὴν νῆσον (Acts 13.6) // through the streets and squares of Jerusalem: Περιδράμετε ἐν ταῖς ὁδοῖς Ἰερουσαλὴμ καὶ ... ζητήσατε ἐν ταῖς πλατείαις αὐτῆς (Jer. 5.1).

A search: for a community of faithful Jesus-believers which led only to Bar-Iesoua: εὗρον ἄνδρα τινὰ μάγον (Acts 13.6) // for one person who acts justly who, if found, will cause God to pardon Jerusalem: ἐὰν εὕρητε ἄνδρα, εἰ ἔστιν ποιῶν κρίμα καὶ ζητῶν πίστιν (Jer. 5.1).

False prophet(s): one is found in Paphos by Barnabas and Saul: εὗρον ... ψευδο-προφήτην Ἰουδαῖον (Acts 13.6) // many are present in Jerusalem: οἱ προ-φῆται προφητεύουσιν ἄδικα (Jer. 5.31, cf. 2.8; 6.13); the Jews have spoken falsely of the Lord: ἐψεύσαντο τῷ κυρίῳ ἑαυτῶν (5.12).

The word of God: is listened to eagerly by Sergius Paulos, the representative of the nations: καὶ ἐζήτησεν ἀκοῦσαι τὸν λόγον τοῦ θεοῦ ... ἐπεὶ ἥδιστα ἤκουεν αὐτῶν (Acts 13.7, 8 D05) // is not heeded by the Israelites and so the nations hear it instead: καὶ εἶπαν· Οὐκ ἀκουσόμεθα, διὰ τοῦτο ἤκουσαν τὰ ἔθνη (Jer. 6.17-18).

Opposition to God: by Bar-Iesoua who attempts to turn the proconsul away from the faith: ἀνθίστατο αὐτοῖς ... ζητῶν διαστρέψαι τὸν ἀνθύπατον ἀπὸ τῆς πίστεως (Acts 13.8) // the Israelites, instead of seeking truth: εἰ ἔστιν ... ζητῶν πίστιν (Jer. 5.1) have turned aside from God and gone away and have refused to turn back: ἐστερέωσαν τὰ πρόσωπα αὐτῶν ἐπὶ πέτραν καὶ οὐκ ἠθέλησαν ἐπιστραφῆναι (5.3); it is their iniquities that have turned away good things: καὶ αἱ ἁμαρτίαι ὑμῶν ἀπέστησαν τὰ ἀγαθὰ ἀφ᾽ ὑμῶν (5.25).

Full of deceit: Paul rebukes Bar-Iesoua for being full of all deceit and fraud, the son of the devil: Ὦ πλήρης παντὸς δόλου καὶ πάσης ῥαδιουργίας, υἱὲ διαβόλου (Acts 13.10) // Jeremiah rebukes Jerusalem for being a false city, all oppression in it: Ὦ πόλις ψευδής, ὅλη καταδυναστεία ἐν αὐτῇ (Jer. 6.6), where the houses are full of deceit: οἱ οἶκοι αὐτῶν πλήρεις δόλου (5.27).

Justice: Bar-Iesoua is the enemy of all righteousness: ἐχθρὲ πάσης δικαιοσύνης (Acts 13.10) // neither the poor nor the wealthy in Jerusalem know the way or judgement of God: οὐκ ἔγνωσαν ὁδὸν κυρίου καὶ κρίσιν θεοῦ (Jer. 5.5).

The ways of the Lord: Paul asks rhetorically when Bar-Iesoua will stop making crooked the Lord's ways which are straight: οὐ παύσῃ διαστρέφων τὰς ὁδοὺς κυρίου τὰς εὐθείας (Acts 13.10) // Jeremiah invites the people to walk in the good way but they refuse: ἴδετε, ποία ἐστὶν ἡ ὁδὸς ἡ ἀγαθή, καὶ βαδίζετε ἐν αὐτῇ ... καὶ εἶπαν· Οὐ πορευσόμεθα (Jer. 6.16; cf. 3.21, they have gone a crooked way, ἠδίκησαν ἐν ταῖς ὁδοῖς αὐτῶν).

The hand of the Lord: Paul warns Bar-Iesoua that the hand of the Lord is about to strike him: καὶ νῦν ἰδοὺ ἡ χεὶρ κυρίου ἐπὶ σέ (Acts 13.11) // the Lord will stretch out his hand against all his people, from the smallest to the greatest: ὅτι ἐκτενῶ τὴν χεῖρά μου ἐπὶ τοὺς κατοικοῦντας τὴν γῆν ταύτην (Jer. 6.12, cf. 6.19, 21).

> *Blindness*: Paul announces to Bar-Iesoua that he will be blind, unable to see the sun: ἔση τυφλὸς μὴ βλέπων τὸν ἥλιον (Acts 13.11) // the people of Israel have eyes but do not see: λαὸς μωρὸς καὶ ἀκάρδιος, ὀφθαλμοὶ αὐτοῖς καὶ οὐ βλέπουσιν (Jer. 5.21).
>
> *For a time*: the blindness that will afflict Bar-Iesoua will only be for a time: ἕως/ἄχρι καιροῦ (Acts 13.11) // the destruction of Israel by the nations will not be total: οὐ μὴ ποιήσω ὑμᾶς εἰς συντέλειαν (Jer. 5.10, 18).
>
> *Immediate*: Bar-Iesoua is affected without any delay: παραχρῆμά τε/καὶ εὐθέως ἔπεσεν ἐπ᾽ αὐτὸν ἀχλὺς καὶ σκότος (Acts 13.11) // the destruction of Israel is imminent: ἐξαίφνης ἥξει ταλαιπωρία ἐφ᾽ ὑμᾶς (Jer. 6.26).

The parallels between the Jews of Israel and Judah in the prophecies of Jeremiah, on the one hand, and Bar-Iesoua as a representative of the Jesus-believing Jews in Paphos, on the other, are direct. There are other parallels between the Gentiles or the nations as the instruments of destruction in Jeremiah's prophecies, and Sergius Paulos as a model of a Gentile who accepts God's word despite the attempts to dissuade him by a Jewish believer. The roles are therefore contrasting: the nations who will attack Jerusalem are not spoken of favourably whereas the comments about the proconsul are all positive. Indeed, his intelligence (Acts 13.7) marks him out as quite the opposite of the people of Israel who 'are not intelligent' (Jer. 5.21, cf. 4.22).

An interesting parallel is found in the opening chapters of the book of Jeremiah when Israel is invited to cross over to Cyprus ('Kittim') and see that there the nations are more faithful to their (non-) gods than Israel to YHWH (Jer. 2.10). This is precisely the result of the belief that the proconsul embraces as a result of what he witnesses and hears: his faith contrasts with the opposition of the Jewish magician.

The essence of Bar-Iesoua's opposition to the message of Jesus can be presumed to be his insistence on the need for Gentiles to observe the Jewish Law, or on the privileged position of Israel with regard to the nations. Either way, he (and the community he represents) has set up obstacles to the entry of the Gentiles into the people of God. Far from preparing the way and making it smooth, the Jewish Jesus-believers have distorted the truth and been opponents of God's justice.

It is worth noting that Jeremiah was a key witness to the last years of the kingdom of Judah, being entrusted with terrible prophecies of destruction against his own people (Jeremiah 1–6); these, however, are counter-balanced by the firm hope of a future restoration of Jerusalem and the Temple (Jeremiah 32–33). In Acts, there is no such promise – the idea of the end of Israel with no hope of future restoration already underlies Acts 12, where the prophecies of Ezekiel concerning first the exile of Jerusalem and then the last times are re-enacted: Herod the Jewish king who attacks the faithful Jewish believers in Jesus is destroyed as if he were the prince of Tyre, the archenemy of Israel; and the Lord is seen as leading his people, represented by Peter, out of the eschatological Temple in a reversal of Ezekiel's prophecy of a restored Israel, whereupon Peter goes 'to another place' in a symbolic gesture that is a sign of exile from Jerusalem identical to that carried out by Ezekiel (Ezek. 12.13).[101] It is therefore no surprise, rather it is in the same line, that Paul is presented in the following chapter of Acts (ch. 13) as re-enacting the prophecies of Jeremiah that show up the falsehood and pretensions of those Jews who oppose God's plan, even while believing in Jesus.

[C] 13.13 *Pamphylia: Perga*

Overview

The third sequence of Section I is brief and succinct in the extreme, being made up of only two sentences. Yet it stands apart from both the preceding and the following sequences since, first, it involves a change of location from Cyprus to Perga back on the mainland, while being also distinct from Antioch of Pisidia to where the narrative moves on in the next sequence. It could have been viewed as an introduction to the four-part sequence in Antioch [D], serving merely as a transition between two important locations, were it not for the crucial piece of information contained in the second element, *viz*: that John (Mark) separated from the group and went back to Hierosoluma. The importance of this information is a second reason for not attaching the sequence to either the one before or after it. As often in the book of Acts, Luke conveys information of the greatest importance in this way.[102] Here, the character of John stands in implicit contrast with Paul: his separating from him is an act not of defiance or weakness for coping with the rigours of the mission but rather arises from a deep theological disagreement over the direction the mission was taking, in which Luke takes the side of John as will become clear in Acts 15.37-39 when the split is reinforced (see *Commentary, ad loc.*).

Structure and Themes

There are just two sentences in the sequence, which form two separate elements, the second corresponding to the first as a comment on it:

    [a] 13.13a   Arrival in Perga of Pamphylia
    [a'] 13.13b   The departure of John

In terms of participants, these are now defined in relation to Paul, though they include Barnabas without his name being mentioned. The narrative of the missionary journey moves on to a different location as Cyprus is left behind and the mainland lying opposite the north coast of Cyprus is reached.

---

101. On the use of Ezekiel in Acts, see *The Message of Acts*, II, Excursus 8, pp. 381–83; and on the assimilation of Herod with the Prince of Tyre, see *Excursus* 9, pp. 383–86.

102. Comparison may be made with the initial presentation of Barnabas in either the D05 text (1.23) or the AT (4.36); or the third Section (III) of the second part of Acts describing the public manifestation of the church in Antioch to Jerusalem (see *The Message of Acts*, II, pp. 321–30, esp. 321).

Translation

Codex Bezae D05

[a]   **13.13a** Setting sail from Paphos, Paul and his circle came to Perga of Pamphylia.

[a']   **13b** John, however, having separated from them, returned to Hierosoluma.

Codex Vaticanus B03

13.13a Setting sail from Paphos, Paul and his circle came to Perga of Pamphylia.

13b John, however, having separated from them, returned to Hierosoluma.

Critical Apparatus

13.13 Ἰωάνης B D ‖ -νν- $\mathfrak{P}^{45.74}$ ℵ *rell.*

The only difference in this verse is the spelling of John (Mark), where both B03 and D05 agree in having the single ν. The single consonant in the name of John-Mark is also found at 12.12 B03 D05, 25 D05*; 13.5 E08 (-νν- B03 D05); 15.37 D05; cf. the single ν in the name of John, the brother of James: 1.13 D05; 12.2 D05.

Commentary

[a] 13.13a *Arrival in Perga of Pamphylia*

13.13a The narrative develops by moving the action away from Paphos, and indeed from Cyprus, with a journey by boat. At the same time, a significant change is made in the description of the participants, for they are presented as 'those around Paul'.[103] This is a clear indication that Paul has now taken on the role of leader in contrast to the directions of the Holy Spirit (cf. 13.2) as well as the earlier narrator's reference to the pair where Barnabas is the first-named (13.7); there is nothing to suggest that Barnabas is happy to take a sub-ordinate role, this interpretation being based on a reading of Acts that assumes all references to Paul to be positive.[104] In fact, not only is Paul regarded as the leader but it seems that a group of followers has gathered around him, since 'the ones around Paul' indicates a larger group than simply Barnabas and John.

Travelling by sea from Cyprus to Pamphylia in Asia Minor, the group would probably have come to land at Attalia (cf. 14.25), a port on the south coast of the area, although it was not impossible to have landed nearer to

---

103. The expression οἱ περὶ Παῦλον is 'a classical Greek idiom' (Bruce, *Text*, p. 259) which describes those who were attached to a teacher or philosopher and included the leader himself (cf. Bailly, περί, *Acc.* A, II: οἱ περί τινα). Mark, according to the AT (but never D05), uses it to describe the non-Jews who went around with Jesus (Mk 4.10 B03, cf. 3.32 B03, 34 B03; see J. Mateos, *Los "Doce" y otros seguidores de Jesús en el Evangelio de Marcos* [Madrid: Cristiandad, 1982], pp. 107–17); Luke also uses it to refer to those disciples who sought to defend Jesus at the time of his betrayal (Lk. 22.49). Cf. οἱ περὶ Πέτρον, Mk 16.1; Ignatius, *Smyrn.* 3.2.

104. Cf., e.g., Bruce, *Text*, p. 259, 'Barnabas is content with second place, a further light on his character'.

Perga itself since it lay close to the navigable river Kestros some six miles inland.[105] Pamphylia was the name of the province lying directly to the west of Cilicia. They did not stop there from what the narrative says at this point, and certainly the account of their return journey through the area on their way back to Antioch suggests that their preaching in Pamphylia on that occasion was for the first time (see *Commentary*, 14.25-26).

[a'] 13.13b *The Departure of John*

13.13b In Luke's writing, the way he refers to characters is a device he uses to convey precise information about them, varying the name or its form according to what he wishes to communicate. This was noted at 13.9, for example, with reference to Paul. In the case of John, on the first two occasions Luke mentioned him, he presented him with the given name of 'Mark': at 12.12 'John, called (καλούμενον) Mark'; 12.25 'John, who had been called (ἐπικλη-θέντα) Mark', where the name 'Mark' refers to his activity as author of an earlier Gospel on which Luke constantly draws.[106] The Greek present participle at the first mention at 12.12 is an indication of his activity at that time when the church was gathered in his mother's house to pray for Peter in prison; the aorist of 12.25 signals, in contrast, that he was not exercising his role when he left Ierousalem with Barnabas and Saul. The third reference to John at 13.6 contained no mention of Mark, as if his role as evangelist was silenced at that point because he was unable to express the truth he had well understood about the universal nature of Jesus' message while Saul/Paul was insisting on regarding the 'synagogues of the Jews' as the primary places to announce the gospel (see *Commentary*, 13.5-6). Now, as John is mentioned for a fourth time, the name Mark is once more omitted, again signifying that he is unable to proclaim the gospel he knew.

As Paul had taken over as the leader by this stage, it would be his ideas and theology that dominated and determined the action in spreading the gospel. So while Barnabas, as was seen in earlier chapters,[107] had the openness of a Hellenist (coming as he did from Cyprus) to the universal message of the gospel, Paul's understanding was in some ways more exclusivist, holding on to the privileged position of Israel within the people of God. It is small wonder, then, that John left Paul and the group that was growing around him, distancing himself[108] from the insistence on taking the gospel to the Jews first.

---

105. See D.A. Campbell, 'Paul in Pamphylia (Acts 13.13-14a; 14.24b-26): A Critical Note', *NTS* 46 (2000), pp. 595–602; but cf. Chilton, *Rabbi Paul*, pp. 118, 279, who prefers to see Attalia as the port of disembarkation.

106. For discussion of these earlier references to John-Mark and his identity as the author of the third Gospel, see *The Message of Acts*, II, pp. 360, 388, 390.

107. Commentary is made on the role of Barnabas and his openness to the Gentiles as an early follower of Jesus in *The Message of Acts*, I. pp. 129–31 (1.23 D05); 298–300 (4.36); II, pp. 196–97 (9.26); 311–14 (11.22-24); 389–91 (12.25).

108. The expression ἀποχωρήσας ἀπ' αὐτῶν is a harsh term that signifies a moving from someone, literally as well as ideologically; however, despite Paul's insinuation at 15.38, there is

He went back home to Hierosoluma, the form of the name Luke gives to the city itself, consonant with John's open-minded views, for he uses this Greek spelling (Ἱεροσόλυμα) to signify the city as a neutral location, as opposed to the Hebrew-derived name Ierousalem (Ἱερουσαλήμ) that denotes the religious and exclusivist centre of Judaism (see *General Introduction*, §VII).

[D] 13.14-52 *Pisidia: Antioch*

General Overview

The sequence that takes place in Antioch of Pisidia is the central one in this section of Acts relating the first phase of Paul's missionary activity. As such, it has a key role to play in the progress of the mission, and in the development of Paul's strategy. John-Mark having left them, Paul and Barnabas go for the first time into a region that has not been mentioned previously with regard to the spread of the gospel, but where their point of contact remains the synagogue. From Antioch, they will leave the region of Pisidia and go to Iconium in the neighbouring area of Phrygia (Sequence [C']).

Structure and Themes

In the synagogue in Antioch, Paul, who had become the leader of the mission (cf. 13.13), will pronounce the first of his speeches recorded by Luke. It is important to note that Luke composes the speeches of his characters in accordance with their individual ways of speaking, and also with their thinking at that time (see *General Introduction*, §VI).

The aim of Paul's first speech is to demonstrate how God has continued his intervention in the history of Israel by raising up Jesus as the Saviour of his people, but also as the means of extending salvation for the first time ever to the Gentiles. A second speech is recorded, given a week later and this time in the name of both Paul and Barnabas, who make a programmatic declaration concerning the change in the status of the Gentiles. The deep hostility on the part of the Jews that their speech provokes forces Paul and Barnabas to leave the area.

The narrative in this sequence is organized around the two successive Sabbaths, creating two parallel sub-sequences each composed of two episodes:

[DA]	13.14-43	The Jews in Antioch
[DA-*A*]	13.14-41	In the synagogue
[DA-*B*]	13.42-43	Jewish response
[DA']	13.44-52	The Gentiles in Antioch
[DA'-*A*]	13.44-49	In the city
[DA'-*B*]	13.50-52	Synagogue response

no reason to interpret it as meaning that John 'deserted' in this instance (*contra* B-A-G, ἀποχω-ρέω).

The second sub-sequence [DA'] corresponds to the first [DA], in so far as both contain a major speech and both show the reaction to the speech, in two separate episodes, [A] and [B].

[DA] 13.14-43 *The Jews in Antioch*

Overview

This scene takes place in the synagogue of Antioch of Pisidia which Paul and his circle visit on their arrival there; it contains a number of parallels with Jesus' visit to the synagogue of Nazareth (Lk. 4.16-30; see *Excursus* 7). Paul takes up an invitation to speak, addressing his speech to the Jews who were present and also to the God-fearers, that is, Gentile members or adherents of the synagogue of whom a number had taken the step of becoming proselytes. In some respects, there are similarities with Stephen's speech (7.2-5, 33); and in others, especially towards the end, with the speeches of Peter, notably the one given in Cornelius' house in Caesarea (10.34-43). The speech shows a certain openness towards the Gentiles, and an understanding of the universal message of Jesus, though Paul in other ways is still thinking in terms of Jesus as the Messiah of Israel (see *Excursus* 5).

Structure and Themes
The sub-sequence is made up of two episodes: the first is largely taken up by Paul's speech in the synagogue of Antioch of Pisidia, and the second by the response to it and the results to which it led:

[DA-*A*]	13.14-41	In the synagogue
[a]	13.14	Arrival of Paul and Barnabas in the synagogue
[b]	13.15	Invitation to speak
[b']	13.16-41a	Paul's speech
[a']	13.41b	Silence
[DA-*B*]	13.42-43	Synagogue response
[a]	13.42	Renewed invitation
[b]	13.43a	Many follow Paul and Barnabas
[b']	13.43b	The spread of the word throughout the city

The narrator's observation that Paul's speech was met with silence is absent from the Alexandrian text. On the structure of the speech itself, see *Excursus* 5.

Translation

Codex Bezae D05

[Aa]   **13.14** Having travelled from Perga, they arrived in Antioch of Pisidia, and having entered into our synagogue on the Sabbath, they sat down.

[b]   **15** After the reading of the Law and the Prophets the synagogue rulers sent to

Codex Vaticanus B03

13.14 Having travelled from Perga, they arrived in Pisidian Antioch, and having gone into the synagogue on the day of the Sabbath, they sat down.

15 After the reading of the Law and the Prophets the synagogue rulers sent to them, saying, 'Men, brothers, if there is one of you who is a speaker or a wise person, or an exhorter, speak to the people'.

[b']
[α] **16** Paul, having stood up and made a sign with his hand, said, 'Men Israelites, and those fearing God, listen. **17** The God of this people, Israel, chose our fathers; for the sake of the people, he made them great during their stay in the land of Egypt and with his arm lifted high he led them out of it. **18** And for 40 years he cared for them in the desert **19** and, having destroyed seven nations in the land of Canaan, he gave as an inheritance the land of the foreigners; **20** and for 450 years he gave judges until Samuel the prophet. **21** Then they asked for a king and God gave them Saul son of Kish, a man from the tribe of Benjamin, for 40 years. **22** When he had removed him, he raised up David for them as a king to whom he said by way of witness, "I have found David the son of Jesse, a man after my own heart who will carry out all my wishes". **23** Accordingly, God, from his seed in conformity with the promise, raised up for Israel a saviour, Jesus, **24** John having previously proclaimed, in anticipation of his arrival, a baptism of repentance to all the people of Israel. **25** When John was accomplishing his task he said, "Whom do you suppose me to be? I am not the one, but look! there is coming after me one whose sandals I am not worthy to loosen from his feet".

[β] **26** Men brothers, descendants of the race of Abraham and those among us fearing God, to us the word of this salvation was sent out. **27** The reason for this is that the ones living in Ierousalem and her rulers, without understanding the writings of the Prophets that are read every Sabbath, and by their act of judging, they fulfilled them. **28** And even though they found no cause of death in him when they judged him, they handed him over to Pilate for execution. **29** As a way of bringing to an end everything that is written about him, they asked Pilate to crucify this man; then, having obtained their request a second time, they

them, saying, 'Men, brothers, if there is among you any word of exhortation for the people, speak'.

16 Paul, having stood up and made a sign with his hand, said, 'Men Israelites, and those fearing God, listen. **17** The God of the people of Israel chose our fathers, and he made the people great during their stay in the land of Egypt and with his arm lifted high he led them out of it. **18** And when for 40 years he endured them in the desert, **19** having destroyed seven nations in the land of Canaan, he gave their land as an inheritance, **20** [all in all] something like 450 years. And after these things, he gave judges until the Prophet Samuel. **21** Then they asked for a king and God gave to them Saul, son of Kish, a man from the tribe of Benjamin, for 40 years. **22** When he had removed him, he raised up David for them as a king to whom he said by way of witness, "I have found David the son of Jesse, someone after my own heart who will carry out all my wishes". **23** From this man's seed God, in conformity with the promise, produced for Israel a saviour, Jesus, **24** John having previously proclaimed, in anticipation of his arrival, a baptism of repentance to all the people of Israel. **25** When John was accomplishing his task he said, "What do you suppose me to be? I am not it, but look! there is coming after me one whose sandals I am not worthy to loosen from his feet".

26 Men brothers, descendants of the race of Abraham, those among you fearing God, to us the word of this salvation was sent out. **27** The reason for this is that the ones living in Ierousalem and their rulers, by not recognizing this man nor understanding the declarations of the Prophets, even though they are read on every Sabbath, in the act of judging him, they fulfilled them. **28** And although they found no cause of death, they asked Pilate to have him executed. **29** When they had brought to an end everything written about him, having taken him down from the tree they laid him in a tomb.

took him down from the tree and laid him in a tomb, **30** and God raised him. **31** This man appeared to the ones while they were going up with him from Galilee to Ierousalem over many days; these people right up to the present have been witnesses of him to the people. **32** And we ourselves announce to you the promise that was made to our fathers, that God has brought this to fulfilment for our children by resurrecting the Lord Jesus, the Messiah. **33** For this is what is written in the first Psalm,

"You are my son,
Today I have fathered you.
Ask of me
And I will give you nations
As your inheritance,
And as your possession
The ends of the earth."

34 When he resurrected him from the dead, no more to return to corruption, he had spoken thus,

"I will give to you
The sure blessings of David".

35 And elsewhere he says,

"I will not give your Holy One
To see corruption".

36 Now David, having served his own generation by the will of God, fell asleep and was added to his fathers and he saw corruption. **37** The one whom God raised up, however, did not see corruption.

[γ]   **38** Let it be known to you, men brothers, that through this man forgiveness of sins is announced and repentance from everything of which you could not be made righteous by the Law of Moses; **39** so everyone believing in this man is made righteous by him with God. **40** Watch out, therefore, that what has been said in the Prophets does not come to pass,

41a "See, those who scoff,
Marvel and vanish,
Because I do a deed in your days
That you will not even believe
If someone declares it to you".'

[a′]   **41b** And they kept silence.
[*B*a]   **42** As they were going out, people were urging that things like this be spoken to them on the next Sabbath.

30 God, however, raised him from the dead, **31** and he appeared for many days to the ones who had gone up with him from Galilee to Ierousalem; these people are witnesses of him to the people.

32 And we ourselves announce to you the promise made to the fathers, that God has brought this to fulfilment for our children by raising Jesus,

33 as indeed it is written in the second Psalm,

"You are my son,
Today I have fathered you".

34 Concerning the fact that he resurrected him from the dead, no more to return to corruption, he has spoken thus,

"I will give to you
The sure blessings of David".

35 And that is why he says in another Psalm,

"I will not give your Holy One
To see corruption".

36 Now as for David, having served his own generation by the will of God, he fell asleep and was added to his fathers and he saw corruption. **37** The one whom God raised up, however, did not see corruption. **38** Let it be known to you, men brothers, that because of this, forgiveness of sins is announced, even everything of which you could not be made righteous by the Law of Moses. **39** Everyone believing in this is justified. **40** Watch out, therefore, that what has been said in the Prophets does not come to pass,

41 "See, those who scoff,
Marvel and vanish,
Because I do a deed in your days,
A deed that you will not even believe
If someone were to declare it to you".'

42 As they were going out, people were asking that on the next Sabbath these things be spoken to them.

| [b] | 43a When the assembly had broken up, many of the Jews and the worshipping proselytes followed Paul and Barnabas as they carried on speaking to them and persuading them to continue in the grace of God. | 43a When the assembly had broken up, many of the Jews and the worshipping proselytes followed Paul and Barnabas who, as they carried on speaking to them, persuaded them to continue in the grace of God. |
| [b'] | 43b And it happened that the word of God went throughout the entire city. | |

Critical Apparatus

13.14 (᾽Αντιόχειαν) τὴν Πισιδίαν B 𝔓⁴⁵·⁷⁴ ℵ A C 453. 1175 *pc* ‖ τῆς Π-ίας D, *Pisidiae* d E H L P Ψ 049. 056. 0142. 33. 1739 𝔐 lat sy co; Chr.

Antioch was an important town, strictly speaking not in Pisidia but just inside the more north-westerly region of Phrygia and in the Roman province of Galatia. Since there was another Antioch well within Phrygia (there were some 16 of them altogether!), it seems that the one Paul visited was known as the Pisidian Antioch because of its proximity to that region; the adjective Πισιδίαν of B03 is not, however, attested elsewhere. Because in the time of Diocletian (295 CE) Antioch was assigned to Pisidia, it has been assumed that the D05 reading is evidence of this reorganization of the provinces (Witherington, *Acts,* pp. 404–405; Metzger, *Commentary,* 1st edn 1975 [but not 2nd edn 1996]). However, as noted by C.J. Hemer (*The Book of Acts in the Setting of Hellenistic History* (ed. C.H. Gempf; Tübingen: J.C.B. Mohr, 1989), p. 228, n. 24), 'Antioch was assigned to Pisidia by Pliny (*Nat. Hist.* 5.24.94), and Ptolemy (*Geog.* 5.4.9) calls the city ᾽Αντιόχεια Πισιδίας'.

Further historical information and helpful photographs of Antioch can be found online at T. Bolen, www.bibleplaces.com/pantioch.htm, n. p. (accessed 12.1.2007).

(καὶ) ἐλθόντες B ℵ* C 81. 1175 *pc* ‖ εἰσελθ- D, *(et) cum introissent* d 𝔓⁷⁴ ℵ² E H L P Ψ 049. 056. 33. 1739 𝔐 latt sy.

The compound εἰσελθόντες in D05 echoes the action of Jesus in the parallel passage of Lk. 4.16 (where the line is accidentally omitted in D05).

(συναγωγὴν) τῇ ἡμέρᾳ τῶν σαββάτων B 𝔓⁷⁴ ℵ *rell, die sabbatorum* d ‖ τὴν ἡμετέραν (ν *erasit* Dˢ·ᵐ·) τῷ σαββάτῳ D* (gig sin sa mae).

This is the second mention of the 'we'-group in the D05 text (cf. 11.28 D05), this time an oblique one, making two additional first person references before the first one attested by both texts at 16.10. There is another additional reference at 21.29 D05 (see *General Introduction,* §VIII).

13.15 (εἴ τίς ἐστιν) ἐν ὑμῖν λόγος παρακλήσεως B 𝔓⁷⁴ ℵ *rell* ‖ λόγου (-ος Dᴬ), σοφίας, ἐν ὑμῖν, παρακλ. D*, *(si quis est) sermo et intellectus in vobis exhortationis* d mae.

In B03, τις functions as an adjective qualifying λόγος, and ἐν ὑμῖν is locational, 'among Paul and his companions' (it is not simply the equivalent of 'you have', which is expressed by the simple dative, without the preposition ἐν [Winer, *Grammar*, pp. 272–73, *contra* B-D-R, §220.1; cf. B-A-G, ἐν, IV.4.a]). In D05, it functions as a personal pronoun and goes with ἐν ὑμῖν ('one of you') which, especially separated from τις, conveys the impression of deference and hesitation. The genitive λόγου of D05 (and possibly the two genitives following, too, as explained in the next paragraph) express a thing possessed or a quality, a use of the genitive that is found on other occasions in the New Testament with a similar force (cf. Mk 5.42: ἦν γὰρ ἐτῶν δώδεκα; see Winer, *Grammar*, p. 244, and cf. Robertson, *Grammar*, p. 497).

The three nouns λόγου, σοφίας and παρακλήσεως can be understood as parallel to each other, expressing three distinct notions. In this case, the meaning of λόγος is general, conveying the sense of 'a person who can speak' (cf. 1 Cor. 2.1; and Lk. 24.19; Acts 7.22; also 13.44b D05 below). Alternatively, σοφίας qualifies λόγου in order to define a particular kind of speech (cf. 1 Cor. 2.4, 13; 12.8). The position of παρακλήσεως at the end of the sentence confers on it a special importance (contrary to Delebecque's view that, having replaced παρακλήσεως by σοφίας, D05 then omitted to remove the second noun [*Les deux Actes*, p. 86]). The whole request is hesitant, as if those asking knew what they wanted (an exhortation from Barnabas, υἱὸς παρακλήσεως, 4.36) but were not bold enough to ask for it directly. The result was that it was Paul, a man of much speech (cf. 13.44b D05, 45 D05) who responded to the request.

13.16 ὁ Παῦλος D ‖ Παῦλος B 𝔓⁷⁴ ℵ *rell.*

The article before the name of Paul is in accordance with the position he has assumed of leader, for it indicates that he was expected to be the person to speak (Read-Heimerdinger, *The Bezan Text*, p. 134).

13.17 (τοῦ λαοῦ) τοῦ Ἰσραήλ B Ψ 1175 bo ‖ Ἰσρ. 181 vg aeth ‖ τούτου Ἰσρ. D, *populi huius Istrahel* d 𝔓⁷⁴ ℵ A C 33. 81. 323. 945. 1270. 1739. 1891. 2344 ‖ τούτου E H L P 049. 056. 614 𝔐.

Israel is normally arthrous in Luke–Acts, except in the genitive where the presence of the article depends on the context. It can be seen from the following list of references that in the expression 'the people of Israel', as well as the synonymous 'sons/house of Israel', Israel is regularly anarthrous, without any other variation between D05 and ℵ01/B03 concerning the presence of the article: arthrous Ἰσραήλ: Lk. 1.68, God of I.; Lk. 2.25, the consolation of I.; Lk. 22.30, judges of I.; Acts 4.8 D05 (*om.* ℵ01/B03), the elders of I.; Acts 28.20 (D05 lac.), the hope of I.; anarthrous Ἰσραήλ: Lk. 1.16; Acts 7.23, 37; 9.15 (D05 lac.); 10.36, the sons of I.; Lk. 2.32, the glory of your people, I.; Acts 2.36; 7.42, the/every house of I.; Acts 4.10; 13.24, the people of I.; Acts 4.27, the nations and people (pl.) of I.; Acts 5.21, the senate of the people of I.

The only variation in the presence of the article before 'the people of Israel' is here at 13.17. In consequence, this articular reading in B03 is anomalous. The demonstrative adjective in the D05 reading belongs with τοῦ λαοῦ, and Ἰσραήλ stands in apposition to the whole phrase (cf. Lk. 2.32).

καὶ (τὸν λαόν) B 𝔓⁷⁴ ℵ Dᴱ *rell* ‖ διά D*, *propter (populum)* d (+ καί: 614. 1611. 2412 gig syʰ; Chrᵖᵗ BarS).

In B03, τὸν λαόν appears to be the object of the verbs that follow to the end of v. 20 – ὕψωσεν, ἐξήγαγεν, etc. However, the plural pronoun αὐτούς in vv. 17, 18 and the plural subject of v. 21 with the corresponding indirect pronoun αὐτοῖς, takes up 'our fathers' from the first clause of v. 17.

With the preposition διά in D05, διὰ τὸν λαόν is a subordinate phrase dependent on ὕψωσεν and, as a result, the object of the verbs is consistently maintained as τοὺς πατέρας ἡμῶν. The phrase is consistent with Jewish theology according to which God acted in favour of Israel because they were his people, 'on account of their being the people' (although Delebecque [*Les deux Actes*, p. 86] finds it 'impossible').

ἐν γῇ Αἰγύπτου B 𝔓⁷⁴ ℵ A 056. 81. 33. 547. 614. 945. 1175. 1505. 1739. 1837. 1891. 2147. 2412. 2495, *in terra Aegypti* d ‖ ἐν τῇ γῇ -πτῳ D ǀ ἐν τῇ -πτῳ Ψ 209 ǀ ἐν γῇ -πτῳ C E H L P 049 𝔐.

The phrase in B03 is similar to that found in the mouth of Stephen at 7.36 D05, ἐν γῇ Αἰγύπτου (ἐν τῇ Αἰγύπτῳ B03), 7.40, ἐκ γῆς Αἰγύπτου, where the reference is made from the point of view of the Israelites who have just escaped from Egypt and are looking back at recent events. The D05 phrase here treats the sojourn in the land of Egypt as a stock fact of history, which indeed it had become.

13.18 (καὶ) ὡς (– E) τεσσερακονταετῆ χρόνον B 𝔓⁷⁴ ℵ *rell* (gig vg) ‖ ἔτη .μ. D, *annis quadraginta* d syᵖ sa mae aeth.— ἐτροποφόρησεν (αὐτούς) B D ℵ C² H L P 049. (056. 0142 –σαν). 614. 1739 𝔐 it vg syʰᵍʳ; Chr Ps-Oecum ‖ ἐτροφοφόρ-, *ac si nutrix aluit eos* d 𝔓⁷⁴ A C* E Ψ 33ᵛⁱᵈ, 181. 1175. 1646. 2127. 2492 *pc* gig syᵖ·ʰ co aeth; CAp Hes Theoph.

It is possible to take ὡς as a subordinating conjunction, meaning 'when' and introducing a clause dependent on the main verb in v. 19, κατεκληρονόμησεν; this is how it has been rendered in the translation provided above because it is the most probable explanation of the B03 text.

Alternatively, ὡς may be understood as a particle of comparison qualifying the time phrase in B03 which is carefully delimited as 'a 40-year period'; it thus underlines the value of 40 as a symbolic number (cf. 5.36, see *The Message of Acts*, I, p. 352; cf. Exod. 16.35; Num. 14.33, 34). An analysis of numbers introduced with ὡς in Luke–Acts found that on three other occasions the adverb 'is omitted by Codex Bezae if the symbol is an obvious one that does not need to be highlighted' (J. Read-Heimerdinger, 'Luke's Use of ὡς and ὡσεί: Comparison and Correspondence as a Means to Convey his Message', in R. Pierri (ed.), *Grammatica Intellectio Scripturae: Saggi philologici di Greco biblico in onore di padre Lino Cignelli, OFM* [Studium Biblicum Franciscanum Analecta 68; Jerusalem: Franciscan Printing Press, 2006], p. 272).

On the other hand, the comparative sense of ὡς is rendered less likely by the fact that the number 40 in B03 is expressed in an adjectival phrase qualifying χρόνον. Besides this factor, Paul, within the context of his appeal to the history of Israel, is not citing the figure as a symbolic one but as one that was taken to be literally true. It is when Israel's years in the wilderness are evoked in presenting later events that the number 40 (or multiples of it) is invested with symbolic value, as it is used to flag up the ancient paradigm.

It is unlikely, in view of the strong traditional association of 40 with the time Israel spent in the desert, that Paul would use ὡς to mean 'approximate'. It is an over-simplification, to the point of error, to say that it is 'more in the style of Luke when numerals are involved to understand ὡς as "about"' (Metzger, *Commentary*, pp. 357–58; cf. the discussion in Read-Heimerdinger, 'Luke's Use of ὡς and ὡσεί'). While that sense is sometimes required, it is not appropriate here where the number 40 is fixed by tradition.

Another possibility is that ὡς could be an adverb meaning 'how', as a residue of the quotation from Deut. 1.31 LXX where the description of God caring for Israel in the desert occurs (ὡς ἐτροφοφόρησέν σε κύριος ὁ θεός σου). This factor raises the question of a further *vl* in the text of Acts concerning the verb of the quotation, whether τροφοφορέω, 'care for', or τροποφορέω, 'endured'; the *vl* reflects similar variation found among the Jewish scriptural texts. The MT of this verse has the more prosaic 'carried' (נשא) which corresponds to τροποφορέω, but most LXX MSS read τροφοφορέω (The *vl* ἐτροποφόρησεν is found in one early LXX papyrus of Deut. 1.31 as well as the Church Fathers, including Origen [C. Dogniez and M. Harl, *Le Deutéronome*, in Harl (ed.), *La Bible d'Alexandrie*, V, 1992), pp. 118–19]; τροποφορέω also occurs as a *vl* in the future tense in the following clause (Rahlfs). As for the verb τροφοφόρεω, it is attested at Deut. 1.31 for the first time in Greek; it only occurs once more in the LXX, at 2 Macc. 7.27 of a mother nursing her child. The sense of God caring for his people in the desert is borne out by the targumic expression that God 'supplied the needs' of Israel in the desert at *Targ. Onq.* Deut. 2.7; 32.10; *Targ. Ps.-J.* Hos. 13.5 (R.P. Gordon, 'The Targumists as Eschatologists', in *Göttingen Congress Volume*, pp. 113–30), which is brought out here by the reading of d05.

Gordon elsewhere ('Targumic Parallels to Acts XIII 18 and Didache X1V 3', *Nov. Test.* 16 [1974], pp. 285–89) takes up the suggestion made by Lake and Cadbury (*English Translation and Commentary*, p. 149) that the forms ἐτροποφόρησεν (read here by B03 and D05) and ἐτροφοφόρησεν (apparently read by d05) are not to be understood as different verbs but simply phonetic variations of the same verb τροφοφορέω in the aorist. This may be the case, but the fact that ἐτροποφόρησεν reflects the MT text of Deut. 1.31 means that it is difficult to be certain.

13.19 καὶ (καθελών) D, *et* d 𝔓⁷⁴ ℵ *rell* ‖ *om.* B 6. 81 *pc* sa.

The omission of καί in B03 may be due to haplography that arose because of the following καθελών (Bruce, *Text*, p. 263; Metzger, *Commentary*, p. 359), but if ὡς is taken as 'when', καί is superfluous (see discussion of previous verse).

(τὴν γῆν) αὐτῶν B 𝔓⁷⁴ ℵ (+ ἀλλοφύλων Dᴱ) *rell* ‖ τῶν ἀλλοφύλων D*, *allophoelorum* d syʰ** mae.

The ambiguity of the referent of αὐτῶν in B03 is avoided by the reading of D05. The term ἀλλόφυλος only occurs elsewhere in the New Testament at Acts 10.28. In the LXX, it is first used at Exod. 34.15 (according to certain witnesses, see Rahlfs) where the context is precisely the entry of the people of Israel into Canaan and YHWH's promise to drive out the inhabitants of the land of which six nations are named (omitting the Gergashites of Deut. 7.1). Elsewhere in the LXX, ἀλλόφυλος is usually a reference to the Philistines, but cf. Isa. 61.5 where it is again a general term for foreigners.

13.20 ὡς (ἔτεσιν) B 𝔓⁷⁴ ℵ *rell*, *quasi* d vg ‖ καὶ μετὰ ταῦτα ὡς Dᴰ E H L P Ψ 049. 056. 1739 𝔐 ‖ καὶ ἕως D* gig.— (πεντήκοντα.) καὶ μετὰ ταῦτα ἔδωκεν B 𝔓⁷⁴ ℵ A C 33. 36. 81. 453. 1175. 2344 *pc* vg ‖ καὶ ἐδ. 614. 1611. 2412 *pc* ‖ (πεντήκοντα) ἔδωκεν D, *dedit* d E H L P Ψ 049. 056. 1739 𝔐.

B03 attaches the time phrase, again prefaced with ὡς (cf. v. 18), to the previous clause, where ὡς could indicate the approximate time taken for the events described in vv. 17-19 (see *Commentary*); it then starts a new sentence with 'After those things', i.e. the time in Egypt and the desert and the conquest of Canaan. The Byzantine MSS, together with Corrector D of D05, begin a new sentence at the start of the verse, attaching the time phrase to the period between the conquest of Canaan and that of the judges. D05 situates the end of the 450 years with Samuel who came after the judges (cf. 1 Kgs 6.1, 480 years from the exodus up to the fourth year of Solomon).

(Σαμουὴλ) προφήτου B 𝔓⁷⁴ ℵ A 81 *pc* ‖ τοῦ πρ. D C E H L P Ψ 049. 056. 1739 𝔐.

With the article, D05 presents Samuel as a prophet known and familiar to his audience; the absence of the article highlights the word 'prophet' as if it were not necessarily expected.

13.22 (ἤγειρεν) τὸν Δαυίδ B 𝔓⁷⁴ ℵ A 33. 1175. 2344 ‖ αὐτοῖς τὸν Δαυ. C E H L P Ψ 049. 056. 614 *pm* ‖ Δαυίδ D.

The absence of the article in D05 alone draws attention to the person of David at this first mention of his name. Comparison may be made with the earlier mention of Saul at 13.21 where the article is retained because he is simply the next person to be listed in the history of God's dealings with Israel. In contrast, with David a critical point is reached in this history, and omitting the article is a way of underlining the new direction Paul's speech takes as he introduces for the first time not just the person of David (from whom Jesus will be descended) but also God's action in raising him up, ἤγειρεν, a verb that will become a *leitmotiv* in the speech (cf. vv. 23, 30, 37).

τὸν τοῦ (Ἰεσσαί) B 𝔓⁷⁴ ℵ *rell* ‖ τὸν υἱόν D, *filium* d e gig vg syᴾ sa mae aeth; Or.— ἄνδρα D, *virum* d 𝔓⁷⁴ ℵ *rell* ‖ *om.* B.

By means of the genitive article, the B03 reading expresses the idea that Saul was the son of Jesse, which D05 spells out by including the word υἱόν. Wilcox identifies the reading of ἄνδρα as a rendering of both the Hebrew and the targumic text of 1 Sam 13.14 underlying Paul's reference to David (*The Semitisms of Acts*, pp. 21–24); the LXX, on the other hand, reads ἄνθρωπον.

13.23 τούτου ὁ θεὸς ἀπὸ τοῦ σπέρματος B ℵ² 𝔓⁷⁴ *rell* | τούτου ὁ θ. ℵ* ‖ ὁ θ. οὖν ἀπὸ τ. σπ. αὐτοῦ D *(deus autem a semine huius* d).

The demonstrative article, which serves as a connective to the new, complex clause in B03, switches the focus to David and underlines the Davidic line of the Messiah. In D05, it is God who is fore-fronted and who remains in focus as the subject of the new clause, just as he has been of the previous sentences since v. 17, except for a brief comment at v. 21a. The connective οὖν serves to round off the first part of his speech.

(κατ' ἐπαγγελίαν) ἤγαγεν B 𝔓⁷⁴ ℵ A E H L P Ψ 049. 056. 0142 𝔐 it vg bo aeth; Ath Chrᵖᵗ Theoph Aug ‖ ἤγειρεν D, *resurrexit* d C 1. 33. 36. 104. 181. 242. 307. 323. 431. 440. 453. 467. 522. 610. 614. 630. 927. 945. 1108. 1241. 1270. 1518. 1611. 1678. 1828. 1838. 1891. 2138. 2298. 2344. 2412 *al* gig w vgᶜᵀ sy sa mae; Chrᵖᵗ Thret Theoph | *om.* 1739.

D05 reads the verb ἐγείρω already used to refer to David (cf. v. 22). It carries the dual sense of 'to raise up' and 'to resurrect' (cf. Peter in Acts 3.15; 10.40). It will be used in the latter sense at 13.30, without needing the clarification of ἐκ νεκρῶν according to D05. B03 avoids any ambiguity here with the neutral verb ἄγω.

σωτῆρα Ἰησοῦν B ℵ A E P C Ψ 056. 81. 104. 440. 453. 614. 927. 945. 1175. 1270. 1611. 1739. 2147. 2344. 2412 *al* vg sy sa bo; Ath Thret ‖ σωτῆρα τὸν Ἰη. D | σωτηρίαν 𝔓⁷⁴ H L 049. 33 𝔐 | εἰς σωτηρίαν 6. 828. 1245 *pc.*

The article before the name of Jesus assumes he is a figure Paul's audience had heard of and were familiar with, i.e. that Paul is not announcing the person of Jesus to them for the first time.

13.24 παντὶ τῷ λαῷ 'Ισραήλ B D, *populo Istrahel* d 𝔓⁷⁴ ℵ² C E Ψ 33. 81. 104. 547. 614. 927. 945. 1175. 1241. 1260. 1611. 1739. 1837. 1891. 2412 *rell* ‖ παντὶ τῷ 'Ισρ. ℵᶜᵒʳʳ·* A 1646ᶜ | τῷ 'Ισρ. H L P 049. 056. 1. 88. 226. 323ᶜ. 330. 440. 618. 1243. 1245. 1505. 1646*. 1828. 1854. 2147. 2492. 2495.

B03 is in agreement with D05 in reading λαῷ before Israel, a reading that the first hand of ℵ01 wrote but corrected to read simply παντὶ τῷ 'Ισραήλ. At the only other occurrence in Luke–Acts of πᾶς with 'Ισραήλ, λαός is read without *vl* (Acts 4.10), as may be expected since λαός justifies the emphasis of πᾶς.

13.25 Τί ἐμὲ (ὑπονοεῖτε εἶναι;) B 𝔓⁷⁴ ℵ A (με 33. 81). 915. 1175 *pc* sa mae aeth; Aug QvDᵖᵗ ‖ Τίνα με D, *quem (suspicamini) me (esse?)* d 𝔓⁴⁵ C E H L P Ψ 049. 056. 1739 𝔐 latt syᵖ·ʰ bo; Chr QvDᵖᵗ.

The difference between the two interrogative pronouns is one of gender, whether neuter ('What?') or masculine ('Whom?'). The masculine tallies better with John's answer (cf. Jn 1.20), and Jesus' own question to his disciples (Lk. 9.20). Either of them could be construed as relative pronouns: 'What/whom you suppose me to be, I am not' (see Winer, *Grammar*, p. 211), though this would cause the parallel with Jesus' question to be lost.

13.26 (γένους 'Αβραάμ) οἱ ἐν ὑμῖν B 𝔓⁴⁵ | καὶ οἱ ἐν ὑμῖν 𝔓⁷⁴ ℵ C E H L P Ψ 049. 056. 614. 1739 𝔐 ‖ καὶ οἱ ἐν ἡμῖν D, *et qui in nobis* d A 81.

B03 somewhat incongruously assimilates the God-fearers with the 'sons of Abraham'. D05 and ℵ01 make a distinction between them, with D05 situating the God-fearers 'among us' – possibly through itacism, though it does accord with the first person plural pronoun in the following main clause (where, in fact, many witnesses other than ℵ01, B03 or D05 read ὑμῖν).

13.27 (οἱ ἄρχοντες) αὐτῶν B 𝔓⁴⁵·⁷⁴ ℵ Dᶠ *rell* ‖ ΑΥΤ.Σ Dᵖ·ᵐ· (= αὐτῆς D*), *eius* d gig sin t vg.

The first hand of D05 is that of the original scribe; the reading of the feminine pronoun refers to 'Ιερουσαλήμ whose rulers were the Temple authorities.

τοῦτον ἀγνοήσαντες B 𝔓⁴⁵·⁷⁴ ℵ (-οῦντες Dᶠ) *rell* ‖ μὴ συνιέντες D*ᵛⁱᵈ, *non intellegentes* d sin aeth.— καὶ τὰς φωνὰς (τῶν προφητῶν) B 𝔓⁴⁵·⁷⁴ ℵ Dᴴ *rell* ‖ τὰς γραφάς D*, *scripturas* d E sin syᵖ.— καὶ (κρίναντες) D, *et* d ‖ *om.* B 𝔓⁴⁵·⁷⁴ ℵ *rell*.

B03 accounts for the condemnation of Jesus by the Jews of Ierousalem on the grounds that they did not know or recognize (the verb ἀγνοέω has a range of meanings) τοῦτον, which should probably be taken to mean Jesus (v. 23, and the subject of ἔρχομαι, v. 25) since he is also the implied object of the following participle κρίναντες; it is not impossible to take it as 'the message', ὁ λόγος, of the previous sentence. τὰς φωνὰς τῶν προφητῶν is apparently also the object of ἀγνοήσαντες, with the sense now of 'not understand' (cf.

Lk. 9.45). On the basis of these two failings, the Jews fulfilled the utterances of the Prophets in their act of judging him. The sentence construction is far from easy because of the apparently double object of ἀγνοήσαντες, as well as the distant objects of both κρίναντες and ἐπλήρωσαν.

D05 does not present any grounds of ignorance for the rulers of Jerusalem, either of Jesus or the Prophets. Instead, the focus is all on the fulfilment of the prophetic writings: they are said to have fulfilled them (which had to happen, cf. Peter, 2.23) without understanding them, and this led them in turn to carry out an act of judgement. καί before the final participle κρίναντες is construed as conjoining it to the participle μὴ συνιέντες in a relation of cause and effect.

13.28 (εὑρόντες) ἐν αὐτῷ D, *in eo* d 614. 1611. 2412 lat sy^{h**} co ‖ *om.* B 𝔓^{45.74} ℵ *rell.*— ἠτήσαντο (ἤτησαν τὸν ℵ* C*) Πιλᾶτον ἀναιρηθῆναι αὐτόν B 𝔓^{45.74} ℵ² C² (D^F) *rell* ‖ κρίναντες αὐτὸν παρέδωκαν Πιλάτῳ ἵνα εἰς ἀναίρεσιν D*, *iudicantes autem eum tradiderunt Pilato ut interficeretur* d 181. 1838.

The B03 version of events is considerably toned down compared to the D05 account: the leaders ask Pilate to execute Jesus even though they can find no justification for it. D05 insists on the fact that the Jewish leaders judged Jesus themselves and then handed him over to Pilate in order for the sentence to be carried out. The presence of ἵνα without a verb following has been explained by Delebecque (*Les deux Actes*, p. 87) as due to the distraction of a scribe who wrote ἵνα in anticipation of a verb; it could equally well be that the subjunctive ᾖ dropped out because of its similarity in pronunciation to the vowel of εἰς: if it were present, the clause would read literally: 'so that he might be for execution'.

13.29 (ὡς δὲ) ἐτέλησαν B 𝔓^{74} ℵ (-σεν D^A, *consummaverunt* d) *rell* ‖ ἐτέλουν D*.— (πάντα) τὰ γεγραμμένα περὶ αὐτοῦ B ‖ τ. π. αὐ. γεγ. εἰσίν D*, *de illo scripta sunt* d (– εἰσίν: D^{s.m.} 𝔓^{45.74} ℵ *rell*).— ἠτοῦντο τὸν Πιλᾶτον τοῦτον μὲν σταυρῶσαι D*, *petierunt Pilatum hunc crucifigi* d (t sy^{hmg} mae) ‖ *om.* B 𝔓^{45.74} ℵ D^{s.m.} *rell.*— καθελόντες B 𝔓^{74} ℵ *rell* ‖ καὶ ἐπιτυχόντες πάλιν καὶ καθ. D (*et impetraverunt iterum et deposuerunt* d t sy^{hmg} mae).— καὶ (ἔθηκαν) D*, *et* d ‖ *om.* B 𝔓^{45.74} ℵ D^{s.m.} *rell.*

B03 views the acts so far as bringing to an end the fulfilment of the prophecies concerning Jesus, following which they removed him from the cross and buried him. D05, in contrast, sees the next events as continuing to fulfil the Scriptures: the Jews' request for crucifixion and their request to remove his body and bury it, underlining Jesus as the topic of the Scriptures by the fronted position of the prepositional phrase περὶ αὐτοῦ and the verb εἰσίν. In that text, μέν is used adverbially, anticipating the second request that is implied in the following clause with καὶ ἐπιτυχόντες πάλιν. The final καί in this sequence, after a participle and before a main verb, underlines the special significance of their placing the body in the tomb (Read-Heimerdinger, *The Bezan Text*, p. 236).

13.30 ὁ δὲ θεὸς ἤγειρεν αὐτὸν ἐκ νεκρῶν B 𝔓⁴⁵·⁷⁴ ℵ *rell* ‖ ὃν ὁ θ. ἤγ. D (*quem deus vero excitavit* d) gig sin (+ *a mortuis*).

The comment in either text is laconic, but in D05 it is extremely so with Jesus, the referent of the relative pronoun, as the pivot between the action of the Jewish leaders on the one hand (they put him in a tomb), and of God on the other (he raised him). For ἐκ νεκρῶν, cf. Lk. 9.7; Acts 3.15; 4.10; 10.41; 13.34; 17.3, 31; for its omission, cf. Lk. 9.22; 24.6, 34; Acts 5.30; 10.40; 13.37. With the relative pronoun, D05 preserves the paratactical style that is typical of kerygmatic proclamations.

13.31 ὃς (ὤφθη) B 𝔓⁷⁴ ℵ *rell* ‖ οὗτος D, *hic qui (visus est)* d.

B03 begins a new sentence, with the nominative relative pronoun linking back to the previous αὐτόν, whereas D05 begins with a demonstrative, now placing Jesus firmly in the spotlight. This is the second of three additional uses of the demonstrative in the Bezan text to refer to Jesus (cf. 13.29, τοῦτον; 13.38, διὰ τούτου).

ἐπὶ ἡμέρας πλείους τοῖς συναναβᾶσιν αὐτῷ ἀπὸ τῆς Γαλιλαίας εἰς Ἰερουσαλήμ B 𝔓⁴⁵·⁷⁴ ℵ *rell* ‖ τ. συναναβαίνουσιν (-βᾶσιν Dˢ·ᵐ·) αὐ. ἀπὸ τ. Γ. εἰς Ἰ. ἐφ' ἡμέρας πλείονας (πλείους Dᴴ⁇) D*, *his qui simul ascenderunt cum eo a Galilea in Hierusalem in diebus pluribus* d.

The aorist participle in B03 views the disciples' journey from Galilee to Ierousalem as a block of action, as it refers to their movements before the death of Jesus (cf. Lk. 18.31); the appearances of Jesus to them thus refer to the time he spent with them in Ierousalem after his resurrection. D05 views the situation differently, with the present participle referring to the time the disciples spent with Jesus, travelling up to Ierousalem from Galilee after his resurrection (cf. Jn 21.1; Mt. 28.16). The period of time Jesus spent in the company of the Eleven is also underlined in Peter's speech according to D05 (Acts 10.41 D05; cf. 1.3).

(οἵτινές) εἰσι B E H L P (σύνεισιν Ψ) 049. 056 𝔐 I νῦν εἰσιν 𝔓⁴⁵·⁷⁴ A C 33. 81. 88. 104. 323. 440. 453. 927. 945. 1175. 1270. 1739. 1837. 1891. 2344 *al* gig syᵖ co I εἰσι νῦν ℵ 36 ‖ ἄχρι νῦν εἰσιν D, *usque nunc sunt* d 255. 614. 1611. 2412 *al* lat syʰ.

The reading of νῦν alone may give the wrong impression that the apostles were only now giving witness in Ierousalem (Metzger, *Commentary*, p. 361). The D05 reading of ἄχρι νῦν, on the contrary, makes it clearer that the apostles have been witnessing from the time of Jesus' resurrection up to and including the present time.

13.32 (πατέρας) ἡμῶν D, *nostros* d E *pc* lat sy^p sa mae aeth; Amb ‖ *om.* B 𝔓^{74} ℵ *rell.*— ἐπαγγελίαν γενομένην B 𝔓^{74} ℵ *rell* ‖ γεν. ἐπ. D, *factam pollicitationem* d 36. 453. 209. 431; Amb Hil.

The omission of the first person pronoun in B03 corresponds to the omission in Peter's speech of the whole phrase πρὸς τοὺς πατέρας ἡμῶν (3.22 D05). The presence of the pronoun, together with the emphatic position of the noun ἐπαγγελίαν at the end of the phrase, and the juxtaposition of the action and the ancestors as the recipients of it, makes more of the ancient promise and its context.

13.33 (ἀναστήσας) ᾽Ιησοῦν B 𝔓$^{45.74}$ ℵ *rell* ‖ τὸν κύριον ᾽Ι. Χριστόν D, *dominum Iesum Christum* d sa mae; Amb ǀ τ. κύρ. ᾽Ιη. 614. 2412 sy^{h**}; Hil.

This is the second of only two references to the resurrection in Acts that directly include the name of Jesus (cf. 4.33). At both places in D05, the full title of Jesus is given. It is typical of the Bezan text to use the full title in formal declarations, though in other contexts the simple name or a short title is used, suggesting that the full title is not merely a reflection of a later Church practice according to which the name of Jesus would always be accompanied by 'Lord' and 'Christ'. It is wrong to say that the full title is characteristic of D05 (*contra* Metzger, citing T.E. Page, pp. 225–26; Barrett, I, p. 646). The full title is also common in the letters of Paul (predating the writing of Acts, let alone the copying of it), who generally refers to Jesus in a stylized way (see Read-Heimerdinger, *The Bezan Text*, pp. 268, 272–73, for an exhaustive examination of the titles of Jesus in Acts).

ὡς καί B 𝔓$^{45.74}$ ℵ *rell* ‖ οὕτως γάρ D, *sicut enim* d.— (ἐν) τῷ ψαλμῷ γέγραπται τῷ δευτέρῳ B 𝔓^{74} ℵ A^2 (A$^{illeg.}$) C Ψ 33. 36. 81. 181. 242. 307. 431. 453. 610. 945. 1678. 1739. 1837. 1891. 1898. 2298. 2344 *al*; (Hil) ǀ τ. ψαλ. τ. δευτ. γέγ. E L P 049. 614 𝔐 it vg; Chr (Ambr^{pt}) Beda^{pt} ǀ τ. δευτ. ψαλ. γέγ. Η 056. 440. 1270. 2147 ǀ τ. ψαλ. γέγ. 1175; (Hes) Beda^{pt} ‖ τ. πρώτῳ ψαλ. γέγ. D, *in primo psalmo scriptum est* d 1175 gig; (Or Oecum) Hil Cass Beda$^{lat\ mss\ acc.\ to}$ ǀ τοῖς ψαλμοῖς γέγ. 𝔓^{45vid} t; (Ambr^{pt}).

There is considerable evidence that in some Hebrew collections of Psalms, the first and the second psalms were joined as one (see Metzger, *Commentary*, pp. 363–64). The practice is attested by some of the Church Fathers as early as Justin Martyr, although the LXX presents them as separate. Zahn suggests that Luke originally wrote in accordance with synagogal practice: 'dem alten jüdischen Gebrauch der Schriftverlesung in den Synagogen entspricht' (p. 443).

(γεγέννηκά σε)· αἴτησαι παρ᾽ ἐμοῦ, καὶ δώσω σοι ἔθνη τὴν κληρονομίαν σου καὶ τὴν κατάσχεσίν σου τὰ πέρατα τῆς γῆς D, *postula a me, et ego dabo tibi gentes hereditatem tuam et possessionem tuam terminos terrae* d vg^D sy^{hmg} mae ‖ *om.* B 𝔓$^{45.74}$ ℵ *rell.*

The quotation from the Psalms continues in D05 with the next verse (Ps. 2.8), thus preparing for the declaration Paul and Barnabas will make at the conclusion of their speech on the following Sabbath. The context of the Psalm quotation is not, however, in accordance with the situation Jesus confronted, nor Paul now, since the next verse (Ps. 2.9) goes on to speak about the nations being given to the king in order that he might 'smash' and 'shatter' them – this discrepancy of context may have caused the verse to be omitted if it were not recognized that in early Judaism scriptural quotations had a significance independent of their context.

13.34 ὅτι (δὲ ἀνέστησεν) B 𝔓⁴⁵.⁷⁴ ℵ *rell* ‖ ὅτε D, *quando* d 255. 614. 1175. 2412 *pc* vg^D gig; Hil.

ὅτι in B03 can be understood as taking up the explanation of the promise, started at v. 33 also with ὅτι; ὅτι could equally well be taken as dependent on εἴρηκεν (Zerwick and Grosvenor, *Analysis*, p. 395), with either a causal sense or meaning 'concerning the fact that'. ὅτε could also have a causal sense, '*avec idée de cause*, comme, puisque' (Bailly, III), or it could be temporal, 'when', in which case the perfect εἴρηκεν should be taken as already achieved at the time of the subordinate verb ἀνέστησεν.

13.35 διότι καὶ ἐν ἑτέρῳ (λέγει) B 𝔓⁷⁴ ℵ A 81*. 1175 (*ideoque et alia* d) | διὸ κ. ἐν (+ τῷ 33. 2344) ἑτέρῳ C E H L P Ψ 049. 056. 33. 81ᶜ. 104. 1739 𝔐 ‖ καὶ ἑτέρως D lat (mae).

B03 links the two quotations with a conjunction of consequence and ties the second one to another psalm. D05 is less specific, spelling out neither the connection between the two quotations nor the source of the second.

13.36 μὲν (γάρ) B 𝔓⁷⁴ ℵ *rell* ‖ *om.* D, *enim* d vg sa.

B03 continues to make the connections between Paul's points explicit, here anticipating the contrast with David that he will make when he shows in v. 37 how the citation refers to Jesus rather than to David.

13.38 ἔστω ὑμῖν B D, *sit vobis* d 𝔓⁷⁴ *rell* ‖ ὑμῖν ἔστω ℵ A 1739.

The word order of ℵ01 places stress on 'you' by placing the pronoun before the verb; its position in D05 and B03, preceding the vocative ἄνδρες ἀδελφοί, has a similar effect.

διὰ τοῦτο B* 𝔓⁷⁴ 36. 61. 326. 436. 1175. 1838. 2344 *al* ‖ διὰ τούτου D, *per hunc* d ℵ A B³ C H⁵ L P Ψ 049. 056. 33. 1739 𝔐 t vg syᵖ co | δι' αὐτοῦ E 218. 255. 425. 611. 642. 808. 1505. 2495 *pc* aeth.

With the neuter demonstrative pronoun in the accusative, B03 presents the grounds for forgiveness as the fact of Jesus being raised from the dead. D05, in contrast, presents the means for forgiveness, using the genitive pronoun which should probably be taken as masculine, referring to Jesus (cf. ὅν as the object of the verb in the previous sentence), but it could also be neuter as in B03.

καὶ (ἀπὸ πάντων) B C² E H⁵ L P Ψ 049. 056. 33. 1739 𝔐 ‖ καὶ μετάνοια D, *et poenitentia* d vgᴰ syʰ** mae ‖ *om.* 𝔓⁷⁴ ℵ A C* *pc* t w vgˢᵗ.

B03 takes ἀπὸ πάντων in apposition to ἁμαρτιῶν, introducing the phrase with an epexegetic καί. D05 relates ἀπὸ πάντων to μετάνοια, which stands in parallel to ἄφεσις.

13.39 (ἐν τούτῳ) οὖν D (*enim* d) 614. 1611. 2412 dem syʰᵐᵍ ‖ *om.* B 𝔓⁷⁴ ℵ *rell.*— (δικαιοῦται) παρὰ θεῷ D, *ad <deum>* d 1611 syʰᵐᵍ mae ‖ π. τῷ θεῷ 614. 2147. 2412 t ‖ *om.* B 𝔓⁷⁴ ℵ *rell.*

With οὖν, D05 draws a conclusion on the basis of Paul's arguments so far, the demonstrative pronoun probably referring to Jesus as before (see v. 38), with the result that it could have a double force: righteousness with God is for everyone believing in Jesus, and it is also by him (rather than by the Law). In B03, ἐν τούτῳ could be neuter, the same referent as the demonstrative pronoun at the beginning of v. 38; together with the absence of παρὰ θεῷ, it causes Paul's conclusion to be rather more impersonal than in the D05 account.

13.41 ἔργον (ὃ οὐ μή) B 𝔓⁷⁴ ℵ A C Ψ 33. 36. 81. 453. 945. 1175. 1270. 1739. 1765. 1827. 2344 *al* vg sa bo ‖ *om.* D d E H⁵ L P 049. 056. 614 𝔐 gig p syᵖ·ʰ aeth.— ἐκδιηγῆται B 𝔓⁷⁴ ℵ Dˢ·ᵐ· *rell* ‖ -γήσεται D*, *exposuerit* d 88. 330. 467. 915. 1241. 1837. 1838.

The repetition of ἔργον in apposition to the first mention of the word is not present in the LXX text of Hab. 1.5 that Paul is quoting, which is to say that B03 departs from it on that point. However, on the tense of ἐκδιηγέομαι, it is D05 that departs from the LXX in using the future indicative instead of the present subjunctive.

καὶ ἐσίγησαν D, *et tacuerunt* d (-σεν: 614. 2412 syʰ** mae) ‖ *om.* B 𝔓⁷⁴ ℵ *rell.*

The silence with which the people in the synagogue receive Paul's proclamation, according to D05, is an indication that they do not accept his words (cf. 15.12, esp. in D05). It may be a conscious echo of Hab. 2.20: 'The Lord is in his holy Temple; let all the earth keep silence before him', since Paul has just cited a prophecy from that book.

13.42 (αὐτῶν) εἰς τὸ μεταξὺ σάββατον ἠξίουν B (bo; Chr) ‖ εἰς τ. μ. σ. E ‖ εἰς τ. μ. σ. παρεκάλουν 36. 307. 453. 610. 1678 ‖ παρ. εἰς τ. μ. σ. 𝔓⁷⁴ ℵ A C Ψ 097. 33. 81. 104. 181. 323. 440. 614. 927. 945. 1175. 1270*. 1611. 1739. 1837. 1891. 2344. 2412 *al* lat syᵖ·ʰ sa mae (aeth); Chrˡᵉᵐ ‖ παρ. τὰ ἔθνη εἰς τ. μ. σ. H⁵ L P 049. 056. 88. 2492 𝔐 ‖ παρ. εἰς τ. ἑξῆς σ. D, *in sequente sabbato* d.

There are several variants involved in this clause: 1) the word qualifying τὸ σάββατον and signifying 'next': D05 is alone in reading the classical adverb ἑξῆς in place of the later word, μεταξύ, that is found in all the other witnesses; 2) the verb signifying that they asked Paul and Barnabas to speak again: B03 is alone in reading ἀξιόω in place of παρακαλέω (E has no verb); παρεκάλουν echoes the request of the synagogue rulers in 13.15 (see above and *Commentary*, *ad loc.*), that some exhortation be spoken to them; 3) the word order of the verb in relation to the time phrase: B03 places the time phrase first, as does a series of minuscules with the alternative verb; all the other readings have the verb first; 4) the subject of the verb: the 𝔐 reading makes it explicit as the Gentiles, contrasting them with the Jews whose synagogue they had been in: (ἐξιόντων δὲ αὐτῶν) ἐκ τῆς συναγωγῆς τῶν Ἰουδαίων.

τὰ (ῥήματα) B 𝔓⁷⁴ ℵ Dᴱ *rell* ‖ *om.* D*.

The absence of the article in the demonstrative phrase in D05 is unusual in Greek but not unknown (see Robertson, *Grammar*, pp. 701–702, who cites Acts 1.5; 24.21 as well as various examples found in inscriptions, though all with the demonstrative in pre-noun position). It may be a way of expressing that the people did not want to hear exactly the same things repeated, but something like them.

13.43 (λυθείσης δὲ) αὐτοῖς ℵ* ‖ *om.* B D d 𝔓⁷⁴ ℵ² *rell.*— τῷ Βαρναβᾷ B 𝔓⁷⁴ ℵ *rell* ‖ Βαρναβᾷ D 216. 1175 mae; Chr.

The dative pronoun in ℵ01* apparently refers to the agent of the passive participle λυθείσης, presumably Paul and Barnabas. The absence of the article before Barnabas in D05 causes them to be viewed as a united pair, acting in harmony (see Heimerdinger and Levinsohn, 'The Use of the Article', p. 29).

ἔπειθον (αὐτούς) B 𝔓⁷⁴ ℵ Dˢ·ᵐ· *rell* ‖ ἐπείθοντο D* (*persuadentes* d) 919.

B03 has the aorist active where D05 has the imperfect middle.

(θεοῦ.) ἐγένετο δὲ καθ' ὅλης τῆς πόλεως διελθεῖν τὸν λόγον τοῦ θεοῦ D (*factum est autem per totam civitatem transire verbum domini* d syʰᵐᵍ) I ἐγ. δὲ κατὰ πᾶσαν πόλιν φημισθῆναι τὸν λόγον E w vg^Θ (mae); Bedaᵐˢˢ ᵃᶜᶜ· ᵗᵒ ‖ *om.* B 𝔓⁷⁴ ℵ *rell*.

The narrative comment with which D05 closes this first sub-sequence [DA] in Antioch refers to the spread throughout the whole city of teaching about God in general and not to the message of Jesus in particular (cf. *Critical Apparatus*, 13.5). According to the pattern regularly maintained elsewhere by D05, the spread of 'the word of God' always occurs among Gentiles since, in the form of the Torah, it has been known by Jews since the very beginning. Receiving the word of God is a necessary prelude to the acceptance of the message of Jesus, as will be seen in Paul's speech the following week (see *Excursus* 1).

The sentence may have dropped out of B03 through haplography: τοῦ θεοῦ ends the previous sentence, and the following one in B03 (see on 13.44 in the following sub-sequence [D´A]).

Commentary

[DA-A] 13.14-41 *In the Synagogue*

[a] 13.14 *Arrival of Paul and Barnabas in the Synagogue*
13.14 From Perga, Paul and his circle (cf. 13.13a) continued their journey for about 100 miles northwards to the city of Antioch, one of many places of this name that had been founded in honour of the Seleucid Antiochus the Great. Antioch was the administrative and military seat of southern Galatia; it will be to churches in this area that Paul will address his Letter to the Galatians. As it lies on a plateau at an altitude of 3,000 ft, separated from the coast by the Taurus mountains, the journey there would have been a difficult one.[109]

It can be deduced from archaeological evidence that the motivation for the choice of Antioch as the next destination was the presence there of the estate of Sergius Paulus in Paphos, and the suggestion that it was under the pro-consul's protection that Paul took his group to Antioch after Paphos has much to commend it, for it is not obvious why he would otherwise have chosen the place.[110]

The first recorded action of Paul and his companions was that they joined in the synagogue meeting on the Sabbath. The structure of the sentence in Greek presents their participation at the synagogue service as their immediate concern.[111] This procedure continues Paul's pattern, established in Salamis (13.5) and Paphos (13.6), of seeking out the Jews first in the places he visited. He will later pursue the same practice elsewhere.

A parallel with Jesus' visit to the synagogue in Nazareth is apparent from the outset: εἰσῆλθεν ... ἐν τῇ ἡμέρᾳ τῶν σαββάτων (Lk. 4.16). The compound verb at the beginning of the sentence in Codex Bezae of Acts 13.14b rein-forces the parallel; however, the continuation makes a significant alteration with an interesting reading that is frequently overlooked by commentators: the synagogue in Antioch of Pisidia was 'our' synagogue. If this reading is correct, the implication is that the narrator of Acts, included among those who accompanied Paul as the 'we'-group, was from Antioch of Pisidia even though he would appear not have been present on this occasion or, if he was, he makes nothing of it. The reading tallies with the conclusion, most probable in the Bezan text, that the narrator of Acts was of Jewish origin (see *General Introduction,* §III).

---

109. For further description of Antioch of Pisidia and of its significance for Paul, see Chilton, *Rabbi Paul,* pp. 117–18, 278–79.
110. Chilton, *Rabbi Paul,* pp. 117–18.
111. The two main verbs, conjoined with καί, are παρεγένοντο ('they arrived') and ἐκάθι-σαν ('they sat down').

Despite the predominantly Gentile nature of the city, there was a strong and influential Jewish presence, to judge from the reaction of the city overall to what happened in the synagogue on the day Paul visited it with his companions. In the synagogue, they took their seats. This would have been the normal position of those attending the synagogue as far as can be judged from archaeological remains.

[b] 13.15 *Invitation to Speak*
13.15 The lessons from the Law (*seder*) and the Prophets (*haftarah*) were the essential reason for the existence of the synagogues in the years before the destruction of the Temple.[112] Passages were selected according to a lectionary, although there is considerable doubt as to the date these were introduced and the form they took.[113] The reading of the Hebrew scrolls would be followed by an interpretation in the vernacular, leading to a homily that would depend closely on the scriptural readings for the day.[114] It is thus permissible to see Paul's speech as fulfilling the role of the expected homily. Although Luke does not say what the readings were on that day, there is evidence in Paul's speech to suggest that the *seder* may have been Deut. 4.25-46 and the *haftarah* 2 Sam. 7.6-16.[115]

It is the synagogue rulers, οἱ ἀρχισυνάγωγοι,[116] who approach Paul's group with a request for a homily addressed 'to the people', that is the Jewish peple. They are addressed as fellow-Jews ('Men brothers') and the formulation of the question is somewhat deferential and indirect, though the form the request takes varies according to the manuscripts of Acts: in the Alexandrian text, they are asked if 'there is a word of exhortation among them'; in the Bezan text, the enquirers seek to know whether among Paul and his companions there is anyone who might be 'a person of speech, or of wisdom, or of exhortation'. The word order of this text places particular emphasis on the final word 'of exhortation' and the tone of respectful deference is especially marked (see *Critical Apparatus* for discussion of the language of the variants). The importance put on 'a person of ... exhortation' seems to indicate that, in Luke's mind at least, Barnabas, the 'son of exhortation' *par excellence* (cf.

---

112. Safrai and Stern, *The Jewish People*, II, pp. 908–944.

113. The two major works on the synagogal lectionary cycles are C. Perrot, *La lecture de la Bible* (Hildesheim: Verlag Dr H.A. Gerstenberg, 1973), and J. Mann, *The Bible as Read and Preached in the Old Synagogue*, I (New York: KTAV, 1940; 2nd edn 1971); II (ed. I. Sonne; Ohio: Hebrew Union College, 1966). It will be seen that there are disagreements between them concerning the identification of readings and their attribution to cycles.

114. A summary of synagogue practice, together with a critical examination of Paul's speech in Acts 13.16-41, is given in J.W. Bowker, 'Speeches in Acts: A Study in Proem and Yelammedenu Form', *NTS* 14 (1967–68), pp. 96–111.

115. Bowker, 'Speeches in Acts', pp. 102–103.

116. The term is a technical one and the plural may indicate that the synagogue was a large one.

1.23 D05; 4.36; 9.31)[117] would have been the person best placed to speak. He will get the opportunity to express his ideas and exert his influence on Paul in the second recorded speech in Antioch (13.46b-47, see *Commentary* below).

[b′] 13.16-41a *Paul's Speech*

It has been observed that there is clear evidence in Paul's speech of Jewish exegetical methods that can only have been known to someone who had been trained in them.[118] It follows that not only was Paul familiar with Jewish ways of thinking and reasoning but so was Luke, who knew how to reproduce a speech that would be an authentic reflection of what Paul said to the synagogue in Antioch of Pisidia.

The structure of the speech helps to follow Paul's arguments through some reasoning that is at times complex, especially for readers not familiar with Jewish exegetical methods (see *Excursus* 5).[119]

[α] 13.16b-25	Exposition 1:	The history of salvation from Abraham to Jesus
[β] 13.26-37	Exposition 2:	The death and resurrection of Jesus
[γ] 13.38-41	Parenesis:	The possibility of forgiveness and final warning

Each of the three sections is marked by a new address; the time to which the contents relates moves from the past (the time of the ancestral promise), through the present (the time of the accomplishment of the promise), to the future (the time of decision and impending disaster).[120]

13.16a As it is, Paul is the one who takes up the invitation, the article before his name in the Bezan text indicating that Luke's addressee would expect him to speak, given the position he had established as leader of the group (see *Commentary*, 13.9, 13). He stands up to speak which, although it is the position adopted by other speakers in Acts (cf. Peter, 1.15; Gamaliel, 5.34; Peter, 15.7; James, 15.13 D05), would appear not to have been the traditional position for the one giving a homily in a synagogue, though it may well be that in the Diaspora local practices were followed.[121] The gesture that he makes with his hand is reminiscent of other occasions on which Luke associates it with a speaker (cf. 12.17; 19.33, 35 D05; 21.40), not all of them for-

---

117. See *The Message of Acts*, I, pp. 129–31 for a discussion of the reading 'Barnabas' at 1.23 D05.

118. See, for example, J.V. Doeve, *Jewish Hermeneutics in the Synoptic Gospels and Acts* (Assen: Van Gorcum, 1953), p. 175: 'in the argument of Acts 13 the work of a schooled rabbi is quite perceptible'.

119. The structure identified here is similar to that proposed by D. Ellul, 'Antioche de Pisidie: Une prédication ... trois credos? (Actes 13,13-43)', *FN* 5 (1992), pp. 3–14. It differs from that suggested by Bowker, 'Speeches in Acts', who sees the first major division at 13.22 with the introduction of the *proem* text and considers the rest of the speech to be the *proem* homily. From a linguistic point of view, the division at v. 22 cuts across a unit of development, and taking vv. 22-41 as one unit ignores the change from exposition to parenesis at v. 38.

120. The time sequence has been well observed and commented on by Ellul, 'Antioche de Pisidie', p. 5.

121. Strack and Billerbeck, *Kommentar*, I, p. 997; IV, p. 185; Schneider, II, p. 131.

mal situations.[122] It may be a means to get his audience to settle down to listen (cf. 13.16b below).

[α] 13.16b-25 *Exposition 1: The History of Salvation from Abraham to Jesus*
Following the opening address, this first exposition is made up of eight descriptive phases and a final, extended one that is more theological in tone:

13.16b	Address
13.17a	Election of the patriarchs
13.17b	Sojourn of Israel in Egypt
13.17c	Exodus
13.18	Crossing of the desert
13.19	Entry into Canaan
13.20	Period of the judges
13.21	Period of the kings
13.22	David, the model king
13.23-25	Jesus, saviour of Israel, preceded by John

In Codex Bezae, following the address, each of the descriptive phases except for v. 17b which is asyndetic, is introduced with καί, and the final peroration at v. 23 with οὖν. In the Alexandrian text, καί is omitted at v. 19 (not ℵ01) and οὖν at the start of the peroration.

The historical schema followed by Paul is similar to that outlined by Stephen (7.2-53) but with noticeable differences. It is to do an injustice to Luke's understanding and skill to suppose that these arise because he wished to avoid repeating things twice or because he had drawn his information from different sources. The divergences between speeches in Acts come about for quite a different reason. Luke of Codex Bezae is writing for Theophilus, the High Priest from 37–41 CE during the years following the death of Stephen and the persecution carried out by Paul as Saul, who had observed at first hand much of what Luke is describing to him;[123] he had a sophisticated and detailed knowledge of how the Scriptures were used according to scholarly Jewish traditions, and understood how the people in the stories Luke was relating thought and spoke. Luke, sharing both his knowledge and understanding, is able to communicate faithfully to his reader the kinds of speeches the characters in his narrative would have made. He takes account of their differing situations, backgrounds, audiences, and the circumstances of their speeches in order to give an accurate representation not only of what they said but also how they said it (see *General Introduction*, §VI).

The main objective of Stephen's speech was to demonstrate how the people of Israel had not obeyed the commandments of God throughout the various stages of their history, most significantly as they were transmitted by Moses.

---

122. The expression κατασείσας τῇ χειρί is exclusive to Luke; it is not exactly the same as that used of a Greek orator (cf. ἐκτείνας τὴν χεῖρα, 26.1).

123. See *General Introduction*, §III for a presentation of Luke as narrator of the book of Acts, and §IV on Theophilus as addressee.

His tone is therefore largely critical, since his goal is to highlight the idolatrous status that the Temple had acquired. Paul's aim will be quite different: his purpose in going through the stages in Israel's history will be to demonstrate how the destiny of Israel had always been in the hands of God and that it was this same God who had given Jesus for the salvation of Israel. The overall tone is, in consequence, positive and, even when he has to deal with the responsibility of the people of Ierousalem for the death of Jesus, he will abstain from launching into any kind of invective.

The goal of Paul's speech, to which he is heading from the beginning, is the declaration of forgiveness in Jesus for everyone and the corresponding prophetic warning to Israel in vv. 38-41.[124]

13.16b Paul addresses the people of Israel, in accordance with the invitation (13.15, πρὸς τὸν λαόν; cf. ᾽Ισραήλ, vv. 17, 23, 24; λαός, vv. 17 × 2, 24, 31; υἱοὶ γένους ᾽Ισραήλ, v. 26), using a typically Lukan term, 'Men Israelites', to designate the people of Israel as the people of the Law and the Temple (cf. Peter, 2.22; 3.12; Gamaliel, 5.35; the Jews from Asia, 21.28).[125] Any proselytes present (cf. 13.43) would be included in this first title since they were regarded as full members of Israel. Paul also uses the term, however, of God-fearers (οἱ φοβούμενοι τὸν θεόν), as if they were a separate category of people (cf. οἱ ἐν ὑμῖν/ἡμῖν φοβούμενοι τὸν θεόν, v. 26). The same term was previously used of Cornelius of Caesarea, and apparently referred to Gentiles who sympathized with the synagogue without becoming proselytes.[126] Despite initially acknowledging their presence among his audience, he will at times in his speech ignore their existence, instead limiting his remarks to the people of Israel.

Paul commands his audience to listen, as if there had been some disturbance.[127]

13.17a The speech opens with the name of God in first place – he is the God of 'this people' of Israel according to the Bezan text, a pejorative term

---

124. Other authors separate 13.38-39 as the single objective of Paul's argument, see J. Kilgallen, 'Acts 13.38-39: Culmination of Paul's Speech in Pisidia', *Bib.* 69 (1988), pp. 480–506.

125. Apart from Luke, only John uses the term ᾽Ισραηλίτης in the sense of a person of integrity (Jn 1.47), and Paul three times (Rom. 9.4; 11.1; 2 Cor. 11.22) in the same strong sense as Luke.

126. See *The Message of Acts*, II, p. 244. There is some disagreement among scholars as to whether God-fearers actually existed as a recognizable group, distinct from both Jews and proselytes; see I. Levinskaya, *The Book of Acts in its Diaspora Setting*, in B. Winter (series ed.), *The Book of Acts in its First Century Setting* (6 vols; Grand Rapids: Eerdmans, 1994–98), V, pp. 51–126. Barrett (I, pp. 629–31) identifies them here either as proselytes, or even as the 'Israelites', rather than a separate group. On the notably social advantages for Gentiles to be attached to synagogues, see J. Lieu, *Neither Jew nor Greek: Constructing Early Christianity* (London: T&T Clark, 2007), pp. 31–68.

127. The imperative ἀκούσατε is only used when there is some agitation among those being addressed: 7.2, Stephen; 15.13, James; 22.1, Paul.

whenever it is used elsewhere.[128] The critical tone contrasts with the positive approbation Paul accords the patriarchs, 'our fathers', that is Abraham, Isaac and Jacob who were chosen by God. It will be seen as the speech progresses that according to Paul the people have strayed away from the destiny for which God had originally chosen their fathers, which accounts for the disdain he expresses here. Like Stephen (cf. 7.2), Paul begins his review of the history of Israel with the patriarchs but, rather than concentrating on the Promise as Stephen did, he focuses attention on the theme of election. With the exception of a brief comment at 13.21a, it is God who takes the initiative as the subject of the sentences right through to the arrival of Jesus, with an additional emphasis through the word order at the mention of Jesus in v. 23 in the Bezan text.[129]

13.17b The next phase in the history of the patriarchs is the time spent in Egypt. According to the Bezan text, God made them great on account of the people, that is, not for their own sake but for the sake of the people of Israel whom they would become.[130] The Alexandrian text understands the sentence differently, taking the people to be directly the object of God's action. This may seem more logical since, throughout the following phases of God's dealings with Israel, it is the people who are the object given that the patriarchs had died. On the other hand, the object pronouns are all plural in agreement with 'our fathers' (αὐτούς/–οῖς, vv. 17c, 18, 21b, 22a), as is the verb in v. 21a. This being so, 'our fathers' come to represent the ancestors in general and 'the people' the nation of Israel as it later came to be.

The verb 'made them great' is used elsewhere only of the exaltation of Jesus (2.33; 5.31) and has the sense of raising up out of an oppressed state, contrasting the stature acquired by the fathers in Egypt with their condition of slavery.

13.17c Paul's summary of the history of Israel continues in epic terms with the account of God leading the ancestors out of Egypt in a demonstration of power. The absence of any mention of Moses is striking, especially compared with Stephen's speech, which paid a great deal of attention to Moses. For Paul, the power of salvation has everything to do with Jesus and nothing to do with Moses and the Law, as will be seen in the later parts of his speech. It must be remembered that Luke constructs this speech to represent Paul's thought, not his own, and there is therefore no need for the ideas expressed in it to agree or coincide with those expressed by other speakers.

---

128. Other occurrences of ὁ λαὸς οὗτος are found at Mt. 13.15 (= Isa. 61.10 LXX); 15.8 (= Isa. 29.13 LXX); Mk 7.6 (= Isa. 29.13 LXX); Lk. 9.13; 21.23; Acts 28.26, 27. The pejorative tone, due to the adjective in post-position, is echoed in the phrase Peter uses when he distances himself from his own people (τοῦ λαοῦ τῶν ᾿Ιουδαίων, Acts 12.11)

129. In D05, the fronting of the subject in the first line of v. 23 underlines the initiative of God: ὁ θεὸς οὖν ... ἤγειρεν.

130. διά + accusative expresses a causal sense, 'on account of', but also a sense of purpose, 'with a view to' (B-D-R, §222.2a), both senses being rendered in English by 'for the sake of'.

13.18 The fourth phase is the 40-year period Israel spent in the desert. 40 years is the traditional period of time ascribed to the wanderings of the people of Israel in the desert, between leaving Egypt and entering Canaan (Deut. 1.3). This is noted, for example, as the length of time for which the Israelites had to eat manna, 'from the 15th day of the second month after they had departed from the land of Egypt' (Exod. 16.2), until they arrived at Canaan (16.35). Codex Bezae, in stating the length of the period without any qualification, is simply repeating the traditional number of years. The qualification ὡς could be an indication that the whole period extended literally beyond 40 years, since elsewhere 40 years is presented as the time the Israelites had to wait before entering Canaan once they arrived near the land, because they complained when they heard from their spies about the fierceness of the inhabitants they would have to overcome (Num. 14.33, 34; cf. Numbers 13). In that case, the 40 years spent in the desert have a symbolic value, expressed by ὡς.

It is more likely that ὡς in the Alexandrian text is to be understood as a conjunction introducing a subordinate clause of time, especially in Codex Vaticanus which does not read καί before the following main verb: καὶ ὡς ... ἐτροποφόρησεν ... καθελὼν ... κατεκληρονόμησεν... (see *Critical Apparatus* for further discussion).

The variant reading concerning the verb, 'cared for' or 'endured', cannot be evaluated on the basis of the Deuteronomy text from which the reference is taken (Deut. 1.31) since the MSS of the LXX vary, too (see *Critical Apparatus*). The sense given by the Latin side of Codex Bezae, that God 'cared like a nurse' for Israel in the desert, reflects the tradition of the Aramaic targums of Deuteronomy and concords better with the positive tone of Paul's account at this point. He has not yet introduced any complaints against Israel. The alternative reading fits better with the tone of Stephen's speech in which he attacks the attitude of the people (Acts 7.38-43).

13.19 The next phase Paul presents is the entry into the land of Canaan, with the extermination of the seven nations (cf. Deut. 7.1-2) and the distribution of the land to the ancestors of Israel (cf. Josh. 14.1). The term attributed to Paul in the Bezan text is the same one Peter used when he first addressed Cornelius (Acts 10.28), and expressed the superiority the Jews felt with regard to the Gentiles.[131] Paul's choice of the word here shows how much he is talking to his Jewish audience from their point of view, for the moment taking no account of the presence of Gentile God-fearers (cf. on 13.16b above).

13.20 The time allocated to the historical periods varies according to the MSS: in the Alexandrian text, the period of approximately 450 years refers to the history of Israel related so far, though exactly which phases are meant is difficult to ascertain since none of the figures given in either the Hebrew or Greek Scriptures corresponds to a total of 450 years.[132] They should perhaps

---

131. See *The Message of Acts*, II, pp. 264–65.
132. See Barrett, II, pp. 633–34 for various suggestions.

be understood as the time in Egypt (400 years) through the wanderings in the desert (40 years) up to the conquest of Canaan (10 years).[133]

The reading of Codex Bezae, taking the 450 years up to the time of Samuel at the end of the period of the judges, is scarcely more comprehensible if it is taken to refer only to the time of the judges, since the time of the judges lasted only 170 years (from 1200–1030 BCE). Even if it is taken to mean the time since the exodus up to Samuel, the number is still inaccurate since 1 Kgs 6.1 speaks of the building of the Temple by Solomon 480 years after the exodus and both Saul and David are said to have reigned for 40 years (Acts 13.22, cf. 1 Sam 13.1; 2 Sam. 5.4; 1 Kgs 2.11). The number of years is unlikely to be literal, in fact: even the 480 years between the exodus and the start of the building of the Temple do not give a satisfactory, literal date for the exodus.[134] Figures cited in such Jewish historic reckonings had a symbolic value (representing, for example, the number of generations) that were not intended to correspond to literal reality, and it is just as likely that the interpretation of 450 years during the early transmission of Acts was figurative in some way. The difficulty felt today with understanding the meaning says more about the limitations of the present-day way of thinking than about the unreliability of the New Testament authors or editors.

This period of the judges, the sixth in Paul's account of the history of Israel, is given an end-time, with the era of Samuel. He was the last of the judges and the first of the Prophets after Moses (cf. 3.24). The association of Samuel with the end of the 450-year-long period during which the fortune of Israel was entirely in God's hands, anticipates a change in tone.

13.21 During Samuel's time, a distinct shift in the history of Israel took place which marked an interruption in the divine initiative, for 'they' asked for a king, thus going against the plan of God (1 Samuel 8). Paul does not develop the notion of disobedience, but takes Saul as a new starting point to move his speech towards his intended goal, which is Jesus. After a brief sentence that has the third person plural as the subject, implying the ancestors of Israel, God is immediately described as acting again in giving them what they wanted. The detail that Saul, with whom Paul shared his past name, was from the tribe of Benjamin just as Paul was (cf. Rom. 11.1; Phil. 3.5), has the effect of silently evoking Paul's own past (cf. Acts 9.4; 22.7; 26.14: 'Saul! Saul!'; see *Excursus* 2).

13.22 Paul passes quickly over Saul's tragic fall to focus attention on David as the model king, raised up by God 'for them', the ancestral fathers whom Paul had introduced at the beginning of his speech as the object of all the divine actions (or 'the people' according to the Alexandrian text, cf. 13.17b). Whereas Stephen had spoken about David in order to introduce the topic of the Temple, Paul has no such interest. His objective is to show how God, who was known to have worked out his plans throughout the history of

---

133. Bruce, *Text*, p. 264; Haenchen, p. 350.
134. See *Jewish Study Bible* on 1 Kgs 6.1, p. 683.

Israel, also had prepared everything for the time he would send the Saviour, in the person of Jesus.

The portrait of David is entirely positive, being the testimony of God himself: Paul takes as a basis for his presentation the text of 1 Sam. 13.14 in a form that combines elements of the MT (or LXX) with elements from the targumic version.[135] What is more, it is prefaced with Ps. 89.21, in such a way as to suggest that Paul was drawing on familiar interpretative traditions in presenting David with these scriptural quotations.[136]

The final statement of the quotation, 'who will carry out all my wishes', corresponds to the targumic form of 1 Sam. 13.14, and constitutes an assurance that David, unlike Saul who did not carry out God's will (cf. 1 Sam. 13.13-14; cf. 28.17-18), will carry out to perfection the orders God entrusts to him.

13.23 These next three verses bring to a conclusion the first exposition setting out the workings of God through the history of Israel. The intermediate conclusion is marked in Codex Bezae with the conjunction οὖν, 'Accordingly', and with 'God' underlined as the subject of the new paragraph. Not so in the Alexandrian text, which has the demonstrative pronoun τούτου, 'of this man [David]', to lead into the presentation of Jesus, thus placing significant emphasis on the Davidic line of the Messiah.

Jesus is presupposed to be known to the synagogue in Antioch, at least in the Bezan text; the omission of the article in the Alexandrian text has the effect of juxtaposing the noun 'saviour' with the name 'Jesus', so bringing out the meaning of the name in Hebrew.[137] He is introduced as 'the seed' of David, 'according to the promise'. The promise that Paul means is not the promise God made to Abraham (cf. Stephen, 7.5) but that made to David – namely, that his posterity should rule for ever, cited in 2 Kgdms (= 2 Sam.) 7.6-16: ἀναστήσω τὸ σπέρμα σου μετὰ σέ (v. 12). It has been suggested, indeed, that this text underlies the whole of Paul's sermon[138] and could even be the *haftarah* reading, which is alluded to throughout Paul's speech. The fact that in the original promise the reference is to a line of descendants, rather than one outstanding person, is something that had already been absorbed into the exegetical use of the promise in Judaism, where the 'seed' could at times be interpreted in the plural as meaning the many kings, or sons, of Israel, and at others as the unique Messianic king. Paul himself will take up the notion of numberless descendants, though only according to the Bezan text, when he goes on to demonstrate in Acts 13.33 D05, and the quotation of 13.34, the universal scope of the promise made to David (see *Commentary* below).

135. Bowker ('Speeches of Acts', pp. 102–104) identifies the quotation of 1 Sam. 13.14 as the introductory text for a *proem* homily.

136. M. Wilcox, 'The Promise of the "Seed" in the New Testament and the Targumim', *JSNT* 5 (1979), pp. 275–93.

137. The Hebrew 'Yehoshua' (also transcribed as 'Joshua') means 'YHWH saves' (cf. Mt. 1.21).

138. Doeve, *Jewish Hermeneutics*, p. 172.

Already in Acts 2.30-31, Peter had applied the promise made to David to the Messiah, on the basis of the dual meaning of the verb ἀνίστημι ('raise up' in the sense of 'bring into being' or in the sense of 'resurrect'),[139] and he had identified the Messiah as Jesus. Paul does not yet in 13.23 make use of the play on the verb ἀνίστημι: the Alexandrian text has the verb ἄγω ('he produced') and Codex Bezae the alternative verb ἐγείρω (which can also have the same dual senses as ἀνίστημι) as an echo of 'he raised up David' (ἤγειρεν [τὸν] Δαυίδ) in 13.22: David was raised up 'as a king' and Jesus as a 'saviour for Israel'. Paul employs the same alternative verb ἐγείρω at 13.30 to refer back to the one God brought into being, at the same time as playing for the first time on the other meaning of 'resurrect' (the Alexandrian text singles out the meaning of 'resurrect' at 13.30). Paul will not introduce the verb ἀνίστημι into his reasoning until he speaks openly and directly about the resurrection in 13.33-37 (see vv. 33, 34). A final use of ἐγείρω will occur at 13.37 (see *Commentary* below).

In his letters, Paul speaks of Jesus as the fulfilment of the promise of the seed, both as the seed promised to Abraham (Gal. 3.16) and the seed of David (Rom. 1.13). It appears that the assimilation of the two was made at an early date in Judaism.[140] The promise made to Abraham, that his seed would be like the dust of the earth (Gen. 13.16) or the stars of heaven (15.5) or the sand on the sea-shore (22.17), is applied to David in Jer. 33.21-22 (in MT, the targum and some MSS of the LXX). The promise of 'seed forever' is likewise associated with David in Ps. 89.5, just after the targum makes an explicit assimilation between Abraham ('my chosen one') and David (*Targ.* Ps. 89.4). The epithet 'chosen one' will again be used of David just prior to the citation Paul makes of this Psalm in 13.22: 'I have exalted one chosen out of my people, I have found David...' (Ps. 89.20-21). The first part of this psalm concludes with a promise that David's descendants would continue forever (Ps. 89.28-38).

It seems, then, that Paul had in mind Psalm 89 as a whole, when he quoted from it in 13.22, and not just an isolated verse. This is, in itself, a typically Jewish use of Scripture. Together with the complex intermingling of scriptural versions, it is evidence that Paul, and by implication Luke, knew well how to conduct sophisticated theological arguments from the Scriptures in accordance with Jewish methods and ways of thinking that his audience would be familiar with and understand. This is no Gentile narrator cobbling together sources in order to give clumsy expression to his own confused theology.

It is important to note Paul's focus on Israel at this point in his speech, just like his restriction of Jesus' role as saviour 'for Israel' (13.23) – it was for the people of Israel that Jesus was intended. This is the first of several similarities between Paul's speech and that of Peter to the household of Cornelius (10.34-43). When Peter explained the good news of Jesus on that occasion, he had

---

139. The link is made explicitly in Acts 2.30 D05 (see *The Message of Acts*, I, pp. 187–89).

140. This is the thrust of the demonstration carried out by Wilcox, 'The Promise of the Seed'.

not yet fully grasped that Jesus was sent by God as much for the nations as for the Jews and without the need for any further action on their part; that is something he came to realize once he saw how God gave the Holy Spirit to the Gentiles he was talking to (10.47; 11.17). So in his speech, despite his listeners being non-Jews (10.2, 35), he presented the message of Jesus as being for the people of Israel (10.36, 42). This limited view of God's purpose in Jesus was corrected in the case of Peter by means of what he witnessed in Cornelius' house, though he only fully grasped how far the traditional hopes and expectations of Israel had to be abandoned after his miraculous release from Herod's prison (cf. his declaration, 12.11).[141] Paul is more ready than Peter was to accept the Gentiles without imposing any condition, but considers Israel to retain the status as the Chosen People into which the nations will be integrated. He will discover in time that the universal message of Jesus does away with the notion of privileged status, but his journey will be both complex and costly, and will not be finished before he reaches Rome.[142]

13.24-25 The last two verses of the first exposition focus on John the Baptist as preparing the way for Jesus, not as an afterthought[143] but as an essential clarification about John's role. Paul brings to an end his presentation of the history of Israel by mentioning the activity of John the Baptist in a positive tone, in contrast to the invective with which Stephen concludes his review of the history of Israel with an attack on the rejection of those who were precursors of the Messiah (cf. 7.51-52).

Given the detailed explanation that Paul makes, John may well have had groups of followers in the area of Antioch who were making false claims for him. The point of Paul's account is to insist that John preceded Jesus and prepared the people for his arrival ([lit.] 'entrance') by preaching a baptism of repentance. This baptism was intended to be for all the people of Israel, not just a select group of initiates, and its purpose was to act as a sign of repentance in preparation for the Saviour of Israel. His role was, nonetheless, clearly preparatory and once Jesus arrived his own ministry began to end.

[β] 13.26-37 *Exposition 2: The Death and Resurrection of Jesus*
The beginning of the second exposition is marked with the repetition of the address given in 13.16b. This section of the speech does not bring in a new character or event but focuses on the person of Jesus introduced at 13.23. The nature of Paul's speech changes here, for he no longer pursues a historical survey but addresses a problem: namely, that the people of Ierousalem have put to death the Messiah. The structure is similar to that of the first exposition

---

141. Peter's gradual discovery of the full scope of Jesus' saving action is explored in *The Message of Acts*, II, throughout the *Commentary* on Acts 10, 11, 12.

142. Paul's spiritual journey will be observed in detail throughout the commentary on Acts 13–28; it is summarized in Rius-Camps, 'Gradual Awakening', pp. 281–96.

143. Barrett, I, p. 637 suggests that Luke (or Paul?) was thinking 'we must not forget to mention the forerunner, John the Baptist'.

in that there are again eight stages following the initial address, which are brought to a conclusion, this time with a series of scriptural proofs. The eight stages are made up of four offences carried out against Jesus in Ierousalem and four witnesses to his resurrection.

13.26	Address
13.27	Offence 1: Judgement of Jesus
13.28	Offence 2: Handing over to Pilate
13.29a	Offence 3: Request for crucifixion
13.29b	Offence 4: Placing in the tomb
13.30	Witness 1: God
13.31a	Witness 2: Jesus himself
13.31b	Witness 3: The first disciples
13.32-33a	Witness 4: Paul and his companions
13.33b-37	Scriptural proofs of Jesus' universal role

13.26 Paul launches into the next part of his speech by taking note for a second time of his audience, addressing them in terms similar to those used at the outset of his speech though in an expanded form. Thus, 'Men Israelites' become 'Men brothers (typically used of Jews among themselves, cf. 13.15), descendants of the race of Abraham', that is, those who represent the first of God's promises made to Abraham of descendants without number. He distinguishes them once more (though not according to Codex Vaticanus) from the God-fearers (see on 13.16b above). The phrase 'among us' tends to confirm that Paul viewed them as a separate group of people. He thereby acknowledges the presence of Gentiles among the assembly, knowing that they are sympathetic to the Jewish religious and ethical practices.

Paul affirms that the message of the salvation he has just mentioned, which was through Jesus (cf. 13.23), was 'sent out to us'. Two points need to be clarified here: first of all, the verb ἐξαπεστάλη has not the sense of the technical verb ἀποστέλλω used to express the idea of mission (cf. 10.36) but a more neutral sense of 'send away'.[144] In consequence, the first person pronoun 'to us' (ἡμῖν) would seem to refer not to the Jews and God-fearers Paul has just addressed as his audience, but to Paul and other Jesus-believers who have received the message that was originally destined for Israel (cf. 13.32, where the emphatic pronoun 'we' [ἡμεῖς] clearly refers to Paul and others who preach the gospel message). Since the message of salvation has been sent away (from Israel, from the Jews in Ierousalem, cf. v. 27) to the believers, Paul is in a position to pass it on to the people in Antioch. He will go on to explain how salvation was to be achieved through Jesus.

13.27 An obvious problem Paul has to deal with is the crucifixion of Jesus, which contradicts the expectations of a triumphant and glorious Messiah. He therefore begins his explanation, introduced with the typical conjunction

---

144. The verb ἀποστέλλω is used in all the Gospels, whereas the compound is used by Luke alone (Lk. × 3 + × 1 D05 + × 1 AT; Acts × 6 + × 2 D05). The sense of ἐξαποστέλλω is given by the prefix ἐξ.

γάρ,[145] by going through the events that brought about Jesus' death. He makes no bones about the identity of those he holds responsible: it was those living in Ierousalem and its (or their, AT) rulers. The form of the name for Jerusalem is that designating the holy city as the religious centre of Judaism, the place of the Temple and the seat of authority.[146] Paul does not mean, then, all the inhabitants of the city but the Jews who lived there and who were part of the spiritual identity of the place as the city chosen by God to be his dwelling place, where the Messiah was expected to arrive and reveal God's glory.[147] The 'rulers' are the authorities of the Temple and the Sanhedrin who ruled supreme in religious affairs among the Jews, despite the presence in Hierosoluma (the secular city) of the government imposed by Rome, and who allowed the Jews to exercise their own internal control in religious matters.

The Jews in Ierousalem benefited from all the knowledge, experience and skill of the most eminent teachers and interpreters of the Scriptures. Nevertheless, they did not know how to interpret the writings of the Prophets, writings that speak of the Messiah and that they would have heard week after week being read in the Sabbath assemblies. The Alexandrian text accounts for their treatment of Jesus on the grounds that they did not recognize or understand Jesus (as the Messiah, taking 'this' to refer back to the person Paul spoke of at some length in 13.23-25). The plea of ignorance is reminiscent of that put forward by Peter, also to explain the treatment of Jesus by the Jewish authorities (cf. 3.17),[148] but it should not be interpreted as an excuse. To the Jewish way of thinking, ignorance constituted a reason for wrong-doing but did not remove the blame for it – all wrong-doing was serious and to be guilty of it unwittingly, if anything, made matters worse (cf. Lev. 5.17). It did not alter the need for amends to be made but rather altered the means demanded in order to make amends. In other words, from a Jewish point of view, the plea of ignorance in the Alexandrian text does not lessen the gravity of the crime of Ierousalem, no more than omitting it in the Bezan text increases the severity of Paul's observations on the Jewish people.[149]

In any case, there was also the matter of the writings of the Prophets. According to the interpretation given to the Alexandrian text in the *Translation* above (the text is notoriously difficult, see *Critical Apparatus*), Paul says that the Jews in Ierousalem not only did not recognize Jesus but they likewise did not understand the utterances of the Prophets, presumably the ones that spoke about the coming of the Messiah; but by their act of judging Jesus, they fulfilled them (in so far as they speak of the dishonourable rejection of the

145. γάρ is frequently used to introduce or link steps in reasoning, without indicating any connection of cause and effect. Here it introduces the justification for Paul's claim that the message of salvation was sent out of Israel to the believers.

146. On the dual terms of Luke, see *General Introduction*, §VII.

147. See *The Message of Acts*, I, *Excursus* 1, pp. 79–87, on the Jewish hopes for the restoration of Israel.

148. See *The Message of Acts*, I, pp. 231–33.

149. This is a flaw in the reasoning of Epp, *The Theological Tendency*, pp. 41–48.

Messiah). The Bezan text has Paul focus entirely on the fulfilment of the Prophets: again according to the interpretation in the *Translation*, the two actions of 'not understanding the prophetic writings' and passing an 'act of judging' are linked in a circumstantial relation: the Jewish leaders judged without understanding the Prophets, and this caused them to fulfil what the Prophets wrote.

Various other ways of interpreting the relations between the participles and the main verb in both texts are possible. What is important is that according to Paul, the fulfilment of the Scriptures was necessary, the Messiah had to die an ignoble death and be a failure from a human point of view (cf. Lk. 24.45-46; Acts 3.17-18), but the agents did not have to be his own people whom he had come to save (cf. Lk. 22.22).

13.28 The second offence of the Jews in Ierousalem was to get Pilate to have Jesus killed even though there were no grounds for the death sentence.[150] The Bezan text develops certain details, twice specifying Jesus by means of the pronoun (ἐν αὐτῷ/αὐτόν), repeating that they themselves had judged him and then, worst of all, spelling out their act of handing Jesus over to a Gentile ruler, Pilate. In his Gospel, Luke underlines the fact that the Jews were unanimous in their decision to hand Jesus over to Pilate (ἅπαν τὸ πλῆθος, Lk. 23.1). The specific purpose, according to the Bezan text, was for his death (the word used by either text, ἀναιρεθῆναι AT/εἰς ἀναίρεσιν D05, makes a connection with Peter's speech to Cornelius, ἀνεῖλαν, 10.39).

13.29a The Alexandrian text considers the Jews' request to Pilate to have Jesus executed as completing what was written about him, a backwards glance to Paul's opening comment that they had fulfilled the Prophets in their act of judging (cf. 13.27). Codex Bezae dwells on yet further details that are viewed as continuing to fulfil the Scriptures. Not only did they hand Jesus over to Pilate for his execution but they also specifically asked for him to be crucified, with the emphatic demonstrative, 'this man' (cf. Lk. 23.18, 21, 23).

13.29b For the Alexandrian text, the prophetic messages about Jesus had been fulfilled with his death and there only remains now for his body to be removed from the cross (the crucifixion has been implied in their request to Pilate, 13.28) and to be placed in a tomb. Peter, in his speech to Cornelius, speaks of the crucifixion in similar terms of 'hanging on a tree' (10.39). Codex Bezae presents even these acts as dependent on the Jews having obtained permission a second time from Pilate in order to take down the body and bury it. This is the fourth and final offence.

Paul's presentation of the facts may be compared with the version Luke presents in his Gospel: there, he describes Joseph of Arimathea as 'a good and righteous man who had not consented to their purpose and deed, and he was

---

150. The innocence of Jesus is repeated three times in the Gospels: 1) Lk. 23.4; Jn 18.38 (Pilate); 2) Lk. 23.14-15 (Pilate and Herod); Jn 19.4 (Pilate); 3) Lk. 23.22; Jn 19.6 (Pilate).

waiting in expectation of the kingdom of God' (Lk. 23.50-51),[151] and he says that it was he who 'asked' (ἠτήσατο) Pilate for the body of Jesus (23.52-53; cf. Jn 19.38). Paul makes no distinction among those responsible for the various stages in Jesus' death, attributing them all to 'those living in Ierousalem and its (their) rulers' (cf. 13.27). That is not to say that he did not realize that Joseph of Arimathea was a good man (as if Luke omitted to tell him). Rather, his point is not to separate those Jews who acted from bad motives from those who were moved by more noble ones (as did Luke in his Gospel), but instead to distinguish between the Jews in Ierousalem who were responsible for all the overall events concerning the death of Jesus, and his disciples to whom Paul will turn in 13.31.

13.30 Having dealt with the death of Jesus, Paul once more brings his speech back to the initiative of God whose intervention in the history of Israel he had followed throughout the first part of his speech. The Alexandrian text continues by simply reintroducing God as the fronted subject of the sentence, so underlining the contrast between the actions of the Jews and the divine action which was to 'raise him up from the dead', using the same verb ἐγείρω as had been used to introduce God's 'raising up' of David (cf. 13.22), but making clear that the alternative meaning of the verb, to 'resurrect', is intended here by including the phrase 'from the dead'. God, then, is the supreme witness to the fact that Jesus was brought back to life after he had been killed and placed in the tomb. Peter makes the same point, directly after mentioning the crucifixion (10.40).

The Bezan text picks up in a more deliberate fashion the narrative thread from the first part of Paul's speech. It was seen that in the Bezan text, Paul not only used the verb ἐγείρω of David at 13.22 but repeated it to speak of God 'raising up' Jesus in 13.23, thus drawing a clear parallel between the two. Now, as Paul uses the verb for a third time, he gives a backward look to his previous use with respect to Jesus at the same time as giving the verb its other meaning of 'resurrect', in other words making an obvious, albeit implicit, play on words. The link in Greek, between the action of the Jews in having Jesus killed and buried, and that of God in both raising him up and resurrecting him, is a simple relative pronoun with no other connecting word, so that the sentence reads literally 'whom God raised/resurrected', ὃν ὁ θεὸς ἤγειρεν. The brief sentence functions as a pivot: on the one hand, it acts as a stark comment to create a double-meaning contrast between God and the Jews, his people: the one they laid in a tomb (the final step in their act of having him killed), was the one whom God had previously raised up as the saviour for Israel; but also, the one they laid in a tomb, God resurrected (cf. the same idea in Peter's speeches, 3.15; 4.10). On the other hand, the sentence anticipates the clause that follows in the next verse.

---

151. ἀγαθὸς καὶ δίκαιος – οὗτος οὐκ ἦν συγκατατεθειμένος (-τιθεμένος D ℵ *al*) τῇ βουλῇ καὶ τῇ πράξει αὐτῶν – ... ὃς προσεδέχετο τὴν βασιλείαν τοῦ θεοῦ.

13.31a The following clause begins, in the Bezan text, with the emphatic demonstrative pronoun, 'this man (οὗτος) appeared...', which corresponds to the relative pronoun of v. 30: 'he whom (ὅν) God resurrected'. In this way, the clause of v. 30, at the same time as linking to the previous discourse as explained above, also starts a new sentence that connects forward with the discourse Paul is about to develop on the resurrection. In the Alexandrian text, the clause begins with a relative pronoun (ὅς) corresponding to the object pronoun (αὐτόν) of the previous sentence. Jesus himself, then, is active in showing himself to his disciples and in this way is a witness to his own resurrection. The disciples are described as those who had gone from Galilee to Ierousalem with Jesus during his lifetime (cf. Lk. 18.31; 23.49; Acts 10.37); these do not just include the Twelve but also many others (cf. Acts 1.21-23 – even Barnabas, 1.22 D05, who is with Paul as he speaks!), although the following verse implies that Paul has in mind a restricted circle. In the Bezan text, the reference is to the journey Jesus undertook after his resurrection, accompanied by his disciples. Though Luke makes no reference to Jesus travelling with his disciples after his resurrection, both Matthew and John speak of his appearing in Galilee to the Eleven (Mt. 26.32, cf. 26.20; 28.7, 10, 16; Jn 21.1). Luke does, on the other hand, present the resurrection appearances as taking place over an extended period of time, specifically 40 days (cf. Acts 1.3; 10.41 D05). Now Luke and Peter may well have given this number for its figurative value,[152] which is not of interest to Paul at this point, but it corresponds in any case to the 'many days' he attributes to the journey. Peter, for his part, also describes as a first hand witness Jesus' appearances to a chosen group of his disciples, probably meaning the Eleven and a small circle of companions (cf. Lk. 24.33), and how they ate and drank with him, and kept company with him according to the Bezan text (Acts 10.41 D05).

Whether before the resurrection (Lk. 9.51, 53; 13.22; 17.11; 19.28; cf. Acts 10.39) or after (Lk. 24.50 [cf. 24.33, 36]; Acts 1.4), the journey ended in Ierousalem, the holy city that Jesus then led his disciples out of (Lk. 24.50). He did not intend them to remain within the confines of the Jewish institution, though they were to announce the good news within it (Lk. 24.47; cf. Acts 1.8) before moving out further and further away from the centre. Paul will demonstrate that he has understood this programme, even though a concern for Ierousalem, which at present is not apparent, will continue to dog him throughout his journeys until he finally reaches Rome.

13.31b The disciples to whom Jesus had appeared over a number of days constitute Paul's third set of witnesses to the resurrection. These same ones are his witnesses to the people, πρὸς τὸν λαόν, that is the Jews. The Bezan text qualifies their witnessing activity, saying that it has continued up to the present time, that it is going on even now. Paul indicates here his view that the scope of the witness of the first disciples of Jesus was to Israel (cf. Gal. 2.7-9), though whether or not they would have agreed with him is not so certain. For

152. See *The Message of Acts*, I, pp. 64–66, on Acts 1.3.

one a thing, Peter himself had been prepared by God to preach the gospel to the Gentiles and was well aware of the fact (10.1–11.18; cf. 15.7b). Barnabas himself, who is with Paul in Antioch of Pisidia as he speaks, had been one of the disciples who had been with Jesus from the beginning of his ministry until his ascension according to Codex Bezae (1.22, 23 D05), and he also was conscious of his role to take the message of Jesus to the Gentiles (cf. on 15.36-39 in Section II below).

13.32-33a The final witnesses are Paul and his companions or perhaps, more realistically, Paul and Barnabas, though it is not unthinkable that 'those around Paul' (13.13) also carried out informal conversations with the people in the places they visited. At this point, Paul brings his speech back to the promise made to 'our fathers', the Bezan text showing how Paul included himself among the Jews of the synagogue, sharing a common ancestry with them, just as did Peter in his speeches to the Jews in Ierousalem according to the same text (2.39 D05; 3.22 D05). The promise in question is the one made to David (cf. 13.23), that God would raise up for him a descendant (or descendants): ἀναστήσω τὸ σπέρμα σου μετὰ σέ, 2 Kgdms 7.12. Paul declares that the promise has been fulfilled for 'our children'. The expected reading would have been 'their children', which is indeed what some manuscripts read,[153] but here Paul is being careful to move on from claiming that the promise made to 'our' Jewish fathers is limited to 'their' Jewish children. Those to whom the promise has been given are, in fact, all those represented in the synagogue of Antioch, both Jews and those Gentiles who fear God; they are the first generation of those who have access to the promise through belief in Jesus, as Paul will explain in the closing elements of his speech. He is looking forward from the present time onwards, as the extended quotation from the Psalm given in the next verse of the Bezan text will demonstrate. Peter makes a similar statement about the promise being 'for us and for our children'[154] in bringing his Pentecost speech to a close, though at that stage he considered the time of the Gentiles to be still in the future (2.39 D05).[155]

In coming back to the promise, Paul now takes up the verb, ἀνίστημι, which he avoided on his first mention of it by playing on the alternative verb ἐγείρω (see on 13.23 above). He makes a clear and open declaration, saying that the promise made to David has been accomplished in Jesus, specifically in his resurrection (or, in the AT wording of this clause and the next, simply in

153. The possessive pronoun is the subject of some variation among the manuscripts, some reading the (apparently) more logical αὐτῶν, others ἡμῖν in apposition to τοῖς τέκνοις. N-A[27] adopts the latter reading: τοῖς τέκνοις [αὐτῶν] ἡμῖν; see Metzger, *Commentary*, p. 362 for the discussion behind the choice.

154. 2.39 D05: ἡμῖν γάρ ἐστιν ἡ ἐπαγγελία καὶ τοῖς τέκνοις ἡμῶν. The AT reads ὑμῖν ... ὑμῶν, which causes Peter to distance himself from his audience. Some have suggested that Paul also said something similar and that the first pronoun ἡμῖν accidentally dropped out (see Barrett, I, p. 645; Bruce, *Text*, p. 268; Metzger, *Commentary*, p. 362).

155. For a discussion of 2.39, see *The Message of Acts*, I, pp. 191–92.

his being brought into existence[156] – see the next paragraph on the quotation
from the Psalm). Codex Bezae associates with the resurrection the dual roles
of Jesus, as Lord and as Messiah. It is often affirmed that it is a scribal feature
of the Bezan text, or the Western text in general, to complete the name of
Jesus with his full titles, as if reflecting later ecclesiastical practice, but the
impression is a false one since there are many occurrences of the name of
Jesus in Acts that the Bezan scribe did not add to (see *Critical Apparatus* for
fuller discussion). At 4.33, the only other reference to the resurrection in Acts
that directly includes the name of Jesus, there seen from the perspective of the
apostles, Codex Bezae again reads the full title. It seems to be that the issue of
the resurrection calls for the title of both Lord and Messiah, because they are
both aspects of what God has done in Jesus, which are demonstrated by means
of the resurrection even though they were already active during his ministry.
Thus Peter, also, associates the fact that it was God who made Jesus Lord and
Messiah with his place at the right of God (2.32-36). Besides, this is Paul's
first declaration of the Lordship and Messiahship of Jesus, which he needs to
underline in order to show how Jesus thus fulfils the promise of a son made
to David.

It is striking that Paul, in all his presentation of Jesus, says not one word
about the life of Jesus, the things he did or taught. This is similar to Peter's
early speeches (cf. 2.14-36, esp. 2.32) but in contrast to his witness to the
Gentile Cornelius where he mentions, in a brief but dense summary, the ministry of Jesus through the power of the Holy Spirit, in 'doing good and healing
all those who were being oppressed by the devil because God was with him'
(10.38). Paul's preoccupation is, first, with the fact that it was God who was
responsible for bringing Jesus into being, just as he was in the case of David,
and secondly, with the resurrection and therefore his rule as Christ, as the
Messiah. These are the things he seeks to bear witness to, which is a somewhat more limited programme than Jesus entrusted to his disciples when he
told them to 'bear witness to me' (1.8).[157]

13.33b The next five verses up to v. 37 are a demonstration from Scripture
that Jesus is a Messiah of all the nations as well as Israel.[158]

Paul first confirms the appointment of Jesus as David's son by citing
the Psalm of enthronement, Psalm 2 according to the LXX but a continuation
of Psalm 1 according to other Jewish traditions. The same words were pronounced at Jesus' baptism according to the Bezan text of Lk. 3.22. Since they
are pronounced both then by a voice from heaven, and now by Paul, without

---

156. Barrett (I, pp. 645–46) excludes the sense of resurrection because Jesus was designated
as the son of God, cited in the Psalm quotation that follows, during his ministry on earth, not after
his resurrection. Cf. Bruce, *Text*, p. 269.

157. See *The Message of Acts*, I, on 1.22 (p. 129) and 2.32 (p. 189).

158. For a thorough examination of the LXX texts, see G.J. Steyn, *Septuagint Quotations in
the Context of the Petrine and Pauline Speeches of the Acta Apostolorum* (Kampen: Kok Pharos,
1995), pp. 168–85.

any other explanation, it can be assumed that they were recognized in Jewish circles as designating the Messiah. In the Alexandrian text, the use Paul makes of the quotation is different from the use he makes in the Bezan text. Where the previous clause of the Alexandrian text reads simply that God has fulfilled the promise 'having raised Jesus', which (see above paragraph) can be taken to mean 'brought him into existence' rather than 'resurrect', the quotation is introduced with ὡς καί ... γέγραπται, 'as indeed it is written...'. The declaration that Jesus is God's son thus relates simply to his being raised up by God, and has nothing to do with his resurrection. The Psalm quotation is made to endorse the son-ship of Jesus.

In Codex Bezae, however, Paul's purpose in citing the Psalm is to demonstrate that he who is David's son also has possession of the nations, so justifying Paul's proclamation that the promise has been fulfilled to both Jews and God-fearers. Thus he introduces the quotation with οὕτως γὰρ ... γέγραπται, 'For this is what is written...'. Furthermore, he does not only cite the verse that declares David as God's son, applying it to Jesus, but he continues the quotation, which goes on to give to David power over the nations. In the original context, David would rule over them as king and destroy them so that they might no longer attack Israel. This idea of destruction is apparently absent from the application of the promise Paul makes to Jesus, but it is nonetheless clearly implied that the time has come for the nations and Israel to be ruled over as one by the Lord Jesus as the Messiah. Because the Jews of Ierousalem put to death the one who was sent as the saviour for Israel, Jesus is enthroned after his resurrection as a universal Lord and Messiah. In what measure Paul continues to view Israel as having the privileged status of the Chosen People of God is not apparent from his speech at this point, though it will become clear that it is an issue that he has by no means yet resolved.

13.34 What Paul needs to convey to his audience is that the promise made to David, like the declaration of son-ship, has been fully realized in Jesus because of his resurrection, and because this resurrection is permanent. Death is equivalent to 'corruption' (διαφθορά), in the sense of returning to the earth (cf. Gen 3.19). For Codex Bezae, the important factor in the promise is that God has also given him the nations (cf. 13.33b D05); this universal aspect is considerably attenuated in the Alexandrian form of Paul's speech, to the point that it is rarely noted.

Paul first of all appeals to a passage from the prophet Isaiah, Isa. 55.3, and then to Ps. 16.10 (15.10 LXX). In the Alexandrian text, these two quotations read as evidence that Jesus has been raised up (13.33a), that he has been resurrected and will not die again (13.34a). The first quotation appears to be addressed to the Jesus-believing community, ὑμῖν, who will receive the sure blessings (τὰ ὅσια) promised to David; and the second gives weight to the first with a causal link (διότι καί), by identifying Jesus as the embodiment of the sure blessings (τὸν ὅσιον) and confirming that his resurrection is definitive.

In the Bezan text, Paul's reasoning process follows a somewhat different path, which has as its starting point the extended quotation of Psalm 2 given in 13.33b. It should be noted that the connection between the Isa. 55.3 text and that from Ps. 16.10 is not made explicit in Codex Bezae. That is because the link is not a logical one but a hermeneutical one that depends, for its sense, on the similarity of wording. The two passages have in common the verb δίδωμι in the future (in the first then the second person), and the key noun ὅσιος, first in the neuter plural, τὰ ὅσια, then the accusative masculine singular, ὅσιον. The verb-noun combination acts as a hook to connect the two passages. The notion expressed by the noun is difficult to translate with a single word in English: it denotes that which is established or ordered or permitted by divine law,[159] so 'blessings' when referring to something given by God to a person, and 'holy one' when referring to a person. In the quotation from both Isaiah and the Psalm, ὅσιος translates the Hebrew חסד. Now, precisely the same term is found in the Hebrew text of 2 Sam. 7.15 (translated in 2 Kgdms LXX by ἔλεος), where YHWH promises his eternal blessing on David: 'I will never withdraw my favour (חסדי) from him'. This is the promise Paul has already referred to (13.23, cf. 13.32) in proclaiming its fulfilment in Jesus. The particular association of texts, all linked in Hebrew by the same term חסד, strongly suggests that the scriptural tradition was known in Hebrew not only by Paul and by Luke but also, obviously, by their addressees, the Jews of the Antioch synagogue and Theophilus respectively.

Despite the similarity in wording, the two passages have a different content and Paul does not cite them as if they both said the same thing. The Isaiah passage is a promise, to anyone who will listen to the good things God has to say, that such a person will be given the blessings (τὰ ὅσια) promised to David, namely that he would be a ruler over many nations. The content of this promise is remarkably like that of Ps. 2.8, just cited in the Bezan text of Acts 13.33b: 'As I have made him a witness of nations, a leader and commander of nations, so you shall summon a nation you did not know, and a nation that did not know you shall come running to you, for the sake of the Lord your God, the Holy One of Israel who has glorified you' (Isa. 55.4-5).[160] The promise

---

159. Bailly, I, 1. For the use of the term ὅσιος in Greek literature, especially in blessings formulae, see H. Jeanmaire, 'Le substantif HOSIA et sa signification comme terme technique dans le vocabulaire religieux', *REG* 58 (1945), pp. 66–89; J. Dupont, 'TA 'OΣIA TA ΠIΣTA (Actes 13,34 = Isaïe 55,3)', in *Études sur les Actes des Apôtres* (Lectio Divina, 45; Paris: Éditions du Cerf, 1967), pp. 337–59.

160. The translation is adapted, according to possible alternative renderings, from the *Jewish Study Bible* (p. 895) which notes: 'In 2 Sam. 7.8-16 and Ps. 89.4, 20-37, God promised to David that his descendants would rule Israel forever as an enduring royal dynasty'. These texts are, of course, exactly the ones adduced by Paul earlier in his speech in Antioch of Pisidia as evidence that God caused Jesus to come into being in order to fulfil the Davidic promises. However, what was not accomplished through David, Deutero-Isaiah applied to all of Israel; whereas Paul, on the other hand, applies it to Jesus as the supreme son of David, the Messiah. Thus, in Paul's reason-

extended by Isaiah to Israel as a whole is interpreted by Paul, on the basis of Ps. 2.8, as fulfilled in Jesus.

13.35 In order for the fulfilment to hold true, Jesus has to be an everlasting Messiah, who will never die. Paul omits the reference to precisely this notion from his citation of Isa. 55.3, which contains the words διαθήκην αἰώνιον, 'an everlasting covenant', in apposition to 'the blessings', but it is so much an aspect of the promise that his hearers must have known it, just as they are supposed to have known the contents of the blessings given to David that Paul likewise does not cite. Paul, then, has to demonstrate that the resurrection of Jesus was definitive and that he would never die again. In a similar way, Peter had taken care to develop exactly the point in his Pentecost speech (2.24-31), using the Scriptures, including an extended citation of Psalm 16 (15 LXX). Paul's proof is limited to one verse from this Psalm, consisting of the declaration made by David that God had given him, his Holy One (τὸν ὅσιον), life and preserved him from death, that is corruption (διαφθορά).

13.36-37 Paul's next task is to explain that the declaration was not actually, permanently, realized in David; by implication, the promise of the first citation could not be realized in David either. In Jesus, on the other hand, God did realize the fact of the Holy One not seeing corruption, and so the earlier promise of ruling over the nations is realized in Jesus. The contrast between David and Jesus is explicitly underlined in the Alexandrian text (μὲν ... δέ). David was king in his own time, entirely in fulfilment of God's purpose (cf. 1 Sam. 15.28-29; 2 Sam. 5.2, 12). An allusion to 1 Kgs 2.10 is made to affirm that David did, indeed, die ('David slept with his fathers and was buried in the city of David'; cf. 2 Sam. 7.12); in consequence, he could not receive the blessings promised to him. In a final, laconic sentence Paul reiterates that Jesus 'did not see corruption', which means that, having died, he was immediately resurrected. For the last time, he uses again the verb ἤγειρεν, echoing the previous uses of the same verb to refer, first, to David as king (13.22), then to Jesus as saviour (13.23); later, to Jesus again (13.30) with the ambiguous meaning now of 'resurrect'. At this final occurrence, when the phrasing used on the last occasion in Codex Bezae is repeated (ὃν ὁ θεὸς ἤγειρεν), the double meaning is strongly apparent, with an intentional play on the fact that God not only brought Jesus into existence but also raised him from the dead.

[γ] 13.38-41a *Parenesis: The Possibility of Forgiveness and Final Warning*
Having set out his demonstration of God's working throughout the history of Israel up to and including the resurrection of the Lord Jesus as the Messiah, Paul now addresses his audience for a final time, drawing conclusions from what he has said so far. There are three parts to his conclusion, each intro-

---

ing, it is because of him (rather than Israel) that 'all humanity ... come to recognize, as a result of her [Israel's] redemption, the one true God' (*Jewish Study Bible*, p. 895).

duced in the Bezan text with the particle οὖν, which takes the listeners through successive steps:

13.38	Announcement of forgiveness and repentance
13.39	Universal justification
13.40-41a	Warning against unbelief

13.38 The address as Paul launches into his conclusion is brief and to the point, limiting those to whom he addresses it to the Jews in the synagogue: 'Men brothers' (cf. 13.15, 26). This restricted address is not carelessness on Luke's or Paul's part, or due to a wish to be brief, but quite deliberate. What Paul has to say here is for the Jews, as will be seen. A similar procedure was noted in Peter's speech at Pentecost where he addressed the first part of his speech to humanity in general but limited the second part to the Jews (2.22, 36).[161]

There is a lesson to be learnt from all that Paul has been saying: 'Let it be known to you...',[162] that on the grounds of the resurrection (διὰ τοῦτο, AT) or through Jesus (διὰ τούτου, Codex Bezae), they have the possibility of forgiveness, and repentance according to the Bezan text. In a circumlocution that summarizes what will become his theological trademark, Paul expresses what exactly they can be forgiven for and repented of, that is, everything that the Law of Moses was incapable of putting right. The term he uses is 'be justified' which, in his writings, acquires something of a technical sense meaning 'be made righteous' (cf., e.g., Rom. 3.9-26). His concern, which emerges throughout his letters, is that the Law of Moses failed to achieve fully the reconciliation of people with God. He does not deny that it had partial value in this respect, suggesting that in some ways the Law did achieve reconciliation and justification with God, but that there were areas that were not affected by the means provided by Moses for making atonement for wrong-doing. How far he actually believed this is open to question since there are apparent contradictions in the evidence from his own writings.[163]

13.39 What is spectacularly new in Jewish terms is Paul's affirmation that this justification is for everyone, on the grounds of faith in Jesus (cf. Rom. 3.22). Peter's conclusion in his speech to Cornelius had been very similar, announcing forgiveness in the name of Jesus 'to all who believed in him' (10.43).

13.40-41a Paul leaves his audience with a stark warning against rejecting what he has said. It now becomes clear why he has addressed the lesson to be drawn from his speech to the Jews alone: it is they who are to take to heart the

---

161. The point is made in *The Message of Acts*, I, pp. 179–80, 184.

162. The expression γνωστὸν ἔστω is used only by Luke in the New Testament (cf. 2.14; 4.10; 28.28).

163. There are undoubtedly points of contact between Paul's speeches in Acts and his letters to different communities. However, to avoid extensive digressions on Paul's theology and Luke's representation of it, detailed comparison will not be made in the *Commentary*. This topic in itself would require another volume.

prophetic warning addressed to Israel in Hab. 1.5. Paul quotes from the LXX text, where the opening line differs from that of the Hebrew text.[164] The people of Israel are addressed in a critical tone: because of their contemptuous attitude, they will marvel at what they see and vanish. The context of Habakkuk's words was the imminent invasion of Israel by the Babylonians whom God would cause to pour into the country of Israel as a terrifying and violent mass and take over all their land and possessions (Hab. 1.6-11). The essential ideas that Paul takes over are that there is about to be a rush of Gentiles to enter Israel and that this is God's doing, his 'work'. He is warning the Jews that if they do not repent or believe in Jesus and, what is more, accept that the possibility of justification with God is also available to the Gentiles, God will carry out his judgement[165] on Israel, which will be overrun and disappear. This is a preoccupation Paul will hold on to – time and time again, he will do all that he can to persuade his own people, the Jews, to believe the universal message of Jesus in order to save them from being annihilated and taken over by the Gentiles.[166] He will have the greatest difficulty in accepting their refusal of the message he preaches, until he finally does so when he reaches Rome.

[a´] 13.41b *Silence*

13.41b The reaction to Paul's speech, and especially to his concluding words, is noted only in Codex Bezae: the assembly is silent.[167] Now silence can sometimes express a positive attitude (cf. 15.12, 13 esp. D05; 21.40), and there may be a conscious echo here of Hab. 2.20 MT: 'The Lord is in his holy Temple; let all the earth keep silence before him', since Paul has just cited a prophecy from that book. Keeping silence (σιγάω) in response to a speech, however, is at times a sign in Luke's writings that the hearers do not want to say anything, because they are not pleased with, nor even know, what is expected or asked of them (cf. Lk. 9.36; 20.26).[168] Their silent response, in effect, puts an end to Paul's speech. It may be compared with the response of Peter's listeners in Ierousalem (some, at least, according to the Bezan text) who, on hearing the

---

164. In the Hebrew text, the prophecy begins by instructing Israel to 'look among the nations, to take note and be amazed'.

165. The notion of God's judgement can be seen from the occurrence of the same phrase, μὴ ἐπέλθη, in Simon Magus' plea that nothing of what Peter had threatened should come upon him (μηδὲν ἐπέλθη, 8.24).

166. The entry of the Gentiles as believers in Jesus does not *ipso facto* mean the exclusion of Israel from the people of God, as stated by Haenchen, p. 55; Schneider, II, p. 141. The idea is rather that if they do not become part of the believing community themselves, then they will be excluded from it and it will be made up of Gentiles.

167. The plural ἐσίγησαν can only refer to the people in the synagogue, and not to Paul (as suggested by Barrett, I, p. 653; Haenchen, p. 355, n. 2) since he was alone in speaking (cf. 13.16a).

168. σιγάω is distinguished in Luke from ἡσυχάζω, which has more positive connotations (cf. Acts 21.40 D05 [B03, σιγάω]; 22.2). The verb σιωπάω also has a negative force in Luke (Lk. 6.9 D05 [AT *om.*]; 19.40 AT [D05 σιγάω]; cf. Mk 9.34; 14.61 AT [D05 σιγάω]).

explanation that Jesus the Messiah had been crucified, were anxious to know
what they should do (cf. 2.37).

[DA-*B*] 13.42-43 *Synagogue Response*

In a new episode, Luke describes the reaction to Paul's speech.

[a] 13.42 *Renewed Invitation*
13.42 It is important to note that Paul and his companions go out of the
synagogue before the meeting finishes (cf. v. 43), as if prompted by the lack
of response to Paul's speech on the part of the people in the synagogue.
Aware of their resistance, manifested by the absence of any kind of discussion
or questioning, they leave. Obviously, if the observation is omitted that the
people were silent after Paul spoke to them about Habakkuk's prophecy, it
becomes difficult to see why they should leave before the synagogue breaks
up, which can explain why some manuscripts interpret the people who speak
in this verse as the Gentiles who met Paul on his way out, while the Jews were
still inside the synagogue (see *Critical Apparatus*).

While they were on their way out,[169] people in the synagogue (probably
the same leaders as gave the initial invitation, cf. 13.15) asked them to return
on the following Sabbath to speak to them again. The general idea is the same
in both texts, but there are subtle and important differences in the way it is
expressed. In Codex Vaticanus, the verb ἠξίουν is the simple verb of request-
ing, in place of the widely attested 'urging' (παρεκάλουν), which takes up the
notion of 'exhortation' from the first invitation at 13.15 (παρακλήσεως). The
Alexandrian text wants 'these things' to be spoken to them the following
Sabbath, referring to the prophetic warning Paul has just given to them. Codex
Bezae leaves the topic more vague, 'the same kind of things', referring to the
ideas of the speech overall.

[b] 13.43a *Many Follow Paul and Barnabas*
13.43a The narration continues by describing, now, what happens when the
synagogue[170] was dismissed. The reaction at this point is more positive: a good
number of the Jews as well as the proselytes 'follow' Paul and Barnabas.
Though Paul is in first place, Barnabas has reappeared as Paul's principal
companion, the two of them (as a united team in Codex Bezae, see *Critical
Apparatus*) representing the task entrusted to them by the Holy Spirit (13.2) of

---

169. The verb ἔξειμι describing their going out of the synagogue is used only by Luke (Acts ×
4), and is a neutral verb, without the connotations of 'exodus' (leaving a place of imprisonment or
slavery, cf. 12.17) that Luke expresses by means of the verb ἐξέρχομαι. The use of the present
participle, alongside the imperfect of the main verb (παρεκάλουν/ἠξίουν), signifies that both
actions were happening together.

170. This is the only occurrence in the Gospels and Acts where συναγωγή does not refer to
the building but to the gathering of the congregation. It corresponds to the verb συνήχθη (13.44)
to describe the gathering of the people of the city (τὸ πλῆθος, 13.45 D05).

taking the gospel away to other lands beyond the sea. This is an altogether better situation than if they adhered to Paul alone.[171] Besides, the verb 'followed' has connotations of following as a disciple.[172] For that reason, Paul and Barnabas are able to persuade them to 'continue in the grace of God', which assumes that they were already on the right path and were to keep going in it. A similar reference to the 'grace of God', manifested in the conversion of many Gentiles in Antioch of Syria, was noted when Barnabas was sent there by the apostles who had heard what was happening there (cf. 11.23).[173] At this point, it is not said explicitly that those following Paul and Barnabas and talking with them believed, as will be said of the Gentiles as a whole after the second speech (13.48).

[b'] 13.43b *The Spread of the Word throughout the City*

13.43b The sentence that sums up the activity in Antioch of Pisidia so far is preserved only in Codex Bezae among the Greek manuscripts. It corresponds to the colophon that follows the second speech in Antioch (13.48-49). The result of the activity of Paul and Barnabas in the city (to be taken as a whole, starting with the synagogue speech and continuing with the discussions that ensued) is that the whole city became aware of the 'word of God'. This phrase has a technical sense in Luke's writings, especially in Codex Bezae where it refers to God's revelation to his creation (see *Excursus* 1). The 'word of God' has hitherto been the privileged possession of Israel and so has been confined to the synagogue in Antioch; but with the activity of Paul and Barnabas, it spreads to the largely Gentile population of the town. That does not mean that they believed it, but that they at least had opportunity to hear it, outside the synagogue. This is an essential prelude to the townspeople hearing the 'word of the Lord' (13.44b; cf. on 13.48, 49 below), the message specifically about or of Jesus, which will be spoken by Paul to the whole city when they gather on the following Sabbath.

Excursus 5

The Structure of Paul's Speech to the Synagogue of Antioch of Pisidia

In the text of Codex Bezae, the structure of Paul's speech can be identified, on the one hand, by the development in his argument and, on the other, by the corresponding connectives (καί, δέ, οὖν, for example) used to link together the various steps in his argument. The connectives are essential linguistic markers that serve as objective signposts for the analysis of the speech: in Codex

---

171. Cf. 'Paul and those around him', 13.13; and 8.6, 12: ἐπίστευσαν τῷ Φιλίππῳ.

172. ἀκολουθέω + dative in the Gospels and Acts has a technical sense of discipleship, which is absent when the person being followed is in the accusative (cf. Mk 14.51 D05, ἠκολούθει αὐτούς).

173. See *The Message of Acts*, II, p. 313.

Bezae, they create a balanced and cohesive framework that tallies with a coherent line of argument.

The overall structure consists of two expositions, rounded off with a parenesis or exhortation. The three sections represent a progressive movement in time, starting in *Exposition* 1 (see *Commentary* 13.16b-25) with the major stages in the history of Israel from Abraham to Jesus; *Exposition* 2 (see *Commentary* 13.26-37), prepared for by the first exposition, focuses on the present time, with Jesus as the main topic; and the final *Parenesis* (see *Commentary* 13.38-41), drawing conclusions from the second exposition, looks forward to the future.

The internal structure of the two expositions is repeated. Each opens with a similar address, to the Jews and the God-fearing Gentiles present in the synagogue. It is followed by eight stages building up to a conclusion, which consists in the first exposition, of the presentation of Jesus and, in the second, of scriptural proofs to demonstrate his universal role.

The *first exposition* consists of a historical survey of Israel, demonstrating how at every stage God was in control and directing events. Paul's goal is to prove that the final event in the long story of Israel's past was the arrival of the Messiah, Jesus. The first eight stages of the history are linked with the connective καί, except at 13.17b where the absence of connective focuses attention on the people of Israel as the object of God's concern. The successive historical eras are presented as a series of events, building up to the final one, the arrival of Jesus, who is introduced with the connective οὖν, 'accordingly'.

The *second exposition* changes in tone, the concern now being to address the seemingly inextricable situation of the present time, caused by the Jewish leaders putting the Messiah to death. The eight stages this time fall into two groups, four offences against Jesus and four corresponding witnesses to his resurrection. The offences follow each other in quick succession, linked with καί except for the principal event, the request for crucifixion at v. 29a, which is marked with δέ. The transition to the series of witnesses is connected to the offences with a relative pronoun that serves as a pivot, keeping the focus on Jesus; it is followed by a series of pronouns linking together the different witnesses. The proofs that conclude the second exposition are introduced with the typical formula οὕτως ... γέγραπται, 'Thus ... it is written' (lit.).

The *parenesis* is addressed to the Jews alone. It draws conclusions from what has been set out in the two expositions. The three steps are introduced with οὖν, the first announcing a hope for the Jews, followed by a declaration that extends this hope to all nations, and concluding with a severe warning that brings the speech overall to a close.

The line of Paul's argument throughout the first exposition and the second up to the scriptural proofs at 15.33-37, presents Jesus as God's plan for Israel: everything is seen from the point of view of the Jews with whom the God-fearing Gentiles present in the synagogue are expected to identify. Once he moves to the citations from the Scriptures, however, Paul picks up a reference to the Gentiles already implied in a text he had alluded to earlier when he first introduced the person of Jesus, namely 2 Sam. 7.15. By a typically Jewish combination of these texts and their application to the present situation, Paul extends the Messiahship of Jesus to the Gentiles, presenting it as an integral part of the eternal plan of God that has, at this present time, finally been realized. Thus, in the final exhortation, he warns the Jews alone that, if they do not avail themselves of the means for salvation offered through Jesus, since this salvation is also now available to the Gentiles Israel will be invaded and outnumbered by the Gentiles entering into God's people.

[DA'] 13.44-52 *The Gentiles in Antioch*

Overview

The second sub-sequence in Antioch of Pisidia mirrors the first ([DA], 13.14-43), although the first was much longer by virtue of the length of Paul's speech. That speech was addressed to the Jews and God-fearers of the local synagogue and pronounced by Paul, who was thus alone responsible for situating Jesus as the Messiah primarily in relation to Israel. The speech in this second sub-sequence is the responsibility of both Paul and Barnabas, working together in harmony, and it is Barnabas who gives Paul the courage and determination to acknowledge the consequences of the Jews' opposition in the city to the message of Jesus. It should be noted that this speech at 13.46-47 does not correspond to the request made to Paul and Barnabas as they were leaving the synagogue, to speak to them again on the following Sabbath (cf. 13.42). That particular speech is noted at 13.44 but its contents are not recorded. The words addressed to the Jews at 13.46-47 are spoken in response to the Jewish reaction to the speech of 13.44.

This second speech recorded by Luke at 13.46-47 represents a turning point in Paul's life and thought, equivalent to Peter's in Acts 12 but with the difference that it is only a first step in the case of Paul (see *Excursus* 11). The essential notions expressed within it, that Israel was chosen first as God's people but the Gentiles were always intended to be included later, will be picked up by James at the Ierousalem meeting (see *Commentary,* 15.14). It should not be assumed that these ideas represent the theology of Luke since he, for his part, aligns himself with the 'we'-group who were more universal in outlook (see *General Introduction,* §VIII). Luke's theology is conveyed through key figures whom he portrays favourably: thus, he is opposed to the idea of the sanctity of the Temple (Stephen, 7.44-50), convinced of God's acceptance of the Gentiles on exactly the same footing as the Jews (Peter, 11.17) and does not hold on to the expectations of a restored Israel (Peter, 12.11).[174]

---

174. The theological positions expressed by Stephen and Peter are explored in *The Message of Acts,* II, *ad loc.*

Luke has recourse in this incident to an exegetical device he already used in the Pentecost scene, whereby the events have a localized, historical reality (taking place on a particular Sabbath in Antioch of Pisidia among Jews and Gentiles of the city) at the same time as a spiritual reality, which is out of time and space and which relates to events that occurred in the beginning of creation. The same phenomenon of a dual register was noted in Acts 2 where the people who were in Ierosualem at Pentecost were seen, on the one hand, to be a literal, historical reality and on the other as a figurative, spiritual one.[175] The underlying paradigm on that occasion was the giving of the Law on Mount Sinai when, according to Jewish tradition, all the nations were present, Israel among all the 70 nations of the earth. The same event is being recalled in the present scene in Antioch as the word of God is received by the Gentiles, as will be seen in the course of the *Commentary*.

There exists a variety of ancient traditions concerning this unique gift from YHWH to his people, often seeking to justify the special place held by Israel as the Chosen People of God. It was, on the one hand, a transmission that occurred by the intermediary of Moses; on the other, it was an event that happened in the beginning of time, at the time of creation. In some versions, it was YHWH who offered his Law; in others, it was the Law personified as Wisdom who walked on the earth and offered herself (see *Excursus* 6). Whichever scenario is followed, a common pattern is clear: when God's teaching (the meaning of Torah) was first given, it was offered to all the nations, but only Israel accepted to obey it and so it was entrusted to them. Because of their fidelity, they were to preserve the Torah and, by virtue of their obedience, attract the nations who would be drawn to them when they saw how they were blessed, and thus come to know and worship the true God. These traditions will be taken up by Paul and Barnabas in the speech Luke has recorded as taking place on the second Sabbath in Antioch of Pisidia (13.46-47); they are equally in evidence in the speech of James in the Ierousalem meeting (15.13-14). Already in his first speech, Paul has alluded to promises that foresee the extension to all nations of the blessings God gave to Israel (13.33b D05, 34, 37, 41). For these to be realized, the nations must receive the word of God, his teachings and commandments. Now, according to the Bezan text of 13.44a, this is precisely what has happened: the word of God has gone throughout the whole city. On that basis, the Gentiles (the nations) can now listen to and understand the word concerning the Lord, Jesus the Messiah (see *Excursus* 1).

Structure and Themes

The events related in the second sub-sequence of the Antioch narrative take place over a period of time that is undefined but seemingly brief. They begin

175. The combination of the historical register alongside a spiritual one as an exegetical device Luke uses to interpret the Pentecost event is examined in *The Message of Acts*, I, on 2.5-8 (pp. 152–64); and on 2.14-40 (pp. 178–92, esp. 179–84).

in a first episode [A] on the Sabbath following Paul's synagogue speech (13.14-41) with Paul's address to the city as a whole [a] and continue, on the same day, with the speech of Paul and Barnabas to the Jews who, fired by their zeal to preserve their privileged heritage, had opposed Paul [b, c]; the conversion of the Gentiles brings the events of that day to a close [c′, b′] but there then follows a general statement [a] which, being linked with καί, serves as a conclusion to the overall episode.

A second episode, [B], follows as a consequence of the first when the Jews, having been unable to put a stop to Paul's message of salvation to the Gentiles by arguments, now turn to physical means [a, b]. How long after the speech of 13.46-47 this happened is not specified – the absence of time markers throughout these episodes (after the opening phrase 'On the following Sabbath') is precisely an indication of the figurative register, which overrides the literal one in this respect. The persecution leads to Paul and Barnabas moving on to Iconium [b′], whereupon the whole sequence [D] is brought to a close with a positive summary statement [c].

The speeches of the first episode, [A], must have taken place in an open space rather than the synagogue, given the number of people ('the whole city') in the audience. The central theme of the speech of which the words are recorded is that the Jews, who were to have drawn the Gentiles to worship of the true God according to the writings of the Prophets and Jewish eschatological expectations, have not fulfilled their role because they have rejected his word. In consequence, Paul and Barnabas will take their message to the Gentiles.

[DA′-A]	13.44-49	In the city
[a]	13.44	The whole city gather to hear Paul
[b]	13.45	The zeal of the Jews
[c]	13.46-47	The speech of Paul and Barnabas
[c′]	13.48a	The Gentiles receive the word of God
[b′]	13.48b	The Gentiles believe
[a′]	13.49	The spread of the word of the Lord
[DA′-B]	13.50-52	Jewish response
[a]	13.50a	The Jews incited the influential citizens
[b]	13.50b	Persecution of Paul and Barnabas
[b′]	13.51	Departure from Antioch to Iconium
[c]	13.52	The situation of the disciples

Translation

	Codex Bezae D05	Codex Vaticanus B03
[Aa]	**13.44** On the following Sabbath, almost the entire city was assembled to hear Paul (he made much talk about the Lord);	**13.44** On the following Sabbath, almost all the city was assembled to hear the word of God;
[b]	**45** and when the Jews saw the assembled crowd, they were filled with zeal and contradicted the words said by Paul, contradicting and blaspheming.	**45** and when the Jews saw the masses, they were filled with zeal and contradicted the things spoken by Paul, blaspheming.

[c]   46 Finally, Paul, speaking boldly, and Barnabas said to them, 'You were the first for whom it was possible for the word of God to be spoken. Since you reject it and judge yourselves not worthy of eternal life, behold, we turn to the Gentiles. 47 For the Lord commanded thus:
  "Behold! As a light I have placed you
    for the Gentiles,
  So that you might be salvation
    to the end of the earth".'

[c'] 48a And on hearing, the nations rejoiced and they received the word of God;

[b'] 48b and they believed, in so far as they were appointed to eternal life.

[a'] 49 And the word of the Lord began to be taken throughout the whole country.

[Ba] 50a The Jews then incited the God-fearing prominent women, as well as the rulers of the city;

[b]   50b and they stirred up great affliction and persecution against Paul and Barnabas and drove them out from their borders.

[b'] 51 As for them, having shaken the dust off their feet at them, they arrived in Iconium.

[c]   52 The disciples were filled with joy and the Holy Spirit.

46 Finally, speaking boldly, Paul and Barnabas said, 'To you it was necessary for the word of God to be spoken first. Since you reject it and judge yourselves not worthy of eternal life, behold, we turn to the Gentiles. 47 For the Lord commanded us thus:
  "I have placed you as the light
    of the Gentiles,
  So that you might be salvation
    to the end of the earth".'

48a On hearing, the nations rejoiced and glorified the word of the Lord;

48b and they believed, as many as were appointed to eternal life.

49 The word of the Lord began to be taken throughout the whole country.

50a The Jews then incited the God-fearing and prominent women, as well as the rulers of the city;

50b and they stirred up persecution against Paul and Barnabas and drove them out from their borders.

51 As for them, after shaking the dust off their feet at them, they went to Iconium,

52 and the disciples were filled with joy and the Holy Spirit.

Critical Apparatus

13.44 (Τῷ) τε B E P 049. 056 𝔐 sy[h] | γε C 1646 | τότε H[5] L ‖ δέ D, *autem* d 𝔓[74] ℵ A C Ψ 33. 81. 88. 323. 440. 547. 614. 945. 1175. 1270. 1739. 1837. 1891. 2147. 2412 *al* latt.

δέ in D05, together with the fronted time phrase, marks a new development in the narrative. τε is probably an example of a phonetic error that occurs on a number of occasions in Acts, especially in ℵ01/B03 (see Read-Heimerdinger, *The Bezan Text*, pp. 205–206; 210–11).

πᾶσα (ἡ πόλις) B 𝔓[74] ℵ *rell* ‖ ὅλη D.

ὅλος in D05 stresses the idea of the city in its entirety (cf. 13.43 D05). ὅλος occurs several times in D05 either as a *vl* for πᾶς (22.5 D05, ὅλον τὸ πρεσβυτέριον) or as an additional reading (Lk. 19.44; Acts 13.43b; 14.6, 7; 19.29). Twice, it is B03 that reads ὅλος where D05 reads πᾶς (Lk. 11.34 B03, πᾶν τὸ σῶμά σου; Acts 2.2, πάντα τὸν οἶκον).

(ἀκοῦσαι) τὸν λόγον τοῦ θεοῦ B* C E H[5] L P Ψ 049. 056 𝔐 vg[cl] sy bo | τ. λ. τ. κυρίου B[2] 𝔓[74] ℵ A 33. 81. 323. 945. 1175. 1739. 1837. 2344 *al* gig vg[st] sa ‖

Παύλου πολύν τε λόγον ποιησαμένου περὶ τοῦ κυρίου D, *(audire) Paulum multum verbum faciens de domino* d (mae).

According to the reading of B03, the people assembled simply to hear the word of God, whereas in the other readings it was the message about Jesus that they came to hear. D05 has them come specifically to hear Paul who, the narrator pointedly comments, made much talk about the Lord. The use of τε to highlight a narrative comment is unusual in Greek but is found elsewhere in Acts (1.15 B03; 2.46; 4.13 B03).

13.45 ἰδόντες δέ B 𝔓⁷⁴ ℵ *rell* ‖ καὶ ἰδ. D, *et cum vidissent* d.— τοὺς ὄχλους B 𝔓⁷⁴ ℵ *rell* ‖ τὸ πλῆθος D (*turbam* d sa mae).

B03 starts a new development at the point when the Jews react to the gathering of the crowds, using ὄχλος in the plural. D05, on the other hand, views the Jews' zeal as part of the same narrative development, and uses the noun τὸ πλῆθος. The word appears frequently in Luke's work (Lk. × 8 [– 1 D05]; Acts × 17 [+ 2 D05]), and in the New Testament otherwise only in Mk × 2 (– 1 D05) and Jn × 2. It denotes a gathering of people or things that have a common identity, unlike ὄχλος, which signifies a more disparate crowd, especially in the plural (cf. 14.11, 13, 18). Here, it corresponds to the idea that the whole city (cf. ὅλη ἡ πόλις, v. 44 D05; cf. v. 43b D05) had gathered for the express purpose of hearing Paul.

τοῖς (+ λόγοις τοῖς E) ὑπὸ (+ τοῦ E) Παύλου λαλουμένοις B ℵ A E Ψ (33). 81. 326. 1837. 2344 *pc* ‖ τοῖς λόγοις (+ τοῖς Dᶠ) ὑπὸ τοῦ Π. λεγομένοις D*, *sermonibus quae a Paulo dicebantur* d ‖ τοῖς ὑπὸ τ. Π. λεγ. 𝔓⁷⁴ C L H⁵ P 049. 056. 097. 1739 𝔐 ‖ τοῖς ὑπὸ Π. λεγ. 614. 2147. 2412.

The dative article in B03 qualifies the passive participle λαλουμένοις and so is neuter; in D05, the article qualifies λόγοις as the subject of the participle λεγομένοις. This is the second additional mention of λόγος in D05 (cf. v. 44).

The absence of the article before Paul in B03 singles out Paul as speaker, as distinct from Barnabas with whom he had previously been named in 13.43a. The article could also have been omitted because ὑπὸ Παύλου is sandwiched in the articular phrase τοῖς ... λαλουμένοις, where another article may have been felt to be too heavy. In D05, Paul has already been identified as the speaker (cf. 13.44), without the article to distinguish him from Barnabas, so that the reference to him here is anaphoric (see Read-Heimerdinger, *The Bezan Text*, pp. 139–43).

ἀντιλέγοντες καὶ (βλασφημοῦντες) D, *contradicentes et* d H⁵ P 049. 056. 097. 614 𝔐 *p* sy^h; Chr ‖ ἐναντιο‹ύ›μενοι καί E gig ‖ *om.* B 𝔓⁷⁴ ℵ A C L Ψ 33. 36. 81. 88. 307. 323. 453. 610. 945. 1175. 1270. 1409. 1505. 1678. 1739. 1837. 1891. 2344. 2495 *al* lat sy^p co aeth.

The repetition of the verb ἀντιλέγω in D05 is superfluous to the meaning, but not to the force, of the narrator's description of the Jews' attack on Paul, who were furious with Paul's preaching to the Gentiles according to this text, rather than simply his popularity as it emerges in the B03 text.

13.46 παρρησιασάμενοί τε B 𝔓⁷⁴ ℵ A C Ψ 81. 323. 440. 1270. 1837. 2344 Ι παρ-οι δέ E L H⁵ P 049. 056 𝔐, *adhibita vero fiducia* d ‖ παρρησι<ασ>άμενός τε D⁽*⁾·ᴬ 242. 917. 1175. 1874 *pc* Ι παρ-ος δέ 1243. 1646.— (ὁ Παῦλος καὶ) ὁ Βαρναβᾶς B 𝔓⁷⁴ ℵ *rell* ‖ Βαρ. D 104. 876. 1108. 1245. 1505. 1518. 1611. 1646. 1838. 1898. 2138. 2495 *pc*; Chr Theoph.

τε as the sentence connective confers a particular importance on the speech of Paul and Barnabas (Levinsohn, *Textual Connections*, pp. 135–36: '…when τε introduces a response, the effect is to give prominence to the response, over against the event which produced it. The response then provides the lead-in to a significant development in the story'; cf. 21.30; 24.10 [D05 lac.]).

In D05, it is Paul especially to whom the singular participle παρρησιασά-μενος refers; at the same time, the use of one article for the two names is an indication that he is regarded as acting in unison with Barnabas when they speak (εἶπαν; cf. on 13.43a above).

(εἶπαν) πρὸς αὐτούς D, *ad eos* d ‖ *om.* B 𝔓⁷⁴ ℵ *rell.*

D05 specifies the addressees of the speech, not because there is any ambiguity but as a means to underline their identity as the Jews who have been opposing Paul's teaching (v. 45), already highlighted by D05 for their actions of contradicting and blaspheming (see above).

(Ὑμῖν) ἦν ἀναγκαῖον πρῶτον λαληθῆναι B 𝔓⁷⁴ ℵ A E H⁵ L P 049. 056. 33. 1739 𝔐 Ι ἀν. πρ. λαλ. C 440 Ι ἦν πρ. ἀν. λαλ. 547ᶜ Ι ἦν ἀν. λαλ. πρ. Ψ Ι ἀν. ἦν πρ. λαλ. 1175 ‖ πρ. ἦν λαλ. D, *oportebat primum loqui* d.

The presence of the adverb ἀναγκαῖον, 'necessary', in B03 operates in conjunction with the place of the other adverb, πρῶτον, before the infinitive it qualifies, to give the sense, 'To you it was necessary … to be spoken first'. The absence of ἀναγκαῖον in D05 results in the structure: ἦν + dative of the person + infinitive, which expresses possibility (Delebecque, *Les deux Actes*, p. 241); with, furthermore, the adverb πρῶτον qualifying the dative pronoun, the meaning is somewhat different: 'You were the first for whom it was possible … to be spoken', which is taken as an allusion to the well-attested Jewish traditions concerning the reasons for the giving of the Torah to Israel in preference to the other nations (see *Commentary,* and *Excursus* 6).

13.47 (οὕτως γὰρ) ἐντέταλται ἡμῖν ὁ (– ℵ) κύριος B 𝔓⁷⁴ ℵ *rell, mandatum dedit nobis dominus* d Ι ἐντέλλεται ἡμ. ὁ κύ. 81. 1175 *pc* ‖ ἐντέταλκεν ὁ κύ. D* (1838) *pc*; Cyr (Cyp).

The reading of B03 is personalized, with regard to the speaker by means of the middle voice of ἐντέλλομαι and with regard to the hearer by means of the first person pronoun: the declaration refers to the command of Jesus to Paul and Barnabas. The reading of D05, in contrast, is more formal and impersonal: the declaration refers to the command of YHWH given, in the active voice ('possible en bon grec', Delebecque, *Les deux Actes*, p. 275), as a prophetic proclamation.

Τέθεικά σε εἰς φῶς ἐθνῶν B 𝔓⁷⁴ ℵ *rell* ‖ Ἰδού φ. τέθ. σε τοῖς ἔθνεσιν D* (φῶς τέθ. σε Dˢ·ᵐ), *Ecce lumen posui te super gentibus* d; Cyp ‖ Ἰδοὺ τέθ. σε εἰς φ. ἐθνῶν E 104.

The variations in the first line of the citation of Isaiah's prophecy (Isa. 49.6) reflect the differing applications made of it. The LXX reads Ἰδοὺ τέθεικά σε εἰς διαθήκην γένους εἰς φῶς ἐθνῶν, which is then completed with the second line as given, without variant, in the text of Acts. It is uncertain to what εἰς διαθήκην γένους refers (cf. 42.6 where it seems to refer to Israel but see *Jewish Study Bible*, p. 867, n. *b-b*), or what is the effect of removing the phrase from the citation. It is also debatable whether in the original prophecy, σε refers to Isaiah himself or to Israel (*Jewish Study Bible*, p. 883). Whatever the case, B03, which reads the LXX text except for the initial Ἰδού, has Paul and Barnabas claim that Jesus applied the prophecy to themselves, given its reading of the first line of 13.47. D05 modifies the LXX text, apart from the opening Ἰδού; the combined effect of conserving Ἰδού and altering the word order to place φῶς before the verb, is to focus on the light as the subject, rather than on the addressee σε. The mention of the Gentiles balances the reference to the light by being placed after the verb. In D05, the pronoun σε may well apply to Israel, in line with the tradition alluded to in the opening sentence of the speech, namely that the Jews were given the Torah in order that they might ultimately enlighten the nations. This is the first indication Luke gives that Paul has any awareness of the Jewish mission to the Gentiles, but without acknowledging yet that it had been specifically entrusted to him by Jesus (compare 9.15 with 22.15 and esp. 26.17-18). For the time being, it remains a general principle, better grasped by Barnabas than by Paul since Paul will continue to seek to evangelize the Jews first and foremost (cf. 14.1 D05, αὐτόν).

13.48 ἀκούοντα δέ B 𝔓⁷⁴ ℵ *rell* ‖ -σαντα δέ Ψ ‖ καὶ ἀκούοντα D, *et cum audirent* d gig.— ἐδόξαζον B 𝔓⁷⁴ ℵ *rell* ‖ ἐδέξαντο D, *exceperunt* d gig mae; Aug Cass.— (τὸν λόγον) τοῦ θεοῦ B D E 049. 88. 323. 453. 1837. 1854. 2492 *pc* saᵐˢ bo; Augᵖᵗ ‖ τὸν θεόν 614. 1245. 1411. 2147. 2412 *pc* syᵖ·ʰ ‖ τοῦ κυρίου 𝔓⁴⁵·⁷⁴ ℵ A C Hˢ L P Ψ 056. 33. 1739 𝔐, *domini* d lat saᵐˢˢ mae; Chr Augᵖᵗ.

The response of the Gentiles follows as a new development in B03, where it is a matter of them glorifying the word of the Lord, that is the gospel of Jesus. In D05, καί introduces the response of the Gentiles as all of a part with the declaration of Paul and Barnabas, as a natural fulfilment of their warning to the Jews: the word of God (the Torah) was first given to Israel (rather than the nations) but now, since they have rejected it, the nations receive it (see *Overview,* and *Commentary, ad loc.* for more detailed theological discussion).

13.49 διεφέρετο δέ B $\mathfrak{P}^{74}$ ℵ *rell* ‖ καὶ διεφ. D, *et promulgabatur* d 522. 945 *pc* p². — δι' (ὅλης) B D $\mathfrak{P}^{45}$ E H⁵ L P Ψ 049. 056. 614 𝔐 ‖ καθ' $\mathfrak{P}^{74}$ ℵ A 33. 181. 242. 326. 383. 467. 522. 927. 945. 1270. 1739. 1837. 1891. 1898. 2298. 2344 *pc*.

Yet again, B03 considers the spread of the gospel to be a new development, whereas D05 views it as part of the previous events.

13.50 καὶ (τὰς εὐσχήμονας) ℵ* E H⁵ L P 049. 056. 614 𝔐 ‖ *om.* B D d $\mathfrak{P}^{45vid.74}$ ℵ² A C Ψ 33. 81. 323. 1175. 1739. 1837. 1891. 2344.

ℵ01* distinguishes between two types of women.

θλῖψιν μεγάλην (– E) καὶ (διωγμόν) D, *tribulationem magnam et* d E (mae) ‖ *om.* B $\mathfrak{P}^{74}$ ℵ *rell.*

The mention of great affliction is no doubt a deliberate echo of 8.1 D05; 11.19, where Paul, as Saul, was responsible for the persecution against the Hellenist believers.

τὸν Παῦλον B $\mathfrak{P}^{45vid.74}$ ℵ *rell* ‖ Παῦλον D mae; Ephr.

The omission of the article before Paul and Barnabas can be explained by the fact that Paul and Barnabas are now seen from the point of view not just of the Jews but also of the distinguished women and the city chiefs in relation to whom they have so far not been mentioned (Read-Heimerdinger, *The Bezan Text*, p. 141).

(ἀπὸ τῶν ὁρίων) αὐτῶν D $\mathfrak{P}^{74}$ ℵ *rell* ‖ *om.* B.

The omission of the possessive pronoun in B03 probably arose through homoioteleuton (ΤΩΝΟΡΙΩΝΑΥΤΩΝ), though the phrase makes sense without it. Other places of *vll* where the genitive pronoun is read only by B03 or D05 are: 1.18 D05; (pl.) 4.5 B03; 5.15 D05; (pl.) 6.3 D05; 7.14 D05, 20 D05, 25 D05, (pl.) 39 B03; 8.28 B03; 10.39 D05; (12.7 D05); 16.16 B03, 34 D05; 18.6 D05; (pl.) 19.9 D05; (pl.) 20.30 D05, 36 B03, 38 B03; 21.21 D05 (*ex err.*?).

13.51 (τῶν ποδῶν) αὐτῶν D, *suis* d E H⁵ L P 049. 056. 614 𝔐 gig sy^{p.h} sa mae aeth ‖ *om.* B $\mathfrak{P}^{74}$ ℵ A C Ψ 33. 81. 927. 945. 1175. 1241. 1739. 1891. 2344.

See the same variant at 13.50 above.

ἦλθον (εἰς ᾽Ικόνιον) B $\mathfrak{P}^{74}$ ℵ *rell* ‖ κατήντησαν D, *venerunt* d.

The verb καταντάω is only used by Luke in Acts (× 9 + 3 D05), and in 1 Corinthians (× 2), Ephesians (× 1) and Philippians (× 1). With its meaning 'come down to, arrive at' (L-J-S, καταντάω, 2), it focuses on the fact of arriving rather than the action of going (cf. 16.8 D05).

13.52 οἵ τε (μαθηταί) B A 33. 945. 1175. 1270. 1739. 1837. 1891 | οἵ γε 𝔓⁴⁵ ‖ οἱ δέ D, *discipuli* vero d 𝔓⁷⁴ ℵ C E H⁵ L P Ψ 049. 056. 614 𝔐 gig vg^D sy^h co.

Introduced with τε, this sentence in B03 stands either as a parenthetical narrative comment (cf. 1.15 B03; 2.46; 4.13 B03; 13.44 B03), or as a significant additional comment (cf. on 13.46 above). δέ is also used in Acts to introduce a parenthetical aside but specifically in anticipation of the events that follow (cf. 1.15 D05; Lk. 24.16), which is not the situation in view here. Its purpose in this verse is rather to signal a contrast, between the forced expulsion of Paul and Barnabas from Antioch and the joy of the disciples in Antioch overall.

Commentary

[DA′-A] 13.44-49 *In the City*

[a] 13.44 *The Whole City Gather to Hear Paul*
13.44 The action follows on from the request, made by the synagogue as Paul and his group were going out, for another speech on the following Sabbath (13.32). The intention was presumably for this to take place in the synagogue, but in the meantime, people all over the city have heard the word of God, in other words, they have heard about the one true God and about his teachings (cf. on v. 43b D05 above); so when the day arrives, it is not just the members of the synagogue who gather[177] but practically the entire city. It is therefore highly unlikely that they met in the synagogue,[178] and more probable that they gathered in an open space in the city. In point of fact, it will become clear in the course of this incident that the whole scene has a dimension that is not in time and space but rather represents a paradigmatic, spiritual reality. This is an important factor to take account of, for it explains some of the apparent contradictions and exaggerations in Luke's narrative at this point.[179] Underlying the events in this scene that unfolds, on the one hand, in a literal, historical dimension, is the fundamental and paradigmatic incident in the history of Israel, the giving of the Torah, which is extended here, in a figurative dimension, to all the nations (see *Overview*). Because of this dual register, the participants in the scene in Antioch are at the same time the local Jews and Gentiles of the city, whilst also representing the people of Israel and all the other nations. Thus, what begins as a reference to 'almost the entire (all the,

177. Luke introduces a clear play on words, the verb 'gathered', συνήχθη, being from the same root as the word for the synagogue, συναγωγή.
178. According to Bruce, 'almost the whole Gentile population turned up at the synagogue' (*Acts*, p. 281); Barrett allows for some spilling out of the synagogue: 'one must suppose, in and around the synagogue' (I, p. 655). If, on the contrary, the meeting takes place in a public place, a similar pattern occurs here to the one that will be later seen in Athens, of discussion taking place in the synagogue with the Jews and the God-fearers, and in the *agora* with the Gentiles (17.17).
179. See Witherington, *Acts*, p. 414, and n. 235.

AT) city' quickly becomes 'the Jews' (οἱ 'Ιουδαῖοι, 13.45) and 'the nations' (τὰ ἔθνη, 13.48).

The Alexandrian text says quite simply that almost all the city gathered to hear the word of the Lord. In that text, the use of the expressions 'word of the Lord' and 'word of God' does not follow a recognized pattern and it is generally assumed that the former is a Christianization of the latter (cf. 13.46, 48).[180] Codex Bezae presents the situation somewhat differently, allowing the narrator to make his own comment on the happenings.[181] According to this text, the city in almost its entirety gathered to hear Paul in particular, whereupon the narrator adds the pointed comment that he talked at length[182] about the Lord. The reference here to 'the Lord' is initially ambiguous, especially from the point of view of the synagogue where it would mean YHWH, but it becomes clear from the Jewish opposition that it was about Jesus that Paul spoke (περὶ τοῦ κυρίου; cf. 13.29a, περὶ αὐτοῦ). The phrase πολὺν λόγον ποιούμενος (lit.) 'making much talk', is also used of Peter according to the Bezan text when, after his 'conversion' at Caesarea, he taught the message he had discovered there, namely that on the basis of faith in Jesus God had accepted the Gentiles just like the Jews (11.2 D05).[183]

It is Paul's speaking here, whether the 'word of God' or 'much talk about the Lord', that corresponds to the request of the synagogue the previous Sabbath, and not the speech of Paul and Barnabas in 13.46-47, which will follow in response to the opposition Paul encounters.

[b] 13.45 *The Zeal of the Jews*

13.45 The participants who now enter on stage are 'the Jews' who will oppose Paul. Commentators quite rightly point out that this designation is too generalized, since in the previous scene, Luke said that many Jews (apart from many proselytes) followed Paul and Barnabas (13.43a), that is, as disciples (see *Commentary* above). The general term, however, is brought in precisely to express the figurative dimension of the scene.

The Jews react to the sight of all the people who had come to hear Paul speaking. Whereas they are described in the Alexandrian text with the plural noun τοὺς ὄχλους, translated here as 'the masses', the Bezan text uses the more specific term, τὸ πλῆθος, which refers to a large number of people who had come together for a particular purpose (cf. 2.6, the great crowd in Ierou-

---

180. Metzger, *Commentary*, pp. 353–54, and n. 2; cf. *Excursus* 1.

181. The intention of the narrator is often apparent in the Bezan wording when it conveys an observation or evaluation on the part of Luke. To dismiss it as 'the Western custom of brightening the text' as does Barrett (I, p. 655), is to miss the significance of the Bezan wording.

182. The phrase πολὺς λόγος occurs four times in the Bezan text of Acts but only the last occurrence is attested by the AT (11.2 D05; 13.44 D05; 18.6 D05; 20.2). A further occurrence is found in the AT at 15.32 where D05 omits the adjective πολλοῦ. It is striking that the three examples not read by the AT arise in a context of scriptural interpretation (at 11.2 D05 by insinuation; at 13.44 D05 and 18.6 D05 explicitly).

183. On 11.2 D05, see *The Message of Acts*, II, pp. 285–87; 292–93.

salem who converged when they heard the sound of people speaking in their languages). This is the case here, where the huge number of people all had one common wish, to hear Paul. The picture painted evokes the prophecy with which Paul had left the Jews, of the nations pouring into Israel (cf. 13.40-41 = Hab. 1.5).

The term Luke uses to describe the reaction of the Jews is ζῆλος, which has the two senses of 'jealousy' and 'zeal'. Now, they may have been jealous because of Paul's success in drawing people to listen to him; but, having identified Paul's opponents as 'the Jews', Luke undoubtedly has a concern not so much with psychological responses as religious ones. As Jews, it must be remembered, these people believed that they had a heritage to preserve for Israel which, before their eyes, is being offered by Paul to Gentiles on a false basis. It was one thing for him to present Jesus as the promised son of David, the Saviour and Messiah of Israel. It is quite another for Paul, a trained Jewish teacher and expert in the interpretation of the Scriptures, to present Jesus as the Lord to nations who have no part in Israel, and to propose to them that they could be justified with God on the basis of simple belief in Jesus without any further steps needing to be taken. When the Jews see this, then, they are filled with zeal for all that they have learnt and believed about being right with God, and about the conditions necessary for Gentiles to be accepted by God.[184]

The content of the Jews' disputes with Paul can be inferred from the proclamation he and Barnabas will make to them. Codex Bezae is again more detailed about their arguments: the Jews specifically contradict the words spoken by Paul – they contradict and blaspheme. The motif of 'word' (λόγος) and 'say' (λέγω) is repeated over and over in the Bezan text of these verses:

13.15	λόγου, σοφίας	λέγετε
13.26	λόγος τῆς σωτηρίας	
13.43b	τὸν λόγον τοῦ θεοῦ	
13.44	πολὺν λόγον	
13.45		ἀντέλεγον
	τοῖς λόγοις	λεγομένοις
		ἀντιλέγοντες
13.46	τὸν λόγον τοῦ θεοῦ	
13.48	τὸν λόγον τοῦ θεοῦ	
13.49	τὸν λόγον τοῦ κυρίου	

Such repetition is not haphazard and empty but, on the contrary, deliberate and full of intended insistence on a theme that lay at the heart of what it meant

---

184. J. Kilgallen ('Hostility to Paul in Pisidian Antioch', *Bib.* 84 [2003], pp. 1–15) expresses it well when he says that the Jews in Antioch 'acted in accord with their insights and education'. Comparison may be made with the High Priests who arrested the apostles when they were teaching in the Temple (5.17-40). Luke said of them, too, ἐπλήσθησαν ζήλου (5.17), which was interpreted as jealousy in the *Commentary* on the passage, because of the parallel with Pharaoh (*The Message of Acts*, I, p. 329); but it could well be that Luke is already playing on the dual sense of the word in Acts 5 and that notion of zeal on the part of the High Priests is also present.

to be the Chosen People of God – that Israel alone among the nations had accepted the word he had spoken (see *Excursus* 6).[185] Now, it is Paul who has been entrusted with the new word of God,[186] in the form of the 'word of the Lord', but the Jews contradict it, word by word, and in contradicting blaspheme, because they speak against that which was given by God.[187]

[c] 13.46-47 *The Speech of Paul and Barnabas*

13.46 The argument reaches its culmination when Paul and Barnabas make a formal pronouncement. It should be noted that this is not the speech that was intended by the synagogue when they asked to hear Paul speak again about the things he had presented to them on the previous Sabbath (cf. 13.42) – that has already taken place (cf. 13.44, esp. D05) and led to the opposition from the Jews.

Here, Barnabas is introduced into the narrative for the first time as a speaker (he is mentioned only indirectly at 13.5 where he and Saul preached in Salamis); in the Alexandrian text, he is viewed separately from Paul (see *Critical Apparatus*), though both are described as 'speaking boldly', a verb used typically by Luke to describe the interpretation of the Scriptures in accordance with the teaching that Jesus is the Messiah.[188] The Bezan text presents them as a united pair, acting in harmony, but applies the participle 'speaking boldly' to Paul alone (παρρησιασάμενος, D05), as if in all his talking he had so far not been as daring and frank as he will be now, backed up as he is by Barnabas. Certainly, what they have to say at this point goes beyond anything Paul has so far been reported as saying. The Bezan text further spells out that they address the Jews who have been contesting Paul and blaspheming.

The speech itself has to be considered in the two texts separately, for the variant readings are closely connected and cannot be dealt with independently of one another. The result is that the speech communicates a different message in the Alexandrian text and in the Bezan text. Taking the Alexandrian version first, Paul and Barnabas say that 'it was necessary' that the word of God was spoken to the Jews first. The term they use is not the divine imperative ἔδει, meaning something that God had ordained, but rather ἦν ἀναγκαῖον, some-

185. As long as it is supposed that Codex Bezae (as part of the so-called 'Western' text) is a free rewriting of Luke's text, the theological purpose behind it will be overlooked and commentators will speak of 'pointless variation' (cf. Barrett, I, p. 655–56).

186. On the existence of the Jewish tradition that a new Torah would be given with the coming of the Messiah, see Ginzberg, *The Legends of the Jews*, VI, p. 438.

187. For a discussion of the terms used in this passage that refer to the interpretation of Scripture, see B.J. Koet, *Five Studies on Interpretation of Scriptures in Luke–Acts* (SNTA 14; Leuven: University Press, 1989), pp. 97–118.

188. παρρησιάζομαι generally means to express oneself openly and frankly, to speak fearlessly. Luke uses it in situations when the speaker is interpreting the Scriptures or talking about Jesus in a Jewish context: Acts 9.27, 29 (Paul); 13.46 and 14.3 (Paul and Barnabas); 18.26 (Apollo); 19.8 and 26.26 (Paul).

thing they considered necessary.[189] The reason for the necessity is not given, but it can be thought that it is the fact that Jesus was the Jewish Messiah, and the good news ought therefore to be given first to the Jews before it was given to anyone else. That is, indeed, becoming established as a pattern as Paul and Barnabas go from place to place. However, the Jews in Antioch have rejected the word of God, refusing to accept what Paul has been proclaiming about the fulfilment of the Scriptures through Jesus and so denying themselves the opportunity of salvation, life in the world to come. The phrasing 'judge yourselves not worthy of eternal life' is seemingly ironic, implying that the Jews could have had a guarantee of eternal life had they considered themselves good enough for it. The phrase 'eternal life' will be taken up by the narrator in describing the reaction to the speech (see on 13.48b below).

As a result, and still in the Alexandrian text, Paul and Barnabas declare that they are going to turn their attention to the Gentiles. In justification of their decision, they apply to themselves (13.47 AT), as if a commandment to them by the Lord Jesus (ἐντέταλται ἡμῖν ὁ κύριος), the words of YHWH recorded by Isaiah, Isa. 49.6. These are quoted following the MT,[190] from a passage that speaks of salvation extending beyond Israel to the ends of the earth. The words were originally addressed to 'My servant', who is variously interpreted in Judaism as Isaiah, or Israel, or a faithful subset of Israel,[191] but whom Paul and Barnabas now understand to be themselves. The sense of the quotation tallies with the citation Paul had used earlier to explain that Jesus was the Messiah for all (13.34, 40-41, cf. 13.39).

Thus, in the Alexandrian text, the decision of Paul and Barnabas refers to the local situation in Antioch where the Jews have refused to accept Paul's preaching about Jesus; and they apply to themselves the Isaiah prophecy about being a light for the Gentiles (Τέθεικά σε εἰς φῶς ἐθνῶν).

The wording of Codex Bezae, on the other hand, causes the speech to be more far-reaching in its scope, relating to the general situation of Israel and the nations, even if on one level it can also be read as applying to the immediate circumstances. First, their opening sentence does not have the word (ἦν) ἀναγκαῖον, 'it was necessary', and the word order brings 'you first' (Ὑμῖν πρῶτον) into prominence: 'You were the first for whom it was possible (dat. + ἦν + inf.) for the word of God to be spoken'. Again, no justification is given for this statement but its logic is familiar to anyone who knows the traditions concerning the gift of the Torah to Israel (see *Excursus* 6): way back in the beginning of time, Israel was the first to receive the word of God because they were the only nation to accept to obey it. Now, however, a dreadful thing has happened: they have behaved like the nations and they have rejected the word of God, the word of salvation (cf. 13.23) that would give

---

189. Cf. Paul's use of the adjective at 2 Cor. 9.5; Phil. 2.25.

190. Most MSS of the LXX include the phrase εἰς διαθήκην γένους, which is not present in the MT and which Steyn (*Septuagint Quotations*, p. 198, n. 211) discounts as a 'possible addition'.

191. *Jewish Study Bible*, p. 883.

eternal life. From a Jewish point of view, all Jews are written in the book of life but can be erased from it for various reasons (cf. Exod. 32.32; Isa. 4.3; cf. Ps. 56.9; 69.29; Mal. 3.16); eternal life is promised to all who devote themselves to the Torah, who accept the Torah and observe the laws.[192]

13.47 In justification of the declaration by Paul and Barnabas that they are turning to the nations, those who had at first been the ones to reject the word of God, they take up the prophecy of Isaiah – however not, in the Bezan text, as commanded to them personally by the Lord Jesus but as a prophecy given to Isaiah about 'my servant' who was to be a light for the nations. The wording of the quotation follows neither the MT nor the LXX: there is an initial 'Behold!' that is also present in the Hebrew text, but the word order brings the noun 'light' into a dominant position (Ἰδοὺ φῶς τέθεικά σε τοῖς ἔθνεσιν). In Luke's Gospel, Simeon had adapted this saying to apply it to Jesus who would be a light for the Gentiles (Lk. 2.32), but precisely the word ἐθνῶν is omitted there by Codex Bezae. In the use Paul and Barnabas make of it here, it is possible to interpret it as applied to Jesus as the servant of YHWH, the Messiah, though they themselves do not make that explicit. It is questionable how established such an interpretation would have been in the first century. In any case, the point being made is that their turning to the Gentiles was in accordance with God's plan of salvation, which Paul had already made even more clear in the Bezan text than the Alexandrian text (13.33, 34, 40-41, cf. 13.39).

A monumental step is being announced by Paul and Barnabas in the Bezan version of the speech. It will be taken up and developed by James after he has heard them reporting at the Jerusalem meeting what God had done among the Gentiles (15.12-21; see *Commentary, ad loc.*). Despite the solemn declaration, Paul will nonetheless continue to insist on going to the synagogue first in every place he visits, and on attempting to bring the gifts of the Gentiles to Jerusalem in order to accomplish the prophecies concerning the eschatological age (cf. Rom. 15.16, 25-27). In other words, although he recognizes that his mission is to the Gentiles, he clings on to the hope that the Jews, his own people, will also accept the message of Jesus and thus fulfil their role of drawing the Gentiles to worship God. Luke follows him on his journey as, twice more (18.6; 28.28), Paul repeats his intention to go the Gentiles, and only on the last occasion in Rome finally abandons his attempts at persuading his own people to accept the message of Jesus. This first affirmation in 13.47 marks the beginning of a long process, which will not become definitive until the third time it is made (see *General Introduction*, §V). The errors Luke discerns in Paul's tactics, especially concerning the special place he accords to the Jews, account for many of the differences between the portrait he draws in his narrative and the one that emerges from Paul's own writings.

---

192. See Ginzberg, *The Legends of the Jews*, I, pp. 81, 86; III, pp. 99, 430. In the Oral Torah, the insistence is particularly on believing in the resurrection of the dead (see J. Neusner, *Judaism When Christianity Began: A Survey of Belief and Practice* [Louisville: Westminster John Knox Press, 2002], pp. 168–71)

[c′] 13.48a *The Gentiles Receive the Word of God*
13.48a Just as there are two distinct texts of the speech Paul and Barnabas addressed to the Jews in Antioch, so there are two distinct descriptions of the reactions on the part of the Gentiles. In the Alexandrian text, following their announcement, the Gentiles (or the nations, since the Greek τὰ ἔθνη has both meanings) rejoiced and glorified the word of the Lord, and a certain number who had been assigned to eternal life believed (see 13.48b below). The response takes place on a local level, at a particular point in time as the Gentiles in Antioch become Jesus-believers.

In Codex Bezae, it is the dimension out of time and space that continues to dominate, just as it did in the speech proclaimed by Paul and Barnabas. The Gentiles, or the nations, received the word of God. The event is dramatic: just as Israel had earlier received the word of God, his teachings and commandments,[193] now the nations also receive the word of God. This is a spiritual reality first and foremost, marking a moment that had been foreseen as part of the Messianic age when the Gentiles would come to know the God of Israel. It places the nations, for the first time in the history of the world as seen from the Jewish point of view, on an equal footing with Israel. It represents something much wider than accepting the word of the Lord, the message of Jesus (see *Excursus* 1), while at the same time being an indispensable foundation for understanding and believing in the one who was sent by the same God who had given them his word.

[b′] 13.48b *The Gentiles Believe*
13.48b The narrator's conclusion in the Bezan text plays, then, on the dual terms of 'reception' and 'rejection'. Equally, there is a play on the phrase 'eternal life' which Paul and Barnabas had used with reference to the Jews who 'judged themselves not worthy of it'. According to the general, figurative register of the narrative as opposed to the historical register, when the word of God was received by the Gentiles, they believed it; they, too, then have eternal life, just as the Jews did already – those who 'were appointed to eternal life' are not a restricted group of the chosen few but all the Gentiles, since God had predestined all Gentiles to eternal life.[194] The moment has now arrived for this to be accomplished.

[a′] 13.49 *The Spread of the Word of the Lord*
13.49 With the observation that the word of the Lord, that is the message of Jesus, began to spread throughout the whole region, the narrator now brings his account back to the historical register. It is a mark of approbation, indicating that what Paul and Barnabas had had the boldness to declare was accurate and therefore bore fruit. They had initially limited their preaching of

---

193. Cf. Deut. 33.3 LXX: ἐδέξατο ἀπὸ τῶν λόγων αὐτοῦ νόμον.

194. It is unjustified to take the relative ὅσοι in a restrictive sense when Luke has no interest in introducing the notion of predestination.

Jesus to the synagogue, but when they open up their audience to include Gentiles and, even more, when they turn from the Jews to the Gentiles, then they are successful in spreading the message they have been appointed by the Holy Spirit to preach, as the Spirit's work (cf. 13.2).

This comment is to be compared with the comment made after Paul's first speech in Antioch the previous Sabbath, when it was said (13.44a) that 'the word of God went through the entire city'. That, it was noted (see *Commentary* above), was a necessary first step for the spread of the word of the Lord, which is now presented as taking place (see *Excursus* 1). Those responsible for taking the gospel message to other places in the area are presumably those who themselves have believed; and it is not an action that occurred just once,[195] but rather they will carry on spreading the news. Paul and Barnabas, meanwhile, have their own journey to make.

[DA'-B] 13.50-52 *Jewish Response*

[a] 13.50a *The Jews Incited the Influential Citizens*
13.50a The spread of the word of the Lord is to be seen as having already started when the Jews in Antioch took action against Paul and Barnabas.[196] Indeed, it was no doubt a factor that contributed to the increase in the Jews' hostility against them and that pushed them to go beyond argument and take action. The Jews enlist the support of two groups of eminent people in the city, those who exercise social power, noble Gentile women who are attached to the synagogue as God-fearers, and those who have political power, the leaders of the city, so probably also Gentiles.

[b] 13.50b *Persecution of Paul and Barnabas*
13.50b The Bezan text makes a link between this persecution of Paul and Barnabas and that of Paul, as Saul, against the Hellenists in Hierosoluma (8.1b D05).[197] This time, however, it will not result in imprisonment or bloodshed, though they will be driven from the region, probably referring to the immediate vicinity of the town.

[b'] 13.51 *Departure from Antioch to Iconium*
13.51 Having been driven out from the borders of Antioch, Paul and Barnabas perform a gesture of shaking the dust from their feet. This was normally a gesture undertaken by Jews when they left Gentile territory so as not to ren-

---

195. The imperfect διεφέρετο expresses ongoing action, which can be understood as having started at this point.

196. The connection between the two events is indicated by the sequence of tenses, where the imperfect διεφέρετο is presented as having already started when the aorist παρώτρυναν occurs.

197. 8.1b D05: διωγμὸς μέγας καὶ θλῖψις, cf. 13.50b D05: θλῖψιν μεγάλην καὶ διωγμόν.

der impure the Holy Land.[198] Jesus extended the significance of the gesture when, in sending the Twelve to preach and heal in Israel (Lk. 9.5, cf. Mk 6.11), and the Seventy to Samaria (Lk. 10.11), he commanded his disciples to shake the dust off their feet if they were rejected by a place, 'as a testimony against them'. In this way, the Jews who reject Jesus were to be treated as Gentiles, a criticism of the harshest order (cf. Acts 18.6).

In the first century CE, Iconium was in Phrygia, part of the Roman province of Galatia, across the border from Pisidia.[199] It was sufficiently important to be given the name of the Roman Emperor Claudius during his rule (41–54 CE), but was a city of some standing already in the Greek Empire.

[c] 13.52 *The Situation of the Disciples*

13.52 The comment about the disciples being 'filled with joy and the Holy Spirit' is a highly positive evaluation, which Luke expresses on only a few occasions (cf. the Ethiopian eunuch, 8.39 D05; Barnabas, 11.23-24). It refers back to the disciples of Antioch as a whole.[200] As a final, backward-looking summary to the sequence overall, the comment indicates that the community of believers in Antioch is well-established, and strengthened by the break Paul and Barnabas had made with the Jews in leaving the city.

Excursus 6

The Gift of the Torah: Jewish Traditions

An awareness of the well-established, and well-documented, Jewish traditions relating to the giving of the Torah is critical to an appreciation of Luke's narrative and the speeches he attributes to Paul and Barnabas in Acts 13.14-50, and later to James in 15.14-21. The traditions emerge repeatedly in the Rabbinic writings in answer to the question that the Gentiles might ask about why Israel alone is a privileged people and how the situation came about: the answer is closely associated with the gift of the Torah to Israel.

The ancient stories concerning this unique gift from YHWH to his people exist in a variety of forms, circulated and transmitted orally before being written down.[202] Though the precise stages of their development are difficult to reconstruct, the same themes and general principles are in evidence: the

---

198. Although removing dust was an act of self-purification, the other side of the coin was that a person thereby indicated that the place being left was impure.

199. Bruce, 'Phrygia', *ABD*, V, pp. 366-67; *Acts*, pp. 276, 279.

200. The comment about the disciples does not refer to those of Iconium since the message of Jesus has not yet been preached there. It is unlikely to refer to those around Paul (cf. 13.13), since the description 'full of joy and the Holy Spirit' is not one predicated of Paul himself who will, for his part, continue to struggle against his mission to take the word of Jesus to the Gentiles (cf. *Commentary*, 13.48).

202. Ginzberg (*The Legends of the Jews*) gives details of a number of these traditions, see esp. I, p. 3; III, pp. 80–82, 126, 142, 350–51, 454; IV, 307–308; VI, pp. 31, 53, 77, 125, 130, 397.

Torah was understood to have been created before heaven and earth; more than 'the Law' as a simple set of regulations, it represents the very wisdom of God;[203] and it was originally intended for all the nations.[204] Two versions of the traditions are selected here to illustrate the Jewish view of the relationship of Israel to the Torah and the situation of the Gentiles.

In the biblical account, the Torah was transmitted by YHWH through the intermediary of Moses on Mount Sinai in the years following the exodus from Egypt. A story derived from Deut. 33.2 tells how, when God first wished to give the Torah to humankind, he approached every nation but each refused to accept it for one reason or another, except for Israel who welcomed it and accepted to obey its commandments. Israel became, in consequence, God's Chosen People, whose role would be to act as a witness for the Gentiles so that they, too, would one day accept the Torah in the same way as the Jews had done. Evidence for this crucial self-understanding of Israel is found in the targumic texts of Deuteronomy 33.2:[205]

> Moses said, 'The Lord was revealed from Sinai to give the Law to his people, the children of Israel. He shone in his Glory on the Mount of Gabla [Edom] to give the Law to the sons of Esau, and when they found written within it: "You shall not be murderers," they did not accept it. And he shone in his Glory to give his Law on the Mount of Paran to the sons of Ishmael. And when they found it was written within it: "You shall not be thieves," they did not accept it. He went back and it was revealed on the Mount of Sinai and with him were myriads of angels. The children of Israel said: "We will do and obey all that is in the Law".'

Other stories speak of a much older event, which took place in the beginning of time when God's Wisdom was first offered to all the nations before it was finally entrusted to Israel. The tradition is found in the book of Ecclesiasticus or Siracides, the work of a certain Ben Sira written in the first quarter of the second century BCE. In key passages of the book, Wisdom is personified as a woman and identified with the Torah. The notion of Wisdom being originally given to all nations is found in the opening chapter (Sir. 1.9-10):[206]

> He [YHWH] himself created her [Wisdom, the Law], and saw and numbered her
> And poured her out upon all his works [i.e. all creation],
> Upon all flesh [i.e. nations] in measure [i.e. not in abundance],
> But without measure does he grant her to them [Israel] that love him.

---

203. Cf. Jn. 1.1-4, which expresses the pre-existence of the Torah: 'In the beginning was the Word [Torah, Wisdom], and the Word was with God and the Word was God. It was in the beginning with God; all things were made through it and without it was nothing made.'

204. Ginzberg, *The Legends of the Jews*, III, p. 197; VI, pp. 32, 33.

205. *Targum Neofiti 1: Deuteronomy* (M. McNamara [ed.]; *The Aramaic Bible*, Va [Edinburgh: T&T Clark, 1997]); *Targum Pseudo-Jonathan: Deuteronomy* (E.G. Clarke [ed.]; *The Aramaic Bible*, Vb [Edinburgh: T&T Clark, 1998]).

206. The English translation is adapted from G.H. Box and W.O.E. Osterley (eds), 'The Book of Sirach', in R.H. Charles *et al* (eds), *The Apocrypha and Pseudepigrapha of the Old Testament in English* (2 vols; Oxford: Clarendon Press, 1963 repr.), I, *Apocrypha*.

Later, she is said to have wandered the earth going from nation to nation and to have chosen the people of Israel as her dwelling place (Sir. 24.7-8, 12):[207]

> With all these [i.e. every people and nation] I sought a resting place
> And said: In whose inheritance shall I lodge?
> Then the Creator of all things gave me commandment
> And he that created me fixed my dwelling place
> And he said, 'Let your dwelling place be in Jacob
> And in Israel take up your inheritance...'.
> And I took root among an honoured people
> In the portion of the Lord and of his inheritance...

Corresponding to the notion of the election of Israel as the people entrusted with the Torah was the idea that at some future date the nations would also be granted understanding and acceptance of it. This new development would be associated with the coming of the Messiah and would result from the Gentiles being drawn to Israel and to the worship of the true God by the testimony of the Jews. This particular development was, however, subject to considerable dispute. It has been seen throughout the examination of the message of Acts according to Codex Bezae that the apostles themselves were uncertain about how they should expect to see it realized.[208] It seems that for many Jews, the idea of the Gentiles ever sharing in the privileges of Israel was abhorrent; others, on the other hand, were more open to the possibility as part of the Messianic hopes, though accepting that Paul and Barnabas, and later James, were right to declare that the time had already come for them to receive the Torah obviously depends on accepting that Jesus was the Messiah.[209]

Excursus 7

Jesus' Mission to Israel and the Mission of Barnabas and Saul to the Gentiles

A series of parallels has been noted in the course of the *Commentary* between the beginnings of the mission to Israel, carried out by Jesus as the Messiah, and the mission to the Gentiles, entrusted to Barnabas and Saul. These follow on from the comparison that was noted between the birth of Jesus and the birth of the church in Antioch in Acts 11.27-30.[210] The comparison brings out the similarities, but also the contrasts, between the work of the teacher and

---

207. Siracides 24 is not available in Hebrew.

208. For example, on the Eleven, see Acts 1.6 (*The Message of Acts*, I, pp. 71–74); on Peter, 2.14b-22 (I, pp. 179–84); 10.34-43 (II, pp. 268–77).

209. On Jewish expectations concerning the Gentiles in the Messianic age, see *The Message of Acts*, I, *Excursus* I, pp. 79–87. Their status in the Rabbinic writings, drawing on earlier traditions, is summarized by Neusner, *Judaism When Christianity Began*, pp. 172–73.

210. The similarities are noted in *The Message of Acts*, II, where they are brought together in *Excursus* 4, pp. 329–30.

that of his disciples, especially Saul/Paul to whom alone the second and third points below refer.[211]

The points of comparison are threefold:

1. *Investiture*

    a. *Jesus* (Lk. 3.1-22): his investiture took place at his baptism by John, the son of Zechariah (3.2b) who was seen carrying out his service as a priest in the Temple (1.23, λειτουργία). John was a prophet of the Most High (1.76) who prepared the way for the Messiah (3.2b-6). The location was the Jordan, a wilderness (3.2b), outside Judaea and away from the religious centre of Ierousalem. Luke sets the historical context by naming the political and religious figures in Israel at the time (3.1-2a): among the former is Herod the tetrarch of Galilee and his brother Philip; the latter are the High Priests Annas and Caiaphas. The Holy Spirit testified to the moment of Jesus' anointing as Messiah (3.22 D05: 'Today I have fathered you').

    b. *Barnabas and Saul* (Acts 13.1-3): their investiture takes place in the Antioch church (13.1-3), away from the Ierousalem church. The historical context is set by the naming of two groups in the church, a total of five prophets and teachers. Among the latter is Menahem, the foster-brother of Herod the tetrarch (13.1). The group was performing an act of worship to the Lord (13.1, λειτουργέω), when the Holy Spirit told them to set apart Barnabas and Saul for his work (13.2). The purpose of their mission only becomes clear as the work unfolds (cf. '[God] opened to the Gentiles a door of faith, 14.27).

2. *Temptation*

    a. *Jesus* (Lk. 4.1-13): Jesus returned from the Jordan full of the Holy Spirit (πλήρης, a permanent state, 4.1) and was led by the Spirit into the wilderness, where he was tempted (πειραζόμενος, 4.2) by the devil for 40 days. Jesus was tempted in three ways to demonstrate to Israel his Messianic role by means of displays of supernatural power and thereby to gain control over the nations (4.3-12); the means included appeal to the Scriptures (4.10-11). Jesus countered the temptations with his first recorded words, and overcame them all (4.13a), and the devil was forced to seek other means to destroy him at a later date ('he went away for a time', ἄχρι χρόνου [καιροῦ, AT]), when he found another opportunity to attack him.

    b. *Saul, as Paul* (Acts 13.6-11): Barnabas and Saul were sent out by the Holy Spirit (13.4) and went to Cyprus. There, they encountered a Jewish false prophet, a magician, called Bar-Iesoua (13.6), whose name has the double meaning of 'son of Jesus' (a disciple), and 'make ready' (translated in Greek as Ἑτοιμᾶς, 13.8a). He represented a false understanding of Jesus' Messianic role, maintaining the privileged status of the Jews – who had to 'prepare the way' for the Gentiles to enter Israel by first receiving the Messiah themselves – and thereby setting up an obstacle to the nations (the Gentiles, represented by the proconsul Sergius Paulus, 13.7) coming to faith in Jesus (13.8b). As such, he also represented the temptation facing Saul (cf. πειρασμός, 15.26 D05) to go first to the Jews with the message of Jesus (13.5a). Saul, filled with the Spirit (πλησθείς, a temporary state) and leaving behind his Jewish past (the name of Saul, 13.10a) as he identified with the Gentiles (with his name of

---

211. The parallel is examined in detail in J. Rius-Camps, *El camino de Pablo a la misión de los paganos. Comentario lingüístico y exegético a Hch 13–28* (Madrid: Cristiandad, 1984), pp. 37–55.

Paul, 13.9a), confronted the tempter, with his first recorded words (13.10b-11), addressing him as 'son of the devil' (13.10b); instead of 'preparing the way' Bar-Iesoua was 'making crooked the straight ways' of the Lord (13.10bc). Paul proclaimed blindness as the Lord's judgement on the false prophet (13.11-12), the same effect that his own fanatical adherence to Judaism had brought on himself (9.8-9). However, he declared the effect on Bar-Iesoua only 'for a time' (ἕως [ἄχρι, AT] καιροῦ, 13.11 D05); he will later succumb to the temptation to go to the Jews first when he goes to the synagogues in other cities until he acknowledges in Rome the truth of the Holy Spirit's warning to the Jews (28.25-29).

3. *First Speech*

a. *Jesus* (Lk. 4.16-30): the setting is the synagogue in his home country of Nazareth (4.16, 24), on the Sabbath (4.16), where he made his first public speech. He stood up to read and was given the scroll of Isaiah; he then sat down to teach, at his own initiative, without waiting for an invitation. He proclaimed the fulfilment of Isaiah's prophecy of the arrival of the Messiah in his own person, omitting the warning about the 'vengeance of the Lord' on his people (4.18-19, cf. Isa. 61.1-2). His teaching was interrupted by the synagogue response, of incredulity and irony (4.22). When he continued, he acknowledged the rejection of his own people, alluding through scriptural examples to the more favourable response of the Gentiles (4.23-27). The response was one of anger, leading to an unsuccessful attempt on his life (4.28-30).

b. *Paul* (Acts 13.16-41): the setting is Antioch of Pisidia, in 'our' synagogue (13.14b D05), on the Sabbath (13.14b), where Paul made his first public speech. After the reading of the Law and the Prophets (13.15), Paul responded to an invitation given to both himself and Barnabas to speak, and did so standing up (13.16a). He proclaimed the arrival of the Messiah in Jesus as the culmination of God's care of his people throughout history (13.23). He was the means for salvation of Israel, on condition of repentance preached by John the Baptist (13.23b-26, 32; cf. 13.38-39, esp. D05). However, in view of the rejection of the Messiah by the Jewish leaders (13.27-29), salvation was now to be announced to the Gentiles, as foreseen by the Scriptures (13.33-37, 39). Paul offered a chance to the Jews to retain their status as the people of God, threatening them that if they did not believe in Jesus, they would be overrun by Gentiles (13.40-41), which would be the 'work' of God. In summary, Paul presented the extension of Messianic salvation to the Gentiles as part of the history of Israel, with the conversion of the Gentiles leading to their integration into Israel; only in the event of the Jews' rejection of the Messiah would Israel be under threat.

The reaction to the speech was initially one of uncertainty (13.41 D05). However, in response to the Jews' request (13.42), Paul spoke again the following Sabbath (13.44), this time to the whole city, and the Jews, hearing his offering of salvation to the Gentiles, opposed him in their zeal to preserve their heritage (13.45). When he persisted and, with the help of Barnabas, even went so far as to give 'the word of God' to the Gentiles, although hitherto the preserve of Israel (13.46-47), they drove the pair out of their city (13.50); subsequently, they will attempt unsuccessfully to kill Paul (14.19-20).

The total picture of the parallels between the apostles and Jesus is considerably more nuanced than is often assumed. The successive elements are of a diverse nature, some of them positive while others are negative. The simple fact of a comparison by no means implies approval, for Luke uses this device to evaluate how the disciples have understood and are carrying out the mission entrusted to them. The diversity of the parallels noted here illustrates Luke's plan of using his first volume, the Gospel, to serve as the model, presenting the person of Jesus as the master; then, in the second volume, the book of Acts, he presents the disciples as they seek to carry out Jesus' teaching, measuring them against the model in order to highlight their successes and also their difficulties.

[C'] 14.1-7b *Phrygia: Iconium*

Overview

The change of setting from Antioch to Iconium at the end of the previous sequence [D] also marks the beginning of a new sequence [C'] in the travel narrative. In actual fact, from the point of view of the content, the division between the sequences is not a clear one and the connection is almost seamless.

The previous sequence in Antioch had reached a dramatic climax with the declaration of Paul and Barnabas that the word of God was being given to the Gentiles (13.46-47). Their proclamation of this turning point in the history of Israel, followed by their expulsion by the Jews from the territory of Antioch, creates the expectation that Paul will not continue with his attempts to persuade his fellow-Jews to accept his message about Jesus. What in fact happens, however, is that he renews his attempts, with consequences similar to those encountered in Antioch. This backward step notwithstanding, a gradual progression in Paul's development throughout this sequence and the next [B'] will be noted with approval by Luke.

Structure and Themes

The sequence in Iconium falls into two episodes, with three elements in the first and four in the second. The setting of the first episode is in the synagogue, whereas in the second it is the broader setting of the town. The Alexandrian text lacks two elements, the final one in each episode, so the structure is given here according to the Bezan text:

[C'-A]	14.1-2	In the synagogue
[a]	14.1	Paul in the synagogue
[b]	14.2a	Persecution by the Jewish leaders
[b']	14.2b	The Lord gives peace
[C'-A⅂	14.3-7b	In the city
[a]	14.3	A positive testimony
[b]	14.4	Division among the crowd
[b']	14.5-7a	Paul and Barnabas escape to Lycaonia
[a']	14.7b	The response of the crowd

The first episode presents Paul speaking in the synagogue with a positive response by a crowd (πλῆθος) of Jews and Greeks [a]; the persecution that ensues when the Jewish leaders incite the Gentiles to oppose them [b]; and the Lord's intervention to resolve the situation [b']. The connective μὲν οὖν introduces the second episode where the opening element portrays Paul and Barnabas testifying in the city and the Lord acting to confirm their message [a]. A split occurs among the population (πλῆθος), who side either with the Jews or the apostles [b]. The Gentiles and the Jews plan to attack the apostles, which causes Paul and Barnabas to flee to Lycaonia in order to resolve the situation; once there, they set about evangelizing [b'], and the response of the crowd (πλῆθος) is positive [a'].

Translation

Codex Bezae D05

[Aa]   **14.1** It happened in Iconium likewise that he entered the synagogue of the Jews and spoke in such a way to them that a great gathering of both Jews and Greeks started to believe.

[b]   **2a** However, the synagogue chiefs of the Jews and the rulers of the synagogue started up among them persecution against the Righteous, and embittered the souls of the Gentiles against the brethren.

[b']   **2b** But the Lord quickly gave peace.

[A'a]   **14.3** So they stayed on for some considerable time and took their boldness of speech from the Lord, who testified to the word of his grace by granting signs and wonders to happen through his hands.

[b]   **4** But there was a split in the city gathering: some were adhering to the Jews while others to the apostles, because of the word of God.

[b']   **5** When an attack was made by the Gentiles and the Jews with their rulers, to insult and to stone them, **6** learning about it they managed to escape to the cities of Lycaonia, to Lystra and Derbe and the whole of the neighbouring district, **7a** and there they were evangelizing.

[a']   **7b** The whole of the assembled crowd was moved at the teaching.

Codex Vaticanus B03

14.1 It happened in Iconium likewise that they entered the synagogue of the Jews and spoke in such a way that a great gathering of both Jews and Greeks believed.

2 However, the Jews who had not been persuaded stirred up

and embittered the souls of the Gentiles against the brethren.

14.3 So they stayed on for some considerable time, taking their boldness of speech from the Lord, who testified to the word of his grace by granting signs and wonders to happen through their hands.

4 But the city gathering was divided, and some were with the Jews, others with the apostles.

5 When an attack was made by both Gentiles and Jews with their rulers, to insult and stone them, **6** learning about it they escaped to the cities of Lycaonia, Lystra and Derbe and the neighbouring district, **7** and there they were evangelizing.

Critical Apparatus

The amount of variation from chapter 14 onwards displays a marked increase compared with the earlier part of the book. This is especially true of the variation in direct speech as opposed to narrative (for specific figures of analysis, see Read-Heimerdinger, *The Bezan Text,* pp. 6–21).

14.1 (εἰσελθεῖν) αὐτούς B 𝔓⁷⁴ ℵ *rell, eos* d ‖ αὐτόν D.

With the singular, D05 directs particular attention on to Paul as the disciples go into the synagogue (cf. v. 3 D05, διὰ τῶν χειρῶν αὐτοῦ [Paul's]), even though mention will be made subsequently of others (cf. v. 2a D05, ἐπήγαγον αὐτοῖς διωγμόν; v. 2b, κατὰ τῶν ἀδελφῶν). B03 does not single Paul out in this way.

(οὕτως) πρὸς αὐτούς D, *ad eos* (πρ. αὐ. οὕτως E syᵖ mae) ‖ *om.* B 𝔓⁷⁴ ℵ *rell.*

D05 commonly specifies the addressee where B03 leaves it implicit (Read-Heimerdinger, *The Bezan Text*, pp. 181–82). Here, αὐτούς is ambiguous, in that the last mentioned persons are 'the Jews' but the following clause suggests that Greeks were also present in the audience. It may be the potential for confusion that caused the pronoun to be omitted in B03.

(ὥστε) πιστεῦσαι B 𝔓⁷⁴ ℵ *rell* ‖ θαυμᾶσαι … καὶ πιστεῦσαι E mae ‖ πιστεύειν D, *crederent* d.

B03 reads the aorist infinitive, viewing the result of the speaking globally, as one of collective belief. With the present, D05 views the result rather as the onset of a process that spread through a large number of people.

14.2 (οἱ δὲ) ἀπειθήσαντες Ἰουδαῖοι B 𝔓⁷⁴ ℵ A C Ψ 33. 81. 323. 440. 1175. 2344 ‖ -θοῦντες Ἰουδ. E H⁵ L P 049. 056. 614 𝔐 ‖ ἀρχισυνάγωγοι τῶν Ἰουδαίων καὶ οἱ ἄρχοντες τῆς συναγωγῆς D, *archysinagogae Iudaeorum et principes synagogae* d (syʰᵐᵍ).

B03 leaves the identity of those who created trouble vague – they were Jews who did not believe, as distinct from the many who did. The verb ἀπειθέω is used twice elsewhere in similar circumstances, cf. 17.5 D05; 19.9; it is equivalent to ἀπιστέω, cf. 17.12 D05; 28.24, where the antonyms πείθομαι and πιστεύω are used.

D05 is specific, as on other occasions (cf. 4.5 D05 B03; 5.35), mentioning the various types of synagogue leaders. Since a distinction is made, the former, οἱ ἀρχισυνάγωγοι, should be understood as referring to men whose function was to conduct worship and whose role was religious in so far as it was internal to the synagogue services; and the latter, οἱ ἄρχοντες, to the men whose role was to supervise affairs in a more general and civil sense. Although it seems that the same person could, and did at times, carry out both functions, they are nonetheless distinct roles (A. Büchler, 'Archon [Archontes or Archonteia]', *Jew. Enc.*, II, pp. 86–87; Schürer, *The History of the Jewish People*, II, pp. 434–46; III, pp. 100–101; cf. Delebecque, *Les deux Actes*, p. 330).

ἐπήγειραν B 𝔓⁴⁵·⁷⁴ ℵ *rell* | ἐπ. διωγμόν E 614. 1611. 2147. 2412 *pc* gig syʰ ‖ ἐπήγαγον αὐτοῖς διωγμὸν κατὰ τῶν δικαίων D, *incitaverunt persecutionem adversus iustos* d (syʰᵐᵍ).

D05 is once again more specific, explaining not only that the Jewish leaders incited persecution against the believers but also that it was 'persecution against the Righteous', where Luke uses a term that challenges the traditional Jewish understanding of who were 'the Righteous' or 'the Just', since they would normally be understood as the faithful of Israel. The second clause, the turning of the Gentiles against the brethren, stands in parallel to the first. The two statements do not, however, simply repeat each other: the first clause refers to an opposition against the Jewish Jesus-believers that the leaders were able to incite among the Jews of the synagogue by virtue of their authority among their own people; and the second, to a more indirect pressure they had to apply in order to stir up the Gentiles attending the synagogue as God-fearers (the two groups were mentioned in that order at 14.1) against the Gentile believers. Luke uses elsewhere a similar procedure, of making two parallel statements that apply to distinct groups of people (cf., e.g., 2.12-13 [*The Message of Acts*, I, p. 164]; 16.4 D05, see *Commentary*, *ad loc.*).

The function of αὐτοῖς is most likely to be a dative of interest (*dativus commodi*, Winer, *Grammar*, p. 265, 4.b), meaning that the persecution the leaders incited among the Jews was in favour of, or with reference to, themselves (this is a Greek construction for which there is no need to see an Aramaism [B-D-R, §192; cf. Metzger, *Commentary*, p. 370]). If αὐτοῖς were to be taken to refer to the believers, with the dative expressing the people against whom the persecution was directed (cf. Bailly, ἐπάγω, II: 'κινδύνους τινί, Isa. 69.2, susciter des périls à quelqu'un'), the expression διωγμὸν κατὰ τῶν δικαίων could be understood as a complete phrase, describing the type of persecution that was instigated rather than simply repeating the indirect object.

Delebecque (*Les deux Actes*, p. 90) takes τῶν δικαίων, in accordance with good Greek, as a neuter ('the things that are right'), giving the meaning 'persecution contrary to what was right'. The explanation on its own is plausible, but it causes the parallel with the following phrase to be lost (Delebecque wrongly attributes ἐπήγειραν to D05 as well as to B03, pp. 330, 406, n. 17).

ὁ δὲ κύριος ἔδωκεν ταχὺ εἰρήνην D, *dominus autem dedit confestim pacem* d a b dem gig p w vgᵐˢ syʰᵐᵍ mae; Cass Beda | ὁ δὲ θεὸς εἰρ. ἐποίησεν E ‖ *om.* B 𝔓⁷⁴ ℵ *rell*.

The presence of the sentence in D05 is explained as a secondary accretion to smooth away the problems of the alternative text (Metzger, *Commentary*, pp. 370–71; Bruce, *Text*, p. 277; Barrett, I, p. 669). The various explanations for the reading without the verse are presented in the *Commentary* on this verse.

14.3 διέτριψαν παρρησιαζόμενοι B 𝔓⁷⁴ ℵ *rell* ‖ διατρίψαντες παρρησια<σά>-μενοι D⁽*⁾·ᴬ (*commorati sunt habita fiducia* d) gig.

The sentence in D05 has no finite verb but two aorist participles, with the support of the Old Latin gig suggesting that it is not simply a scribal error: 'Le διατρίψαντες de D, soutenu par g[ig], est l'écho d'une structure de phrase aujourd'hui perdue; ces deux témoins n'ont aucun verbe principal dans la phrase' (Boismard and Lamouille, II, p. 97; *pace* Delebecque, *Les deux Actes*, pp. 90–91). Another occurrence of the same structure is found at 3.5 D05, where the verb εἶναι is to be supplied (B-D-R, §468.2, and n. 3; cf. M.S. Smith, 'Grammatically Speaking', in Muraoka and Elwode [eds], *Sirach, Scrolls and Sages*, pp. 278–332).

The omission of a syllable in παρρησιασάμενοι was also seen in D05 at 13.46.

(μαρτυροῦντι) τῷ λόγῳ B D 𝔓⁷⁴ ℵ² *rell* ‖ ἐπὶ τ. λ. ℵ* A syᵖ.— διδόντι (σημεῖα) B D 𝔓⁷⁴ A E H⁵ P 049. 056. 33 𝔐 l καὶ δ. C L 88. 104. 323. 945. 1175. 1739. 1891 *pc* ‖ -τος ℵ (+ καὶ 81). 1505. 2492. 2495.

N-A²⁷ places ἐπί in square brackets. The simple dative τῷ λόγῳ of B03 and D05 makes 'the word of his grace' (preached by Paul and Barnabas) the object of the Lord's testifying; in these manuscripts, it is the same Lord who causes (διδόντι, dat.) signs and wonders to happen. ℵ01 presents the situation differently: the Lord testifies 'on the word of his grace', in other words, he confirms it; and it is his grace (διδόντος, gen.) that gives signs and wonders to happen.

(διὰ τῶν χειρῶν) αὐτῶν B 𝔓⁷⁴ ℵ Dᴬ/ᵖ·ᵐ·? *rell, eorum* d ‖ αὐτοῦ D*.

The singular of D* is striking because it goes against the plural participles at the beginning of the sentence. This may be another occasion when Paul is implicitly singled out (cf. 13.46 D05; 14.1 D05), the plural τῶν χειρῶν also being used of Paul alone at 19.11 (but cf. singular διὰ χειρὸς Βαρναβᾶς καὶ Σαύλου, at 11.30, where the singular expresses the unity of the pair). It is possible, in view of the striking similarity between 14.3-4 and 4.29-30, that the singular pronoun is intended to refer to 'the Lord' (cf. ἐν τῷ τὴν χεῖρα [+ σου D05] ἐκτείνειν [+ σε B03] εἰς ἴασιν καὶ σημεῖα καὶ τέρατα γίνεσθαι; cf. also Lk. 23.46: εἰς χεῖρας σου παρατίθημι [-μι D05] τὸ πνεῦμά μου; 24.50: ἐπάρας [+ δὲ D05] τὰς χεῖρας αὐτοῦ [– D05] εὐλόγησεν αὐτούς).

14.4 ἐσχίσθη δὲ (τὸ πλῆθος) B ‖ ἦν δὲ ἐσχισμένον D, *divisa autem erat* d syᵖ.

B03 describes the split among the people of the city with the aorist, as an event that occurred. D05 describes it rather as a state of affairs (periphrastic perf.) that existed. (Barrett [I, p. 670] states in error that 'D already has ἐσχίσθη in v. 2'.)

οἱ (δέ) B 𝔓⁷⁴ ℵ *rell* ‖ ἄλλοι D, *alii* d.— (ἀποστόλοις) κολλώμενοι διὰ τὸν λόγον τοῦ θεοῦ D, *propter verbum dei* d syʰᵐᵍ (mae) ‖ *om.* B 𝔓⁷⁴ ℵ *rell*.

ἄλλοι in D05 makes a stronger contrast with the first group of people, reinforced by the additional comment about the second group.

14.5 (τῶν ἐθνῶν) τε καὶ ᾿Ιουδαίων B $\mathfrak{P}^{74}$ $\aleph$ *rell* ‖ κ. τῶν ᾿Ι. D, *et Iudaeorum* d.

With the repetition of the article and the absence of τε, D05 views the Jews as a separate group of people.

14.6 καὶ (κατέφυγον) D*, *et fugerunt* d ‖ *om.* B $\mathfrak{P}^{74}$ $\aleph$ D$^{s.m.}$ *rell.*

Adverbial καί in D05 underlines the main verb (Read-Heimerdinger, *The Bezan Text*, pp. 208–11); the notion of completeness expressed by the prefix κατα- is thus reinforced, and the success of the escape is expressed in the translation by 'managed to'.

εἰς (Λύστραν) D*, *in (Listra)* d C* ‖ *om.* B $\mathfrak{P}^{74}$ $\aleph$ D$^{s.m.}$ *rell.*— (τὴν περίχωρον) ὅλην D, *totam* d E lat (mae) ‖ *om.* B $\mathfrak{P}^{74}$ $\aleph$ D$^{s.m.}$ *rell.*

The scope of the area where Paul and Barnabas escaped to is carefully delineated in D05, with the repetition of the preposition and the adjective ὅλην.

14.7 (εὐαγγελιζόμενοι ἦσαν.) καὶ ἐκινήθη ὅλον τὸ πλῆθος ἐπὶ τῇ διδαχῇ D, *et commota est omnis multitudo in doctrinis* d b (h) w vg$^{\Theta}$ (mae) ‖ (εὐαγγελιζόμενοι ἦσαν) τὸν λόγον τοῦ θεοῦ. καὶ ἐξεπλήσσετο πᾶσα ἡ πολυπληθία ἐπὶ τ. δ. αὐτῶν E ‖ *om.* B $\mathfrak{P}^{74}$ $\aleph$ *rell.*

The response of the crowd is not specified in B03. The term πλῆθος is typically Lukan (cf. *Critical Apparatus*, 13.45) and is used especially to denote a large group of people who share a common interest (as distinct from ὄχλος, a disparate group). The verb κινέω is used again, also in the passive, at 21.30.

Commentary

[C′-A] 14.1-2 *In the Synagogue*

[a] 14.1 *Paul in the Synagogue*

14.1 As the narrative zooms in on the events in Iconium, the setting is once more the synagogue. According to most manuscripts, both Paul and Barnabas go to the synagogue and speak to those gathered there. Codex Bezae singles out Paul, placing on him the responsibility for maintaining the pattern (κατὰ τὸ αὐτό)[212] of visiting the synagogue when they arrive at a new place. This persistence is contrary to the solemn recognition he had given (together with

---

212. The expression κατὰ τὸ αὐτό is ambiguous. It can mean 'together' (B-A-G,, κατά, II, 5, b, α), but that meaning is excluded in the Bezan text where Paul alone goes into the synagogue. The sense of 'in the same way' (as before) is also possible (Bruce, *Text*, p. 277) and is strongly suggested by the equivalent expression in the parallel scenes at Lk. 4.16: εἰσῆλθεν κατὰ τὸ εἰωθὸς αὐτῷ ἐν τῇ ἡμέρᾳ τῶν σαββάτων εἰς τὴν συναγωγήν, and also at Acts 17.2: κατὰ τὸ εἰωθὸς τῷ Παύλῳ εἰσῆλθεν πρὸς αὐτούς.

Barnabas) in Antioch, namely, that the rejection of the message of Jesus by the Jews had a significance that went far beyond the local situation in Antioch (see *Commentary*, 13.44-48). Despite acknowledging the object of his mission as being henceforth the Gentiles (13.46), he persists in attempting to use his power of speech to persuade his fellow-Jews to accept the gospel message. The tactic seems to be part of his conviction that for Israel to maintain its distinct identity and existence, the Jews must first accept Jesus as the one sent by God, and so draw the Gentiles to the same truth (cf. his speech in Antioch, 13.33-41, esp. his warning 13.40-41). Only much later, when he makes his first defence speech in Jerusalem (22.21), will Luke let his audience know that Jesus had sent Paul specifically to the Gentiles but that Paul resisted his command.

The singling out of Paul by the Bezan text achieves the effect of making quite clear that Paul is responsible for the decision to go to the synagogue. That is not to say necessarily that he went alone, but simply that he took it upon himself to speak there, as he had spoken in the synagogue of Antioch (cf. 13.16). When Paul speaks in accordance with the plan of God, Luke has him acting in harmony with Barnabas (cf. 13.2, 46), but when he acts out of his own understanding and plans, he is presented as acting alone.

With the unnecessary qualification of the synagogue as 'of the Jews', Luke distances himself from Paul's strategy, just as he had done when relating Paul's visit to Salamis (13.5a). The Bezan text specifies that Paul spoke 'to them', yet another insistence on his concern to present the Jews with the message of Jesus.[213] In the event, a large group[214] including Greeks as well as Jews will be convinced by his speaking. The Alexandrian text (with the aorist verb) presents the step of belief as a completed action, as a block event; the Bezan text is more nuanced, using the continuous present verb to express how belief spread progressively through the crowd. A similar occurrence had taken place in Antioch where both Jews and Gentile proselytes had followed Paul and Barnabas (13.43). Here, however, there is a noteworthy difference, for the non-Jews are referred to as 'Greeks',[215] implying that they were not as yet attached to Judaism as proselytes. They may have been God-fearers with a keen interest in Jewish worship and beliefs, whom Paul specifically addressed in

213. The Greek πρὸς αὐτούς expresses the idea that Paul sought to establish a relationship with the Jews in the synagogue rather than address them in an impersonal way (for which Luke uses the dative pronoun; see Read-Heimerdinger, *The Bezan Text*, pp. 176–82).

214. The term πλῆθος is distinguished in Luke's writings from ὄχλος, referring as it does to a group of people who have gathered for a particular purpose as opposed to simply a mass of people (cf. *Commentary*, 13.45). At 14.1, it anticipates the later use of the term to refer to the people of the city at 14.4, 7 D05.

215. The distinction between 'Jews' and 'Greeks', where the latter term is the equivalent of 'Gentiles', has already appeared in Acts (11.19-20 D05), and will re-appear at 16.1-3; 17.10-12 D05; 18.4; 19.10, 17; 20.21, 24 D05; 21.27-28. It is a typically Pauline expression: cf. Rom. 1.16; 2.9, 10; 3.9; 10.12; 1 Cor. 1.24; 10.32; 12.13; Gal. 3.28; Col. 3.11. The choice of the name here may well reflect the status of Iconium as a Greek city (Witherington, *Acts*, p. 418, citing W.M. Ramsay, *Cities of Paul* [Reprint; Minneapolis: James Family Christian Pub.; n.d.], p. 359).

the synagogue in Antioch (13.16, 26), but they are identified here by their Gentile status of Greeks, rather than by their closeness to Judaism.[216] Some progress has thus been made, for in Antioch it was not until Paul had first of all addressed the synagogue that the Gentiles of the city had been drawn to listen to him (cf. 13.44, esp. D05).

[b] 14.2a *Persecution by the Jewish leaders*

14.2a Opposition to Paul was mounted by the Jews, and not just to Paul but to all 'the brethren' (τῶν ἀδελφῶν), those who believed in his message. The Alexandrian text identifies the agitators as those who did not accept Paul's message and who roused the Gentiles to hostility against the believers. The Greek expression, ἐκάκωσαν τὰς ψυχὰς τῶν ἐθνῶν, conveys the idea that the Jews put ideas into their minds to cause them to react negatively against them. Codex Bezae goes further in singling out the leaders in particular – both those who were synagogue rulers (οἱ ἀρχισυνάγωγοι) and who exercised their role in relation to synagogue worship, and those who had a more general organizational function (οἱ ἄρχοντες) and who therefore had a political importance.[217] The dual terminology appears to be pointless, until it is recognized that the double insistence serves the purpose of stressing that it was the leaders 'of the Jews' who were responsible for instigating persecution, and that all the weight and power of the Jewish leadership was put behind it; the contrast made by the Bezan text with the power of the Lord in countering their attack (14.2b) will be all the stronger. The Jewish leadership en bloc roused their fellow-Jews (see *Critical Apparatus*) to hostility against the believers in Jesus, and also used their power to poison the minds of the Gentiles against them.

The persecution in Iconium echoes that stirred up against Paul and Barnabas in Antioch (cf. 13.50). The situation here, however, is more complex, for the persecutors include Gentiles as well as Jews, and those persecuted also include Gentiles as well as Jews. The parallel statements in Codex Bezae reinforce the double statements: the synagogue leaders stirred up the Jews to persecute the Jewish Jesus-believers (the Righteous) and caused the Gentiles to react against the Greek brethren. The conflict here is broad, between believers and non-believers rather than between Jews zealous to preserve their inheritance and Jews who proclaimed a new teaching (cf. 13.45, esp, D05, and *Commentary, ad loc.*). Luke makes it clear that the real objects of attack are 'the Righteous' or 'the Just', a term common in Judaism to refer to those who fulfilled the goal of 'righteousness'.[218] The parallelism in Codex Bezae powerfully brings out the reversal of roles, equating the Righteous with 'the brethren'.

---

216. Lieu (*Neither Jew Nor Greek*, pp. 31–47) identifies the social advantages of association with the synagogue.

217. The distinction between 'religious' and 'political' is seen from a non-Jewish point of view, i.e. Roman in this instance, for the two aspects were closely connected in Jewish public life.

218. The concept of צדק underpins the ethical and legal code of the Torah, referring to the nature of relationships of people among themselves and with God.

[b′] 14.2b *The Lord Gives Peace*

14.2b The situation is left unresolved in the Alexandrian text, so that commentators suggest various explanations and conjectures to account for the continuing presence of Paul and Barnabas in a city where the climate of opposition to their teaching and to the community growing around them is so generalized and strong.[219] According to the Bezan text, the attempt by the synagogue leaders to destabilize the new movement is countered by the intervention of the Lord. The 'Lord', ὁ κύριος, refers to the resurrected Jesus who is identified increasingly in Acts as the κύριος of the LXX, that is, YHWH as opposed to Elohim.[220] The care with which Jesus watches over the mission he entrusts to his followers can be noted not only here but at various critical points in its development.[221] Just how he intervenes will be detailed in the following verse, preparing for the renewed hostility which, next time, will have more drastic consequences.

[C′-A′] 14.3-7b *In the City*

[a] 14.3 *A Positive Testimony*

14.3 The continued presence of Paul and Barnabas in Iconium despite the persecution is perhaps best explained, as far as the Alexandrian text goes, by the suggestion that the mention of trouble in 14.2 in fact is meant to anticipate the more detailed description of events in vv. 4-5 (see on 14.2 above). There still remains the problem, nonetheless, of the typically Lukan resuming formula, μὲν οὖν, at v. 3 and the corresponding δέ at v. 4.[222] Since its function is to introduce an event that follows on from the previous one, in accordance with it, v. 3 in the Alexandrian text must be taken as developing from v. 1, and

219. All tastes are catered for: v. 2 is a parenthesis, so v. 3 really follows on from v. 1; or v. 3 is a redactional gloss incorporated into the text at a later date; or the order of vv. 2 and 3 was interchanged; or Luke inserted v. 3 into his source material; or v. 2 refers to the persecution of v. 5 and is placed by Luke beforehand in anticipation of what will follow. J. Hugh Michael ('The Original Position of Acts 14.3', *ET* 40 [1928–29], pp. 514–16) suggests that '14.3 stood originally right in the middle of 13.48'. J. Taylor (*Les Actes des Deux Apôtres*. V. *Commentaire historique* [Act 9.1–18.22], [ÉBib, NS, 23; Paris: J. Gabalda, 1998], pp. 166–170) argues that 14.1-2, 5-6 belong to the first redaction of Luke, and vv. 2-4 to the second.

The presence of μὲν οὖν ... δέ in vv. 3-4 is a controlling factor in the debate, for elsewhere in Acts it has been observed to mark a break between incidents rather than continuity, with οὖν nevertheless making a connection back to the previous event (see Levinsohn, *Textual Connections*, pp. 137–50, esp. 145–46).

220. Read-Heimerdinger, *The Bezan Text*, pp. 278–97. Cf. M. Barker, *The Great Angel: A Study of Israel's Second God* (London: SPCK, 1992), who identifies YHWH as a distinct divine being in First Temple Judaism, a theological understanding that was revised in the post-exilic period.

221. Cf. *The Message of Acts*, I, p. 201 on 2.47b; II, pp. 308–309 on 11.21; p. 363 on 12.17a; in this volume, *Commentary*, 16.14; 18.9. Cf. also 23.11.

222. Of the 40 (+ 3 D05) occurrences of μὲν οὖν in the New Testament, one is found in Luke (3.18) and 28 (31 D05) in Acts.

v. 4 must pick up from v. 2.[223] Accordingly, in the Alexandrian text, the unfolding of events follows an alternating pattern: the mission encounters a high level of success first in the synagogue and then in the city (vv. 1, 3); but the Jews of the synagogue instigate hostility towards the believers (v. 2), which leads to a split among the people of the city between those supporting the apostles and those supporting the Jews (v. 4); the result is fierce opposition from a combined force of Jews and Gentiles against the believers (either in general, or Paul and Barnabas in particular, see on 14.5-6 below).

In the Bezan text, the narrative follows a different pattern. There are, in fact, two distinct scenes, the first in the synagogue and the second in the city, with the two-fold intervention of Jesus serving as a link between them. In the synagogue, Paul's preaching meets with an exceptional level of success among Jews and Greeks. However, trouble arises when the synagogue leaders take a united stand against the believers, inciting the Jews against them and causing the Gentiles to be hostile to them, too. The climate of hostility and suspicion is settled by the rapid intervention of Jesus, though the details of his action are not given. Consequently, Paul and Barnabas are able to stay on in Iconium and are made bold to speak about the Lord who confirms their message by miraculous signs and wonders. The attack from the townspeople that ensues is of a different nature from the initial persecution that occurred in the context of the synagogue, as will be seen (14.5 below).

The description of the action of the Lord in Iconium here at 14.3 is forceful. Paul and Barnabas are made bold to speak about him: the verb Luke uses has the technical sense in his writing of giving innovative and daring interpretations of the Scriptures in accordance with the truth about Jesus,[224] so it may be assumed that they are not simply proclaiming the good news about Jesus but are doing so in the context of the Jewish prophecies and expectations, particularly insisting on 'his grace' (cf. 13.43). Jesus himself gives confirmation to what they are saying, by the manifestation of supernatural 'signs and wonders', which may include healings from physical diseases as well as release from the oppression of unclean spirits. The description of the activity of Paul and Barnabas working in harmony with Jesus is strikingly similar to the prayer for such divine corroboration, made in Ierousalem by the apostles in response to the threats against them by the Temple authorities (4.29-30; cf. 5.12-16). The singular 'his hands' in Codex Bezae may be another occasion of singling out Paul as the one taking the lead (cf. 19.11-12); alternatively it may refer to 'the hands of the Lord' (cf. Lk. 23.46).[225]

223. This is the observation of Levinsohn, *Textual Connections*, pp. 145–46; cf. Zerwick and Grosvenor (*Analysis*, p. 397) who view v. 2 as a parenthesis.

224. Cf. 13.46, where the verb is used of Paul who, together with Barnabas, takes a step never taken before of declaring that the word of God is to be given to the Gentiles (see *Commentary, ad loc.*).

225. At 11.30, the singular διὰ χειρὸς Βαρναβᾶ καὶ Σαύλου expresses the unity between Barnabas and Saul at that point when they were in Antioch. Paul's leading role is emphasized in contrast by the singular at 14.3 if, indeed, the reference is to his hands.

[b] 14.4 *Division among the Crowd*

14.4 As a result of the preaching and the supernatural activity, the city was divided. The suggestion is that prior to the arrival of Paul and Barnabas, the residents were generally united, despite being a mixed population of Jews and Greeks. Now, however, some of the people opt to side with Paul and Barnabas and others to side with the Jews, though the split was not a simple Gentile–Jew one but resulted in a mixture of supporters for both parties. The Alexandrian text presents the division as an event that occurred, while the Bezan text presents it as a state that resulted from the preceding events:[226] on the one hand, the previous extreme hostility stirred up by the Jewish synagogue leaders among the Jews and the Gentiles (14.2) and, on the other, the positive response of many in the synagogue, reinforced by the intervention of the Lord in an endorsement of the message preached in the city (14.3).

For the first time in Luke's writing, the term 'apostles' is given to disciples who did not belong to the Twelve/Eleven; it will be used once more, but only by the Alexandrian text, at 14.14. It is often assumed that the title hitherto reserved for the Twelve representatives of the tribes of Israel is now extended to include other representatives, in other words, the designation remains a reference to a closed group. However, note should be made how, on the contrary, Luke has often employed the verb ἀποστέλλω, 'send', to refer to those sent by God or by Jesus to accomplish a mission that was distinct from the specific mission to Israel for which Jesus chose the Twelve.[227] By extending the term 'apostles' to two sent out by the Holy Spirit (cf. 13.4) on an alternative mission, Luke thus removes the previous restriction on the scope of the term.[228] It is noteworthy that Paul is not called an apostle in the later stages on his mission, when he is no longer following the direction of the Holy Spirit.

The reason for the split among the population is made explicit in Codex Bezae: the two groups of people were 'adhering'[229] to one side or the other because of the word of God. The same issue as had provoked zeal and violence in Antioch (cf. 13.45, 46, 48) has yet again caused great tension and conflict. It is worth recalling the specific sense Luke gives to the 'word of God' as opposed to the 'word of the Lord' (see *Excursus* 1). The 'word of God' designates communication from God to humankind, originally entrusted to the Jews in the form of the Torah, and only once people have received the word of

226. The aorist in the AT here denotes an event, in contrast to the periphrastic perfect of the Bezan text which describes a state of affairs.

227. The verb ἀποστέλλω is used notably of the Seventy(-Two) disciples sent to Samaria (Lk. 10.1, 17), presented by Luke, and only Luke, as the alternative to the mission to Israel that had just been entrusted to the Twelve.

228. On the role of the Twelve after the death of Jesus, see the analysis of J. Rius-Camps and J. Read-Heimerdinger, 'After the Death of Judas: A Reconsideration of the Status of the Twelve Apostles', *RCatT* 29 (2005), pp. 305–34. Cf. the use of ἀπόστολος in Paul's letters: 1 Cor. 9.1-2; 2 Cor. 8.23; Gal. 1.1.

229. The Greek verb κολλάω literally means 'stick like glue' (L-J-S, κολλάω, II).

God are they in a position to receive the 'word of the Lord', the specific message about Jesus and/or his teaching. Paul and Barnabas made a solemn declaration in Antioch, that the time had come for the word of God to be given to the Gentiles, proclaiming that Jesus as the Messiah was a universal ruler, that he was for the Gentiles as well as for the Jews. A number of Jews in Antioch had been inspired with zeal to protect their privileged inheritance, and to oppose Paul's teaching even though it represented God's plan for the world. They thereby, according to Paul and Barnabas, rejected the word of God and denied their own right to the life that accompanied it.[230]

The conflict in Iconium, according to Codex Bezae, has the same basis as the trouble in Antioch. It is not just a dispute over the Messiahship of Jesus that is the root of the problem, but rather what Paul and Barnabas are teaching about the word of God – hitherto it was the preserve of the Jews and now, since the time of Paul and Barnabas in Antioch, it is proclaimed as belonging also to the Gentiles.

[b'] 14.5-7a *Paul and Barnabas Escape to Lycaonia*
14.5-6 A fresh attack is prepared by Gentiles and Jews alike. It is implied that the object of attack is Paul and Barnabas, although it is not impossible that all the believers are again targeted (cf. 14.2). This is all the more likely in the Bezan text, where specific comment is made about the movements of Paul and Barnabas in Lystra (14.7c D05) compared with the general statements made just beforehand (14.6; see on 14.7c below). Nevertheless, if the believers generally had to flee at this point, they were later able to return (cf. 14.21).

In the Alexandrian text, the Gentiles and Jews are grouped together as one and they are accompanied by their respective leaders. The distinction made between the two groups in the Bezan text causes the leaders to be more probably associated with the Jews alone; and on the basis of the distinction, the two actions of insulting and stoning can be viewed as equally distinct, with the Gentiles being responsible for the insults (having had their minds previously poisoned against the believers by the Jews), and the Jews with their leaders for the stoning, which is a means of Jewish attack that has already been noted (with reference to Stephen, 7.58-59; cf. Lk. 13.34, par. Mt. 21.35). The Jews have finally succeeded in obtaining what they set out to achieve after the synagogue preaching (cf. 14.2), but the temporary peace brought about by the Lord gave time for a believing community to be established in Iconium (cf. 14.21-23).

Paul and Barnabas learn of the plot and fully realize the consequences of it.[231] This realization is more than a simple discovery of what is planned against them, for the Greek also implies a new awareness of the situation – of the determination of the Jews to put a stop to their work, even to the point

---

230. See *Commentary*, 13.14-50, esp. 13.33-35, 39, 41, 44-48.

231. On the two other occasions that the participial form of the verb συνεῖδον is found in the New Testament, it is a question of a full realization: Acts 5.2 (Sapphira has full knowledge of her husband's deceit); 12.12 (Peter has a full awareness of his liberation).

of drawing on Gentile support when need be. They consequently have to get themselves right away from Iconium[232] and go to a district where no mention is made of a Jewish synagogue – on the contrary, the only Jews spoken of in the next sequence will be seen to meet in the open air. Their destination is the cities of Lystra and Derbe in Lycaonia, and the area round about, the whole area as Codex Bezae specifies. These will be the two cities that are the focus of the following narrative sequence, [B'].

14.7a The activity of Paul and Barnabas is underlined with another periphrastic construction, which is more forceful than the simple imperfect.[233] It may be observed how Luke has been progressively more specific in his choice of vocabulary to describe the preaching activity, as the area of their speaking widened: in the synagogue, they (or just Paul according to the Bezan text) 'spoke' (14.1); in the city, they boldly spoke 'the word of his grace' (14.3); and now in the (whole, D05) region of Lycaonia, they 'were evangelizing', that is, they were announcing the good news.

This statement, and the following one that describes the response to their preaching, stand as a general comment on their visit to the area, the following verses from 14.7c D05 onwards presenting the scene in greater detail.[234]

[a'] 14.7b *The Response of the Crowd*

14.7b In the Alexandrian text, no response to the evangelization carried on by Paul and Barnabas is recorded. The comment recorded in the Bezan text may have been omitted because it seems superfluous unless it is understood as a general comment. It serves the further purpose of marking a progression throughout the sequence, so that the term πλῆθος acquires the technical sense of a body of people distinct from the synagogue (cf. its use in this sense at 13.45 D05): without the article first, Luke uses it at 14.1 to describe an identifiable group of people among the synagogue attenders; then, at 14.4, it refers to a group made up of people within the city of Iconium; finally, here at 14.7b D05, the scope has widened even more to include people from an entire region. Luke insinuates the universal appeal of the message preached by Paul and Barnabas, as opposed to the deliberately exclusive nature of the synagogue teaching.

[B'] 14.7c-20 *Lycaonia: Lystra*

Overview

This is the penultimate sequence of the first phase of the mission to the Gentiles, which takes place in the new setting of Lystra. It develops one aspect of the evangelizing and teaching activity of Paul and Barnabas in Lycaonia

---

232. The completeness of their escape is suggested by the perfective prefix of the verb καταφεύγω, reinforced as it is in D05 by the adverbial καί before it.

233. Cf. the periphrastic perfect of 14.4a D05, and the periphrastic imperfect of 14.4b D05.

234. The same process of 'zooming' was observed at 1.3-14, on which see *The Message of Acts*, I, p. 47.

summarized at 14.6-7b. This is the first location in which there is no mention of local Jews, and so equally, the first time that no preparation for the gospel has been made in the city through the witness of the Jews. The initial event in Lystra is the healing of a lame man outside the city gates, symbolizing the power of Jesus to give spiritual health to the worshippers of pagan gods. The outcome is not entirely successful, although some disciples are made. It leads to a new attack from the Jews who travel from the last two places visited by Paul and Barnabas, namely Antioch and Iconium. The incident gives Paul the impetus to make another step in distancing himself from his fellow-Jews, while also serving as a transition to move Paul and Barnabas on to Derbe, the second city mentioned in the general summary of 14.6-7b.

Structure and Themes
There are two episodes, the first presenting the main action, while the second is a development arising out of it:

[B'-A]	14.7c-18	The healing of the lame man
[a]	14.7c	Paul and Barnabas stay in Lystra
[b]	14.8	The man born lame
[c]	14.9a	The lame man listens to Paul
[d]	14.9b-10a	Paul orders him to stand and walk
[e]	14.10b	The man gets up and walks
[e']	14.11	The acclamation of the crowds
[d']	14.12	Hermes and Zeus
[c']	14.13	Attempts of the priests to offer sacrifice
[b']	14.14-17	The reaction of Paul and Barnabas
[a']	14.18	Their difficulty in preventing sacrifice
[B'-A']	14.19-20	The Jewish attack on Paul
[a]	14.19a	The arrival of Jews from Iconium and Antioch
[b]	14.19b	The stoning of Paul
[b']	14.20a	He goes back into the city
[a']	14.20b	Departure to Derbe

According to the text of Codex Bezae, the first episode, [B'-A], has at its centre the healing of the lame man and the enthusiastic response of the crowds. The action takes place outside the city, at the gates. The second, [B'-A'], is set within the city; it illustrates the response of hostile Jews, who come from Antioch and Iconium, where Paul has already made enemies among them, to put him to death. It is noteworthy that in Codex Bezae, Lystra is mentioned both in the opening element of the sequence (14.7c D05) and in the penultimate one (14.20a D05), underlining its unity; the second reference is absent from the Alexandrian text.

Translation

Codex Bezae D05	*Codex Vaticanus B03*
[Aa] **14.7c** Paul and Barnabas stayed on in Lystra.	

[b]   **8** A certain man used to sit there who had been unable to use his feet from the womb of his mother, and who had never walked at all.

[c]   **9** This man heard Paul speaking, feeling full of fear.

[d]   **10a** Paul, looking intently at him and seeing that he had faith to be healed, said to him in a loud voice, 'To you I say in the name of the Lord Jesus: Stand upright on your feet and walk'.

[e]   **10b** And at once, without further ado, he sprang up and walked.

[e']   **11** When the crowds saw what Paul had done, they raised their voices in Lycaonian saying, 'The gods have become like mortals and have come down to us'.

[d']   **12** (Barnabas they called Zeus, but Paul Hermes, since he was interpreting the message.)

[c']   **13** The priests of the local Zeus Propolis, bringing bulls and garlands to them at the gates, wished to sacrifice with the crowds.

[b']   **14** When Barnabas heard, and Paul, tearing their clothes they rushed right out into the crowd, crying out and shouting, **15** 'Men, what is this that you are doing? We are mortal men just like you, and we proclaim to you the good news of God, so that you would turn from these powerless things to the living God, the one who made heaven and earth and the sea and all things in them, **16** who in past generations allowed the various nations to go their own ways; **17** and certainly, he did not leave himself without a witness, since he has performed good to you, giving you rain from heaven and fruitful seasons, and filling your hearts with food and gladness.'

[a']   **18** And by saying these things, they only just managed to stop the crowds from sacrificing to them.

[A'a]   **19a** While they stayed on teaching, some Jews came from Antioch and Iconium;

[b]   **19b** and, having intimidated the crowd and stoned Paul, they dragged him outside the city, supposing him to be dead.

8 In Lystra, a certain man used to sit, unable to use his feet and lame from his mother's womb, and who had never walked.

9 This man was listening to Paul speaking.

10a And he, looking intently at him and seeing that he had faith to be healed, said to him in a loud voice, 'Stand upright on your feet'.

10b And immediately, he leapt up and walked;

11 and when the crowds saw what Paul had done, they raised their voices, in Lycaonian, saying, 'The gods have become like mortals and have come down to us'.

12 (They called Barnabas Zeus, but Paul Hermes, since it was he who was the interpreter of the message.)

13 The priest of the Zeus who was in front of the city, bringing bulls and garlands to the gates, wished to sacrifice with the crowds.

14 When the apostles Barnabas and Paul heard, tearing their clothes they rushed out into the crowd, crying out and saying, **15** 'Men, what is this that you are doing? We also are mortal men, just like you, and we proclaim good news, that you turn from these powerless things to a living God, who made heaven and earth and the sea and all things in them, **16** who in past generations allowed all the nations to go their own ways; **17** and yet he did not leave himself without a witness, since he has done good to you, giving you rain from heaven and fruitful seasons, and filling your hearts with food and gladness.'

18 And by saying these things, they only just managed to stop the crowds from sacrificing to them.

19a From Antioch and Iconium came Jews;

19b and, having won over the crowd and stoned Paul, they started dragging him outside the city, supposing him to be dead.

[b′]   20a But his disciples surrounded him   20a But the disciples surrounded him
          and he got up and went into the city of   and he got up and went into the city;
          Lystra;
[a′]   20b and the next day he went out with   20b and on the next day he went out
          Barnabas to Derbe.   with Barnabas to Derbe.

Critical Apparatus

14.7c Ὁ δὲ Παῦλος καὶ Βαρναβᾶς διέτριβον ἐν Λύστροις D, *Paulus autem et Barnabas moras faciebant in Lystris* d E b h w vg^Θ mae ‖ *om.* B 𝔓^74 ℵ *rell.*

B03 omits a second consecutive sentence (cf. *Critical Apparatus*, 14.7b), which opens a new sequence in D05. Apart from John (Jn 3.22), Luke is alone in the New Testament to use the verb διατρίβω (Acts × 7, + 2 D05: 14.7c, 19).

14.8 (ἀνήρ) ἀδύνατος ἐν Λύστροις τοῖς ποσὶν ἐκάθητο χωλός B ℵ* 1175 ‖ ἐν Λ. ἀδ. τ. ποσ. ἐκ. χωλ. 𝔓^74 ℵ^2 A C H L P Ψ 049. 056. 33. 1739 𝔐 vg ‖ ἀδ. τ. ποσ. ἐκ. χωλ. E ‖ ἐκ. ἀδ. τ. ποσ. D, *sedebat adynatus a pedibus* d gig h.— τῆς (μητρός) D* ‖ *om.* B 𝔓^74 ℵ D^{s.m.} *rell.*

B03 specifies at this point that the location is Lystra, where D05 has made it clear in the previous sentence (omitted by B03, see above). The position of ἐν Λύστροις underlines the location, disrupting as it does the phrase describing the man's infirmity. The word order of D05 focuses attention of his lack of movement (ἐκάθητο) rather than on the cause of it.

The presence of χωλός in B03, together with the absence of the article before μητρός, creates a phrase identical to that used to introduce the lame man at the Beautiful Gate in Jerusalem (cf. 3.2), which the present incident mirrors (for the phrase ἐκ κοιλίας μητρὸς [αὐτοῦ], cf. also Mt. 19.12; Lk. 1.15; Gal. 1.15). For the article before μητρός in D05, cf. Jn 3.4, εἰς τὴν κοιλίαν τῆς μητρὸς αὐτοῦ, where the dual article reflects the emphasis of Nathaniel's question. The article is typically omitted in genitival phrases in Acts when the phrase in question is a set expression, as is the case here (Heimerdinger and Levinsohn, 'The Use of the Article', p. 30). Exceptionally including the article consequently has the effect of highlighting the word μητρός. Since the 'mother' here, as at 3.2, represents the biological ancestry of the man, the reason for highlighting it in the story of the man at Lystra would seem to be his Gentile origin (as opposed to the Jewish origin in every instance of the anarthrous phrase elsewhere). See *Commentary* for further discussion of the symbolic representativity of the lame man.

(οὐδέποτε) περιεπάτησεν B 𝔓^74 ℵ A C Ψ 33. 81. 88. 104. 323. 945. 1739. 1891. 2344 ‖ -πεπατήκει D E H L P 049. 056 𝔐.

The pluperfect in D05 insists on the fact that the man had never walked, because that was his state; the aorist of B03, in contrast, refers to an action that had never taken place.

14.9 (οὗτος) ἤκουεν B C P 049. 056. 1. 6. 226. 323. 330. 440. 536. 915. 927. 1241. 1243. 1245. 1828. 1854. 2492 *pc* ‖ -σεν D, *audivit* d 𝔓⁷⁴ (οὐκ -σεν ℵ) A E H L Ψ 33. 81. 88. 104. 547. 614. 618. 945. 1175. 1270. 1505. 1611. 1646. 1739. 1837. 1891. 2147. 2344. 2412. 2495 h vg syᵖ bo.— (Παύλου) λαλοῦντος ὑπάρχων ἐν φόβῳ D, *possidens in timore* d (h) ‖ λαλοῦντος B 𝔓⁷⁴ A *rell* ‖ λέγοντος ℵ 2147.

B03 portrays the man as listening to Paul over a period of time. D05 portrays his listening as an event (for which 'heard' is a more apt translation) without reference to duration, but qualifies him as having been afraid when he heard him.

ὃς ἀτενίσας αὐτῷ B 𝔓⁷⁴ ℵ *rell* ‖ ἀτ. δὲ αὐ. ὁ Παῦλος D, *intuitus autem eum Paulus* d (gig h syᵖ mae aeth) ‖ πρὸς ὃν ἀτ. ὁ Π. E.

D05 marks a new development with δέ, and specifies Paul by name. B03, having not read the previous adjectival phrase describing the man's fear, continues with the subject relative pronoun to switch to Paul who has just been mentioned in that text.

14.10 (φωνῇ·) Σοὶ λέγω· ἐν τῷ ὀνόματι τοῦ κυρίου Ἰησοῦ Χριστοῦ D C 33. 323. 945. 1739 *pc* (E, Ψ, 6. 36. 1175 *al*, 614 h t vgᶜ syᵖ·ʰᵐᵍ co aeth; Irˡᵃᵗ Theoph Cass) ‖ *om.* B 𝔓⁷⁴ ℵ 𝔐 gig vg syʰ boᵖᵗ.— (ὀρθὸς) καὶ περιπάτει D syʰᵐᵍ mae ‖ *om.* B 𝔓⁷⁴ ℵ *rell*.

D05 has Paul pronounce a formal declaration, using the full title of Jesus, which is typical of D05 in solemn situations (see Read-Heimerdinger, *The Bezan Text*, pp. 272–74). Furthermore, the instruction to walk as well as to stand is included in D05 but not B03.

(καὶ) ἥλατο καί (– B) B 𝔓⁷⁴ ℵ *rell* ‖ εὐθέως παραχρῆμα ἀνήλ- (ἀνήλλ- Dᶜ) καί D* syᵖ·ʰᵐᵍ mae ‖ παρ. ἐξήλλ- καί E.

The use of the compound verb ἀνάλλομαι D05 is unique in the New Testament, although the verb is found occasionally in other writings.

The juxtaposition in D05 of the two adverbs expressing immediacy has the effect of stressing how the healing followed instantly from Paul's command. A combination of the same adverbs is found in the WT at 9.18 (D05 lac.; see *The Message of* Acts, II, *Critical Apparatus*, p. 182). The absence of insistence in B03 is in line with the relative prominence given to the reaction of the crowd in the following sentence (see below).

14.11 (οἵ) τε B 𝔓⁷⁴ ℵ A 36. 453. 1837 *pc* ‖ δέ D, *autem* d C E H L P Ψ 049. 056. 33. 1739 𝔐 gig vg syʰ sa mae.

The conjunction τε in B03 gives prominence to the event it introduces, and so has the effect of downplaying the healing of the lame man in favour of the response of the crowd (see comment above). This is the first occurrence of τε in a series of three (cf. 14.12, 13), observed elsewhere in Acts (cf. 2.43-46) where D05 reads δέ each time. With δέ in D05 here, the healing is portrayed as the climax of the first part of the story, with the reaction of the crowd providing the corresponding response.

(ἐπῆραν) τὴν φωνὴν αὐτῶν B 𝔓⁷⁴ ℵ² A C E H L P Ψ 33. 614. 1739 𝔐 I αὐ. τ. φ. 049. 056. 1. 104. 330. 448. 1854. 2147. 2492 I τ. φ. ℵ* II φ. αὐ. D 1838.

The absence of the article can be accounted for by the fact that the anarthrous phrase ἐπῆραν φωνήν is a stock one. It is found in the LXX with the article (Judg. 2.4; 9.7; 2 Kgdms 13.36), and in the New Testament only in the work of Luke, where there are both arthrous and anarthrous references: Lk. 11.27; 17.13; Acts 2.14 (arthrous); 4.24; 14.11; 22.22 (arthrous). The arthrous form of the phrase may arise here at 14.11 B03 because of the qualification that the people spoke in their own language of Lycaonia, so undoing the set nature of the phrase (cf. 2.14, where in D05 Peter raises his voice *first*; and 22.22, where the people interrupt Paul to raise *their* voice to prevent him using *his* voice).

τοῖς (ἀνθρώποις) D 1 *pc* sa mae II *om.* B 𝔓⁷⁴ ℵ *rell*.
The article in D05 before ἀνθρώποις possibly causes the reference to be more specifically applied to Paul and Barnabas than humans in general.

14.12 (ἐκάλουν) τε B 𝔓⁷⁴ ℵ *rell* II δέ D 181. 242. 467. 945. 1739. 1854. 1891. 2492 *pc* e gig; Chr.

B03 introduces with τε additional information about the identity of Paul and Barnabas as gods, whereas D05 uses δέ to signal a parenthesis, anticipating the following development (Levinsohn, *Textual Connections*, pp. 123–27; cf. 91). This is the second of three successive statements introduced with τε in B03 (cf. 14.11, 13).

τὸν Βαρναβᾶν B 𝔓⁷⁴ ℵ A C* 81. 88. 614. 1175. 2412 I τ. μὲν Βαρ. C² E H L P Ψ 049. 056. 1739 𝔐 II Βαρναβᾶν D.

The importance of Barnabas is highlighted in D05 by the absence of the article before his name, especially in contrast to the presence of the article before the name of Paul; the arthrous reference to Paul indicates that he is the implicit topic of the narrative throughout this incident.

Δία B ℵ A C P Ψ 049. 33ᵛⁱᵈ. 945 𝔐 II Δίαν D P⁷⁴ E H L 056. 81. 88. 440. 547. 1175. 1739. 2344 *al.*

Although Δία is the usual accusative form of the name of Zeus, in D05 it is declined in line with the accusative form of Ἑρμῆν, the name given to Paul. The variety of support suggests that it was not merely accidental but a valid alternative.

ἐπειδὴ (αὐτὸς ἦν) B D 𝔓⁷⁴ ℵ² *rell* ‖ ἐπεί ℵ 927.

ℵ01 also reads ἐπεὶ δέ against ἐπειδή in B03 at Lk. 7.1 (D05 words the sentence differently, without either form of the conjunction). From Luke's use elsewhere (cf. ἐπεί Lk. 1.34; ἐπειδή Acts 13.8 D05, 46; 14.12; 15.24), it may be suggested that ἐπειδή implies a stronger sense of cause and effect than does ἐπεί. (This would explain why some manuscripts at 13.46 attest a correction of ἐπειδή to ἐπειδὴ δέ [ℵ01ᶜ D05ᴮ] rather than to ἐπεὶ δέ which is, indeed, the reading of other manuscripts – to have made the correction ἐπεὶ δέ would have weakened the force of ἐπειδή.)

ὁ (ἡγούμενος) B 𝔓⁷⁴ ℵ *rell* ‖ *om.* D C* 056. 467. 1518.

The presence of the article in B03 before ἡγούμενος causes this noun to be the subject and Paul (αὐτός) to be the complement, so that the statement answers the question 'who was the interpreter of the message?' and not 'what was Paul?'. D05, in contrast, does answer this second question: ἡγούμενος functions as a present participle in a periphrastic construction, ἦν ἡγούμενος, and so focuses on Paul's activity rather than the identity of the interpreter.

14.13 ὅ τε ἱερεύς B 𝔓⁷⁴ ℵ A 945. 1175. 1270. 1739. 1891. 2344 | τότε ἱερεύς C | ὁ δὲ ἱερεύς E H L P 049. 056. 614 𝔐 ‖ οἱ δὲ ἱερεῖς D, *sacerdotes autem* d.— τοῦ Διὸς τοῦ ὄντος πρὸ (πρὸς C*) τῆς πόλεως B 𝔓⁷⁴ ℵ A C² E H L P 049. 056. 1739 𝔐 ‖ τ. ὄντος Δ. πρὸ πόλ. D*, *qui erant Iovis ante civitate\<m>* d | τ. ὄντος Δ. πρὸ τῆς πόλ. Dᶜ 614. 1611. 2412.— (ταυροὺς) αὐτοῖς D*, *eis* d ‖ *om.* B 𝔓⁷⁴ ℵ Dˢ·ᵐ· *rell.*— ἐνέγκας B 𝔓⁷⁴ ℵ *rell* ‖ -καντες D, *adferentes* d gig vgˢᵁ aeth; Ephr.— ἤθελεν θύειν B 𝔓⁷⁴ ℵ A C E L P Ψ 056. 33. 1739 𝔐 ‖ ἤθελον ἐπιθύειν D, *volentes immolare* d h | ἤθελον θύειν H 049. 1. 81. 323. 330. 618. 1243. 1270. 1505. 1828ᶜ. 1854. 2492.

There are several small differences in the portrayal of the scene outside the city gates. Where B03 presents just one priest of Zeus, D05 has more than one (sing./pl. noun ὁ ἱερεύς/οἱ δὲ ἱερεῖς; participle ἐνέγκας/ἐνέγκαντες; verb ἤθελεν/ἤθελον). Furthermore, B03 uses the conjunction τε to introduce the specific information that will lead to the next development in the narrative (v. 14). It stresses the fact that the god (probably a statue and temple) was outside the city, just in front of it, τοῦ Διὸς τοῦ ὄντος πρὸ τῆς πόλεως. D05 lays emphasis rather on the fact that the priests were connected with the local Zeus (τοῦ ὄντος Διός), whose name may have been Propolis (for the use of the participle of εἶναι to mean 'local', cf. 5.17; 13.1; Bruce, *Text*, p. 322; Lake and Cadbury, *English Translation and Commentary,* p. 165; the varying position of ὄντος does not make any real difference to the sense but rather the focus, cf. B-D-R §474.5, a, c).

These priests intended to offer sacrifices to Barnabas and Paul (αὐτοῖς), since they were perceived as gods, with the compound verb ἐπιθύειν (as opposed to the simple θύειν in B03) also confirming the idea that the sacrifices were to be offered towards a specific person. The compound verb is sometimes found with the specific meaning of 'offering an additional sacrifice' (cf. Bruce, *Text*, p. 322); if that is what is meant here, the idea is that the sacrifice to Barnabas and Paul was to be in addition to the sacrifice normally offered.

14.14 ἀκούσαντες δὲ οἱ ἀπόστολοι (Βαρναβᾶς καὶ Παῦλος) B 𝔓⁷⁴ ℵ *rell* ‖ ἀκούσας δέ D, *cum audisset autem* d (gig h syᵖ; Aug).

The surprising singular in D05, with the unusual order of 'Barnabas and Paul', suggests that it is the reaction of Barnabas that is in focus, though he acted in unison with Paul (plural verb forms follow, and plural possessive pronoun αὐτῶν). Barnabas is not singled out in B03, where the plural participle is used; they are also called 'apostles' in this text (cf. 14.4).

(τὰ ἱμάτια) ἑαυτῶν B ℵ² A 33. 1270. 1854 ‖ αὐτῶν D 𝔓⁷⁴ ℵ* C E H L P Ψ 049. 056. 614 𝔐.

The reflexive pronoun in B03 makes clear that Paul and Barnabas tore their own garments (as a reaction against blasphemy; see H.J. Cadbury, 'Dust and Garments', in F.J. Foakes Jackson and K. Lake, *The Beginnings of Christianity*, V (London: Macmillan, 1933), pp. 269-77 [271]).

καὶ (ἐξεπήδησαν) D*, *et* d ‖ *om.* B 𝔓⁷⁴ ℵ Dˢ·ᵐ· *rell*.

The adverbial καί in D05 confers dramatic importance to the act of rushing out into the crowds (Read-Heimerdinger, *The Bezan Text*, pp. 208–210; cf. 14.6 above).

14.15 (καὶ) λέγοντες B 𝔓⁷⁴ ℵ Dᴰ *rell* ‖ φωνοῦντες D* (*clamantes et vociferantes* d).

In line with the dramatic emphasis given to the action of Barnabas and Paul, the verb φωνέω is also more expressive than λέγω.

καὶ (ἡμεῖς) B 𝔓⁷⁴ ℵ *rell* ‖ *om.* D d (𝔓⁴⁵) 049. 1175. 1854. 2492 gigᶜ h; Chr.— (εὐαγγελιζόμενοι) ὑμᾶς B 𝔓⁷⁴ ℵ *rell* ‖ ὑμῖν τὸν θεόν D, d it? mae; Irˡᵃᵗ.— ἐπιστρέφειν B 𝔓⁷⁴ ℵ *rell* ‖ ὅπως ... ἐπιστρήψητε D, *ut ... convertamini* d (E) it; Irˡᵃᵗ Var.— ἐπὶ θεὸν ζῶντα, ὃς ἐποίησεν B 𝔓⁷⁴ ℵ² A C E Ψ 33. 81. 88. 104. 323. 945. 1175. 1270. 1739. 1891. 2344 ‖ ἐπὶ τὸν (– ℵ*) θ. τὸν ζ., ὃς ἐπ. 𝔓⁴⁵ ℵ* H L P 049. 056. 1. 226. 330. 440. 547. 614. 618. 1241. 1245. 1611. 1646. 1828. 1837. 1854. 2147. 2412. 2492. 2495 ‖ ἐπὶ τ. θ. ζ. τὸν ποιήσαντα D (h).

The focus of the elements of the speech varies from one text to another. In B03, Barnabas and Paul first draw attention to their presence (καὶ ἡμεῖς); they are proclaiming good news in a general sense, the content of the proclamation being left unspecified; their purpose is expressed by the infinitive ἐπιστρέφειν; the goal of the conversion is presented as a living god, without the article, who is further qualified with the relative pronoun as having created heaven and earth. In D05, there is a stronger focus on the content of the good news, God, who is specified as the object of proclamation; the purpose is more forcefully expressed by the adverb ὅπως and the subjunctive verb; God is again specified as the goal of conversion with the anaphoric article (*pace* Boismard and Lamouille [II, p. 100]: 'D a une leçon double, avec le redoublement de τὸν θεόν'), and his role as creator is presented as a defining aspect, with the articular participle τὸν ποιήσαντα (cf. 4.24; 17.24; Ps. 145.6 LXX).

14.16 πάντα (τὰ ἔθνη) B 𝔓⁴⁵·⁷⁴ ℵ *rell* d ‖ κατά D*.

πάντα τὰ ἔθνη in B03 could be understood as including Israel since they were one of the seventy nations who were thought of as peopling the earth. D05 uses τὰ ἔθνη with the more usual Jewish sense of 'the Gentiles', with κατά having here a distributive force, 'throughout'.

14.17 καίτοι B 𝔓⁷⁴ ℵ² A C* 33. 69. 81*. 945. 1175. 1739. 1891. 2344 ‖ καίτοιγε ℵ* C² H L P Ψ 049. 056. 614 𝔐 ‖ καίγε D, *et quidem* d 𝔓⁴⁵ E gig vg.

The same variants are found at 17.27 where, however, B03 agrees with D05 (καίγε B D Ψ 33 𝔐; Ir^lat). While καίτοι introduces a concessive statement (B-D-R, §§425, n. 1; 450.3), καίγε emphasizes its content (§439.2 and n. 3).

αὐτὸν ἀφῆκεν B 𝔓⁴⁵ ℵ* A E 6 *pc* ‖ ἑαυτὸν ἀφ. 𝔓⁷⁴ ℵ² C H L P Ψ 049. 056. 33. 1739 𝔐 ‖ ἀφ. ἑαυτόν D, *reliquit seipsum* d h.

B03 highlights the pronoun by placing it before the verb, whereas D05 does it by using the reflexive form.

ἀγαθουργῶν B 𝔓⁷⁴ ℵ A C Ψ 33. 81. 945. 1175. 1739. 1891. 2344 ‖ ἀγαθοποιῶν D, *benefaciens* d E H L P 049. 056. 614 𝔐.

The compound verb ἀγαθουργέω of B03 has the nuance of 'perform, or work, good', a rare verb (see Bailly, *ad loc.*) used only once in the New Testament at 1 Tim. 6.18, of people; it is not found in the LXX. D05 has the verb 'do good', ἀγαθοποιέω, which is used several times elsewhere in the New Testament, always of people; however, it is also found in the LXX, where God is the subject (e.g. Num. 10.33; Ps. 125.4). D05, in other words, allows Paul's words to reflect scriptural language, even though he is talking to a Gentile audience, whereas B03 avoids this, even to the point of using a rare alternative verb.

ὑετοὺς διδούς B D 𝔓⁴⁵ C E H L P 049. 056. 614 𝔐 ‖ δ. ὑε. 𝔓⁷⁴ ℵ A Ψ (33^illeg). 81. 927. 945. 1270. 1739. 1891. 2147. 2344.

The word order of both B03 and D05 places the gift of rain (ὑετούς) in close proximity to the mention of its origin (οὐρανόθεν); by placing the participle διδούς first, ℵ01 causes both the rain and the seasons to be associated with an origin in the heavens.

τὰς (καρδίας) B 𝔓⁷⁴ ℵ D^F *rell* ‖ *om.* D*.

In general, when καρδία is followed by the possessive pronoun or a name, it has the article; however, at Lk. 1.17, 51 the article is omitted despite the pronoun. In the LXX, likewise, although the article is generally present before καρδία followed by a pronoun, there are a number of anarthrous examples (e.g. 1 Kgdms 10.26; 29.10; 3 Kgdms 8.47, 58; 12.27, 33; Ps. 13.1; 14.2).

14.18 μόλις (κατέπαυσαν) B 𝔓⁷⁴ ℵ *rell* ‖ μόγις D 1175 *pc* co^gr.

The two words mean 'hardly, with difficulty, only just', with μόγις the earlier of the synonyms, used by Homer and later by Plato; both arise, however, in later Hellenistic literature. At Lk. 9.39, the same *vl* is found, with B03 again reading μόλις and D05 with ℵ01 μόγις; D05 also reads μόγις at Lk. 23.53. Cf. *vl* at Rom. 5.7.

14.19 Ἐπῆλθαν δέ B (𝔓⁷⁴ⁱˡˡᵉᵍ) ℵ A H L P Ψ 049. 056. 0142. 1. 104. 226. 330. 547. 614. 618. 1241. 1243. 1505. 1611. 1828. 2147. 2412. 2492. 2495 ar gig vg sy^p.h sa bo aeth ‖ Ἀπ- δέ 𝔓⁴⁵ ‖ Διατριβόντων (+ δὲ D^B) αὐτῶν καὶ (– C) διδασκόντων ἐπῆλθον D* (*Moras facientes eos et docentes supervenerunt autem* d) C E 6. 33. 36. 69. 81. 88. 323. 325. 326. 436. 440. 453. 630. 927. 945. 1175. 1270. 1646. 1739. 1837. 1877. 1891 *al* h sy^hmg mae; Cass Beda^mss acc. to—ἀπὸ Ἀντιοχείας καὶ Ἰκονίου Ἰουδαῖοι B 𝔓⁷⁴ ℵ (+ τινες: E 467) *rell* (+ *quidam* vg) ‖ ἀπὸ Ἀντ. κ. Ἰκ. 𝔓⁴⁵ ‖ τινες Ἰουδ. ἀπὸ Ἰκ. κ. Ἀντ. D (*Iudaei ab Iconio et Antiochia* d) h (sy^p.hmg) mae; Ephr^pt.

B03 moves directly into the next development of the story, causing the arrival of Jews from Antioch and Iconium to follow on immediately from the attempts of the crowds to sacrifice to Paul and Barnabas. The word order brings the places into focus, implicitly contrasting them with Lystra where the action takes place. With an additional genitive absolute clause D05 presents, on the contrary, the interaction of Paul and Barnabas with the crowds as continuing (cf. 14.7c D05) for some time before some (τινες) Jews came to Lystra. Since Paul and Barnabas are in focus in this clause, it is between them and the Jews that a contrast is made, by virtue of the word order, rather than between the cities. The absence of connective to introduce the genitive absolute (added by Corrector B) is unusual in Luke's work, though not unknown (cf. Lk. 8.49: ἔτι αὐτοῦ λαλοῦντος; Acts 10.44: ἔτι λαλοῦντος τοῦ Πέτρου; Boismard and Lamouille comment: 'D d sont les seuls à omettre la particule δέ; une telle absence de liaison n'est pas étrangère au style du TO' (II, p. 101). It may cause the reference to staying on in Lystra to refer to the whole time (cf. 14.7c), not a new span of time (see Read-Heimerdinger, *The Bezan Text*, pp. 248–49).

The different order in which the names of the towns from which the Jews came to Lystra are cited reflects a difference in point of view: B03 gives them in the order in which they had appeared in the narrative, starting with the one furthest away from the Lystra story; D05 gives them in order of their geographical proximity to Lystra, starting with the closest.

(καὶ) πείσαντες Β 𝔓⁴⁵ᵛⁱᵈ·⁷⁴ ℵ *rell* ‖ ἐπισείσαντες D, *instigassent* d h sy^hmg.

According to B03, the Jews won the crowds over so that they joined forces with them against Paul; D05 has the Jews urging the crowds on, probably with the idea that they used scare tactics (L-S-J, 1, ἐπισείω).

ἔσυρον Β 𝔓⁷⁴ ℵ A C H P 049. 056. 33. 81 *pm* ‖ ἔσυραν D E L 614. 945. 1739 *pm*.

B03 reads the imperfect of σύρω, D05 the aorist (cf. 17.6 where the same *vl* is found). The imperfect is probably to be interpreted as inceptive: 'they started dragging…'.

νομίζοντες αὐτὸν τεθνηκέναι Β 𝔓⁴⁵·⁷⁴ ℵ *rell* ‖ νομίσαντες αὐ. τεθνηκέναι C 323. 927. 945. 1270. 1739. 1891. 2344 ‖ νομίσαντες αὐ. τεθνᾶναι E H L P 049. 056 𝔐 ‖ νομίζοντες τεθνᾶναι αὐ. D, *existimantes mortuum esse eum* d.

Both B03 and D05 read the present participle of νομίζω. Both the long and the short forms of the perfect active infinitive are attested outside the New Testament (for examples, see B-A-G; L-J-S, θνήσκω).

14.20 κυκλωσάντων δὲ τῶν μαθητῶν αὐτόν Β 𝔓⁷⁴ ℵ A C Dᴮ (– αὐτόν Ψ) 33ᵛⁱᵈ. 81. 614. 927. 1175. 1611. 1646. 1837. 2147. 2344. 2412 ‖ κυ. δὲ αὐτὸν τ. μαθ. (+ αὐτοῦ E) H L P 049. 056. 1739 𝔐 ‖ κυκλώσαντες δὲ τῶν μαθητῶν (! οἱ μαθηταί, cf. d vg^F; Ephr) αὐτοῦ D* (+ αὐτόν 𝔓⁴⁵ᵛⁱᵈ, *circumeuntes enim discipuli eius* d).

The nominative participle read by D05 must be presumed to be an error for the genitive, since there is no nominative subject. The genitive pronoun αὐτοῦ is, however, possible, leaving the object of the participle (Paul, expressed by αὐτόν in B03) implicit.

Λύστραν D d ‖ *om.* Β 𝔓⁷⁴ ℵ *rell*.

The name of the city is unnecessary from the point of view of clarity, but it contributes to the coherence of the narrative from the structural point of view.

τῇ (ἐπαύριον) Β 𝔓⁴⁵·⁷⁴ ℵ Dˢ·ᵐ· *rell* ‖ τήν D*.

D* reads the accusative article rectified by a later corrector. This is the only example in the New Testament of ἐπαύριον with the accusative, so it would seem to be an error, although there are other instances of the accusative expressing a point of time rather than duration (e.g. Acts 20.16; cf. Robertson, *Grammar*, pp. 470–71).

Commentary

[B′-A] 14.7c-18 *The Healing of the Lame Man*

[a] 14.7c *Paul and Barnabas Stay in Lystra*
14.7c The opening statement of this new sequence is absent from the Alexandrian text, along with the final statement that brought the previous sequence to

a close. The result is that in the Alexandrian text, the narrative continues directly from the portrayal of Paul and Barnabas (last referred to as 'the apostles', 14.4) as announcing the good news 'in Lystra, Derbe and the surrounding district' (14.7a) to the presentation of the lame man in Lystra (14.8). In Codex Bezae, in contrast, the narrator treats the initial description of their evangelizing in the new area as a preliminary summary, including the overall result (cf. 14.7b, above), before focusing on incidents in Lystra in particular.

From what can be ascertained from Luke's narrative, and from what is known from archaeological evidence, there were no Jews in the city of Lystra. It was a Roman colony belonging to the interior province of Galatian Lycaonia, about 25 miles south-west of Iconium, and surrounded on all sides by other Roman provinces of Asia Minor: Phrygia, Pisidia and Cilicia. Paul and Barnabas' arrival here was precipitated by their expulsion from Iconium, which has the positive effect of forcing them to speak directly to Gentiles without concerning themselves with visiting the Jewish synagogue. From the point of view of announcing the gospel, however, it poses the difficulty that their hearers have had no preparation from being introduced to the peculiarly Jewish concepts of God or morality.

Paul and Barnabas are mentioned by name in the Bezan opening sentence, for the first time since the end of the Antioch sequence (cf. 13.50). In fact, throughout the Lystra scenes, proper names will figure prominently.[235]

[b] 14.8 *The Man Born Lame*

14.8 The role of the lame man is to be a representative of a type, indicated as elsewhere in Acts[236] by the adjective τις, 'a certain'. He serves as an illustration of how Paul adapted his message to a purely Gentile audience. As is often noted, there are many parallels between the healing of this man and that of the lame man who sat at the Beautiful Gate in Ierousalem (cf. 3.2-10),[237] and more distantly, that of the paralytic in the Gospel of Luke (Lk. 5.18). The total incapacity of the man to walk – he had never walked,[238] being lame from the time of his mother's pregnancy, not as an accident of birth or during his lifetime – symbolizes the inability of the people of Lystra, the worshippers of Zeus, to stand upright and walk in a spiritual sense. Like the man at the Temple, he was born with the inability to walk – neither the Ierousalem Temple nor the cult of Zeus gave freedom or strength of movement to its followers. In comparison, however, the lame man at the Temple in Ierousalem had his

235. Paul and Barnabas: 14.7c D05; Barnabas and Paul: 14.12, 14; Paul: 14.9a, 9b D05, 11, 19; the Lord Jesus Christ: 14.10; Zeus and Hermes: 14.12; Zeus: 14.13: Lystra: 14.7c D05/8 AT; Iconium and Antioch: 14.19 (in reverse order AT). The paralytic, in contrast, does not bear a name.

236. Cf. 3.2; 5.1, 34, 36; 8.9; 9.10, 33, 36, 43; 10.1, 5, 6; 13.6.

237. *The Message of Acts*, I, p. 210–17.

238. The pluperfect tense of D05 expresses particularly forcefully the fact that the man had never been 'in a state to walk'; see *Critical Apparatus*.

friends to carry him to the gate of the Temple so he could ask for alms (3.2); likewise, the paralytic in the Gospel also had his friends to find a way to get him through the crowds to Jesus (Lk. 5.18-19). Here in Lystra, it is simply said that the man 'used to sit' (ἐκάθετο, cf. καθήμενος AT [καθεζόμενος D05], Acts 3.10).

[c] 14.9a *The Lame Man Listens to Paul*

14.9a The man must have sat at the gates of the city, where there was a temple to Zeus (cf. 14.13), for that is where he heard Paul speaking and, listening to him, had been full of fear according to Codex Bezae. This detail will be import-ant in assessing Paul's style of preaching to the Gentiles.

[d] 14.9b-10a *Paul Orders Him to Stand and Walk*

14.9b In the case of the paralytic in the Gospel, Jesus responded to the faith of those who brought him (Lk. 5.20); as for the lame man at the Temple, it was he who took the initiative in seeking out Peter and John (Acts 3.2-5). Now, positively, it is Paul who makes the first move, not without first weighing up the situation of the man: the verb used to express Paul's looking at the man (ἀτενίζω) is only used by Luke in the context of a communication with a spiri-tual dimension.[239] He thus ascertains his faith, in other words his believing response to the message he had heard about Jesus, which allows him to make the next move.

14.10a The healing command in the Alexandrian text is abrupt and con-tains no mention of the name of Jesus. The wording of the Bezan text begins with a phrase found elsewhere in Luke, 'I say to you',[240] and continues with an invocation of the name of Jesus, using the full title as is usual in the Bezan text when Jesus is referred to in formal situations.[241] Paul's way of referring to Jesus should be compared to the invocation by Peter (and John) for the healing of the lame man at the Temple gate, for there the name was 'Jesus Christ the Nazorene' (3.6). The term Nazorene is a reference to the Davidic Messiah which, though meaningful in a Jewish context, has little sense in a wholly Gentile environment.[242] Here, Paul uses the title 'Lord' in associa-tion with Jesus Christ. The three aspects – Lord, Jesus, Christ – are identical

239. For the occurrences of the verb ἀτενίζω and its force, cf. 3.3, *The Message of Acts*, I, pp. 206, 312–13.

240. Σοὶ λέγω: cf. Lk. 5.24 = Mk 2.11; Lk. 7.14; Mk 5.41.

241. It is a widely held misconception that the Bezan text generally completes the name of Jesus with his full title of the Lord Jesus Christ. In fact, this is only the case in formal or liturgical situations (Read-Heimerdinger, *The Bezan Text*, pp. 262–74). That Paul also frequently uses the full title is evidence that the practice cannot be restrictively attributed to later church usage.

242. See *The Message of Acts*, I, p. 14, on Peter's invocation of Jesus and an analysis of the name 'Nazorene'. Cf. also J. Rius-Camps, '"Nazareno" y "Nazoreo" con especial atención al Códice Bezae', en R. Pierri (ed.), *Grammatica intellectio Scripturae: Saggi filologici di Greco biblico in onore di padre Lino Cignelli, OFM* (Studium Biblicum Franciscanum Analecta 68; Jerusalem: Franciscan Printing Press, 2006), pp. 183–204.

to those found in the preaching of the Hellenists to the non-Jews in Antioch.[243] Paul proclaims Jesus, the Messiah who had been rejected by the leaders of Judaism and by many of his own people, the Jews, as the Lord; by virtue of his resurrection, he continues to be alive and to give life and wholeness to those who believe in him.

Paul commands the man to stand upright (ὀρθός), which has figurative connotations of changing his behaviour so that it is 'right'.[244] The Bezan text also includes Paul's command to walk, as in the parallels of 3.6 and Lk. 5.23 (Mk 2.9), anticipated by the narrator's comment that the lame man had never walked (14.8, esp. D05).

[e] 14.10b *The Man Gets Up and Walks*
14.10b Both texts record that the man got up and walked, in the same way as the man at the Beautiful Gate did (cf. 3.8).[245] His jumping up contrasts with the former sitting position that he was condemned to adopt at the gate of the city, by the temple of Zeus. The Bezan text particularly underlines the immediate effect of Paul's command with a double adverbial expression, 'at once, without further ado'. The first of these adverbs is found both when the paralytic is healed by Jesus (Lk. 5.25) and the lame man by Peter (Acts 3.7). In Peter's case, however, it is striking that he assisted the man to get up, as if he were not convinced of the power of his words; Paul, like Jesus, has no such hesitation.[246]

[e'] 14.11 *The Acclamation of the Crowds*
14.11 There is a certain grotesqueness in the scene that follows (14.11-18). It is, in fact, a fine theological irony, which underlies the symbolic content of the people and their reactions. The crowds of the town appear for the first time, hitherto merely represented by the lame man (cf. on 14.8 above). The repeated use of the plural 'crowds' in this scene (four times in Acts 14) gives the impression of a general, unidentified mass of people. They speak in Lycaonian, which immediately draws attention to a problem: Paul, who clearly did not speak the local language, has announced the gospel message to the people of the place in a language that was not their native tongue. The result is that the powerful miracle that has taken place among them has not produced a real change of values but rather a syncretistic mix. Despite the existence of faith (cf. 14.9b), which was sufficient for the healing to take place, the understanding of what Paul has been saying has only been partial. The confusion is simi-

---

243. See 11.20, εὐαγγελιζόμενοι τὸν κύριον Ἰησοῦν Χριστόν (esp. D05; see *The Message of Acts*, II, p. 308). Cf. also 8.16 D05; 10.36; 11.17; 15.11 D05, 26; 16.31 D05; 19.5 D05; 20.21 D05, 24 D05, 35 D05; 21.13 D05, and esp. 28.31.

244. ὀρθός is a predicative adjective equivalent to an adverb, a practice that is found frequently in the work of Luke: Lk. 21.34; 24.22; Acts 3.11; 12.10; 20.6 D05; 27.19; 28.13; cf. B-D-R, §243.1.

245. ἥλατο AT, aorist of ἅλλομαι, as at 3.8b AT; ἀνήλατο D05, cf. ἐξαλλόμενος, 3.8a.

246. The comparison is noted in the *Commentary* on 3.7 in *The Message of Acts*, I, pp. 214–15.

lar to that witnessed by Philip in Samaria, in the incident concerning Simon Magus.[247]

The cacophony of voices in this scene gives a striking impression of confusion: on the one hand, there is Paul shouting 'with a loud voice'[248] in Greek, and on the other, the crowds 'raising their voices' in Lycaonian.

[d'] 14.12 *Hermes and Zeus*

14.12 Despite speaking in Lycaonian, the people of Lystra do not identify Paul and Barnabas with local Phrygian deities but with gods from the Greek pantheon. There was apparently a temple to Zeus at the gates of the city, as already noted (on 14.8 above, and cf. on 14.13), with local men acting as priests. It was very possibly because of the foreignness of Paul and Barnabas, and consequently their speaking in Greek, that they were most naturally associated with Greek gods. Luke's account of the particular roles assigned to each is full of irony: Barnabas, who did not speak and perhaps cut a solemn, prophetic figure, is designated as the father of the gods, Zeus; Paul, who had done the talking, is seen as fulfilling the role of Hermes, the spokesman and interpreter of Zeus.

Barnabas thus is viewed as the supreme god, whose commands and teachings were communicated through his messenger, Paul. Therein lies Luke's irony for, even though it was on the basis of their confused understanding, the Gentiles in Lystra have placed Paul and Barnabas back in the order in which the Holy Spirit chose them (13.2) and in which Sergius Paulus had asked to speak to them (13.7). Paul had been responsible for reversing the roles, being the one to respond to the invitations to speak as far back as Paphos in the early stages of their ministry together (cf. 13.9), so that he had become the dominant figure (cf. 13.13, 15; and see *Commentary, ad loc.* for each of these verses in chapter 13) and will retain that role until Barnabas finally separates from him (15.36-39).[249]

Paul and Barnabas do not yet react to the acclamations of the crowds, since they do not understand what is being said in Lycaonian. Their inability to understand the people of Lystra, as also the people's incomplete compre-

---

247. Simon Magus's offer of money in exchange for power was also an indication that, despite his attachment to Philip, there had not been a fundamental change in values; cf. *The Message of Acts*, II, p. 144, on 8.18-19.

248. μεγάλη φωνῇ, 14.10: Luke always uses this expression in situations of tension: of those who are demonized (Lk. 4.33; 8.28; Acts 8.7); lepers (Lk. 17.15); joyful disciples (19.37); the excited crowd of Jews demanding the death of Jesus (23.23) or Stephen (Acts 7.57); Jesus (Lk. 23.46) or Stephen (Acts 7.60) as they died; Paul to the Philippian jailer (16.28); and, finally, Festus proclaiming Paul mad (26.24).

249. From the time of the Paphos visit, Paul's name is always cited first before that of Barnabas (13.43, 46, 50; 14.7c D05); and after this brief reversal (14.12, 14), his name will again appear first (cf. 14.20; 15.2a, 2b). Throughout the whole of this first phase of the mission, it is Paul who takes the lead in acting or speaking (13.16-41, 44 D05, 45, 46; 14.1 D05 [αὐτόν, sing.], 3 D05 [αὐτοῦ, sing.], 9-10).

hension of what Paul has said, is symbolic of the mutual lack of understanding between Jews and Gentiles of each other's cultures and ways of thinking. Paul, as a well-trained rabbi with a profound grasp of Judaism, did not know how to communicate with the local people who had their own cultural and religious attitudes. As seen in the case of the lame man, Paul's speeches inspired fear more than anything else; and Paul, for his part, was misled by his superficial discernment of the man's faith which was, certainly, sufficient for him to be healed but not so profound or radical as to lead to a decision to follow the Lord Jesus Christ whom Paul preached. Consequently, instead of a total acceptance of what Paul was preaching, there was an attempt to interpret Paul and Barnabas in terms of the existing religious belief system. Luke's message, in other words, is that it is not enough to release people from whatever holds them immobile and imprisoned, but that a total change of values and mentality is required. There had incontestably been a physical healing, even in the name of Jesus according to the Bezan text, but this on its own was not evidence of a proper understanding of him or of adherence to him as Lord.

[c'] 14.13 *Attempts of the Priests to Offer Sacrifice*
14.13 If Paul and Barnabas do not understand the shouts of the crowd as they express their admiration and gratitude, the priest (or priests in Codex Bezae) of Zeus does understand. According to the Alexandrian text, he brought bulls and garlands (probably to decorate the bulls who were to be sacrificed) to the gates of the city where the temple was situated. Together with the crowds, he intended[250] to offer a sacrifice to the men who were gods in human form. The Bezan account differs in several ways: there are several priests, which is a typical practice known to have existed at the great temples;[251] they serve the local cult of Zeus, who seems to be called by the name of Propolis;[252] they bring the bulls out to Barnabas and Paul, making clear that it is to them that they intend to offer sacrifices.

[b'] 14.14-17 *The Reaction of Paul and Barnabas*
14.14 The detail provided by the Bezan text in the previous verse, that the priests were wanting to offer sacrifices to Barnabas and Paul, accounts for their sudden and violent reaction at this point. Until now, they had not understood what was being said about them; but once preparations begin for sacrifices to be made to them, they realize what is happening – Barnabas first, but Paul, too. That sacrifices were being prepared in a more general sense at the local temple (as in the AT) does not account so fully for the horrified reaction of 'the apostles' as they are called here by the Alexandrian text (cf. 14.4). The

---

250. The force of the imperfect ἤθελεν here is in the fact of wanting to sacrifice, although the goal was not achieved.

251. Bruce, *Text*, p. 282; Metzger, *Commentary*, p. 374.

252. The phrase in Greek meaning 'in front of the city' can be interpreted in the Bezan text as the proper name of the god – see *Critical Apparatus*.

order 'Barnabas and Paul' is indicative of the responsibility Barnabas now assumes in protesting against the sacrifices, with the unusual leading role taken by him highlighted in the Bezan text (see *Critical Apparatus*).

Their response is to tear their clothes, as a sign of their absolute refusal to accept the divine honours being given to them, treating them as blasphemy.[253] They then rush into the crowd, shouting now even louder than before (cf. on 14.11 above) in order somehow to make their voices heard and to convey their message clearly. The wording of the Bezan text is particularly expressive at this point (see *Critical Apparatus*).

14.15 According to the narrator, the speech is proclaimed by both Barnabas and Paul. The fact that only Paul will be attacked (cf. 14.19b) is therefore difficult to account for in the Alexandrian text, for there the attack follows on directly from this speech; in the Bezan text, a more general context is given at 14.19a, where mention is made of Paul and Barnabas staying in Lystra and teaching; since teaching has been seen to be Paul's personal ministry (cf. 13.1 *Commentary*), it is more coherent that the attack from the Jews should be directed specifically at Paul alone.

The speech opens with the single word 'Men', a style of address that is only found when Paul speaks to an audience made up solely of Gentiles and without mentioning their place of origin.[254] It is followed by a rhetorical question, intended as a plea to make the people stop what they are about to do.[255] In much the same way as Peter at Cornelius' house (cf. 10.26), Barnabas and Paul protest that they are men just like their admirers (ὁμοιοπαθεῖς ἐσμεν ὑμῖν ἄνθρωποι), inverting the terms used to praise them (οἱ θεοὶ ὁμοιωθέντες ἀνθρώποις). Their proclamation of the good news takes up the verb from 14.7a (εὐαγγελιζόμενοι) and is expressed differently in the two texts. In the Alexandrian text, it is a general proclamation, an invitation to the people of Lystra to turn from their worthless idols to a god who is alive and who is the creator of the universe, which is described in the characteristic terms of 'heaven, earth, sea and everything in them' (cf. Exod. 20.11; Ps. 145.6 LXX). The Bezan text is more specific about the object of the proclamation, as the one and only

---

253. Cf. the High Priest who tore his clothes when he heard Jesus acknowledge that he was the Messiah, because he took it as blasphemy (Mk 14.63-64 [par. Mt. 26.65]). Luke does not record this gesture in his Gospel account, although in other respects he follows Mark in this scene. It is as if he wished to save the detail for a scene in Acts, as happens on other occasions; see Cadbury, 'Dust and Garments', pp. 271–72.

254. The term of address is reserved for Gentiles, here and at 27.10, 21, 25. The occurrence at 7.26 in the AT (ἄνδρες, ἀδελφοί ἐστε) is therefore an exception, since it is addressed by Moses to fellow-Jews, but D05 reads differently: τί ποιεῖτε, ἄνδρες ἀδελφοί;

255. Luke has other speakers use a similar rhetorical question in an attempt to stop some activity: τί ποεῖς; in the singular (10.26 D05), or τί ποιεῖτε; in the plural (7.26 D05; 21.13). See Zerwick and Grosvenor, *Analysis*, p. 398, who propose two possible interpretations: '*what is this that you are doing?*' (as pred. τί may be used w. ταῦτα, cf. Lk 15:26, Jn 6:9); equally possible, *why are you doing this?*'. However, the following context, 'And by saying these things, they only just managed to stop the crowds from sacrificing to them', suggests it expresses an immediate future.

God (τὸν θεόν, with the article) who stands in contrast to the plurality of the 'powerless things';[256] this God to whom the people should turn is further defined as the creator.

14.16-17 The message proclaimed by Barnabas and Paul is a new one, it marks the beginning of a new age though it is couched in thoroughly Jewish language (cf. Ps. 147.8; Jer. 5.24). In order to make the link between this new era and what had gone before, they go on to explain how God had previously left the nations without teaching or commandments, yet not without his provision for them through the natural gifts of the seasons and their fruits; by these means he had shown his care for the nations.

This short and simple speech is the first outline of their teaching to Gentiles who had no prior knowledge of Judaism. There is no reference to Jesus, to his mission or to his central message. Nonetheless, Paul's command to the lame man was explicitly given in the name of Jesus according to the Bezan text (14.10 D05), and in both texts the verb 'evangelize' (14.7a) implies that the good news of the gospel was announced in some way or other. That the nature of the speech should be different from previous speeches does not mean that it is merely a Lukan invention; it is simply that the audience in Lystra is quite different from any previously encountered.

[a′] 14.18 *Their Difficulty in Preventing Sacrifice*
14.18 The conjunction καί leading into the narrator's comment on the incident conveys the impression of the tussle between the people on the one hand, and Barnabas and Paul on the other. The words they addressed to the crowd, being in Greek as they were, are only just successful in calming the townspeople and preventing them from going ahead with offering them sacrifices. The people had been so impressed by the miracle of healing that they felt impelled to sacrifice despite the words spoken to them by Barnabas and Paul – for, in fact, they could barely understand what was being said to them.

The problem is that Barnabas and Paul have an obvious difficulty in knowing how to communicate with people with whom they have no common language, literally or figuratively. So at this point, the people in Lystra have been given the ability to 'walk' through the healing of the lame man who represents them, but have yet to learn the 'right' way (cf. 14.10).

[B′-A′] 14.19-20 *Jewish Attack on Paul*

[a] 14.19a *The Arrival of Jews from Iconium and Antioch*
14.19a There is an implied change of setting here from outside the gates (cf. 14.13) to inside the city (cf. 14.19b). The change is more readily accounted for by the statement in Codex Bezae that Paul and Barnabas stayed on teach-

---

256. μάταιος expresses a strongly negative idea, conveying the general sense of empty and useless; see μάταιος, B-A-G, subst.; L-J-S, I, 1. It is used of false gods in the LXX (Esth. 4.17 p; Jer. 2.5; 8.19; 3 Macc. 6.11).

ing after the attempts of the people to sacrifice to them. Alternatively, since the comment echoes the opening words of the sequence in the Bezan text (cf. 14.7b, 7c), it could refer to all the time Paul and Barnabas spent in Lystra, not just after the attempt to sacrifice to them (see *Critical Apparatus*). Here occurs yet another instance where the narrative of the Alexandrian text lacks coherence,[257] so creating the 'more difficult' reading. The Bezan reading may be explained (and is by commentators) as a later attempt to clarify the story; on the other hand, it must be noted that the coherence of the Bezan text of Acts in general is seen not just in the story line but in the interplay between scenes, the portrayal of the characters, the linking back to the Gospel of Luke, the allusions to the Jewish Scriptures, and the overall theological message.[258] Coherence is so much an integral feature of the Bezan narrative that it cannot all have been added in at a later date. It is more likely that the incoherence of the Alexandrian text was introduced as modification to an earlier text was made.

According to the Alexandrian text, Jews apparently came to Lystra directly as a result of Paul's healing of the lame man and the resultant acclamation of him and Barnabas in the city. The Bezan text indicates a further period of teaching by Paul and Barnabas in the city before a group of certain Jews arrived, thus providing more reason for them to make the journey and giving them more time to do so. They travelled no small distance, Antioch of Pisidia being some 100 miles away and Iconium lying between there and Lystra. They obviously had strong motives for going to the trouble of travelling to a Gentile city, and the fact that the only Jews mentioned in this scene travelled in from outside confirms the impression that there was no local Jewish community in Lystra. These Jews had already stirred up animosity against Paul and Barnabas in both towns, driving them out of Antioch (13.50) and attempting to stone them in Iconium (14.5-6).

[b] 14.19b *The Stoning of Paul*

14.19b On this third occasion of persecution, the aim of the Jews from Iconium and Antioch turns out to be to get rid of Paul in particular. Unlike the people of Lystra (cf. on 14.10 above), the Jews consider him to be the real force behind what was going on. Where Barnabas and Paul had had difficulty in restraining the crowds (14.18), the Jews are successful in persuading them to join in their attacks according to the Alexandrian text; the Bezan text expresses the idea that the Jews used scare tactics to intimidate the crowd. In any case, they no doubt spoke a language they all could understand – they are sufficiently in tune with the mentality of the local people that they get them to turn against the very men they had been worshipping as gods so that, at the very least, even if the local people do not join in neither do they prevent the Jews from stoning Paul. That he is singled out implies that the Jews took

257. An earlier example of a lack of coherence in the AT was seen in this sequence at 14.2.

258. This is a major conclusion of the linguistic analysis of the Bezan text of Acts carried out by Read-Heimerdinger, *The Bezan Text*, see esp. pp. 350–52.

some trouble to convince the crowds not only that he deserved death but also that it was he, rather than Barnabas, who was responsible for whatever crime the Jews portrayed him as guilty of. Some manuscripts[259] include an explanation of how the Jews managed to get the Lystran crowds to turn against their heroes: 'while they (the apostles) were discussing with boldness, they convinced the crowds to stand away from them, saying that they were speaking no truth but that everything was false. And having persuaded the crowds...' The language of the sentence is Lukan but its absence in D05 raises questions about its authenticity. The idea that Paul and Barnabas were caught up in 'discussing' (διαλεγομένων) 'with boldness' (παρρησία) is typical of the Acts narrative,[260] but the first term is a negative comment on Paul's tactics because of his reliance on human eloquence, while the second expresses a positive evaluation – the contradiction that therefore results in placing the two terms side by side is another reason for questioning the validity of the reading.

Since the stoning takes place within the city, it would appear that the Jews fell in with the local, Gentile custom rather than their own regulations, which stipulated that stoning must take place outside the city walls. Only once the stoning is over and Paul is presumed dead, will his body be removed outside the city.

[b'] 14.20a *He Goes Back into the City*

14.20a Luke packs a considerable amount of information into this brief sentence. On the level of the narrative events, he says that Paul gets up and goes back into the city, with the circumstantial comment that his (the, AT) disciples had surrounded him. It is precisely in that detail that there lies a wealth of implicit comment. The previous element [b] had described how Paul has been as good as killed by his own people, the Jews, but now in this corresponding element, with the support and protection of the believers in Jesus (expressed figuratively by their action of 'surrounding' him), he is brought back to life. These disciples may be thought of as Gentiles from Lystra who had accepted the message about Jesus and who formed, as such, the beginnings of a Christian community in Lystra despite the general lack of understanding on the part of the townspeople. The description of them as 'his [Paul's] disciples' in Codex Bezae is reminiscent of the reference to 'those around Paul' after he left Paphos (cf. 13.13), but the disciples here in Lystra are more likely to be local people than companions who had been travelling around with Paul – the detail in the Bezan text that it was into Lystra that Paul went once he had been surrounded by the disciples and had got up, suggests that it was because of the

---

259. διαλεγομένων αὐτῶν παρρησία ἔπεισαν (ἀνέπ- C) τοὺς ὄχλους ἀποστῆναι ἀπ' αὐτῶν λέγοντες ὅτι Οὐδὲν ἀληθὲς λέγουσιν ἀλλὰ πάντα ψεύδονται. (καὶ πείσαντες τοὺς ὄχλους...) (C) 6. 36. 81. (104. 326.) 453. 945. 1175. 1739 al (h) sy^hmg mae.

260. διαλέγομαι: Acts 17.2, 17; 18.4, 19, 28 D05; 19.8, 9; 20.7, 9; 24.12, 25.— παρρησία: Acts 2.29; 4.13, 29, 31; 6.10 D05; 16.4 D05; 28.31.— παρρησιάζομαι: Acts 9.27, 28; 13.46; 14.3; 18.26; 19.8; 26.26.

disciples that he was enabled to return, which would be a natural consequence if they were from the town themselves. The name of the city in the Bezan text echoes the beginning of the sequence (cf. 14.7c D05, 8 B03) as it is brought to a close.[261]

In spite of this total rejection of Paul by the Jews, who go so far as to attempt his murder, Paul himself will continue to try, one way or another, to win them over to the gospel as he pursues his mission in the later stages.

[a'] 14.20b *Departure to Derbe*

14.20b The sequence concludes with a transitional statement that serves to move Paul and Barnabas on to the next place of their missionary activity, Derbe, which had already been mentioned in the anticipatory summary of the sequence at 14.6. Note should be made of the verb, ἐξῆλθεν, 'go out', which is used typically by Luke of occasions when an 'exodus' is made, in the sense of a spiritual journey away from the institution of Judaism (cf. Jesus, Lk. 22.39, [cf. Lk. 9.31]; Peter, Acts 12.17). Paul's 'exodus' is the final element in this brief scene, and corresponds to the arrival of the Jews in Lystra at the opening of it, [a] 14.19a. It is their attempt on his life that prompts this step, one more in the distance he gradually puts between himself and the Jews (cf. ἐξῆλθεν used of Paul at 15.40 when another step is made).

[A'] 14.21-27 *Return to Antioch of Syria*

Overview

This closing sequence of the section relates how Paul and Barnabas return to Antioch of Syria from where the section began (cf. 13.1). It is as succinct as the opening one, [A] 13.1-3, to which it corresponds, summarizing how the initial order of the Holy Spirit to the church in Antioch, and to Paul and Barnabas in particular, had been carried out successfully. The only place whose name is not mentioned in the list of regions or cities they stop at on the return journey is Cyprus. Its omission may confirm the impression obtained by the final elements of the Cyprus sequence where, in Codex Bezae at least, it was evident that Sergius Paulus had not become a disciple of Jesus though he had believed in God (cf. 13.12 and *Commentary, ad loc.*).

The number of verbal similarities between the closing sequence and the opening one is striking: ἐν Ἀντιοχείᾳ // εἰς Ἀντιόχειαν | κατὰ τὴν οὖσαν ἐκκλησίαν // κατ' ἐκκλησίαν | τῷ κυρίῳ // τῷ κυρίῳ | εἰς τὸ ἔργον ὃ προσκέκλημαι αὐτούς // εἰς τὸ ἔργον ὃ ἐπλήρωσαν | νηστεύσαντες καὶ προσευξάμενοι // προσευξάμενοι μετὰ νηστειῶν | καὶ ἐπιθέντες τὰς χεῖρας αὐτοῖς // χειροτονήσαντες δὲ αὐτοῖς.

---

261. The contribution made by the repeated name of Lystra to the structural harmony of the sequence means that it is not as strange as Boismard and Lamouille state: 'une expression telle que "la ville de Lystres" serait étrange en fin de récit' (II, p. 101).

This is the only sequence in the section in which Paul and Barnabas are not named. In the first two sequences, they are named in the order Barnabas and Saul ([A] 13.1, 2; [B] 13.7). Following the change of Saul to Paul, it is he who is named first in the central sequences ([C] 13.13; [D] 13.46; [C'] 14.7b). The first order is resumed with the identification of Barnabas as Zeus and Paul as Hermes in the penultimate sequence ([B'] 14.12, 14) though it is Paul who finally dominates when the two are mentioned by name for the last time ([B'] 14.20b).

Structure and Themes
The sequence follows a linear structure as the main protagonists travel along a direct route to return to their point of departure, from Derbe to Antioch of Syria:

[a]	14.21-22	Start of the return journey from Derbe
[b]	14.23	Lystra, Iconium and Antioch
[c]	14.24	Arrival in Pamphylia
[d]	14.25	Perga and Attalia
[e]	14.26	Departure for Antioch of Syria
[f]	14.27	Report in Antioch

Each of the places they had stopped at on the mainland (cf. 13.13) is named as they pass through them in turn and build up the churches that had been established there.

The conjunction in the Alexandrian text at 14.21 is τε which, if intended, links the start of the return journey to the previous element (14.20b) rather than beginning a new sequence here. However, since no new episode is indicated elsewhere in the Alexandrian text between 14.21 and the end of the return journey at 14.27, it is likely that this τε is to be read as δέ. The paragraph break indicated by N-A[27] at 14.24 is not supported by the conjunction καί in the text adopted there. Likewise, the following sequence begins at 14.28 with δέ, and not 15.1.[262]

Translation

Codex Bezae D05	Codex Vaticanus B03
[a]　**14.21** While they were evangelizing the people in the city, and having made many disciples, they made a start to return	**14.21** When they had evangelized that city, and having made a considerable number of disciples, they returned to

262. Commentators divide the text in a variety of ways, often ignoring the distinct functions of καί and δέ. For example, Barrett (I, p. 689) follows the same division as N-A[27], viewing the travelling through Pisidia as the start of the return journey, although the start was, in fact, back in Lystra (14.21); Fitzmeyer (p. 534) recognizes the break at 14.21, but not 14.28; Bruce (*Text,* p. 287) and Witherington (*Acts,* p. 450) indicate a break only at 15.1. Lake and Cadbury (*English Translation and Commentary,* p. 169) regard 14.27–15.2 as a separate, brief paragraph: this has the advantage, at least, of keeping together the two imperfect verbs (διέτριβον, 14.28 ... ἐδίδασκον, 15.1) which, linked with καί as they are, indicate concurrent action.

to Lystra, Iconium and Antioch, **22** where they went about strengthening the souls of the disciples, above all encouraging them to remain in the faith and saying 'It is through many difficulties that we have to go to the kingdom of God'.

[b]   **23** When they had appointed for them elders in each of the churches, they prayed, indeed with fasting, and committed them to the Lord in whom they believed.

[c]   **24** Having gone through Pisidia, they came to Pamphylia;

[d]   **25** and after speaking the word in Perga, they went down to Attalia where they were evangelizing them,

[e]   **26** and from there they sailed away to Antioch from where they had been commended to the grace of God for the work which they had accomplished.

[f]   **27** When they arrived and had gathered the church together, they announced what God had done for them with their souls, namely, that he had opened a door of faith for the Gentiles.

Lystra, and to Iconium and to Antioch, **22** where they went about strengthening the souls of the disciples, and encouraging them to remain in the faith, saying 'It is through many difficulties that we have to enter into the kingdom of God'.

23 When they had appointed for them elders in each of the churches, they prayed with fasting and committed them to the Lord in whom they had believed.

24 And having gone through Pisidia, they came to Pamphylia;

25 and after speaking the word in Perga, they went down to Attalia,

26 and from there they sailed away to Antioch from where they had been commended to the grace of God for the work which they had accomplished.

27 When they arrived and had gathered the church together, they announced what God had done with them, namely, that he had opened a door of faith for the Gentiles.

Critical Apparatus

14.21 Εὐαγγελισάμενοί τε τὴν πόλιν ἐκείνην B 𝔓⁴⁵ ℵ²(*om.* ℵ*: *h.t.* πόλιν ... πόλιν 1241) C L Ψ 049. 056. (33). 1739 𝔐 | -ζόμενοί τε τ. πόλ. ἐκ. 𝔓⁷⁴ A H P 88. 330 *pc* | -ζόμενοι δέ τ. πόλ. ἐκ. E (1243) ‖ Εὐαγγελιζόμενοι δὲ τοὺς ἐν τῇ πόλει D (*Evangelizantes autem in illa civitate* d gig h syᵖ).

The three variant readings in this clause function together. B03 links the start of the return journey to the previous sentence with τε. If this is the particle intended (that is, it does not arise through phonetic confusion with δέ, see *Structure and Themes* above; cf. Read-Heimerdinger, *The Bezan Text*, pp. 205–206), it tends to accord greater importance to Paul and Barnabas' return to Lystra (the main verb of this clause) than their journey to Derbe (the action of the previous clause), and causes the visit to Derbe to take on a secondary importance. As a connective, τε should probably not be taken in association with the following καί to mean 'both ... and'. The aorist tense of the participle εὐαγγελισάμενοι has the same effect of playing down the importance of the visit to Derbe, for it stands as a simple statement of the action undertaken in there before the return journey to Lystra was made. Furthermore, the object of the participle is 'that town', viewed as a collective noun without an overt reference to the people.

D05, in contrast, separates this new sentence from the previous one with δέ, and thus allows the start of the return journey to mark the beginning of a new sequence that groups together its various components. The present tense of the participle causes the action of evangelizing to be viewed as still ongoing while the preparations for the return journey were underway. Ropes' comment (*Text*, p. 137) that the 'aorist [εὐαγγελισάμενοι] alone yields a possible sense' is unjustified, given that the present participle concords with the imperfect ὑπέστρεφον in D05 at the end of the sentence (see below). Finally, the object of the evangelization is made personal, with the article τούς denoting the inhabitants of the city rather than the place as an impersonal location.

(μαθητεύσαντες) ἱκανοὺς ὑπέστρεψαν B 𝔓⁷⁴ ℵ *rell* ‖ πολλοὺς -φον D (*plures reversi sunt* d).— εἰς τὴν Λύστραν καὶ εἰς ̓Ἰκόνιον καὶ ̓Αντιόχειαν B 81 | εἰς τὴν Λ. κ. εἰς ̓Ικ. κ. εἰς ̓Αντ. 𝔓⁷⁴ ℵ A C E Ψ 33^{vid}. 2344 | εἰς Λ. κ. εἰς ̓Ικ. κ. εἰς ̓Αντ. 945. 1175. 1739. 1891 | εἰς τὴν Λ. κ. ̓Ικ. κ. ̓Αντ. H L P 049. 056. 226*. 614 𝔐 ‖ εἰς Λ. κ. ̓Ικ. κ. ̓Αντ. D 226ᶜ. 323.

The variants in the second participial clause and the main verb are coherent with the distinct readings of the first clause according to the particular manuscripts. B03 qualifies the number of new disciples made as ἱκανούς, a stronger word than πολλούς. It then relates the return journey with a global aorist, maintaining attention on Lystra by marking it out with the article, compared with Iconium and Antioch which are anarthrous. Throughout the successive clauses of 14.20-21 in the B03 text, the return to Lystra is the eventual goal – the absence of the name of the city in 14.20 (see *Critical Apparatus*) means that the episode is only properly closed once it is mentioned in v. 21.

D05 continues in its readings here to mark the start of a new narrative sequence. The adjective πολλούς is appropriate to describe the people of the city who have been mentioned in the previous clause (see above). The return journey is then signalled with an imperfect verb, where the action, being concurrent with that of the present participle εὐαγγελιζόμενοι (see above), is viewed as 'beginning'. In the presentation of the three towns they returned to, there is no particular focus on Lystra, the episode there having been brought to a close with the reference to the town by name at 14.20a.

14.22 παρακαλοῦντές τε D ℵ² | καὶ παρ. A C 88. 104. 383. 467. 522. 614. 876. 913. 915. 945. 1175. 1518. 1611. 1739. 1765. 1799. 1838. 1891. 2138. 2147. 2298. 2412 *al* h p² vg^D; Chr Theoph Oecum ‖ παρ. B 𝔓⁷⁴ ℵ* *rell* d.

By linking the two participles with τε, D05 presents the action of encouragement as an action that is additional to that of strengthening.

εἰσελθεῖν (εἰς τὴν βασιλείαν) B 𝔓⁷⁴ ℵ D^B *rell*, *introire* d ‖ ἐλθεῖν D*.

The compound verb in B03 focuses on the action of entering the kingdom of God, where the simple verb of D05 focuses rather on the going there. The wording of D05 echoes that of the thief on the cross who asks Jesus to remember him at the time when he goes to his kingdom, ὅταν ἔλθῃς εἰς τὴν βασιλείαν σου (Lk. 23.42 – ὅταν + aor. subj. indicates some future time, whenever that might be).

14.23 προσευξάμενοι δέ D, *autem* d Ι καὶ πρ. Ψ 88. 323. 614. 1611. 2147. 2412 ΙΙ πρ. B 𝔓⁷⁴ ℵ *rell*.

The particle δέ following προσευξάμενοι in D05 has the function of clarifying that the prayer was accompanied with fasting (cf. B-D-R, §447.1c), similar to the function of καί but with a stronger force.

(εἰς ὅν) πεπιστεύκεισαν B 𝔓⁷⁴ ℵ C* *rell* ΙΙ -κασιν D (*crediderunt* d) C² 536. 1838 (καὶ -κασιν: 614. 913. 1108. 1518. 1611. 1799. 2138. 2147. 2412).

B03 uses the pluperfect (without the past augment, cf. 4.22 B03 D05; Bruce, *Text*, p. 286) to refer to a change of state that had been experienced by the people in the past, at the time of Paul and Barnabas' earlier visit in fact. This is the only occurrence of the pluperfect of the verb πιστεύω in the New Testament. The perfect in D05 draws attention more to their present state, resulting from their previous action of believing (for the definition of the perfect aspect as expressing a state, see Young, *Intermediate New Testament Greek*, pp. 126–29). The form is often used by John (Jn 3.18; 6.69; 8.31; 11.27; 16.27; 20.29) and by Luke (Acts 15.5; 16.34; 18.27; 19.18; 21.20, 25).

14.24 καὶ διελθόντες B 𝔓⁷⁴ ℵ *rell* ΙΙ δι. δέ D, *regressi autem* d b co.— εἰς (τὴν Πισιδίαν) ℵ ΙΙ *om.* B D d 𝔓⁷⁴ A *rell*.— (ἦλθον) εἰς τὴν Παμφυλίαν B 𝔓⁷⁴ ℵ C E 81. (1175). 2344 ΙΙ εἰς Π. D A H L P Ψ 049. 056. 614. 1739 𝔐.

With the connective δέ, D05 once more views the move out of Pisidia and on into Pamphylia as a new development in the narrative whereas B03, with καί, regards it as part of the same unit. This makes the B03 reading of τε at 14.21 suspect (see above), for it means that the last conjunction δέ in this sequence is at 14.20, with the result that all the stages between Paul going back into Lystra and his arrival with Barnabas in Antioch (14.27) are grouped together as one development and there is no paragraph break (see Levinsohn, *Discourse Features*, p. 31 on the function of δέ to signal a new development in a story). The preposition εἰς before Pisidia in ℵ01 suggests that Antioch is not viewed as belonging to the province (cf. *Critical Apparatus*, 13.14).

14.25 ἐν (+ τῇ 𝔓⁷⁴) Πέργῃ B D, *apud Pergen* d 𝔓⁷⁴ ℵ² C E Ψ 33. 1739 𝔐 ΙΙ εἰς τὴν (– τὴν A) Πέργην ℵ* A 81.

The first hand of ℵ01 views the town of Perga as the people of the place, to whom (εἰς) Paul and Barnabas speak, rather than the place within which (ἐν) they speak.

(τὸν λόγον) τοῦ κυρίου ℵ A C Ψ 33. 81. 88. 181. 326. 614. (– τοῦ 927). 1270. 1409. 1837. 2147. 2344. 2412 *al* it vg syᵖ·ʰ** Ι τ. θεοῦ 𝔓⁷⁴ E gig boᵐˢ ΙΙ *om.* B D d H P L 049. 056. 1739 𝔐 vgᵐˢ co (aeth); Chr.

With the qualification τοῦ κυρίου, ℵ01 specifies that the word is the gospel. The occurrence of τὸν λόγον without any qualification is rare in Luke–Acts (cf. Lk. 1.2; Acts 4.4; 8.4; 10.36, 44; 11.19; 16.6 AT; 17.11). It suggests that Paul and Barnabas did not just announce the gospel to Jews who already knew the 'word of God', but spoke to Gentiles, too, who knew neither the word of God nor the word of the Lord (see *Excursus* 1). On their previous visit, no mention is made of any preaching in the city.

(᾽Αττάλειαν) εὐαγγελιζόμενοι αὐτούς D, *evangelizantes eos* d 257. 383. 614. 1799. 2147. 2412 *pc* sy^{h**} mae ‖ *om.* B 𝔓^{74} ℵ *rell.*

Attalia, the sea port, had not been mentioned on the outward journey, so again this is the first mention of any preaching there.

14.26 (κἀκεῖθεν) ἀπέπλευσαν D B² 𝔓^{74} ℵ A C E L P 049. 056. 1739 𝔐 ‖ ἀνέπλ- H Ψ ‖ *om.* B*.

The omission of the verb in B03* treats the travel from Perga through Attalia and on to Antioch as one stage in the journey. The absence of the participial clause εὐαγγελιζόμενοι αὐτούς (see above) makes this possible. In contrast, D05 treats the two places, Perga and Attalia, as quite separate.

14.27 (καὶ) συναγαγόντες B 𝔓^{74} ℵ *rell* ‖ συνάξαντες D.

B03 uses the classical, 2nd aorist form of ἄγω, whereas D05 has the later, 1st aorist form (Delebecque, *Les deux Actes*, p. 94).

ἀνήγγελλον B 𝔓^{74} ℵ A C Ψ 81. 1175. 1739. 1837. 1891 ‖ ἀνήγγειλον D, *renuntiaverunt* d H L P 049. 056. 614 𝔐 ‖ ἀπήγγειλαν E 242. 323. 927. 1270. 2492 *pc* gig vg; Chr.— (ὅσα) ἐποίησεν ὁ θεός B A C E H P L Ψ 049. 056. 81. 1175 𝔐 ‖ ὁ θ. ἐπ. D, *deus fecit* d 𝔓^{74} ℵ 36. 104. 242. 257. 431. 453. 457. 522. 614. 618. 913. 945. 1108. 1505. 1518. 1611. 1739. 1799. 1891. 2138. 2298. 2412. 2495.— μετ᾽ αὐτῶν B 𝔓^{74} ℵ *rell* ‖ αὐτοῖς (– D^{s.m.}) μετὰ τῶν ψυχῶν αὐτῶν D*, *illis cun animabus eorum* d (gig).

The announcement by Paul and Barnabas is presented differently in the two texts. B03, with the imperfect, portrays it as something going on over a period of time; then, in the contents of the announcement, the action carried out by God is set alongside the collaboration of Paul and Barnabas by virtue of the word order that places ὁ θεός next to μετ᾽ αὐτῶν. In D05, the focus is on the fact of announcing (aorist aspect) rather than the duration (imperfect); and the juxtaposition of αὐτοῖς and μετὰ τῶν ψυχῶν αὐτῶν places Paul and Barnabas in the spotlight: God did things for them and with their collaboration (see *Commentary* for a discussion of the term ψυχῶν). The phrase μετὰ τῶν ψυχῶν αὐτῶν is generally considered to be Semitic 'and is linguistically equivalent to μετ᾽ αὐτῶν in the usual text. The preceding αὐτοῖς is less easy to account for, but it probably represents the Aramaic proleptic pronoun, which is superfluous in Greek' (Metzger, *Commentary*, p. 338). As Delebecque points out (*Les deux Actes*, p. 94), if the words in D05 simply mean 'with them', it may be asked why it was necessary to introduce a Semitism at this point. Concerning αὐτοῖς, the dative is used elsewhere to refer to the beneficiaries of God's action (cf. Lk. 1.25, 49; 8.39a, 39b; Acts 16.40; cf. 9.13), just as μετ' αὐτῶν elsewhere refers to those who work with him (Acts 15.4; cf. δι' αὐτῶν, 15.12).

Commentary

[a] 14.21-22 *Start of the Return Journey from Derbe*

14.21 The action in this verse first continues in Derbe where Paul and Barnabas had fled from Lystra (14.20b). This town marks the furthest point of their journey for it is here that they will turn round and begin to retrace their steps. The Alexandrian text presents the evangelization of the town together with the making of disciples, on the one hand, and the start of the return journey, on the other, as two separate events that are consecutive in time. The focal point of the sentence is Lystra to which they return and which, as the last mentioned town, is still in mind, so to speak, with Iconium and Antioch accorded secondary importance (see *Critical Apparatus* for discussion of the Greek). Codex Bezae, however, views the evangelization as taking place at the same time as preparations were being made for the start of the return journey; Derbe is the focal point, with Paul and Barnabas' preaching described as addressed to the people themselves rather than impersonally to the town; and Lystra is simply the first of the three towns that were to be visited with Iconium and Antioch, cited in geographical order and given equal prominence. By either account, by the time Paul and Barnabas left Derbe, they had made many disciples (a considerable number, AT) there, so that they leave on a positive note with apparently no attacks or other negative effects to interfere with the success of their mission.

14.22 In the towns they re-visit, their concern is to build up the disciples whom they had left there on the earlier visit. The fact that no hostility at all is noted throughout the return journey suggests that Paul and Barnabas did not engage in public preaching this time but concentrated their attention on the believers. Thus, they 'were strengthening their souls', an important action previously undertaken only by Peter, when he also visited various places on his way to Jerusalem (cf. 11.2), so a positive comparison is being made.[263] They also encourage them to persevere in their new-found faith, exhortation that was no doubt all the more necessary in view of the persecution they were liable to suffer. Indeed, they spell this out, the switch to direct speech underlining the statement that hardship is inevitable, 'it is necessary' (lit. δεῖ). This impersonal construction is used in Acts to express a divine necessity, something that belongs to fulfilling God's plan.[264]

---

263. For discussion of the significance of Peter's action, see *The Message of Acts*, II, pp. 291–93.

264. For similar use of δεῖ to express the divine plan, cf. Lk. 2.49; 4.33; 9.22; 12.12; 13.14, 33; 17.25; 19.5; 22.37; 24.7, 26, 44; Acts 1.16, 21; 3.21; 4.12, 36; 5.29; 9.6, 16; 11.24; 15.5; 16.30; 17.3; 18.21 D05; 19.21; 21.22 D05; 23.11; 25.10; 27.24, 26.

The kingdom of God is presented in both texts as a future reality, with the Alexandrian text focusing on the entry, and the Bezan text more on the going there as it echoes the plea of the thief at the crucifixion who asked Jesus to remember him 'at the point when you go to your kingdom' (Lk. 23.42; see *Critical Apparatus*).

[b] 14.23 *Lystra, Iconium and Antioch*
14.23 Paul and Barnabas do not leave the disciples in Lystra, Iconium and Antioch without first establishing some kind of governing body whom Luke refers to as 'elders' (πρεσβύτεροι). This is the first time that the term is used clearly of the organization of churches, earlier occurrences having referred to the Jewish leaders in Ierousalem (4.5) or to the leaders of 'the brethren in Judaea' (11.30) where it is not clear how far these people were distinguished from people who had a role as Jewish leaders more generally. At Antioch, mention was made of 'prophets and teachers' (13.1) who would have played a leading part in the church there. In places far away from the first churches in Antioch and Ierousalem, it may have been deemed both wise and necessary to recognize more formally a group of members who were appointed to oversee the church affairs. The arrangement was that each local church was independent and had its own leadership. They were selected by Paul and Barnabas who, no doubt aware of their precarious situation without more knowledgeable teachers to guide them, made a special point of praying and even fasting before finally entrusting the churches to Jesus whom they had come to acknowledge as Lord.[265]

The action of committing the disciples to the Lord has strong parallels with the action of the church in Antioch of Syria, who prayed for Barnabas and Saul in a similar way at the outset of their mission (see *Overview* above).

[c] 14.24 *Arrival in Pamphylia*
14.24 The next step of the journey takes Paul and Barnabas through Pisidia where Antioch was located (see *Commentary*, 13.14 on the geographical location), and on to Pamphylia. The successive stages are now only briefly summarized.

[d] 14.25 *Perga and Attalia*
14.25 On the outward journey, no preaching in Perga of Pamphylia was recorded. It was there, in fact, that John had separated from them (13.13). This

---

265. The referent of the object pronoun αὐτούς following the verb παρέθεντο is ambiguous: it is usual not to repeat the pronoun when the referent is the direct object of two successive verbs (χειροτονήσαντες, παρέθεντο), so the natural interpretation would be that the pronoun refers here to the disciples in general (αὐτοῖς, as the indirect object of χειροτονήσαντες); on the other hand, the participle προσευξάμενοι intervening between the two verbs χειροτονήσαντες and παρέθεντο may call for the reference to the elders to be repeated with the accusative pronoun (see Read-Heimerdinger, 'The Tracking of Participants', pp. 439–55). Nonetheless the following clause, in which αὐτούς are qualified as having believed in the Lord, does suggest a broader meaning than the elders alone.

time, Paul and Barnabas speak 'the word', which, unusually for Luke's writings, has the qualification neither 'of God' nor 'of the Lord'. Luke uses the former to refer to communication between God and people in general, such as had been entrusted to the Jews in the Torah, whereas the latter is more specific and means the message or teaching of Jesus (see *Excursus* 1). The absence of qualification here suggests that they spoke to both Jews and Gentiles as appropriate. This understanding fits well with the general phrase 'in Perga' (ἐν Πέργῃ).

From Perga, which is some six miles inland, they went down to Attalia, the sea-port which was not mentioned by name on the outward journey (see *Commentary*, 13.13 on the outward route from Cyprus). According to Codex Bezae, they also announced the good news, εὐαγγελιζόμενοι, to the people of the town. The Greek verb εὐαγγελίζομαι was first used by the narrator[266] of the preaching of Paul and Barnabas in the area of Lystra and Derbe (14.7a), where it was noted that for the first time, having been driven out of the synagogue, they found themselves in an area where there were no Jewish communities (cf. *Commentary*, 14.7a). It was subsequently used in addressing the Gentile audience at Lystra (14.15) and at Derbe (14.21). 'Evangelizing' will continue (15.35; 16.10, 17 D05; 17.18 AT) to denote a positive evaluation of Paul's activity in particular.

[e] 14.26 *Departure for Antioch of Syria*
14.26 Finally, they set off for Antioch of Syria. This had been their starting point, where the Holy Spirit had singled them out 'for the work to which I have called them' (13.2), and which they have now accomplished. The church fasted and prayed for them, before laying hands on them and letting them go (13.3). This verse stands in perfect parallel to the initial statement of their departure, as if to underline that the obedience and trust of the Antioch church as a whole is compensated by their safe return.

[f] 14.27 *Report in Antioch*
14.27 The return of Paul and Barnabas to Antioch marks the success of their venture. They have overcome opposition from Jewish Jesus-believers who were proclaiming a false message to Gentiles (Cyprus); from the synagogue leaders (Antioch and Iconium); and from Gentiles stirred up by Jews (Antioch, Lystra and Derbe). Once back, they gather together the Christian community, for which Luke uses the verb generally associated with the synagogue (συναγαγόντες/συνάξαντες) rather than the usual 'call together',[267] as if to

---

266. Cf. 13.32 where Paul uses εὐαγγελίζομαι to proclaim God's fulfilment of the promise to Israel in Jesus.

267. προσκαλέομαι: 13.2, 7 AT (cf. 5.40; 6.2; 16.10; 20.1 D05; 23.17, 18, 23); συγκαλέομαι: 13.7 D05 (cf. 5.21; 10.24; 28.17).

indicate how the body of the church was replacing, or had replaced, that of the Jewish synagogue in Antioch.[268]

Paul and Barnabas report to the church their experiences, essentially 'what God did'. There are two distinct aspects to their report, the one concerning themselves and the other concerning the Gentiles. The two balance each other and will be alternately the centre of attention in the following section. Their own personal experience is related in indirect speech, as an awareness of God working for them (or possibly 'in them'), with their collaboration. They are conscious of having worked themselves, but at the same time of having been able to carry out what they set out to do because God was working on their behalf and using them to achieve the goals. The Greek expression in the Bezan text 'with their souls' may or may not be an echo of a Semitic expression (see *Critical Apparatus*) but its purpose in any case is to underline their personal contribution. Luke's insistence on the word 'soul' throughout this passage is striking (cf. 14.2, 22).[269]

As the report moves into direct speech, the most important aspect of what God has done is underlined by the switch from indirect speech, a technique that has been observed on other occasions, most recently at 14.22.[270] In the briefest of statements, the new step that has been taken in the spread of the gospel message is summarized: God has opened a door of faith to the Gentiles. No mention of the Jews, of any interest on their part in the preaching of Paul and Barnabas (although it was noted in Antioch, 13.43, and in Iconium, 14.1a), is made. For them, the 'door of faith' into the community of the people of God was already open. But for the Gentiles, things were different. They had been excluded from the people of God under the Law of Judaism unless they submitted to conditions of access for proselytes (cf. 13.16, 43); yet, what Paul and Barnabas have witnessed in the course of their activity among the Gentiles is that God has reversed the situation so that they, too, have been given and have received the word of God (13.46-48; 14.4), they have seen miracles worked (14.3, 10), they have believed in the Lord (14.1, 22), and they have access to 'the kingdom of God' (14.22). It may be recalled that the exact

268. συνάγω had been used at 13.44b (in the passive, συνήχθη), precisely when it was a question of the whole city gathering on the Sabbath in the manner of the synagogue on the previous Sabbath.

269. 14.2: ἐκάκωσεν τὰς ψυχὰς τῶν ἐθνῶν; 14.22: ἐπιστηρίζοντες τὰς ψυχὰς τῶν μαθητῶν. In the battle of strength between the Jews and the apostles (14.4), the former had a pernicious influence on the Gentiles by 'embittering their souls', and the latter engaged 'their souls' in the struggle while exercising a positive influence on the believers by 'strengthening their souls'.

270. The same pattern of indirect speech followed by a critical statement in direct speech occurs in the exhortation of the disciples on the return journey. It was seen earlier at Acts 1.4-5 (*The Message of Acts*, I, p. 68) and will be noticed again at 17.3 (where the first ὅτι introduces the content of παρατιθέμενος, and the second a sentence in direct speech). Luke frequently uses ὅτι to preface direct speech in Acts: cf. 2.13; 5.23, 25; 6.11; 14.22; 15.1, 5; 16.36; 17.3, 6; 18.13; 19.21; 25.8; 26.31; 28.25.

nature of the work which the Holy Spirit was envisaging when Barnabas and Saul were first set apart was not made clear (cf. 13.2). That was because no one could have anticipated, or even conceived of, the enormous change that was about to take place. The Jewish believers knew from the writings of the Prophets that the Messiah would reach out to the Gentiles (cf. 13.33b D05, 34, 39b), but it was not seen as a present reality nor was it known how it would come about. What Paul and Barnabas have to report in Antioch is that the opening up of the kingdom of God to Gentiles by the Messiah has finally been realized, in ways that were neither foreseen nor expected, and that they have been not only witnesses to the process but also participants in it.

II. THE JUDICIAL REVIEW IN IEROUSALEM
14.28–15.41

General Overview

Section II of this third part of Acts is situated between the first phase of the mission to the Gentiles (Section I, 13.1–14.27) and the second (Section III. 16.1–18.23). It is here that Luke places the meeting in Ierousalem that was organized by the leaders of the church there in order to sort out the problems posed by the Gentiles when they became believers. In so far as the Jesus-believers were still considered to be part of Judaism, this supposed that the Gentiles must submit to the usual conditions imposed on proselytes, of circumcision and acceptance of the Jewish Law, in order to gain admission to the communities of believers: the Church was a group within Israel and therefore its members had to be Jews, or become Jews and live like them. However, this view of the Church as part of Israel, which maintained the privileged status of the Jews with regard to the Gentiles, was beginning to shift, in some quarters at least.

It had already been challenged in Caesarea (10.1-48), with the gift of the Holy Spirit to the Gentiles without any preliminary rites or other demands. Peter had seen clearly then that Gentiles did not have to become members of Israel in order to be acceptable to God. Likewise, in Antioch, Gentiles were part of the local church alongside Jews, without apparently being circumcised or accepting to follow the Law (11.19-26). Finally, Paul and Barnabas had gone out from the Antioch church and many Gentiles had become believers in other countries, where they had not been required to submit to any conditions either (13.4–14.25).

Between the views represented by Peter and by Paul, nonetheless, there was a critical difference, which would become a key factor in the debate in Ierousalem. Peter maintained that there was no distinction between Jew and Gentile, that each was equally acceptable to God and that the Law was of no value to either (15.10-11a). Paul saw the matter otherwise, as he set out in his speech in Antioch of Pisidia: Gentiles, by their acceptance of the Messiah, become part of Israel; Israel remains the people of God, into whom the Gentiles can now enter by virtue of their faith in Jesus as Lord and Saviour (13.32-33, esp. D05). True, circumcision and the Law are not necessary for Gentiles; nevertheless, Israel, according to Paul's way of thinking, retains its importance and identity – but, and it is a significant 'but', the conversion of the Jews to belief in Jesus is essential if they are not to be overrun by the influx of Gentiles (13.39-41).

Luke will make increasingly clear over the coming chapters that according to his own understanding of Jesus' message, which he believed to be in tune with the Holy Spirit, Paul was wrong: Israel ceased to have a privileged status but was, on the contrary, as Peter maintained, one nation among many, and all were equal.[1] Luke's presentation of Paul, in consequence, has as its goal to make this factor clear. This explains why he is not afraid to contradict some of the things Paul had said in his letters. It is not that he was not familiar with Paul's views or did not understand them; nor that he deliberately sought to misrepresent him, or to distort the facts for the sake of his story: where his account differs from that of Paul, he is showing the Paul that his friends and companions witnessed at the various points of his spiritual journey. For Luke knows that Paul himself evolved in his understanding of the significance of Israel and of being Jewish, and also that this progress was made only at considerable cost.

Into this scene steps James, active for the first time in Acts, though he has previously been mentioned by name by Peter at 12.17; and before that, he was present as one of the brothers of Jesus at 1.14. His theological understanding of Israel and the Gentiles represents yet another strand of interpretation (for all, in the end, are to do with the exegesis of the Jewish Scriptures), more conservative than that of Paul in maintaining the relevance of the Law for both Jewish and Gentile believers, as will be seen in this chapter. James does, however, take a decisive step for the Church is ruling that circumcision is not necessary for Gentile brethren. This is a radically new position, which constitutes a break with traditional Jewish teaching. Hence, although the meeting takes place in Ierousalem, where circumcision and the Law are taught as indispensable requirements, the decree that comes out of it represents a freer attitude, so that the apostles and elders responsible for it will henceforth be associated with Hierosoluma (16.4).

The beginning of Section II is marked at 14.28 with the conjunction δέ in Greek. The sentence at 15.1 does not begin a new paragraph since the connective καί that links it to the previous sentence conjoins sentences within a paragraph but not across paragraph boundaries (cf. the discussion in the *Overview* [*Structure and Themes*] to the last sequence of Section I, [A'], 14.21-27).[2]

---

1. In identifying a position held by Luke that goes beyond the position adopted by Paul and that is even more radical in its view of Israel than the one he strives to realize, we differ from Chilton, who presents Paul's vision as in tune with divine revelation (*Rabbi Paul. An Intellectual Biography* [New York: Doubleday, 2004], e.g., pp. 75–80, 89–90, 119, 128, 145).

2. This was the conclusion of Levinsohn, *Textual Connections*, pp. 96-99, who made a detailed examination of all the sentence links in Acts and analysed their function in structuring the narrative. He concludes that καί introduces new characters, as at 15.1, when they enter the narrative to interact with the Christian leaders already on stage.

Structure and Themes

The section is made up of four sequences, all concerned with the issue of the admission of Gentiles into the Church. The question is introduced in the opening sequence [A], which is set in Antioch. The action then transfers to Ierousalem [B], where the problem is examined in detail and a resolution decided upon. The corresponding sequence [B'] presents the application of the decision in Antioch. However, disagreement continues through to the final sequence [A'], still set in Antioch and still with the issue of the Gentiles as its underlying cause:

[A]	14.28–15.2	Conflict over the tradition of Moses
[B]	15.3-29	Examination of the case
[B']	15.30-35	The application of the decision
[A']	15.36-41	Conflict over John-Mark

A number of characters, some of them new to the narrative of Acts, play an important role in the events of this section. Paul and Barnabas, however, remain present throughout and provide a constant point of reference. It may be noted that the transition to this new section begins with them spending time in Antioch (14.28, Διέτριβον δὲ χρόνον οὐκ ὀλίγον), a transition that will be repeated at the end of the third sequence (15.35, Παῦλος δὲ καὶ Βαρναβᾶς διέτριβον ἐν Ἀντιοχείᾳ). The parallel statements show how the great debate provoked by the disciples who insisted on imposing circumcision is viewed as a digression, essentially challenging the legitimacy of the work Paul and Barnabas have been carrying out among the Gentiles. On the other hand, it may also be noticed that just as the arrival of the people from Judaea will interrupt their stay in Antioch, so will Paul's later decision to re-visit the churches they had founded.

[A] 14.28–15.2 *Conflict over the Tradition of Moses*

Overview

The first sequence is set in Antioch where Section I ended (cf. 14.26-27). The issues of circumcision and keeping of the Law are raised by visiting brethren from Judaea, in much the same way as they had been raised with Peter some time earlier (cf. 11.2b-3). These issues are made explicit for the first time in the context of the mission of Paul and Barnabas.

Structure and Themes

Paul and Barnabas remain in focus as the central characters. However, new characters arrive from Judaea and enter into the narrative, ones not hitherto mentioned. It is they who introduce the topic of circumcision and the Law with respect to Gentile believers in Jesus. Their basic tenets are briefly stated and the opposition they aroused in Paul and Barnabas is described, with Paul's position clearly stated in the Bezan text. Again in the Bezan text, it is the people from Judaea who send Paul and Barnabas to Ierousalem, and not the Antioch church as in Codex Vaticanus:

> [a]   14.28   Paul and Barnabas stay in Antioch
> [b]   15.1   Visitors from Judaea
> [b′] 15.2a   Paul and Barnabas oppose their teaching
> [a′] 15.2b   They send Paul and Barnabas to Ierousalem

Translation

Codex Bezae D05

[a]   **14.28** They stayed on for quite some time with the disciples.

[b]   **15.1** And some people who had gone down from Judea were teaching the brethren, 'Unless you are circumcised and keep on walking by the tradition of Moses, you cannot be saved'.

[b′] **2a** A quarrel started up, and Paul and Barnabas had a not insignificant debate with them (for Paul said that they should remain exactly as they were when they believed and insisted strongly on it).

[a′] **2b** The people who were from Ierousalem ordered them – Paul and Barnabas – and some others to go up to the apostles and elders in Ierousalem, in order to be judged in submission to them over this question.

Codex Vaticanus B03

14.28 They stayed on for quite some time with the disciples.

15.1 And some people who had gone down from Judea were teaching the brethren, 'Unless you are circumcised according to the tradition of Moses, you cannot be saved'.

2 Since there was a serious disturbance and Paul and Barnabas had a not insignificant debate with them,

they decided that Paul and Barnabas, as well as some others from among them, should go up to the apostles and elders in Ierousalem regarding this question.

Critical Apparatus

15.1 (περιτμηθῆτε) τῷ ἔθει τῷ Μωϋσέως B 𝔓⁷⁴ ℵ A C Ψ 81 | τ. ἔθ. Μωσέως E H L P 049. 056. 33. 1739 𝔐 ‖ καὶ τ. ἔθ. Μωσέως περιπατῆτε D d syʰᵐᵍ sa mae; Irˡᵃᵗ ᵛⁱᵈ Didasc CAp.

Whereas in the B03 text the conditions imposed on the Gentiles by the people from Judaea are limited to circumcision in accordance with Mosaic custom, the D05 text singles out circumcision as one particular issue from the Mosaic code of conduct, which the Gentiles are required to follow in its entirety. The dative article before Moses in B03 has the effect of adding explanatory information to qualify the custom. The anarthrous name in D05 is the genitive; it is typical in stock expressions, such as 'the custom of Moses', to omit the article before the name (cf. τὸ ὄνομα Ἰησοῦ Χριστοῦ: 3.6; 4.10; 16.18; τὸ βάπτισμα Ἰωάννου: 1.22; 18.25; 19.3).

15.2 γενομένης δὲ στάσεως B ℵ C L Ψ 81. 927. 945. 1175. 1243. 2147 | γεν. οὖν στ. 𝔓⁷⁴ A E H P 049. 056. 0294. 614 𝔐, *facta ergo seditione* d ‖ γεν. δὲ ἐκτάσεως D.— τῷ Βαρναβᾷ B 𝔓⁷⁴ ℵ *rell* ‖ Βαρναβᾷ D.— πρὸς αὐτούς B 𝔓⁷⁴ ℵ *rell, ad eos* d ‖ σὺν αὐτοῖς D sa mae.

The B03 reading of στάσις (translated as *seditio* by d) is found elsewhere in Luke's writings, always with the sense of 'uprising, insurrection' (cf. Lk. 23.19, 25 B03; Acts 19.40; 23.7 [D05 lac.], 10 [D05 lac.]; 24.5 [pl., D05 lac.]). The D05 reading of ἔκτασις means 'mental tension' (as at Acts 3.10 D05; see L-S-J, ἔκτασις, I, 3).

The absence of the article before Barnabas causes him to be viewed as being in harmony with Paul, forming a united pair (Heimerdinger and Levinsohn, 'The Use of the Article', p. 29). The difference in preposition before the third person pronoun may well be occasioned by the difference in the noun (στάσις, ἔκτασις), πρός indicating an engagement between the two parties and σύν suggesting more of a conflict.

ἔλεγεν γὰρ ὁ Παῦλος μένειν οὕτως καθὼς ἐπίστευσαν διϊσχυριζόμενος D (*dicebat autem Paulus manere sic sicut crediderunt* d b gig w vg⁰) sy^hmg mae; (Ephr) ‖ *om.* B 𝔓⁷⁴ ℵ *rell*.

The explanatory clause is absent from B03; the versional support for its presence in D05 is widespread.

ἔταξαν ἀναβαίνειν Παῦλον καὶ Βαρναβᾶν καί τινας ἄλλους ἐξ αὐτῶν (ἐξ αὐ. ἀλ. ℵ) B 𝔓⁷⁴ ℵ *rell* (ar c dem) e (l) p (ro) aeth; Amph Chr Hier ‖ οἱ δὲ ἐληλυθότες ἀπὸ Ἰερουσαλὴμ παρήγγειλαν αὐτοῖς τῷ Παύλῳ καὶ Βαρναβᾷ καί τισιν ἄλλοις ἀναβαίνειν D, *qui autem venerunt ab Hierusalem statuerunt eis Paulo et Barnabae et quosdam alios* (!) *ascendere* d gig ph w sy^hmg (mae).— (εἰς Ἰερουσαλὴμ) ὅπως κριθῶσιν ἐπ' αὐτοῖς (-ῶν D^C) D, *ut iudicent super eos* d (following περὶ τοῦ ζητήματος τούτου, 257. 383. 614. 1799. 2147. 2412 *pc* sy^h**) ‖ *om.* B 𝔓⁷⁴ ℵ *rell*.

According to B03, it was the church community in Antioch who took the decision to send Paul and Barnabas to Ierousalem, accompanied by others from the church (ἐξ αὐτῶν). The responsibility for sending them to Ierousalem in D05 lies with those who had come from there; their specific purpose in ordering them to go is for them to be judged by the Church leaders.

Commentary

[a] 14.28 *Paul and Barnabas Stay in Antioch*
14.28 Once Paul and Barnabas arrive back in their home church, as it were, they stay on there without any immediate intention of going away. The sentence is usually considered to bring the previous episode to a close, whereas the conjunction (δέ) in fact ties it to the following episode and so makes it the opening statement of the new section (see *Overview*).

Luke describes the length of their stay with an understatement, underlining that it lasted some time, the imperfect tense in Greek expressing here the indefiniteness of the period of time they spent with the disciples, 'the church' of Antioch.[3] They apparently had no reason to think that any trouble was brewing. The question of the admission of the Gentiles into the Church had already been dealt with in Ierousalem after Peter's experience in Caesarea, when he had explained to those who challenged him (11.2-3) how he had been taken by surprise by the intervention of God himself in giving the Holy Spirit to Gentiles whom he, too, would have previously considered as unfit to be considered on the same footing as Jews (11.2a, 15-17; cf. 10.19-20, 44-48). Barnabas was almost certainly present at that meeting in Ierousalem and, since he had already accepted the Gentile believers in Antioch on behalf of the Ierousalem church (cf. 11.22-23), he would not have been expecting any problem to be raised at this stage. As for Paul, he was in Tarsus at the time but would have been made fully aware of what had gone on.

[b] 15.1 *Visitors from Judaea*

15.1 The stay of Paul and Barnabas in Antioch is interrupted by the arrival of some people from Judaea, a small group (τινες, 'some'). That Luke gives their place of origin as Judaea is an indication of their religious tendencies, for Judaea in his work stands for exclusive Judaism. Although it is not stated at this stage in the story that they are Jesus-believers, it becomes clear over the course of the story that they were indeed disciples, from the Pharisee party (cf. 15.4b, esp. D05, 24).

Having reached Antioch, they begin teaching in competition, as it were, with Paul and Barnabas.[4] The use of the term 'brethren' (τοὺς ἀδελφούς) to describe those whom they address reflects their point of view as fellow-believers. They have taken the trouble to travel to Antioch because they are opposed to the conduct of the church in Antioch, namely their failure to impose conditions on the Gentiles who wish to enter the Church in a wider sense. They categorically maintain the position that Gentiles must be circumcised, in accordance with the 'custom of Moses', that is the teaching that the rite of entry for any Gentile who would become part of Israel was circumcision (cf. Exod. 12.48). Codex Bezae goes further: once the rite of circumcision was accomplished, the Gentile must continue to respect the custom of Moses in general.

This is presented as the necessary condition for salvation. From a Jewish perspective, salvation was only possible for those who belonged to Israel, of which following the tradition of Moses was the hallmark. Some within the

---

3. While Luke uses the verb μένω frequently along with the other Gospel writers, he is almost alone to use the verb διατρίβω, as he does here, to indicate a stay in a place for a certain length of time.

4. The sequence of tenses is to be noted: the ongoing action of Paul and Barnabas is expressed by the imperfect, διέτριβον, and is interrupted by the travelling to Antioch of the men from Judaea, κατελθόντες, aorist, who, once in Antioch, teach over a period of time, ἐδίδασκον, imperfect.

Church continued to uphold that teaching, contrary to the promise made by the angel to Cornelius and manifested through the events in his house in Caesarea ('[Peter] will speak words to you by which you may be saved', 11.14).[5]

In the light of this insistence, it is evident that the Church was still understood to be a part of Judaism, otherwise there would be no sense in anyone expecting its adherents to follow Jewish customs. The issue at stake is the condition of entry for those Gentiles who join this branch or sect of Judaism. Paul had attempted in his speech in Antioch to explain that the time had come for Gentiles to have the same access to God as had hitherto been the privilege of Jews, in other words, for them to be integrated into Israel. The basis for this claim was that Jesus was the one who fulfilled the ancient promises, not just that a Messiah would be sent to rule Israel but also to gather in the Gentiles (13.32-39, 46-47, see *Commentary, ad loc.*). It was precisely this teaching that so angered the Jews in Antioch and Iconium (13.45; 14.2, 5, 19; see *Commentary, ad loc.*), because it posed a direct challenge to the unique status of the Jews, and caused them to attempt to silence Paul by killing him.

[b′] 15.2a *Paul and Barnabas Oppose their Teaching*
15.2a The teaching of the men from Judaea provokes a serious conflict in the church, among the brethren whom they were teaching. The Greek term describing this conflict refers, in the Alexandrian text, to a revolt or an important disturbance; the Bezan text is less dramatic in speaking about tension or disagreement (see *Critical Apparatus*). In either case, it is expressed in a debate that takes on considerable proportions, as Paul and Barnabas talk with the church about the issues raised. The Bezan text presents Paul and Barnabas here as united (see *Critical Apparatus*), and further clarifies the substance of the debate, attributing it to Paul's insistence that believers, whether Jew or Gentile, should remain as they are, circumcised or uncircumcised respectively. The insistence of Paul is expressed with a rare verb that only Luke uses in the New Testament, twice in relation to Peter and his persistence (Lk. 22.59; Acts 12.15).[6] On respecting the rest of the Mosaic tradition, nothing is said.

[a′] 15.2b *They Send Paul and Barnabas to Ierousalem*
15.2b The outcome of the argument is that Paul and Barnabas end up being sent to Ierousalem to talk about the question with the apostles and the leaders there. Whether they were sent by the church or by those who had come from Judaea is at first sight ambiguous in the Alexandrian text, where either one is grammatically possible. The use, however, of the loaded term Ἰερουσαλήμ,

---

5. See *The Message of Acts*, II, pp. 299–300.
6. διϊσχυρίζω. The two scenes involving Peter correspond to each other, in that in the first someone insists for the third time that he had been among those who knew Jesus; and in the second, it is Rhoda, the servant girl, who insists for the third time that Peter is at the door (see *The Message of Acts*, II, p. 262, and cf. *Excursus* 5, pp. 365–68).

'Ierousalem', to refer to the place where the apostles and elders are to be found, is a clue that it is the visitors who are responsible for the arrangement. The church in Antioch is free from the Jewish authority of the holy city, for which Ierousalem is the name Luke uses, as opposed to Hierosoluma ('Ιερο-σόλυμα) when he means the city in a neutral, non-religious sense (see *General Introduction*, §VII). In contrast, the people who are demanding circumcision continue to hold on to the ways of thinking associated by tradition with the Jewish institution, represented by its centre in Ierousalem. They view the apostles and the elders as still part of that system and therefore as based in the holy city, the religious centre. The very choice of verb, 'go up' (ἀναβαί-νειν), expresses the idea of going to the holy place.[7]

Their decision to send Paul and Barnabas (this time mentioned as a united pair), together with some others from the local church, to talk with the Ierou-salem church authorities about the issue of circumcision is evidence that they are happy to accept them as leaders, for they would not otherwise have referred Paul and Barnabas to them. The two groups, the apostles and the elders, are viewed by them as forming a single body (one preposition and one article in Greek).[8] The apostles have occupied a position of leadership since the beginning (4.35; 5.1; cf. 8.14; 11.1), though something of a shift took place with the election of the Seven Hellenists (6.2, 6). It may be for the pur-pose of material tasks that the 'elders' emerged as a separate and identifiable group, for they are first mentioned as the people in Judaea to whom Paul and Barnabas take gifts during the famine (11.29-30).[9] Now, for the first time, they are seen in close association with the apostles, as leaders on a par with them. On future occasions in this section, the elders will be again associated with the apostles (cf. 15.4a, 6, 22, 23). In two additional instances, however, the Bezan text mentions the elders on their own (15.4b, 11b), and it will become apparent that it is this group that was of especial importance for those who were insisting on circumcision (see *Commentary, ad loc.*).[10]

In the Bezan text, the intention of the visitors is even clearer – first, it is said explicitly that it is they who order Paul and Barnabas to go up to Ierou-salem with some others. These visitors are precisely from Ierousalem them-selves.[11] Their purpose is furthermore spelt out: it is so that the Antioch church leaders be judged by the apostles and the elders over the issue of the

---

7. Cf. Lk. 18.10; Acts 18.22; 25.1. See *Critical Apparatus* 13.4, on the opposite verb, κατα-βαίνω.

8. πρὸς τοὺς ἀποστόλους καὶ πρεσβυτέρους.

9. See *The Message of Acts*, II, pp. 326–29. The apostles had been previously associated only with 'the brethren in Judaea' (11.1), though it is clear from ch. 12 that they belong to the church of Ierousalem where the elders are found.

10. The apostles will not be mentioned again in Acts after the last reference at 16.4. The elders, on the other hand, will reappear under the leadership of James at 21.18 as those in charge of the Ierousalem church.

11. The stative aspect of the perfect, οἱ ἐληλυθότες, expresses their identification with the place.

Mosaic Law (cf. 15.1, circumcision and following the tradition of Moses).[12] They thus not only respect the authority of the Ierousalem leaders but presumably also expect to have a reasonable chance of being vindicated by them. In any case, they view the Antioch church as being under their authority and dependent on their judgement.[13]

[B] 15.3-29 *Examination of the Case*

Overview

The second sequence describes in detail the development of the dispute over the Gentiles, between the Antioch church represented by Paul and Barnabas, on the one hand, and the Ierousalem church, on the other, where it emerges that there are different opinions.

According to Codex Vaticanus, the meeting takes place in Hierosoluma (Ἱεροσόλυμα, 15.4a B03), in order to examine the question of the conditions to be imposed on the Gentiles who became believers: its aim will be to reach agreement between the leaders of the church in Antioch and that in Ierousalem about the practice to be followed (15.2b AT). According to Codex Bezae, on the other hand, the meeting is of a more judicial nature, called for the purpose of the leaders in Ierousalem (Ἱερουσαλήμ, 15.4a D05 א01; cf. additional mention of Ierousalem, 15.2b D05) judging the position upheld by Paul and Barnabas (15.2b D05). The Vaticanus reading at 15.4a tallies better with Paul's description of a meeting in Jerusalem (Hierosoluma, Ἱεροσόλυμα) in his letter to the Galatians (Gal. 2.1-10). However, although this factor may indeed have played a part in the textual modifications, no attempt will be made here to match Paul's letters with the account of Acts – it may be hoped that once the text of all of Luke's narrative concerning Paul has been scrutinized in detail, and its particular coherence observed in Codex Bezae, the ground will have been prepared for a fresh look at the question of the agreement between Paul and Luke on historical matters.[14]

---

12. The way the visit of Paul and Barnabas is presented in Codex Bezae contrasts with Paul's presentation of his visit in Gal. 2.2. Whether the same visit is in question is a matter of much scholarly debate. If Paul is referring to the visit of Acts 15, the discrepancy between Luke's and Paul's descriptions can be accounted for by the need Paul felt to insist on his spiritual freedom.

13. The construction ἐπ' αὐτοῖς expresses the dependency on the apostles and elders; cf. L-S-J, ἐπί, B. With dat.: I, 1, g: 'in dependence upon, in the power of'. The construction with the genitive expresses, in contrast, the idea of being judged by someone.

14. The closer agreement between the AT of Acts 15 and Gal. 2.1-10, which both portray a Paul who is not subject to any human authority, could be accounted for by the modification of the primitive text by an editor (or by disciples of Paul) who wished to smooth out the discrepancies. The Bezan readings in this respect are the more difficult ones; and yet, in the studies carried out on the problem of matching the account of Acts with the letters of Paul, it seems easier to charge Luke with carelessly using erroneous sources, of being ignorant of the facts, or of deliberately toning down the conflict between Paul and James, than to accept the authenticity of the Bezan narrative which, taken overall, provides a picture of Paul torn in different directions by the

Once the people from Antioch arrive in Ierousalem, it turns out that there are two sharply contradictory opinions about the Gentiles: there is the view of some of the Pharisee believers, that circumcision and Law-keeping are necessary for all; and there is the view of Peter, that they are absolutely not, that Jews and Gentiles are equally accepted by God without any prior conditions. Barnabas and Paul's testimony backs up the view and experience of Peter. The role taken on by James is to reconcile the two opposing stands, which he attempts to do by continuing to uphold Israel's privileged position but saying that the time for the Gentiles to come in has arrived, for which they must respect the essentials of the Law: this is his judgement.

It is important to be clear whose view the decree represents: it is not Luke's in Codex Bezae, for he shows, by the use of 'in the Spirit' at 15.7 D05, that he approves instead Peter's view, namely that God has accepted the Gentiles without any prior conditions whatsoever. In order to interpret James, it is of no help to ask how it fits with views expressed elsewhere in Luke's work, since Luke deliberately constructs the speeches according to what the individual speakers would have said at that time (their understanding being open to modification), and not what he wants them to say (see *General Introduction*, §VI).

Structure and Themes

The theme throughout the sequence is the terms on which Gentiles should be admitted to the Church. The first four elements set the scene, transferring the action from Antioch to Ierousalem and re-stating the principal arguments of the two opposing sides. They are matched by four more elements, which present the successive stages of the meeting convened to settle the matter:

[a]	15.3	The journey from Antioch to Ierousalem
[b]	15.4a	Arrival in Ierousalem
[c]	15.4b-5	The objections raised by Pharisee believers
[d]	15.6	The meeting of the apostles and the elders
[d']	15.7-11	Peter's speech
[c']	15.12	The testimony of Barnabas and Paul
[b']	15.13-21	James' speech and verdict
[a']	15.22-29	The ratification of James' verdict

The tightly-knit nature of this sequence can be seen in the distribution of the vocabulary over the various testimonies and speeches, whether reported by Luke directly or indirectly (the different formats indicate corresponding elements):

The position of the APOSTLES:
1. PAUL AND BARNABAS: ἐκδιηγούμενοι *τὴν ἐπιστροφὴν τῶν ἐθνῶν*, 15.3

emerging problem of the Gentiles, and carrying out actions that sometimes contradicted his words. In other instances, when it is Codex Bezae that presents the smoother account, commentators and textual critics alike are quick to attribute its text to a scribe's attempt at harmonization, such are the prejudices that reign against this manuscript.

2. PETER: maintains that ἀφ' ἡμερῶν ἀρχαίων he was chosen so that ἀκοῦσαι τὰ ἔθνη τὸν λόγον τοῦ εὐαγγελίου καὶ πιστεῦσαι, 15.7
3. BARNABAS AND PAUL: ἐξηγούμενοι ὅσα ἐποίησεν ὁ θεὸς ... ἐν τοῖς ἔθνεσιν, 15.12

The reponse of JAMES:

1. Major premiss: SIMEON explained (ἐξηγήσατο) how <u>in the beginning</u> (πρῶτον) God took a people *from the nations*, ἐξ ἐθνῶν, a PEOPLE (ΛΑΌΝ): PRECEDENCE OF ISRAEL, 15.14
2. Minor premiss: thus will agree (συμφωνήσουσιν, fut.) the words of the PROPHETS, 15.15: restoration of the TENT OF DAVID = ISRAEL, 15.16, so that *the rest of humanity*, πάντα τὰ ἔθνη ἐφ' οὓς ἐπικέκληται τὸ ὄνομά μου, may seek God, 15.17
3. This has been the plan of the Lord <u>forever (ἀπ' αἰῶνος</u>), 15.18
4. Conclusion of JAMES: I therefore rule, Μὴ παρενοχλεῖν τοῖς ἀπὸ τῶν ἐθνῶν ἐπιστρέφουσιν ἐπὶ τὸν θεόν, ἀλλὰ ἐπιστεῖλαι, that the PRECEDENCE OF ISRAEL is to be respected, 15.19-21

Translation

Codex Bezae D05	*Codex Vaticanus B03*
[a] **15.3** So, having been given provisions for the journey by the church, they passed both through Phoenicia and through Samaria, relating in detail the conversion of the Gentiles and they caused great joy to all the brethren.	**15.3** So, having been given provisions for the journey by the church, they passed through both Phoenicia and Samaria, relating in detail the conversion of the Gentiles and they caused great joy to all the brethren.
[b] **4a** When they arrived in Ierousalem, they were handed over grandly to the authority of the church, of the apostles and of the elders, since they were speaking out about what God, with their collaboration, had done.	**4a** When they arrived in Hierosoluma, they were received by the church, and the apostles and the elders, and they announced what God had done with their collaboration.
[c] **5** Those who had ordered them to go up to the elders intervened, saying (they were certain people from the party of the Pharisees who had believed), 'It is necessary to circumcise them and, indeed, to order them to keep the Law of Moses'.	**5** Some people from among the party of the Pharisees who had believed intervened, saying, 'It is necessary to circumcise them and also order them to keep the Law of Moses';
[d] **6** The apostles and elders assembled to see about this matter.	**6** and so, the apostles and the elders assembled to see about this matter.
[d'] **7a** When there had been much argument, Peter stood up in the Spirit and said to them,	**7a** When there had been much debate Peter, having stood up, said to them,
[α] **7b** 'Men, brothers, you know that ever since the days of old God's choice for us was that through my mouth the Gentiles would hear the message of the gospel and believe. **8** Now, he who knows the heart, God, witnessed to them, when he gave upon them the Holy Spirit just as to us, **9** and he made no distinction between us and them, cleansing their hearts by faith.	**7b** 'Men, brothers, you know that from the early days God chose from among you that it should be through my mouth that the Gentiles would hear the message of the gospel and believe, **8** and God who knows the heart witnessed to them, when he gave to them the Holy Spirit just as to us, **9** and he made no distinction between us and them, cleansing their hearts by faith.

[β] **10** So now why do you put God to the test by placing a yoke on the neck of the disciples that neither our fathers nor we have been strong enough to bear? **11** Instead, we will continue believing that it is through the grace of the Lord Jesus Christ that we are saved, in just the same way as they are.'

[c′] **12** Since all the elders gave their agreement to what Peter had said, all the meeting fell silent and listened to Barnabas and Paul explaining what signs and wonders God had done among the nations through them.

[b′] **13** After they had been silent, James got up and said,

[α] **14** 'Simeon explained, just as God in the beginning visited the nations to take from them a people for his name, **15** so, indeed, the words of the Prophets will concord, just as it is written, **16** "After these things, I will go back and will rebuild the tent of David which has fallen, and the ruins of it I will rebuild, and I will set it up **17** so that the rest of humanity may seek God, even all the Gentiles on whom is called my name", says the Lord. He will do these things. **18** His work has been known to the Lord forever.

[β] **19** Therefore, my judgement is that we should stop troubling those who turn from the Gentiles to God, **20** but we should write to them to abstain from the pollutions of idols, illicit sexual relations and blood, and whatever they do not wish to happen to themselves, stop doing to others. **21** For from ancient times Moses has had in every city people proclaiming him, that is in the synagogues where he is read every Sabbath.

[a′] **22** Then it was decided by the apostles and the elders with the entire church to choose and send men from among them to Antioch, together with Paul and Barnabas – Judas whom they called Barabbas and Silas, leading men among the brethren – **23a** after writing a letter for them to take by hand, which contained the following:

[α] **23b** 'The apostles and the elders who are brethren, to those in Antioch, Syria and

10 So now why do you put God to the test by placing a yoke on the neck of the disciples that neither our fathers nor we have been strong enough to bear? **11** Instead, we believe that it is through the grace of the Lord Jesus that we are saved, in just the same way as they are.'

12 All the meeting fell silent and listened to Barnabas and Paul explaining what signs and wonders God had done among the nations through them.

13 After they had been silent, James answered saying,

14 'Simeon has explained how God first visited the nations to take from them a people for his name, **15** and with this the words of the Prophets agree, just as it is written, **16** "After these things, I will return and will build again the tent of David which has fallen, and the remains of it I will rebuild, and I will set it up **17** so that the rest of humanity may seek the Lord, even all the Gentiles on whom is called my name", says the Lord who has been making these things **18** known forever.

19 Therefore, my decision is that we should stop troubling those who turn from the Gentiles to God, **20** but we should write to them to abstain from the idol sacrifices, illicit sexual relations, meat cooked in its juices and blood. **21** For from ancient times Moses has had in every city people proclaiming him in the synagogues, where he is read every Sabbath.

22 Then it was decided by the apostles and the elders with the entire church to choose and send men from among them to Antioch, together with Paul and Barnabas – Judas whom they called Barsabbas and Silas, leading men among the brethren – **23a** after writing, for them to take by hand,

23b 'The apostles and the elders who are brethren, to the brethren in Antioch,

[β]

Cilicia, the brethren who are from the Gentiles, greetings! **24** Since we heard that certain people who had gone out from us disturbed you with their talk, unsettling your minds, though we did not give them instructions, **25** we have decided, after becoming of one mind, to choose and send to you men, with your beloved Barnabas and Paul, **26** men who have given up their life on account of the name of the Lord Jesus Christ to every trial. **27** So we have sent Judas and Silas, who will themselves tell you by word of mouth what follows.

[γ]

28 For the decision of the Holy Spirit and of ourselves is that no other burden is to be put on you than these: it is essential **29** to abstain from idol sacrifices, blood and illicit sexual relations; and whatever you do not wish to happen to yourselves, not to do to another; do well by keeping yourselves away from these things, sustained by the Holy Spirit. Farewell!'

Syria and Cilicia who are from the Gentiles, greetings! **24** Since we heard that certain from among us troubled you with their talk, unsettling your minds, though we did not give them instructions, **25** we have decided, after becoming of one mind, to send to you men whom we have chosen with our beloved Barnabas and Paul, **26** men who have given up their lives on account of the name of the Lord Jesus Christ. **27** So we have sent Judas and Silas, to tell you themselves the same things by word of mouth.

28 For the decision of the Holy Spirit and of ourselves is that no other burden is to be put on you than these things that are essential: **29** that you abstain from idol sacrifices, blood, meat cooked in its juices and illicit sexual relations; if you keep out of trouble with these things, you will do well. Farewell!'

Critical Apparatus

15.3 (καὶ) Σαμάρειαν B 𝔓⁴⁵·⁷⁴ (Σ-ρίαν ℵ) *rell* ‖ τὴν Σαμαρίαν D H 049 (Σ-ρειαν 1. 69. 104. 330. 383. 440. 876. 1828. 1838. 1854. 2147. 2492) *pc*; Theoph.

In D05, the two regions of Phoenicia and Samaria are treated as distinct by means of the repeated article, whereas B03 groups them together.

ἐκδιηγούμενοι B D 𝔓⁷⁴ ℵ² *rell* ‖ διηγούμενοι ℵ* 104.

The prefix ἐκ-, absent from the ℵ01 reading, confers the added sense of telling 'in detail' (cf. 13.41).

15.4 (εἰς) Ἱεροσόλυμα B 𝔓⁴⁵·⁷⁴ A Ψ 81. 88. 614. 927. 1175. 1270. 1505. 1837. 2147. 2412. 2495 *pc* gig vg ‖ Ἱερουσαλήμ D d ℵ C E H L P 049. 056. 1739 𝔐 vgᴰ sa; CAp.

D05 is consistent in the distinction it makes between Ἱεροσόλυμα as the name of the geographical location, and Ἱερουσαλήμ to designate the Jewish institution centred in Jerusalem (see *General Introduction*, §VII). The use here of Ἱερουσαλήμ is in keeping with the earlier mention of the holy city at 15.2b D05. It is specifically from the church that continues to be associated with the Jewish religious institution that the people come insisting on circumcision, and to that church that Paul and Barnabas go. See *The Message of Acts*, II, pp.

118–19 on 8.1b, and p. 364 on 12.17b, for a fuller discussion of the presence of distinct communities in Jerusalem.

παρεδέχθησαν B ℵ 𝔓⁴⁵ᵛⁱᵈ·⁷⁴ A Ψ 33ᵛⁱᵈ. 81. 326. 1175. 1837 *pc* | ἀπ- E H L P 049. 056. 1739 𝔐 | προσ- 927. 1270 | ὑπ- 36. 453 *pc* | ἀπεδέχθησαν μεγάλως C 6. 257. 383. 614. 1108. 1611. 1704. 1799. 2147. 2412, *excepti sunt mire* d syʰ** sa; Amb Cass ‖ παρεδόθησαν μέγως (παρεδέχθησαν μεγάλως Dᴮ) D*.— ἀπό (τῆς ἐκκλησίας) B C 36. 431. 453. 1175 *pc* ‖ ὑπό D ℵ 𝔓⁴⁵ᵛⁱᵈ·⁷⁴ A E H L P Ψ 049. 056. 33. 1739 𝔐.

In this one sentence there are several differences between B03 and D05: the verb παρεδέχθησαν or παρεδόθησαν; the presence of the adverb μέγως; and the preposition ἀπό or ὑπό. The D05 reading has its own coherence (*pace* Delebecque, *Les deux Actes*, p. 95, who believes it to be a copyist's error).

The verb read by B03, παραδέχομαι, meaning to 'receive, welcome', is not common in the New Testament, and when it is used elsewhere the object is always a thing, not a person (cf. Mk 4.20; Acts 16.21; 22.18; 1 Tim. 5.19), except for Heb. 12.6 (citing Prov. 3.12) and here at 15.4 B03. When it is a question of receiving persons, Luke always uses the alternative ἀποδέχομαι, a verb only used by him in the New Testament (Lk. × 2; Acts × 5 + 1 D05), except at Acts 2.41 ℵ01/B03 (οἱ … ἀποδεξάμενοι τὸν λόγον αὐτοῦ; D05: οἱ … πιστεύσαντες τὸν λόγον αὐτοῦ). The aorist passive of παραδίδωμι read by D05* means that the brethren from Antioch were 'handed over' to the church in Ierousalem, in a negative sense (cf. Lk. 9.44; 18.32; 21.16; 22.22; 24.7; Acts 28.17) rather than a positive one (cf. Lk. 4.6; 10.22; Acts 14.26; 15.40), so that they were placed under its authority – which is consistent with the purpose of the visit to Ierousalem according to 15.2b D05, namely that those who were not insisting on circumcision should be judged by the apostles and the elders there.

For this understanding, ὑπό is the proper preposition, indicating 'under' the authority of the Ierousalem church. With the verb παρεδέχθησαν, ὑπό has the alternative sense of 'by', introducing the agent of the passive verb, a sense that is conveyed by ἀπό in B03. As the preposition introducing the agent of a passive verb, ἀπό represents a later development that Luke does not generally adopt (see Read-Heimerdinger, *The Bezan Text*, pp. 184–87). It is irrelevant to compare it with the Semitic construction (cf. Metzger, *Commentary*, p. 378), since the change from ὑπό to ἀπό following passive verbs was taking place in Hellenistic Greek outside the biblical texts, until ὑπό ceased to be used altogether to introduce the agent.

The reading μέγως in D05* is not a contraction of μεγάλως, but is an adverb formed from the root of an 'old noun (μέγη) μέγα = *greatness*' (Moulton and Howard, II, p. 160). The adjectival form from the same noun (μέγας, μέγα, μέγαν) is found at Jn. 21.11 D05* (μέγων).

ἀνήγγειλάν τε (– ℵ* | δὲ 614. 2412) B 𝔓⁷⁴ ℵ² A C E H L P Ψ 049. 056. 33. 1739 𝔐 ‖ ἀπ<α>γγείλαντες D* 𝔓⁴⁵ᵛⁱᵈ vg | ἀπήγγειλάν τε Dˢ·ᵐ· 323, *renuntiaverunt* d.— (ὅσα) ὁ θεὸς ἐποίησεν μετ' αὐτῶν B 𝔓⁷⁴ ℵ A C E H L P Ψ 049. 056. 33. 945. 1739 𝔐 vg ‖ ἐπ. ὁ θ. μ. αὐ. D, *fecit deus cum illis* d 𝔓⁴⁵ 614. 618. 2147. 2412 gig | ἐπ. μ. αὐ. ὁ θ. 81. 323.

B03 reads the finite form of the verb ἀναγγέλω (cf. 14.27), linked with the connective τε, to create a clause that is distinct from the previous one describing the reception of the travellers from Antioch by the church in Ierousalem. D05, in contrast, has the verb ἀπαγγέλλω (cf. 4.23; 11.2 D05) in the form of a participle, which is dependent on the main clause describing the handing over of the travellers from Antioch to the church in Ierousalem.

The variant of the final clause concerns the place of the verb ἐποίησεν in relation to the subject ὁ θεός. In both B03 and D05, the word order is the reverse of what each text reads at 14.27 (see *Critical Apparatus, ad loc.*). This time, it is D05 that juxtaposes ὁ θεός and μετ' αὐτῶν, underlining thereby the aspect of collaboration. The placing of ὁ θεός before the verb in B03 underlines, in comparison, the role of God.

15.5 ἐξανέστησαν δέ B 𝔓⁴⁵ᵛⁱᵈ·⁷⁴ ℵ *rell* ‖ οἱ δὲ παραγγείλαντες αὐτοῖς ἀναβαίνειν πρὸς τοὺς πρεσβυτέρους ἐξαν. D, *qui autem praeceperunt eis ascendere ad presbyteros surrexerunt* d (syʰᵐᵍ).— τινὲς τῶν (– τῶν 𝔓⁴⁵ 1646) ἀπὸ τῆς αἱρέσεως τῶν Φαρισαίων πεπιστευκότες λέγοντες B 𝔓⁷⁴ ℵ *rell* ‖ λέγοντές τινες ἀπὸ τ. αἱρ. τ. Φ. πεπ. D 𝔓⁴⁵ᵛⁱᵈ (syʰᵐᵍ).

The variants here concern the identity of those in Ierousalem who insist on circumcision for the Gentiles. B03 introduces them without further ado as 'some people from among the party of the Pharisees who had believed', that is some of the Pharisees who were Jesus-believers. D05 begins by identifying them as the people who had gone to Antioch; and adds the further description in an emphatic position, after the participle λέγοντες. The description differs slightly from the B03 text: they are 'certain people from the party of the Pharisees who had believed'. The genitive article τῶν in B03 has the effect of underlining their identity as Pharisees, an emphasis that is expressed more forcefully through the word order in D05.

(παραγγέλλειν) τε B ℵ *rell*, *(praecipiendum)que* d ‖ δέ D.

The particle δέ in D05 is a marker of intensity (B-D-R, §557.1c; cf. 14.23 *Critical Apparatus*), stronger than τε though even this confers importance on the second of the two infinitives.

15.6 (συνήχθησάν) τε B 𝔓⁴⁵·⁷⁴ C Ψ 33. 81. 1175. 1505. 2344. 2495 *pc* vg ‖ δέ D, *autem* d ℵ A E H L P 049. 056. 1739 𝔐 gig vgᴵᴹ sy | *om.* 0173. 326.— (οἱ ἀπόστολοι καὶ) οἱ πρεσβύτεροι B 𝔓⁴⁵·⁷⁴ ℵ *rell* ‖ πρεσβ. D.

The use of τε in the B03 text to connect the assembling of the apostles and elders to the Pharisees' protest ties the meeting closely to the Pharisees' intervention, as a response to it. δέ in D05 and ℵ01 presents the assembly of the apostles and elders as a new development (cf. Levinsohn, *Textual Connections*, pp. 135–36).

B03 distinguishes at this point between the apostles and the elders, with the repetition of the article, as elsewhere in the sequence (cf. 15.4, 22, 23). D05 considers the apostles and elders to form a single unit (as at 15.2b and 16.4). The reason for the alternative presentations is discussed in the *Commentary, ad loc.*).

15.7 (πολλῆς δὲ) ζητήσεως B 𝔓⁴⁵·⁷⁴ ℵ A Ψ 33. 81. 945. 1175. 1646. 1739. 1837. 1891. 2344 ‖ συν- D, *altercatio* d C E H L P 049. 056. 614 𝔐 l vg.

With the prefix συν-, the noun has the sense of an argument more than a simple discussion (συνζητέω, Lk. 22.23; 24.15; συνζήτησις, Acts 28.29).

ἀναστὰς Πέτρος B 𝔓⁷⁴ ℵ Dᴴ *rell* ‖ ἀνέστησεν ἐν πνεύματι Π. D*, *surrexit in spiritu Petrus* d l | ἀναστὰς Π. ἐν πν. ἁγίῳ 257. 614. 1799. 2412 syʰᵐᵍ; (Tert Ephr) Cass.— καὶ (εἶπεν) D*, *et* d l ‖ *om.* B 𝔓⁷⁴ ℵ *rell*.

The presence and action of Peter at this stage in the narrative are treated in the B03 text as not unusual. The participle ἀναστάς preceding a verb of speaking is a common way of introducing an important speech in Acts (cf. 1.15; 13.16; 15.13 D05; with aor. part. σταθείς: 2.14; 17.22). Attention is drawn in D05, however, to both his presence and his action, first with the finite verb rather than the particcple, and secondly, with the expression ἐν πνεύματι, unique in Acts (see Read-Heimerdinger, *The Bezan Text*, p. 160) and, indeed, in the New Testament. The meaning of it is discussed in the *Commentary*.

(ἀρχαίων) ἐν ὑμῖν ἐξελέξατο ὁ θεός B 𝔓⁷⁴ ℵ A C 0294. 33. 36. 81. 88. 181. 436. 630. 927. 945. 1175. 1270. 1739. 1891 *al* ar (bo; Irˡᵃᵗ) CAp Chr | ἐν ἡμῖν ἐξ. ὁ θ. Ψ 326. 629. 1837. 2344 l vgʷʷ; (Rebapt) | ἐν ἡμῖν ὁ θ. ἐξ. Dᴬ, *in nobis deus elegit* d 323. 614. 1611. 2147. 2412 *pc* gig | ὁ θ. ἐν ὑμῖν ἐξ. 226. 440. 547. 618 | ὁ θ. ἐν ἡμῖν ἐξ. E H L P 049. 056. 0142 𝔐 (lat) syʰ ‖ ἡμῖν ὁ θ. ἐξ. D* 614. 2412. (056. 0142) | ὁ θ. ἐξ. 69. 189. 2492 *pc* vgˢᵁ syᵖ sa aeth.— διὰ τοῦ (στόματος) B 𝔓⁷⁴ ℵ Dᶜ *rell* ‖ διά D* E 69*. 618.

According to B03, Peter refers to God choosing him among the apostles and the other early disciples, ὑμῖν, to speak to the Gentiles. In D05, reading ἡμῖν, he refers to a decision made for Israel, for the Jewish people, by God in the days of old, a reference to the beginning of the history of Israel (ἀπό with the aorist ἐξελέξατο has the sense 'as from, as early as'). B03, not at ease with this reference to the Jews, would have updated Peter's claim to apply it to the more recent history of the disciples.

The absence of article before στόματος in D05 causes the phrase to be a fixed expression (cf. LXX: Deut. 8.3; 3 Kgdms 17.1; 2 Chron. 35.22; 36.21,

22; Ps. 49.16; Prov. 27.21) and lessens the particular force of it, so that Peter becomes a tool rather than important in his own right.

15.8 καὶ ὁ καρδιογνώστης θεός B 𝔓⁷⁴ ℵ *rell* ‖ ὁ δὲ καρ. ὁ θ. D, *qui autem corda novit deus* d.

In B03, the reference to ὁ καρδιογνώστης θεός picks up the earlier reference to God in the opening statement of Peter's speech (15.7), with this new sentence adding further information (καί) about God's plan for the Gentiles. The connective δέ in D05 treats the new sentence as a development, building on the previous one, according to Luke's habitual use of δέ: this can be explained by the fact that D05, unlike B03 (see above), presents the choice of Peter as a decision that formed part of God's plan in an earlier time; the time of his witnessing to the Gentiles, in contrast, is the present time, so that the two parts of his plan are distinct. The word order of D05 confers emphasis on ὁ καρδιογνώστης, treating it as a noun.

(δοὺς) αὐτοῖς C E 0294. 1739 𝔐 l vg syʰ sa boᵐˢˢ aeth; Irˡᵃᵗ Rebapt Amb ‖ ἐπ' αὐτούς D, *super eos* d (ˢ Ψ) ‖ *om.* B 𝔓⁴⁵ᵛⁱᵈ·⁷⁴ ℵ A 33. 81. 1175. 2344 *pc.*

The omission of the pronoun in B03 can be accounted for by the fact that the previous pronoun αὐτοῖς can also be understood as serving the second verb, the participle δούς, and thereby paralleling the following first person pronoun ἡμῖν. D05 prefers the prepositional phrase in place of the dative, to express the idea of movement of the Spirit upon the people rather than a simple gift of God to them.

(ἡμῶν) τε καὶ αὐτῶν B 𝔓⁷⁴ ℵ *rell* ‖ καὶ αὐ. D, *et ipsos* d.

τε in B03 distinguishes more sharply between the two sides than καί on its own.

15.11 (τοῦ κυρίου ᾿Ιησοῦ) Χριστοῦ D C Ψ (+ ἡμῶν 33). 36. 69. 453. 467. 522. 876. 945. 1175. 1739. 1765. 1891. 2298 *pc* it syᵖ boᵖᵗ aeth; Irˡᵃᵗ Aug Theoph ‖ *om.* B 𝔓⁷⁴ ℵ A E 𝔐 vgˢᵗ syʰ sa boᵖᵗ.— πιστεύομεν B 𝔓⁷⁴ Dˢ·ᵐ· *rell, credimus* d ‖ -σομεν D* ℵ.

It is typical of D05 to include the full title of Jesus in statements of a formal nature, such as is appropriate to the solemn purpose of the meeting (cf. 1.22 D05, see *The Message of Acts*, I, p. 129). In other circumstances, D05 is content to use the name alone or a short title (see Read-Heimerdinger, *The Bezan Text*, pp. 272–74).

The future of D05* and ℵ01 marks the beginning of a duration, referring to the change in attitude that Peter and his companions underwent following what they saw in Cornelius' house in Caesarea, and that Peter insists they will maintain, despite the attempt of others to impose the Law.

15.12 ἐσίγησεν δέ Β 𝔓⁷⁴ ℵ *rell* it vg (syᵖ) saᵐˢˢ bo aeth; (Bas) CAp Hes (Thret) Hier ‖ συγκατατεθεμένων δὲ τῶν πρεσβυτέρων τοῖς ὑπὸ τοῦ Πέτρου εἰρημένοις ἐσίγ. D, *desponentes autem presbyteros quae a Petro dicebantur silevitque* d (l) syʰ**; Ephr.

N-A²⁷ gives in error the present participle συγκατατιθεμένων as the reading of D05, in place of the perfect participle ΣΥΝΚΑΤΑΤΕΘΕΜΕΝΩΝ. In this participial clause, D05 indicates the agreement of the elders with Peter's speech.

(ἤκουον) Βαρναβᾶ καὶ Παύλου ἐξηγουμένων Β 𝔓⁷⁴ ℵ Dᴴ *rell* ‖ Βαρναβᾶν κ. Παῦλον ἐξηγούμενοι (*sic*) D*, *Barnabam et Paulum exponentes* d.

The accusative of D05*, followed by the surprising nominative of the present participle, may indicate that the gathering heard Barnabas and Paul speaking without, however, really listening to what they were saying.

15.13 ἀπεκρίθη Ἰάκωβος λέγων Β 𝔓⁷⁴ ℵ *rell* ‖ ἀναστὰς Ἰ. εἶπεν D, *surgens Iacobus dixit* d syᵖ.

The variant readings in each verse of James' speech contribute to the overall sense and should not be taken in isolation. B03 presents James as responding to what Peter had said, understanding his reference to 'Simeon' to be Simon Peter. D05, on the other hand, has him get up to speak, as Peter had done before him, but not in answer to anyone, because his reference to Simeon is not to Simon Peter but to Simeon the Just. See *Commentary* for further development of this interpretation, and see also the next variant.

15.15 (καὶ) τούτῳ Β 𝔓⁷⁴ ℵ Dᶜ *rell* ‖ οὕτως D, *sic* d gig sa; Irˡᵃᵗ.— συμφωνοῦσιν Β 𝔓⁷⁴ ℵ Dᶜ *rell*, *consonat* d ‖ -νήσουσιν D*.

The differences here arise from the alternative interpretations of James's reference to Simeon (see above). In line with B03's understanding that he is talking about what Peter has just said concerning the events in Caesarea (τούτῳ), James cites the Prophets as agreeing with (συμφωνοῦσιν, present) Peter's account of the election of the Gentiles. However, in D05, James has summarized the interpretation of the Torah given by Simeon the Just and goes on to cite what Simeon said about the Prophets, that they will (οὕτως συμφωνήνουσιν, future) concord with its teaching.

15.16 μετὰ ταῦτα Β 𝔓⁷⁴ ℵ Dˢ·ᵐ· *rell* ‖ μ. δὲ ταῦ. D*, *post haec autem* d 1874.— ἀναστρέψω Β 𝔓⁷⁴ ℵ *rell* ‖ ἐπι- D, *convertar* d vgᵐˢ.

δέ of D05 expresses the notion that the Prophets build on the teachings of the Torah, not just repeat them. The D05 verb follows Jer. 12.15 LXX.

(τὰ) κατεστραμμένα (-εμμένα Β) ℵ Ψ 33. 326. 1837 *pc;* (Eus) ‖ ἀνεσκαμ- Ε 547 ‖ κατεσκαμ- D 𝔓⁷⁴ A C L P 049. 056. 1739 𝔐.

The same *vl* is found in Amos 9.11 LXX: κατεστραμμένα Α^c Q*, κατεσκαμ-
B Q^a. Both are perfect participles. The former verb, καταστρέφω, has the sense
of destroy a city (Bailly, 1) while the latter, κατασκάπτω, has the same
meaning, though with greater intensity (Bailly, 2 'saper, miner, *d'où* détruire
de fond en comble').

15.17 (τὸν) κύριον B 𝔓⁷⁴ ℵ *rell* ‖ θεόν D, *deum* d b c vg^Θ; Rebapt.

Most MSS of Amos 9.12 LXX continue from ἀνθρώπων to καὶ πάντα
directly; but B03 follows A02, where τὸν κύριον is a reference to YHWH,
which D05 never uses from the point of view of Gentiles (see Read-
Heimerdinger, *The Bezan Text*, p. 286).

ποιῶν (ταῦτα) B 𝔓⁷⁴ ℵ* Ψ *pc*, *faciens* d ‖ ὁ ποιῶν ℵ² A C D^H E H L P 049.
056. 33. 1739 𝔐 sy^h; Eus ‖ ποιήσει D*.

B03 continues the citation from Amos 9.12. The D05 reading (described
as a 'leçon impossible' by Delebecque [*Les deux Actes*, p. 96]), may be understood as an emphatic declaration by James, prefacing his final citation from
the Prophets in the D05 text. It is unlikely to have arisen through homoioteleuton, whereby the relative pronoun was omitted because it resembled the
end of the previous word (ΚΥΡΙΟΣΟΣ), since the divine title is abbreviated in
D05 to ΚΣ.

15.17/18 ταῦτα γνωστὰ ἀπ' αἰῶνος B ℵ C Ψ 33. 81. 323. 630. 1175. 1505.
2344 *al* co; Didasc Eus ǀ τ. πάντα γν. ἀπ' αἰ. 36. 307. 453. 610. 1678. 1739.
1891 ǀ τ. πάντα ἅ ἐστιν γνωστὰ αὐτῷ ἀπ' αἰ. 945 *pc* (aeth) ‖ ταῦτα· γνωστὸν
ἀπ' αἰ. ἐστιν (– 𝔓⁷⁴ A) τῷ κυρίῳ τὸ ἔργον αὐτοῦ D 𝔓⁷⁴ A lat (sy^{hmg}; Ir^{lat}) ǀ
ταῦτα (+ πάντα H 056 𝔐 sy^h, ᵞE L P 049)· γνωστὰ ἀπ' αἰῶνός ἐστι τῷ θεῷ
πάντα τὰ ἔργα αὐτοῦ E H L P 049. 056. 0142. 614 𝔐 (gig) sy^{(p).h}; CAp Chr.

Where B03 concludes the exposition of James' speech with a participial
phrase (see above) summarizing the plan of God (ταῦτα) as 'known from long
ago', D05 first of all attaches ταῦτα to an independent statement (see above),
and has an additional concluding sentence. In either case, there may be an
allusion to Isa. 45.21. The significance of the variant is evaluated in the *Commentary*.

15.20 (τῆς πορνείας) καὶ πνικτοῦ B 𝔓⁷⁴ A Ψ 33. 81 *pc*; Didasc CAp (PsCl) ǀ κ.
τοῦ πν. ℵ 𝔓⁴⁵ C E H L P 049. 056. 1739 𝔐 lat sy^{p.h} sa (bo) aeth; Or^{lat.pt} Chr ‖
om. D d gig; Ir^{1739mg.lat} Tert Aug Ambst Ephr.

D05, with a range of patristic support, does not include the requirement for
abstention from πνικτός. It is similarly absent in D05 from the letter setting out
James' judgement (15.29), and from James' speech to Paul (21.25). The
meaning of the term and the reason for its absence in D05 is examined in the
Commentary.

(αἵματος), καὶ ὅσα μὴ θέλουσιν ἑαυτοῖς γίνεσθαι ἑτέροις μὴ ποιεῖτε (-εῖν ar Ir) D, *et quae volunt non fieri sibi, aliis ne faciatis* d ar (sa aeth); Arist Ir[1739mg.lat] (*itaq\<ue\> quod tibi fieri ab aliis non vis, tu alio ne feceris* Didasc[fgVer lat*]) Eus[1739mg] (Ephr[comm]) | (πορνείας), κ. ὅσα ἂν μὴ θέλωσιν αὐτοῖς γίν. ἑτ. μὴ ποιεῖν 323. 440. (ˢ945. 1739). 1891 *pc* ‖ *om.* B 𝔓[45.74] א *rell* lat sy[p.h] bo; Or[lat.pt] CAp Chr.

The form of the so-called 'Golden Rule' is not an invention of the scribe of D05 who thought to create a negative form of the teaching of Jesus (cf. Mt. 7.12; Lk. 6.31). On the contrary, it is a saying well-attested in Jewish writings, where it is cited as the answer of Hillel in response to the request from a Gentile to teach him the Law quickly: 'Do nothing to your neighbour that you would hate to have done to you! This is the entire Torah; all the rest is merely interpretation' (Sab. 31a, noted by G. Vermes, in Schürer, *The History of the Jewish People*, p. 467). Other Jewish writings testify to the saying: e.g., Tob. 4.15; Ep. Arist. 207; Philo, *Hypothetica* I, Eusebius, *Praeparatio Evangelica* 8.7.6; T. Naph. [Heb.] 1.6; Targ. Y. I Lev. 19.18 (cf. Strack and Billerbeck, *Kommentar*, I, p. 460). Further attestation is found in *The Teaching of the Two Ways*, which forms the basis of the *Didache* (*Did.* 1.2); *Agraphon* 37, in A. Resch, *Agrapha. Aussercanonische Schriftfragmente*, pp. 60–61; Clement of Alexandria, *Stromata*, 2.23: 139.2.

The sentence is repeated in the letter written to Antioch according to D05 (cf. 15.29 below), with similar support.

(κατὰ πολιν) ἔχει D ‖ *om.* B 𝔓[45.74] א *rell.*— ἔχει (ἐν ταῖς συναγωγαῖς) D* (ἔ\<χει\> D[p.m]) B *rell* ‖ *om.* D[s.m].

B03 reads ἔχει once, whereas D05 repeats the verb, in order to clarify that where Moses has people proclaiming him in every city is precisely in the synagogues (Scrivener explains: 'l. 2 *init.* ε *eras. s. m.: literae ferè tres* [χει?] *deperditae inter* ε *et* εν', p. 444).

15.22 (τότε) ἔδοξε B 𝔓[74] א D[s.m.] *rell* ‖ ἐδόξασεν D*.

D05* has the archaic form of the aorist.

τῷ (Παύλῳ) B 𝔓[74] א A E Ψ 81. 1175. 1270. 1739. 1891 (+ τῷ Βαρναβᾷ 33. 614. 945. 1611. 1837. 1891. 2147. 2344. 2412) ‖ *om.* D H L P 049. 056 𝔐.

With the article before Paul but not Barnabas, B03 views them as a unit; the same is true of D05 where there is no article. The article has the function of treating the information as expected (everyone knew them, and that they would go back to Antioch), and thus causes the focus of the sentence to be the new information, that is, that chosen men would go with them. The absence of the article in D05 causes all the information to be viewed as new – that the church had decided to send chosen men, together with Paul and Barnabas, to take a letter to Antioch. At 15.25, the article is omitted before the names of Barnabas and Paul, in that order.

(τὸν καλούμενον) Βαρσαββᾶν B 𝔓⁷⁴ ℵ *rell* ‖ Βαραββᾶν D, *Barabbas* d.

D05 reads the name of the criminal released in place of Jesus ('the son of the father'), as mentioned at Lk. 23.18; B03 has the same name as given (not D05) to Joseph ('the son of the Sabbath'), one of the candidates put forward to replace Judas (cf. 1.23 AT).

15.23 (γράψαντες) διὰ χειρὸς αὐτῶν B 𝔓³³ᵛⁱᵈ·⁴⁵ᵛⁱᵈ·⁷⁴ ℵ* A 629 *pc* l vg bo aethᵖᵗ ǀ δ. χει. αὐ. τάδε ℵ² E P 049. 056. 0142. (χειρῶν 33). 1739 𝔐 syᵖ·ʰ; CAp Chr ǀ δ. χει. αὐ. ταῦτα 1505. 2495 ‖ ἐπιστολὴν δ. χει. αὐ. περιέχουσαν τάδε D, *epistulam per manus suas continentem haec* d ǀ δ. χει. αὐ. ἐπιστ. περ. τάδε C ar c gig w vgᵐˢ (– περ. sa) aethᵖᵗ ǀ δ. χει. αὐ. ἐπιστ. καὶ πέμψαντες περ. τάδε 614. 2147. 2412 *pc* syʰᵐᵍ ǀ ἐπιστ. δ. χει. αὐ. ἔχουσαν τὸν τύπον τούτου Ψ.

The reading of B03 is clear as it stands, yet many manuscripts have a sentence that is more complete in one way or another. The D05 reading confers greater importance on the formulation of the verdict in a letter, which is appropriate enough in the context. It also introduces the ambiguity that the letter was actually written by Judas and Silas ('through their hand'), rather than simply delivered by them. The possibility of confusion in B03 is reduced by the omission of the word 'letter', and may explain why it dropped out.

ἀδελφοῖς τοῖς ἐξ ἐθνῶν (χαίρειν) B 𝔓⁷⁴ ℵ *rell* ‖ τ. ἐξ ἐθ. ἀδ. D, *qui sunt ex gentibus fratribus* d.

The word order of B03 is neutral, whereas D05 emphasizes the Gentile origin of the addressees of the letter, to distinguish them from the Jewish Jesus-believers (*pace* Boismard and Lamouille, II, p. 106, according to whom, 'L'archétype de D omettait l'expression τοις εξ εθνοις [*sic!*]; le scribe de D l'a réinsérée à une mauvaise place').

15.24 (ἐξ ἡμῶν) ἐξελθόντες D, *exeuntes* d 𝔓³³·⁷⁴ ℵ² A C E H (L) P Ψ 049. 056. 33. 1739 𝔐 latt syᵖ·ʰ (sa) bo aeth; Irˡᵃᵗ Orˡᵃᵗ Socr Pac ‖ *om.* B ℵ* 88. 915. 1175; CAp Amph Chr Ps-Vig.— ἐτάραξαν (ἡμᾶς) B 𝔓⁷⁴ ℵ Dˢ·ᵐ· *rell* ‖ ἐξετάρ- D*, *perturbaverunt* d.

D05 provides the detail that the trouble-makers were not just from the Ierousalem church (or even the leadership, if ἡμῶν is to be taken in the narrow sense of the authors of the letter), but that they had 'gone out' from them, so underlining their membership of the church. B03 describes them as having 'troubled' the Gentiles in Antioch, whereas D05, with the compound of the verb, has the stronger 'disturbed, upset'.

15.25 (ἡμῖν) ἐκλεξαμένοις B 𝔓⁴⁵ᵛⁱᵈ A L Ψ 33. 1739 𝔐ᵖᵗ latt (syᵖ) ‖ -μένους (ἄνδρας) D, *electos* d ℵ C E H P 049. 056 𝔐ᵖᵗ syʰ; Irˡᵃᵗ CAp Amph Chr Socr.

B03 reads the dative participle, agreeing with ἡμῖν. D05 has the participle in the accusative, referring to the subject of the infinitive πέμψαι, as at 15.22.

15.26 (ἀνθρώποις) παραδεδωκόσι τὰς ψυχὰς αὐτῶν B 𝔓⁷⁴ ℵ *rell* ‖ -δώκασιν τὴν ψυχὴν αὐ. D, *qui tradiderunt animam suam* d bo^mss; Ir^lat.— (Χριστοῦ) εἰς πάντα πειρασμόν D E, *in omni temptationi* d 257. 383. 614. 1799. 2147. 2412 e l sy^hmg ‖ *om.* B 𝔓⁷⁴ ℵ *rell.*

B03 reads the perfect participle, agreeing with ἀνθρώποις. D05 reads the perfect indicative which should be preceded by a relative pronoun (*qui tradiderunt* d); alternatively, the D05 reading is a copyist's mistake (α > ο). The singular of D05, 'who gave up *their life*', links the two participants closely together. The reading εἰς πάντα πειρασμόν (cf. Lk. 4.13) may be an allusion to the threat of being killed (cf. 20.19; 21.31), but the wider sense of the word ψυχή, which refers not only to physical life but to one's whole being, suggests a willingness to forgo one's own interests and plans (cf. Jesus who 'lays down his life' as the good shepherd, Jn. 10.11,15). In that sense, it allows the overall comment in D05, παραδεδώκασιν τὴν ψυχὴν αὐτῶν εἰς πάντα πειρασμόν, to be taken as a reference to the readiness of Paul and Barnabas to be placed under the authority of the Ierousalem church and to be judged by the leaders there, and thus confirms the *lectio difficilior* of 15.4 D05 (cf. 21.31).

15.27 ἀπαγγέλλοντας τὰ αὐτά B 𝔓⁷⁴ᵛⁱᵈ ℵ A C Dᴮ E H P L 049. 056. 33. 1739 𝔐 ‖ -γελοῦντας ταῦτα D*, *haec* d 𝔓³³ Ψ 88. 181. 257. 467. 614. 913. 915. 1108. 1175. 1611. 1646. 1799. 1898. 2412 *pc* sy^p.h sa aeth; Didasc Chr.

B03 reads the present participle where D05 uses the future; both have a final sense (cf. Zerwick, *Biblical Greek*, §284: 'The question may be raised, whether the present participle may not at times stand for the future one indicating the end in view'). The same variant occurs at 17.15.

The pronoun in B03 refers to the 'same things', that is, Judas and Silas are to explain orally what is written in the letter overall. In D05, the demonstrative pronoun is used, anticipating the decision regarding the Gentiles that follows.

15.28 (ἔδοξεν γὰρ) τῷ πνεύματι τῷ ἁγίῳ B 𝔓³³·⁷⁴ ℵ A Ψ 33. 81. 927. 1270. 1837. 2344 ‖ τῷ ἁγ. πν. D, *sancto spiritui* d C E H P L 049. 056. 1739 𝔐 e gig l; Ir^lat Or Cyp Cyr Hes^lat.

Luke varies the word order of the phrase for the Holy Spirit according to the context (see Read-Heimerdinger, *The Bezan Text*, pp. 151–72 for an exhaustive analysis of the phrase in Luke's writings). The B03 expression is usually found in the context of a new explanation or instruction (cf. 13.2; 15.8); it may be the formal setting of the letter, whose purpose is to communicate information, that is behind the choice of wording. The D05 phrase, on the other hand, is reserved for situations where the Spirit communicates with, or relates to, Christian believers, in an intimate way (cf. 1.8; 15.29 D05; 16.6), as is appropriate here.

(μηδὲν) πλέον B 𝔓³³·⁷⁴ ℵ *rell* ‖ πλεῖον D Ψ 945. 1739. 1891.

Both forms are found in Hellenistic Greek as the comparative neuter of πολύς (B-A-G, πολύς, II).

(πλὴν) τούτων τῶν ἐπάναγκες B 𝔓³³ᵛⁱᵈ ℵ² C Dᴮ? H Ψ 049. 69. 81. 88. 104. 614. 945. 1175. 1270. 1505. 1739. 1854. 1891. 2412. 2492 *al, haec quae necesse est* d; Irˡᵃᵗ ‖ τῶν ἐπάναγκες (ἐξαν- 𝔓⁷⁴) A 36. 453. 1241. 1611 *pc*; Cl ‖ τῶν ἐπάναγκες τούτων E L P 056 𝔐 ‖ τούτων· ἐπάναγκές <ἐστιν> D* ℵ* 33. 1837. 2344 *pc*.

As the text stands in B03, the neuter adjective ἐπάναγκες is being used as an adverb with a plural article which, while theoretically not impossible, is a construction not found with this adverb elsewhere; if the article is intentional, ἐπάναγκες has to be understood as standing for a general noun, and the infinitive ἀπέχεσθαι that follows has the force of an imperative. Alternatively, it is possible that the article in B03 is the result of dittography, in which case the text should be punctuated in such a way that ἐπάναγκες begins a new sentence, listing the contents of τούτων (as in D05 and ℵ01); cf. Delebecque (*Les deux Actes*, p. 97): 'le texte court [B03] semble fautif en écrivant τῶν, par dittographie, après τούτων, qui doit être suivi d'un point en haut'.

The absence of the article in D05 is viewed by Metzger (*Commentary*, p. 386) as a possible instance of haplography. Such a view ignores the sense that is given by the D05 reading as it stands, where the equivalent of a colon follows τούτων, and a new sentence begins with ἐπάναγκες (the verb ἐστιν is implicit), followed by the infinitive (cf. Bailly, ἐπάναγκες). In this way, D05 distinguishes between the decision of the Holy Spirit (μηδὲν ... βάρος) and that taken by the assembly (πλὴν τούτων· ἐπάναγκές <ἐστιν> ἀπέχεσθαι...).

15.29 (αἵματος) καὶ πνικτῶν B ℵ* A* C 81. 614. 1175. 1611. 2147. 2412 *pc* (co) aeth; Cl Orˡᵃᵗ ᵖᵗ CyrJᵐˢˢ Amphᵖᵗ Socr Gaud Hierᵖᵗ·ᵐˢˢ ᵃᶜᶜ· ᵗᵒ Cassian ‖ κ. -οῦ 𝔓⁷⁴ ℵ² A² E H L P Ψ 33. 1739 𝔐 (lat) syᵖ·ʰ; (Orˡᵃᵗ ᵖᵗ) CAp CyrJ Diod Amphᵖᵗ Did? Chr Sev Cyr Ambstᵐˢˢ ᵃᶜᶜ· ᵗᵒ Ps-Vig ‖ *om.* D d l aethᵖᵗ; Ir¹⁷³⁹ᵐᵍ·ˡᵃᵗ Tert Cyp Pac Hierᵖᵗ Ambst Aug.

The absence of καὶ πνικτῶν in D05, with some versional and a range of patristic support, has already been noted at 15.20 (see above), and the issue is examined in detail in the *Commentary* on that verse.

(πορνείας), καὶ ὅσα μὴ θέλετε ἑαυτοῖς γίνεσθαι (γέν- 614. 2412) ἑτέρῳ (-οις 323. 945. 1739. 1891 *al* syʰ** Ir) μὴ ποιεῖν (-εῖτε Dᴱ 614 *pc* ar q sa Ir Cyp) D*, *et quaecumque non vultis vobis fieri aliis ne feceritis* d 42. 51. 234. 242. 323. 429. 464. 614. 945. 1739. 1891. 2412 *pc* ar l p ph w vgᵐˢ syʰ** sa aeth; Ir¹⁷³⁹ᵐᵍ·ˡᵃᵗ Eus¹⁷³⁹ᵐᵍ Cyp ‖ *om.* B 𝔓³³·⁷⁴ ℵ *rell* c dem e gig p ph ro w vg syᵖ bo; Tert Cl Orˡᵃᵗ CAp CyrJ? Diod Amph Did? Chr Sev Socr Cyr Ambst Pac Gaud.

The sentence concluding the advice of the letter in D05 is similar to the judgement with which James concluded his speech (cf. 15.20 above).

ἐξ ὧν (διατηροῦντες) B 𝔓³³·⁷⁴ ℵ *rell* ‖ ἀφ' ὧν D, *a quibus* d 323. 614. 945. 1739. 1891. 2412 e vg; Ir^lat Tert.— (εὖ) πράξετε B 𝔓³³ ℵ A (E) P Ψ 049. 056. 33. 1739* 𝔐 d latt sa bo; Cl Or^lat CAp Did? Chr Socr Pac Ps-Vig ‖ -ξατε 𝔓⁷⁴ C L 2344 ar aeth; (Amph) ‖ -ξατε φερόμενοι ἐν τῷ ἁγίῳ πνεύματι D (*agitis ferentes in sancto spiritu* d) 1739^c (l); (Ir^{1739mg.lat}) Tert Cass Ephr.

The prepositional phrase ἐξ ὧν in B03 follows directly from the list of four types of activities to which the relative pronoun ὧν relates. When the verb διατηρέω is used in the LXX with the preposition ἐκ (cf. Prov. 21.23), the meaning is 'to keep out of trouble'. This sense is appropriate in referring to a list of wrong practices from which the Gentiles are being asked to refrain. In the D05 text, an injunction in the form of a traditional, general precept follows the list (see previous *vl*), and the relative pronoun ὧν thus refers to a more complex package than a list of wrongdoings. In this context, διατηρέω ἀπό has the sense of 'keep away from'.

B03 uses the indicative future of the verb πράσσω, D05 the aorist imperative.

Commentary

[a] 15.3 *The Journey from Antioch to Ierousalem*

15.3 The new sequence begins with a typically Lukan formula, μὲν οὖν, whereby he ties it to the previous agreement to send representatives from Antioch to Ierousalem (15.2b), and looks forward at the same time to their arrival at the church there (15.4a, introduced with the corresponding δέ).[15] In accordance with what was decided, or even ordered in the Bezan text, by the people who had come from Judaea, the travellers are given the necessary provisions for their journey[16] by their local church and are seen making their way, first through Phoenicia then Samaria, between which the Bezan text makes a clear distinction.

Although the principal travellers are Paul and Barnabas, other people from Antioch accompany them (cf. 15.2b); nothing is said of them throughout the whole sequence, but their constant presence in the background should be

---

15. μὲν οὖν is usually found at the beginning of a new sequence in Acts (see 13.4, *Critical Apparatus*), where οὖν is retrospective and μέν introduces the first of two events that are in accordance with what has gone before, while looking forward to the second one, introduced with δέ.

16. The verb προπέμπω can have the meaning of either 'escort' or 'give provisions' for a journey; cf. 20.38 where the sense is 'escort': προέπεμπον δὲ αὐτὸν εἰς [ἐπὶ D05] τὸ πλοῖον; but at Rom. 15.24; 1 Cor. 16.6, 11; 2 Cor. 1.16; Tit. 3.13, both senses are possible and, indeed, are not mutually exclusive. Either sense would be acceptable here, but the idea of the church equipping their representatives with what they need for their journey, which is being undertaken under duress, so to speak, is particularly fitting; this may include people going some of the way with them.

borne in mind.[17] The group takes advantage of their journey to meet with the communities of disciples along the way. Phoenicia was the coastal region, stretching from Syria in the north to Galilee in the south, with Samaria to the south-east en route to Jerusalem. It was already mentioned as one of the places visited by Hellenistic disciples, where they had only spoken to Jews about Jesus (cf. 11.19).[18] Samaria, likewise, has been mentioned as a region visited by the Hellenist disciples, and especially by Philip (8.1, 5, 9) and, subsequently, by Peter and John (8.14, 25). In view of the evangelization that had been carried out, it is evident that there were believers in these areas; though nothing has been said about any organized churches as such, it may well be that they had formed identifiable groups of Jesus-believers, but as far as can be deduced they were still considered, and considered themselves, to be part of Judaism.

At the time Samaria and Phoenicia were introduced into the narrative, the gospel had not yet been given to Gentiles, and it would seem from the comments made here that this was a new phenomenon for the believers with whom the Antioch representatives met. For indeed, Paul and Barnabas, and their companions, explained to them in detail what had been happening among the Gentiles, their 'conversion',[19] and in so doing 'caused great joy'. So, even if this reaction seems to indicate that there were as yet no Gentiles among them, they were nevertheless open and well-disposed to accept the mission to the Gentiles without any kind of opposition.

This account of the way Paul and Barnabas made use of the journey to Ierousalem to meet with the disciples along the way and pass on the news about the Gentiles mirrors that given in Codex Bezae – but not the Alexandrian text – about Peter's identical actions on his journey from Caesarea to Jerusalem, which for him meant Hierosoluma but which he was also visiting with the purpose of giving to the authorities an explanation of the conversion of the Gentiles (11.2 D05).[20]

[b] 15.4a *Arrival in Ierousalem*
15.4a The account of the arrival in Jerusalem of Paul and Barnabas is quite different in the two texts. The Alexandrian text speaks of Hierosoluma, a neutral designation without any sense of it being the centre of Jewish authority (see *General Introduction*, §VII). Codex Bezae, in contrast, gives the name as

---

17. Paul (Gal. 2.1) mentions taking the Gentile disciple Titus with him, along with Barnabas, to Jerusalem on one occasion when he discussed the question of circumcision with the leaders there. Whether Paul is referring to the same visit as the one narrated in Acts 15 is a matter that is too complex to be discussed here.

18. Acts 11.19 is discussed in *The Message of Acts*, II, pp. 306–307.

19. This is the only use of the noun ἐπιστροφή in the New Testament, though Luke uses the cognate verb ἐπιστρέφειν in the sense of a spiritual conversion × 9 in Acts (3.19; 9.35; 11.21; 14.15; 15.19; 26.18, 20; 28.27), in addition to three uses with a more physical sense.

20. The Bezan reading of 11.2 is examined in detail in *The Message of Acts*, II, pp. 291–94.

Ierousalem, which tallies with the earlier references to the men who had come to Antioch – they had gone down from 'Judaea' (15.1), from 'Ierousalem' (15.2a D05); they were insisting on a view that was in line with Jewish teachings, and it was they who sent Paul and Barnabas to 'Ierousalem' (11.2b) to be judged there (D05). Everything speaks of a context that is thoroughly Jewish and it is in accordance with the nature of the problem that the matter should be examined within the setting of Jewish authority, such as Ierousalem represents in Luke's work according to Codex Bezae.

The Alexandrian text has the visitors received by 'the church, the apostles and the elders', that is, the community as a whole and in particular the two distinct teams of leaders (cf. 15.2b, *Commentary*). Having been welcomed, they go on to describe to the church what God has been doing in Antioch, with their collaboration.

In Codex Bezae, the situation is full of tension. The visitors from Antioch were handed over, by those who had ordered them to go up to Ierousalem (15.2b), and placed under the authority of the Ierousalem church, with its two groups of leaders. This handing over, moreover, was done with a certain degree of ceremony and display of power (μέγως). It is thus apparent that the 'mother church' continues to be regarded as the main authority, retaining power over believers from other church communities; as much was implied by the order that the Antioch brethren should be 'judged' by the Ierousalem leaders (15.2b D05). This view is, of course, in contradiction with the way the Holy Spirit had worked directly through the church in Antioch to appoint Barnabas and Paul (Saul) for the mission to the Gentiles, without any question whatsoever of the Ierousalem church ratifying the appointment (cf. 13.1-3). That does not mean that Luke (or the Bezan editor) was confused, or mixed up his sources, or did not notice the contradiction. It does mean that the narrator is quite deliberately underlining fundamental differences in the concept of the Church held by distinct groups of believers. Some are quite free from the belief in the traditional status of Ierousalem as the centre of religious authority, while others still operate within Jewish categories of thinking and view the apostles and elders of the Ierousalem church as having authority over the churches everywhere. It is precisely this difference of understanding that lies behind the argument over the Gentiles.

That Paul and Barnabas accepted being handed over to the Ierousalem church in this way is a demonstration of their willingness to forgo their religious freedom for the sake of the gospel. In order to preserve the essence of the teaching of Jesus for the Gentiles – that all are acceptable before God without circumcision and without taking on the Law (cf. 15.2a D05) – they are prepared to do what is necessary to explain to the Ierousalem church what they have witnessed God doing through their ministry. The notion of 'handing over (lit.) their life for the sake of our Lord Jesus Christ' comes up in the letter that emerges from this meeting (cf. 15.26),[21] and may be a recognition by the apostles and elders of the sacrifice Paul and Barnabas made in appearing before the Ierousalem church.

The terms used to describe how they reported what God had been doing are similar to those with which Luke relates how Paul and Barnabas had given an account of the conversion of the Gentiles when they arrived back in Antioch after the first phase of the missionary journey (14.27; cf. also 21.19).[22] From the reaction of the Pharisee believers that follows, it is apparent that they also spoke about the same topic in Ierousalem. Luke's silence about the exact content of their report here is significant, as if to indicate the degree of caution they were exercising in order not to provoke problems, or even through a lack of boldness.

In Codex Bezae, it is, in fact, even as they are speaking about what had been going on among the Gentiles that the people from Antioch are brought under the authority of the Ierousalem church.[23] It is precisely in this matter that they are not permitted to have a free say or speak openly. This connection explains the intervention of the Pharisee believers in the next sentence.

[c] 15.4b-5 *The Objections Raised by Pharisee Believers*

15.4b-5 What Paul and Barnabas were relating is quickly challenged by certain members of the Ierousalem church. They are described as being believers from the sect of the Pharisees. The Bezan text identifies them with those people who had caused the disquiet in Antioch; so far, it had been said only that they were from Judaea (15.1) or Ierousalem (15.2b), but they are now defined more exactly as members of the Pharisees. The word order of the Bezan text places heavy emphasis on their identity,[24] which is considerably less strong in the Alexandrian text (see *Critical Apparatus*). Luke has already indicated that there was support for the apostles from the Pharisee Gamaliel in the early days of the church (cf. 5.34-39, esp. D05),[25] but this is the first

---

21. The verb παραδίδωμι is used in Codex Bezae of the visitors of Antioch who are 'handed over' to the Ierousalem church, and in both texts of Barnabas and Paul who 'handed over their lives (life, D05) for the sake of the Lord Jesus Christ' at 15.26.

22. 14.27: παραγενόμενοι ... τὴν ἐκκλησίαν ἀνήγγελλον ὅσα ἐποίησεν ὁ θεὸς μετ' αὐτῶν (ἀνήγγειλον ὅσα ὁ θεὸς ἐποίησεν αὐτοῖς μετὰ τῶν ψυχῶν αὐτῶν, D05), cf. 15.4: παραγενόμενοι ... τῆς ἐκκλησίας ... ἀνήγγειλάν τε ὅσα ὁ θεὸς ἐποίησεν (ἀπαγγείλαντες ὅσα ἐποίησεν ὁ θεὸς D05) μετ' αὐτῶν.

23. The relationship between the main verb παρεδόθησαν in the aorist and the dependent participle ἀπαγγείλαντες in the present is seemingly one of reason – 'they were handed over because they were speaking out'. A relationship of attendant circumstances ('while they were speaking out') could be envisaged but hardly justifies the action of the main verb.

24. The emphasis is conferred by placing the description of the speakers after the introductory formula 'they reacted saying...'. The same device was noted at 1.15 when Peter got up to address the 120 in the upper room (see *The Message of Acts*, I, p.118); and will be observed again at 15.20 (see *Commentary, ad loc.*).

25. The role of Gamaliel in supporting the apostles is examined in *The Message of Acts*, I, pp. 345–55.

explicit mention of Pharisees who had become Jesus-believers. In Luke's Gospel, the Pharisees had represented fierce opposition to Jesus, not even accepting to be baptized by John (Lk. 7.29-30). Far from rejoicing at what Paul and Barnabas reported, as the people in Phoenicia and Samaria had done (cf. 15.3), they now oppose the practice that was being carried out in Antioch of not subjecting Gentile believers to circumcision and the Mosaic Law. As Pharisees, they have a special interest in the Torah and the detail of its interpretation.[26]

According to Codex Bezae, we now learn that it was specifically to the elders that these Pharisee believers had ordered Paul and Barnabas to go, in order to be judged in Ierousalem. That this emerges only now suggests that they had previously attempted to conceal who their supporters were but that it becomes clear once the party are in Ierousalem. In Antioch, the elders had been mentioned together as one body with the apostles; on the arrival of the people from Antioch in Ierousalem, they were distinguished as two separate bodies; and now the distinction between them is seen to be important, for it is the elders in particular who are concerned with the issue of the admission of the Gentiles. This information tallies with the impression gained from chapter 12, where the miraculous release of Peter, the leader of the apostles, from prison in Ierousalem (12.3-17) was seen to be a metaphor for his release from the traditional expectations and aspirations of Judaism. Though nothing was said specifically about the rest of the apostles, it may be surmised that he convinced them of his experience. In any case, already then a group of believers under the leadership of James was seen to exist as a distinct group (cf. 12.17), who did not share in the freedom enjoyed by those in the church who were praying for Peter's release (and were therefore presumably already free themselves; cf. 12.5, 12-17).[27] The role of James, it would now appear, is to head the elders – it is he who speaks on their behalf, just as Peter speaks on behalf of the apostles. His position will become clear when he makes his speech at the meeting that follows.

These are the two points that the Pharisee believers are concerned about. In Antioch, only the requirement for circumcision was noted by the Alexandrian text, though the Bezan text was insistent from the beginning on the two aspects of circumcision and following the Law of Moses (see *Commentary*, 15.1). Here, they present them as a divine command, with the impersonal verb δεῖ, 'it is necessary', which often translates the will of God (cf. 14.22). The intention lying behind these conditions to be imposed on the Gentiles who believe in Jesus needs to be clarified. At 15.1, it was expressed in terms of salvation: 'Unless you are circumcised and keep on walking by the tradition of Moses, you cannot be saved'. According to the Jewish understanding,

---

26. On the characteristics of the Pharisees as a group concerned with the strict observation of the Law, see Schürer, *History of the Jewish People*, II, §26, pp. 381–403.

27. Peter's escape from prison as a metaphor for his freedom from Jewish messianic expectations is analysed in depth in *The Message of Acts*, II, pp. 321–68.

expressed here by the Pharisees, being saved means belonging to Israel. When Gentiles accepted the word of God and believed in Jesus, they were considered to be entering Israel, to be taking part in something that was inherently Jewish. It is therefore quite natural that the conditions of entry should be discussed. The Pharisees want to maintain the requirements that were laid down in the Torah and that are a fundamental expression of what it means to be the People of God: the physical sign of circumcision, and the spiritual sign of adherence to the commandments of Moses, the Torah. Contrary to these ancient and essential defining features of Israel, others, notably Paul in Antioch, have been allowing Gentiles to enter Israel without accepting either of them. Where the apostles and the elders stand is about to become evident.

[d] 15.6 *The Meeting of the Apostles and the Elders*
15.6 The meeting of the leaders arises out of the opposition of some of the church to the Antioch brethren. The apostles and elders are treated as one group by most manuscripts, as at the first mention of them at 15.2b but in contrast to the distinction between them when they are presented in the context of Ierousalem (15.4, cf. 15.23). Codex Bezae, on the other hand, continues to regard them as distinct groups, which reflects the reality of the situation expressed in the Bezan detail that it was 'the elders' to whom the Pharisee believers had ordered Paul and Barnabas to go (cf. 15.4b D05).

Whether as two separate groups or a united body, they proceed to meet together to examine the question of the conditions for the entry of the Gentiles into the Church.[28] It is not clear if other members of the Ierousalem church were present at this meeting. At 15.12, mention is made of 'the multitude' (lit.; τὸ πλῆθος), but in the Bezan text in particular this could simply mean all those present at the meeting rather than the church as a whole. The church is indeed named as endorsing what the apostles and elders will decide (cf. 15.22), but this may well come after the meeting has taken place.

During the meeting, which takes up the second half of this sequence, the difference of opinion held by the apostles, on the one hand, and the elders, on the other, will become apparent. Peter will speak as the representative of the apostles, and James will pronounce a verdict as the representative of the elders (see *Overview*; *Structure and Themes*). Between their speeches, Barnabas and Paul will give their evidence. Once the disagreement between the two parties is identified, it is clear that this order of events represents a trial, albeit without the formality of a court of law.

[d'] 15.7-11 *Peter's Speech*
15.7a The meeting begins in an atmosphere of argument and questioning (ζήτησις [συν- D05]), the disagreement expressed more strongly in Codex Bezae where the prefix συν- of the Greek verb expresses the idea that they

---

28. Note the singular construction ἰδεῖν περί + genitive.

were discussing 'with each other', that is the apostles with the elders. The implication is that there were strongly held, opposing views. Finally, Peter prepares to put forward his view. The Alexandrian text brings him into the narrative at this point as if his presence were expected, using a typical formula to introduce a speaker (see *Critical Apparatus*).[29] He has, in fact, not been heard of since he 'went to another place' (12.17) after reporting to the church who were praying for him how the Lord had sent his angel to rescue him from prison, a narrator's comment that draws on a scriptural reference to the prophetic gesture of Ezekiel in leaving Ierousalem like an exile (Ezek. 12.3).[30] The metaphorical nature of that comment is apparent in the fact that he is now found in Ierousalem with the other apostles but, as his speech will demonstrate, he remains free of the Jewish Messianic expectations of a restored kingdom of Israel, which depended for their realization on the continuing privileges and supremacy of Israel under the rule of the Davidic Messiah. It was through his symbolic release from Herod's prison that he was freed from this traditional mentality.[31]

Codex Bezae brings Peter back into the narrative with a more dramatic introduction. First, the verb 'he stood up' has more force as a finite verb than the participle of the Alexandrian text; secondly, he is said to be 'in the Spirit'. This is a comment full of positive endorsement, which Luke uses, with considerable restraint, to express his approval and agreement with what is said (cf. Peter, 4.8; Stephen, 6.10 D05; Paul, 13.9). It is an indication that, according to Luke, the contents of the speech are in accordance with the teaching of Jesus. Peter's role at this point in acting as the mouthpiece of the Spirit for the other leaders is, indeed, in harmony with Jesus' commandment to him just before his death – Jesus warned him that Satan had asked to 'sift [the disciples] like wheat' but that he had prayed that Simon's faith 'would not fail' (Lk. 22.31-32a), and furthermore that when he 'turned again' he must 'strengthen the brethren', καὶ σύ ποτε ἐπιστρέψας στήρισον (σὺ δὲ ἐπίστρεψον καὶ στήριξον D05) τοὺς ἀδελφούς σου (22.32b). The realization of that prophetic commandment is noted only by Codex Bezae, at Acts 11.2 when Peter was on his way to tell 'the brethren in Judaea' (11.1) about what had happened in Caesarea. Through God's giving of the Holy Spirit to the Gentile Cornelius and his household without any prior action on their part, Peter had finally understood that the Gentiles were accepted by God in the same way as the Jews (cf. 10.47; 11.17); as he went to speak about this in Judaea, he 'strengthened the brethren' in the villages on the way, as he 'announced the grace of God'.[32]

29. The absence of the article before Peter's name in Greek arises because he has been 'offstage', so to speak, since his last appearance at 12.17 (Heimerdinger and Levinsohn, 'The Use of the Article', pp. 21–22).

30. See *The Message of Acts*, II, pp. 381–83 on the use Luke makes of the prophecies of Ezekiel in Acts 12.

31. See *The Message of Acts*, II, pp. 340–73 for this interpretation of Acts 12.

32. The Bezan text of 11.2 is analysed in *The Message of Acts*, II, pp. 285–87; 291–94; and the realization of Jesus' commandment to Peter in *Excursus* 5, pp. 365–68.

This is precisely the message he will repeat to those gathered to examine the question of the admission of the Gentiles into the Church, continuing to fulfil Jesus' command to him to 'strengthen the brethren'.

His speech is not so much a defence in the judicial sense, which could easily be refuted, but more a prophetic declaration vindicating those who are accused of doing wrong and giving irrefutable evidence on behalf of the Gentiles, in exactly the way promised by Jesus (cf. Lk. 21.15). By its very brevity and conciseness, typical signs of Luke's approval, this last speech of Peter's constitutes a faithful declaration of Luke's own understanding of Jesus' teachings, of what is commonly called his 'theology'. Little wonder, then, that in the Bezan text he is careful to preface it with 'in the Spirit'.

Peter's speech, as is customary, has two parts: the first, an *Exposition* ([α], 15.7b-9) where, for the third time in Acts, the perfect equality between Jews and Gentiles is affirmed, based on the experience of Cornelius in Caesarea, when Peter was 'converted' to the Gentile cause (cf. 10.9-48; 11.4-17); the second part is a *Parenesis* ([β], 15.10-11), in which Peter categorically rejects the Law of Moses as a basis of salvation, stating his belief in the sole validity of the grace of the Lord Jesus Christ for both Jews and Gentiles.

[α] 15.7b-9 *Exposition*

15.7b Peter addresses his audience as 'Men, brothers', an address found elsewhere in the context of a gathering of disciples.[33] The exact sense of his opening sentence varies according to the manuscripts. He refers to the role God assigned to him 'from the days of old' (lit.), namely to be the one through whom the Gentiles might hear the gospel message and believe, a fact that, he says, his audience are well aware of. According to the Alexandrian text, God singled him out 'from among you' – that is, the disciples Peter is addressing, and the reference to 'the early days' means the early days of the Church. With the reading 'us' in place of 'you' in Codex Bezae, 'us' is a reference to the Jewish people, and the 'days of old' a reference to God's plan from the beginning of time – that Peter should be the one to proclaim first the good news of Jesus to the Gentiles was God's plan for Israel from the days of old.

---

33. ἄνδρες ἀδελφοί is found in an intimate context, usually a church or synagogue: 1.16 (Peter to the disciples in the upper room); 2.37 (the Jews in Ierousalem to Peter and the other apostles); 13.15 (the Antioch synagogue rulers to Paul and Barnabas), 26 (Paul to the people in the Antioch synagogue); 15.7 (Peter to the Ierousalem meeting), 14 (James to the same meeting); cf. ἀδελφοί alone at 20.18 D05 (Paul to the Ephesian elders); 21.20 (sing.; James to Paul). When the audience is specifically Jewish, ἄνδρες Ἰσραηλῖται is more common: 2.22; 3.12; 5.35; 13.16; 21.28. Note the combined address, ἄνδρες ἀδελφοὶ καὶ πατέρες: 7.2 (Stephen to the Sanhedrin); 22.1 (Paul to the people in Ierousalem). To unbelieving Gentiles, ἄνδρες is used on its own or with the name of the town: 14.15 (Paul to the people of Lystra); 17.22, ἄνδρες Ἀθηναῖοι (Paul to the Athenians); 19.25 (Demetrius to the Ephesians); 19.35, ἄνδρες Ἐφέσιοι (the town clerk to the Ephesians).

This presents the facts from the Jewish perspective, acknowledging that what has happened is part of God's eternal intention for his people.[34]

15.8-9 Peter goes on essentially to summarize what he had said to the apostles following his experience in Caesarea (cf. 11.3-17). His description of God as 'the heart knower'[35] (lit.; emphasized in Codex Bezae) introduces the idea that it is not the external condition of a person that God considers, but the internal state, exactly as he had realized when he was sent by the Holy Spirit to Cornelius' house: 'God is not a respecter of persons, but in every nation the one fearing him and performing works of righteousness is acceptable to him' (10.34-35). For Peter, the irrefutable proof of the truth of this assertion is the fact that God gave the people in Caesarea the Holy Spirit, without any prior condition. In actual fact, Peter had been beginning to preach about forgiveness but, before he had even had a chance to mention repentance (as he had done when speaking to the Jews in Ierousalem, 2.38-40), the Holy Spirit interrupted him and fell on all of Peter's audience (10.44).[36] God, in other words, made no distinction between the Jews and the Gentiles, as Peter had observed at the time in Caesarea and when he related the incident in Ierousalem.[37]

The links with the Gospel of Luke, the first volume of his work, are clearly in evidence here, where the Pharisees and the scribes in the Gospel are paralleled by the Jesus-believers from the party of the Pharisees in Acts; and the tax-collectors and sinners in the Gospel are represented in Acts by the uncircumcised Gentiles.[38] Peter would have observed Jesus' relationships with both groups in the Gospel on many occasions, even though it was not until he was in the house of Simon the Tanner in Joppa that he finally understood that 'pure' and 'impure' have no meaning as external distinctions: 'What God has declared clean, you must not continue to call common', AT; 'What God has declared clean for you, do not continue to call common', D05 (10.15; cf. 11.9). This was in contradiction to the traditional understanding of the Law (cf. Lk. 11.39-41; Mt. 23.25-26), and as such, a radical element in Jesus' teaching that a change had taken place. It is apparent from this episode in Acts, that there were elements in

34. The succession of three aorist verbs – ἐξελέξατο ... ἀκοῦσαι ... πιστεῦσαι – expresses the timeless nature of God's plan.

35. The same term καρδιογνώστης is used in the disciples' prayer for the replacement of Judas (1.24).

36. The interruption to Peter's speech at 10.44 is striking. It is discussed in *The Message of Acts*, II, pp. 277–78.

37. Peter's account here, especially the Bezan phrase ἐπ' αὐτούς, may be compared with 10.44 (ἐπέπεσεν [ἔπεσεν D05] ἐπὶ πάντας) and 11.15 (ἐπ' αὐτοὺς [αὐτοῖς D05] ὥσπερ [ὡς D05] καὶ ἐφ' ἡμᾶς).

38. The connections between the attitude of the Pharisees towards Jesus over his dealings with the tax-collectors and sinners, and that of the circumcision party towards Peter over his dealings with the Gentiles, are examined in Rius-Camps, *De Jerusalén a Antioquía: Génesis de la iglesia cristiana. Comentario lingüístico y exegético a Hch 1–12* (Córdoba: El Almendro, 1989), pp. 276–79.

the church in Ierousalem who still had not come to terms with the change. They persisted in the traditional notion that for Gentiles to fully enter the community of believers, the Church, they must go through the rituals laid down for proselytes who wished to enter Israel.

[β] 15.10-11 *Parenesis*

15.10 Peter now moves on (νῦν οὖν) to the exhortation, in which he draws conclusions from his brief, but dense, exposition. He takes up the words Moses used when he rebuked the people of Israel for putting God to the test in the wilderness when they were thirsty and had no water: 'Why do you put God to the test?' (Exod. 17.2). The way that their grumbling tested God was that it questioned his presence with them (cf. 17.7). The parallel with the present scene in Ierousalem is that here the Pharisee Jesus-believers are challenging God's acceptance of the Gentiles, wanting to prove it by imposing on them the conditions of the Law of Moses. What they called a divine imperative (δεῖ, 15.5), Peter calls a 'test' of God. The test is unjustified, he points out, because even the Jews have not been able to follow the Law, neither 'we', the Jewish Jesus-believers or the Jews in general, nor the ancestors of Israel. Stephen had said much the same thing to the Sanhedrin some years earlier (cf. 7.53). Peter calls the Law a 'yoke', a device that not only was a burden to the animals who carried it but also prevented any kind of freedom.[39]

15.11 Peter concludes by taking his opposition to the Law even further, further than he had done before in his account of the events in Caesarea (cf. 11.2-17). Not only is the Law not necessary for the salvation of the Gentiles, it is even not the means of salvation for the Jews. The means is 'the grace of the Lord Jesus (Christ, D05)'. The position of this phrase at the front of the sentence is emphatic, contrasting grace with the Law insisted upon by Peter's opponents. It qualifies the infinitive 'be saved',[40] and underlines how the basis of salvation for both Jews and Greeks is identical. In his earlier speech, he had concluded that God gave the same gift to the Gentiles when they believed as to the Jews when they believed (11.17). He now rephrases the comparison, so that the point of reference is the Gentiles: the salvation of the Jews is on the same basis as that of the Gentiles, it is through grace. The impact of such a statement must have been enormous: it is equivalent to saying that belonging to Israel is not necessary, exactly the opposite of what the Pharisee believers were claiming (cf. on 15.5 above).

The manuscripts vary over the tense of Peter's affirmation, the Alexandrian text reading the present, 'we believe', and Codex Bezae reading the

---

39. Paul uses the same term 'yoke' of the Law in Gal. 5.1. Rabbinic writings also refer to the Law as a yoke, but speak of it in positive terms (see Strack and Billerbeck, *Kommentar*, II, pp. 608–610).

40. Barrett's suggestion (I, pp. 719–20) that the phrase διὰ τῆς χάριτος τοῦ κυρίου Ἰησοῦ [Χριστοῦ, D05] could be interpreted as qualifying the verb πιστεύω does not take account of the emphatic force of the fronted position of the phrase.

future, 'we will believe'.[41] The future here expresses an intention to continue doing what has already been begun. It may also have the effect of making the following infinitive, σωθῆναι, 'to be saved', apply to the future: 'we will continue believing that we will be saved'. In point of fact, however, the tense of the infinitive is undefined,[42] and can be interpreted as future whether the main verb be present or future, as it can also be interpreted as a present ('we are saved').

For Peter, then, the matter is clear: God does not make the keeping of the Law a condition for salvation, no more for Jews than for Gentiles. The question of circumcision is implicitly included as an aspect of Law-keeping, though Peter does not focus on it particularly. It took the conversion of the Gentiles for Peter (and others who share his conviction) to realize that belonging to Israel does not serve as a guarantee of salvation.

[c'] 15.12 *The Testimony of Barnabas and Paul*
15.12 A comment in the Bezan text at 15.5 revealed that it was the elders who were intended to be the judges of the position being maintained in Antioch concerning the Gentiles (see *Commentary* above). For a second time now, and again only in the Bezan text, the elders are seen to be the key figures, in the remark that they in particular came to agree with what Peter had said.[43] This is a critical observation, for it indicates that at this point Peter, who was the representative of the apostles, had the support of the other group among the leaders. His words had been inspired by the Spirit (according to Codex Bezae, cf. 15.7 D05), and have been successful in communicating a solution to the problem, in favour of the Gentiles. When James makes his summing up speech, he will have a reduced margin for negotiation.

The agreement of the elders has the effect of settling the atmosphere of the meeting, so that the whole gathering are silent and listen to what Barnabas and Paul have to say. In the Alexandrian text, where the remark about the elders' agreement is absent, the silence following Peter's speech is ambiguous: was it a supportive silence or a hostile one?[44] It leaves the ruling over the Gentiles entirely in the hands of James, for there has been no previous indication of how the people gathered felt about what Peter had said.

The dominant role of the elders will be seen once more in the Bezan text when they are cited as the people responsible for the letter sent to the churches

41. The verb πιστεύω is intransitive here, followed by the aorist infinitive. It does not have the force of 'believe in, have faith in' (*contra* J. Nolland, 'A Fresh Look at Acts 15.10', *NTS* 27 [1980], pp.105–115 [113]).

42. The aorist aspect is not limited to any time, the focus being on the action rather than the time.

43. The Greek is the perfect participle, συγκατατεθεμένων, expressing a state reached (see *Critical Apparatus*).

44. Silence as a response to a speech indicates on occasions that the audience do not know how to reply (cf. 13.41 D05, and *Commentary, ad loc.*).

(cf. 15.41 D05). Even though a later comment refers to both apostles and elders (16.4 D05), in line with the earlier references to the leadership in Ierousalem (cf. 15.2b, 4), the repeated singling out of the elders in the Bezan text contributes to the impression that will be finally confirmed when Paul visits Jerusalem in chapter 21, namely that it is the elders who are exercising the controlling power in the leadership of the Church. The apostles are now still active at this stage as joint leaders, but they are losing their authority and, indeed, will not be referred to again after the last mention of the letter at 16.4.

Once Peter has made his speech, the way has been prepared for the representatives from Antioch to make their case. Barnabas and Paul are mentioned in the reverse order to that which has been used so far in this incident (cf. 15.2). The order can be explained from the context, for Barnabas had close ties with the church in Ierousalem, having been delegated by the apostles to investigate the news they were hearing about the conversions of Gentiles in Antioch (cf. 11.22). He had responded in an entirely positive way to what he found and, on that occasion, the apostles had not questioned his judgement. He had taken the initiative to fetch Paul from Tarsus. Although it is true that Paul took over as leader once the mission was underway (cf. 13.13; and esp. 15.2a D05), from the point of view of the Ierousalem church, Barnabas was the more important of the two and it is to be expected that he should be named first since the scene is being viewed through their eyes. Moreover, the order 'Barnabas and Paul' maintains the order in which they were named by the Holy Spirit (13.2) for the work which they now relate.

The silence of the assembly (not just of the elders but of everyone present, according to the presentation of the Bezan text) permits Barnabas and Paul to talk uninterrupted by the arguing and confusion that had characterized their earlier attempt (cf. 15.4, 5a) and the start of the meeting (cf. 15.7a). Now they have a chance to tell the story of the Gentiles again, giving the evidence not just of God's approval but even of his intervention, through the miracles that were performed through them. The term 'signs and wonders' is a hendiadys, equivalent to 'miraculous signs', and is found in the Jewish Scriptures (cf. for example, Exod. 7.3; 11.9-10 LXX). Luke uses it frequently in his second volume, where it has a positive force (Acts 2.19, 22, 43; 4.30; 5.12; 6.8; 7.36; 14.3), unlike in the Gospels of the other writers (cf. Mt. 24.24; Mk 13.22; Jn 4.48). It is a figurative expression of the endorsement God gives in the end times (cf. 2.19) to the activity carried out in both Israel and among the nations in the name of Jesus.

It is surprising to note that this is the last time that mention will be made in Acts of 'signs and wonders', when so far they have accompanied all the main characters who have played a part in the history of salvation: Moses (7.36); Jesus (2.22; 4.30); the apostles (2.43; 5.12); Stephen (6.8); Paul and Barnabas (14.3). It is as if this last mention marks the high point of the mission to the Gentiles, which will be compromised from now on – first, by the regulations imposed in the Jerusalem decree, and secondly, by the separation of Barnabas from Paul. Its subsequent absence needs to be considered alongside the absence of the Holy Spirit from all of Paul's speeches from now on. Not once will the Spirit be seen to inspire or support what Paul says, neither in his mission nor in his defence.[45] In other words, a problem is posed here in this sequence of the narrative, which will take up the second half of the book as it is investigated, developed, and at last resolved in the final verses (cf. chapter 28).

[b'] 15.13-21 *James' Speech and Verdict*

15.13 The silence with which 'all the meeting' listened to Barnabas and Paul was already mentioned before they spoke, and is now underlined in a repeated reference to it. The significance of the silence is that they will have been able to explain in depth what they had seen happening, without being interrupted or challenged. Among those listening attentively to Barnabas and Paul and agreeing with Peter's affirmations (according to the Bezan text, 15.12a D05), was James as one of the elders.

The role of James in the narrative so far has been shadowy: starting with an indirect reference to him as one of 'the brothers of Jesus' (1.14),[46] the narrator then presents him through the mouth of Peter, as an absent, and somewhat unknown, figure, in the phrase 'James and the brethren' (12.17). In the Gospel, Jesus did not consider him as one of his disciples (cf. Lk. 8.19-21); he would have possibly witnessed the rejection of Jesus by the synagogue in their home town of Nazareth. All that can be deduced from these references is that a) at some point he changed to become a disciple of Jesus; b) he has been in the company of the disciples in Ierousalem since the time of Jesus' ascension; c) he has not been part of the church in Hierosoluma that is free of the traditional Jewish expectations concerning the restoration of Israel;[47] and d) he plays the part of the leader of a separate group of believers, the elders, who remain attached to Jewish ways of thinking. By the end of this chapter, his theological position will have become clearer, as will his role as the leading authority of the Jerusalem church. The picture will be further added to at his next appearance as the leader of the church, with elders alongside him but not the apostles (21.18).

Paul, in his letter to the Galatians, will speak of James as the brother of the Lord (Gal. 1.19), and also as one of the 'pillars' of the Church alongside Cephas (Peter) and John (2.9). He makes it clear that, as far as he is concerned, James

---

45. The absence of the Holy Spirit in the trial scenes of Paul is a significant interpretative key that will be explored in detail in the final volume of *The Message of Acts*.

46. The identification of James, the leader of the Ierousalem church, as one of the brothers of Jesus is due to tradition, tallying with Paul's reference to him in Gal. 1.19. For more information on the tradition, see B.D. Chilton and J.N. Neusner, *The Brother of Jesus: James the Just and His Mission* (Louisville: Westminster John Knox, 2001). Cf. M. Barker, *The Great High Priest: The Temple Roots of Christian Liturgy* (London: T&T Clark, 2003), pp. 27–29.

47. The position of James is investigated in *The Message of Acts*, II, p. 364.

represents the 'circumcision faction' (2.12-13) who was responsible for causing upset in the Antioch church.[48]

The meaning of James' speech is quite different according to the text in which it is read. The variant readings in each verse contribute to the overall sense and should be taken in combination with each other, starting with the way the narrator introduces James as the next speaker. The Alexandrian text presents him as responding (ἀπεκρίθη ... λέγων) to what has been said so far, in particular to the speech of Peter to whom he will refer as 'Simeon'. The Bezan text, in contrast, has already indicated his positive reaction to Peter's speech (15.12a), and has him getting up now to make his own, independent contribution (ἀναστὰς ... εἶπεν) without referring to Peter as a previous speaker (see *Critical Apparatus*).

His speech is constructed along classical lines of rhetoric as are many of the key speeches in Acts, with an *Exposition* ([α] 15.14-18) in which he sets out arguments from 'Simeon' and from Scripture, and a *Parenesis* ([β] 15.19-21) in which he pronounces his judgement (D05; decision, AT).

[α] 15.14-18 *Exposition*

15.14-17a James begins by demanding the attention of the meeting, speaking as one with authority. Contrary to the common reading of James' speech, it is evident from what he actually says that he does not agree with Peter about the Gentiles and, while accepting to drop the requirement for circumcision, he will nevertheless attempt to impose a form of the Law of Moses on them. It is possible to see this even in the Alexandrian text, but the speech does not seem to be interpreted in this way by exegetes working from the Alexandrian text.

The key to the difference in the interpretations of James' speech lies in the identity of Simeon, the name with which he begins his exposition: 'Simeon has explained (ἐξηγήσατο) how God first visited the nations to take from them a people for his name...'. It is almost universally assumed that 'Simeon' here refers to Peter who had been the first to express his view about the Gentiles,[49] and that is, indeed, how the editors of the Alexandrian text appear to understand James: that Peter had explained the beginning of how God had taken from among the Gentiles a people (the household of Cornelius) for his name (to belong to him, to be believers in Jesus). For all that it seems

---

48. Paul's evaluation of Peter in this context is a matter deserving of detailed examination, not least for the way it fits in with what Luke says. The present analysis, however, is deliberately restricted to the portrait Luke presents, so as not to obscure Luke's purpose in his narrative.

49. There are occasionally others who take Simeon to be a reference to Simeon of Luke 1.25, 34 (notably Chrysostom, *In Acta Hom.*, 33.1). For discussion, see R. Riesner, 'James's Speech (Acts 15.13-21), Simeon's Hymn (Luke 2.29-32), and Luke's Sources', in J.B. Green and M. Turner (eds), *Jesus of Nazareth: Lord and Christ* (Grand Rapids: Eerdmans, 2002), pp. 263–278; J. Lagrand, 'Luke's Portrait of Simeon (Luke 2.25-35)', in J. Hills (ed.), *Common Life in the Early Church* (Harrisburg, Pennsylvania: Trinity Press International), pp. 175–85; R.W. Wall, *Acts of the Apostles* (New Interpreter's Bible, 10; ed. L.E. Keck; Nashville: Abingdon Press, 2002).

the natural way to understand the reference, this interpretation is not without its difficulties. First, Peter is never called Simeon by Luke. It could be thought that Luke puts in the mouth of James the Aramaic form of the name since he was addressing Jews (cf. 2 Pet. 1.1 Συμεών, according to some manuscripts [Σίμων, B03 *et al.*]), but elsewhere Luke attributes the Greek form of the name to Aramaic speakers conversing among themselves (e.g. Lk. 22.31; 24.34).

A more serious problem is that James' summary does not correspond to what Peter said. Peter did not say that God took people from among the Gentiles to be Jesus-believers, but that God chose him from the early days to speak to the Gentiles about the gospel, that God demonstrated his acceptance of the Gentiles, that the Law is an impossible burden for anyone to bear, and that for both Jews and Gentiles alike salvation is through the Lord Jesus Christ (see on 15.7-11 above). So James's Simeon is *not* saying the same thing as Peter.

Staying with the Alexandrian text, James goes on in 15.15-17a to cite support from the writings of the Prophets for the ideas he attributes to Peter: the three texts he appeals to speak of the restoration of Israel, the 'tent of David', after the return from exile (Jer. 12.15); the assimilation into the restored kingdom of the Gentiles who believed in the God of Israel (Amos 9.12); and the fact that the divine plan is not a new idea but valid from the days of old (probably an allusion to Isa. 45.21), so giving strength to his arguments. In other words, Israel continues to preserve their ancestral privileges as the Chosen People who, having fallen into disarray, are to be renewed and strengthened under the rule of the Davidic Messiah, at which time the other nations will be drawn to Israel and to YHWH, in so far as YHWH has chosen them. This insistence on the status of Israel is, like James' opening summary, in contrast to the simple point made by Peter when he concluded that belonging to Israel was no longer of relevance since salvation was solely on the basis of faith in the Lord Jesus. It apparently reflects James' view that the Church constitutes the rebuilt Israel into which the Gentiles are now entering, all believing in Jesus as the Messianic son of David.

Looking now at the Bezan text of the speech, it may be noticed that the construction of the exposition is different from that of the Alexandrian text. According to the usual interpretation, as given above, the word καθώς after ἐξηγήσατο (has explained) must be taken as meaning 'how', even though this is an almost unknown use of the word. However, in Codex Bezae, there is the word οὕτως corresponding to καθώς, and the future tense of the verb 'agree' follows it, so that the sentence reads: 'Simeon explained, just as God in the beginning ... so, indeed, the words of the Prophets will concord'. In view of the future tense, it is evident that the teaching about God's election of Israel predates the writings of the Prophets, and cannot therefore be attributed to Peter.

There is, however, a Simeon who fits perfectly with James' argument and who serves him well in the conclusion he wishes to arrive at. It is Simeon II, known as 'the Just', the well-known and highly revered High Priest between

226 and 198 BCE. It is precisely this historical figure who, in Jewish tradition, was regarded as an interpreter of the Scriptures of the highest order. His teaching has not survived directly in written form since it was transmitted orally, but the memory of him and of his reputation has been preserved in the book of Ecclesiasticus or Siracides, the work of a certain Ben Sira written in the first quarter of the second century BCE. In the final chapters of his book, which Ben Sira dedicates to the 'Praise of the Fathers of All Times' (Sir. 44.1 Heb.), considerable space is devoted to Simeon. He is presented as the epitome of wisdom: he is 'the pride of his people' (50.1 Heb.) and by means of a highly allegorical account of the fortification of the Temple and Jerusalem, is closely associated with the Torah as the saviour and protector of Israel and her holiness (50.1-4).[50] He is the latest of the descendants of Aaron cited by Ben Sira as having been entrusted with the commandments and authority of Moses (cf. 45.5, 17). The high esteem in which Ben Sira holds Simeon is that of a disciple for his master, and explains why the theology and ideology of the book is said to transmit that of Simeon himself.[51]

It is within the book of Siracides that the well-known Jewish teaching is found concerning the election of Israel to be God's Chosen People, a teaching already discussed with reference to the speech of Paul and Barnabas in Antioch of Pisidia, for they also referred to it (cf. 13.46; see *Excursus* 5). There are two places where Ben Sira draws on the tradition, in describing first, how God, at the beginning of creation, gave Wisdom (embodied in the Torah) to all nations but in abundance to Israel (Sir. 1.9-10); and secondly, how God, again at the beginning of time, chose Israel from among all the nations to be the dwelling place of Wisdom (24.7-12). Later Rabbinic writers evoke this tradition to justify the privileged status of the nation of Israel as God's Chosen People. As James says, 'Simeon explained [as recorded by Ben Sira] just as God in the beginning [of time] visited the nations [all 70 of them] to take from them a people [Israel] for his name...'. The phrase that James uses here, 'a people for his name', occurs in all the Palestinian targums of Exod. 19.5, which read, 'You shall be a people for my name', in place of the MT, 'You shall be my special possession'.[52] In diverse ways, James is

---

50. See B. Barc, *Les arpenteurs du temps: Essai sur l'histoire religieuse de la Judée à la période hellénistique* (Lausanne: Editions du Zèbre, 2000), pp. 137–43. Barc contends that for Ben Sira the definitive, single redactor of the Torah was none other than Simeon II.

51. According to recent study of Siracides, an intimate connection can be established between Simeon as High Priest and Ben Sira, in both their attitude to the Law and its interpretation (Sir. 50.27c). In addition to the work of Barc cited above, see the detailed analysis of O. Mulder, *Simon the High Priest in Sirach 50. An Exegetical Study of the Significance of Simon the High Priest as Climax to the Praise of the Fathers in Ben Sira's Concept of the History of Israel* (Leiden: Brill, 2003), pp. 363–70.

52. See *Targ.* Lev. 20.26, cited by R. Le Déaut, 'Targumic Literature and New Testament Interpretation', *Biblical Theology Bulletin* 4 (1974), pp. 243–89 (261); see also *A Rabbinic Anthology* (C.G. Montefiore and H. Loewe [eds]; London: Greenwich Editions, 1940), pp. 76–84.

drawing on traditional teaching, which may have been in oral form but would have been familiar to his audience as first century Jews as it was to him.[53]

Since Paul and Barnabas already drew on this tradition in their speech to the people of Antioch (cf. 13.46b-47; certainly in the Bezan text, though it is debatable whether the editor of the Alexandrian text recognized what they were doing), it goes almost without saying that, in their explanation here in Ierousalem of their work among the Gentiles, they would have developed in detail their understanding of what God was doing among the Gentiles in terms with which their audience were familiar. The Jewish leaders themselves would have wanted to know how the new happenings fitted in to the scheme of history that they believed to be the plan of God for the world. It may be observed that James begins his speech with the same verb that is used of Barnabas and Paul, when they 'explained'. As well as straightforward 'explanation', the verb can be used of 'interpretation', either of the Scriptures or of events in such a way as to make clear God's purpose and plan.[54] Barnabas and Paul, like Simeon before them, interpret what they have witnessed in terms of God's initial plan.

On this understanding, James is not describing God's election of the Gentiles to be his people (as the interpretation of Simeon as Peter requires) but the election of Israel to be his special people. In alluding to the ancient tradition, however, he also presupposes its next stage according to which the nations, who were initially intended to know God's Law but rejected it, will one day, under the rule of the Messiah, be granted the grace to receive it.[55] It is precisely this idea that is expressed in the prophecies James cites as he pursues his thinking about Israel's position. It was seen above that the Alexandrian text has James say that the Prophets agree (συμφωνοῦσιν, present) with what he has just summarized as Peter's opinion (τούτῳ), that is, they back up the notion that God has called the Gentiles to enter into his people. Codex Bezae articulates the connection differently. Both the first statement about election of Israel and the second about the inclusion of the Gentiles are attributed to Simeon's teaching – he explained that just as (καθ-ώς) God initially chose Israel from among the nations (according to his interpretation of the Torah), so (οὕτως) the words of the Prophets will agree (that is, concord, συμφωνήσουσιν, future, after the writing of the Torah) in their promises of the other nations eventually being brought into the Chosen People.

15.17b-18 According to the Alexandrian text, James concludes the first part of his speech with a participle clause that continues as part of the prophetic

---

53. That James knew the Siracides traditions and was inspired by them is apparent from his Epistle (see R. Bauckham, *James* [London: Routledge, 1999], pp. 74–85).

54. Cf. Jn 1.18. B-A-G, ἐξηγέομαι.

55. The corresponding notions of reception and rejection of the Torah are presented in conjunction with one another at various critical points in the Scriptures (e.g. Deut. 30.15-20).

citations, in which 'the Lord' is a reference to YHWH.[56] In the Bezan text, however, James concludes his exposition with a personal comment, affirming his confidence that the Lord will do what is promised in the Prophets, based on the fact that the drawing in of the Gentiles is part of the eternal plan of the Lord. Even in the second mention of 'the Lord' in the Bezan wording, it is unlikely that James intends it to refer to Jesus, despite the evidence for the transfer of the identity of 'the Lord' (κύριος in LXX) from YHWH to Jesus as early as Peter's speech at Pentecost (2.36).[57] The use of the word 'work' (ἔργον) echoes the same word used twice before with reference to the Gentiles: first, at the calling of Barnabas and Saul (Paul) by the Holy Spirit for 'the work' among the Gentiles (cf. 13.2); and again, in the warning Paul gave to the Jews of Antioch concerning the invasion of Israel by the Gentiles if they continued to refuse the Messiah sent by God (13.41). For James, the turning of the Gentiles to God is only part of a greater work, namely the rebuilding of Israel.

[β] 15.19-21 *Parenesis*

15.19 Having set out, according to the Alexandrian text, the prophetic evidence that supposedly confirms Peter's testimony that God had accepted the Gentiles, James goes on to state his decision on the matter of the conditions of their entry into the Church – this, at least, is how the verse is interpreted by most commentators. The transition takes on a more formal nature in Codex Bezae where James, without any reference to Peter, had produced his own arguments based on oral and written traditions that reaffirmed the privileged status of Israel whilst allowing that the long-foreseen time had arrived for the Gentiles to be brought into the Chosen People; he now, therefore, makes his judgement in accordance with the purpose for which Paul and Barnabas had been sent up to Ierousalem according to the Bezan text (cf. 15.2b).

The difference between the two texts, in a verse that is without variant readings, arises from the verb James uses to express his opinion, κρίνω, for it has the two senses in Greek of 'decide' or 'judge'.[58] While the Alexandrian text is generally taken to express a 'decision', the coherence of the Bezan text requires the meaning of a 'judgement'. The same difference in interpretation

---

56. The anarthrous reference to 'the Lord' in the expression λέγει κύριος used by James occurs frequently in the same expression in the LXX. The second reference in the additional sentence read by D05 is more likely to have the article because it is anaphoric than because it is intended to refer to Jesus.

57. See *The Message of Acts*, I, p. 190.

58. Cf. Bailly, κρίνω, II, 1, 'décider, trancher' and II, 3, '*par extension* juger, estimer, apprécier'; L-S-J, κρίνω, II, 2, 'decide disputes ... decide a contest' and II, 4, 'judge of, estimate'. Zerwick and Grosvenor, *Analysis*, p. 401, interpret the verb as 'judge best', and the same verb in the same context at 16.4 as 'decide, determine, make (a decision etc.)' (p. 403). This tendency to water down the force of James' intervention is seen in the quotations of Ireneus (*propterea ego secundun me iudico*) and Ephraem (*et de hoc [quantum stat in potentia] mea confirmo verba Shmavonis*), cited by L. Cerfaux and J. Dupont, *Les Actes des Apôtres* (Paris: Éditions du Cerf, 1953), p. 158; cf. Epp, *The Theological Tendency*, p. 104.

will affect the later expression ἔδοξεν (cf. 15.22, 25, 28, 34 D05), which literally means no more than 'it seemed', but can be used in the opening formula of a decree with the sense of 'it has been decided'.

In point of fact, in both texts the sense of 'I judge' is appropriate, for the following reasons:

1. James begins his summing up with the adverb διό (an adverb frequently used by Luke though practically absent from the other Gospel writers),[59] followed by the emphatic personal pronoun placed before the verb, ἐγὼ κρίνω, in contrast to the way Peter began his *parenesis* with a plea to his audience (νῦν οὖν τί πειράζετε, v. 10);

2. the same declaration, ἐγὼ κρίνω, is found at Acts 7.7, a literal quotation of Gen. 15.14 concerning the divine judgement of Egypt;[60]

3. the verb κρίνω is used of the decree in two later references, with the sense of a judgement (16.4 AT; 21.25);

4. the verb κρίνω is found frequently in Acts, almost exclusively in a judicial sense, in the active to refer to the sentence of a judge or a court (Acts 3.13; 7.7; 13.27, 28 D05; 17.31; 23.3; 24.6 *vl*; 25.25; 26.6; 27.1); and in the middle or passive to clarify the reason for someone to have been judged (23.6; 24.21; 26.6), or the court by which someone is judged (15.2 D05; 25.9, 10, 20);

5. the tone of James' conclusion is one of an order: 'we should stop troubling ... but we should write to them to abstain...';[61]

6. the repetition of James' declaration virtually word for word in the letter (compare vv. 19-20 with vv. 28-29), and the reminder of it later by James and the elders when speaking with Paul (cf. 21.25), indicates that it carries the weight of a verdict;

7. the appeal to Moses (Μωϋσῆς γάρ...) means not only that the Jewish Law corroborates what James says, but also that Peter's view that the Law is an intolerable burden, is invalid even though, as far as Codex Bezae is concerned, the elders had previously agreed with him.

The first part, then, of James' verdict is that pressure should no longer be put on the Gentiles to be circumcised and to follow the Law of Moses (cf. 15.1 [esp. D05], 5). The verdict so far sounds positive.

15.20a There is, however, a second part that shows how far James, despite the concessions he makes to the Gentiles, continues to maintain the validity of the Jewish Law. He lists a variety of practices from which the Gentiles must be ordered to abstain. The list varies from one text to another, and a great deal has been written on the meaning and force of the various practices and the

---

59. Apart from Mt. 27.8, διό only appears in Luke's writing, either on its own (Lk. 7.7; 14.19 D05, 20 D05; 16.8 D05; Acts 15.19; 20.26 *vl*, 31; 25.26; 26.3; 27.25, 34) or reinforced with καί (Lk. 1.35; Acts 10.29; 13.35 *vl*; 24.26).

60. Similar formulas are found throughout the LXX: Ps. 74.3; Isa. 49.25; Ezek. 20.36 A02; Dan. 3.96 (spoken by Nebuchadnezzar, καὶ νῦν ἐγὼ κρίνω, translated by Theodotian as καὶ ἐγὼ ἐκτίθεμαι δόγμα).

61. μὴ παρενοχλεῖν: 'μή with pres. inf. *that we should stop troubling*' (Zerwick and Grosvenor, *Analysis*, p. 401); ἀλλὰ ἐπιστεῖλαι αὐτοῖς τοῦ ἀπέχεσθαι, where ἐπιστέλλω + inf. aor. takes on the sense of 'commander ... ordonner de' (Bailly, ἐπιστέλλω, 2).

significance of the textual difference. Much of the debate turns on whether the practices are of a ritual nature or of an ethical one, but from a Jewish point of view (which is the one from which James is speaking), the regulations on which they depend can only be ethical:[62] the defilement brought on by disobeying them is permanent (see *Excursus* 8). As such, they are of far more consequence than rules for behaviour that will enable the Jews and the Gentiles to live in better harmony.

Without the mention of πνικτοῦ, as in Codex Bezae, the three practices James mentions are the three essential things that a Jew must always follow in every circumstance, even if threatened with death; they are all contained in Leviticus 17–20 where Moses is given a series of commandments for all the people of Israel: idols (17.2-9; 19.4; 20.2-6, 27), illicit sexual relationships (ch. 18; 20.10-21) and bloodshed (17.2-4, 10-14).[63] These laws are absolutely binding; infringement of them incurs permanent defilement and carries the penalty of exclusion from Israel and even death if they are infringed (17.4, 9, 10, 14; 18.29). The Gentiles, according to James, should be required to respect the same mandatory laws.

The presence of καὶ πνικτοῦ poses two problems: first, as to its meaning, and secondly, as to the reason for its inclusion in the list here. The customary interpretation of the term πνικτός is that it is a reference to the killing of animals by strangling, despite there being no specific mention in the Law of this method among the regulations for preparing animals for food.[64] If the sense of 'strangled' is taken, as a reference to meat killed by a means that is not permitted, then the prior order to abstain from 'blood' must mean something other than the eating of non-kosher meat (otherwise James is simply moving from the general command to a specific example). If the alternative meaning of 'blood' as murder is taken, as suggested by the list with only three practices (see above), then the occurrence of a reference to the regulations for the slaughter of animals in the midst of a list of moral regulations is odd.

However, πνικτός does not only, or even principally, mean 'strangled' in non-biblical texts but rather 'suffocated, stifled', a sense that may well be intended by the Alexandrian text although it is doubtful that James himself would have found it necessary to mention it.[65] The meaning of πνικτός as

---

62. The discussion by Barrett, II, pp. 730–36 sets out the various positions clearly and illustrates the usual understanding of the distinction between ritual and ethical. Cf. M. Simon 'The Apostolic Decree and its Setting in the Ancient Church', *Bulletin of the John Rylands Library* 52 (1970), pp. 437–60.

63. See, e.g., *Sheb.* 35a.49f; *t. Shabb.* 16.14.

64. Some take πνικτός to be equivalent to θνησιμαῖον ἢ θηριάλωτον ('what dies of itself or is torn by wild animals') of Lev. 17.15. The defilement incurred through this practice is, however, unlike the moral defilement incurred by the other three practices in James' list, for it is temporary and can be reversed by following the ritual set out in the same verse (cf. 17.16).

65. See L-S-J, πνίγω, I, 1. 'strangle'; II, 1. 'cook in a close-covered vessel'; πνικτός, 1. 'strangled'; 2. 'air-tight'; Bailly, πνίγω, 1. 'etrangler, étouffer, suffoquer'; 2. particularly, 'faire

'suffocated' appears to have been applied to a method of cooking meat (as opposed to slaughtering the animal), whereby the meat was cooked in a closed pan in its own juices without any additional liquid.[66] It was, for example, particularly popular in Alexandria according to Philo, who commanded Jews to avoid such gluttony.[67] Could the order attributed to James, that the Gentiles abstain from πνικτός, be a reference to the same culinary practice? It would have been added at a very early date by an editor (a community) aware that Gentiles were in the habit of eating meat prepared in this way and wanting to stop them doing so, either in order not to cause offence to their Jewish fellow Jesus-believers or in order not to lead them astray. In this case, the reference to πνικτός introduces a dietary issue relevant for table-fellowship into the list of James' concerns.

The first item, 'the pollutions of idols', has also been interpreted as a dietary rather than a moral regulation, referring to the eating of food sacrificed or otherwise offered to idols. Paul alludes to such a practice (1 Cor. 8.1-4), advising the disciples in Corinth that it is not harmful as long as it does not cause offence to a fellow-believer (cf. 8.7-13).To interpret James in the same way, however, is to hear him with Christian ears – it could well be that that is how the Alexandrian text heard him, adjusting the list of requirements accordingly (see also on 15.20b below), but if that is so it merely underlines how the Bezan text yet again was written from a Jewish perspective that the Alexandrian text attenuated.

15.20b The Jewish perspective of Codex Bezae is confirmed by the summary James adds to his list of essential requirements, for the formula that he uses corresponds to the traditional Jewish summary of the law for a proselyte (Tob. 4.15; Sir. 31.15; see *Critical Apparatus* for further detail). In appending it to the list, he passes from indirect speech to direct, a literary procedure that has been noted elsewhere as peculiarly Lukan and as conferring emphasis on the words in direct speech.[68] These words in James' case contain an imperative verb in the present tense, which expresses the sense of 'stop doing' (cf. v. 19), and are addressed to the Gentile believers.

The absence in the Alexandrian text of the Jewish summary of the Law for Gentiles is further evidence that the text of James' speech has been adapted to a Christian, rather than a Jewish, context.

15.21 The appeal to Moses with which James concludes is a justification for, and a comment on, the list of conditions to be imposed on the Gentiles

---

cuire dans un vase clos'; B-A-G, πνικτός, 'in secular Greek only with another meaning: = "steamed, stewed, baked"'.

66. The same term is used in French, 'cuire [la viande] à l'étouffée'.

67. Philo, *Spec. Leg.* IV, 23.122, using the compound ἀποπνίγω: '... strangling (ἄγχοντες) their victims and stifling (ἀποπνίγοντες) the essence of life ... burying the blood, as it were, in the body' (*The Works of Philo* [trans. C.D. Yonge; Peabody, MA: Hendrickson, 1998]).

68. Passage from indirect to direct speech without any introductory preface was noted at 14.22 (see *Commentary, ad loc.*).

(connected in Greek with the conjunction γάρ). Although the list is generally regarded as a set of 'concessions', that is, as a generous readiness to place on the Gentile believers a lesser burden than the whole Law, they must be weighed against the evaluation of the Law that Peter gave in his speech: Peter had said that the Law was a insupportable yoke that was useless for salvation; James requires the Gentiles to observe the mandatory regulations of the Law, as well as its general ethos, on the grounds that it is an ancient heritage that Jews everywhere have always adhered to and that can be readily heard wherever Gentiles might find themselves. By his insistence on the Law, James clearly not only continues to maintain its validity but considers it to be the norm for Gentile believers as well as Jews. Gentiles are being brought into Israel, identified and regulated by the Law of Moses.[69]

The contrast between the attitude of James to the Law and that of Peter is yet again a demonstration that James does not agree with Peter and that considerable tension must underlie this meeting. Peter believes that God accepts the Gentiles on the basis of what he knows of their hearts, faith in Jesus being the only requirement for salvation (cf. 15.10-11); the proof is that God gave them the Holy Spirit without any prerequisite rituals or behaviour. James wishes to take measures to make sure that the hearts of the Gentiles will be maintained in an acceptable state by ordering them to obey the essentials of the Law. He makes no mention whatsoever of the Holy Spirit, nor of Peter's denunciation of the Law, nor of the grace of the Lord Jesus Christ. On the contrary, he has stressed the restoration of the Davidic kingdom and the continuing validity of the Torah for Jews. He has not insisted on the need for the Gentiles to be circumcised, and in this respect has, indeed, made a concession that constitutes a radical departure from traditional Jewish teaching. It is because of this step that he will later be viewed as being in Hierosoluma (cf. 16.4) and no longer in the Jewish centre of Ierousalem. For this reason, the decree that comes out of the meeting is not associated with Ierousalem, and the mere (theologically) neutral title of the 'Jerusalem decree' has been preferred for the present work.

The important shift from Ierousalem notwithstanding, James has not shifted at all in his view of the special status of Israel compared with the other nations. The conditions that he imposes on the Gentiles presuppose their prior acceptance of Judaism.

[a'] 15.22-29 *The Ratification of James' Verdict*

The final element in the sequence includes a series of steps that culminate in the setting out of James' judgement in the form of a letter to the Gentiles. In order for these steps to be taken, several things are assumed to have happened

---

69. The point is well made by P. Borgen, *Early Christianity and Hellenistic Judaism* (Edinburgh: T&T Clark, 1996), pp. 233–51, although his conclusion that the decision taken in Jerusalem should not be viewed as a decree does not take account of the authority enjoyed by James within the Church .

that are not mentioned explicitly, or not in detail: first, James' verdict was approved (15.28; maybe there was no opportunity to challenge it); secondly, his idea to write to the Gentile believers was accepted (15.23b); thirdly, the letter was written (15.23a) and addressed specifically to the Gentile disciples in the areas of Antioch, Syria and Cilicia (15.23b); and finally, men were elected to take the letter to Antioch (15.22, 23a D05, 25, 27).

By making no mention of further discussion or debate, Luke implies the power of authority held by James. While making a concession with regard to circumcision, he has gone against Peter's position with regard to the status of the Law (inspired though it was by the Spirit, cf. 15.7 D05), and simultaneously worked against the approval of Peter's position that the elders expressed according to Codex Bezae. Whereas 'all the meeting' (τὸ πλῆθος) had listened in silence to Barnabas and Saul following the elders' approval of Peter's speech, they have apparently all been swayed by James to accept a compromise. No one is said to have argued with him or disagreed with his verdict. Luke himself, however, cannot have been so happy with an outcome that contradicted the outcome that should have resulted from a speech expressing the will of the Spirit, and his own silence about the matter is eloquent.

15.22-23a The concluding stage of the meeting is introduced with the conjunction τότε, which Luke typically uses to indicate the result or outcome of a situation that brings an episode to a close.[70] The unanimity of the church in undertaking the action that follows is strikingly highlighted by the list of the three separate groups of which it was composed following the verb at the beginning of the sentence: the apostles and the elders, together with the whole (Ierousalem) church (cf. the same distinct elements listed at 15.4). In reality, the decision in all likelihood would have been put forward by the apostles and the elders (it is they who are the authors of the letter) and agreed to by the body of the church.

The leaders with the church take a decision – this is the force of the impersonal Greek verb ἔδοξεν in a judicial context (lit. 'it seemed good').[71] They will communicate the verdict to the Antioch church, and will do so by sending with Paul and Barnabas two of their leaders as representatives of the local church. Of the two men chosen nothing more is known at this stage than their names: Judas, who is currently known[72] in the church as Barsabbas ('son of the Sabbath') according to the Alexandrian text, and as Barabbas ('son of the father')[73] according to Codex Bezae; and Silas who is simply named as such. More information will be given concerning these men in due course as the

---

70. Read-Heimerdinger, *The Bezan Text*, pp. 211–25.

71. Bailly, δοκέω, IV; L-S-J, δοκέω, 4, b.

72. The present passive participle of (ἐπι)καλέω expresses a name that is actively being used or acquired (cf. 1.23, Joseph Barabbas [AT]/Barnabas [D05]; 12.12, John Mark). The aorist participle in contrast is used when the function is not active (cf. 4.36, Joseph Barnabas; 12.25, John Mark).

73. *EWNT*, I, pp. 471, 478.

story unfolds. Meanwhile, it is said that they will personally communicate ('by their hand') what the church has written, of which both the form ('a letter') and the contents ('as follows') are underlined in the Bezan text.

Judas and Silas will go to Antioch with Paul and Barnabas, who are named in the order in which they appeared when the dispute over the Gentiles was first mentioned (cf. 15.2). This is the order that Luke adopts when he refers to them as the narrator, reflecting the dominant position that Paul had assumed following the mission in Cyprus.

The letter is made up of three parts: [α] an extended *Address* (15.23b), [β] an *Introduction* preparing for the decree (15.24-27), [γ] the *Decree* itself (15.28-29).

[α] 15.23b *Address*

15.23b The opening of the letter gives information about both the writers of it and its addressees. The writers are listed again (cf. 15.4, 6 [AT], 22) as two distinct groups, the apostles and the elders.[74] The elders are specifically named as 'brethren', so clarifying their status as Jesus-believers (see also 16.4, πρεσβυτέρων τῶν ἐν Ἱεροσολύμοις, and 20.17, τοὺς πρεσβυτέρους τῆς ἐκκλησίας) and distinguishing them from the non-believing Jewish elders (cf. 4.5, 8, 23). These are the two groups who had spoken in the meeting, Peter representing the apostles and James the elders and, while they are now in agreement, they are independent of one another in the sense that they had had to come to an agreement rather than being intrinsically united (as they were when they decided to call the meeting, cf. 15.6 D05).

The recipients are also addressed as 'brethren', those believers among the Gentiles, with the Bezan word-order stressing their origin as non-Jewish (see *Critical Apparatus*). The locations specified were contained within the area of the Roman province of Syria. Luke presents the three places as a single block (with one article prefacing all three in Greek), the whole of a well-delimited region.[75] Antioch is named first on account of the importance the capital of Syria had acquired for the Gentile believers; next comes the region of Syria, probably including the district of Phoenicia; and finally the region of Cilicia, where Paul's home town of Tarsus was located. The choice of these three regions, and only these three, is important, for it means that the decree was not addressed to the Gentiles beyond this territory. There were, of course, Gentile believers in other areas, such as Pisidia and Phrygia, as Paul and Barnabas would have related. The limitation put on the addressees suggests that the authority of James as leader of the Jerusalem church did not go beyond these three regions.

---

74. Both groups are prefaced with the article, signalling their separate identities, unlike 15.2, 6 D05 where they act as one body.

75. Zerwick and Grosvenor, *Analysis*, p. 401: 'one art. doing duty for three regions, a certain unity marking them off from other places and so possibly delimiting the area where the decrees would be operative'.

[β] 15.24-27 *Introduction*

15.24 The introduction constitutes a formal prologue, which bears unexpected marks of resemblance to the prologue with which Luke prefaces his whole work (Lk. 1.1-4; see *Excursus* 9).[76] Its purpose is to make clear that those who had gone to Antioch and troubled (AT)/disturbed (D05) the Gentile believers were without authority. It is nevertheless acknowledged that they belonged to the Ierousalem community, as the Bezan text makes especially clear: they 'had gone out from us'. The way that the leaders say that they had heard of the activity of these trouble-makers only indirectly (15.24) suggests that they had not been aware of what they were doing until after the event; this fits with their insistence that they had given them no orders to go to Antioch. The letter does not say, however, that the leaders were quite unaware that there had been any discussion in the Ierousalem church about the issues raised by the Gentile believers and, even if no one actually instructed them to go and teach the Gentiles about circumcision and the Law, it is clear that the Pharisees who went to Antioch were confident that they would receive support from the elders at least (cf. 15.2b [esp. D05], 4b and 5a D05). The apostles, on the other hand, represented as they were by Peter with his conviction that there was no need for the Gentiles to become Jews, would not have backed the efforts of the Pharisees. The fact that they are always named first before the elders, in the letter itself as well as in the narrative (cf. 15.2b, 4, 6, 23; 16.4), is a sign of the greater weight of their authority in relation to that of the elders. Their disappearance from the narrative following the distribution of the letter to the Gentiles (cf. 21.18-19, where only the elders are mentioned) is unlikely to be unrelated to the conflict that existed over the Gentile question. In any case, it was at some time after this point that the elders took over sole responsibility for the Jerusalem church, and Luke's silence about what became of the apostles is entirely typical of his narrative art as a means to let his audience know that there was a serious problem. The issue will be examined in relation to 21.17-26.

15.25 Despite the underlying tension, they had reached unanimity over the procedure to be followed, namely to choose two of their leaders to accompany Paul and Barnabas back to Antioch and to communicate to the Gentiles the result of the trial. The complete agreement concerning this was already signalled by the narrator in the address of the letter (cf. 15.22-23a: 'the apostles and the elders with the entire church'); the Greek construction, 'having become of one mind' (lit.), shows that the unanimity was only arrived at after previous disagreement.[77] The decision is expressed by an impersonal construction (ἔδοξεν ἡμῖν), also used at 15.22 to convey the unanimity of the people. It will

---

76. Cf. B-D-R, §464, n. 4: These two passages are the only places where Luke constructs a 'period' proper.

77. γενομένοις ὁμοθυμαδόν: the aorist participle is dependent on the aorist finite verb ἔδοξεν in a relationship of prior action.

be used for a third time in this passage, to communicate in the letter the outcome of the meeting, where unanimity is singularly lacking (cf. on 15.28 below).

Barnabas and Paul are mentioned in the order in which they were presented as speaking in the Ierousalem meeting. (cf. 15.12). Barnabas was closer than Paul to the church in Ierousalem, having been sent out by the apostles to see what was happening in Antioch when news of the Gentile conversions reached them (cf. 11.22). It was Barnabas who later, once he was in Antioch, had gone off in search of Paul and brought him back from Tarsus. It is, therefore, natural that the leaders should think of him as the leader of the pair. That, of course, was the order in which the Holy Spirit also chose them for their mission (cf. 13.2). The letter reflects, in other words, the perspective of the writers and suggests a certain conflict with the way Paul saw himself as the leader and acted as spokesman (cf. 13.13, 16, 43, 44, 46, 50; 14.1 D05, 3 D05, 7, 9, 11, 19, 20; 15.2).

Further description is given of Barnabas and Paul. Though the Alexandrian text refers to them as 'our beloved', fully associating them with the Jerusalem church, the Bezan text speaks of them as 'your beloved', identifying them with Antioch instead.

15.26 In both texts, nonetheless, their worth is acknowledged: they have 'given up their lives on account of the name of the Lord Jesus (Christ, D05)'. As a phrase on its own, the expression usually means that they have given themselves up to death, and the perfect tense of the verb in Greek implies that they are indeed dead, which is clearly not the case.[78] With the qualification of the Bezan text, 'in every trial', and especially with the singular 'life' in place of the plural 'lives' (see *Critical Apparatus*), the meaning is more obviously that they are prepared as a united team to set aside their own desires and well-being in whatever difficulties might arise in the course of promoting the good news of Jesus – including the good news for the Gentiles that he is equally their Lord and Messiah, for which Paul and Barnabas had accepted to be 'handed over' to the Ierousalem church (cf. 15.4a D05, where the same verb, παραδίδωμι, is used of them as here).

15.27 The purpose of sending Judas and Silas, who are not described in any more detail in the letter, is for them to announce orally, presumably explaining in more detail, the contents of the letter. Their function then is not only to be the bearers of the letter but also, as representatives of those who formulated it, to interpret the decree that it contained.

[γ] 15.28-29 *The Decree*
15.28 Finally, the letter gets down to setting out the all-important verdict of the Jerusalem leaders concerning the Gentiles. It was noted that Luke twice

---

78. 'παραδοῦναι τὴν ψυχήν is not usually applied to a man who is still alive' (Metzger, *Commentary*, p. 386, citing Lake and Cadbury).

presents the previous decision, to send representatives with a letter to Antioch, as unanimous (cf. 15.22, 25): this next decision, where the same impersonal construction is used as on the other two occasions (ἔδοξεν + dat., 'For the decision of...'), is not unanimous. It reflects the compromise that was reached between the two opposing positions of Peter, who spoke through the Spirit (noted only by Codex Bezae, 15.7 D05), and James who did not. The tension is evident in the introductory formula, 'For the decision of the Holy Spirit and of ourselves', which is followed by a summary of the two points of view. The first was communicated by the Spirit speaking through Peter: 'no ... burden is to be put on you'; the second was expressed by James: '... other ... than these (things, AT) ...'. Peter had made it clear that requiring the Gentiles to follow the Law of Moses was to put God to the test by 'placing a yoke on the neck of the disciples' (15.10). The verdict of James, on the other hand, was that the Jewish believers should indeed stop troubling the Gentile disciples (about circumcision), but that they should instead (the force of ἀλλά in Greek) tell them to respect the essential requirements of the Law (and obey its main principle, according to Codex Bezae).

The decision, then, about what is to be required of the Gentiles was not a joint decision, taken unanimously. It was a compromise between two opposing positions. The question is whether there can be any satisfactory compromise when the Spirit has made clear what is the way of God. The decision to impose on the Gentiles the condition that they should follow the Law, however minimal the conditions, as if they were foreigners living in Israel, goes against the nature of the Holy Spirit who is, on the contrary, a Spirit of freedom (cf. 2 Cor. 3.17; Jn 8.32, 36). That the letter could have been written, however, in the name of both the apostles and the elders means that Peter, together with the other apostles, must have accepted this compromise. Is this the kind of wavering that Paul refers to in his letter to the Galatians (Gal. 2.11-14)?[79]

The Alexandrian text presents the regulations that the Gentiles must observe as '[no other burden than] these things (τουτῶν, neuter plural) that are essential...', reducing to a minimum, in other words, the aspects of the law that the Gentiles must follow. The Bezan text words (and therefore punctuates) the sentence differently, saying '[no other burden than] these: it is essential...' – the force of this wording is all the stronger for saying that some burdens ('these', τούτων, referring to βάρος) do have to be imposed.

15.29a Furthermore, the Bezan wording reflects in a quite precise way the understanding referred to above (see on 15.20) that there were three ethical regulations of the Law that, whatever the cost, Jews must never go against even if circumstances made all the others impossible to maintain. These three

---

79. The question is posed here to suggest that the comparison of Paul's letter to the Galatians with the Acts narrative necessitates a reading of the Acts text that goes beyond the surface story to take account of all the implicit information that Luke supplies. To answer the question is a separate study in its own right.

– idolatry, forbidden sexual relations and bloodshed – are the ones listed as the essential requirements for Gentiles who believe in Jesus. The list of requirements is the same as that given by James in his speech to the meeting (cf. 15.20), with the same variant reading (presence or absence of πνικτῶν, 'meat cooked in its juices'. Only the order of the list differs, with both texts inverting the position of 'blood' and 'illicit sexual relations', so that the reference to the cooking of the meat comes in third position each time in the Alexandrian text.

The summary of the Law for Gentiles that James appended to the list according to the Bezan text is present again in the letter, with certain differences between the two statements of it:

1. 3rd person followed by negative imperative // 2nd person followed by negative infinitive;
2. indirect speech followed by direct // direct speech followed by indirect;
3. plural 'to others' // singular 'to another'.

With typical stylistic awareness, Luke adapts the Law summary to the situation in which it is stated (James' verdict about the Gentiles // the letter addressed to them).

15.29b The closing sentence of the letter is straightforward in the Alexandrian text, following on directly from the list of the three forbidden practices. The verb used, διατηρέω, with the preposition ἐξ, 'out of', has the implications of 'keep out of trouble' (see *Critical Apparatus*), as is reflected in the translation, and the whole sentence has the force of a conditional statement, commending the Gentiles *if* they do as they are instructed. In the Bezan text, the concluding sentence takes the form of a final command, 'do well', accompanied by two conditions, 'by keeping yourselves away from these things' and 'sustained by the Holy Spirit'. The first is negative and makes explicit the means to 'do well', relating not just to the list of forbidden practices but the summary of the Law as well. The second condition is positive, the only positive expression in the instructions to the Gentiles: their obedience is made possible because they are strengthened by the Holy Spirit, with the Greek expression for 'the Holy Spirit' the one Luke reserves for the Spirit's activity among the disciples, the same one as that used in the introduction to the instructions of the letter.

In fact, the introduction mentioned 'the Holy Spirit and ourselves', the first associated with the requirement for 'no burden to be placed' on the Gentiles, and the second with the essential demands and the summary of the Law. In the concluding command to 'do well', the inverse order of persons is suggested: the Gentiles are to refrain from all the stated practices by the decision of the apostles and elders; they are to be sustained by the Holy Spirit. The chiastic inversion underlines the contradiction implicit in the letter: the confusion of the binding nature of the legal demands, on the one hand, and the freedom given by the Holy Spirit, on the other.

The letter ends with a final customary salutation, 'Farewell!'

Excursus 8

Ritual and Ethical Laws

The distinction between ritual and ethical laws is an important one for it allows the consequences of following them on the one hand, or breaking them on the other, to be understood more clearly. The reason for which James selected three particular aspects of behaviour from which the Gentiles should abstain also becomes more apparent in turn.

If the purpose of Torah in general, and of the individual laws in particular, is to enable right relationships to be maintained between the people and God and among the people themselves, then the overarching goal of the one following Torah can be defined as becoming holy, indeed, like God himself.[80] Infringing the teachings brought on a state of impurity that had to put right in a variety of ways. The significance of the different commandments and the effects of disregarding them may have varied from one period to another, but certain features of the situation in the first century while the Temple was still standing can be discerned. The vast majority of the biblical laws were to do with maintaining a state of purity that rendered a person fit to enter the Temple, to encounter God's presence – that is ritual purity. Ethical or moral purity was of a different nature and threatened the land of Israel itself and the very presence of God there. The distinctive characteristics of the ritual and ethical considerations may be summarized as follows: [81]

Ritual Considerations	*Ethical Considerations*
1. Defilement results from contact with natural sources or processes;	Defilement results from committing grave sins, notably idolatry, illicit sexual relations and murder;
2. Defilement is inevitable, contracted in the course of daily living;	Defilement is largely avoidable, contracted by a deliberate intention;
3. Defilement does not arise from or constitute sin;	Defilement always arises from sin and makes the person a sinner;
4. The defilement is often contagious;	The defilement is not contagious;
5. The effect on the person is short-lived;	The effect on the person is long-lasting, or even permanent;
6. The sanctity of the Temple is threatened if a ritually impure person enters;	The sanctity of the land of Israel and of God's presence there is threatened;
7. The means to remove defilement are ritual acts – bathing, waiting, sacrifice.	The means to remove defilement is punishment or sacrifical atonement, exile or possibly death.

The status of the Gentiles in relation to the purity regulations was a matter of serious dispute during the Second Temple period.[82] In so far as they were wor-

---

80. See J. Neusner, *Judaism When Christianity Began: A Survey of Belief and Practice* (Louisville: Wetsminster John Knox Press, 2002), pp. 45–48.

81. The criteria for distinguishing between ritual and ethical laws are adapted from J. Klawans, 'Concepts of Purity in the Bible', *Jewish Study Bible*, pp. 2041–47.

82. Klawans, 'Concepts of Purity', pp. 2046–47.

shippers of idols, they were considered to be in an inherent state of moral impurity, they were sinners by nature – this accounts for the Jews' avoidance of social contact with them and, more specifically, the resistance met by the early Jewish Jesus-believers when they sought to ignore the boundaries that had separated the Gentiles from the people of Israel. The problem was not that the Gentiles would transmit their sinfulness as if by contagion, but rather that they might influence the Jews to follow their practices.

Excursus 9

*The Prologue of Lukes' First Volume and
the Introduction to the Jerusalem Decree of the Second Volume*

Between the prologue that stands right at the beginning of Luke's work (Lk. 1.1-4) and the introduction to the letter from the Jerusalem church in the middle of the second volume (Acts 15.24-27), there is a surprising but striking similarity of structure that has all the marks of being intentional.[83] In each passage, there is a *protasis* made up of three components, followed by a corresponding *apodosis*, also with three components, brought together in a concluding summary. The parallels between the members of the protasis are ones of contrast, while between the members of the respective apodoses they are parallels of similarity. The summary statement at the end of both the prologue and the introduction to the letter consists of a single statement that declares the purpose of the writing in each case. In the table below, corresponding elements that display verbal similarity are given in capitals, and those that are marked by difference are given in italics:

Protasis	*Luke's Prologue*	*Jerusalem Decree*
1.	SINCE ('Ἐπειδήπερ) MANY PEOPLE (πολλοί) *have undertaken to compile* an ACCOUNT (διήγησιν)	SINCE ('Ἐπειδή) we have heard that CERTAIN PEOPLE (τινες) who had gone out from us *disturbed you* with their WORDS (λόγοις)
2.	of the things that *have been accomplished* among us,	*unsettling* your minds,
3.	just as they were passed on to us by those who were *eyewitnesses* from the beginning and who became *keepers* of the word,	though we did not give them *instructions*,
Apodosis		
1.	I HAVE DECIDED also (ἔδοξεν κἀμοί)	WE HAVE DECIDED (ἔδοξεν ἡμῖν)
2.	*after investigating* EVERYTHING CAREFULLY (πᾶσιν ἀκριβῶς) afresh,	*after becoming* OF ONE MIND (ὁμοθυμαδόν),
3.	TO WRITE IT DOWN FOR YOU (σοι γράψαι) in an orderly manner, most Excellent *Theophilus*,	TO SEND TO YOU (πέμψαι πρὸς ὑμᾶς) men, with your beloved *Barnabas* and *Paul* ...
Purpose		
	so that you may recognize the soundness	So we have SENT (ἀπεστάλκαμεν)

---

83. The similarities are so striking that they are pointed out in B-D-R, §464, n. 4.

of THE TEACHINGS (λόγων) about which you have been informed.	Judas and Silas,to tell you by WORD of mouth (διὰ λόγου) what follows.

That Luke should have composed the prologue to his two volumes in a rhetorical style well-suited to the nature of his work is not out of the ordinary. What is surprising, is the repetition of the same rhetorical device in the centre of the second volume in a letter written by the apostles and elders of the Jerusalem church. The elements of contrast underline the difference between the situation of Theophilus prior to Luke's writing to him, when he had been informed by many people who were faithful recorders of what had happened with regard to Jesus, and the situation of the recipients of the Jerusalem letter, when they had received the visit of a few people who acted without authority and advocated disturbing teachings with regard to Jesus.

On the other hand, the elements of similarity highlight the fact that both writings share the same objective: to confirm for Theophilus the truth of what he has heard, and to correct for the communities represented by Paul and Barnabas the errors that they had heard.

[B′] 15.30-35 *The Application of the Decision*

Overview

This sequence corresponds to the previous one [B] in which the conditions for the entry of the Gentiles into the Church were decided. The decree that had been written by the apostles and elders in Jerusalem (15.23-29) has had the effect of freeing them from Ierousalem and bringing them to Hierosoluma (cf. 16.4). For that reason, Ierousalem is no longer an appropriate term to refer to the church in Jerusalem once James' judgement has been accepted. On the other hand, it is to run ahead of Luke to refer to it by the name of Hierosoluma before 16.4. In this interim period, we therefore have chosen to use the English spelling of Jerusalem. The decree is now handed over, preparing the way for its delivery to other communities in the subsequent narrative (cf. 15.41; 16.4). The future role of Silas as the companion of Paul is likewise prepared for, in the Bezan text, by presenting his decision to stay in Antioch instead of returning to Jerusalem.

Structure and Themes

The elements of this brief sequence follow in rapid succession, all conjoined with δέ. The first three deal with the delivery of the letter from Jerusalem, which is received with muted satisfaction; in contrast, the oral ministry of Judas and Silas is wholly positive. The second three elements resolve the presence in Antioch of the people who had brought the letter: Judas and Silas, on the one hand, Paul and Barnabas on the other.

[a]	15.30	Delivery of the letter to Antioch
[b]	15.31	Rejoicing at the exhortation

Translation

Codex Bezae D05

[a]   **15.30** So the men, having been sent off, went down to Antioch in a matter of days and, gathering everyone together, they handed in the letter.

[b]   **31** When they had read it, they rejoiced at its exhortation.

[c]   **32** Judas and Silas, who were themselves prophets, when they were full of the Holy Spirit they exhorted the brethren with their words and strengthened them.

[c']   **33** When they had been there for a while, they were sent off in peace by the brethren to those who had sent them.

[b']   **34** Silas, however, decided they would remain; but Judas went, alone.

[a']   **35** Paul and Barnabas stayed on in Antioch, teaching and announcing – with many other people – the good news of the word of the Lord.

Codex Vaticanus B03

15.30 So the men, having been sent off, went down to Antioch and, after gathering everyone together, they handed in the letter.

31 When they had read it, they rejoiced at its exhortation.

32 Judas and Silas, who were themselves prophets, exhorted the brethren with their many words and strengthened them.

33 When they had been there for a while, they were sent off in peace by the brethren to those who had sent them;

35 and Paul and Barnabas stayed on in Antioch, teaching and announcing – with, indeed, many other people – the good news of the word of the Lord.

Critical Apparatus

15.30 (ἀπολυθέντες) ἐν ἡμέραις ὀλίγαις D*, *in diebus paucis* d (l) ‖ *om.* B 𝔓³³·⁷⁴ ℵ Dˢ·ᵐ· *rell.*

The presence of a time detail in D05, absent from B03, can also be observed at, e.g., 2.1 D05; 3.1 D05; 16.11 D05; 19.9 D05.

(καὶ) συναγαγόντες B 𝔓³³·⁷⁴ ℵ Dᴮ *rell, et cum collegissent* d ‖ -άγοντες D* 2492.

The aorist participle in B03 expresses the time sequence, with the handing in of the letter taking place after the church was assembled. In D05, though the facts remain the same, the present participle conveys a greater sense of urgency.

15.32 (Ἰούδας) τε B 𝔓³³ ℵ *rell, quoque* d ‖ δέ D 𝔓⁷⁴ 88. 1646. 1854.

If τε in B03 is intentional (i.e. it is not due to phonetic confusion), the clause it introduces is presented as additional information (Levinsohn, *Textual Connections*, pp. 127–29). In D05, the activity of Judas and Silas is presented as a new development with δέ.

(ὄντες) πλήρεις πνεύματος ἁγίου D, *pleni spiritu sancto* d ‖ *om.* B 𝔓³³·⁷⁴ ℵ *rell.*

The comment by the the narrator in D05 on Judas and Silas is a positive one, endorsing their activity (cf. Stephen, 6.10 D05; Peter, 15.7 D05).

(διὰ λόγου) πολλοῦ B 𝔓³³·⁷⁴ ℵ *rell* ‖ *om.* D d.

B03 qualifies the speaking of Judas and Silas as 'much'.

15.34 ἔδοξε δὲ τῷ Σιλᾷ (-εᾷ D d) ἐπιμεῖναι αὐτούς D*, *placuit autem Sileae sustinere eos* d C 33 (πρὸς αὐτούς Dᴬ ‖ αὐτόθι 945 ‖ -οῦ 36. 88. 242. 257. 307. 323. 383. 431. 453. 467. 522. 536. 610. 614. 915. 1108. 1175. 1409. 1611. 1739. 1678. 1799. 1891. 1898. 2147. 2298. 2344. 2412 *al* it vgᵐˢˢ syʰ** sa boᵐˢˢ aeth; Cass Ephr) ‖ *om.* B 𝔓⁷⁴ ℵ A E H L P Ψ 049. 056. 69. 81 𝔐 dem e p vgʷʷ·ˢᵗ syᵖ bo; Chr.— μόνος δὲ 'Ιούδας ἐπορεύθη D, *solus autem Iudas profectus est* d ar gig l ph ro (+ εἰς 'Ιερουσαλήμ w vgᶜˡ); Cass ‖ *om.* B 𝔓⁷⁴ ℵ A C E H L P Ψ 049. 056. 33. 1739 𝔐 dem e p vgʷʷ·ˢᵗ syᵖ bo; Chr.

B03 omits any mention of a split between Silas and Judas. The third person accusative pronoun relating to Silas in the D05 clause is the subject of the infinitive ἐπιμεῖναι. Apart from C04 and 33, other witnesses appear to have considered it to be anomalous, interpreting the sentence in different ways: the Latin page d5 translates the verb as *sustinere*; Corrector A of D05 supplies the preposition πρός; other Greek manuscripts and versions take it to be an error for the locative αὐτοῦ (cf. 21.4, ἐπεμείναμεν αὐτοῦ [D05 lac.; d5 *mansimus apud eos*), although the locative pronoun is superfluous given that the prefix ἐπι- already expresses the local sense of the verb (Moulton and Howard, p. 312). The omission of the sentence by many other witnesses may have arisen because of the harshness of the conflict evident in the D05 text, or because αὐτούς was perceived as an anomaly.

15.35 Παῦλος δέ B 𝔓⁷⁴ ℵ *rell* ‖ ὁ δὲ Παῦ. D, *Paulus vero* d.

The article prefacing the joint names of Paul and Barnabas in D05 is an indication that they have remained in focus, as a united pair, throughout this scene.

μετὰ καὶ (ἑτέρων) B ℵ Dᴱ *rell* ‖ καὶ (– Dˢ·ᵐ· 1739*) μετά D*, *et cum* d.

The particle καί is adverbial in both texts, with the position after μετά in B03 conferring even greater emphasis on the participation of 'many others' in the activity of evangelization in Antioch.

Commentary

[a] 15.30 *Delivery of the Letter to Antioch*
15.30 The new sequence follows on directly from the preparation of the letter for the Gentiles, in accordance with what has been decided. Luke uses a typical formula in Greek to introduce two actions to which the decision of the

apostles and elders leads: the first in the opening sentence (μὲν οὖν),[84] and then the second one in the next verse (δέ).

The immediate action is the departure of the men who had been chosen to deliver the letter for Antioch. The return journey has several marks of contrast with the journey from Antioch to Ierousalem (cf. 15.3): on the outward journey, it was said that the church in Antioch had provided for the travellers, and on the return simply that they were 'sent off'; the journey to Ierousalem was made via the churches of Phoenicia and Samaria, where the news of the conversions of the Gentiles had caused great joy, while the journey back to Antioch was made directly, 'in few days' (lit.). It would have been logical for those going to Antioch to call in on the brethren again, to tell them what had been decided in Jerusalem. The fact that they did not was no doubt a deliberate choice, for it would have most likely caused considerable delay, not only to explain to these people the decision but also to justify the conditions that were to be imposed on the Gentiles. Those returning to their home town and home church would have wanted to get there as quickly as possible to pass on the news.

Once in Antioch, the people who had gone down from Jerusalem gathered together 'the multitude' (lit.), that is, all the members of the church, not just the leaders or the Gentiles.[85] In Codex Bezae, the tense of the participle confers a sense of urgency on the meeting (see *Critical Apparatus*), as if to say that they wasted no time in getting on with it.

[b] 15.31 *Rejoicing at the Exhortation*
15.31 The reaction in Antioch when the letter was handed over is again subtly contrasted with the reaction of the brethren in Phoenicia and Samaria when they heard about the Gentiles. There the news had 'caused great joy'; now, in Antioch, when they read the letter the people 'rejoiced', which would seem quite positive were it not for the comparison with the earlier response.

The detail that they rejoiced 'at the exhortation' is of particular interest, especially since the corresponding verb, 'exhorted', will be taken up in the next verse with reference to the prophetic activity of Judas and Silas under the influence (according to Codex Bezae) of the Holy Spirit. The noun παρά-κλησις, 'exhortation, encouragement', is always associated in Luke's writings with the activity of the Holy Spirit.[86] In the letter according to the Alexandrian

---

84. The same formula is used on many occasions in Acts to present two actions that arise from the previous sequence, cf. 15.3.

85. πλῆθος is used in the sense of the whole assembly, Jew and Gentile, leaders and ordinary people, elsewhere in Acts (cf. 13.45, the city of Antioch of Pisidia; 14.4, the city of Iconium; 15.12, the meeting in Ierousalem).

86. παράκλησις is used of Barnabas, who is said to be 'a good man, full of the Holy Spirit and faith' (11.24); indeed, it is the meaning of the name given to him (1.23 D05; 4.36). Elsewhere in Acts, it is used of the Holy Spirit directly (9.31); and, together with σοφία, of the spiritual message Paul and Barnabas might have for the synagogue in Antioch of Pisidia (13.15). The verb

text, there is scarcely an exhortation – instead, there is a list of essential legal requirements, which consist of four practices that are to be avoided, and a conditional statement telling the Gentiles that they 'will do well' if they refrain from these practices (cf. 15.28-29). At most, the conditional statement could be understood as a weak exhortation. In contrast, the letter according to Codex Bezae contains a clear exhortation associated, what is more, with the Holy Spirit, even though, there also, it is interwoven with legal requirements (which are even more extensive in the Bezan text than in the Alexandrian text, cf. 15.29 D05): the Gentiles are ordered to 'do well' by means of avoiding the various practices, 'being sustained by the Holy Spirit'. The combination of legal and spiritual commands reflects the confusion in the minds of the leaders in Jerusalem, who struggle to detach themselves from the requirements of the Law and to accept the empowering freedom of the Spirit.

Luke has been careful, in the Bezan text, to demonstrate this confusion, and also the conflict between the apostles, represented by Peter, who insisted that the Law had no more value, and the elders, represented by James, who decreed that the Law was to be followed in its essential aspects. It is in keeping with the nuanced picture he has painted that he restricts now the rejoicing of the church in Antioch to the positive aspect of the letter, the exhortation associated with the Holy Spirit. It may be imagined that if the exhortation had not been mixed up with legal demands, the rejoicing would have been greater; but it is not because some aspects of the Jerusalem decree are contrary to the Spirit that all of it is to be rejected.

[c] 15.32 *Judas and Silas Exercise their Gifts as Prophets*

15.32 The exhortation of the letter is developed by Judas and Silas as they speak as prophets, filled with the Holy Spirit according to Codex Bezae. As elsewhere in Luke's work,[87] this detail is an expression of his positive evaluation of their contribution to the building up of the church in Antioch. The verb 'strengthened' is a significant one in Luke's vocabulary, for it was used first of Peter when, after his realization that the Gentiles were accepted by God as equals to the Jews, he 'strengthened' the brethren on his way to Hierosoluma (11.2 D05). It was used in similar circumstances of Paul and Barnabas, who strengthened the brethren in Phoenicia and Samaria with news of the Gentile conversions as they also travelled to Ierousalem (15.3). Here, for the third time, the act of strengthening is associated with the entry of the Gentiles into the Church. What Judas and Silas had to say, then, was in accordance with the Holy Spirit. Later, Silas will seemingly again exercise his prophetic gifts when he accompanies Paul on the later stages of the mission.

παρακαλέω, when it does not simply express a request (e.g. 9.38; 16.9), is also used of Barnabas (11.23); and of Judas and Silas who were 'full of the Holy Spirit' (15.32 D05).

87. Cf. Peter, 15.7a, and the *Commentary, ad loc.*

[c'] 15.33 *The Dismissal of Judas and Silas*

15.33 The positive role of Judas and Silas continues to be expressed as they are finally sent back to the apostles and elders. Their stay in Antioch lasted some time, and had a calming effect on the church, since they were sent off 'in peace'. The picture is one of harmony and agreement, overriding the negative aspects of the Jerusalem decree.

[b'] 15.34 *Silas Stays in Antioch, Judas Returns to Jerusalem*

15.34 Codex Bezae introduces at this point a note of uncomfortable tension. Judas and Silas, having accomplished the task for which they went to Antioch, are now free to leave. In the briefest of statements, the Bezan text makes clear that Silas decided they should not go back to Jerusalem;[88] Judas apparently disagreed since he did go back, but alone (μόνος, stressed in the Greek). The two short sentences, both introduced with δέ, are effective in insinuating the conflict that was continuing to simmer in Antioch, a conflict that will burst out afresh in the final sequence of this section (see 15.36-41 below).

Silas so far has always been the second name of the pair (cf. 15.22, 27, 32); Judas was the leader and was described as 'the son of the Sabbath' (AT) or 'of the father' (D05). The name of Judas represents the very essence of Judaism and it is he who goes back to Jerusalem, where the church continues to maintain traditional teachings and practices of Judaism, including Temple worship and sacrifices (cf. 21.20-24, 26). He is, indeed, 'the son of the father' in the sense of representing those who uphold the faith of their ancestors. It should be noted, nonetheless, that there has been a shift within the Jerusalem church, for it will no longer be associated with Ierousalem but Hierosoluma (cf. 16.4, *Commentary*). The decision taken by James and agreed by the apostles and elders has caused a significant step to be taken in detaching the church from the traditional Jewish way of thinking, by re-formulating the conditions for the entry of the Gentiles so that circumcision in particular was no longer required.

Silas, whose name has affinities with the original name of Paul,[89] will henceforth play an important role as the companion of Paul (cf. 15.40). He may have wanted to stay in Antioch to keep an eye on the situation he could foresee arising between Paul and Barnabas.

[a'] 15.35 *Paul and Barnabas Stay On in Antioch*

15.35 Finally, the narrator turns his attention, and that of his addressee, back to Paul and Barnabas who have been present all through this section, though

---

88. Only the Greek of Codex Bezae has an accusative-infinitive construction, which translates as: 'Silas decided that they would remain'. Other witnesses interpret the clause as meaning 'Silas decided to remain there', which involves altering the Greek pronoun (see *Critical Apparatus*) and lessens the flagrant disagreement with Judas who does not stay in Antioch.

89. Σιλᾶς, Σιλέας is the Greek form of a name that 'is perhaps derived from the Aramaic form of "Saul"' (*EWNT*, III, p. 580; cf. B-D-R, §§53.3b, n. 7; 125.2, n. 6).

without directly intervening since their opportunity in Ierousalem to explain their experiences among the Gentiles (15.12). In the Alexandrian text the article is omitted before both names as the pair are brought back into focus after the departure of Judas and Silas; in D05 a single article presents Paul and Barnabas as a united pair (see *Critical Apparatus*). Once the letter had been handed over and Judas had gone back to Jerusalem, they stayed on in Antioch for an unspecified length of time, expressed with the imperfect verb in Greek (διέτριβον), in just the same way as in the opening sequence of Section II when Paul and Barnabas wanted to stay with the disciples in Antioch (cf. 14.28, 'they stayed on [διέτριβον] for quite some time with the disciples'). On the previous occasion, they had been interrupted by the arrival of the Pharisee brethren who came insisting on the need for circumcision and the Law. Now, too, their stay will again be interrupted, as will become clear in the following section; this time it will be Paul himself who unsettles the situation, wanting to go back to the places where they had gone together in the first stage of their mission. For the time being, while they remain in Antioch they teach and announce the good news of the word of the Lord, that is the message of Jesus (see *Excursus* 1). For this latter activity, they are assisted by many other people, an indication that other disciples, too, have the ability and the confidence to pass on the gospel message. In fact, this had been a mark of the Antioch community since the early days, for it was there that men from Cyprus and Cyrene had gone, speaking for the first time to Greeks about the Lord Jesus Christ (cf. 11.20).

[A′] 15.36-41 *Conflict over John-Mark*

Overview

The start of the new sequence is marked by a time detail (Μετὰ δέ τινας ἡμέρας, 'After some days'). This final sequence of Section II corresponds to the opening sequence [A] 14.28–15.2, in so far as each one introduces a new conflict concerning the Gentiles. In 14.28–15.2, the cause of the conflict was made explicit; here, it will be merely insinuated, only becoming clearer as the narrative moves on in the following section.

The conflict in this sequence concerns Paul and Barnabas, and the immediate reason for the disagreement is John-Mark's presence with them as they go back to visit the churches they had established during the first stage of the mission. It is almost universally assumed that Barnabas is the guilty party, for the simple reason that Paul is considered to be infallible. That is not at all the view of the narrator of Acts according to the Bezan text, as will be seen increasingly in the final part of Acts once Paul becomes determined to visit Jerusalem before going to Rome, an action that Codex Bezae severely criticizes.[90] Moreover, throughout the Bezan text, Barnabas is an exemplary hero, modelled on the patriarch Joseph, starting from his first appearance at 1.23.[91] He serves as a guide for Paul, encouraging him and introducing him to Jesus-believers, notably in Ierousalem (9.27), and in Antioch (11.25-26). He was a Hellenistic Jew who, in common with the Hellenist disciples of Jesus in general, had a clear understanding of the universality of the gospel message.[92] It should be remembered that the order in which the Holy Spirit chose two from among the church in Antioch to undertake the mission to the Gentiles was Barnabas first, then Paul as Saul (cf. 13.2). John-Mark (the cousin of Barnabas according to Paul's letter to the Colossians, 4.10) also demonstrates his grasp of the universal aspect of Jesus' teaching, as the son of Mary in whose house the church was praying for Peter's deliverance from Jewish Messianic expectations (12.12),[93] and also as the author of the second Gospel.[94]

Paul in contrast, for all that he insists frequently on his belief that Gentiles do not need to be circumcised or follow the Law, continues to think in terms of Israel as the Chosen People and as the point of reference for the conversion of the Gentiles to the Lord. This was apparent in his speech to the synagogue in Antioch of Pisidia (13.15-41, see *Commentary, ad loc.*) and will continue to be revealed in certain key actions throughout the second and third stages of his mission to the Gentiles (for example, in Lystra, 16.3; in Cenchrea, 18.18; in the Temple, 21.26).

The conflict between Paul and Barnabas is made evident throughout this sequence by two linguistic devices that Luke uses typically to underline contrast between participants. One is the absence of the article before the name of the person; the other is the placing of the name before the verb, as near to the front of the sentence as possible. By the consistent use of these two devices, Codex Bezae presents a picture of heightened tension compared with the Alexandrian text (see *Critical Apparatus*).[95] Indeed, these few verses in Codex

---

90. The theme of Paul's disobedience with regard to his final visit to Jerusalem is examined in detail by Rius-Camps, 'The Gradual Awakening of Paul's Awareness of his Mission to the Gentiles', in T. Nicklas and M. Tilly (eds), *Apostelgeschichte als Kirchengeschichte. Text, Traditionen und antike Auslegungen* (BZNW, 122; Berlin-New York: Walter de Gruyter, 2003) pp. 281–96.

91. The character of Barnabas is studied by J. Read-Heimerdinger, 'Barnabas in Acts: A Study of his Role in the Text of Codex Bezae', *JSNT* 72 (1998), pp. 23–66. The first mention of his name at Acts 1.23 in Codex Bezae is discussed in *The Message of Acts*, I, pp. 129–31. His role is further explored with reference to 4.36 (II, pp. 298–301).

92. The role of the Hellenists in representing accurately the universality of Jesus' teaching is explored in *The Message of Acts*, II, pp. 27–31.

93. See *The Message of Acts*, II, p. 360.

94. For the identification of John-Mark as Mark the evangelist, see Rius-Camps, 'Qui és Joan, l'anomenat "Marc"?', *RCatT* 5 (1980), pp. 297–329.

95. The question of the article before the names of persons in Acts is studied exhaustively by Read-Heimerdinger, *The Bezan Text*, pp. 116–44; modification to the usual word order for the sake of highlighting is discussed in general terms, pp. 68–70.

Bezae, 15.36-41 D05, display an exceptionally high concentration of linguistic markers that signal conflict.

Structure and Themes

The final sequence centres on the fierce disagreement that causes a definitive split between Barnabas and Paul [d]. The first three elements [a b c] present the build-up to the separation, and the last three [b′ c′ a′] the results of it. The correspondences between the elements of the ascending movement and those of the descending movement are marked: both [a] and [a′] refer to Paul's visit to the churches; the positions of Barnabas and Paul are restated in the same order [b - b′], [c - c′] each time.

[a]	15.36	Paul's proposal to visit the brethren
[b]	15.37	Barnabas' intention to take John-Mark
[c]	15.38	Paul's opposition
[d]	15.39a	The split between Barnabas and Paul
[b′]	15.39b	Barnabas's departure to Cyprus with Mark
[c′]	15.40	Paul leaves Antioch with Silas
[a′]	15.41	Paul visits the churches in Syria and Cilicia

Translation

Codex Bezae D05

[a]   **15.36** After some days, Paul said to Barnabas, 'Come on, let us go back and visit the brethren who are in every city, among whom we announced the word of the Lord, to see how they are'.

[b]   **37** Barnabas was resolved to take along with them John who was recognized as Mark.

[c]   **38** Paul, however, did not wish to, saying that the one who had withdrawn from them from Pamphylia onwards and had not accompanied them to the work to which they had been sent, this man he forbade to be with them.

[d]   **39a** There developed sharp disagreement with the result that they separated from each other.

[b′]   **39b** Then Barnabas, taking Mark, sailed to Cyprus.

[c′]   **40** Paul, having welcomed Silas, left after being commended to the grace of the Lord by the brethren.

[a′]   **41** He went through Syria and through Cilicia, strengthening the churches and handing over the commands of the elders.

Codex Vaticanus B03

15.36 After some days, to Barnabas Paul said, 'Come on, let us go back and visit the brethren in all the cities in which we announced the word of the Lord, to see how they are'.

37 Barnabas wanted to take along, in addition, John called Mark.

38 Paul, however, held that the one who had withdrawn from them from Pamphylia onwards and had not gone with them to the work, they were not to take this man along.

39a There developed sharp disagreement with the result that they separated from each other,

39b and that Barnabas, taking Mark, sailed away to Cyprus.

40 Paul, having choosen Silas, left after being commended to the grace of the Lord by the brethren.

41 He went through Syria and Cilicia, strengthening the churches.

Critical Apparatus

15.36 (εἶπεν) πρὸς Βαρναβᾶν (+ ὁ 33. 69. 1175. 1837. 2344) Παῦλος B 𝔓⁷⁴ ℵ A C Ψ 81 ‖ ὁ (+ D) Π. πρὸς Βαρ. D, *ait Paulus ad Barnaban* d E H L P 049. 056. 1739 𝔐 gig l vg^w.

The article before Paul in D05, reinforced by his position in the sentence, is an indication that he remains in focus (cf. 15.35 D05 above), and that Barnabas in comparison is not now the centre of attention; the effect is to portray Paul as the dominating character at this point. In the Alexandrian text, both participants continue to have equal narrative status.

(ἀδελφοὺς) κατὰ πόλιν πᾶσαν B 𝔓⁷⁴ ℵ A C 33. 69. 927. 1270 ‖ κ. π. πόλ. H L P 049. 056 𝔐 ‖ τοὺς κ. πᾶ. πόλ. D 36. 257. 383. 431- 453. 614. 618. 913. 1518. 1611. 1799. 2138. 2147. 2412 *pc* l sy^p-h** .— ἐν αἷς (κατηγγείλαμεν) B 𝔓⁷⁴ ℵ *rell* ‖ ἐν οἷς D, *penes quos* d.

According to B03, Paul's proposal is focused on the cities in which the message has been announced, whereas by means of the three *vll* of D05 (the repetition of the article τούς, the word order of πᾶσαν πόλιν and the masculine relative pronoun οἷς), the proposal in that text is focused on the brethren to whom the message has been announced.

15.37 (Βαρναβᾶς δὲ) ἐβούλετο B 𝔓⁷⁴ ℵ A C E Ψ 33. 81. 104. 323. 614. 945. 1175. 1270. 1611. 1739. 1891. 2344, *volebat* d ‖ -εύσατο H L P 049. 056 𝔐 ‖ -εύετο D gig.— (συμπαραλαβεῖν) καὶ τὸν Ἰωάννην B ℵ 81. 88. 614. 1611. 2412 *pc* ‖ καὶ Ἰω. 𝔓⁷⁴ A C E Ψ 049. 36. 1175. 1241. 1505 *pm* ‖ τὸν Ἰω. H L P 056. 33^vid. 424 *pm* ‖ Ἰωάνην D / Ἰωάννην 323. 1739. 1891 *al*, *Iohannen* d l p vg^mss sa.— (τὸν) καλούμενον B 𝔓⁷⁴ ℵ* A E H L P 049. 056 𝔐 ‖ ἐπικ- D, *qui cognominatur* d ℵ² C Ψ 33. 81. 614. 1175. 1241. 1505. 1739 *al*.

B03 uses the verb βούλομαι in the imperfect, 'he wanted'; D05 has the verb βουλεύομαι in the aorist, which takes on the sense of 'decided, resolved' (see Bailly, βουλεύομαι, '*avec l'inf.* décider de'). B03 plays down the significance of Barnabas' wish further, by saying that he 'wanted to take along, in addition, John called Mark', where the name of John is arthrous since he has already been mentioned as the companion of Barnabas and Paul. D05 is more categorical and the conflict is more evident: he 'was resolved to take along with them John who was recognized as Mark'; the absence of the article before John is an indication that the choice was not expected (Read-Heimerdinger, *The Bezan Text*, p. 129).

The force of the distinction between the verb καλέω and the compound ἐπικαλέω lies in the fact that Luke consistently uses the latter to refer to the function of a character that is either active (present, cf. Barnabas, 1.23; John-Mark, 12.12; 15.37) or dormant (aorist, cf. Barnabas, 4.36; John-Mark, 12.25).

15.38 ἠξίου Β 𝔓⁷⁴ ℵ *rell* ‖ οὐκ ἐβούλετο λέγων D, *nolebat dicens* d l (syᵖ aeth).

Once again, B03 plays down the tension, saying that Paul 'held that', (ἀξιόω, 'consider fitting', B-A-G, 2a; with the imperfect conferring the sense of insistence). D05 is more categorical in expressing Paul's opposition to Barnabas, using the verb βούλομαι.

(τὸν) ἀποστάντα Β 𝔓⁷⁴ ℵ *rell* ‖ -στήσαντα D (-στατήσαντα Α ǀ *hiis qui discesserunt* d!).

B03 reads the intransitive second aorist participle of ἀφίστημι. If the first aorist of D05, ἀποστήσαντα, is transitive, it is obviously erroneous since there is no complement (cf. Delebecque, *Les deux Actes*, p. 98, 'impossible parce que transitif'). However, the D05 reading may be compared with the first aorist participle διαστήσαντες at 27.28 where it is clearly intransitive. On that basis, there is a case for accepting the D05 reading here as displaying an accepted, though rare, use. In any case, it is the *lectio difficilior*, which is more likely to have been corrected by other manuscripts than to be a corruption of the intransitive form of an exemplar.

(συνελθόντα) αὐτοῖς Β 𝔓⁷⁴ ℵ *rell* ‖ om. D (*simul venerunt* d!).— (ἔργον) εἰς ὃ ἐπέμφθησαν D, *in quo missi erant* d c w vgᶜᴹᴿᵀ ‖ om. Β 𝔓⁷⁴ ℵ *rell*.

The absence of the dative pronoun αὐτοῖς in D05 is accounted for by the presence of the phrase εἰς ὃ ἐπέμφθησαν in that text, rendering the pronoun unnecessary.

μὴ συμπαραλαμβάνειν τοῦτον Β 𝔓⁷⁴ ℵ ǀ μὴ -λαβεῖν τ. Η L Ρ 049. 056 𝔐 ǀ τοῦτον μὴ -λαμβάνειν 𝔓⁴⁵ᵛⁱᵈ gig vg*cl ‖ τ. μὴ εἶναι σὺν αὐτοῖς D (*hunc non adsumerent secum* d).

The wording of B03 considers the presence of John-Mark with Paul and Barnabas from the point of view of their action, they being the subject of the infinitive συμπαραλαμβάνειν, and τοῦτον being the direct object. In contrast, the wording of D05 focuses on the action of John-Mark, he being the subject, as the accusative pronoun τοῦτον, of the infinitive εἶναι. The Latin page d5 is a conflation of both readings.

15.39 τόν τε (δέ Η 049. 1. 330 d boᵐˢˢ) Βαρναβᾶν παραλαβόντα τὸν Μᾶρκον ἐκπλεῦσαι Β 𝔓⁷⁴ ℵ *rell* ‖ τότε Βαρναβᾶς παραλαβὼν τ. Μᾶρ. ἔπλευσεν D a b c gig vgᴰ (*Barnabas vero adsumpto Marco navigaverunt* d).

In B03, the sentence continues to be dependent on the conjunction ὥστε, in parallel to the previous infinitive ἀποχωρισθῆναι, as an additional result. The subject of the infinitive ἐκπλεῦσαι is thus in the accusative. D05, on the other hand, marks a new sentence with the conjunction τότε expressing a concluding result of a previous scene (Read-Heimerdinger, *The Bezan Text*, pp. 212–13; 218–19), with the verb having a finite form and the subject in the nominative. The verb is the simple πλεύω, rather than the compound ἐκπλεύω of B03. The absence of the article before Barnabas maintains the contrast between him and Paul (as in vv. 37, 38), whereas in B03 the presence of the article has the effect of lessening the conflict (*The Bezan Text*, p. 130).

15.40 ἐπιλεξάμενος (Σιλᾶν) B $\mathfrak{P}^{74}$ ℵ *rell* ‖ -δεξάμενος D, *suscepit* d.

B03 reads the verb ἐπιλέγομαι, 'choose', whereas D05 reads ἐπιδέχομαι, 'welcome', suggesting that Silas was ready to accompany him.

(τῇ χάριτι) τοῦ κυρίου B $\mathfrak{P}^{74}$ ℵ A D^E 33. 81. 181. 1409. 1837. 2344 ar c dem p ph^2 m vg$^{ww.st}$ sa ‖ τοῦ θεοῦ $\mathfrak{P}^{45}$ C E H L P Ψ 049. 056. 614. 945. 1175. 1241. 1739 $\mathfrak{M}$ a b gig p ph* w vg^{BW} sy$^{p.h}$ bo; Chr Thret ‖ κυρίου D*, *domini* d.

The expression τῇ χάριτι τοῦ κυρίου is arthrous in B03 as also the Corrector E of D05; the anarthrous form in the first hand of D05 corresponds to the fixed expression of the LXX.

ὑπό (τῶν ἀδελφῶν) B $\mathfrak{P}^{74}$ ℵ *rell* ‖ ἀπό D, *a (fratribus)* d.

ὑπό is the correct preposition to introduce the agent of the passive verb παραδοθείς. When ἀπό replaces ὑπό, it is with verbs of sending, especially with the prefix ἀπό-. Since D05 is consistent in following this rule (see Read-Heimerdinger, *The Bezan Text*, pp.184–87), the preposition ἀπό here can be seen to express the departure of Paul from the brethren who commended him to the grace of the Lord.

15.41 (διήρχετο δὲ) τὴν Συρίαν καὶ τὴν Κιλικίαν B D Ψ 88. 1646 ‖ τ. Συ. κ. Κι. ℵ A C E H L P 049. 056. 614. 945. 1175. 1241. 1739 $\mathfrak{M}$ ‖ διὰ τῆς Σ-ας κ. τῆς Κ-ας $\mathfrak{P}^{45}$.

B03 and D05 treat the two areas of Syria and Cilicia as quite distinct, while ℵ01 groups them together.

(ἐκκλησίας) παραδιδοὺς (-δόντες sy^{hmg}; Ephr) τὰς ἐντολὰς τῶν πρεσβυτέρων D (*tradens autem mandatum presbyterorum* d, *praecipiens custodire praecepta apostolorum et seniorum* a ar b c dem gig ph ro w vg^{mss} sy^{hmg}; Ephr) ‖ *om.* B $\mathfrak{P}^{41.(74)}$ ℵ *rell*.

In D05, Paul is said to hand over 'the commands of the elders', in accordance with earlier readings of D05 that emphasized the role of this group (cf. 15.5 D05, 12 D05).

Commentary

[a] 15.36 *Paul's Proposal to Visit the Brethren*
15.36 The previous sequence concluded with a positive and harmonious picture of Paul and Barnabas, and many others, teaching in Antioch and announcing the good news of the gospel there. No end was specified for this situation, but it does not last long since, 'after some days', Paul has the idea to

go back to see the brethren he had got to know with Barnabas during their
earlier missionary activity. The two texts present differently the way he makes
the suggestion to Barnabas.

In the Alexandrian text, the spotlight falls, as it were, equally on both
Barnabas and Paul as they are mentioned without the article in Greek;[96] at
the same time, the position of Paul after Barnabas ('said to Barnabas Paul',
lit.) disrupts the expected order of the speaker before the addressee, and thus
maintains Paul as the dominant figure. The plan he puts to Barnabas is that
they should visit the brethren in all the places where they had preached the
word of the Lord, the message of Jesus (see *Excursus* 1).

In the introduction to Paul's plan in Codex Bezae, the leading role of Paul
is underlined even more than in the Alexandrian text. At 15.35, a single article
had presented Paul and Barnabas as a united pair (see *Critical Apparatus, ad
loc.*); now the article is maintained before Paul as he takes the initiative to
formulate a plan, and its omission before Barnabas has the effect of disrupting
the harmony and equality between them.[97] According to the Bezan text, it is the
brethren who are very much the centre of Paul's concern: he refers to them as
'[those] who are in every city' and '[those] among whom' they had preached
the word of the Lord.

Whether in the Alexandrian text or Codex Bezae, the tone of Paul's words
is not one of an invitation,[98] nor of a simple exhortation, but of a command.[99]
His intention is not to take the mission to the Gentiles to new countries but to
go back to the places where they already knew there were believers. The
motive behind his strategy is not yet made clear – he simply wants to see
'how they are'. The real reason will be seen (especially in the Bezan text)
once Paul arrives in the cities where he wanted to see the brethren (see 16.4
Commentary).

96. Names of persons in Greek are normally prefaced with the article; omission of the article
has the effect of drawing attention to the person for one reason or another. Several examples of
this are seen throughout the sequence (see comments in the *Overview* above). At 15.35, the article
was omitted before both names in the AT (see *Critical Apparatus, ad loc.*) as the pair were
brought back into focus after the departure of Judas and Silas, with whom they were contrasted
because they stayed in Antioch.

97. Although at 15.35 and 15.36 the name of Paul has the article but not that of Barnabas, the
reason for the omission of the article before Barnabas is different in each case because of the different grammatical roles of the two names: at v. 35, the two names are in the nominative, conjoined by καί; at v. 36, Paul is in the nominative and Barnabas is preceded by a preposition. If
Paul and Barnabas continued to be working together in harmony, the article could be expected to
be maintained before his name; it may also be that without the article, Barnabas is one person
among the 'many others', highlighted as Paul singles him out to talk to him.

98. The particle δή, more intensive than δέ, has already been seen at 5.8 D05*; 13.2 (cf. 6.3
A02; Lk. 2.15).

99. The aorist subjunctive ἐπισκεψώμεθα (cf. Lk. 2.15) is the equivalent of an aorist imperative: cf. Acts 6.3; 13.2.

[b] 15.37 *Barnabas' Intention to Take John-Mark*

15.37 Barnabas is now singled out in the spotlight as his reaction to Paul's plan is presented,[100] the connective δέ preparing for an element of discord. According to the Alexandrian text, Barnabas expresses his wish to take John along with them, too, the term καλούμενον, 'being called' (lit.), introducing the name Mark by which he was known (cf. 'Judas called Barabbas/Barsabbas, 15.22). The name of John is prefaced with the article, a sign that his association with Paul and Barnabas continued to be an active memory. He had gone with them when they had first gone out from Antioch (13.5b), but had left them once they were in Pamphylia and gone back to Hierosoluma (13.13), the unstated reason being that he did not agree with Paul's methods and dominance (see *Commentary, ad loc.*). He may have been in Antioch at this time, since he will leave from there with Barnabas before the end of the sequence.

The feelings of Barnabas are expressed more forcefully in the Bezan text, where he is said to have decided to take John along with them, not in addition but as a person who was indispensable in Barnabas' judgement; the reason for his decision is made evident in the description of John as ἐπικαλούμενον, using the present tense of the participle that has been used at other places in Acts to designate the recognition of the function of a character (see *Critical Apparatus*; also *Excursus* 2). The role of John, as was noted when he was first introduced in chapter 12,[101] is as the keeper of the gospel for which he is known as 'Mark', the name under which he will go to Cyprus with Barnabas (cf. 15.39b). This function had not been acknowledged when Barnabas and Paul had taken him along with them to Antioch (12.25, where the aorist participle ἐπικληθέντα was used to indicate an inactive function), nor when he had accompanied them from Antioch on their earlier journey where he is simply referred to as 'John' (cf. 13.5, 13); here in Antioch, however, his role is again actively recognized.

Barnabas obviously has a reason for wanting John to accompany him and Paul as they go back to visit the communities founded on the first visit, and in the Bezan text it is made clear: he is to be with them in his function as Mark, maintaining the truth of the gospel in those places where Barnabas must have missed his presence on the earlier journey, as Paul repeatedly went to the synagogues giving precedence to the Jews over the Gentiles in contradiction to the universal message of Jesus. Now that Paul is in possession of the decree from the apostles and elders, which strengthens his position to some extent, it is no wonder that Barnabas insists on having the back up of John-Mark in order to combat Paul's attitude to the Jews. It will become clear once Paul arrives in the cities they had previously visited that Barnabas was not wrong in anticipating trouble.

---

100. The name of Barnabas is the first word in the sentence and the article is omitted (see Read-Heimerdinger, *The Bezan Text*, pp. 128–29).

101. John-Mark's earlier appearances are discussed in *The Message of Acts*, II, pp. 360, 390, with reference to 12.12 and 12.25 respectively.

[c] 15.38 *Paul's Opposition*

15.38 The confrontation between Barnabas and Paul continues, with the Greek connective δέ again marking the opposition between them. Now, the name of Paul is singled out, as was that of Barnabas at the beginning of the previous sentence.[102] The imperfect tense of the Greek verb (though a different verb in each text) gives the sense of a repeated insistence, echoing the imperfect describing the position of Barnabas in 15.37. This was not a quick disagreement but an argument that was maintained over some time.

In the Bezan text, he opposes Barnabas's decision with his own will, and this is where the heart of the conflict lies. In justification, he invokes the fact that he had left them in Pamphylia and so from that point on had not accompanied them while they were carrying out the work for which they had been sent. The reference is to their commissioning by the Holy Spirit, ratified by the church in Antioch (13.2-4). His refusal is categorical, referring to John-Mark with a disrespectful 'this man'[103] and forbidding him to be with them.[104] He makes no comment on John-Mark's reasons for having withdrawn from them early on in the mission, nor on Barnabas' reasons for wanting him to be with them now. It is this silence that has caused Paul's opposition to be interpreted as justified but, as always, Luke's silence is eloquent and needs also to be listened to.

As before, the conflict is somewhat attenuated in the Alexandrian text account, where Paul is said to have 'held' (in the sense of 'thought appropriate') that they should not take John-Mark with them, on the same grounds as in the Bezan text but without any mention of their being 'sent' to their work. He takes up the same verb as Barnabas used (συμπαραλαμβάνω, 'take along'), stating his position as a straightforward opposition to the wish of Barnabas.

[d] 15.39a *The Split between Barnabas and Paul*

15.39a Things finally come to a head, when the conflict is so intense that Luke refers to it as a παροξυσμός, 'sharp disagreement'.[105] Paul and Barnabas, despite being chosen as a pair by the Holy Spirit (cf. 13.2-4), 'separate from each other'. It is no coincidence that Luke uses exactly the same verb (ἀπο-χωρέω) to describe this separation as the one he used when John-Mark separated from them in Pamphylia (cf. 13.13). The difference is that this time it is John-Mark who is the cause of the split, but the repetition of the verb is a way

---

102. Not only is the name the first word in the sentence, preceding even the verb, but it is again anarthrous, signalling the ongoing conflict between Paul and Barnabas.

103. Both texts read the demonstrative pronoun τοῦτον, but its position at the front of the sentence in D05 confers on it a more marked note of disrespect.

104. The negative infinitive expresses a prohibition: '*il défendait*: ce verbe traduit l'infinitif d'ordre μὴ εἶναι' (Delebecque, *Les deux Actes*, p. 99).

105. Louw and Nida, *Greek-English Lexicon*, p. 440, παροξυσμός: 'a severe argument based on intense difference of opinion'.

of signalling that the reason behind the division, for Barnabas as much as for John-Mark, is the impossibility for John to exercise his function as Mark while Paul is in charge of the mission.

[b′] 15.39b *Barnabas's Departure to Cyprus with Mark*

15.39b Following the separation, Barnabas and Paul will go their separate ways. The Alexandrian text links Barnabas' departure for Cyprus with John-Mark directly to the split, as a second result of the intense disagreement that follows on from the first (see *Critical Apparatus*). Codex Bezae, on the other hand, presents it as the final outcome of the preceding narrative, so according it greater prominence.

Cyprus is Barnabas' native country (cf. 4.36), as well as being the first place visited on the initial journey with Paul but where no new disciples were made, although there are various indications that there were already believers there.[106] This departure across the sea, intensified with the compound verb 'sailed away' in the Alexandrian text, marks the definitive exodus of Barnabas from the confines of Judaism.[107] It is significant that John-Mark is referred to only by his adopted name of Mark at this point: he finally enjoys full freedom to exercise his function, in the company of Barnabas. It may be justifiably supposed that Cyprus was only the beginning of their joint venture and that the whole of the earlier journey will be repeated in due course, for Barnabas has already expressed the concern that Mark should visit also the other communities founded by Paul and himself.

Neither of these two characters, the one representing the prophetic gifts of encouragement and exhortation and the other the proclamation of the gospel, will be referred to again by Luke, a sure sign that their activity is in full harmony with the message of Jesus as presented by Luke in his first volume (see *General Introduction*, §II).

[c′] 15.40 *Paul Leaves Antioch with Silas*

15.40 Just as the name of Barnabas was placed at the front of the previous sentence in the Bezan text (following the initial connective which must stand in first position in Greek), so now the name of Paul stands as the first word

---

106. In Salamis, although 'the word of the Lord' was proclaimed in the synagogues, there is no report of belief in Jesus. In Paphos, the episode concludes with the proconsul believing but, according to the Bezan text, the object of this belief is limited to God, which is not the same as belief in Jesus, and he was not baptized (see *Commentary, ad loc.*). However, the Hellenist disciples who left Hierosoluma at the time of Stephen's death had gone to Cyprus among other places, preaching the gospel to Jews (11.19); and it was 'men from Cyprus and Cyrene' who had first preached the gospel in Antioch to Gentiles (11.20).

107. The sea represents the direction of an exodus, in the sense of a departure from religious enslavement, in Luke's writings: cf. Lk. 5.27 D05; 17.2, 6; Acts 10.6, 32; 17.14; 27.30, 38, 40; 28.4. See *The Message of Acts*, II, pp. 248, 261 on the force of the symbol for Peter in Caesarea.

in the new sentence.[108] The contrast between them is thus underlined, as also Barnabas' choice of Mark is contrasted with Paul's choice of Silas. Although Silas has already been present in the narrative, he has not been anticipated as Paul's choice.[109] The Bezan text recorded that he had stayed in Antioch (15.34) without giving any explanation for his decision; that the same text now says that Paul 'welcomed Silas', would seem to indicate that it had something to do with Paul and that he was already disposed to work alongside him.

As Paul leaves with Silas, he is entrusted to 'the grace of the Lord' by the church in Antioch, just as Barnabas and Saul had been when they first left Antioch for their mission (cf. 14.26). Thus it is clear that the church gives them their support and understands that they will need the help of the Lord for what they propose to do. That is not the same as saying that they give them approval – on the contrary, the more they understand about Paul's plan, which goes contrary to the plan of Jesus, the more they will realize that he needs divine grace.

[a′] 15.41 *Paul Visits the Churches in Syria and Cilicia*

15.41 The narrative continues in the singular, viewing Paul's journey with Silas as being under his leadership and at his initiative. He goes through the two regions named in the letter from Jerusalem, both Syria and Cilicia. Although his original plan had been to visit the brethren 'in all the cities' where they had preached the good news, he obviously does not want to be in the same places as Barnabas and Mark. His route to the various places therefore follows the reverse itinerary, going via the north rather than the south.[110] In fact, neither Syria nor Cilicia was mentioned as having been visited with Barnabas, but taking them as starting points has the further advantage of their being able to deliver the letter addressed to the Gentiles in these places. It presumably allowed Paul to visit his home town of Tarsus, too (cf. 9.11, 30; 11.25).

In these regions, Paul undertakes two activities in the churches. The first is to strengthen them, in the same way as Peter strengthened the brethren on his journey between Caesarea and Hierosoluma (cf. 11.2 D05); likeweise Paul and Barnabas, the disciples in Lystra, Iconium and Antioch of Pisidia; and Judas and also Silas, the brethren in Syrian Antioch. The other activity, related only by the Bezan text, is to give them the Jerusalem letter, described as 'the com-

---

108. Both names are anarthrous in D05, underlining yet again the contrast between them (Read-Heimerdinger, *The Bezan Text*, p. 130).

109. The fact that nothing prepares for Paul's choice of Silas accounts for the absence of the article before his name (Read-Heimerdinger, *The Bezan Text*, p. 129); it is also a way of contrasting him with Barnabas' choice of Mark in the previous verse.

110. In the first century, before the capture of Jerusalem by the Romans, Syria was the province that stretched to the north of Judaea, reaching as far as the capital of Antioch; Cilicia lay at its north-western border, stretching westwards along the south coast of Asia Minor (*Atlas of the Bible*, pp. 170–74).

mands of the elders'. This description of the letter betrays yet again (cf. 15.5 D05, 12 D05) the leading role played by the elders, under the direction of James, in deciding the conditions for the entry of the Gentiles into the Church. It is becoming clearer that transmitting the contents of the letter is a key motive for Paul's journey, when he will hope to show to the Jews he goes to meet that the conditions for the admission of the Gentiles can be justified from the Scriptures and have been agreed in Jerusalem.

General Overview

The third section of this part of Acts takes up the theme of Paul's journeys, also the theme of the first section. Between the two, there has been the meeting with the apostles and the elders in Ierousalem to settle the question of the conditions for the admission of the Gentiles into the Church (14.28–15.29). The outcome of the meeting was set out in a letter addressed to the Gentiles of Antioch, Syria and Cilicia (15.23b-29). Following its delivery to the brethren in Antioch (15.30-31), Paul took it to the churches of Syria and Cilicia, accompanied by Silas who was one of the two leaders sent from Jerusalem (no longer called Ἰερουσαλήμ, cf. 15.30-35, *Overview*) to take the letter to Antioch (15.40-41, cf. 15.22, 32-34). Barnabas had not accompanied him because he had separated from Paul and gone to Cyprus with John-Mark (15.36-39). The split was caused by the fierce disagreement over Barnabas' decision (15.37 D05; wish, AT) that John-Mark should go with them when Paul had expressed his intention to go back to visit the churches they had founded on their earlier journey (Cyprus, Antioch of Pisidia, Iconium, Lystra and Derbe). Indeed, with Barnabas and Mark having gone to Cyprus (15.39b), Paul had taken the northerly route overland, visiting the churches of Syria and Cilicia (15.41) and delivering the letter from Jerusalem (D05).

Once Paul is on his way, and after visiting the northerly regions that he had been to with Barnabas, he is seen heading westwards, though the reason for this direction is not apparent until much later when, in the fourth part of Acts at 19.21, Paul reveals that he knew it was God's plan for him to go to Rome. A series of divine interventions occurs meanwhile, in the early verses of this section, to keep him moving along a westerly route until he finally crosses over the sea into Macedonia. The majority of this section will take place in Macedonia and Greece.

At the very point of crossing over from Asia to Macedonia, the 'we'-group appear, for the first time in the narrative of the Alexandrian text but for a second, or even third, time in the text of Codex Bezae (cf. 11.28; 13.14). Their role will be to act as prompts and guides to Paul in order to keep him focused on the mission to the Gentiles that has been entrusted to him (see *General Introduction*, §V).

The end point of the section, and also the third part of Acts, has been identified at 18.23 by noting the inherent unity of the narrative from 18.24 to the end of the book of Acts, as discussed in the *General Introduction*, §XII.

Structure and Themes

As in the first section that dealt with the journey undertaken by Barnabas and Paul (13.1–14.27), the progress in the narrative in this section is again marked by successive stages in the journey. This time, Paul is the leader from the start, accompanied by Silas then also Timothy (16.3), and briefly by an anonymous group referred to as 'we' (16.10-17; see *General Introduction*, §VIII). Eight sequences are identified, with the first [A] and the last [A'] forming introductory and concluding narrative passages. Several sequences are composed of smaller episodes arranged in a variety of patterns. The two central sequences, [D-D'], represent the climax of Jewish opposition to Paul and Silas in this section.

[A]	16.1-4	Prolegomena
[B]	16.5-10	Crossing into Macedonia
[C]	16.11-40	Macedonia I: Philippi
[C-*A*]	16.11-12	Journey to Philippi
[C-*B*]	16.13-15	Lydia
[C-*C*]	16.16-24	Imprisonment
[C-*B'*]	16.25-34	The Philippian jailor
[C-*C'*]	16.35-39	Release from prison
[C-*A'*]	16.40	Departure from Philippi
[D]	17.1-9	Macedonia II: Thessalonica
[D']	17.10-13	Macedonia III: Beroea
[C']	17.14-34	Greece I: Athens
[C'-*A*]	17.14-15	Journey to Athens
[C'-*B*]	17.16-18	Paul in the synagogue and in the market place
[C'-*B'*]	17.19-34	Paul in the Areopagus
[B']	18.1-17	Greece II: Corinth
[B'-*A*]	18.1-11	In the synagogue
[B'-*A'*]	18.12-17	Before the proconsul Gallio
[A']	18.18-23	Epilogue

[A] 16.1-4 *Prolegomena*

Overview

These verses at the beginning of the second phase of the mission to the Gentiles form a preparatory sequence, which sets the scene for the expansion of the mission beyond the territory covered during the earlier stage. The mention of 'those nations' in the opening clause of Codex Bezae serves as a bridge to move the narrative on from the previous section, which had concluded with the naming of Syria and Cilicia. The circumcision of Timothy, a son of mixed Jewish–Gentile parentage, constitutes a new strategy devised by Paul to prepare for his continuing attempts to win over his fellow-Jews to belief in

Jesus as the Messiah: he shows that he is ready to encourage those believers of Jewish origin to continue to adhere to the Jewish Law.

Structure and Themes

The main point of interest in this preparatory sequence is Paul's meeting of Timothy and his circumcision of him. The theme of circumcision was raised in the previous section by the insistence of some of the Pharisee believers on the need to circumcise the Gentile disciples (cf. 15.1, 5). Here, the idea is taken further, by raising the question of circumcision among Jewish believers.

The action takes place in Derbe, Lystra and Iconium, the furthest cities visited by Paul and Barnabas during the first phase of the mission, but now returned to at the outset of his return visit.

[a]   16.1a   Paul's arrival in Derbe and Lystra
[b]   16.1b-2 Introduction of Timothy
[c]   16.3a   Paul wishes to take Timothy with him
[c']   16.3b   Circumcision of Timothy
[b']   16.3c   Timothy's parentage
[a']   16.4   Preaching and transmission of Jerusalem decree

Translation

Codex Bezae D05

[a]   **16.1a** Having gone through those nations, he went down to Derbe and Lystra.

[b]   **1b** There, there was a certain disciple by the name of Timothy, the son of a Jewish woman believer but of a Greek father, **2** who was well spoken of by the brethren in Lystra and Iconium.

[c]   **3a** This man, Paul wanted him to go out with him;

[c']   **3b** and he took him and circumcised him because of the local Jews in that place

[b']   **3c** (for his father, they all knew that he had been Greek).

[a']   **4** Going through the cities, they preached to them and delivered to them with all boldness the Lord Jesus, the Messiah, at the same time delivering also the commands of the apostles and elders who were in Hierosoluma.

Codex Vaticanus B03

16.1a He went down both to Derbe and also to Lystra.

1b There was a certain disciple there by the name of Timothy, the son of a Jewish woman believer but of a Greek father, **2** who was well spoken of by the brethren in Lystra and Iconium.

3a This man, Paul wanted him to go out with him;

3b and he took him and circumcised him because of the local Jews in that place

3c (for they all knew that his father had been Greek).

4 As they were travelling through the cities, they delivered to them for their observance the rules that had been decided by the apostles and elders who were in Hierosoluma.

Critical Apparatus

The text of chapter 16 has a high incidence of variant readings, with over a third (34.6%) of the Bezan text affected by variation, which is second only to the 40% of variant text found in chapter 18. Around half of that variation is made up of material not read by the Alexandrian text, a proportion that is exceptionally high compared with other chapters of Acts (overall, the Bezan text of Acts is only 6.6% longer than the AT – the usual figure of 10% that is bandied around is an exaggeration of the calculations based on a reconstituted, fictitious 'Western' text; see Metzger, *Commentary*, p. 223). A further third of the variation in chapter 16 is made up of alternative material (that is, it exists in the AT but in a different lexical or grammatical form); the remaining variation is made up of word order differences, or material present in the AT but not in D05. (All figures are taken from Read-Heimerdinger, *The Bezan Text*, pp. 6–21, where further comparison of the amount of variation in the narrative compared with speech is presented.)

16.1 Κατήντησεν δέ B 𝔓^{45.74} ℵ *rell* ‖ Διελθὼν δὲ τὰ ἔθνη ταῦτα κατ. D (*Pertransiens gentes istas* d) a (b gig) vg^{DO} (sy^{hmg}; Cass).— καὶ εἰς Δέρβην B 𝔓^{45vid} A Ψ 33^{vid}. 36. 69. 181. 242. 257. 431. 453. 467. 522. 614. 913. 1108. 1175. 1270. 1595. 1611. 1739. 1799. 1891. 1898. 2138. 2298. 2344. 2412. 2495 *al* sy^h | *om.* 𝔓⁷⁴ ‖ εἰς Δέρ. D, *Derben* d ℵ C E H L P 049. 056 𝔐 latt sy^{p.hmg}; Cass.— καὶ εἰς Λύστραν B 𝔓^{45.74} ℵ A Ψ 81. 181. 257. 467. 614. 913. 1108. 1175. 1505. 1518. 1611. 1799. 1838. 1898. 2138. 2344. 2412. 2495 sy^{hmg}; Theoph ‖ καὶ Λύσ. D C E H L P 049. 056. 1739 𝔐 gig vg sa.

A series of variants characterizes the opening of the new section. D05 links it closely with the previous sentence, referring to Syria and Cilicia, which Paul visited when he left Antioch with Silas, as τὰ ἔθνη ταῦτα; the towns of Derbe and Lystra are then introduced without particular highlighting, as being the cities he was heading for according to his plan set out in the last sequence (cf. 15.36); the single preposition εἰς groups the cities as a unit, because they are the combined goal of Paul's journey according to the plan in his mind.

B03 omits any reference to the areas of Syria and Cilicia (as it had also omitted any reference to the delivery of the commands of the elders in those places, cf. 15.41), and therefore underlines the arrival of Paul in the next cities, treating each one as independent with the repetition of not only the preposition εἰς but also καί.

ἦν ἐκεῖ B 𝔓^{45.74} ℵ *rell, erat ibi* d ‖ ἐκ. ἦν D.

The variant involves simply the word order. The placing of the adverb before the verb in D05 underlines the location and thus stresses that Timothy was already there, in the area of Derbe and Lystra (according to B03, in Lystra alone since the town was named independently in the previous sentence), as a disciple. The description of Timothy that follows in 16.2 indicates that the area he was associated with was general and wide (Lystra and Iconium), and yet also specific (ἐν τοῖς τόποις ἐκείνοις, v. 3).

The word order of D05 may, possibly, express a play on words, already noticed at 7.4 (*The Message of Acts*, II, pp. 51, 73), that frequently occurs in the Hebrew Bible in order to hide the unutterable name of the divine in two successive steps: 1) the consonants שם represent the word 'name' (*shem*) or 'there' (*sham*), according to the vocalization, and 2) יהוה, the consonants for the name of God, also represent the third person of the verb 'to be'. In consequence, the phrase ἐκεῖ ἦν is found in the LXX as a translation of the Hebrew device to express the name, and presence, of God (cf. 1 Samuel 19.3). Here in Acts 16.1b, there is a suggestive echo of the hidden meaning of ἐκεῖ ἦν in the next two words presenting Timothy, ὀνόματι Τιμόθεος, where ἐκεῖ (representing שם, 'name') corresponds to ὀνόματι, and Τιμόθεος, meaning 'honouring God', corresponds to ἦν (representing יהוה, YHWH).

16.3 (ᾔδεισαν γὰρ) ἅπαντες B 𝔓⁴⁵ᶜʲ· ᴬˡᵃⁿᵈ ℵ A E H L P Ψ 040. 056. 33. 1739 𝔐 ‖ πάντες D, *omnes* d 𝔓⁷⁴ C 69. 181. 255. 917. 1175. 1646. 1828. 1874. 1898 *pc* vg .— ὅτι Ἕλλην ὁ πατὴρ αὐτοῦ (ὑπῆρχεν) B 𝔓⁷⁴ ℵ A C Ψ 36. 69. 81. 181. 242. 431. 453. 467. 522 945. 1175. 1739. 1837. 1891. 1898. 2298. 2344 *pc* vg co ‖ τὸν πατέρα αὐτοῦ (+ ἅπαντες 257. 383. 614. 913. 1505. 1518. 1611. 1799. 1838. 2138. 2147. 2412. 2495) ὅτι Ἕλλην D, *patrem eius quod Graecus esset* d 𝔓⁴⁵ᶜʲ· ᴬˡᵃⁿᵈ E H L P 049. 056. (614) 𝔐 gig syᵖ.

B03 (with ℵ01) has a tendency to read ἅπας against πᾶς in D05 at places of variant reading, so stressing 'all without exception' (see Read-Heimerdinger, 'The Distinction between ἅπας and πᾶς in the Work of Luke', forthcoming).

B03 expresses the matter concerning Timothy's father in an indirect statement, saying that 'they knew that...', where the imperfect tense ὑπῆρχεν would normally signify that 'he had been' Greek, that is, that he is no longer living. D05 uses the typically Greek construction of prolepsis to express the same facts more forcefully: the subject of the content clause (introduced by ὅτι) is first stated as the object of the main clause (Delebecque, *Les Deux Actes*, pp. 205–206, who cites several other instances of the same construction, even more common in the D05 text than in the AT).

16.4 ὡς δὲ διεπορεύοντο (τὰς πόλεις) B 𝔓⁴⁵·⁷⁴ ℵ *rell* ‖ διερχόμενοι δέ D, *circumeuntes autem* d (gig; Ephr).

The introduction to the sentence is expressed by an imperfect verb in a circumstantial clause of time in B03, and with a present participle of the same verb in D05.

παρεδίδοσαν αὐτοῖς B 𝔓⁴⁵ᵛⁱᵈ·⁷⁴ ℵ *rell* ‖ ἐκήρυσσον καὶ παρ. αὐ. (– κ. παρ. αὐ. syʰᵐᵍ; Ephr) μετὰ πάσης παρρησίας τὸν κύριον Ἰησοῦν Χριστόν D, *praedicabant et tradebant eis cum omnem fiduciam dominum Iesum Christum* d (syʰᵐᵍ; Ephr).— φυλάσσειν τὰ δόγματα τὰ κεκριμένα ὑπὸ τῶν ἀποστόλων B 𝔓⁴⁵ᵛⁱᵈ·⁷⁴ ℵ *rell* ‖ ἅμα παραδιδόντες καὶ τὰς ἐντολὰς (+ τῶν Dᴱ) ἀποστόλων D*, *simul tradentes et mandata apostolorum* d.

B03 has Paul and Silas undertake one action, that of delivering the letter, expressed as 'the rules decided by the apostles...', so that the churches would observe them.

D05 sees them as undertaking two actions, presented in a double structure that is highly emphatic. First, the actions are stated on their own with two finite aorist verbs – ἐκήρυσσον καὶ παρεδίδοσαν. Then, they are re-stated: first, with the manner of the preaching described, and the contents specified; then, with the repetition of the second verb as a present participle, and again its contents specified. The contents of the preaching is potentially ambiguous, in that the Greek phrase τὸν κύριον Ἰησοῦν Χριστόν can be construed as one single component ('the Lord Jesus Christ'), or as two with the verb εἶναι implied ('that the Lord was Jesus, the Messiah'); in so far as the message was directed to a Jewish audience (rather than the churches), it is more likely that Luke intended the phrase to be read in the second way, as a declarative statement with its two components. The content of the letter they handed over is expressed more simply than in B03, as 'the commands of the apostles...'.

Commentary

[a] 16.1a *Paul's Arrival in Derbe and Lystra*

16.1a Paul and Silas now move on from Syria and Cilicia to put into action Paul's plan of returning to visit the brethren in the cities where he had previously announced the gospel with Barnabas (cf. 15.36). The northern itinerary followed, starting with the towns of Derbe and Lystra which had been at the end of the previous journey, was no doubt dictated in part by the presence of Barnabas and Mark in Cyprus (cf. 15.39), which had been the previous starting point (cf. 13.4-12); it also made a natural progression from Syria and Cilicia where they had gone to deliver the letter (cf. 15.41). These two regions were the only places apart from Antioch, where the letter had already been delivered (cf. 15.30-31), to which the letter was addressed, but it will be seen in 16.4 that Paul and Silas will extend the scope of the letter by taking it to other towns they visit. Codex Bezae underlines the anomaly, inherent in this step because it is unauthorized, by spelling out not only that the commands had been delivered in Syria and Cilicia (cf. on 15.41 D05 above) but also that it was after going 'through those nations' (the ones to which the letter was addressed) that they arrived in Derbe and Lystra. This is now a new region, that of Lycaonia, of which no mention is made in the letter.

Geographically, Derbe and Lystra were accessible overland from Cilicia by way of the Cilician Gates through the Taurus Mountains. Derbe would have been the first city arrived at, with Lystra some distance away. Their association depends more on their both belonging to Lycaonia (cf. 14.6) than on their proximity (see on 16.2 below).

[b] 16.1b-2 *Introduction of Timothy*

16.1b Once in the area of Derbe and Lystra,[1] a new character is introduced into the narrative and an event concerning him is related, which is all the more

---

1. It is unwarranted to take the adverb 'there' [ἐκεῖ] as referring only to the last-named place, especially in the Bezan text where the two cities are viewed as a single unit (see *Critical Apparatus*, 16.1). Cf. Bruce, *Text*, p. 307.

dramatic for being quietly understated. The character is introduced with the same phrase, καὶ ἰδού (literally 'and behold'), that introduces other characters in Acts who, as they are encountered for the first time by a character already on stage, signal a fresh development in the narrative (cf. Lk. 2.25 B03; 5.12; 7.37; 9.30, 38; 10.25 B03; 13.11; 14.2; 19.2; 23.50; 24.4; Acts 1.10; 3.2 D05; 8.27; 12.7). His name is Timothy, and as well as being a person in his own right, he is a disciple who represents a certain category of people, as indicated by Luke's typical use of the adjective 'a certain' (τις).[2] It is interesting to note that just such a character, who is both emblematic and real, is presented at the outset of all three of the three phases of Paul's mission: Bar-Iesoua (D05; Bar-Jesus, AT) in the beginning at Paphos (13.6); Timothy in Lystra, here (at 16.1); and Apollos (Apollonius, D05) as the final phase begins in Ephesus (18.24). Each one sets the tone for the progress of that particular stage of the mission – this was observed in the case of the Jewish false prophet in Paphos, who represented the temptation facing Paul as he went from city to city to accord a privileged status to the Jews in his presentation of the gospel (see *Commentary*, 13.6-12; *Excursus* 7).

16.2 In the case of Timothy, it will be the difficulty posed by his mixed parentage that marks out the issues that Paul will have to confront as he moves to new areas with a predominantly Gentile culture. His mother was a Jewish Jesus-believer whereas his father, who may not have been still alive (cf. on 16.3 below), was Greek. That his mother had married a Gentile says much about her openness, since such marriage was forbidden according to the Jewish Law.[3]

Timothy was well known and well thought of by the brethren in Lystra, and also Iconium, now mentioned for the first time in this phase of the mission (cf. 13.51–14.5 for the earlier mention). These two towns were close to each other, even though in different districts, and at some distance from Derbe.[4] Putting together the geographical information of 16.1 and 16.2, it emerges that a) Timothy was in Derbe and Lystra, viewed as a single area in the Bezan text, and that b) his good reputation was established in Lystra and Iconium. Where he was from specifically is ambiguous – possibly Derbe, and he was also known to the brethren of Lystra and Iconium; or Lystra and Iconium and was not known in Derbe because it was far away. He represents, in other words, at least two of the three communities founded during the first phase of the mission in these places. At Iconium, mention was made earlier of both Jews and Gentiles (cf. 14.1, 2, 5), whereas in Lystra, only Gentiles were portrayed (cf. 14.19, where Jews came to Lystra from Iconium and Antioch to stir up

---

2. This device has already been recognized on a number of occasions previously; cf. in the earlier chapters of this third part of Acts: 13.6, the Jewish false prophet; 14.8, the lame man in Lystra.

3. Mixed marriages were, according to the available evidence, rare; cf. M. Goodman, *Rome and Jerusalem: The Clash of Ancient Civilisations* (London: Allen Lane, 2007), pp. 119–21.

4. C.J. Hemer, *The Book of Acts in the Setting of Hellenistic History* (ed. C.H. Gempf; Tübingen: J.C.B. Mohr, 1989), p. 110 and n. 23.

trouble among the Gentiles); Derbe was mentioned only briefly without any detail about the nature of the people Paul and Barnabas had dealings with (cf. 14.21a). Since Timothy is a representative disciple, it can be inferred that the churches he was connected with were composed both of Jews and Gentiles who co-existed in close harmony and who formed new disciples, such as Timothy.

[c] 16.3a *Paul Wishes to Take Timothy with Him*
16.3a Whether or not Paul already knew Timothy from his earlier visit is not clear – the introductory formula, καὶ ἰδού, of 16.1b tends to suggest that this was a first meeting. His desire that Timothy should accompany him is presented by Luke in an abrupt and bald statement, linked simply by the demonstrative pronoun τοῦτον to the previous narrative[5] and with the verb in the aorist (ἠθέλησεν, 'he wanted'). The reason for Paul's wish for Timothy to be with him is to be interpreted in the light of his representative role, and the strategy Paul has worked out for his mission. Timothy will be a companion, certainly, but he will be a companion who will serve as an example for the Jews whom he still intends to convince of the truth of the gospel.

[c'] 16.3b *Circumcision of Timothy*
16.3b As will be seen, Paul will continue to seek out Jews in the places he visits, with the goal of persuading them to believe in Jesus, and to accept the Gentile believers in their communities. In the area where Timothy is known, there had been ferocious attacks on Paul on the part of the local Jews who, in the end, had given up Paul for dead (cf. 14.2, 5, 19). It was seen (*Commentary, ad loc.*) that the reason for their hostility was his teaching that the Gentiles were to be integrated into the People of God without undergoing any preliminary ritual. He needs to prove to the Jews that as far as the Jewish Jesus-believers are concerned, he is not advocating that they renounce the Jewish Law.[6] Timothy will be the proof – though associated with mixed communities, he is a disciple who remains faithful to his Jewish parentage. This is what Paul now symbolically demonstrates by circumcising him.

[b'] 16.3c *Timothy's Parentage*
16.3c The reason for the circumcision is linked to the public knowledge among the Jews of Timothy's Gentile parentage. By circumcising Timothy, Paul makes it abundantly clear that the perspective of Judaism dominates (circumcision is a requirement) and overrides the Gentile point of view (circumcision is not

---

5.   The use of the demonstrative to link a new sentence to the preceding narrative is rare in Acts (cf. 1.14; 8.26b; 13.7b; 14.9; 16.3, 17; see Read-Heimerdinger, *The Bezan Text*, p. 246). While it avoids the repetition of the relative pronoun (cf. ὅς, 16.2), its effect, especially combined with the aorist ἠθέλησεν, is to create a solitary sentence that stands out from the narrative context.

6.   Paul's acceptance of the Law for Jewish Jesus-believers is confirmed at his meeting with James and the Jerusalem elders in 21.18-26.

necessary). The possibility mentioned above that Timothy's father was dead at this point (cf. on 16.2) confirms the suggestion that his Gentile past no longer has any influence over his behaviour. In the same way, the Jews in the mixed churches are not to be governed by the value system of the Gentiles but continue to be subject to the Law. Paul's aim, then, in circumcising Timothy is to demonstrate to the Jews that he does not consider the Law to have lost its validity for Jews when they believe in Jesus as Lord and Messiah.

In the event, beyond the immediate area (see on 16.5 below) Timothy will not be seen directly serving his purpose, since he is not mentioned again in connection with Paul, only with Silas and then only in passing (cf. 17.14, 15; 18.5), or later with Erastus but again in passing (19.22). This may well be the result of the fact that Paul's plans are indeed seen to be thwarted, as three times in the following narrative he will be directed by divine intervention away from the places he was intending to evangelize (cf. 16.6-10 below).

[a′] 16.4 *Preaching and Transmission of Jerusalem Decree*
16.4 The journey of Paul and Silas, now with the additional company of Timothy, is picked up from 16.1a, as the group is seen travelling through the cities previously mentioned, that is, Derbe, Lystra and Iconium. According to the Alexandrian text, they passed on to them 'the rules that had been decided by the apostles and elders', so that they (presumably the churches) would observe them – the Gentile believers did not have to follow the whole Law of Moses in all its detail, but they did have to respect the three essential imperatives (to refrain from murder, illicit sexual relations and idolatry) and conform to the ethical outlook of the Law (see *Commentary* on 15.19-21, 28-29).

Codex Bezae presents two distinct actions undertaken by the group which are set out in a characteristically Lukan pattern to underline the dual nature of their activities: they are stated first in summary form and then expanded on in turn (see *Critical Apparatus*). In the *Translation*, the text is translated literally to show how there existed side by side the actions of both preaching and delivering. The preaching about the Lord relates to a Jewish audience, with the qualification 'with all boldness' one that is entirely positive for Luke because it is an indication that the Scriptures were interpreted in the radically new way that the teaching of Jesus required (cf. 4.29; 28.31).[7] The content of their preaching was that the Lord (κύριος, known to the Jews already as YHWH) was Jesus, and that he was the Messiah, the one sent by God to save Israel.

The 'delivering', on the other hand, is directed at the churches and relates to the contents of the letter that had been addressed to the Gentiles of 'Antioch, Syria and Cilicia'. This is clarified as the verb 'deliver' is repeated and mention is made (more simply than in the AT) of the 'commands of the apostles and elders'. For the second time (cf. 16.1a D05), Luke draws atten-

---

7. The phrase is examined with reference to its earlier occurrences in Acts 4 in *The Message of Acts*, I, pp. 261–62, 278, 280.

tion to the fact that Paul and Silas pass on these instructions to communities beyond the regions specified in the letter.

It is interesting to note that here for the first time the apostles and elders are associated with Hierosoluma and no longer with Ierousalem as they have been until now (cf. 15.2b D05, 4 D05; see *General Introduction*, §VII, on the dual system of terminology adopted by Luke). It is as if by taking a firm stand against the imposition of circumcision on the Gentiles, the leaders of the Church finally have moved away from the views of the Jewish religious authorities, represented by Ierousalem, and have become free of their constraints. This, in fact, is the last time the apostles are mentioned in the book of Acts, always an indication in Luke's work that his characters have reached a full understanding of Jesus' teaching (cf. Peter, 12.17).[8] The elders will be met again, under the leadership of James, at 21.19-25 but there, too, they will be associated with Hierosoluma (cf. 21.17) as they continue to maintain that circumcision is not required of the Gentile believers (21.25).

[B] 16.5-10 *Crossing into Macedonia*

Overview

The mission of Paul, supported by Silas and now also accompanied by Timothy, moves on in this sequence towards Macedonia, to the north-west of Galatia where he has been working so far. The direction his journey takes, however, is not according to his own plan but rather is prompted by divine intervention correcting the route he planned. This will be seen three times in the form of a) the Holy Spirit, b) the Spirit of Jesus, and c) a man from Macedonia, all of them concurring in their goal to get Paul to travel in the direction of Rome, which he will reveal later is the destination he knows he is intended to go to (19.21).

In this sequence, the 'we'-group is introduced into the narrative. This is their first appearance in the Alexandrian text, but in Codex Bezae they were already introduced at 11.28 (and referred to obliquely, it seems, at 13.6; see *General Introduction*, §VIII). Their purpose will be to interpret for Paul his vision of the man from Macedonia (16.10), although that particular role is not apparent in the Alexandrian text of the verse. Now that Barnabas is no longer there with Paul to exercise a corrective influence over Paul's inclination to deviate from the direction of the mission that is intended by God, another group of people take over his function. They will stay in the narrative until Paul is arrested for creating a disturbance in the city of Philippi reappearing, after a considerable interval of time, in Greece when they will accompany Paul on his journey to Jerusalem and once more serve to endorse the guidance

---

8. Peter's release from a Jewish mentality is discussed with reference to Acts 12.5-17 in *The Message of Acts*, II, pp. 340–73.

of the Holy Spirit (21.13-15), though on that occasion they will fail to persuade him to obey the divine leading.

Structure and Themes

The headings of the elements follow the narrative of the Bezan text which differs in focus from the Alexandrian text in these verses (see *Critical Apparatus*). After a positive summary of the churches in Syria and Cilicia [a], the narrative continues to follow the route of Paul's journey, referring to three adjacent regions (Galatic Phrygia, Asia and Mysia) which take him progressively westwards and where he is prevented from turning aside or stopping to evangelize [b, c]. Finally, the arrival at Troas on the western coast [d] stands as a turning point: a dramatic and decisive divine intervention occurs [c'], which requires explanation [b'] and interpretation [a'] with the help of the 'we'-group who are introduced at this point. Troas, where the second half of the sequence is situated, is thus a place of special importance since the course of the mission from now on will take on a significantly new direction.

[a]	16.5	The growth of the churches
[b]	16.6	Travel through Galatic Phrygia
[c]	16.7	Prohibition to go to Bithynia
[d]	16.8	Travel through Mysia to Troas
[c']	16.9	Paul's vision of a man from Macedonia
[b']	16.10a	Paul's explanation of the vision to the 'we'-group
[a']	16.10b	The interpretation of the vision

Translation

Codex Bezae D05

[a] **16.5** So the churches were strengthened and increased in number daily.

[b] **6** They went through the region of Galatic Phrygia, though they were prevented by the Holy Spirit from speaking the word of God to anyone in Asia.

[c] **7** When they were at the border of Mysia, they wanted to make their way to Bithynia, and the Spirit of Jesus did not allow them.

[d] **8** Having gone through Mysia, they reached Troas.

[c'] **9** And in a vision in the night there appeared to Paul like a man, a certain Macedonian, standing before his face, beseeching and saying, 'Cross over into Macedonia and help us'.

[b'] **10a** So when he got up he related to us the vision;

[a'] **10b** and we understood that the Lord had called us to evangelize the people in Macedonia.

Codex Vaticanus B03

16.5 So the churches were strengthened in their faith and increased in number daily.

6 They went through the region of Galatic Phrygia, though they were prevented by the Holy Spirit from speaking the word in Asia.

7 Having arrived at the border of Mysia, they attempted to travel to Bithynia, and the Spirit of Jesus did not allow them.

8 Having gone along the edge of Mysia, they went down to Troas.

9 And a vision in the night appeared to Paul: a certain Macedonian man was standing and beseeching him and saying, 'Cross over into Macedonia and help us'.

10a When he saw the vision,

10b straightaway we sought to go out to Macedonia, inferring that God had called us to evangelize them.

Critical Apparatus

16.5 (ἐστερεοῦντο) τῇ πίστει Β 𝔓⁷⁴ ℵ *rell* ‖ *om.* D d; Ephr.

B03 qualifies the manner in which the churches were strengthened, namely in faith; D05 leaves the manner undefined and thus open to a more general interpretation.

16.6 μηδενὶ (λαλῆσαι) D, *nemini* d gig; Ephr Spec ‖ *om.* Β 𝔓⁷⁴ ℵ *rell.*— (τὸν λόγον) τοῦ θεοῦ D, *dei* d gig vg^DEO sy^P bo aeth; Ephr Spec ‖ *om.* Β 𝔓⁷⁴ ℵ *rell.*

D05 has two details that are not included in B03: first, the refusal to allow Paul and his companions to speak in Asia is more categorical since they could speak to no one; and secondly, the contents of their speaking is defined as the 'word of God'.

16.7 ἐλθόντες (δέ) Β 𝔓⁷⁴ ℵ *rell* ‖ γενόμενοι (-ην D*) D^H, *cum venissent* d.

The verb of B03, ἔρχομαι, expresses movement, whereas that of D05, γίνομαι, expresses the state of being in a place. The original hand of D05 reads an erroneous feminine accusative.

ἐπείραζον Β 𝔓⁷⁴ ℵ *rell* ‖ ἤθελαν D, *volebant* d sy^P aeth.— εἰς τὴν Βιθυνίαν Β 𝔓⁷⁴ ℵ *rell* ‖ εἰς Β. D 2298.— πορευθῆναι Β ℵ Α Ε Ψ 69. 81. 1175. 1837. 2344 ‖ -εσθαι D, *abire* d 𝔓⁷⁴ C H L P 049. 056. 1739 𝔐.

According to B03, Paul and his group would have actually attempted to go to Bithynia, whereas according to D05 it said simply that they wished to do so, where the form ἤθελαν represents the imperfect (ἤθελον) of the verb θέλω (Scrivener, p. xlvi; Moulton and Howard, *Grammar*, p. 194).

The difference in the tense of the infinitive (aor. B03, pres. D05) arises from the difference in the choice of the main verb preceding it, with B03 presenting the travel to Bithynia as a global event and D05 as a progressive journey. The result is that B03 presents the group as undertaking an external action, and that D05 focuses on the earlier stage of the interior thoughts and desires. The same focus on the inner motives and wishes of the protagonists of the narrative is seen elsewhere in D05 (Peter, 11.2b D05; Paul, 19.1 D05).

With the article, B03 views Bithynia as a normal choice of destination, whereas D05 presents it more as a plan that would not be necessarily expected.

16.8 παρελθόντες (δέ) Β 𝔓⁷⁴ ℵ *rell* ‖ διελ- D, *cum transissent* d gig vg sy^h.— κατέβησαν (εἰς Τρῳάδα) Β 𝔓⁷⁴ ℵ *rell, descenderunt* d ‖ κατῆλθον Ψ ‖ κατήντησαν D.

The prefix of the first verb varies (cf. 13.6), with the result that B03 describes the route as going along the border of Mysia whereas D05 presents it as going through the province. As for the second verb, κατήντησαν of D05 is also read at 13.51 D05, as a variant for ἔρχομαι in B03. It has the sense of 'reach' and so refers more to the arrival at Troas than the journey there. καταβαίνω in B03 expresses the idea of going down to a sea-port (cf. 13.4 D05, *Commentary, ad loc.*).

16.9 (καὶ) ὅραμα Β 𝔓⁷⁴ ℵ *rell* (*visum* d) ‖ ἐν ὁράματι D e syᵖ; Irˡᵃᵗ Cass.— τῷ Παύλῳ ὤφθη Β 𝔓⁷⁴ ℵ Dˢ·ᵐ· Ε Ψ 33. 69. 81. 181. 242. 945. 1175. 1739. 1837. 1891. 2344 *al* vg ‖ ὤφθη (ἐφάνη 614. 1505. 1611. 2412. 2495 *al*) τ. Π. D*, *apparuit Paulo* d A C gig (614) 𝔐 gig syᵖ aeth; Ephr.— διὰ νυκτός Β D A 6. 36. 88. 1175 *pc* ‖ δ. τῆς ν. ℵ 𝔓⁷⁴ C E H L P Ψ 049. 056. 33. 1739 𝔐.— ὡσεὶ (ἀνήρ) D, *quasi* d syᵖ sa; Ephr ‖ *om.* Β 𝔓⁷⁴ ℵ *rell.*— Μακεδών τις ἦν (ἑστώς) Β 𝔓⁷⁴ ℵ A C Dᴱ 33. 69. 81. (945). 1175. 1739. 1837. (1891). 2344 *al* Ι τις Μακ. ἦν 630 (– τις 431. 1891) syʰ Ι τις ἦν Μακ. H L P 049. 056. 614 𝔐 ‖ Μακ. τις D* E 209. (1241). 1311 syᵖ aeth; Ephr (Chr).— κατὰ πρόσωπον αὐτοῦ D, *anti faciem eius* d 257. 383. 614. 1799. 2147. 2412 *pc* (syʰ**) sa ‖ *om.* Β 𝔓⁷⁴ ℵ *rell.*

A series of variants combines to present differently Paul's vision. B03 first has the vision as the subject that appeared to Paul, with Paul highlighted in the pre-verb position, and then goes on in an independent sentence to describe the vision of a certain Macedonian man. D05 presents the man himself as appearing to Paul (not highlighted in pre-verb position) 'in a vision', describing him as 'like' a man from Macedonia and standing before Paul. For other occurrences of the expression κατὰ πρόσωπον αὐτοῦ, cf. Lk. 2.31; Acts 3.13; 25.16. By these various features, the man is more in focus in the D05 account than in that of B03.

καὶ (παρακαλῶν) Β 𝔓⁷⁴ ℵ A C E 33. 81. 88. 614. 618. 927. 945. 1175. 1270. 1505. 1611. 1739. 1891. 2147. 2344. 2412. 2495, *et* d gig ‖ *om.* D H L P 049. 056 𝔐 aeth; Ephr Chr.— αὐτόν Β 𝔓⁷⁴ ℵ *rell* ‖ *om.* D d 1022. 1245 gig; Ephr Chr.

In D05, the Macedonian is the subject of the main verb ὤφθη of which Paul is the indirect object (see above), as well as of the two participles παρακαλῶν καὶ λέγων of which Paul is also the implied object; the pronoun is not generally repeated after the verb παρακαλέω or verbs of saying if it has already been specified (see Read-Heimerdinger, 'The Tracking of Participants with the Third Person Pronoun', pp. 442–43). The different construction in B03, however, means that the Macedonian is not the subject of ὤφθη, and thus Paul needs to be specified as the object of the participle παρακαλῶν, which, furthermore, requires a connection to the previous main verb ἦν with καί.

16.10 ὡς δὲ τὸ ὅραμα εἶδεν Β 𝔓⁷⁴ ℵ *rell* ‖ διεγερθεὶς οὖν διηγήσατο τ. ὁρ. ἡμῖν D, *exsurgens ergo enarravit visum nobis* d sa.

D05 makes explicit that Paul related the vision to his companions, the 'we'-group, here introduced for the first time in the present context, though obliquely with the dative pronoun. B03 leaves this information implicit. These *vll* account for the following ones.

εὐθέως ἐζητήσαμεν ἐξελθεῖν εἰς Μακεδονίαν συμβιβάζοντες (ὅτι) B 𝔓⁷⁴ ℵ *rell* ‖ καὶ ἐνοήσαμεν D, *et intellegimus* d.— (προσκέκληται ἡμᾶς) ὁ θεός B 𝔓⁷⁴ (– ἡμᾶς ℵ*) ℵ² A C E Ψ 33. 36. 81. 181. 307. 453. 610. 945. 1175. 1678. 1739. 1837. 1891. 2344 *al* it vg bo; Hier ‖ ὁ κύριος D, *dominus* d H L P 049. 056. 614 𝔐 c (gig) sy^{p.h} sa; Ir^{lat} Chr.— (εὐαγγελίσασθαι) αὐτούς B 𝔓⁷⁴ ℵ *rell* ‖ τοὺς ἐν Μακεδονίᾳ D, *qui in Macedonia sunt* d.

Following on from the previous variant, B03 now introduces the 'we'-group with the first person plural of the verb ζητέω, suggesting that Paul is included in the group as they seek without further ado to go to Macedonia in accordance with their understanding (συμβιβάζοντες, present participle) that God called them to evangelize them (as elsewhere in Luke, the third person plural pronoun is to be understood as meaning the inhabitants of a place, cf. Delebecque, *Les deux Actes*, p. 209). The choice of the verb συμβιβάζω is potentially ambiguous: as a transitive verb, it expresses in its figurative sense the idea of 'convincing, instructing, advising' someone (Bailly, 2; B-A-G, 3), which implies that the 'we'-group acted as guides to Paul (as in D05, see below), though without him being specified as the object of the verb; it can also be used intransitively, with the sense of 'inferring, concluding', (Bailly, 3; B-A-G, 2), which is probably the sense intended here – even though the aorist participle could be expected (since logically the deduction must have been made before taking the decision to go to Macedonia), it is possible to envisage the inferring being concomitant with the decision to go to Macedonia.

D05, in contrast, has the 'we'-group first interpret Paul's vision as meaning that the Lord (Jesus, in the form of the Macedonian man) had called them (including Paul) to evangelize the people in Macedonia. D05 thus accords the 'we'-group a more active role in helping Paul move on to Macedonia. B03 avoids identifying the Lord as a man, as elsewhere (cf. 7.55; Read-Heimerdinger, *The Bezan Text*, pp. 290, 291, 293).

Commentary

[a] 16.5 *The Growth of the Churches*

16.5 The start of a new sequence is marked with the same formula, μὲν οὖν, that Luke uses on other occasions to indicate two situations or events that arise out of the previous narrative.[9] The first in this instance is the positive state of the churches in the area revisited by Paul once the instructions from the apostles and elders had been handed over to them. These had a beneficial effect since the churches are said to be strengthened (in faith, AT) and to increase in number on a daily basis. The implication is that the Jewish hostility Paul and Barnabas experienced in the region on their earlier visit is no longer a threat to their existence. Indeed, the rapid growth of the churches may well have been due to the conversion of Jews who felt able to enter the

9.   On the use of μὲν οὖν as a pericope marker, see note on 15.30.

church now that the Gentile issue had been settled satisfactorily and it was clear that they themselves could continue to follow the Law. Timothy will have served a useful purpose in this respect.

[b] 16.6 *Travel through Galatic Phrygia*

16.6 The second event that follows on from the preaching activity in the area of Derbe, Lystra and Iconium, and the passing on to the churches there of the apostles' and elders' instructions, is that Paul, Silas and Timothy move on westwards, through the next district of Phrygia, that part that had been absorbed into the wider province of Galatia. This is the most probable meaning of the area described in the text as 'the Phrygian that is (καί) Galatian region' (lit.).[10] Within that region was probably situated the city of Antioch of Pisidia (cf. 13.14-50).

The plan appears to have been to continue west and to stop to evangelize the adjacent province of Asia, but the group was directed by the Holy Spirit not to do this. The Bezan text is categorical in expressing the obstacle to the group's undertaking any preaching there at all, using the term the 'word of God', which characteristically refers to speaking to Gentiles (see *Excursus* 1), and thereby suggesting that Paul had intended to open up new fields of mission in the area. This, in itself, would have been a positive step (as opposed to the negative strategy of seeking out Jews to talk to about the gospel), but it seems that it was particularly important for Paul to continue heading west without any obstacle to hold him back. How the guidance of the Spirit was made known is not specified, though it may be imagined that Silas, being a prophet (cf. 15.32), may well have served as an instrument to communicate the divine purpose. Alternatively, it may have been believers from the churches they visited who were alert to the leading of the Spirit and passed it to Paul and his companions.

[c] 16.7 *Prohibition to Go to Bithynia*

16.7 The result was that, since the group did not stop in Asia, they arrived at the border of Mysia.[11] There, they wanted (or even attempted, according to the

---

10. Grammatically, καί between the two names could mean that they refer to two distinct regions, though if this were intended the plural χώρας would be expected (cf. 12.20 D05; cf. also 18.23, where Galatia and Phrygia are distinguished as two adjacent regions). The borders of the Roman provinces between Syria in the east and the Aegean sea in the west were subject to considerable change under Roman rule, and the borders of Phrygia in particular are hard to define because it was constantly being split up and redistributed to various rulers, or attached in one way or another to neighbouring districts (see F.F. Bruce, 'Phrygia', ABD, V, pp. 366–67). By the first century BCE, the western part of it lay in Asia and the eastern part in Galatia, which was itself originally a separate province to the north-east of Phrygia but had been expanded by the addition of territory in the south and west, including Lycaonia, Pisidia and Pamphylia, so that in the wider sense of Galatia, the cities of Derbe, Lystra and Iconium were all included in it (S. Mitchell, 'Galatia', *ABD*, II, pp. 870–72). Some commentators understand Galatia here in Acts 16.6 as meaning the smaller province in the north, but the conclusion of the most recent studies is that Luke means the Galatic area of Phrygia (Hemer, *Hellenistic History*, p. 112, and n. 28).

11. The preposition κατά with a place name in the accusative has the sense of 'on the edge of' or 'close to' (Bailly, κατά, B, II, 3, 'dans le voisinage de').

AT) to turn northwards and go into Bithynia, as if anything would be preferable to keeping on heading west! Once more, the intentions of the group are prevented from being carried out, this time by the Spirit of Jesus. This is a unique reference to the Spirit of Jesus, though the direct association of the Holy Spirit with Jesus is clear in Luke's work (cf. Lk. 24.49, esp. D05; Acts 2.33). It is each time more striking that Paul is meant to be following a specific goal in his mission, with first an obstacle (κωλυθέντες, 16.6) and now a prohibition (οὐκ εἴασεν) to keep him on the right course. The work he is carrying out had initially been entrusted to him by the Holy Spirit (13.2, 4), with the prophet Barnabas named first as his fellow-worker. Since Paul's refusal to accept the beneficial presence of John-Mark with them (see *Commentary*, 15.36-41), he had lost the influence of Barnabas to keep him following his assigned goal.

It is again not stated how the prohibition of the Spirit of Jesus was expressed. As in the previous instance, it is likely to have been through prophecy, revealed to the group collectively or to one of the members individually; according to the presentation of the situation in Acts, there are not as yet any communities of believers in the area.

[d] 16.8 *Travel through Mysia to Troas*
16.8 The central element of the sequence bring the action to Troas, a coastal city at the western tip of Mysia, whose principal importance for the journey of the missionary group lies in the fact that it was from there that ships crossed the northern part of the Aegean to go from Asia to Macedonia. According to the Alexandrian text, the route to Troas seems to have been along the coast, where there is indeed a known road connecting the coastal cities. Codex Bezae speaks of passing 'through Mysia', crossing the country by an inland route, perhaps via Pergamum or by some other, less travelled, path.[12] The fact of making for Troas does look, in any case, as if it were a deliberate choice of destination because it was the next town that would take Paul towards Rome. It will need further persuasion, however, to get him to continue westwards with his journey.

[c'] 16.9 *Paul's Vision of a Man from Macedonia*
16.9 Whereas the two previous interventions to keep Paul on the right road have been to stop him from being diverted from the end goal, there is now a third intervention whose purpose is positive, to encourage him to keep going in the direction he has been shown. This time, a fuller description is given to explain how Paul was guided by a vision he saw.

The account of the vision differs according to the manuscripts (see *Critical Apparatus*), though in the essentials they agree – it happened during the night, though how long the group stayed in Troas or where they stayed is not specified. The vision consisted of a man from Macedonia begging Paul (addressed

---

12. Hemer, *Hellenistic History*, pp. 112–13, n. 29; cf. W.P. Bowers, 'Paul's Route through Mysia. A Note on Acts 16.8', *JTS* 30 (1979), pp. 507–11.

in the singular) to cross over to Macedonia to help them; once more, the adjective τις, 'a certain', is used of a person who is a representative of a type, in this case more than a person in his own right.[13] In Codex Bezae, the man is more in focus as he is seen standing before Paul, and he is described as one 'like' a man. The identity of the man is not given, but this is a typical characterization of YHWH when he appears to a person in human form.[14] The position of the one like a man is particularly striking, recalling Stephen's vision of the 'son of man standing at the right hand of God' (7.56).

The plea of the Macedonian illustrates yet again how it is the Gentiles who take the initiative in moving the proclamation of the gospel into their territory (cf. Sergius Paulus who invites Saul and Barnabas so that he can hear the word from them, 13.7). He begs Paul to 'cross over' to Macedonia, using a verb that is rare in the New Testament but that recurs frequently in the LXX as a technical term to speak of the crossing of the Jordan into the Promised Land, or the crossing of the Red Sea to escape out of Egypt.[15] It is, in this sense, a term that designates a critical moment in the life of a person or a people, a crossing over a boundary with the idea of 'no return'. This is what Paul is invited to do, in leaving behind the land with which he has been familiar and to which he has been attached and taking the definitive step of moving into wholly new territory, that of the Gentiles.

The call for help from the Macedonian is the same as that of the father of the epileptic boy in Mark's Gospel (Mk 9.22), which Luke did not use in his gospel but reserved for this moment. In so far as the man is Jesus himself, he is taking the position of the king in the parable recorded in Matthew's Gospel (Mt. 25.31-46), where Jesus identifies himself with the poor and the sick and, as such, is helped when his servants help those in need.

[b'] 16.10a *Paul's Explanation of the Vision to the 'We'-Group*
16.10a It is at the point following Paul's vision that the 'we'-group are brought into the story. The Alexandrian text has just one clause in this verse, saying that when Paul saw the vision we, recognizing the meaning of the vision as a call from God, set about going[16] to Macedonia. For the Alexandrian text, this is the first time that the 'we'-group have been mentioned, though why they were in Troas or where exactly Paul met them is not said. The Bezan text presents a more complex and more detailed picture of events. First, Paul is seen waking up[17] and explaining the vision to 'us'. In so far as the verb is meant

---

13. Cf. the comments on τις at 16.1b above.
14. See M. Barker, *The Great Angel: A Study of Israel's Second God* (London: SPCK, 1992), pp. 7–8.
15. διαβαίνω is found at Lk. 16.26 (crossing of the 'great chasm') and Heb. 11.29 (crossing of the Red Sea). In the LXX, it is used to refer to the crossing of the Jordan at, e.g., Num. 32.7, 29, 30, 32; 33.51; 35.10; Deut. 3.21, 25, 27, 28; 4.22a, b, 26; Jos. 1.2, 11, 14); it is twice used of the crossing of the Red Sea (Num. 33.8; Jos. 4.23–5.1).
16. The verb is ἐξελθεῖν, the verb of the exodus, see *Commentary*, 15.40.
17. διεγερθείς, used also of Jesus in the boat during the storm, Lk. 8.24, the only two occurrences in the New Testament of the verb διεγείρω with the meaning of 'wake up'.

to be taken literally, this implies that 'we' were sleeping close by. So he did not, in other words, respond to the vision when he saw it (unlike in the AT), but turned to other people to relate it without having grasped its meaning. This is apparent from the wording of the following clause in the Bezan text.

[a′] 16.10b *The Interpretation of the Vision*

16.10b In a Bezan second clause, it is then 'we' who interpret the vision, identifying the man as 'the Lord', meaning Jesus. It should be noticed that the Alexandrian text avoids assimilating the man with Jesus, by referring to 'God' instead of 'the Lord'. The conclusion of the 'we'-group in the Alexandrian text is expressed as a plural present participle ('inferring/concluding') which probably includes Paul. In the Bezan text, there is a separate finite verb in the first person plural (ἐνοήσαμεν) which, even though it too includes Paul, distinguishes between Paul alone who is the subject of the previous verb διηγήσατο, 'he related' and 'we' who participated with him in understanding the vision. The 'we'-group, in other words, play a more important role in interpreting the vision, a role that will be seen again when the 'we'-group attempt to persuade Paul to accept Agabus' warning not to go to Ierousalem (21.12-14, esp. D05).

In both texts, the awareness of the divine call is expressed with a perfect verb, προσκέκληται. The reference is not so much, or not just, to the specific call that Paul had heard that night (which would have been expressed with an aorist verb) but to the overall calling throughout the series of revelations of the divine will that had been given during the recent stages of the journey: the Holy Spirit had prevented them from delaying in Asia, the Spirit of Jesus had not allowed them to go to Bithynia.[18]

The call is to 'evangelize' the people of Macedonia. The activity of evangelizing consists in 'announcing the good news', a feature of public proclamation that Luke has presented since the time of John the Baptist (Lk. 3.18) and which, when the content is not specified, has as its object the message about Jesus.[19] The call had been addressed to Paul alone, confirming that he is the leader of the mission and responsible (and answerable) for it, but the plural verbs from now on, and throughout the following description of the journey to Macedonia, indicate that Luke does not think of him as undertaking the mission alone.

[C] 16.11-40 *Macedonia I: Philippi*

Overview

The start of the second phase proper of the mission begins in this sequence, since the action of the preliminary verses, 16.1-10, was either located in famil-

---

18. On the stative aspect of the perfect expressing an overall event, see R.A. Young, *Intermediate New Testament Greek* (Nashville, TN: Broadman & Holman, 1994), p. 126.

19. Of the 54 occurrences in the New Testament of the verb, Luke has over half of them: Lk. × 10; Acts × 15 (+ 14.25 D05; 16.17 D05). When the contents of the proclamation are not specified, the addressees are in the accusative (cf. Lk. 3.18; Acts 8.25, 40; 14.15, 21, 25 D05; 16.10).

iar territory or, during the journey, was not allowed to develop into missionary activity. Once Paul and his companions arrive in Philippi, a Roman colony where any Jews were a small minority,[20] the mission to the Gentiles becomes the central concern, though Paul does not give up so easily his preoccupation with the conversion of the Jews. The 'we'-group will continue to be present in the narrative up to the point when Paul and Silas are imprisoned for allegedly proselytizing; since the 'we'-group do not share Paul's outlook or his over-riding concern with the Jews, which Luke evaluates negatively according to the Bezan text (see *General Introduction*, §V), they are not implicated in the offences of Paul and Silas and disappear from the narrative until their presence is invoked again to bring Paul back into line with God's plan for him.

There is, in fact, a complex interplay of metaphorical levels in this long sequence, though many of their features are absent from the Alexandrian text. Reading from the Bezan text, the prison represents, on the one hand, the attitude of Paul and Silas to the Jewish teachings, which hold them bound and prevent them from freely speaking to the Gentiles in terms that are acceptable to them. God, however, intervenes to release them from prison, at which point they are enabled to successfully announce the way of salvation to their jailor. Their definitive release the next day, on the other hand, is not obtained on valid grounds, for Paul appeals to their status as Roman citizens with no mention of the Lord or their service of him.

At the same time, there is a number of possible clues that suggest Luke in the Bezan text constructs this scene on an underlying paradigm, according to which the Roman magistrates of the city re-enact the prophecy of Psalm 2 (see *Excursus* 10 for details), which speaks of the nations attacking 'the Lord and his anointed' – they employ the people under them (the sergeants and the jailor) to carry out their attack, but are duly terrified by God's intervention in the earthquake – first the jailor, then the magistrates themselves. Because Jesus has been made the Son of God and has been given the nations to rule over, he has prevented their plot coming to fruition. The jailor represents the Gentiles who submit to God and finally come to rejoice and trust in him.

Structure and Themes

The unity of this long sequence derives from the location since all the action takes place in Philippi. There are, however, six episodes, which are each identified by a change in person and local setting.

[C-*A*] and [C-*A'*] act as an introduction and conclusion to the sequence respectively, narrating the arrival and departure of the disciples from Philippi. [C-*B*] concerns the conversion of Lydia, a Gentile God-fearer who is attached to the synagogue, while [C-*B'*] corresponds to this episode in relating the conversion of the jailor, a Gentile with no connection with the synagogue. The two episodes that relate the imprisonment [C-*C*] and the release from prison [C-*C'*] alternate with the conversion scenes.

---

20. Hemer (*Hellenistic History*, p. 114) points out that this may have been due to the fact that the city was not a commercial centre.

[C-A] 16.11-12   Journey to Philippi
  [a]   16.11-12a   Arrival in Philippi
  [a′]   16.12b   Stay in Philippi
[C-B] 16.13-15   Lydia
  [a]   16.13a   A place of prayer
  [b]   16.13b   Conversation with the women
  [c]   16.14   Lydia accepts what Paul was saying
  [b′]   16.15a   Baptism and invitation to stay in her house
  [a′]   16.15b   Her insistence
[C-C] 16.16-24   Imprisonment
  [a]   16.16   A slave girl meets us
  [b]   16.17   Her acclamation of Paul and the 'we'-group
  [c]   16.18a   Repetition over several days
  [d]   16.18b   Paul orders the spirit to come out of her
  [e]   16.18c   The spirit comes out of her
  [e′]   16.19   Her masters drag Paul and Silas before the rulers
  [d′]   16.20-21   Their accusation to the magistrates
  [c′]   16.22a   The crowd join in
  [b′]   16.22b-23   The magistrates throw them into prison
  [a′]   16.24   The jailor ensures security
[C-B′] 16.25-34   The Philippian jailor
  [a]   16.25a   Paul and Silas praise God
  [b]   16.25b   The prisoners listen to them
  [c]   16.26a   An earthquake
  [d]   16.26b   The doors open and the chains fall off
  [e]   16.27   The jailor is about to kill himself
  [f]   16.28   Paul stops him
  [g]   16.29   The jailor falls at the feet of Paul and Silas
  [h]   16.30   He asks them about salvation
  [h′]   16.31   Paul and Silas tell him to believe in the Lord Jesus Christ
  [g′]   16.32   They speak the word of the Lord to all in his house
  [f′]   16.33a   The jailor treats their wounds
  [e′]   16.33b   The jailor's baptism
  [d′]   16.34a   He prepares a feast
  [c′]   16.34b   He rejoices
[C-C′] 16.35-39   Release from prison
  [a]   16.35a   The meeting of the magistrates
  [b]   16.35b   They were afraid
  [c]   16.35c   They order the release of the prisoners
  [d]   16.36   The jailor transmits the order
  [e]   16.37   Paul's response to the magistrates
  [d′]   16.38a   The sergeants report his words
  [c′]   16.38b   The magistrates are afraid
  [b′]   16.39a   The magistrates speak to Paul and Silas
  [a′]   16.39b   They urge them to leave the city
[C-A′] 16.40   Departure from Philippi
  [a]   16.40a   Paul and Silas go to Lydia
  [b]   16.40b   They report to the brethren
  [a′]   16.40c   They depart from Philippi

The complex and detailed internal structural patterns are striking throughout this sequence, and mark a change from previous patterns.[21] The narrative becomes more concerned with small observable facts, resulting in a great number of structural elements.

Translation

Codex Bezae D05	Codex Vaticanus B03
[Aa] **16.11** On the next day, having been led away from Troas, we ran a straight course to Samothrace, and on the next day to Neapolis, **12a** and from there to Philippi, which is the chief colony city of Macedonia.	**16.11** Having put out to sea from Troas, we ran a straight course to Samothrace, then on the next day to Neapolis, **12a** and from there to Philippi, which is a leading city of the part of Macedonia, a colony.
[a′] **12b** We prolonged our stay in this city for some days.	**12b** We prolonged our stay in this city for some days,
[Ba] **13a** However, on the day of the Sabbath, we went outside the gate by the river where it seemed there was a place of prayer.	**13a** and on the day of the Sabbath, we went outside the gate by a river where we supposed there was a place of prayer.
[b] **13b** Having sat down, we started to speak with the women who had come with us.	**13b** Having sat down, we started to speak with the women who had gathered.
[c] **14** And a certain woman called Lydia, a seller of purple goods from the city of Thyatira, a worshipper of God, listened, and the Lord opened her heart to give heed to what was said by Paul.	**14** And a certain woman called Lydia, a seller of purple goods from a city, Thyatira, a worshipper of God, was listening, and the Lord opened her heart to give heed to what was said by Paul.
[b′] **15a** When she had been baptized and all her household, she begged us, saying, 'If you have judged that I am faithful to God, come into my house and stay',	**15a** When she had been baptized and all her household, she begged us, saying, 'If you have judged that I am faithful to the Lord, come into my house and stay',
[a′] **15b** and she put pressure on us.	**15b** and she put pressure on us.
[Ca] **16** It came about that as we were going to prayer, a certain slave girl who had a spirit of divination came up to us (she was someone who brought her masters much gain by this spirit in telling fortunes).	**16** It came about that as we were going to the place of prayer, a certain slave girl who had a spirit of divination came to meet us (she was someone who brought her masters much gain by telling fortunes).
[b] **17** This girl, as she followed behind Paul and us, then started shouting out, saying, 'These are the slaves of the Most High God, and they are announcing to us the good news of the way of salvation'.	**17** This girl, as she followed behind Paul and us, started shouting out, saying, 'These men are slaves of the Most High God, these men who are proclaiming to you the way of salvation'.
[c] **18a** She continued doing this over many days.	**18a** She continued doing this over many days.
[d] **18b** Having turned to the spirit, and being very annoyed, Paul said, 'I order you in the name of Jesus Christ to come out of her',	**18b** Having become very annoyed and having turned to the spirit, Paul said, 'I order you in the name of Jesus Christ to come out of her',

---

21. The change is noted by Witherington (*Acts*, p. 486), who attributes it to the fact that the 'we' sections now begin, but the detail and complexity continues even in the prison scenes where the 'we'-group are absent.

[e]	**18c** and immediately it came out.	**18c** and it came out at that very hour.
[e′]	**19** When the masters of the slave girl saw that they had been deprived of their profit that they used to have through her, they seized hold of Paul and Silas and dragged them into the market place to the rulers;	**19** And her masters, having seen that the hope of their profit had gone out, seized hold of Paul and of Silas and dragged them into the market place to the rulers;
[d′]	**20** and having brought them to the magistrates, they said, **21** 'These men are throwing our city into confusion, being Jews and announcing to the Gentiles things that are not lawful for us to receive nor do, being Romans'.	**20** and having brought them to the magistrates, they said, **21** 'These men are throwing our city into confusion, being Jews and announcing customs that it is not lawful for us to receive nor to do, being Romans'.
[c′]	**22a** And a large crowd joined together against them, shouting out.	**22a** And the crowd joined together against them.
[b′]	**22b** Then the magistrates, tearing off their garments, commanded them to be flogged **23** and having inflicted on them many blows, they threw them into prison, ordering the jailor that they were to be kept securely.	**22b** Then the magistrates, tearing off their garments, commanded them to be flogged **23** and having inflicted on them many blows, they threw them into prison, ordering the jailor to keep them securely.
[a′]	**24** Having received such an order, he threw them into the inner prison and secured their feet in the stocks.	**24** Having received such an order, he threw them into the inner prison and secured their feet in the stocks.
[*B′*a]	**25a** Around the middle of the night, Paul and Silas were singing hymns to God in prayer.	**25a** Around midnight, Paul and Silas were singing hymns to God in prayer.
[b]	**25b** The other prisoners were listening attentively.	**25b** The other prisoners were listening attentively.
[c]	**26a** Suddenly, there was a great earthquake so that the foundations of the jail were shaken.	**26a** Suddenly, there was a great earthquake so that the foundations of the jail were shaken.
[d]	**26b** At once, all the doors opened and all the bonds were loosened;	**26b** All the doors opened and all the bonds were undone.
[e]	**27** and the jailor, having woken up and seeing the doors of the prison open and having drawn his sword, was about to kill himself, assuming that the prisoners had escaped.	**27** The jailor, having woken up and seeing the doors of the prison open, having drawn his sword was about to kill himself, assuming that the prisoners had escaped.
[f]	**28** But Paul called out in a loud voice, saying, 'Don't do yourself any harm, for all of us are here'.	**28** But in a loud voice Paul called out, saying, 'Don't harm yourself, for all of us are here'.
[g]	**29** Asking for lights, he sprang in and, in a state of trembling, he fell before Paul and Silas at their feet;	**29** Asking for lights, he sprang in and, having started to tremble, he fell before Paul and Silas;
[h]	**30** and he led them out when he had secured the rest and said to them, 'Masters, what must I do to be saved?'	**30** and having led them out, he said, 'Masters, what must I do to be saved?'
[h′]	**31** They said, 'Believe in the Lord Jesus Christ and you will be saved, you and your household';	**31** They said, 'Believe in the Lord Jesus and you will be saved, you and your household'.
[g′]	**32** and they spoke to him the word of the Lord, together with everyone else in his house.	**32** and they spoke to him the word of God, together with everyone else in his house.

[f'] **33a** And taking them at that very hour of the night, he released them from their blows;

33a And taking them at that very hour of the night, he washed their wounds;

[e'] **33b** and he, for his part, was baptized and all his family, immediately;

33b and he was baptized, he and all of his family, immediately,

[d'] **34a** and also, having brought them up into his household, he went so far as to set a meal before them.

34a and having brought them up into his household, he set a meal before them.

[c'] **34b** And he was rejoicing with all his household, having become a believer in God.

34b And he rejoiced with all his household, having believed in God.

[*C*'a] **35a** When it was day, the magistrates came together, united in purpose, in the market place,

35a When it was day, the magistrates

[b] **35b** and remembering the earthquake that had happened, they were afraid;

[c] **35c** and they sent the sergeants to say, 'Release those men whom you received yesterday'.

35c sent the sergeants saying, 'Release those men'.

[d] **36** And the jailor went in and reported the words to Paul: 'The magistrates have sent for you to be released. So now, go out and go on your way.'

36 The jailor reported these words to Paul: 'The magistrates have sent for you to be released. So now, go out and go on your way in peace.'

[e] **37** But Paul said to them, 'Innocent as we are, they beat us in public, uncondemned men, we who are Roman citizens, and threw us into prison, and now, they throw us out in secret? Oh no! Let them come themselves and bring us out.'

37 But Paul said to them, 'They beat us in public, uncondemned men, we who are Roman citizens, and threw us into prison, and now, they throw us out in secret? Oh no! Let them come themselves and bring us out.'

[d'] **38a** So the sergeants reported to the magistrates themselves these words, which were spoken for the magistrates.

38a So the sergeants reported to the magistrates these words.

[c'] **38b** They, hearing that they were Romans, were afraid,

38b They were afraid when they heard that they were Romans.

[b'] **39a** and having gone to the prison with many friends, they begged them to go out, saying, 'We did not know, regarding your case, that you were good men'.

39a And they went and they begged them,

[a'] **39b** And having led them out, they begged them, saying, 'Go right out of this city, in case they gather to present themselves again to us, shouting against you'.

39b and, having led them out, they asked them to go away from the city.

[*A*'a] **40a** Having gone out of the prison, they went to Lydia's house;

40a Having gone from the prison, they went into Lydia's house;

[b] **40b** and seeing the brethren, they reported what the Lord had done for them, by way of encouraging them;

40b and seeing the brethren, they encouraged them;

[a'] **40c** and they went out.

40c and they went out.

Critical Apparatus

Within this sequence, the penultimate episode [C-*C*] (16.35-39) displays a high density of textual variation.

16.11 Ἀναχθέντες οὖν B C H L P 049. 056. 1739 𝔐 gig syʰ saᵐˢˢ; Irˡᵃᵗ I ᾽Αν. δέ 𝔓⁷⁴ ℵ A E Ψ 6. (33). 69. 81. 181. 326. 1175. 1409. 1837. 1898. 2344 *pc* it vg saᵐˢ bo aeth; Chr Theoph II Τῇ δὲ ἐπαύριον ἀχθέντες D*, *alia die perducti* d (ἀναχ- Dᴱ 257. 383. 614. 1799. 2147. 2412 syʰᵐᵍ).

B03 links the next stage of the journey back to the vision by means of the connective οὖν, and the deponent passive of ἀνάγω, with the sense of 'put out to sea' (B-A-G, ἀνάγω, 3; cf. 13.13; 18.21; 27.21). In D05, the connective δέ introduces a new time frame; and the link is made back to the previous scene with the verb ἄγω which, in the passive, refers to the action of the Lord in leading the group away from Troas through the vision given to Paul (cf. 16.9-10): cf. Lk. 4.1. The same alternative verbs are found at Acts 28.11 (D05 lac.): ἤχθημεν H 049. 056. 6. 33. 326. 1891. 2464 *pm*, for ἀνήχθημεν *rell*.

τῇ δὲ ἐπιούσῃ B 𝔓⁷⁴ ℵ *rell* II καὶ τῇ ἐπ. ἡμέρᾳ D, *et sequenti die* d gig l vg.— (εἰς) Νέαν πόλιν B 𝔓⁷⁴ ℵ A Dᴱ 467. 1175. 1739. 1838 *pc* aeth II Νεάπολιν D*, *Neapolin* d C E H L P 𝔐 gig vg syᵖ sa bo aeth.

B03 conjoins Samothrace with the next leg of the journey with the connective δέ, perhaps to underline the fact that the party did not stop in Samothrace but continued. D05 reads the more expected καί to indicate a continuous chain of events.

The spelling of Neapolis in B03, as two words, conforms to classical usage, but examples of a single word as in D05 are to be found in ancient literature or inscriptions (Hemer, *Hellenistic History*, p. 113, esp. n. 30).

16.12 (ἥτις ἐστὶν) πρώτη (-ης [Clericus cj.] vgᵐˢˢ) τῆς (– B) μερίδος τῆς Μακεδονίας πόλις, κολωνία B H L P 049. 056. 614 𝔐 I πρ. τῆς μερ. Μακ. πόλ., κολ. 𝔓⁷⁴ ℵ A C Ψ 33. 36. 69. 81. 88. 323. 547. 945. 1175. 1837. 1891. 2344 *pc* I πρ. μερὶς Μακ., πόλ. κολ. E a b dem p² vgᵂ sa II κεφαλὴ τῆς Μακ., πόλ. κολ. D, *caput Macedoniae, civitas colonia* d syᵖ I πρ. τῆς Μακ., πόλ. κολ. 614. 618. 1241. 1505. 1611. 1739. 2412. 2492. 2495 *pc* syʰ.

B03 describes Philippi as a first, or leading, city, πρώτη πόλις; what is not clear, however, is what it is the first city of. μερίς means a part or portion, and can be used as a technical term meaning 'district', but that use has to be discounted here since Macedonia was not a district but a province made up of four districts (Witherington, *Acts*, pp. 488–90, esp. 489, n. 77). The omission of the article before μερίδος could be due to haplography, especially since the reading is without support. Witherington then, taking the sense of μερίς as 'portion', suggests 'a first (or leading) city of (that) portion of Macedonia'. The problem with this suggestion is that the article, even if it is read, has to be taken as the equivalent of a demonstrative. The conjectured final sigma of πρώτη (see Metzger, *Commentary*, pp. 394–95) causes it to agree with μερί-δος rather than πόλις, which has the advantage of allowing the sense of district for μερίς ('a city of the first district of Macedonia)'.

D05 omits any reference to μερίς, saying that Philippi was a, or the, κεφαλή of Macedonia. If this word is taken in the sense of 'capital', the information is wrong, since Thessalonica was the capital. The weaker meaning of 'chief' fits better, especially if taken as qualifying the whole phrase and not just the name of Philippi: the chief colony city of Macedonia.

16.13 Τῇ τε (ἡμέρᾳ) B 𝔓⁷⁴ ℵ A C E H L P 049. 056 𝔐 ‖ Τῇ δέ D, *Die autem* d Ψ 33. 242. 323. 383. 440. 467. 522. 614. 913. 945. 1505. 1518. 1611. 1739. 1799. 1837. 1891. 2138. 2147. 2344. 2412. 2495 e vg syʰ sa bo; Chr Theoph.

τε in B03 has the effect of presenting the previous sentence as preliminary information (Levinsohn, *Textual Connections,* pp. 132–35). This is to detract, however, from the emphasis on the verb conferred by the periphrastic imperfect (ἦμεν ... διατρίβοντες). By introducing the next movement with δέ, D05 accords to the previous one its full importance at the same time as marking a rupture with it (see *Commentary*).

(παρὰ) ποταμόν B 𝔓⁷⁴ ℵ *rell* ‖ τὸν π. D 618. 1311. 1838 *pc*; Theoph.— (οὗ) ἐνομίζομεν προσευχὴ (εἶναι) B *pc* | -ετο (-ζεν 𝔓⁷⁴) -χή 𝔓⁷⁴ A* E H L P 056. 1739 𝔐 | -ετο εὐχή 049. 69. 1854. 2492 | -ζομεν (-ζεν ℵ) προσευχήν ℵ A² C Ψ 33. 81. 181. 1837. 1898. 2344 *pc* sa bo aeth ‖ ἐδόκει προσευχή D, *oratio ... videbatur* d it vg syᵖ·ʰ·.

The article before ποταμόν in D05 identifies the river as the one defined by the following clause – the one where it seemed there was a place of prayer. B03 is more vague about the river, and at the same time presents the knowledge of the place of prayer directly through the eyes of the 'we'-group. The noun προσευχή should be in the accusative in B03, as it is in ℵ01.

(ταῖς) συνελθούσαις B 𝔓⁷⁴ ℵ² H L P Ψ 049. 056. 33. 1739 𝔐 | συνελ. ἡμῖν ℵ* C E ‖ συνεληλυθυίαις D, *quae cumvenerint* d.

B03 reads the aorist participle, referring to the fact of the women having gathered there, versus the perfect of D05, referring to their present state of being gathered, as if they had come there for a particular purpose. In view of the perfect tense, it is perhaps more reasonable to take the verb συνέρχομαι as meaning that the women had 'accompanied' Paul and his companions (B-A-G, 2; cf. Lk. 23.55).

16.14 τῆς (πόλεως) D ‖ *om.* B 𝔓⁷⁴ ℵ *rell*.— (τὸν) θεόν B 𝔓⁷⁴ ℵ Dᵖ·ᵐ· *rell, deum* d ‖ κύριον D*.— ἤκουεν B 𝔓⁷⁴ ℵ A C Dˢ·ᵐ·E H P 1. 69. 81. 226. 323. 440. 547. 945. 1175. 1241. 1243. 1245. 1646. 1739. 1828. 2492, *audiebat* d ‖ -σεν D* L Ψ 049. 056. 33. 88. 104. 181. 330. 383. 467. 522. 614. 618. 913. 915. 927. 1108. 1270. 1505. 1518. 1611. 1837. 1838. 1854. 1891. 1898. 2138. 2147. 2344. 2412. 2495 *pc* vg; Chr Oecum Theoph.

The first variant is the omission in B03 of the article before the city, which happens several times elsewhere, though directly before the name rather than the noun πόλις (cf. Salamis, 13.5).

According to Scrivener (p. 444, col. 3, fol. 481b), 'κ. elot. sub θ in θν p.m.': i.e. D^{p.m.} wrote ϴ over the original κ. In view of the fact that elsewhere in Acts, the divine title with respect to Gentiles, even God-fearing ones, is always θεός (cf. 16.15a; Cornelius, 10.2, 3), that is most likely to be the correct reading here.

The imperfect of B03 presents the Lord as opening her heart while she was listening. The aorist of D05, on the other hand, presents the two actions as an overall event.

(ὑπό) Παύλου B D ($\mathfrak{P}^{74}$) ‖ τοῦ Παύ. ℵ A C E H L P Ψ 049. 056. 33. 1739 𝔐.

The absence of the article in both B03 and D05 presents Paul as seen through the eyes of Lydia for whom Paul is a new acquaintance (Heimerdinger and Levinsohn, 'The Use of the Article', pp. 31–32). It further distinguishes the things spoken by Paul from what was spoken by the group as a whole (cf. ἐλαλοῦμεν, 16.13b).

16.15 πᾶς (ὁ οἶκος) D, *omnis* d 257. 522. 536. 913. 1270 (gig) vg^{CT} w sa^{ms} bo^{mss}; Cass ‖ *om.* B $\mathfrak{P}^{74}$ ℵ *rell*.

The all-inclusiveness of D05 echoes similar phrases in the narrative concerning Cornelius 10.2; 11.14 (cf. comparable phrases with ὅλος at 7.10, Pharaoh; 18.8, Crispus). Metzger's comment that 'the Western text characteristically expands the narrative by adding πᾶς', is quite unjustified as far as D05 is concerned: there are more additional occurrences of πᾶς in ℵ01/B03 (+ 13) than in D05 (+ 11; see Read-Heimerdinger, 'The Distinction between ἅπας and πᾶς in the Work of Luke').

(τῷ) κυρίῳ B $\mathfrak{P}^{74}$ ℵ *rell, domino* d ‖ θεῷ D.

D05 consistently uses θεός to refer to the divine from the point of view of Gentiles (cf. on 16.14 above; Read-Heimerdinger, *The Bezan Text*, p. 286).

16.16 τὴν (προσευχήν) B $\mathfrak{P}^{45.74}$ ℵ A C E Ψ 33. 81. 1175. 1739 1891. 2344 ‖ *om.* D H L P 049. 056. 615 𝔐.

B03 understands the text as meaning that Paul and his companions were on their way to the place of prayer (cf. 16.13a), but D05 says, more controversially, that they were going to prayer (that is, to participate in the activities of the local Jewish meeting place, represented in Philippi by the προσευχή).

(πνεῦμα) πύθωνα B D* $\mathfrak{P}^{74}$ A C* 81. 326. 1837. 2344 vg ‖ -νος $\mathfrak{P}^{45}$ C^3 D^A E H L P Ψ 049. 056. 33. 1739 𝔐 gig sy^{hmg(gr)}.

Some MSS including the Corrector A of D05 read the genitive 'a spirit of (a) python', rather than the accusative, which either stands in apposition, 'a spirit, a python', or functions as an adjective, 'a python spirit'.

ὑπαντῆσαι (ἡμῖν) B* 𝔓⁴⁵·⁷⁴ ℵ C E Ψ 33. 36. 81. 181. 431. 453. 467. 1175. 1838. 1898. 2344 *pc* ‖ ἀπ- D, *obviam fieri* d A B² H L P 049. 056. 1739 𝔐.

Both compounds have a similar meaning of 'go to meet', with the same variant reading between ℵ01 and B03 at Lk. 17.12 (where D05 has a different phrase); at the other occurrence in Luke, B03 and D05 agree in reading ὑπαν-τάω (Lk. 8.27).

(κυρίοις) αὐτῆς B 𝔓⁴⁵·⁷⁴ ℵ *rell, suis* d ‖ *om.* D 917. 2412.— διὰ τούτου (μαντευομένη) D*, *per hoc* d ‖ *om.* B 𝔓⁴⁵·⁷⁴ ℵ Dˢ·ᵐ· *rell.*

D05 supposes that it is clear that the masters are those of the young girl. It makes explicit, on the other hand, that the profit she brought them was by means of the spirit (τούτου, gen. neut. pro.).

16.17 (κατακολουθοῦσα) Παύλῳ B *pc* ‖ τῷ Παύ. D 𝔓⁴⁵·⁷⁴ ℵ 1891 *rell.*— (καὶ ἡμῖν) ἔκραζεν B 𝔓⁴⁵·⁷⁴ ℵ *rell* ǀ -ξεν 1. 36. 618. 1175. 1241. 1505. 1518. 1739ᶜ. 2344. 2495 *pc* vgᵀ; Lcf Theoph ‖ καὶ (– Dˢ·ᵐ·) ἔκραζεν (-ον D*) Dᴴ, *et clama-bat* d.

The absence of the article before Paul in B03 causes him to be seen from the point of view of the slave girl, for whom this is a first encounter (cf. on Lydia at 16.14 above). However, the insistence on the presence of both 'Paul and us' suggests that Paul is not being mentioned (or not only mentioned) from the point of view of the slave girl but that of the narrator, specifically for the purpose of distinguishing between the characters at this point (see *Commentary* for further discussion); this accounts for the presence of the article in D05.

D05 underlines the main verb ἔκραζεν (the original hand reads a plural ending) by means of the adverbial καί before it, as several times elsewhere (Read-Heimerdinger, *The Bezan Text*, pp. 208–10).

(Οὗτοι οἱ) ἄνθρωποι B 𝔓⁴⁵·⁷⁴ ℵ Dᴱ *rell* ‖ *om.* D* d gig; Lcf Chr.

With the word ἄνθρωποι, B03 predicates of 'these men' that they 'are slaves of the Most High God'; D05 singles out 'these' (and not someone else) as being 'the slaves...'.

(οἵτινες) καταγγέλλουσιν B 𝔓⁴⁵·⁷⁴ ℵ *rell* ‖ εὐαγγελίζονται (-τες D*) Dˢ·ᵐ·, *evangelizant* d gig syᵖ boᵐˢˢ; Lcf.— ὑμῖν B D, *vobis* d 𝔓⁷⁴ ℵ E 36. 104. 226. 307. 330. 453. 610. 1175. 1409. 1611. 1739. 1854. 1891 *pc* ar c dem gig l p w vg syᵖ·ʰ·ᵖᵃˡ bo aeth; Orˡᵃᵗ Eustath Lcf ‖ ἡμῖν A C H L P Ψ 049. 056. 33. 614 𝔐 e ph ro sa; Orᵍʳ Chr.

The reading of εὐαγγελίζοντες in D05* is due to homoioteleuton, arising because of the previous word οἵτινες (and possibly originally written as ΕΥΑΓ-

ΓΕΛΙΖΟΝΤΕ [Ε = ΑΙ]). It is to be rejected since Luke never uses the verb εὐαγγε-λίζομαι in the active voice. The compound verb in B03 has much the same sense but without being a technical term for the proclamation of the gospel, in the way that the verb of D05 is.

The reading of ὑμῖν in both B03 and D05 is also to be considered erroneous and arising through itacism (*pace* Metzger, *Commentary,* p. 396), at least in D05 since exegetes are content to accept it in the usual text: there, the slave girl is addressing Paul and the demonstrative οὗτοι refers to the 'we'-group alone (cf. previous variant); by ἡμῖν the slave girl means herself and those whom she represents, παιδίσκη τις (v. 16; see *Commentary*). The only other people mentioned that she could have been speaking to are τοῖς κυρίοις (vv. 16, 19), but there is no indication that they are present in this scene in D05.

16.18 διαπονηθεὶς δὲ Παῦλος καὶ ἐπιστρέψας τῷ πνεύματι (εἶπεν) B 𝔓⁴⁵·⁷⁴ ℵ A ‖ διαπ. δὲ ὁ Παῦ. κ. ἐπ. τ. πν. C E H L P Ψ 049. 056. 33. 1739 𝔐 ‖ ἐπιστρέ-ψας δὲ ὁ Παῦ. τ. πν. κ. διαπ. D (*conversus autem Paulus in spiritu et cum indoluisset* d); Ambr.

The article is omitted before Paul in B03 as the focus switches back to him after a temporary focus on the slave girl (cf. 16.17, where the article was also omitted in B03 as he was viewed through the eyes of the slave girl). In D05, Paul has been in focus throughout this scene (unlike the previous scene with Lydia, where she was the main concern in D05, cf. on 16.14 above).

The order of the two aorist participles differs in B03 and D05. Although little, if anything, can be inferred about the time sequence of successive aorist participles preceding a finite verb (since, being timeless, they may denote coincident action, see, e.g., Robertson, *Grammar,* pp. 1112–14), B03 seems to have understood the two verbs as expressing successive action and preferred to present the more logical sequence of Paul becoming troubled and then turning to the spirit. The order in D05, in contrast, does not express time sequence: it presents the main action supporting the finite verb (εἶπεν) as Paul's turning (ἐπιστρέψας) to the spirit, and his distress (διαπονηθείς, where the aorist expresses an inner state as a global situation and not as a past event) as a pivot that accounts for his action of 'turning and saying'.

The Latin page d5 has understood τῷ πνεύματι as a reference to the spirit of Paul.

τῷ (ὀνόματι) D H L P Ψ 049. 056 𝔐 ‖ *om.* B 𝔓⁷⁴ ℵ A C E 33. 81. 614. 927. 945. 1270. 1505. 1611. 1739. 1837. 1891. 2344. 2412. 2495.— ἐξελθεῖν (ἀπ' αὐτῆς) B 𝔓⁴⁵·⁷⁴ ℵ *rell* ‖ ἵνα ἐξέλθῃς D, *ut exeas* d e gig; Lcf ‖ ἔξελθε 33ᵛⁱᵈ.

The omission of the article in B03 is the only occasion when ὄνομα in the phrase ἐν τῷ ὀνόματι Ἰησοῦ Χριστοῦ is anarthrous (cf. 2.38; 3.6; 4.10, 18; 6.8 D05; 8.16; 10.48; 14.10 D05; 15.26; 18.8 D05; 19.5, 13, 17; 21.13; see Read-Heimerdinger, *The Bezan Text,* pp. 256–71).

The construction of ἵνα + subjunctive in D05 is a feature of Koine Greek, in place of the classical infinitive.

(καὶ) ἐξῆλθεν αὐτῇ τῇ ὥρα B 𝔓⁴⁵ᵛⁱᵈ·⁷⁴ ℵ *rell* ‖ εὐθέως ἐξ. D saᵐˢ aeth.

The phrase of B03, αὐτῇ τῇ ὥρα, is exclusive to Luke (Lk. × 6; Acts × 2 [– 16.18 D05]). On the other hand, εὐθέως is found in Matthew × 12, Mark × 27 D05 only (AT reads εὐθύς); John × 3; Luke × 15 (Lk. × 6; Acts × 9 [+ 13.11 D05; 14.10 D05; 16.18 D05; 19.6 D05]). The B03 expression is more emphatic, and more solemn in tone.

16.19 καὶ (– A*) ἰδόντες B A* ǀ ἰδόντες δέ 𝔓⁴⁵·⁷⁴ ℵ A² *rell* ‖ ὡς δὲ εἶδαν D (*cum vidissent* d).— (οἱ κύριοι) αὐτῆς B 𝔓⁴⁵·⁷⁴ ℵ A² *rell* ‖ τῆς παιδίσκης D, *eius puelles[ae]* d.

In the text of B03, the connective καί, the present participle ἰδόντες, as well as the genitive pronoun αὐτῆς referring to the slave girl, all function together to portray the slave girl's owners as present on the scene when she was shouting out (cf. 16.18). In D05, the connective δέ, the subsidiary time clause and the genitive of the noun τῆς παιδίσκης, all combine, on the contrary, to portray the masters as absent. This factor reinforces the interpretation that the girl's words in D05 were addressed to Paul in particular.

(ὅτι) ἐξῆλθεν ἡ ἐλπίς B 𝔓⁴⁵·⁷⁴ ℵ *rell* (*ispes et* d!) ‖ ἀπεστερῆσθαι D.— (τῆς ἐργασίας αὐτῶν) ἧς εἶχαν δι' αὐτῆς D, *(reditus eorum) quem habebant per ipsam* d ‖ *om.* B 𝔓⁴⁵·⁷⁴ ℵ *rell.*

In a clause of indirect speech, B03 reads a conjugated verb ἐξῆλθεν, with the subject ἡ ἐλπίς. D05 has a perfect passive infinitive (of ἀποστερέω, cf. 1 Tim. 6.5; Winer, *Grammar,* pp. 426-27, 718), of which the implied subject is the same as that of the main verb, that is the masters (cf. 4.16 D05; 27.10 [D05. lac.]; B-D-R, §397.5, n. 13). *Contra* Delebecque (*Les deux Actes,* p. 102) who notes that ἀπεστερῆσθαι 'est une faute de copiste' and with Blass and Rehkopf corrects it unnecessarily to ἀπεστέρηνται.

τὸν (Σιλᾶν) B 𝔓⁴⁵·⁷⁴ ℵ A² *rell* ‖ *om.* D C 88. 618. 915. 919. 1898 *pc.*

By the omission of the article before Silas in D05, he is viewed as forming a united pair with Paul. B03 usually (but cf. 17.4 B03) retains the article with Silas when he is mentioned with Paul, so maintaining his separate identity (and that of Paul; cf. 16.29 B03; and 17.10, 14, where τε has a similar effect of reinforcing the distinctiveness of the characters already indicated by the presence of the article before each name). In the D05 text, a tension between Paul and Silas will become apparent in chapter 17, at which point the double article is used (cf. 17.4, 10, 14; see Read-Heimerdinger, *The Bezan Text,* pp. 136–37).

16.21 (καταγγέλλουσιν) ἔθη B 𝔓⁷⁴ ℵ Dˢ·ᵐ· *rell* ‖ τὰ (– 2412*) ἔθνη D*, *gentes* d 2412*.

τὰ ἔθνη in D05 may be a scribal error. On the other hand, it could be considered as an accusative of the persons addressed by the verb καταγγέλλω, as often happens with the verb εὐαγγελίζομαι (Acts 5.42; 8.35; 11.20; 13.32; 14.25 D05). The translation follows this option.

(ἔξεστιν) ἡμῖν παραδέχεσθαι οὐδὲ ποιεῖν Ῥωμαίοις οὖσιν B 𝔓⁷⁴ ℵ *rell, nobis recipere nec facere Romani cum simus* d ‖ ἡμᾶς -δέξασθαι οὔτε π. Ῥω. ὑπάρχουσιν D.

ἡμᾶς in D05 could be taken as the subject of the aorist infinitive παραδέξασθαι, in which case the dative phrase Ῥωμαίοις ὑπάρχουσιν is not in apposition to it but directly dependent on οὐκ ἔξεστιν.

The aorist infinitive in D05 contrasts with the following present infinitive ποιεῖν, read by both texts: receiving the things that are being announced is viewed as a single act, whereas doing them is viewed as progressive. With the present infinitive of the two verbs, B03 does not make the distinction.

The distinction between οὐδέ and οὔτε is in general terms the same as between δέ (disjunction) and τε (continuity), though in view of the many *vll* it is apparently not respected (Winer, *Grammar*, pp. 611–12, 615–16). Here, the negation is continued from οὐκ ἔξεστιν, with the two infinitives being connected with the second negative particle. If the value of the forms is being recognized, then B03 views the two actions as distinct, whereas D05 views them as belonging together: 'οὐδέ and μηδέ add negation to negation, whilst οὔτε and μήτε divide a single negation into parts' (p. 612; cf. 17.29 D05).

The *vl* ὑπάρχω for εἶναι occurs frequently in D05 in Luke's work, the former stating more strongly the existence of what is affirmed (cf. ὑπάρχω for γίνομαι 16.29 below).

16.22 (καὶ) συνεπέστη ὁ ὄχλος κατ' αὐτῶν B 𝔓⁷⁴ ℵ *rell* ‖ πολὺς (+ D d gig syᵖ sa aeth; Lcf) ὄχλος συνεπέστησαν κ. αὐ. κράζοντες D, *multa turba supervenerunt adversus eos clamantes* d.

By presenting the crowd with the anarthrous article, B03 continues, as before with the owners (cf. 16.19 above), to portray the participants in this scene as already present when the slave girl was shouting out (cf. 16.17). D05, again in line with 16.19, brings the crowd on stage only at this point (no article), describing them as numerous (πολύς) and referring to them in the plural (συνεπέστησαν ... κράζοντες) in keeping with the reference to their number. The D05 reading πολὺς ὄχλος συνεπέστησαν is attested by a Malkite liturgical text in Palestinian Syriac (M. Black [ed.], *Rituale Melchitarum*, pp. 17–18). The agitation of the crowd is intensified in D05 by the participle κράζοντες.

καὶ (οἱ στρατηγοί) B 𝔓⁷⁴ ℵ Dᴴ *rell* ‖ τότε D*, *tunc* d syᵖ.

With καί, B03 continues to present the scene as one continuous movement (cf. on 16.19, and the previous variant); with τότε, D05 introduces the following scene as a response to the accusations of the owners of the slave girl.

16.23 (πολλὰς) δέ B 6. 81. 181. 1175. 2147. 2495 *pc* e bo ‖ τε D 𝔓⁷⁴ ℵ *rell*.

D05 uses τε to link together closely the various steps in the punishment dealt by the magistrates, having started a new development in the narrative with the previous clause (see above variant). B03, which had not made such a break there, makes it here instead. From the point of view of the narrative flow, the D05 sequence is more coherent.

(ἀσφαλῶς) τηρεῖν B 𝔓⁷⁴ ℵ *rell* ‖ -ρεῖσθαι D, *servari* d.

For the aorist passive infinitive of D05, cf. 24.23; 25.4, 21. The passive maintains Paul and Silas as the subject (as below, see next variant).

16.24 ὅς (παραγγελίαν) B 𝔓⁷⁴ ℵ *rell* ‖ ὁ δέ D, *qui* d syᴾ sa boᵐˢˢ.— (τοὺς πόδας) ἠσφαλίσατο αὐτῶν εἰς τὸν ξύλον B 𝔓⁷⁴ ℵ C* 33. 81 ‖ αὐ. ἠσφ. εἰς τ. ξύλον C² E H L P Ψ 049. 056. 614. 1739 𝔐 ‖ αὐ. ἠσφαλίσαντο ἐν τῷ ξύλῳ D* (-σατο Dˢ·ᵐ·, *pedes eorum conclusit in ligno* d gig vg; Lcf).

As the jailor becomes the new subject (having been the indirect object of the previous clause, 16.23), B03 refers to him with the nominative relative pronoun, and he continues to remain in focus as the subject of the two finite verbs (ἔβαλεν ... ἠσφαλίσατο). D05 marks a new development (δέ) and also switches focus to the jailor with the article ὁ standing for the noun; the switch is only temporary, however, for with the plural verb ἠσφαλίσαντο it moves back once more to Paul and Silas, in keeping with the concern shown in the previous variant. Here, ἀσφαλίζω, a semi-deponent verb, is used in a passive sense (L-S-J, ἀσφαλίζω, 1, a: 'some of these tenses are used in pass. sense'); the τοὺς πόδας αὐτῶν is the subject, in the accusative because it represents a part of the overall subject, Paul and Silas (cf. Winer, *Grammar*, p. 287: 'the accusative came to be used with passive verbs, in general, to indicate the more remote object, and especially the *part* of the subject which is in the state or condition indicated by the verb').

The position of the possessive pronoun after the verb in B03 throws the spotlight on to the jailor's act of fastening the feet.

The preposition εἰς can be explained by the jailor's act of putting the feet into the stocks, just as ἐν in D05 can be understood as referring to the final position of the feet in the stocks. In general, variation between the two prepositions can be justified by the context (see Read-Heimerdinger, *The Bezan Text*, pp. 192–97).

16.25 Κατὰ δὲ τὸ (– ℵ) μεσονύκτιον B 𝔓⁷⁴ ℵ Dᶜ *rell* ‖ Κ. δ. μέσον τῆς νυκτός D*, *Circa mediam vero noctem* d.

The expression of B03 is found at Lk. 11.5; Acts 20.7. That of D05 is found at Acts 27.27, and close to the form at Exod. 12.29 LXX (μεσούσης τῆς νυκτός) referring to the night of the Passover, which is being echoed in this scene of deliverance (see *Commentary*).

ὁ (Παῦλος) D *pc* ‖ *om.* B 𝔓⁷⁴ ℵ *rell.*

The presence of the article before Paul in D05 also serves Silas, presenting them together as a pair (as at 16.19 [*om.* B03 ℵ01], 29 [*om.* ℵ01]); it indicates that they have been maintained as the focus of attention, unlike in B03 where, as was seen in the *vll* of 16.23, 24, attention had switched to the jailor.

16.26 ἠνεῴχθησαν δέ B gig; Cyr Lcf Cass ‖ ἤν. δὲ παραχρῆμα D C 69. 88. 1175. 1739. 1837 ‖ ἠνοίχθησαν δὲ π. ℵ 𝔓⁷⁴ A E 33. 81 ‖ ἀνεῴχθησάν τε/δὲ π. H L P Ψ 049. 056. 614 𝔐, *apertaeque sunt statim* d.

D05 includes the adverb παραχρῆμα, as elsewhere in Acts (cf. 5.5 D05; 14.10 D05).

(τὰ δεσμὰ) ἀνέθη B 𝔓⁷⁴ ℵ² Dˢ·ᵐ· *rell* ‖ ἀνελύθη D*, *relaxata sunt* d ℵ*; Chr ‖ ἐλύθη 1838 *pc.*

Both verbs are rare with the transitive sense of 'loosen' (B-A-G, ἀνίημι 1; ἀναλύω, I), that of B03 found only at Acts 27.40 in Luke's writing, and that of D05 not used elsewhere. The verbs are not frequent in the LXX either, though transitive usage is more common with ἀνίημι.

16.27 ἔξυπνος δέ B 𝔓⁷⁴ ℵ *rell* ‖ καὶ ἔξ. D, *et exomnis* d. — καὶ (ἀσπασάμενος) D* ‖ *om.* B 𝔓⁷⁴ ℵ Dˢ·ᵐ· *rell* d.

The connective δέ in B03 presents the switch back to the jailor as a new narrative development (cf. on vv. 25, 26 above), whereas καί of D05 views it as part of a series of events following the quake.

B03 does not express the connection between the participles (asyndeton); the three successive occurrences of καί in D05 (cf. the previous variant) evoke a greater sense of panic.

16.28 (ἐφώνησεν δὲ) Παῦλος μεγάλη φωνῇ B *pc* ‖ ὁ Π. μεγ. φ. 181. 431. 927 ‖ ὁ Π. φ. μεγ. 36. 180. 629. 927 gig ‖ μεγ. φ. Παῦ. 𝔓⁷⁴ Ψ, *magna voce Paulus* d ‖ μεγ. φ. ὁ Παῦ. A 1875. 1898 ‖ φ. μεγ. ὁ Παῦ. D C³ E H L P 049. 056. 614. 1739 𝔐 ‖ φ. μεγ. Παῦ. ℵ C* 33. 88 *pc.*

As the jailor had been in focus in the previous clause in B03 (by virtue of δέ at 16.27 above), the switch to Paul is now marked with the absence of the article and the position of his name immediately next to the verb. In D05, he has always been the focus of the story (see Heimerdinger and Levinsohn, 'The Use of the Article', p. 28) and therefore his name not only has the article but is positioned at the end of the clause.

The word order of D05 (noun–adjective) is usual with an anarthrous noun, and assumes that the loudness of Paul's voice is natural in the circumstances. The placing of the adjective in first position in B03 therefore has the effect of underlining the loudness of Paul's voice (cf. 14.10, μεγάλη φωνῇ, where the loudness is emphasized as Paul has to shout above the crowd; see Read-

Heimerdinger, *The Bezan Text*, pp. 90–93). It is yet another device used to highlight the presence of Paul in this scene.

τι (κακόν) D ‖ *om.* B 𝔓⁷⁴ ℵ *rell* d.

τι, though unnecessary for the sense, has an emphatic force in D05.

16.29 αἰτήσας δὲ φῶτα (εἰσεπήδησεν) B 𝔓⁷⁴ ℵ *rell* ‖ φῶ. δὲ αἰτ. D, *lumen vero petens* d.— (ἔντρομος) γενόμενος B 𝔓⁷⁴ ℵ A C³ E H L P 049. 056. 33. 1739 𝔐, *factus* d ‖ ὑπάρχων D C* Ψ 181. 257. 614. 913. 927. 1108. 1505. 1518. 1611. 1799. 1898. 2138. 2412. 2495; Chr.

D05 places the noun φῶτα in an emphatic position at the front of the new sentence.

The verb ὑπάρχω is again used by D05 (cf. 16.21 above), this time against γίνομαι of B03.

(προσέπεσεν) πρὸς τοὺς πόδας D*, *ad pedes* d l s vg^AC (b c dem gig p vg^IMOT sy^{p.h**} sa bo; Lcf Chr Cass) ‖ *om.* B 𝔓⁷⁴ ℵ D^{s.m.} *rell*.— τῷ (Σιλᾷ) 𝔓⁷⁴ ℵ A C³ E H L P Ψ 049. 056. 33. 1739 𝔐 ‖ *om.* B D C* 1646.

πρὸς τοὺς πόδας in D05* serves as an adverb qualifying προσέπεσεν, which itself governs the names τῷ Παύλῳ καὶ Σιλᾷ in the dative (the phrase is usually followed by the name or pronoun in the genitive, cf. Mk. 5.22; 7.25; Jn 11.32; Lk. 10.39 B03; Acts 5.10). Comparison may be made with Lk. 5.8 D05, προσέπεσεν αὐτοῦ τοῖς ποσίν.

The name of Silas is preceded yet again by the article in ℵ01, treating him as distinct from Paul (cf. 16.19), whereas D05 continues at this point (now supported by B03) to view them as forming a united pair.

16.30 (καὶ) προαγαγών (προάγων ℵ*) B 𝔓⁷⁴ ℵ² *rell, cum produxisset* d ‖ προήγαγεν D.

B03 reads the aorist participle of προάγω, anticipating the finite verb ἔφη; D05 reads a finite verb, conjoined to εἶπεν with καί (see below).

(ἔξω) τοὺς λοιποὺς ἀσφαλισάμενος D (*ceteros custodivit* d sy^{p.h**}).— ἔφη B 𝔓⁷⁴ ℵ *rell* ‖ καὶ (– D^{s.m.}) εἶπεν αὐτοῖς D*, *et dixit illis* d.

D05 specifies that the jailor led Paul and Silas outside only after making sure the other prisoners could not escape, thus indicating that the earthquake had loosened the bonds of everyone in the prison.

B03 uses here the imperfect ἔφη, found only occasionally as a verb of speaking in Acts (cf. 1.4 D05; 2.38; 7.2; 8.36; 10.28, 30, 31; 11.28 D05; 16.37; 17.22; 19.25 D05, 35; 21.37; 22.2 [not D05], 27 B03, 28; + 11 occurrences in passages that are missing in D05). D05 has the more common εἶπεν here; furthermore, the text specifies the addressee with the dative pronoun αὐτοῖς referring to Paul and Silas (cf. αὐτούς in the previous clause), a clarification arising from the mention just made of the other prisoners in D05.

16.31 ('Ιησοῦν) Χριστόν D C E H L P Ψ 049. 056. 1739 𝔐 sy sa aeth || *om.* B
𝔓⁷⁴ ℵ A 33. 81. 1243. 2344 *pc* gig vg bo.

It is typical of D05 to use the full title of Jesus in declarations of salvation,
though the use of the full title is not a generalized tendency since it is not
found in all situations (see Read-Heimerdinger, *The Bezan Text*, pp. 264, 267,
271).

16.32 (τὸν λόγον) τοῦ θεοῦ B ℵ* 255 *pc* || τοῦ (– D) κυρίου D, *domini* d 𝔓⁴⁵·⁷⁴
ℵ² A C E H L P Ψ 049. 056. 33. 1739 𝔐 it vg sy^{p.h.pal} sa bo; Lcf Epiph Chr |
om. 1891 ar.

The phrase τὸν λόγον τοῦ θεοῦ of B03 is in keeping with Luke's custom of
using this expression when the word is addressed to Gentiles for the first time.
The expression in D05, τὸν λόγον κυρίου, is unique in Acts, in that κυρίου is
anarthrous, though it is the common expression in the LXX (Read-Heimerdinger,
The Bezan Text, p. 297). It may be that κύριος is being highlighted by the
absence of the article here because the word is salient, precisely because Paul
and Silas do not go through their normal practice of offering τὸν λόγον τοῦ
θεοῦ to a Gentile before speaking τὸν λόγον τοῦ κυρίου (see *Commentary*).

16.33 ἔλουσεν (ἀπὸ τῶν πληγῶν) B 𝔓⁴⁵·⁷⁴ ℵ D^B *rell* || ἔλυσεν D*, *solvit* d. Given

It looks as if D05* uses λύω through phonetic confusion with λούω. Given
the noun πληγή, meaning 'a blow', and by extension 'the wound resulting
from a blow' (cf. Bailly, πληγή, I, 1; III), the verb of B03 makes more
sense. A figurative meaning is possible, however, given the underlying symbolism of the account (on which see *Commentary*).

(καὶ) ἐβαπτίσθη αὐτός B 𝔓⁷⁴ ℵ *rell* || αὐ. ἐβ. D, *ipse baptizatus est* d.— (καὶ)
οἱ αὐτοῦ ἅπαντες B ℵ 614. 1243. 1505. 2147. 2412. 2495 *pc* || οἱ αὐ. πάντες
D, *et eius omnes* d 𝔓⁷⁴ C E H L P Ψ 049. 056. 1739 𝔐 | ὁ οἶκος αὐ. ὅλος 𝔓⁴⁵
vg^{cl} bo^{ms} | οἱ οἴκιοι αὐ. πάντες A.

The position of the emphatic pronoun αὐτός before the verb sets the baptism of the jailor in contrast with his action of treating the wounds of Paul and
Silas. Its position in B03 conjoins it directly with the members of the household,
οἱ αὐτοῦ ἅπαντες.

The pronoun ἅπαντες in B03 insists on the entirety; it arises seven times
in B03 as a *vl* for πᾶς in D05 (and twice in D05 against πᾶς in B03; Read-
Heimerdinger, 'The Distinction between ἅπας and πᾶς in the Work of Luke').

16.34 καὶ (ἀναγαγών τε) D^{p.m.}, *et* d || *om.* B 𝔓⁷⁴ ℵ D^{s.m.} *rell*.

καί ... τε as read by D05 is highly unusual, but it is not unknown in classical Greek (examples from Thucydides are cited by Dennison, *Greek Particles*,
pp. 535–56). τε serves as the connective, while καί is adverbial, here emphatic
because the action of the jailor is exceptional (as highlighted again by a second
adverbial καί in the following line, see below).

(εἰς τὸν οἶκον) αὐτοῦ D 𝔓⁷⁴ ℵ A E H L 049. 056. 614 𝔐 ‖ *om.* B 𝔓⁴⁵ C P Ψ 81. 88. 547. 614. 945. 1241. 1270. 1505. 1646. 1739. 1891. 2412. 2495.

The possessive adjective in D05 is not necessary for the sense, but it establishes a) the contrast between αὐτούς (Paul and Silas) and αὐτοῦ (the jailor); b) the parallel with Lydia (cf. 16.15, εἰς τὸν οἶκόν μου).

καὶ (παρέθηκεν) Dᵖ·ᵐ·, *et* d ‖ *om.* B 𝔓⁷⁴ ℵ Dˢ·ᵐ· *rell.*

The pattern of καί between a participle and a finite verb is a characteristic of D05, which serves to underline the second action because it signals a moment of exceptional dramatic importance (Read-Heimerdinger, *The Bezan Text*, pp. 208–10).

(καὶ) ἠγαλλιάσατο B 𝔓⁷⁴ ℵ A C E H L Ψ 049. 33. 81. 88. 104. 614. 945. 1175. 1241. 1270. 1505. 1611. 1646. 1739. 1891. 2147. 2344. 2412. 2495 ‖ -ᾶτο D, *exultabat* d C* P 056 𝔐 e (gig) syᵖ sa boᵐˢˢ; (Lcf).

B03 reads the aorist of ἀγαλλιάομαι, whereas D05 reads the imperfect.

πανοικεί B 𝔓⁷⁴ ℵ *rell* ‖ σὺν τῷ οἴκῳ αὐτοῦ D (*cum tota domu sua* d).

The adverb of B03 is not found elsewhere in the New Testament, nor in the LXX. The expression of D05 is equivalent, and by its wording maintains the insistence on the whole household of the jailor.

(πεπιστευκὼς) τῷ θεῷ B 𝔓⁷⁴ ℵ *rell* ‖ ἐπὶ τὸν θεόν D ‖ τ. κυρίῳ 88. 915. 917. 1898. 2401 c (*in domino* d) gig s vg^D sa aeth; Lcf Chr.

The preposition ἐπί in D05 makes it clear that the jailor has acquired faith in God, an important step for a Gentile seen from a Jewish point of view. Without the preposition, the dative τῷ θεῷ may mean the same thing but the point is not made so forcefully. The reading of d5 also has the effect of removing the force of the message underlying the wording of D05.

16.35 (γενομένης) ἀπέστειλαν οἱ στρατηγοί B 𝔓⁴⁵ᵛⁱᵈ·⁷⁴ ℵ *rell* lat syᵖ·ʰ·ᵖᵃˡ co aeth; Chr ‖ -στάλκασιν 614. 1505. 1611. 2147. 2412. 2495 ‖ συνῆλθον οἱ στρ. ἐπὶ τὸ αὐτὸ εἰς τὴν ἀγορὰν καὶ ἀναμνησθέντες τὸν σεισμὸν τὸν γεγονότα ἐφοβήθησαν καὶ ἀπέστειλαν D, *convenerunt magistrati idipsud in foro et rememorati sunt terraemotum qui factus est timuerunt et transmiserunt* d (syʰᵐᵍ); Ephr.

B03 may have shortened the sentence by homoioteleuton (ἀπέστειλαν B03, at the beginning of the phrase // ἀπέστειλαν D05, at the end). Without it, the narrative lacks coherence, since no reason is suggested for the magistrates deciding to release their prisoners.

(τοὺς ῥαβδούχους) λέγοντες B 𝔓⁷⁴ ℵ *rell* ‖ -τας D, *dicentes* d.

According to B03, it is the words of the magistrates, οἱ στρατηγοί, that are reported, whereas in D05 it is those of the sergeants, τοὺς ῥαβδούχους (an identical variant is seen at Lk. 24.34). By the same variant, the addressee of the words spoken changes: in B03, the magistrates order the sergeants to release the men; in D05, the sergeants tell the jailor to release them.

(ἐκείνους) οὓς ἐχθὲς παρέλαβες D, *quos externa die suscepisti* d 383. 614. 1799. 2147. 2412 sy^h ‖ *om.* B 𝔓^74 ℵ *rell* lat sy^(p).pal co aeth; Chr.

In B03, the demonstrative ἐκείνους, without any further qualification, can be read as denigrating. Not so in D05 where a descriptive clause complements the preposition.

16.36 ἀπήγγειλεν δὲ ὁ δεσμοφύλαξ (ἀρχιδεσμ- 𝔓^74) B 𝔓^74 ℵ *rell* ‖ καὶ εἰσελθὼν ὁ δεσμ. ἀπ. D, *et ingressus optio carceris renuntiavit* d (sy^p).— (τοὺς λόγους) τούτους 𝔓^74 ℵ A E H L P Ψ 049. 056. 33. 1739 𝔐 ‖ *om.* B D 𝔓^45vid C 1891.

B03 starts a new development with δέ, since the jailor now comes back on-stage in this text; in D05, he had already been implied as the addressee of the words of the sergeants (2nd person sing., παρέλαβες), and the narrative continues with καί (see on 16.35 above). The demonstrative τούτους qualifies τοὺς λόγους, words that were initially addressed to the sergeants according to B03, but presumably passed on to him. In D05, the demonstrative is superfluous, for the words were addressed to him directly.

D05 includes the circumstantial detail that the jailor went in (to the prison), indicating that he carried out the order given to him by the sergeants. Again, since the jailor only now comes back into the story in B03, the detail is unnecessarily specific.

Ἀπέσταλκαν (οἱ στρατηγοί) B 𝔓^45.74 ℵ 1175^c ‖ -τάλκασιν D E H L P Ψ 049. 056. 614. 1739 𝔐 ‖ -τειλαν C 81; Theoph.

D05 reads the correct form of the perfect, which tended to be assimilated in the third person plural with the weak aorist ending as B03 illustrates (cf. ἀπέστειλαν, 16.35).

(πορεύεσθε) ἐν εἰρήνῃ B 𝔓^45vid.74 (εἰς εἰρήνην ℵ) *rell* lat sy^p.h co aeth Chr ‖ *om.* D d gig.

The jailor in D05 issues a brusque command to go, without the softening of the order 'in peace', which was not part of the magistrates' order.

16.37 Ἀναιτίους (δείραντες) D, *Anetios caesos* d sy^p aeth; Cass ‖ *om.* B 𝔓^45.74 ℵ *rell*.

Paul's insistence on his innocence in D05 is concordant with his indignation at the treatment he and Silas have received.

16.38 τοῖς στρατηγοῖς B 𝔓^45.74 ℵ D^s.m. *rell* ‖ ΑΥΤΟΙΣΟΙΣΤΡΑΤΗΓΟΙΣ D*.— (ταῦτα) τὰ ῥηθέντα πρὸς τοὺς στρατηγούς D, *quae dicta sunt ad praetores* d (sy^p) ‖ τοῖς ῥαβδούχοις 𝔓^45 ‖ *om.* B 𝔓^74 ℵ D^s.m. *rell*.

D05* appears to have read ΑΥΤΟΙΣΟΙΣΤΡΑΤΗΓΟΙΣ for ΑΥΤΟΙΣΤΟΙΣΣΤΡΑΤΗΓΟΙΣ, through haplography.

The emphatic dative pronoun αὐτοῖς underlines the magistrates as the intended recipients of Paul's words, as does the following adjectival phrase in D05, which takes up πρὸς αὐτούς from 16.37a.

ἐφοβήθησαν δὲ ἀκούσαντες ὅτι Ῥωμαῖοί εἰσιν B 𝔓45vid.74 ℵ A 33. 69. (81). 945. 1175. 1739. 1837. 1891. 2344 I καὶ ἐφ. ἀκ. ὅτι Ῥω. εἰ. E H L P Ψ 049. 056. 614 𝔐 II οἱ δὲ ἀκ. ὅτι Ῥω. εἰσιν ἐφ. D, *cum autem audierunt quia Romani sunt timuerunt* d syᵖ.

The word order of B03 confers particular importance on the fact of Paul and Silas being Roman. In D05, this fact is downplayed by being expressed in a participial clause preceding the main verb; in addition, the initial articular pronoun signals that this sentence is an intermediate step, preparing for the more important following action, the speech of the magistrates to Paul and Silas (see next variant). The initial articular pronoun and position of the verb at the end of the clause in D05 emphasizes the fear of the magistrates and especially the cause of it.

16.39 (καὶ) ἐλθόντες παρεκάλεσαν αὐτούς B 𝔓45vid.74 ℵ *rell* II παραγενόμενοι μετὰ φίλων πολλῶν εἰς τὴν φυλακὴν παρ. αὐ. ἐξελθεῖν εἰπόντες· Ἠγνοήσαμεν τὰ καθ' ὑμᾶς ὅτι ἐστὲ ἄνδρες δίκαιοι D, *cum venissent cum amicis multis in carcerem rogaverunt eos exire dicentes: Ignoramus adversum vos quoniam estis viri iusti* d I ἐλθόντες εἰς τὴν φυλακὴν παρ. αὐ. ἐξελθεῖν εἰπόντες· Ἠγν. τ. καθ' ὑμ. ὅτι ἐσ. ἄν. δίκ. 257. 383. 614. 1799. 2147. 2412 vgᴿ² syʰ**; (Ephr).

The narrative in B03 concludes in a matter-of-fact way, explaining how the magistrates did what Paul had asked.

D05 has a number of circumstantial details, which express with more force the magistrates' fear and insistency, the significance of which is examined in the *Commentary*. First, the magistrates are said to have gone to the prison with many friends and, once there, to have begged the two prisoners to go out, explaining that they had not realized that they were 'good men'. The same term δίκαιοι is used of the disciples at 14.2 D05.

(καὶ ἐξαγαγόντες) ἠρώτων ἀπελθεῖν ἀπὸ τῆς πόλεως B 𝔓74 ℵ A 33. 81. 945. 1175. 1739. 1891. 2344 I ἠρ. ἐξελθεῖν ἀπὸ τ. πόλ. 𝔓45vid E H L P Ψ 049. 056 𝔐 II παρεκάλεσαν αὐτοὺς λέγοντες· Ἐκ τῆς πόλ. ταύτης ἐξέλθατε, μήποτε πάλιν συστραφῶσιν ἡμῖν ἐπικράζοντες καθ' ὑμῶν D, *rogaverunt eos dicentes: De civitate ista exite, ne forte iterum convertantur ad nos clamantes adversum vos* d I καὶ ἐκ ταύτης τῆς πόλ. ἐξέλθετε, μή πως ἐπιστραφῶσι πάλιν οἱ ἐπικρ. καθ' ὑμ. 257. 383. 614. 1799. 2147. 2412 vgᴿ² syʰ**; Ephr.

The details continue in D05: having led them out of the prison, they again insist on the urgency for them to get out of the city, in case the local people start up another complaint against them. B03 expresses it more tamely as a 'request', 'to go away from the city'.

16.40 ἀπὸ (τῆς φυλακῆς) B ℵ 945. 1739. 1891 *pc* ‖ ἐκ D 𝔓⁷⁴ A E Ψ 33. 614 𝔐.

The choice of the preposition is in accordance with the wording of the request of the magistrates in each text (see previous variant).

εἰσῆλθον B 𝔓⁴⁵·⁷⁴ ℵ *rell* ‖ ἦλθον D, *venerunt* d 1175 e gig sa aeth; Cass.

The compound verb of B03 reiterates the sense conveyed by the preposition πρός following it, that they went into her house.

(ἰδόντες) παρεκάλεσαν τοὺς ἀδελφούς B 𝔓⁴⁵ᵛⁱᵈ·⁷⁴ ℵ A 33. 81. 181. 1175. 1898 ‖ τ. ἀδ. διηγήσαντο ὅσα ἐποίησεν κύριος αὐτοῖς παρακαλέσαντες (-σαν τε Dˢ·ᵐ·) αὐτούς D*, *fratres narraverunt quanta fecit dominus cum eis exhorti sunt eos* d b (gig) vgᴰ; (Cass) ‖ τ. ἀδ. παρακαλέσαντες αὐτούς E H L P Ψ 049. 056. 1739 𝔐.

B03 notes that Paul and Silas saw the brethren, exhorted them and departed. D05 has the additional information that the manner of exhortation was by reporting 'what the Lord did with them' (cf. 14.27; 15.4, 12).

Commentary

[C-A] 16.11-12 *Journey to Philippi*

[a] 16.11-12a *Arrival in Philippi*

16.11-12a The opening verses of the sequence serve as an introduction to the narrative that takes place in Philippi relating, as they do, the sea-crossing from Troas (cf. 16.10). The start of the new sequence is signalled more overtly in the Bezan text with the time phrase, 'On the next day'.

As the group leave Troas, in Codex Bezae they are presented as being 'led away', in accordance with the divine promptings that have brought them to this point. The sea voyage is smooth, progressing without any obstacle from Troas to the island of Samothrace,[22] and then on the next day to Neapolis on the mainland, the port that served Philippi some 10 miles inland. The successive stages of the journey (Troas, point of departure – Samothrace, an island – Neapolis, port of arrival – Philippi, leading city and final destination) echo those of the initial journey of the mission to Cyprus (13.4-6: Selucia – Cyprus – Salamina – Paphos), but with an important difference for, on the earlier occasion, Barnabas and Saul had stopped in Salamina to go to 'the synagogues of the Jews' before making for the final destination of Paphos whereas now, the group go directly to Philippi without any diversion on the way.

Not only does opening time detail in Codex Bezae make clear that the obedience to the divine call was immediate but it also, in combination with the fol-

---

22. The verb εὐθυδρομήσαμεν is used only by Luke, here and at 21.1 referring to an analogous sea-crossing.

lowing time marker, 'on the next day', provides a framework of three days for the journey. 'Three days' here, as elsewhere, marks the passage from death to life as Paul undertakes his 'exodus' away from the confines of Judaism (see *Commentary*, on 15.40). The presence of the 'we'-group is important, for their role will be the mouthpiece of the Holy Spirit when Paul is being led by his own goals and understanding rather than the divine plan (see on 16.16-24 below).

Philippi was a Roman colony, the leading one according to Codex Bezae, and as such represented a Gentile city as far as Paul's mission was concerned, where relatively few Jews would be found. The only comparable city from the first phase of the mission was Lystra. The significance of Philippi for Paul's final destination of Rome (cf. on 16.6,7 above) is that it lay on the Via Egnatia, an ancient road that ran from the west across Macedonia as the main route to Rome and that the disciples would have travelled along from Neapolis.[23] Paul has been set on the right road, but it will be his choice as to whether he stays on it.

[a′] 16.12b *Stay in Philippi*

16.12b Luke underlines the determination of the group to remain in Philippi before heading onwards, by using a periphrastic construction to express the verb 'stay'[24] and a demonstrative phrase to refer again to the city, ἐν ταύτῃ τῇ πόλει, 'in this city'.

[C-B] 16.13-15 *Lydia*

In this episode, Paul is seen to gravitate, contrary to the divine leading related in the previous sequence [B], towards those people who had a Jewish background, as he is drawn back to the safety of his own experience. The 'we'-group will serve to highlight his weakness as Luke distances them from him.

[a] 16.13a *A Place of Prayer*

16.13a The opening of a new division in the narrative is not apparent in the Alexandrian text where, on the contrary, the connective τε treats the previous sentence as preliminary material leading up to a more important event, that of going outside the city gates on the Sabbath, by a river where we 'supposed there to be a place of prayer'. The connective δέ in the Bezan text views the event as marking a new development, which indeed it is: there is first a new time indication, the Sabbath, and secondly a new location, a 'place of prayer'.[25]

---

23. Photos of Philippi and the Via Egnatia can be seen at http://www.bibleplaces.com/philippi. htm

24. The periphrastic construction in place of the imperfect has the effect of underlining the action of the participle, here διατρίβοντες.

25. προσευχή was the term regularly used to designate a synagogue building, until the first century CE when the meaning of the term συναγωγή began to change from denoting a group of people to denoting the actual building where they met (Josephus, *Life*, 277; M. Hengel, 'Proseuche

Instead of staying in the city, where the Gentiles would be, the group now go out of the city, outside the gates, to a meeting place for Jews.[26] There is thus a hiatus with the previous direction the mission was taking, in so far as the Jews have come back into the picture, both by the way the day is presented, and by the identification of the location. In the Bezan text, it seems that Paul and his group had heard about the place of prayer while they were in the city, and that they had been told, presumably by Jews, that it was beside the river; in the Alexandrian text, it is rather that the group go to a river outside the city, working on the assumption that they would find a place of prayer there without any prior contact with any Jews.

[b] 16.13b *Conversation with the Women*
16.13b Once at the place of prayer, Paul and his companions sit down and start to speak. This is the attitude of a teacher in the synagogue (cf. Jesus, Lk. 4.20; see also *Commentary*, 13.16). The audience is portrayed as women who had gathered there, in the Bezan text with an expectant purpose – it is even possible to understand the verb in the Bezan text as meaning that the women had accompanied Paul and his companions to the place.[27] These are likely to be the same people who had told them about the meeting place and indicated to him where it was (cf. on 16.13a above). The incident certainly does not have the marks of an unexpected happening that took place without any kind of preparation.

[c] 16.14 *Lydia Accepts What Paul was Saying*
16.14 One of the women of the group was 'a certain' Lydia, once more a person who represents a type as well as being a real person in her own right.[28] She is defined first by her name, then by her occupation, which was a seller of purple goods. Thirdly, her place of origin is specified, Thyatira, a city in the province of Asia and specifically in the region of Lydia like the name of the

---

und Synagoge', in G. Jeremias, H.-W. Kuhn and H. Stegemann (eds), *Tradition und Glaube. Das frühe Christentum in seiner Umwelt* (Göttingen: Vandenhoeck und Ruprecht, 1971), pp. 157–84; E. Schürer, *The History of the Jewish People in the Age of Jesus Christ* [3 vols; rev. and ed. G. Vermes, F. Millar and M. Black; Edinburgh: T&T Clark, 1973], II, 425–26, 439–40; E.M. Smallwood, *The Jews under Roman Rule: From Pompey to Diocletian* [Leiden: E.J. Brill, 1976], p. 133). It is possible that the same meaning is intended by the occurrence of the word in D05 at 18.18 (Cenchrea). The proximity to the river (and the sea at Cenchrea) is typical of the location chosen for synagogues, to facilitate ritual washings (cf. Josephus, *Ant.* XIV, 258).

26. The expression repeats the direction 'outside': ἐξήλθομεν ἔξω, as in Lk. 22.62 after Peter had denied Jesus.

27. The verb συνέρχομαι means 'to assemble', but frequently has the sense of 'to travel with someone', even when the person thus accompanied is not specified (B-A-G, 2; cf. Lk. 23.55; Acts 1.21; 9.39; 10.23, 45; 11.12; 15.38; 21.16; 25.17).

28. Cf. on Timothy, 16.1b. Here, the word order of τις before the name of Lydia confers a particular importance on her, since the usual order is name + τις (see Read-Heimerdinger, *The Bezan Text*, pp. 99–100).

woman; yet even though she was not from Philippi, she had a house there, as will be seen (16.15). Finally, she is a God-fearer, a Gentile who was sympathetic towards the Jewish religion without having become a proselyte.

At the outset of the incident, the whole group had been seen speaking with the women (ἐλαλοῦμεν, 'we started to speak'), and it was to them that Lydia listened (ἤκουσεν, D05; ἤκουεν, AT; see *Critical Apparatus*). However, a subtle shift takes place following this verb – although she listened to 'us' speaking, she took particular notice of what Paul said. He is carefully distinguished from the rest of the speakers by the technique of omitting the article before his name (see *Critical Apparatus*). That Lydia was able to respond to Paul was because the Lord 'opened her heart', expressed with a verb that implies a thorough comprehension.[29] She is alone among the group of women in the way she reacted positively to Paul, which suggests that the other women may have been Gentiles, people whom Lydia had brought along to the place of prayer to hear Paul and his companions speak.

Now, it will be seen in the narrative that follows that the message Paul preached was not entirely in tune with the message preached by the 'we'-group who, as has already been pointed out (see *Commentary*, 16.10, and see *General Introduction*, §VIII) are more in line with the radical nature of Jesus' teaching. The discrepancy is not explained at this point because it has already become apparent in the course of his teaching and activities throughout the previous narrative from chapter 13. Paul was observed, for example in his speech to the synagogue in Antioch of Pisidia (see esp. *Commentary* on 13.14-41; 14.1), to maintain the privileged status of the Jewish people and to view the Gentiles as being grafted into Israel, through the coming of the Messiah, as part of the restoration of Israel in the end days. The message repeatedly communicated through the Spirit, or taught by other divine representatives, has underlined, in contrast, the end of Israel's hopes of restoration as a privileged nation and the complete equality of Gentiles and Jews (see *Commentary*, 15.7-11 on Peter's speech).[30] As an example of his Jewish stance, Paul was prepared to pass on the commands of the letter, which required Gentiles to observe the essential requirements of the Law, beyond even the areas named in the letter (see on 16.4 above).

In the case of Lydia, she pays especial attention to Paul's words, and is enabled by God to understand his teaching. He has spoken to her, however, as to one attached to Judaism, and not as a Gentile. This is a backward step for Paul, made apparent by the careful presentation of Lydia's origin – she does

---

29. The verb διανοίγω is found in a similar situation in Lk. 24.31 AT, 32 AT, 45, where the prefix δια- expresses the completeness of the verb (cf. J. Read-Heimerdinger and J. Rius-Camps, 'Emmaous or Oulammaous? Luke's Use of the Jewish Scriptures in the Text of Luke 24 in Codex Bezae', *RCatT* 27 [2002], pp. 23–42).

30. Earlier evidence in Acts of these teachings is found, for example, in 12.1-17 (*The Message of Acts*, II, pp. 331–73); see also *The Message of Acts*, I, *Excursus* 1, 'The Restoration of Israel: Two Conflicting Plans', pp. 79–87. They are discussed in detail in Rius-Camps and Read-Heimerdinger, 'After the Death of Judas: A Reconsideration of the Status of the Twelve Apostles', *RCatT* 29 (2005), pp. 305–34.

not belong to Philippi but to Asia from where Paul was specifically prevented from speaking the word of God (16.6b)! This evaluation of Paul's preaching by Luke obviously depends on a comprehension on the part of the addressee of the geographical place names he mentions, including the name of Lydia, which insists on her origin in the region in Asia of the same name. Thus it is seen that although Paul has been brought to Philippi by means of three divine promptings, contrary to his own inclinations to remain on the other side of the sea, he falls back on to the territory with which he is familiar and talks with people with whom he has at least some common language and with whom he shares both a conceptual and scriptural framework. No mention has been made of any conversation Paul had had so far with the local people of Philippi. The difficulty he and Barnabas had experienced in talking to the Gentile population of Lystra (14.7-20, see *Commentary, ad loc.*) accounts for his preference to be with people with whom he can communicate more easily. In the next scene, when the masters of the slave-girl state their complaints against Paul and Silas, it becomes even clearer that their preaching in the city was presented in terms of Judaism (see on 16.20-21 below).

The contrast between the talking of the 'we'-group and that of Paul is brought out by the repetition of terms in a chiastic pattern: ἐλαλοῦμεν ('we started to speak') – ταῖς ... γυναιξίν ('to the women') ‖ τις γυνή ('a certain woman') – τοῖς λαλουμένοις ὑπὸ τοῦ Παύλου ('what was said by Paul'). The contrast will be made more overt in the next sequence [C] by the girl with the spirit of divination. Initially, Paul cannot be distinguished from the other persons meant by the first person plural verb, and this is not accidental – the 'we'-group can be understood on one level to represent the good side of Paul, that part of him that does understand the universal teaching of Jesus and that cares about the salvation of the Gentiles for their own sake and not just as part of the salvation of his own people, the Jews.

For all that Paul's message was restricted in scope, that does not prevent the Lord from using what he says to bring her to an acceptance of his teaching about the Messiah, no doubt made on the basis of Scripture as on previous occasions when he spoke to Jews or God-fearers. That her faith is in some way limited is nevertheless about to become apparent and to pose a problem for others in Paul's company whose teaching differed from his because it reflected a more open view of the Gentiles.

[b'] 16.15a *Baptism and Invitation to Stay in her House*
16.15a The success of Paul's preaching results in the baptism not only of Lydia but also of her entire (according to Codex Bezae) household. Their family association means, however, that the community they form in Philippi is one of outsiders (since she is from Thyatira), and one that starts from a basis of Judaism since she had been a sympathetic God-fearer. The situation is similar to that of the God-fearer Cornelius in Caesarea who was also baptized with all

his household (cf. 10.24, 44, 48) with, however, the significant difference that in Caesarea the people received the Holy Spirit.

That Lydia's conversion is not complete in some sense is evident from her insistent plea to Paul and the 'we'-group that they stay in her house – in fact, more than that, she urges them to stay as part of her household, for the Greek word οἶκος used for 'house' is exactly the same as that found in the previous clause ('she was baptized and all her household'), rather than the word Luke uses to mean the building, οἰκία. Note that following her baptism she addresses the whole party (see ἡμᾶς, 'us', at the end of the verse), and voices to them a doubt concerning their response to her: 'If you (plural) have judged that I am faithful to God...' – this is the wording of the Bezan text (the AT has 'the Lord'), where the choice of the words 'faithful to God' rather than 'belief in the Lord' (for example) signals an incomplete conversion, an attachment to the God of Israel but not faith in the Lord Jesus.[31] She states the condition in the most general of terms, without any reference to Jesus.

Lydia's insistent invitation to Paul and the 'we'-group to enter her household is striking, suggesting that they at first refused.

Her doubt could arise from the fact that she is a Gentile. Will Paul and his company now accept her as a faithful Jew and agree to enter her house(hold)? Is her conversion to belief in Jesus good enough for her no longer to be viewed as unacceptable company for a Jew such as is Paul (and Silas and Timothy and 'we')? Her question means that she has understood Paul's message to be about becoming a Jew; that she views the speakers as Jews. It is a sign of how little she has grasped, or understood from Paul's teaching, of faith in Jesus who considered no one to be unfit for social contact.

Her attitude stands in contrast to the wholly positive account of the jailor into whose house(-hold) Paul and Silas will go and even eat without any doubt or hesitation (16.34). The difference may reflect the progress made by Paul and Silas by that stage, as they have begun to understand, by means of God's intervention, that the Gentiles have equal status to Jews.[32]

[a'] 16.15b *Her Insistence*

16.15b That there was indeed hesitation is confirmed by the pressure she is forced to put on the group to stay in her house.[33] The reluctance, on the part of

---

31. A similar incompleteness was noted with respect to Sergius Paulus who, according to Codex Bezae, 'believed in God' (the AT has simply 'believed') as a result of what he saw happen to the Jewish magician. In his case, however, there is no mention of any understanding of the faith, nor of baptism.

32. There are interesting parallels between Lydia's invitation to Paul and his companions to stay in her household and the scene where Lot invites the two angels to stay with him. In both cases, the host has to insist (Acts 16.15: παρεβιάσατο, cf. Gen. 19.3: κατεβιάζετο [παρεβιάζετο, A03: cf. 19.9, παρεβιάζοντο, in a physical sense]); and in both cases, there is a contrast with a positive character who shows up the weakness of the other (cf. Abraham, Gen. 18.1-33, whose generosity and disinterested intercession for the people of Sodom contrast with the passivity and self-seeking of Lot, 18.6-8; see *Jewish Study Bible*, pp. 39–42).

33. The verb παραβιάζομαι expressing the insistence of Lydia is used only once more in the New Testament, of the disciples who pressed Jesus to go into the house with them in Oulam-

the 'we'-group at least, may well have been due to a desire to avoid such an open association with people from a Jewish background in a city where their mission was to preach to the Gentiles. In the event, only at the end of the whole episode will Paul and Silas be seen going to her house (16.40), without the 'we'-group who will shortly disappear from the scene.

[C-C] 16.16-24 *Imprisonment*

The situation resulting from the incident of the previous episode [C-B] is that Paul has succeeded in creating a Jesus-believing community in Philippi on the basis of foreign Gentiles who had previously been attracted to Judaism. The contrast between the scope of Paul's teaching, which was restricted to Jewish terms and concepts, and that of the 'we'-group, which was more universal, caused an underlying tension. The contrast now becomes clearly evident through the spiritual awareness of a slave-girl, and causes Paul severe difficulties. The significance of the presence of the 'we'-group is signalled through the repetition of the first person plural pronoun three times from vv. 16-17a, the last time distinguished from Paul, and then as the second person plural pronoun in the words of the girl (v. 17b).

The double centre [e ‖ e'] of this episode will be the exorcism of the slave girl performed by Paul, which results in an outcry by the girl's owners, and eventually the imprisonment of Paul and Silas in the most secure prison of the city.

[a] 16.16 *A Slave Girl Meets Us*
16.16 The next incident takes place on another day, and this time on the path going to the place of prayer or, more controversially as Codex Bezae has it, to prayer, that is to participate in the activities at the local Jewish meeting place by the river. The day may well have been another Sabbath. The account continues to be given in the first person plural, which designates the 'we'-group but includes, initially at least, Paul also.

Another new character is introduced who comes to meet them as they were on their way. She is a slave-girl, again a representative of a type as Lydia was in the previous incident, but unlike Lydia she is not named and, moreover, the adjective indicating her representative status is placed after the noun.[34] The combination of these factors means that the focus of the narrative remains on the main protagonists, Paul and the 'we'-group, and does not switch to the slave-girl. Her role is to act as a catalyst for the action of the episode but she is

---

maous (Emmaus, AT; Lk. 24.29) where they, too, had their eyes opened (partially at least, cf. Lydia, on Acts 16.14 above) to understand how the Scriptures spoke about Jesus (Lk. 24.32, cf. vv. 27, 31).

34. Usually, τις is placed after the noun it qualifies in Acts, the usual position for the non-emphatic adjective (Read-Heimerdinger, *The Bezan Text*, pp. 99–100). When, exceptionally, it is placed before the noun, as in the case of Lydia (16.14; cf. 3.2; 17.34; 21.10), it highlights the person as being of significance in their own right.

not important to the story as a person in her own right. What is said about her is that she had 'a Python spirit' (lit.), where 'Python' refers to the underworld symbol of Delphi through whom the priestess of Apollo reputedly delivered oracles, so that the spirit is one of divination that enables the girl to tell fortunes.[35] Because she was a slave girl, her ability was a valuable source of income for her masters who thus benefited from the spirit in her.

It should be noted that unlike in the previous scene where Paul and his companions took an active part in meeting with the women at the place of prayer, the slave-girl takes the initiative and comes to meet them. This has been the repeated pattern with respect to contact between Paul and Gentiles (cf. the invitation from Sergius Paulus, 13.7b; the call from the one like a Macedonian, 16.10a).

[b] 16.17 Her Acclamation of Paul and the 'We'-Group
16.17 Having come to meet the group on the path going to the place of prayer, the slave-girl starts to follow behind them. At this point, Paul and the 'we'-group are pointedly distinguished from one another by the narrator, though the two are kept in equal focus[36] as the girl shouts out. Her shouting is underlined in the Bezan text (see *Critical Apparatus*), the reason for which lies in what she says and whom she is addressing.

According to the usual interpretation of the Alexandrian text, the girl shouts out to any who are listening (assuming the path to be crowded with people, including her masters, cf. 16.19 AT, 22 below), announcing that 'these men [Paul and his companions] are slaves of the Most High God' and advertizing their cause by letting the people around know that they are proclaiming to them (ὑμῖν, 'to you') the 'way of salvation'. The use of the second person pronoun causes her to be viewed as separate from the rest of the people, presumably because of her spiritual state. Her recognition of the God whom they were serving echoes that of the demoniac of Gerasene in Luke's Gospel (Lk. 8.26-39, esp. v. 28).

The Bezan text presents a somewhat different situation. The girl singles out 'These' (as distinct from someone else) as 'the slaves of the Most High God'. The parties in question, in the light of the previous episode where Paul was seen to be teaching a message more restricted to an audience familiar with Judaism, are the two just mentioned: Paul and the 'we'-group'. The owners of the slave-girl are not necessarily present (cf. 16.19 D05), and though there may have been other passers-by on the path no mention is made of them. Rather her words are addressed to Paul, as she lets him know that it is the 'we'-group, and not he, who serve the Most High; they are the ones, she

35. μαντευομένη, the only occurrence in the New Testament of this word with its 'pagan connotation' (Bruce, *Text*, p. 315).

36. In D05, Paul is not seen from the point of view of the slave girl since the article is maintained; he is thus distinguished from the 'we'-group but not given prominence (cf. Paul without the article at 16.14 D05, where he is mentioned as distinct from the 'we'-group and from the point of view of Lydia).

says, who announce correctly the good news about the way of salvation 'to us', that is the Gentiles. In this version of the story, the girl is identified with the rest of the local population and not alienated from them, exactly as the representative adjective τις, 'a certain' (see on 16.16 above), indicates. The use of the verb εὐαγγελίζομαι in the Bezan text, with the technical sense of announcing the gospel that it acquires in Luke's writings, corresponds to the interpretation of Paul's vision in Troas (see *Commentary*, 16.10b). The spiritual insight of the girl is, compared with that seen in the Alexandrian text, acute and goes further than simply identifying God whom the disciples serve.

[c] 16.18a *Repetition over Several Days*
1618a The girl's following of Paul and his companions, and her shouting out of the same thing, happened repeatedly over a period of time, but apparently did not cause Paul to modify his outlook or his strategy.

[d] 16.18b *Paul Orders the Spirit to Come Out of Her*
16.18b That Paul understands the point being made by the slave-girl results in the end in his becoming extremely annoyed by her. So he turns to her as she follows behind him and orders the spirit to come out of her. His annoyance, according to the Bezan word order, qualifies his tone as he speaks to her, rather than being given as the reason for his action. He speaks in the name of Jesus Christ, taking from him as the Messiah the authority over the spirit of divination.

[e] 16.18c *The Spirit Comes Out of Her*
16.18c The response is immediate, as expressed in different ways by both texts. However, the success of Paul's order is no evidence of it having been the right thing to do. This would not be the only instance of healing or exorcism in the name of Jesus mentioned in Luke's work that was not right.[37] Paul has, in fact, abused his spiritual authority to silence the voice that spoke on behalf of the Gentile population of Philippi to tell him that his companions were the ones announcing the good news of the gospel to the Gentiles.

[e'] 16.19 *Her Masters Drag Paul and Silas before the Rulers*
16.19 The presentation of the scene in the Alexandrian text makes it possible to think that the masters of the girl witnessed the incident, for the narrator continues without signalling a new development (with καί) to say that they saw that their hope of financial gain had 'gone out', referring apparently to the spirit. Indeed, in the Alexandrian text, the narrative consists of one long unit of development from the point of Paul's addressing the spirit at 16.18b to the moment that Paul and Silas are secured in the stocks in prison at 16.24b (see *Critical Apparatus* for the variation concerning the successive sentence links). The Bezan text begins a new paragraph with a fresh time marker, and presents

---

37. Cf. Lk. 8.28-33; 9.40.

the owners of the girl as finding out about their loss after the exorcism had taken place. Their complaint, that they had been 'deprived of their profit that they used to have through her' is ironic in so far as Luke has let the audience know that the prophetic spirit of the girl spoke the truth and was therefore a precious sign to the local population to point them to the people from whom they could hear the message of salvation – but that is probably not what the owners themselves had in mind. Similarly, the accusations they will make to the magistrates (16.20-21) will again contain more truth than they are aware of.

It is to the magistrates in the Agora or market place, with its function as a meeting place for judicial purposes,[38] that the slave-girl's masters take Paul now, together with Silas. Silas' presence has not been directly mentioned since he was named as Paul's choice of companion as he left Antioch (15.40) at the end of the previous narrative sequence. That he is seized along with Paul, however, shows that he was associated with him in his teaching, and not with the 'we'-group who no longer have any part in the narrative. From this point, the 'we'-group will leave Paul, just as Barnabas did when he took Mark to Cyprus (15.39). They will reappear at 20.6, at the point when Paul is about to leave Philippi for Hierosoluma (cf. 20.16 D05).

[d'] 16.20-21 *Their Accusation to the Magistrates*
16.20-21 The authorities of the city are organized in a hierarchy: generically, they are referred to as the 'rulers' among whom there are three levels: the magistrates (στρατηγοί, encountered here) who represented the emperor in a Roman colony and would normally be termed *duoviri*, the sergeants or 'lictors' (ῥαβδοῦχοι, 16.35c), and the jailor (δεσμοφύλαξ, 16.23). The three tiers stand for the totality of the system, with the sergeants and the jailor acting in various positions of subservience to carry out the orders of the magistrates.

The accusations the masters make against Paul and Silas are that they, who are Jews, are troubling the peace of Philippi, the *pax romana*, by advocating customs that are forbidden to them, who are Romans. It is entirely possible that the majority of the free inhabitants (so not the slave-girl) were, indeed, Roman citizens, for from the first century BCE it was increasingly common for citizenship to be granted by the local Roman authorities to the population of the colonies.[39] The balance of the sentence conveys the point forcefully that Paul and Silas are perceived as proselytizing, of trying to convert Roman citizens to Judaism. This view of their activity, seen from the standpoint of non-Jewish observers, confirms the impression already gained from Lydia, that Paul's teaching about Jesus was expressed in Jewish terms (see on 16.14 above).

[c'] 16.22a *The Crowd Join In*
16.22a From the point of view of the Alexandrian text, bystanders have been present on the scene from the time the slave-girl was shouting out about Paul

38. The Agora served as an area for public business, which included commerce but also the hearing of civil law cases.
39. Goodman, *Rome and Jerusalem*, pp. 163–66.

and his companions (cf. 16.17), addressing her words to them (ὑμῖν, 'to you'). These local inhabitants are now portrayed as 'the crowd', and they joined in with the owners of the girl in complaining against the disciples.

In the Bezan text, there may have been local bystanders in the scene on the path going to the place of prayer, but they are not explicitly mentioned. They were, however, represented by the slave-girl as Gentiles who are not acquainted with Judaism and who were included in the pronoun 'to us' (ἡμῖν, 16.17b D05). Now, in the market place, they are presented for the first time as a 'large crowd' who add their complaints to the masters', shouting out just like their representative, the slave-girl, had done (cf. 16.17 D05, where the verb is underlined).

[b'] 16.22b-23 *The Magistrates Throw Them into Prison*
16.22b-23 The magistrates inflict a series of punishments on Paul and Silas. They strip them[40] and order them to be flogged (ῥαβδίζειν), an order that would be carried out by the 'lictors' or sergeants (ῥαβδοῦχοι, cf. 16.35); after a thorough beating, they put them in prison, with instructions to the jailor to make sure they were securely held. In this way a new character, who is to become the focus of the following incident, is introduced obliquely into the narrative. His role is to execute the orders of the magistrates, the rulers who attack the disciples. The significance of this point is examined in *Excursus* 10.

The treatment to which Paul and Silas were subjected was possible because they were viewed as foreigners, without the right to defend themselves or to a fair trial, to which Roman citizens were entitled.

[a'] 16.24 *The Jailor Ensures Security*
16.24 The jailor duly carries out his orders, putting them into the innermost part of the prison, probably meaning a dungeon, and fixing their feet in the stocks so that there was no possibility of escape. Just as with Peter in Acts 12, every effort is made to ensure that the prison is secure (see *Excursus* 11).[41] In symbolic terms, the prison illustrates the lack of spiritual liberty experienced by Paul and Silas, bound hand and foot, as it were, to Judaism through the focus they have given to their mission. Their attitude on behalf of the Jewish people has resulted in a state of enforced inactivity and, consequently, powerlessness with respect to the Gentiles.

[C-B'] 16.25-34 *The Philippian Jailor*

This episode corresponds to the episode [C-B], 16.11-15, of which the conversion of Lydia was the main topic, just as now it is that of the jailor. The

---

40. Here, unlike at 14.14, the tearing off of the clothes is a preliminary to flogging. Cf. H.J. Cadbury, 'Dust and Garments', in F.J. Foakes Jackson and K. Lake (eds), *The Beginnings of Christianity*, V (London: Macmillan, 1933), p. 271.

41. Cf. 12.4, 6: see *The Message of Acts*, II, pp. 339, 352.

action builds up to the climax [h ‖ h'], consisting of the jailor's question about salvation and the words of Paul and Silas in response.

The paradigmatic value of Psalm 2, if indeed it is being used in this sequence (see *Overview* and *Excursus* 10), is developed extensively in this episode, in which most of the suggested parallels are to be found.

[a] 16.25a *Paul and Silas Praise God*

16.25a The state of mind of Paul and Silas while they are in prison is reported by the narrator in positive terms. Even though it is because they had gone against the plan God had for the mission, by proclaiming the gospel in Jewish terms, that they find themselves in the prison, they nevertheless display exemplary faithfulness to God as they pray and sing his praises during the night. The term 'sing hymns' (ὕμνουν) may be the first one that serves as a cue for allusions to Psalm 2 (*Excursus* 10).

The time is described in the Bezan text with a phrase similar to that used of the exodus of the Israelites from Egypt (cf. μεσούσης τῆς νυκτός, Exod. 12.29 LXX). As will be seen, Paul and Silas are about to undergo a sort of exodus themselves.

[b] 16.25b *The Prisoners Listen to Them*

16.25b In their attitude of prayer and praise, they serve as an example to the other prisoners who 'were paying attention to them'. The verb, which is often translated as 'listen', is not the usual one for the activity of listening (ἀκούω – for example, used of the women listening at the place of prayer, or of Lydia listening to Paul), but has a stronger force (ἐπακροάομαι, a hapax of the New Testament, not found in the LXX). Luke's choice of it here may be to give a second clue to the activation of Psalm 2 (see *Excursus* 10), though it is unclear how it functions.

[c] 16.26a *An Earthquake*

16.26a The sudden, and massive, earthquake that occurred shakes the foundations of the prison. In its suddenness and violence, it is reminiscent of the day of Pentecost when the Spirit arrived: there was a sudden 'sound from heaven, like that of wind, a violent one, being driven in and it filled all the house...' (2.2). An even stronger parallel is created with the day when the Temple (referred to in biblical language as ὁ τόπος, 'the place') was shaken prior to the second outpouring of the Holy Spirit (4.31), an event that was linked with Psalm 2.2 in the same way as the earthquake in Philippi will be seen to be linked with it (see on 16.35 below); and the outpouring of the Spirit enabled the disciples 'to speak the word of God with boldness to all those who wished to believe'. The same verb σαλεύω, 'shake', is used in both places, with its implications of God's judgement on the place that is shaken.[42] Here, it is the very foundations of the prison in which Paul and Silas are bound, immobile

---

42. See *The Message of Acts*, I, pp. 278–79, for examination of the implications of the earthquake at 4.31.

and powerless. As was noted on 16.24, the prison is an outer manifestation of their inner state, of being constrained by their attachment to Jewish ways of thinking or presenting the good news about Jesus. This constraint, which renders them ineffective and helpless, is being broken by the action of God and they, too, will be free to speak to the jailor (16.31).

[d] 16.26b *The Doors Open and the Chains Fall Off*
16.26b Within the physical realm, the result of the earthquake is that the security of the prison is, 'at once' as Codex Bezae specifies, destroyed: all the doors that were holding the prisoners inside were opened and everything that bound the prisoners, such as the stocks in which Paul and Silas were fastened, was loosened. All the prisoners, in consequence, are free though no one escapes.

[e] 16.27 *The Jailor is About to Kill Himself*
16.27 The jailor appears in the narrative for the second time and becomes at this point the key character of the story. He is a representative, at the lowest of the three levels (see on 16.20 above), of the Gentile authorities who have opposed Paul and Silas. The narrative in the Bezan text over the following verses picks up speed as it builds towards Paul's intervention in the next verse. The Alexandrian text presents the narrative at this point more as successive developments (see *Critical Apparatus*).

It is interesting to note that all the Gentiles who appear in Philippi are presented with an indication of their social status, and of their place in a social hierarchy: Lydia who, as a merchant trader, was autonomous; the slave girl with her masters; the magistrates with the lictors under them; the jailor, also subordinate to them and responsible for the prisoners under his charge. In this instance, the jailor believes that he has failed in his duty to guard the prisoners securely because when he sees all the doors open (ἀνεῳγμένας, where the perfect expresses the finality of the event), he fears the worst and believes that all the prisoners have fled (ἐκπεφευγέναι, again the perfect). Aware of the shameful and unbearable consequences of this state of affairs, he saw killing himself as the only way of escape for himself.

On the level of the symbolism of the prison, the prisoners represented for the jailor his last hope of hearing the good news. As a Gentile, represented by the slave-girl (see on 16.16 above), he had already lost the hope of foreseeing a better future through the message announced by the 'we'-group (cf. 16.19); and now, he believes that those who potentially had the message that would bring him release from his situation of servitude have abandoned him, even though he was guarding them so carefully.[43]

---

43. The semantic field of 'guarding' is richly represented in this episode: φυλακή × 5 (+ 1 D05); δεσμοφύλαξ × 3; τηρέω × 1; δεσμωτήριον × 1; δέσμιος × 2; δεσμός × 1; ἀσφαλίζομαι × 1 (+ 1 D05); ἀσφαλῶς × 1. The observation that the jailor was sleeping (ἔξυπνος, 16.27) stands in stark contrast.

[f] 16.28 *Paul Stops Him*

16.28 At the dramatic moment at which the jailor has his sword drawn, on the point of killing himself, Paul shouts out, taking charge of the situation as he realizes the importance of the presence of the prisoners for their guard.

[g] 16.29 *The Jailor Falls at the Feet of Paul and Silas*

16.29 The response of the jailor to Paul's reassurance is presented again in the Bezan text as a rapid succession of actions, culminating in his question to them at 16.30b; the sense of panic and drama is less evident in the Alexandrian text of these two verses (see *Critical Apparatus*).

The first response of the jailor to Paul's announcement was to call for lights – the placing of the word at the front of the new sentence highlights its symbolic significance for the jailor's inner, spiritual quest. The word φῶς used here for 'light' is the same term of Isaiah's prophecy of Isa. 49.6, cited by Barnabas and Paul when they proclaimed the role of Israel to be a light to the Gentiles (13.47 D05, see *Commentary* above). The jailor then rushes into the dungeon prison in a state of some agitation, and falls at the feet of Paul and Silas. This attitude of servitude expresses his awareness of his dependence on them for his own safety. He attributes his own safety, dependent on the fact that no one has escaped, to their presence in the prison.

[h] 16.30 *He Asks Them about Salvation*

16.30 As the narrative rushes on, in the Bezan text the jailor is seen making sure the other prisoners are safely locked up again before taking Paul and Silas outside, where he addresses them with the same term of superiority and authority that was used of the masters of the slave girl (κύριοι, cf. 16.19), as he asks them the critical question: 'What must I do to be saved?' On one level, he may be simply enquiring about his physical wellbeing, conscious of some role played by Paul and Silas, or by their god, in the earthquake but also in his good fortune to have all the prisoners present. The verb σῴζω, 'save', does not necessarily refer to spiritual salvation but is the usual term for rescue from natural danger.[44] On another level, he may be expressing his awareness that an earthquake represented divine judgement and his belief that Paul and Silas held the key to being rescued from the death that would result from it. Finally, speaking for the Gentiles in Philippi, he is enquiring about salvation in an eternal dimension, for which Paul and Silas have been entrusted with the good news. The impersonal verb δεῖ (lit. 'it is fitting') is used typically by Luke to refer to the divine plan, so conferring a note of dramatic irony on the jailor's question since, being ignorant of the divine plan behind the gospel of Jesus Christ, he is asking more than he realizes.

[h'] 16.31 *Paul and Silas Tell Him to Believe in the Lord Jesus Christ*

16.31 Now that Paul and Silas have been released from all their bonds, and have freedom to speak without expressing themselves from the perspective of

---

44. B-A-G, σῴζω, 1.

Jews or Israel, the dramatic climax of the story is reached as Paul and Silas, finally, present the good news in simple terms for the first time in Philippi. Their answer to the jailor's question is the same as Philip's message to the Ethiopian eunuch (8.37, not all MSS), or that of Peter to the meeting in Ierousalem (15.11) – he is to believe in the Lord, Jesus, with Codex Bezae specifying in addition, that they also present him as the Christ (cf. Peter, 15.11 D05). Not only will he himself be saved by this simple act of belief, but also all the persons in his household whom he represents.

[g'] 16.32 *They Speak the Word of the Lord to All in his House*

16.32 At the point when Paul and Silas are outside the prison, talking with the jailor, it appears that other people come to join them, people who were 'in his house'. Here, Luke distinguishes between the 'household' (οἶκος) of the previous verse and the physical building (οἰκία) from where people came and with whom Paul and Silas talked.[45] They speak 'the word of God', according to the Alexandrian text, which is in line with the distinction Luke makes (though not consistently in the AT, see *Excursus* 1) between 'the word of the Lord', as the specific message concerning Jesus, and 'the word of God', which refers to teaching about God in a more general sense, and precedes the transmission of the word of the Lord to Gentiles. The Bezan reading here, 'the word of the Lord', is thus highly exceptional – indeed, this is the only occasion in the whole of Acts when a Gentile is given the word of the Lord without prior mention of the word of God (cf. the next and final use of the term 'word of God' in Corinth at 18.11). The Greek indicates that Luke was aware of the unique nature of the reference (by omitting the article before the word 'Lord', see *Critical Apparatus*), and that he knew what he was doing when he chose to use it here. The fact that Paul and Silas did speak the word of the Lord to the jailor is precisely a positive sign: for once, they have gone straight to the gospel without taking the preliminary steps of first ensuring that the foundation of the word of God had been laid. There is no mention of the Jerusalem letter or the commands of the elders.

[f'] 16.33a *The Jailor Treats their Wounds*

16.33a The jailor responds to the good news announced to him by Paul and Silas by treating their wounds there and then. The reading of the Alexandrian text is the most obvious here, that the jailor washed their wounds (literally, their 'blows', cf. 16.23, that is, the wounds they had received from the blows). The text of Codex Bezae may have been meant to have the same reading, but it in fact reads, by the addition of a vowel, 'he released them from their blows' (see *Critical Apparatus*). In the same way as the Alexandrian text is a condensed way of expressing that he 'washed them from the effect of the blows inflicted on them', so the Bezan text could have the meaning that he 'released them from the effect of the blows inflicted on them'. He did this by responding

---

45. Cf. the comments on Lydia's household at 16.15a above.

positively to their speaking about Jesus in terms comprehensible to Gentiles, and so soothing, in a figurative sense, the wounds inflicted on them because of the negative response to their preaching when it had been carried out in Jewish terms.[46] He thus removes any trace of their captivity.

[e'] 16.33b *The Jailor's Baptism*

16.33b The positive tone of the account continues as the jailor is baptized without any further delay, along with all the members of his family. The reciprocity of the act, with his 'washing' in baptism corresponding to the washing of the prisoners' wounds, is evident in the reading of 16.33a in the Alexandrian text, though not in the Bezan text. The result of the baptisms is the beginnings of a purely Gentile community of local people from Philippi, corresponding to that founded by Lydia made up of God-fearers from Asia (cf. on 16.15a above).

[d'] 16.34a *He Prepares a Feast*

16.34a The jailor's next step is highly significant, and unexpected, as signalled by the Bezan text. He first of all 'takes up' (ἀναγαγών) Paul and Silas into his family, not just into the house but into his 'household' (cf. comments on 16.32 above). His gesture may be compared with that of Lydia (16.15a, b), which is similar except that she expressed doubt about the disciples' willingness to go into her household, and had to be insistent with her request. In the case of the jailor, there is no doubt and no hesitation, as the jailor even goes so far as to prepare for them a meal. He has 'restored them' to their dignity as free people, the figurative meaning of the verb 'take up', which is emphatically underlined in Codex Bezae (see *Critical Apparatus*).[47] They, for their part, have fully accepted his status as one like them, in no way a foreigner with whom social contact was forbidden.

At some point following the meal, in so far as it refers to a literal event, Paul and Silas must have returned to the prison since they are found there the next day. It can be presumed that the jailor did not keep them out of the prison permanently, knowing the consequences if he did so, but took them back with the other prisoners whom he had previously secured (cf. 16.30 D05). In fact, it will be seen (16.37) that Paul and Silas have not yet been freed from their own inner imprisonment.

[c'] 16.34b *He Rejoices*

16.34b The account of the jailor's faith in God is completed with a final note about his rejoicing in that fact, with all of his household. His belief is expressed in emphatic terms, describing a permanent change of state that has resulted in faith in the one God. This corresponds to the full trust that was promised in

---

46. There are parallels in the action of the jailor with the parable of the Good Samaritan: he 'bandaged the wounds' of the man after he had fallen into the hands of robbers who 'stripped him and beat him' (Lk 10.30, 34).

47. B-A-G, ἀνάγω, 4; Bailly, ἀνάγω, II, 'élever [quelqu'un à une dignité]'.

the Psalm on which this incident is perhaps being modelled (cf. Ps. 2.12: μακάριοι πάντες οἱ πεποιθότες ἐπ' αὐτῷ, see *Excursus* 10).

[C-C'] 16.35-39 *Release from Prison*

This episode corresponds to the previous one, [C-C], 16.16-24, in which Paul and Silas are put in prison. According to the Bezan text, the structure has at its centre [e] Paul's words to the magistrates which, far from being words of salvation (cf. his words to Lydia, 16.14, or to the jailor, 16.31), are words of human protest and indignation. Consequently, while the events will result in the release of Paul and Silas from prison, a backward step has been taken in so far as Paul has lost an opportunity to announce the gospel to Gentiles because of his need to defend himself against injustice.

This passage is one of those that attest the most variation in the whole of Acts, with much of the criticism of Paul as well as several possible allusions to Psalm 2, absent from the Alexandrian text.

[a] 16.35a *The Meeting of the Magistrates*
16.35a A new episode begins with four changes indicated in the Bezan text, though only the first two in the Alexandrian: the time is the next day, the characters are the magistrates, the place is the market place, and the topic is their gathering there. In the course of the scene, it will be apparent that even though Paul and Silas had been taken into the jailor's house during the night, they are to be found in the prison the next morning (cf. 16.36 D05, 39a D05, 40).

The magistrates gather together in the market place, according to Codex Bezae, with a particular intention, which was presumably to pursue the case of Paul and Silas that they had not investigated the previous day in view of the uproar caused by the crowd (cf. 16.22, esp. D05). The phrase describing their coming together repeats exactly the words of the disciples in Ierousalem as they reflected on the treatment meted out to them by the authorities there, citing Ps. 2.2: '[The kings of the earth took position, and] the rulers gathered, all with a common purpose (οἱ ἄρχοντες συνήχθησαν ἐπὶ τὸ αὐτό), against the Lord and his anointed (the king or Messiah)'[48] (Acts 4.26). On that occasion, the reference to the Psalm was followed by an earthquake in Ierousalem (4.31), anticipating a clear parallel with the scene in Philippi. Then, the disciples had given a new interpretation to the Psalm by applying it to Israel as well as the nations,[49] whereas now it refers only to the rulers (cf. 16.19) of the Gentiles uniting 'against the Lord and his anointed', represented by Paul and Silas. Their plan, however, has already been undone in advance.

The subjugation of the Gentiles to the Lord's anointed, promised in Ps. 2.8-10, was introduced by Paul in his speech to the synagogue in Antioch of

---

48. The Hebrew מָשִׁיחַ becomes, in post-biblical literature, the term used to refer to the ideal Davidic king, the Messiah; and in the LXX, χριστός.

49. On 4.26, see *The Message of Acts*, I, pp. 274–75.

Pisidia, according to Codex Bezae (Acts 13.33b D05) where he cites Ps. 2.8 (see *Commentary, ad loc.*). There, the reference to the Psalm was entirely positive, and was by way of demonstrating that Jesus, as the Lord's anointed, the Christ, would take possession of the nations in the sense of being the means of salvation for them as well as for the people of Israel. Paul, however, did not go on to apply the idea of God taking revenge on the nations for their attacks on Israel. It is now, in contrast, that that idea comes to the fore.

Indeed, it is the allusion to the prophecy at this point that suggests that the entire episode may be intended to be seen as an outworking of Psalm 2, as the passage takes up terms and concepts expressed within it (see *Excursus* 10). The general picture is that of Jesus as the Lord's anointed who has been given to the Gentiles as their ruler (Ps. 2.8-10); if they attack the Lord, they will be punished and made to fear him (2.4-5), but if they submit to him and accept him as their ruler, they will rejoice as they trust in him (2.10-12).

[b] 16.35b *They were Afraid*

16.35b This element is not attested by the Alexandrian text. It makes most sense when taken together with the previous one (also absent from the AT): although the magistrates had come together with the purpose of carrying out some further action against Paul and Silas, when they 'remembered' the earthquake they thought better of their intention. Clearly, it was hardly possible that they might have 'forgotten' the earthquake, which had happened during the night and must have left traces of destruction all around.[50] The point of using the verb 'remember', however, seems to be that it expresses the stronger sense of recalling the prophecy of the Psalmist (see above, 16.35a) as the magistrates of Philippi re-enacted it, for the Psalm goes on to warn the Gentile rulers that the Lord will turn against them in his anger for their attacks and will bring on them all kinds of destruction so that they will be afraid (Ps. 2.5, 9-11, see *Excursus* 10). They, of course, would be quite unaware of how they were living out the prophecy, but it is Luke's aim according to the Bezan text to demonstrate how the Scriptures are fulfilled because the divine plan controls the situation, not because people consciously carry it out. The Alexandrian text loses the possible link to Psalm 2 by omitting these two elements that allude to it.

[c] 16.35c *They Order the Release of the Prisoners*

16.35c The narrative of the Alexandrian text is brief and to the point: the magistrates order the sergeants to free 'those men', where the reference to Paul and Silas echoes the complaint made against 'those men' by the slave masters (16.20). The Bezan text continues to be more detailed and specific: they send the sergeants to order the jailor to free 'those men whom you received yesterday'.

---

50. In any case, that the magistrates saw signs of physical destruction assumes that the earthquake was a literal event – this may be to misunderstand Luke's metaphorical purpose. Whether the archaeological evidence for the prison in Philippi shows that it was close to, or under, the Agora is open to interpretation; see T. Bolen, http://www.bibleplaces.com/philippi.htm

[d] 16.36 *The Jailor Transmits the Order*

16.36 The jailor passes on the order to Paul, with the Bezan text making clear that he went into the prison. The omission of this detail in the Alexandrian text may be due to the apparent contradiction with the account of their exit from the prison and their visit to the jailor's house during the night (cf. 16.30, 33-34). He reports the magistrates' words faithfully (ἀπόλυσον ‖ ἀπολυθῆτε), though the Alexandrian text softens the command to leave the prison by having the jailor add his own 'in peace', which concords better with the friendly relationship he had established with them during the night but contradicts the urgent and brusque nature of the magistrates' concern.

[e] 16.37 *Paul's Response to the Magistrates*

16.37 Paul's reaction was no doubt not what the magistrates expected. Addressing his words to the magistrates ('to them', a feature to which Codex Bezae will draw attention twice more, cf. 16.38a D05), but through the jailor who is to be the bearer of his response, he contests the attempt to hush up the case. He puts forward four (three in the AT) anomalies: they are innocent (Bezan text); they were humiliated in public so should not be released in secret; they had no trial so are uncondemned, yet have been locked up in prison; and above all, they are Roman citizens, the crucial factor. The play on words is forceful: the magistrates first threw them into (ἔβαλαν) prison publicly (δημοσίᾳ) and now throw them out (ἐκβάλλουσιν) secretly (λάθρᾳ).

The appeal to their Roman citizenship is, on the one hand, a positive indication that Paul now no longer portrays himself as a Jew but acknowledges an aspect of his identity that causes him to be like the Gentiles – like the slave-masters and the people of Philippi in general, he is a citizen of the Empire. This is the first of the three appeals Paul will make to his Roman citizenship, and the first overt association, albeit indirect, of Paul with Rome (cf. 22.25-29; 23.27). His insistence on his identity as a Roman citizen will be made with increasing force, a narrative device Luke uses to reflect his growing awareness of the ultimate destination of his mission in Rome.

On the other hand, that Paul makes use of this fact in order to insist on the innocence of himself and Silas, and on the injustice that has been done to them, is out of place in the present circumstances. His refusal to leave the prison makes an unnecessary statement on his part: they have been released from prison by the action of God, by the demonstration of his anger and power in the earthquake which has forced the rulers of Philippi to give up their attack on the disciples. However, instead of accepting their offer of freedom, brought about by the work of God, Paul stubbornly insists that the magistrates themselves come to take them out (ἐξαγαγέτωσαν) of the prison. The choice of the verb ἐξάγω, the verb *par excellence* of Exodus, means that Paul makes the Gentile rulers responsible for his 'exodus' from the bonds of his Jewish ways of thinking, on the grounds of his Roman citizenship. Although he had been prepared to come to the assistance of the jailor who panicked in the aftermath of the earthquake (cf. 16.27-29), when it is a question of the higher authorities Paul seeks to protect his position and his rights.[51] His protest about their mistreatment, making the magistrates afraid of the consequences from the higher powers of the Empire, not the divine ones, is his own way of defending himself, which he will make use of again later when he is arrested in Ierousalem, once more as part of his own self-defence (cf. 22.25-29).

[d'] 16.38a *The Sergeants Report his Words*
16.38a The sergeants take (from the jailor) Paul's answer back to the magistrates, the Bezan text underlining twice more (cf. 16.37) that it was to them that his words were addressed. The effect of this is to show how Paul is concerned with the magistrates in their position at the top of the hierarchy, and how he sets up a challenge to their authority in order to obtain release for himself and Silas. The vocabulary used to refer to Paul's words is remarkable (τὰ ῥήματα ταῦτα τὰ ῥηθέντα), for the terminology is quite different from that used on other occasions when the gospel is spoken, for which the terms λόγος / λαλέω are used (cf., most recently, 16.13b-14). Luke's choice of words here makes abundantly clear that what Paul spoke for the benefit of the magistrates was in no way the gospel, underlining how he has missed an opportunity to testify to God's liberating power by his human need to insist on his innocence and his rights. The Alexandrian text, meanwhile, attenuates the criticism by the absence of several readings in this verse.

[c'] 16.38b *The Magistrates are Afraid*
16.38b Having been made afraid by the earthquake, according to the Bezan text (cf. 16.35b D05), the magistrates now have a second reason for fearing, namely the news that Paul and Silas are Roman citizens and that they have therefore acted contrary to their rights. This fear, however, unlike the fear provoked by the earthquake, which led them to revoke their order of imprisonment, does not move the city authorities to take any further steps towards God but will simply cause them to ensure personally that the decision they had already arrived at is carried out. It has no effect in helping them to question, much less understand, the teaching of Paul and Silas for which they imprisoned them in the first place. The wording of the Bezan text makes this sentence simply an intermediate step, preparing for their speech as highly significant (see *Critical Apparatus*).

[b'] 16.39a *The Magistrates Speak to Paul and Silas*
16.39a The Alexandrian text winds up the incident with a brief summary: the magistrates complied with Paul's request by going themselves to take them

---

[51] On Paul's consciousness of his status 'among the elite of his world', see J.H. Neyrey, 'Luke's Social Location of Paul: Cultural Anthropology and the Status of Paul in Acts', in B. Witherington (ed.), *History, Literature and Society in the Book of Acts* (Cambridge: Cambridge University Press, 1996), pp. 251–79.

out of the prison, and they asked them to leave the city (16.39b). Codex Bezae continues to be considerably more detailed: they took 'friends' with them,[52] adding to their number not with a show of strength to intimidate the prisoners but to bolster their own courage in confronting a threatening situation; they went right into the prison, where they begged them to leave and justified themselves on the grounds that they had been unaware that they were good men (δίκαιοι). The choice of vocabulary is curious, for instead of referring to Paul's claim to Roman citizenship, the magistrates declare the two prisoners to be honest and good men. Since Paul's own declaration of their innocence hardly constitutes proof of the matter, it is clear that the conclusion drawn by the magistrates is drawn on other grounds, namely the occurrence of the earthquake. They obviously have associated the earthquake with Paul and Silas and see it as a sign of divine retribution for having imprisoned innocent men. They make no excuse, however, for having mistreated Roman citizens without following the correct legal procedure. It is as if, for the time being, Paul's awareness of being Roman, and therefore identifying with the Gentiles, has only just begun and does not yet have any impact on the Gentiles themselves.

The magistrates' choice of the term δίκαιοι to describe Paul and Silas has, from a Jewish point of view, a further significance for, as was pointed out with reference to its previous occurrence at 14.2 D05, it also means 'righteous' in the sense of a maintaining a right relationship with God and with other people and, as such, is the goal of every Jew.[53] There is thus a certain irony in the Gentile authorities' application of it here to Jewish prisoners, precisely when Paul has appealed to his rights on purely human grounds, and avoided all opportunity to speak of the God who has freed them from the prison by means of the earthquake, even though the magistrates themselves had interpreted it correctly as a sign of divine intervention on their behalf. On this occasion, he has failed to demonstrate that they were δίκαιοι from a Jewish point of view.

[a'] 16.39b *They Urge Them to Leave the City*
16.39b The magistrates go on to comply with Paul's requirements by leading him and Silas out of the prison. The narrator repeats the verb used by Paul in the imperative (ἐξαγαγέτωσαν, 16.37), showing how they led the disciples away from their place of captivity, just as the Lord had led the Israelites out of their captivity in Egypt, and thus created the circumstances for them to accomplish their own 'exodus'. The difference is that in this case, Paul has demanded

---

52. φίλος is a characteristic term of Luke (Mt. × 1; Jn × 6; Lk. × 15; Acts × 3 (+1 D05), used three times in scenes with Gentiles (Lk. 7.6; Acts 10.24; 19.31).

53. Luke uses the term δίκαιος often, to designate a person who is faithful to God: in the singular, it is used of Simeon (Lk. 2.25); of Jesus (23.47; Acts 3.14; 7.52; 22.14); of Joseph of Arimathea (Lk. 23.50); of the centurion Cornelius (Acts 10.22); in the plural, Lk. 1.6, 17; 5.32; 14.14; 15.7; 18.9; 20.20; Acts 14.2 D05; 16.39 D05; 24.15. The inclusion of the noun ἄνδρες (not essential in Greek) has the effect of underlining δίκαιοι as a personal characteristic (cf. B-A-G, ἀνήρ, 4)

a human agent, to demonstrate his own social standing, which allows him to be under the authority of no one.

Codex Bezae places heavy emphasis on the fact that they not only ask them (ἠρώτων, the imperfect, expressing repeated action) to go away from the city (ἀπελθεῖν) but that they even beg them (παρεκάλεσαν, as at v. 39a) to go right out of it (ἐξέλθατε), just as the jailor had told them to go out of the prison (ἐξελθόντες, v. 36). Furthermore, they give the reason that they are worried they might be called upon a second time by the local people with a complaint against the disciples. The reason that this happened the first time was that Paul and Silas had been preaching the gospel in Jewish terms; the magistrates, always more knowing that they realize,[54] are concerned that they might simply go back to doing what they had been found doing in the city before, that is, talking to the Gentiles about Jewish customs. There is, indeed, a real danger of this happening, for Paul and Silas have not yet fully overcome their tendency to see things through Jewish eyes, as will be seen immediately after they leave the prison, and in a variety of ways throughout the subsequent chapters of Acts.

[C-A'] 16.40 *Departure from Philippi*

The final episode, in which Paul and Silas leave Philippi, corresponds to the initial one [C-A] (16.11-12) in which Paul and Silas were seen arriving in the city. It develops out of the magistrates' pleas in 16.35-39 for them to 'go out' (ἐξέρχομαι) of the city, and takes up this verb in both 16.40a and 16.40c.

[a] 16.40a *Paul and Silas Go to Lydia*
16.40a The magistrates had insisted with considerable force that Paul and Silas should 'go out' of Philippi. In the event, Paul and Silas do not immediately leave the city but first 'go out' (ἐξελθόντες) of the prison and then make their way to Lydia's house where there was a community created by the Gentile God-fearers (cf. 16.15).

[b] 16.40b *They Report to the Brethren*
16.40b There, they saw the brethren and encouraged them. Codex Bezae specifies that their encouragement consisted of reporting what the Lord had done for them. The phrase has been seen before when Paul met with disciples after experiencing the work of the Lord (cf. 14.27; 15.4). It is to be expected that they told them about their experience in the prison and of the conversion of the jailor, which may have led to further developments in Philippi though they are not recorded in Acts. When Paul is later found at Philippi, it is again with

---

54. This unawareness on the part of the characters is the point of dramatic irony: the audience know by now that Paul and Silas have not carried out their mission to the Gentiles in the way that they were intended to do; the magistrates do not know this, so that when they voice their concern about a repeat of the first incident they are actually saying more than they intend.

the 'we'-group; he has spent Passover there, before setting off back for Hiero-soluma (20.6, cf. 20.16).

[a'] 16.40c *They Depart from Philippi*
16.40c Finally, after this one last contact with Jesus-believers who had previous links with Judaism, Paul and Silas do what the magistrates had begged them to do, and they go out (ἐξῆλθαν) of the city.

Paul and Silas thus leave the first city where they have had opportunity to announce the gospel to Gentiles, having created, first, a community made up of people who were already attracted to Judaism and presided over by Lydia; and another, made up of Gentiles with no contact with Judaism and presided over by the jailor.

Excursus 10

Psalm 2 in Acts

Psalm 2 has been cited or alluded to in Acts twice before chapter 16, at 4.25-28 and 13.33. In Luke's Gospel, there was already an earlier citation of the Psalm at the baptism of Jesus, but only in Codex Bezae (Υἱός μου εἶ σύ, ἐγὼ σήμερον γεγέννηκά σε, 'You are my son, today I have fathered you', Lk. 3.22 D05). There, the voice from heaven establishes that Jesus is the Messiah, that is, the anointed one, as well as the fulfilment of the promise made to David that his son would sit on his throne for ever (cf. 2 Sam. 7.6-16, and see *Commentary*, 13.23, 33). The reference in the Gospel thus creates a basis on which further use of the Psalm can be built: Jesus is the Messiah and God's son.

The first appeal to the Psalm in Luke's second volume is made by the disciples when they realize how the opening verses, Ps. 2.1-2, have been fulfilled in the combined attack on Jesus made by the Jewish authorities represented by Herod, and the Roman rulers represented by Pilate (Acts 4.28-29). The same interpretation is made by Paul in his speech to the synagogue in Antioch of Pisidia as he works through the offences against Jesus (13.27-29), though it does not become apparent that he is alluding to Psalm 2 until he makes explicit quotation of it in 13.33. The verse he cites is the same as that heard at Jesus' baptism according to Lk. 3.22 D05, applying the declaration of son-ship to Jesus. In the Bezan text of his speech Paul continues the quotation with the following verse, Ps. 2.8, thereby announcing that Jesus is the Messiah not only of Israel but also of the nations, and introducing into his exposition the notion of the Gentiles being brought under his rule (Acts 13.33b D05). He further repeats this idea by his reference to Isa. 55.3 (Acts 13.34), a statement that prefaces in the Isaianic context a promise of rule over the Gentiles (Isa. 55.4-5), which Paul applies to Jesus as the resurrected Messiah (see *Commentary*, 13.33-37 for detailed analysis of Paul's use of these texts).

It may well be that in the Bezan text of Acts 16.11-40, Psalm 2 is being drawn on for a third time, though if this is the case it is not being quoted but alluded to. Certainly, its application to the opposition of the Gentiles to Jesus, who is the Messiah and the Son of God, has already been well established from the previous references, so that if the allusion is intentional in Acts 16 its re-enactment in the context of the attack of the rulers of Philippi on Paul and Silas has been prepared for. Throughout the passage, there are many verbal parallels, some *verbatim*, and additional parallels of themes and concepts; both types are more evident in the text of Codex Bezae, as the following analysis demonstrates. The order of allusions will be followed in the Acts account according to the Bezan text, indicating the references to the Psalm and citing the Greek when the allusion is a verbal one.

Acts 16

The slaves (οἱ δοῦλοι) of the Most High are announcing (εὐαγγελίζονται D05) the way of salvation (ὁδὸν σωτηρίας), 16.17b

Paul spoke in the name of Jesus Christ (Χριστοῦ), 16.18

The masters (οἱ κύριοι) dragged Paul and Silas to the rulers (ἐπὶ τοὺς ἄρχοντας), 16.19

The masters accused Paul and Silas of throwing their city into confusion (ἐκταράσσουσιν), 16.20

They accused them of announcing (καταγγέλλουσιν) to the Gentiles (τὰ ἔθνη) things that they are forbidden to do, 2.21 D05

A great crowd joined together against Paul and Silas (συνεπέστησαν κατ' αὐτῶν), 16.22 D05

The magistrates tore the clothes off (περιρήξαντες) Paul and Silas, 16.22b

The magistrates ordered [the lictors, τοὺς ραβδούχους, 16.35] to flog (ῥαβδίζειν) Paul and Silas, 16.22b

Paul and Silas were praying and singing hymns (ὕμνουν), 16.25

Their bonds (τὰ δεσμά) were loosened, 16.26b

The jailor was trembling (ἔντρομος), 16.29b

He fell at the feet (προσέπεσεν πρὸς τοὺς πόδας) of Paul and Silas, 16.29b D05

They told him to believe in the Lord Jesus Christ (τὸν κύριον Ἰησοῦν Χριστόν), 16.31 D05

Psalm 2

The kings and judges of the earth are to 'be slaves' (δουλεύσατε, 2.11) to the Lord, or they will perish from the way of righteousness (ἐξ ὁδοῦ δικαίας, 2.12). The Son proclaims (διαγγέλλων, 2.7) the Lord's decree

The kings and rulers come against the Lord and his anointed (χριστοῦ), 2.2

The kings and rulers (οἱ ἄρχοντες) come against the Lord (κατὰ τοῦ κυρίου), 2.2

The Lord will throw the kings and rulers into confusion (ταράξει), 2.5b

The Gentiles (ἔθνη, 2.1) conspire against the Lord, who will give them (ἔθνη, 2.8a) to his son as his heritage. His son proclaims (διαγγέλλων, 2.7) the Lord's decree

The Gentiles conspire and the peoples plot; the kings of the earth and the rulers gather together against the Lord and his anointed (κατὰ τοῦ κυρίου καὶ τοῦ χριστοῦ αὐτοῦ), 2,1-2

The kings and rulers said 'Let us tear their bonds apart' (Διαρήξωμεν), 2.3

The Son will break the nations (Gentiles) with a rod (ἐν ῥάβδῳ) of iron, 2.9a

Psalms were sung (cf. διάψαλμα), 2.2b

The kings and rulers will burst the bonds (τοὺς δεσμούς), 2.3a

The kings and judges of the earth are to rejoice in him [the Lord] with trembling (ἐν τρόμῳ), 2.11b

The kings and judges of the earth are to do homage to the Son (רשׁק, lit. kiss the feet, Heb. [παιδεύθητε, seize hold of discipline, LXX]), 2.10

The kings and rulers come against the Lord (τοῦ κυρίου) and his anointed (τοῦ χριστοῦ), 2.2b

The jailor rejoiced (ἠγαλλιάσατο), 16.34b	The kings and judges of the earth are to rejoice (ἀγαλλιᾶσθε), 2.11b
He had become a believer in God (πεπιστευ-κὼς ἐπὶ τὸν θεόν), 16.34b D05	Blessed are those who put their trust in him [the Lord] (οἱ πεποιθότες ἐπ' αὐτῷ), 2.12b
The magistrates [= rulers, οἱ ἄρχοντες, 16.19b] gathered together (συνήχθησαν ἐπὶ τὸ αὐτό), 16.35a D05	The rulers gathered together (οἱ ἄρχοντες συνήχθησαν ἐπὶ τὸ αὐτό), 2.2b
The magistrates were afraid (ἐφοβήθησαν), 16.35b D05	The kings and rulers are to serve the Lord with fear (ἐν φόβῳ), 2.11a
They said, 'We did not know you are righteous (δίκαιοι) men', 16.39b D05	They might perish from the way of righteousness (ἐξ ὁδοῦ δικαίας), 2.12

As can be seen from the above list, there are 18 elements in the Acts story that correspond to Psalm 2, all direct verbal tallies (some verbatim) as well as the general reference to 'singing hymns to God' at Acts 16.25, which serves as a general cue to activate the Psalm paradigm. Eight of the parallels in Acts are absent or less exact in the Alexandrian text.

Despite the extent of the parallels, some doubt as to whether an allusion to Psalm 2 is intentional must be voiced. Some of the parallel terms are ones that commonly occur in both Acts and the Scriptures (e.g. the Gentiles, the Lord, the rulers). Several are not being used in the same way in each context. On the other hand, nowhere else in the New Testament is this collection of verbal parallels with Psalm 2 to be found. Furthermore, the thematic parallel of the attack by the Gentiles on Paul and Silas as representatives of the Lord anointed and the corresponding reaction of God in terrifying the Gentiles provides an entirely appropriate context for an application of Psalm 2 to the events in Philippi. Finally, the echoes of the earthquake in Acts 4 as God's response to the opposition to the apostles, when the apostles explicitly applied Psalm 2 to their situation, are evident in the Philippi scene and give reason for suspecting that the use of the Psalm as a paradigm in Acts 16 is, indeed, deliberate.

Excursus 11

The Prison of Peter and the Prison of Paul and Silas

There are interesting parallels between the imprisonment of Peter by Herod in Jerusalem, and that of Paul and Silas by the magistrates in Philippi. The repetition of scenes by successive characters is a device Luke uses to bring out the similarities between them, but also the differences.[55] Thus, the outcome of the first scene involving Peter was presented as wholly positive whereas that

---

[55] In this respect, Luke's use of repetition or re-enactment goes beyond the straightforward construction of parallels that was a feature of classical Greco-Roman history writing (see G.W. Trompf, *The Idea of Historical Recurrence in Western Thought: From Antiquity to Reformation* [Berkeley: University of California Press, 1979], where he recognizes with clarity how Luke's use of recurrence is to some extent distinct from Hellenistic practice, but nevertheless assumes the internal parallels in his two volumes to be positive [e.g. pp. 122–28]).

of the second involving Paul and Silas has more negative aspects to it. The following parallels may be noted:

The Prison of Peter (Acts 12)

Peter was being kept in the prison (ἐτηρεῖτο ἐν τῇ φυλακῇ) ... between two soldiers, bound with two chains ... two guards in front of the door were guarding the prison (φύλακες πρὸ τῆς θύρας ἐτήρουν τὴν φυλακήν), 12.5a, 6b

In that night Peter (τῇ νυκτὶ ἐκείνῃ) was sleeping between two soldiers, 12.6a

There was much prayer (πολλὴ προσευχή) in earnestness from the church to God (πρὸς τὸν θεόν) concerning Peter, 12.5b

And behold (καὶ ἰδού), the angel of the Lord came and stood by Peter, 12.7a

And a light (φῶς) shone out in the chamber, 12,7b

Nudging Peter's side, the angel woke him up (κοιμώμενος), 12.7c, cf. 12.6a

And the chains (αἱ ἁλύσεις) peeled off from Peter's hands, 12.7d

The angel said to Peter, 'Put your cloak (τὸ ἱμάτιον) around you', 12.8c

He was taken out through the first and the second prison (διελθόντες ... πρώτην καὶ δευτέραν φυλακήν), 12.10a

The Iron gate (τὴν πύλην τὴν σιδηρᾶν) leading to the city opened (ἠνοίγη) of its own accord for Peter and the angel, 12.10b

Herod had killed James with the sword (μαχαίρᾳ), 12.2

Peter, having been freed, reported to the community in Mary's house how the Lord had brought him out of the prison (διηγήσατο αὐτοῖς πῶς ὁ κύριος αὐτὸν ἐξήγαγεν ἐκ τῆς φυλακῆς), 12.17a

Peter did not go back to the church of Ierousalem but ordered the community to report these things to James and the brethren (τοῖς ἀδελφοῖς), 12.17b

After going out (καὶ ἐξελθών [for the third time, cf. 12.9, 10c]) he went to another place, 12.17c

When day came (Γενομένης δὲ ἡμέρας), there was a commotion among the soldiers over what had become of Peter, 12.18

The Prison of Paul and Silas (Acts 16)

The jailor (ὁ δεσμοφύλαξ) received the order to keep (τηρεῖσθαι) securely Paul and Silas ... he secured their feet in the stocks, 16.23-24

Around the middle of the night (κατὰ τὸ μέσον τῆς νυκτός), Paul and Silas were singing hymns, 16.25a D05

Paul and Silas were singing hymns to God in prayer (προσευχόμενοι ὕμνουν τὸν θεόν). The other prisoners were listening attentively, 16.25a

Suddenly (ἄφνω), there was a great earthquake so that the foundations of the jail were shaken, 16.26a

The jailor asked for lights (φῶτα), 16.29a

The jailor awakened out of sleep (ἔξυπνος), 16.27a

And from all the prisoners the bonds (τὰ δεσμά) were loosened, 16.26b

The magistrates had torn off the garments (τὰ ἱμάτια) of Paul and Silas, 16.22b

The jailor had thrown them into the inner prison (εἰς τὴν ἐσωτέραν φυλακήν), 16.24b

At once, all the doors (αἱ θύραι πᾶσαι) of the prison opened (ἠνεῴχθησαν), 16.26b, 27a

The jailor having drawn his sword (τὴν μάχαιραν), was about to kill himself, 16.27b

Paul and Silas, having gone out of the prison, went to Lydia's house and seeing the brethren, they reported what the Lord had done for them (διηγήσαντο ὅσα ἐποίησεν κύριος αὐτοῖς), 16.40 D05

Paul and Silas went back to Lydia's house to see the brethren (τοὺς ἀδελφούς) by way of encouraging them, 16.40b

They went out (καὶ ἐξῆλθαν [for the second time, cf.16.40a]), 16.40c

When it was day (Ἡμέρας δὲ γενομένης), the magistrates ... remembering the earthquake that had happened, were afraid, 16.35

The chief points of similarity are that both accounts stress the careful attempts to make sure the prisoners were kept in the utmost security, in the innermost prison. The release happens during the night on each occasion, thanks to divine intervention while prayer is being made. The bonds are miraculously loosened and the doors of the prison are opened. The escape causes a disturbance among the Roman authorities on each occasion. Following their release, Peter on the one hand, and Paul and Silas on the other, recount to the church their deliverance, which represents something of a personal exodus from the restrictions of Judaism (this is the force of the repeated verb ἐξέρχομαι in each case).

The effects of Peter's deliverance from Herod's prison are, however, far-reaching and permanent in a way that they are not in the case of Paul and Silas. Peter recognizes the work of the Lord in freeing him, not just from the physical prison but from 'all the expectations of the people of the Jews' (12.11), that is, the hopes of a Messianic restoration of Israel. Although he goes to the part of the church that was praying for him (because they had already experienced this liberation) and tells them about the escape, he does not go to the other part of the church under the authority of James that remains more closely attached to Jewish hopes and ways of thinking.

In the account concerning Paul and Silas, there is no recognition on their part of the intervention of the Lord in freeing them from the prison of the Gentiles. On the contrary, it is the Roman authorities who interpret the earthquake as a sign of divine displeasure with their action. Moreover, Paul and Silas do not avail themselves of the freedom that the opening of the prison gives them, nor even of the magistrates' order to leave the prison, but continue to wait inside until the magistrates come to take them out themselves. Paul's insistence on their human rights and status as Roman citizens is symbolic of his continuing attachment to his social position among the Gentiles as if it were of more value than his being an envoy of the Lord Jesus, on a mission of the Holy Spirit. Although he takes advantage of the situation in the night to speak to the jailor about the Lord, he will continue to maintain his strategy of trying to convince the Jews first about the truth of the Messiah in order to prepare the way for the Gentiles to enter into the restored Israel.

It is the differences between Peter's release from prison and that of Paul and Silas that show up the weaknesses of the latter and justify the continuation of the narrative, which will follow Paul as he makes further progress in his grasp of the full truth of the freedom offered by Jesus from any notions of national or social privilege.

[D] 17.1-9 *Macedonia II: Thessalonica*

Overview

Paul and Silas have been persuaded by the city authorities to leave Philippi to avoid risking a repeat occurrence of the trouble caused when people among the local population complained to them that the disciples had been trying to convert them to Jewish ways. This was the first city where they had stopped after crossing into Macedonia in response to the man's call to come and help the people there. Because they continued their practice of announcing the gospel in essentially Jewish terms, their success in meeting the Macedonian's request was limited: they first founded a community made up of Gentiles who had been sympathizers with Judaism, and only after divine intervention when they were in prison was another, made up of Gentiles, created.

This sequence located in Thessalonica is closely related to the following one [D′] that takes place in Beroea, because Jews from Thessalonica go to Beroea once the narrative there is underway. The pair of sequences stands together at the centre of Section III of this third part of Acts. Each presents a scene in the synagogue with a positive outcome among Jews and also Gentiles, which leads to a second scene in which Jews stir up opposition. The importance of the two sequences as the structural centre of the narrative is that they bring to a climax the consequences of Paul's mission strategy, of taking the gospel to the Jews first before the Gentiles.

Structure and Themes

In Thessalonica, Paul will continue his practice of teaching in the synagogues, preaching to Jews and God-fearers from the basis of the Scriptures. His work will meet with a measure of success among Jews and Gentiles alike, but will be attacked by hostile Jews who denounce them to the Roman authorities as opponents of Caesar.

The sequence is made up of two equal halves, the first describing Paul's synagogue teaching and its positive results, and the second the attack of unbelieving Jews of the city:

[a]	17.1	Journey to Thessalonica
[b]	17.2a	Paul goes to the synagogue
[c]	17.2b-3	He lectures for three Sabbaths
[d]	17.4a	Some Jews are persuaded
[e]	17.4b	Many Gentiles and women join Paul and Silas
[e′]	17.5a	Other Jews set the city in uproar
[d′]	17.5b	They look for Paul and Silas in Jason's house
[c′]	17.6-7	They drag Jason and others to the authorities
[b′]	17.8	They disturb the authorities and the crowd
[a′]	17.9	Jason and the others pay a caution

The division of the sequence into elements, and the titles assigned to them, follow the Bezan text.

Translation

Codex Bezae D05

[a]　**17.1** Having gone through Amphipolis, they then went down to Apollonis, and from there to Thessalonica where there was a synagogue of the Jews.

Codex Vaticanus B03

17.1 Having gone through Amphipolis and through Apollonis, they went to Thessalonica where there was a synagogue of the Jews.

[b]	**2a** And according to his custom, Paul became involved with them.	**2a** According to Paul's custom, he became involved with them,
[c]	**2b** On three Sabbaths, he lectured to them, **3** expounding from the Scriptures that the Christ had to suffer and to rise from the dead, and alongside that submitting that 'This is the Christ, Jesus, the one whom I proclaim to you'.	**2b** and on three Sabbaths, he lectured to them from the Scriptures, **3** expounding and submitting that the Christ had to suffer and to rise from the dead, and that 'The Christ is this man, Jesus whom I am proclaiming to you'.
[d]	**4a** And some of them were persuaded.	**4a** And some of them were persuaded
[e]	**4b** And, by the force of their teaching, many of the God-fearers and a great number of Greeks and not a few wives of the leading citizens threw in their lot with Paul and with Silas.	**4b** and threw in their lot with Paul and Silas, as did also a great number of the Greek God-fearers, together with not a few of the leading women.
[e′]	**5a** However, the Jews who were not persuaded, having collected together some wicked men from the rabble, created a disturbance in the city;	**5a** However, the Jews, becoming zealous, and by taking to themselves from the rabble some wicked men and gathering a crowd, they started to create a disturbance in the city;
[d′]	**5b** and setting on the house of Jason, they tried to look for them, to bring them out to the people's assembly.	**5b** and setting on the house of Jason, they tried to look for them, to bring them to the people's assembly.
[c′]	**6** Since they did not find them, however, they dragged Jason and some brethren to the politarchs, shouting and saying, 'These are the men who have turned the world upside down, and they have come here, **7** and Jason has taken them in', and 'All these men act contrary to the decrees of Caesar, saying that there is another king, Jesus'.	**6** Since they did not find them, however, they dragged Jason and some brethren to the politarchs, shouting, 'These men, who have turned the world upside down, have come here, too, **7** and Jason has taken them in, and all these men act contrary to the decrees of Caesar, saying that there is another king, Jesus'.
[b′]	**8** And it disturbed the magistrates and the crowd.	**8** They disturbed the crowd and the magistrates as they listened to these things,
[a′]	**9** When they heard these things and had taken security from Jason and the others, they let them go.	**9** and when they had taken security from Jason and the others, they let them go.

Critical Apparatus

The overall amount of textual variation in this chapter is unremarkable, it being considerably less than that of both chapters 16 and 18. However, the proportion of additional material to alternative material in Codex Bezae compared with Codex Vaticanus is unusual in that there is significantly less of the former than the latter, a reversal of the pattern usually seen in the preceding chapters. In fact, after an unusually high amount of additional material in the next chapter, chapter 18, the trend observed in chapter 17 will continue in the final chapters of Codex Bezae as the proportion of additional material steadily decreases (see Read-Heimerdinger, *The Bezan Text*, pp. 11–16 for precise figures).

17.1 (Διοδεύσαντες δὲ) τὴν Ἀμφίπολιν (πόλιν ℵ*) καὶ τὴν Ἀπολλωνίαν B 𝔓⁷⁴
(ℵ) A 81. 88. 945. 1175. 1739 | τὴν Ἀμφ. κ. Ἀπολ. H L P Ψ 049. 056. 33. 945.
1739 𝔐 | τὴν Ἀπολ. καὶ τὴν Ἀμφ. E ‖ τὴν Ἀμφ. D.— ἦλθον εἰς τὴν Θεσσα-
λονίκην B 547 | ἦλθον εἰς Θ. ℵ A E H L P Ψ 049. 056. 33. 945. 1739 𝔐 ‖ καὶ (–
Dˢ·ᵐ·) κατῆλθον (+ καὶ Dᶜ) εἰς Ἀπολλωνίδα (-νία Dᵖ·ᵐ·?) κἀκεῖθεν εἰς Θ. D*.

In D05, Scrivener identifies a dot over the δ of Ἀπολλωνίδα (indicating
that δ is erroneous), which the first hand may have perhaps placed uninten-
tionally: *'puncto p. m. supra δ in απολλωνιδα forsan casu posito'* (p. 445). It
is unlikely that Ἀπολλωνία is the correct reading, since the accusative Ἀπολλωνίαν would be required as in B03. Ἀπολλωνίδα in D05 is the accusative of
Ἀπολλωνίς.

B03 has two stages to the journey, the first being the travel through Amphipolis and Apollonia, which are distinguished by separate articles but linked as
the destination of the participle διοδεύσαντες, and the second the journey to
Thessalonica. D05 views the journey as having three stages: the first was the
passing through Amphipolis, the second the going down (using κατέρχομαι)
to their primary goal of Apollonia (underlined with both the omission of the
article, and with the adverbial καί before the finite verb, on which see Read-
Heimerdinger, *The Bezan Text*, p. 209), and the third, the continuation of the
journey on to Thessalonica. Amphipolis is treated as expected information,
probably because it would be known as a town on the Egnatian Way between
Philippi and Thessalonica; since the same was true of Apollonia, that could also
account for the article before the name in B03. (Some MSS read the article
before συναγωγή in this verse, but not D05, contrary to Barrett, II, p. 809.)

17.2 κατὰ δὲ τὸ εἰωθὸς τῷ Παύλῳ B 𝔓⁷⁴ ℵ *rell* ‖ καὶ (– Dˢ·ᵐ·) κατὰ τ. εἰ. ὁ Παῦλος
D, *et secundum consuetudinem Paulus* d (e gig vg syᵖ aeth).— καὶ ἐπὶ σάββατα
τρία διελέξατο B 𝔓⁷⁴ ℵ A 33. 81. 88. 945. 1175. 1739. 1891 | κ. ἐπὶ σ. τ. διελέγετο
H L P 049. 056 𝔐 ‖ ἐπὶ σ. τ. διελέχθη D (+ καὶ E Ψ 181. 257. 383. 431. 614. 1108.
1505. 1518. 1611. 1799. 1898. 2138. 2147. 2298. 2412. 2495; Chr.

The links between the sentences of 17.1-3 vary between B03 and D05.
After the initial sentence of v. 1, B03 introduces Paul's going to the synagogue in Thessalonica as a new development (δέ) and links to it with καί his
debating on three Sabbaths. D05, on the other hand, links the second sentence
to the opening one with καί, and then has no link (asyndeton) before the third.
Since the function of asyndeton is to draw attention to the sentence that follows (Read-Heimerdinger, *The Bezan Text*, pp. 246–53), D05 treats Paul's
lecturing in the synagogue on three Sabbaths as of special importance, because
on this occasion it was what he said that was especially significant.

Concerning the deponent verb διαλέγομαι, B03 reads the usual middle
aorist, while D05 has the passive found only in Attic texts.

ἀπὸ (τῶν γραφῶν) B 𝔓⁷⁴ ℵ *rell* ‖ ἐκ D, *de* d.

There are several variant readings concerning ἀπό/ἐκ in B03 and D05
(Read-Heimerdinger, *The Bezan Text*, pp. 188–92): ἀπό has the sense here of

Paul starting from the Scriptures in his teaching and going beyond them; ἐκ, on the other hand, has Paul taking his teaching from ('out of', lit.) the Scriptures. The idea that he taught about the death and resurrection of Christ by demonstrating this truth from the Scriptures is made clearer with the preposition ἐκ (see *Commentary*).

17.3 τὸν (Χριστόν) B 𝔓⁷⁴ ℵ *rell* ‖ *om.* D.

With the article before Χριστόν, B03 treats the Christ as a known or expected topic of Paul's teaching in the synagogue, which it was as far as Luke or his addressee were concerned; the absence of the article, in contrast, treats the topic as something new, thus viewing it from the point of view of the members of the synagogue.

(οὗτός ἐστιν) ὁ Χριστὸς ὁ ᾽Ιησοῦς B sa? I ὁ Χρ. ᾽Ιη. H L P Ψ 049. 056. 0142. 1739 𝔐 sa?; Theoph I ὁ Χρ. 919 ‖ Χρ. ᾽Ιη. D, *Christus Iesus* d 𝔓⁷⁴ A 33. 81. 226. 1646. 1838. 2344 *pc* c dem gig 1* p ro w vg^{ww.st} sy^h aeth; Chr^{lem} I ᾽Ι. Χρ. ℵ 257. 614. 913. 1108. 1505. 1611. 1765. 2138. 2147. 2412. 2495 *pc* ar l² ph vg^{cl} bo? I ᾽Ι. ὁ Χρ. E 36. 307. 431. 453. 1518. 1678. 1799 *pc* e bo?; Chr.

The omission of the article before Χριστός in D05 is in accordance with the fact that it is the complement of the verb ἐστίν, the complement being naturally salient (indicated by the absence of the article) since it is new information. In retaining the article, B03 accords more importance to the fact that the reference to Χριστός is anaphoric, since he has just been mentioned.

The article before ᾽Ιησοῦς in B03 identifies Jesus as the one Paul is proclaiming, and causes the whole phrase ὁ ᾽Ιησοῦς ὃν ἐγὼ καταγγέλλω ὑμῖν to stand in apposition to οὗτος; the absence of the article in D05 causes the name of Jesus alone to stand in apposition to οὗτος, and the relative clause beginning ὃν to qualify ᾽Ιησοῦς further.

17.4 (καὶ) Σιλᾷ B ‖ τῷ Σιλέᾳ D 𝔓⁷⁴ ℵ *rell.*— τῇ διδαχῇ D, *doctrinae* d ‖ *om.* B 𝔓⁷⁴ ℵ *rell.*

The manuscript D05 reads the dative ΣΙΛΛΙΑ with the correction ΣΙΛΕΑ (D^{Kmg}), just like the dative ΣΙΛΕΑ at 15.34 D05 (cf. 16.29 D05, ΣΙΛΛ).

The article before the name of Silas treats him as distinct from Paul. Hitherto in D05, Paul and Silas had been viewed as a united team (16.19 D05, 29 D05).

Without resorting to conjectural readings, the dative τῇ διδαχῇ in D05 qualifying the verb προσεκληρώθησαν can be interpreted as a dative of means, 'on the grounds/by the force of their teaching'.

τῶν τε σεβομένων B 𝔓⁷⁴ ℵ *rell* ‖ πολλοὶ τῶν σεβ. D, *multi caelicolarum* d sy^p; Ephr Cass.— ῾Ελλήνων (πλῆθος) B ℵ E L P Ψ 049. 056. 614. 1739 𝔐 p vg^{mss} sy^{p.h} sa bo^{mss} aeth; Chr ‖ καὶ ῾Ελ. D 𝔓⁷⁴ A 33. 81. 181. 2344 *pc* lat bo I *om.* 36. 307. 453. 610. 1678.— γυναικῶν τε (τῶν πρώτων) B 𝔓⁷⁴ ℵ *rell* ar e; Chr ‖ καὶ γυναῖκες D, *et mulieres* d lat sy^{p.h} (aeth); Cass.

B03 identifies two groups: 1) 'a great number of the Greek God-fearers', 2) 'not a few of the leading women' (where τῶν πρώτων has to be taken as gen. pl. fem., referring to γυναικῶν, equivalent to γυναικῶν τῶν εὐσχημόνων of 17.12b B03). D05 identifies three groups: 1) 'many of the God-fearers', 2) 'a great number of Greeks' and 3) 'not a few wives of the leading men (of the city)' (where τῶν πρώτων is a gen. pl. masc., as at 13.50b, and equivalent to τῶν εὐσχημόνων ἄνδρες καὶ γυναῖκες of 17.12b D05).

17.5 ζηλώσαντες δὲ οἱ Ἰουδαῖοι καὶ προσλαβόμενοι B 𝔓⁷⁴ ℵ A E Ψ 33. 69. 81. 104. 323. 547. 614. 927. 945. 1175. (1241). 1270. 1505. 1611. 1739. 1837. 1891. 2147. 2412. 2495 | προσλαβόμενοι δὲ οἱ Ἰουδ. οἱ ἀπειθοῦντες H L P 049. 056 𝔐 || οἱ δὲ ἀπειθ- Ἰουδ. συστρέψαντες D (*adsuptis vero Iudaeis convertentes* d).— (προσλαβόμενοι) τῶν ἀγοραίων ἄνδρας τινὰς πονηροὺς καὶ ὀχλοποιήσαντες ἐθορύβουν B 𝔓⁷⁴ (τινὰς ἄνδρας: ℵ Ψ H L P 049. 056. 1241 𝔐) 33. 81. 927. 945. 1175. 1270. 1505. 1739. 1901 *al* vg (sy) co (προσλ. + οἱ ἀπειθ-: 614. 1241. 1505. 1611. 2147. 2412. 2495 | πον. + ἀπειθήσαντες E) || τινὰς ἄνδρας τ. ἀγ. πονηροὺς ἐθορύβουσαν D (*quosdam viros forenses subdoles turbabant* d).

The presentation of events, describing how some Jews create a disturbance in the city, is somewhat different in B03 and D05. In B03, the Jews in general are responsible for the trouble, their motive being that they were zealous (or jealous, ζηλώσαντες, see *Commentary*); two steps are then presented – they take (προσλαβόμενοι) from the rabble some wicked men, and gather a crowd (ὀχλοποιήσαντες, the only occurrence of the word in the New Testament) – as a means to creating a disturbance (imperfect, ἐθορύβουν) in the city. In D05, there is no mention of zeal, and the Jews who created the problem are specified as being those who were not persuaded (ἀπειθήσαντες, cf. ἐπείσθησαν, 17.4a); the collecting together (συστρέψαντες) of wicked men represents a single step replacing the two of B03, with the adjective πονηρούς in an emphatic position at the end of the participial clause; and the disturbance is presented as an event (aorist, ἐθορύβουσαν) rather than an ongoing (or incipient) process.

The Latin page d5 attests a conflation of the two accounts.

(αὐτοὺς) προαγαγεῖν B 𝔓⁷⁴ ℵ A Ψ 33. 81. 323. 440. 927. 945. 1175. 1505. 1611. 1739. 1891. 2147. 2495, *producere* d | προσ- E 614. 1270. 2412 | ἀνα- L | ἀγαγεῖν H P 049. 056 𝔐 || ἐξ- D *pc* syᵖ⁽⁺⁾ sa aeth.

προαγαγεῖν of B03 expresses the sense of the Jews bringing Jason forward for trial (cf 12.6; *The Message of Acts*, II, p. 345). D05 focuses, in contrast, on the efforts of the Jews to get Jason out of the house (ἐξαγαγεῖν).

17.6 βοῶντες (ὅτι) B 𝔓⁷⁴ ℵ *rell* || βοῶντες καὶ λέγοντες D, *clamantes et dicentes* d b gig w vgᴰᴿ aeth.— (οὗτοί) εἰσιν D*, *hi* d Ψ 33. 1243 a c dem gig p w vgᵐˢˢ syᵖ aeth || *om.* B 𝔓⁷⁴ ℵ Dˢ·ᵐ· *rell*.

By means of the second participle, D05 distinguishes between two separate complaints contained within the direct speech that follows: 1) Οἱ τὴν οἰκουμένην ἀναστατώσαντες οὗτοί εἰσιν ... ’Ιάσων, and (καί) 2) Οὗτοι πάντες πράσσουσιν ... ’Ιησοῦν. B03 treats the complaint as a single one, and more-over, with the omission of the verb εἰσίν, lessens the force of the first part of the complaint.

17.7 ἕτερον λέγοντες εἶναι (’Ιησοῦν) B 𝔓⁷⁴ ℵ A 33. 36. 81. 181. 242. 257. 323. 431. 453. 522. 614. 913. 945. 947. 1108. 1175. 1241. (1243). 1270. 1505. 1518. 1739. 1799. 1611. 1838. 1891. 1898. 2138. 2298. 2344. 2412. 2495 gig vg; Theoph ‖ λέγ. ἕτ. εἶναι D, *dicentes alium esse* d H L P Ψ 049. 056 𝔐 ‖ λέγ. εἶναι ἕτ. E e.

In the final sentence of the complaint, D05 underlines by the word order the claim by the disciples that they have a king who is not Caesar.

17.8-9 ἐτάραξαν δέ B 𝔓⁷⁴ ℵ *rell* ‖ καὶ ἐτάραξεν D, *et concitaverunt* d gig sa bo.— τὸν ὄχλον (τὴν πόλιν E) καὶ τοὺς πολιτάρχας B 𝔓⁷⁴ ℵ *rell* ‖ τοὺς πολ. κ. τ. ὄχλον D, *principes et turbam* d gig syᵖ.— ἀκούοντας ταῦτα. καὶ λαβόντες B 𝔓⁷⁴ ℵ *rell* ‖ ἀκούσαντες (-σαντα Dᴮ) τ. καὶ λαβ. D*, *audientes haec et accipientes* d ‖ ἀκούοντες τ. καὶ λαβ. 614. 1505. 1611. 2412

B03 and D05 understand the two sentences following the direct speech in different ways. With the first connective δέ and the second καί, B03 views the two sentences as being two elements of a new development following the speech. The first is that the Jews (cf. 17.5) disturbed the crowd and the magistrates as these people listened (accusative present participle) to what they had to say; the subject then changes in the second sentence, as the magistrates release the brethren after taking bail from Jason.

D05 presents the speech as an impersonal singular subject, which disturbed (ἐτάραξεν) the magistrates and the crowd, linking the verb with καί to the speech itself. A new sentence is introduced without any connective, and starts with two parallel nominative participles ἀκούσαντες ... καὶ λαβόντες, referring to the magistrates alone. The asyndeton underlines the fact that the action of the magistrates does not respond to what the Jews expected or hoped for.

Commentary

[a] 17.1 *Journey to Thessalonica*

17.1 Paul and Silas begin their journey away from Philippi by travelling onwards along the *Via Egnatia*, the main route across Macedonia towards Rome (cf. on 16.11 above). They went through Amphipolis, and also Apollonia according to the Alexandrian text, presumably stopping there overnight as they headed towards their destination of Thessalonica, a journey of some 100 miles. Codex Bezae suggests, on the contrary, that Apollonia was their initial chosen des-tination where they intended to stay longer, and perhaps did, before con-tinuing in due course to Thessalonica. The reason they went on to Thessalonica is made explicit: there was a synagogue there.[56] That Luke qualifies it as 'a synagogue of the Jews' is an expression of his disapproval of Paul's pattern of working, as has been noted previously (see on 13.5; 14.1), the unnecessary qualification drawing attention to Paul's practice of seeking out Jews instead of going to the Gentiles.

The naming of three geographical locations is a narrative device, used several times by Luke, to set up landmarks along the way and to indicate that the journey is progressing towards a goal (cf. 13.4-5; 14.21, 25-26; 16.6-8, 11). Thessalonica was the capital city of the second district of Macedonia (cf. 16.12, *Critical Apparatus*, on Philippi) and was remarkable for the cult of the Emperor that was practised there,[57] a fact that is relevant for the accusations brought against Paul in this city.

[b] 17.2a *Paul Goes to the Synagogue*

17.2a Luke comments that it was Paul's practice, as if it were not already clear, to go to the synagogue, and not just to go into the building or to attend the service but to 'get involved'[58] with the people there. He is still driven by the need to convince his fellow-Jews of the truth of the gospel, believing that this is essential for the continuing status of Israel into which the Gentiles will be grafted (see *Commentary*, 13.33-41).

[c] 17.2b-3 *He Lectures on Three Sabbaths*

17.2b-3 Paul's close contact with the synagogue is illustrated by the fact that on three successive Sabbaths, he held debates there. The verb Luke uses to describe his activity refers to lecturing that leads to discussion, especially contentious debate.[59] This reflects a change in strategy that Paul will adopt from now on in his conversations, principally with Jewish audiences. Instead of presenting Jesus as the culmination of the history of Israel, the fulfilment of the Promise given by the Father (cf. the speech to the synagogue in Pisidian Antioch, 13.16-41), he will focus on two issues that were particularly controver-

---

56. ὅπου has a causal force (Zerwick, *Biblical Greek*, §217: 'one may well suspect a causal sense and conclude that Paul did not stop at Amphipolis or Apollonia because there was no synagogue there').

57. For some of the evidence of the imperial cult in Thessalonica, see Witherington, *Acts*, p. 503.

58. εἰσῆλθεν with the preposition πρός (αὐτούς) indicates a degree of familiarity.

59. When the verb διαλέγομαι is used in Acts, it expresses the strong sense of 'discuss, conduct a discussion', rather than the simple sense of 'speak, preach' (B-A-G, διαλέγομαι, 1, cf. 2). Of the 13 (14 D05) times it is found in the New Testament, 10 (11) of the occurrences appear from this point on in Acts, with Paul as the subject except once: 17.2, 17; 18.4, 19, 28 D05 (Apollonius); 19.8, 9; 20.7, 9; 24.12, 25. Elsewhere, it occurs at Mk 9.34; Heb. 12.5; Jude 9. The alternative verb διαλογίζομαι has the sense of 'consider, reason' or 'consider and discuss' (esp. with πρός + acc., 'among themselves') and even 'argue' (B-A-G, διαλογίζομαι, 1, 2); it is used × 16 in the New Testament (of which Lk. × 6), and the cognate noun διαλογισμός × 14 (Lk. × 6) but neither are used in Acts. That Luke always chooses διαλέγομαι in preference to διαλογίζομαι in Acts suggests that he intended it to convey the stronger sense of the verb (cf. Zerwick and Grosvenor, *Analysis*, pp. 407, 412).

sial: the suffering of the Messiah, and the identity of the Messiah as Jesus. He will no longer preach or proclaim the gospel but come to rely on his powers of persuasion.

The importance of Paul's teaching as he set out his position is highlighted in Codex Bezae by introducing the sentence without any connective (see *Critical Apparatus*), thus anticipating a speech that is especially significant. The two essential topics he spoke about are signalled by the two participles that precede the speech (διανοίγων, 'expound'; παρατιθέμενος, 'set out, submit'). The relationship of the participles to the main verb before them and the content of the teaching following them is slightly different in the two texts. According to the Alexandrian text, he started from the Scriptures and then went on to develop his explanation with further discussion. The phrase 'from the Scriptures' (ἀπὸ τῶν γραφῶν) qualifies the finite verb διελέξατο, 'he lectured'; the two participles διανοίγων καὶ παρατιθέμενος then clarify the manner of Paul's lecturing, and the two ὅτι clauses the content of the lecturing:

> διελέξατο αὐτοῖς ἀπὸ τῶν γραφῶν
>   διανοίγων καὶ παρατιθέμενος
>   ὅτι τὸν Χριστὸν ἔδει παθεῖν
>   καὶ ὅτι Οὗτός ἐστιν ὁ Χριστός, ὁ Ἰησοῦς ὃν ἐγὼ καταγγέλλω ὑμῖν

The first content clause is in indirect speech, the second in direct speech, where the transition from one to the other is a device that highlights the direct speech and that has been observed elsewhere (cf. 1.4-5; 14.22, 27).

In the text of Codex Bezae, the preposition before 'the Scriptures' is ἐκ, 'out of', and as such qualifies not all of Paul's lecturing but only the first aspect of it, his 'expounding'. The verb Luke uses here for 'expound', διανοίγω, usually has a literal meaning, 'to open up'. Luke is alone in using the verb in a figurative sense, and each time in connection with the Scriptures (cf. Lk. 24.31, 32, 45).[60] It expresses well the sense of Paul drawing out of the Scriptures the evidence relating to Christ's death and resurrection. The second participle, 'submitting', thus refers to a separate issue, the content of the words in direct speech. Accordingly, each participle has a corresponding element introduced with ὅτι, the first in indirect speech and the second in direct speech:

> διελέχθη αὐτοῖς
>   ἐκ τῶν γραφῶν διανοίγων
>   ὅτι Χριστὸν ἔδει παθεῖν καὶ ἀναστῆναι ἐκ νεκρῶν
>   καὶ παρατιθέμενος
>   ὅτι Οὗτός ἐστιν Χριστός, Ἰησοῦς, ὃν ἐγὼ καταγγέλλω ὑμῖν

In other words, he explained from the Scriptures that the Christ had to suffer and rise from the dead; and, alongside that explanation, in parallel, he presented his claim that the one whom he was announcing, Jesus, was the Christ.

---

60. The verb sometimes has the literal meaning of opening up a passage between two masses of land so as to create a way through, for example (Bailly, διανοίγω, 2, 'ouvrir de façon à faire communiquer').

The order of the sentence in Greek, setting out the two parallel participles first, followed by the two parallel components of the speech that correspond to them, is typical of Lukan rhetorical style noted on a number of occasions.[61]

The presentation of the Messiah as one who suffered contradicts the expectation of a triumphant and powerful king who would come to liberate Israel from her enemies, the Gentiles. From that point of view, if Jesus was the Messiah, his coming was a failure. The alternative model is, nevertheless, to be found in the Jewish Scriptures (cf. Isa. 42.1-9; 49.1-6; 50.4-9; 52.13–53.12), as Jesus himself was at pains to explain to his disciples after his death and resurrection when he interpreted to them Moses and the Prophets and showed how the death of the Messiah (ἔδει παθεῖν τὸν Χριστόν), and his subsequent glorification, were part of the divine plan (Lk. 24.26, 44, 46). It is likewise on the death and glorification through the resurrection that Paul focuses in his lectures in the synagogue of Thessalonica.

The second step is to persuade his audience that the Messiah foreseen in the Jewish Scriptures is none other than Jesus. The focus in each text is again subtly different: Paul's point in the Alexandrian text answers the question, 'Who is the Christ', saying the Messiah (the Christ) whom he has argued had to die and rise again is 'this man', the Jesus about whom he is talking with them. In the Bezan text, Paul's declaration answers the question, 'Who is this man, Jesus whom I am proclaiming to you?', by saying he is the Messiah, the Christ.

[d] 17.4a *Some Jews Are Persuaded*

17.4a There is a positive response to Paul's lecturing in the synagogue, with 'some of them' being convinced by what he said. It becomes clear with the next clause that the people referred to here are Jews. Codex Bezae will later distinguish them from other Jews who were not persuaded by Paul's teaching (cf. 17.5 below). In the Alexandrian text, the subject of the verb also includes the categories of Gentiles mentioned in the second half of the verse.

[e] 17.4b *Many Gentiles and Women Join Paul and Silas*

17.4b In the Alexandrian text, the subject of this clause is the same as that of the previous one in the first half of the verse (see above), that is some of the Jews and two groups of Gentiles: numerous God-fearing Greeks and also a good number of leading women. They all 'threw in their lot' with Paul and Silas, with Luke using a verb (προσκληρόω) that has the idea of sharing the same fate or circumstances.

In the Bezan text, the first clause of 17.4a refers only to 'some of them', that is some of the Jews in the synagogue. This second clause is a new action with three new subjects: many of the God-fearers (by definition, Gentiles); a great number of Greeks (by implication, with no previous attachment to the synagogue); and wives of the leading men of the city (also Gentiles, of high standing and connected by marriage with the Roman city authorities). The reason for which these Gentiles

---

61. Cf., e.g., 17.6 D05 below.

decide to join in with Paul and Silas is that they were impressed by the teaching of each of them. For the first time in the Bezan text, the pair are presented here as independent, rather than forming a united team.

[e'] 17.5a *Other Jews Set the City in Uproar*

17.5a A final group of people did not respond positively to Paul's message: these are the Jews who, unlike those of 17.4a, are not swung over by what he said and seek to create trouble for the disciples. The Alexandrian text describes them as becoming 'zealous', a description that has been applied before to Jews who opposed Paul's teaching, those in Antioch of Pisidia at 13.45 where it was noted that the cause of their zeal was their desire to maintain the purity of their religion and, in particular, to resist Paul's message that with the coming of Jesus as the Messiah, salvation and the word of God had been extended to the Gentiles. That may be presumed to be the motivation for the attack of the Jews here in Thessalonica, too. The verb ζηλόω could in fact be taken to mean 'be jealous' rather than 'be zealous', but since there is every reason to suppose that the opposition of the Jews to Paul had a religious motive, rather than simply being due to their envy of his success, the interpretation of 'zealous' is to be preferred here.

The Bezan text does not comment on their motive but refers to them only as Jews who were 'not persuaded' (ἀπειθοῦντες), as distinct from the group in 17.4a who 'were persuaded' (ἐπείσθησαν), that is, they accepted the arguments Paul put forward for Jesus as the Messiah.

The action of these Jews is to use some disreputable men from among the local layabouts to create a disturbance. The picture in the Alexandrian text is somewhat reinforced by the detail that they (probably a combination of the Jews as well as the men they had got to join them) also gather a crowd together who add to the commotion in the city. The purpose in creating an uproar would be to demonstrate to the authorities that Paul and Silas were having a disruptive effect on the city as a whole, that it was an incident of major importance.

[d'] 17.5b *They Look for Paul and Silas in Jason's House*

17.5b The plan was to find Paul and Silas so they could take them to the 'people', referred to with the term δῆμος, which can designate simply a 'mob' but, in view of the developments in this instance, it probably has the more specific sense here of a citizens' parliament[62] that had power to intervene in civil cases. In order for the Jews to bring their complaints to the assembly, they needed to have the accused men. Clearly, it is believed that Paul and Silas are sheltering in Jason's house, but that Jason is one of their adherents only emerges in the men's complaints. His name is Greek but that says nothing about whether he is a Jew or a Gentile since it was common for Jews of Hellenistic origin to

---

62. B-A-G, δῆμος, 2, though the entry includes the comment, 'it is poss. that *crowd* is the meaning in all pass. in Ac'.

have Greek names. Given that so little is said about him, it is curious that he figures prominently in the scene, being mentioned by name four times.

[c'] 17.6-7 *They Drag Jason and Others to the Authorities*

17.6 Paul and Silas are apparently well hidden, whether in Jason's house or elsewhere, for they are not found. It is consequently Jason and 'some brethren' who are dragged out instead. In view of the wording of the accusations made to the authorities, it appears that these brethren are not from Thessalonica but are associates of Paul and Silas, all of whom were staying in Jason's house.

The Jews and their supporters take Jason and the brethren to the local magistrates, referred to as 'politarchs', a term particularly associated with Macedonia that qualifies them as non-Roman authorities.[63] Once there, they shout out[64] their accusations. These are formulated in strong terms, which are all the more striking because they are made by Jews against other Jews – for even though they have not managed to find Paul and Silas, it is against the brethren who are associated with them ('these men') that they allege offences of a most serious nature from the point of view of the Roman Empire.

There are, in fact three allegations, of which the first two are grouped together as one charge and the third stands apart. The two separate charges are distinguished in the Bezan text, as on other occasions, by the two verbs that introduce the direct speech (cf. 17.3 above, for example). The first allegation is that the brethren, 'these men' who represent the group led by Paul and Silas, have 'turned the world upside down',[65] a grave accusation that they have disrupted the peace of the whole Empire, the *pax romana*. A similar complaint was made against Paul and Silas in Philippi, but there it was made by the Gentile slave masters and related only to the city (cf. 16.20). Here, it relates to the whole of the inhabited world, suggesting that the Jews in Thessalonica were aware of the activity of Paul and Silas in other places; this is confirmed by the way they present the other brethren whose reputation has already been heard of before they arrived in Thessalonica, especially in the Bezan phrasing.

17.7 As for Jason, his offence, which is part of the first charge, consists in having sheltered the group while they were staying in Thessalonica.

The second, separate, charge relates to the proclamation of Jesus as a king, of which 'all these men' – the brethren they have found, and Jason, and no doubt any others who include Paul and Silas, too – are guilty. The Jewish attackers interpret their teaching about Jesus as setting him up as an alternative king to Caesar, contrary to the imperial decrees.[66] The Bezan word order

---

63. See Hemer, *Hellenistic Setting*, p. 115, n. 35 for bibliography.

64. The verb βοάω conveys the idea of shouting for help rather than just making a noise, and of the 13 times it is used in the New Testament, seven occurrences are in Luke's work.

65. The verb ἀναστατόω will be used again at 21.38 to query Paul's role in another uprising against the Empire.

66. Exactly what these decrees (δόγματα) were is a matter of debate and speculation. It may be that the term is being used loosely to refer to the supreme authority of the Emperor. Witherington (*Acts*, pp. 507–508) makes interesting suggestions, linking them to the promises of a future kingdom of God expressed in Paul's letters to the Thessalonians.

places particular emphasis on the fact that Jesus is considered to be an alternative ruler (see *Critical Apparatus*).

[b′] 17.8 *They Disturb the Authorities and the Crowd*
17.8 The serious nature of the charges means they cannot be ignored. The steps that followed are presented once more in slightly different ways in the Alexandrian and the Bezan texts. According to the former, something of a disturbance was created by the Jews among the crowd, whom they had brought with them (cf. 17.5a AT), and among the politarchs as they listened to what they were saying. The Bezan text, on the other hand, has an impersonal verb to say simply that 'it', the allegations in general, disturbed the politarchs, as also the crowd who happened to be there since the Bezan text has not already mentioned them (cf. 17.5a D05).

[a′] 17.9 *Jason and the Others Pay a Caution*
17.9 The connections between the sentences that follow the Jews' accusations are not immediately clear in the Alexandrian text but can be deduced. The disturbance the Jews create (see 17.8 above) is presented as a new development (δέ), with the Jews as the plural subject of the verb (ἐτάραξαν); the next sentence has a change of subject implied, as 'they' (now the politarchs presumably) let Jason and the others (the brethren) go (ἀπέλυσαν) once they have taken security from them. Since the connective (καί), which introduces this final step, does not signal contra-expectation but continuity, it was apparently viewed as an effective solution to have Jason and the other brethren pay a sum of money and 'bind them over' to guarantee peace.

The Bezan text presents the decision of the politarchs to let Jason and the others go as not corresponding to the expected outcome. A new sentence starts with the participial clause 'having heard (ἀκούσαντες) these things', where, as in the Alexandrian text, the politarchs are assumed to be the new subject, but here there is no connecting word back to the previous statement (that what the Jews said disturbed them). The action of this sentence thus stands as quite disconnected from the outcome expected: the authorities do not throw the accused into prison, as they had done in Philippi, but receive a guarantee that peace will be maintained and let them go. The reason for this may well be hinted at in the list at 17.4b D05 of the people who had joined Paul and Silas, for Codex Bezae includes 'wives of the leading citizens', men who would include, if not the politarchs precisely, people of the same social circle.

The situation at this stage of Paul's mission is that he still has not carried out the plea of the Macedonian to preach the gospel to Gentiles. It is true that some Gentiles have responded to his teaching, but he has not fundamentally altered his pattern of aiming his proclamation of the gospel primarily at Jews, and doing it in a Jewish context. Any Gentiles that might have joined him are a side effect, not his main goal. The communities that are founded are, with the exception of that of the Philippian jailor (whose basis is not entirely secure, cf. on 16.36 above), always related to the synagogues, even though they are made up of Jews and Gentiles. The result is that both in Philippi and in Thessalonica, Paul's missionary activity is causing disruption because the local Jews perceive it as a threat to their own self-understanding and their continued enjoyment of a privileged status that they were accorded in the Empire as Jews.

The accusations brought against Paul and Silas do not lead to their being charged with any offence. Both in Philippi and in Thessalonica, they are allowed to go free. The 'security' that Jason and the others pay on their behalf means that they effectively put an obstacle in the way of the missionary activity of Paul and Silas; even though they have accepted their message and are believers, they do not give their full backing to the mission.

[D'] 17.10-13 *Macedonia III: Beroea*

Overview

This sequence acts as a kind of mirror to the previous one [D], which was set in Thessalonica. The action now moves on to another city, Beroea, where the incidents unfold in rapid succession. The brevity of the passage is indicative of its importance, since Luke typically makes his statements short when he wishes to draw attention to their significance.

Structure and Themes
The sequence of events is very similar to that in Thessalonica. The setting is initially the synagogue, where there is a noticeably positive response, but this incites the anger of some Jews, in this case some from Thessalonica, who come to stir up agitation among the local population. The result is that Paul and Silas have to leave the city.

    [a] 17.10a The brethren send Paul and Silas to Beroea
    [b] 17.10b They go straight to the synagogue
    [c] 17.11   A positive response
    [c'] 17.12 Belief and unbelief
    [b'] 17.13a Jews from Thessalonica come to Beroea
    [a'] 17.13b They stir up the crowds

The two central elements create a narrative focus on the response to the visit of Paul and Silas to the synagogue once they arrive in Beroea from Thessalonica. Corresponding to their role is that of the Jews from Thessalonica who react by creating a disturbance to counteract the missionary activity.

Translation

Codex Bezae D05	*Codex Vaticanus B03*
[a] **17.10a** Immediately, when it was night, the brethren sent Paul and Silas to Beroea;	**17.10a** Immediately, when it was night, the brethren sent Paul and Silas to Beroea;
[b] **10b** once they had arrived, they took themselves off to the synagogue of the Jews.	**10b** once they had arrived, they took themselves off to the synagogue of the Jews.

[c]	11 These people were noble-minded, unlike those in Thessalonica, seeing as they received the word with all eagerness, daily examining the Scriptures, to see if these things were really so.	11 These people were more noble-minded than those in Thessalonica, seeing as they received the word with all eagerness, daily examining the Scriptures, to see if these things could really be so.
[c′]	12 Some of them believed (though some did not believe); and from among the Greeks, especially those of distinction, both men and women, a considerable number believed, too.	12 Many from among them believed, not a few of the distinguished Greek women, and men, too.
[b′]	13a When the Jews from Thessalonica, however, knew that the word of God had been proclaimed to Beroea and that people had believed, they actually went to the town;	13a When the Jews from Thessalonica, however, knew that in Beroea also the word of God had been proclaimed by Paul, they went there too,
[a′]	13b and there, they persisted in disturbing the crowds and throwing them into confusion.	13b disturbing the crowds and throwing them into confusion.

Critical Apparatus

17.10 (εὐθέως) διὰ νυκτὸς ἐξέπεμψαν B D 𝔓⁴⁵ᵛⁱᵈ·⁷⁴ Ψ 33. 69. 104. 323. 945. 1270. 1739. 1891. 2344 | ἐξ. δ. ν. ℵ | δ. τῆς ν. ἐξ. E H L P 049. 056. 614 𝔐 | ἐξ. A 81.— τόν τε Παῦλον B 𝔓⁷⁴ ℵ *rell* || τὸν Παῦ. D, *Paulum* d 1799. 2147 *pc* e gig vg.

B03 distinguishes sharply between Paul and Silas with not only the repeated article, as in D05, but also the particle τε (cf. a similar distinction at 16.19 B03, 29 B03).

17.11 εὐγενέστεροι τῶν ἐν Θεσσαλονίκῃ B 𝔓⁴⁵·⁷⁴ ℵ *rell, nobiliores qui Tessalonicae sunt* d || εὐγενεῖς τῶν ἐν τῇ Θεσ. D dem p*.

B03 reads the comparative adjective followed by the genitive pronoun to indicate the people with whom the Beroeans are being compared. In D05, which has the simple adjective, the genitive case of the pronoun has the force of 'unlike' (Delebecque, *Les deux Actes*, p. 106).

τὸ (καθ' ἡμέραν) B H L P 049. 056. 1. 6. 69. 226*. 330. 440. 547. 618. 927. 1175. 1243. 1245. 1270. 1646. 1828. 1854. 2147. 2492 *pm* || om. D 𝔓⁴⁵·⁷⁴ ℵ (A *illeg.*) E Ψ 0120. 33. 36. 81. 88. 104. 181. 226ᶜ. 242. 257. 323. 431. 453. 467. 522. 614. 913. 915. 945. 1108. 1505. 1611. 1739. 1799. 1837. 1891. 1898. 2138. 2298. 2344. 2412. 2495 *pm*; Chr.

The pronoun before καθ' ἡμέραν is exceptional (cf. 2.46 B03, 47; 3.2; 16.5; 19.9).

(εἰ) ἔχοι ταῦτα οὕτως B 𝔓⁷⁴ ℵ A Dᴴ H L P Ψ 049. 056. 614. 1739 𝔐, *si habeant haec ita* d | τ. οὕτ. ἔχοι 𝔓⁴⁵ 0120. 69. 181. 1175. 1898 *pc* vg syᵖ || ἔχει τ. οὖτ. D* E 1. 36. 88. 181. 242. 453. 913. 915. 945. 1241. 1505. 1518. 1898. 2147. 2495 Theoph Oecum.

The optative of B03 expresses the indefiniteness of the indirect question; the indicative of D05 presents a real possibility.

17.12 πολλοὶ μὲν οὖν ἐξ αὐτῶν ἐπίστευσαν B ℵ A H L P Ψ 049. 056. 33. 1739 𝔐 (– μὲν οὖν 614*. 1412 Ι – μὲν 1505. 1611. 2147. 2495 Ι – οὖν E 1828), *multi ergo ex his crediderunt* d Ι πολ. μὲν οὖν ἐπ. ἐξ αὐ. 𝔓⁴⁵ᵛⁱᵈ 945 ΙΙ τινὲς μὲν οὖν αὐ. ἐπ. D.

The account of those who responded with belief is a little different in each text. B03 begins by specifying πολλοὶ ... ἐξ αὐτῶν, referring to the Jews in the synagogue (cf. οὗτοι, 17.11). D05 also begins with a reference to the Jews, but is more nuanced, saying only that 'some' of them believed. The following variant will qualify this information.

τινὲς δὲ ἠπίστησαν D, *quidam vero credere noluerunt* d 383. 614. 1799. 2147. 2412 ΙΙ *om.* B 𝔓⁷⁴ ℵ *rell.*

D05 qualifies the previous comment on the response of the Jews, by adding that some did not believe.

καὶ τῶν Ἑλληνίδων (Dᴮ) γυναικῶν (Dᴱ) τῶν εὐσχημόνων καὶ ἀνδρῶν οὐκ ὀλίγοι (ἀνδ. οὐκ ὀλ. Dᴴ) B 𝔓⁷⁴ ℵ Dᶜᵒʳʳˢ· *rell* ΙΙ κ. τ. Ἑλλήνων καὶ τ. εὐσχ. ἄνδρες καὶ γυναῖκες ἱκανοὶ ἐπίστευσαν D*, *et Graecorum et non placentium et viri et mulieres pleres crediderunt* d.

B03 continues by describing other people who believed as οὐκ ὀλίγοι, where the litotes contrasts with the positive πολλοί referring to the Jewish believers. These are distinguished Greek citizens, the women being highlighted in comparison with the men.

D05, having made clear that some Jews did not believe, continues like B03 to mention the distinguished Greek citizens, with the difference that it repeats the verb ἐπίστευσαν because of the intervening clause, and it treats the men and women equally. It would be possible grammatically to understand the Greeks and the distinguished people as two different groups, but it is perhaps more natural to interpret the καί between them as adverbial and to take the two words in apposition. It is striking how successive correctors of D05 have sought to bring the text into line with B03.

17.13 τῆς (Θεσσαλονίκης) B 𝔓⁴⁵ ℵ A H L P Ψ 049. 056. 33. 1739 𝔐 ΙΙ *om.* D 𝔓⁷⁴ E 242. 614. 913. 945. 1108. 1505. 1611. 2138. 2412. 2495 *pc.*— (καὶ) ἐν τῇ Βεροίᾳ κατηγγέλη ὑπὸ τοῦ Παύλου ὁ (Dᴱ) λόγος τοῦ (Dᴱ) θεοῦ ἦλθον B 𝔓⁷⁴ ℵ *rell* ΙΙ λόγος θεοῦ κατ. εἰς Βεροίαν καὶ (– Dˢ·ᵐ·) ἐπίστευσαν, καὶ ἦλθον εἰς αὐτήν (– Dˢ·ᵐ·) D*, *verbum dei adnuntiatum est in Beroeam et crediderunt, et venerunt in eam* d.

The article before the name of Thessalonica in B03 is anaphoric, as it is before Beroea in the following subordinate clause. The absence of the article in D05 draws attention to the contrast between Thessalonica, on the one hand, and Beroea (also without the article) on the other.

The clause expressing the content (ὅτι) of what the Jews from Thessalonica knew is worded differently. B03 contrasts Thessalonica with Beroea by fronting the name of the second town before the verb; the focus of the Jews' concern is Paul's activity, his announcing of the word of God; on account of this, they went to Beroea. The focus of their concern in D05 is the word of God, that it is being proclaimed to Beroea (where the preposition εἰς has the effect of personifying the town) and that the people there believed the word. The absence of articles in the phrase λόγος θεοῦ highlights it, because in the synagogue the expected phrase would be ὁ λόγος τοῦ κυρίου (see *Excursus* 1).

The action of the Jews in both cases was to go to Beroea, an action that D05 again underlines with the preceding adverbial καί (see Read-Heimerdinger, *The Bezan Text*, pp. 208–10) and the pronominal phrase εἰς αὐτήν to make explicit that they undertook the action of going to Beroea.

(σαλεύοντες) καὶ ταράσσοντες τοὺς ὄχλους B 𝔓⁷⁴ ℵ A 33. 69. 81. 104. 323. 614. 945. (1175). 1270. 1505. 1611. 1739. 1837. 1891. 2147. 2344. 2412. 2495 lat | τ. ὄχλ. κ. ταρ. Ψ | τ. ὄχλους 𝔓⁴⁵ E L P 049. 056 𝔐 aeth; Chr | τὸν ὄχλον H | κ. ταράσσοντες (ΤΑΣΣΟΝΤΕΣ D*) τοὺς ὄχλους οὐ διελίμπανον Dᴮ (*et turbantes multitudinem non cessabant* d syᴾ).

D05 reinforces the action of the Jews from Thessalonica, suggesting that their troubling of Beroea continued over a period of time.

Commentary

[a] 17.10a *The Brethren Send Paul and Silas to Beroea*
17.10 The result of the security given to the authorities by Jason and the other brethren (see 17.9 above) is that Paul and Silas are no longer free to continue their missionary activity in Thessalonica. At the same time, the outcome of their appeal to the politarchs would not have satisfied the Jews, and it is probably to avoid their further persecution that the brethren in Thessalonica now help Paul and Silas to leave the city during the night, getting them away without the Jews being aware of their departure or of their destination. For the first time in the Bezan text, a hint of tension between Paul and Silas is given as the two are named as separate individuals and no longer as united partners of a team. Further evidence for this tension will be seen in the following sequence [C'].

It is to Beroea that they travel, an important town to the west of Thessalonica but, significantly, south of the Via Egnatia that Paul and Silas, in the company of Timothy, had been travelling along toward Rome (see on 16.11–12a above). The action of the brethren, like that of those who will accompany them out of Beroea (see 17.14-15), serves to protect Paul and Silas and yet, at the same time, to divert them from the right route for their journey. In other words, the opposition stirred up by Paul's teaching in the synagogue, and the guarantee extracted from some of the brethren that peace would be maintained, has resulted in his moving away from the path his mission was supposed to be following. It will be a long time before he finally finds his way back on to it.

[b] 17.10b *They Go Straight to the Synagogue*
17.10b Paul's overriding concern with conveying the message concerning Jesus to his fellow-Jews is seen yet again as, despite his experience in Thessalonica, he goes with Silas to the synagogue as soon as they arrive in Beroea. The combination of the participle παραγενόμενοι, 'having reached', and the rare verb ἀπῄεσαν,[67] expresses the intensity of his preoccupation. Note that the synagogue is again referred to as 'the synagogue of the Jews', a sign of Luke's disapproval as he underlines Paul's concern (see also 13.5; 14.1; 17.1).

[c] 17.11 *A Positive Response*
17.11 The activity of Paul and Silas in the synagogue appears to have continued the pattern laid down in Thessalonica (cf. 17.2-3), for here the people present are seen examining the Scriptures in order to find out if what they were saying could be justified. They are favourably compared with the Jews of Thessalonica where, although some were said to have been persuaded by Paul (17.4a), there was a forceful group of Jewish opponents who expended considerable energy in stirring up the townspeople against them (17.5-9). While the Bezan text is absolute in presenting the Beroean Jews as 'noble-minded' and those of Thessalonica as not so, the Alexandrian text makes a more relative presentation, saying simply that those in Beroea were 'more' noble-minded that the others. Their superiority is manifested in their encounters day after day (compared with the three weekly ones in Thessalonica) to study the Scriptures relating to the Messiah that Paul has been discussing.

[c'] 17.12 *Belief and Unbelief*
17.12 The visit of Paul and Silas to the synagogue resulted, if the Alexandrian text is followed, in a notable success – this is the first outcome, which is signalled with the connective μὲν οὖν, anticipating a second signalled with δέ, which is the arrival of Jews from Thessalonica (17.13). According to the Alexandrian text, many of the members believed and they were joined by a good number of Greek women and men from the higher ranks of society, with an emphasis on the women; no negative reaction is noted. In the Bezan text, on the other hand, the account is more nuanced. Some of the synagogue members are said to have believed (rather than 'many') and this positive news is then immediately counter-balanced by the corresponding, parenthetical statement that some did not believe.[68] Moving on, however, to consider the response among

---

67. This is the only occurrence of the verb ἄπειμι in the New Testament, where the prefix ἀπ- expresses the sense of 'they went off' to the synagogue, that is, they did not settle before doing so.

68. δέ links this statement to the context as a parenthesis, and not as the δέ corresponding to μέν of the first clause – this will follow in v. 13.

the Gentiles, the same types of people are mentioned in Codex Bezae, though with an equal consideration given to the men and the women and with a greater number of people estimated. The community of believers that is thus formed in Beroea is a mixed one, made up of both men and women and with a relatively strong representation from the upper social class among the Gentiles.[69]

The same divided response among the Jewish audience was noted in the Bezan text at Thessalonica (where, there too, the number of Gentiles was observed to be particularly large, cf. 17.4a, 4b, 5 in D05). A similar pattern had already been seen in Iconium (14.1) and will be seen again in Ephesus (19.8-9), and finally at Rome (28.24) where Paul will, in the end, accept the futility of giving precedence to the Jews. It may be observed that the pattern is found at each stage of the mission, with the two sets of contrasting verbs πιστεύω ‖ ἀπιστέω (believe ‖ disbelieve) and πείθω ‖ ἀπειθέω (persuade ‖ not persuade) functioning as parallel synonyms, so that in both Iconium (ὥστε πιστεῦσαι ‖ οἱ δὲ ἀπειθήσαντες) and Rome (οἱ μὲν ἐπείθοντο ‖ οἱ δὲ ἠπίστουν), the words are interchangeable. Paul is convinced that if, anywhere in the Empire, he can get the Jews to accept Jesus as the Messiah, this will have an impact on Jews elsewhere and the chain reaction will facilitate the mission to the Gentiles. This had been the hope and expectation set up by such prophecies as Ps. 2.8; Isa. 2.2-4.[70]

[b′] 17.13a *Jews from Thessalonica Come to Beroea*
17.13a The second outcome of the activity of Paul and Silas in the synagogue (17.10-11; cf. the first at 17.12) is that the Jews in Thessalonica heard about it and came to Beroea. In both texts (though in different ways, see *Critical Apparatus*), the cities of Thessalonica and Beroea are set in contrast to each other. The interest of the Thessalonian Jews in what was going on in Beroea explains why Paul and Silas were helped to get out of Thessalonica by night, in an attempt to escape the notice of the local Jews. In the end, they heard about what had happened – the Alexandrian text places the accent on Paul's activity in proclaiming the word of God, which appears to be a simple reference to his preaching the gospel. The Bezan text is more specific: the focus is the word of God, and the fact that it had been proclaimed and believed in Beroea, without any mention of Paul himself. This concern is consistent with what was seen in relation to the trouble caused in Antioch of Pisidia when 'the word of God went through the entire city' (13.43b D05) or when 'the nations received the word of God' (13.48 D05; see *Commentary*,

69. Among those who respond to Paul's teaching are often noted people from the higher social classes, including women (cf. 17.4, 12, 34 D05; 28.7, 17). The Jews likewise, when they seek support for their attacks on him, enlist people of high social standing (cf. 13.50, in Antioch of Pisidia).
70. These texts may be compared with the prophecy from Isaiah cited by Paul and Barnabas when they spoke to the Jews in Antioch of Pisidia: Isaiah (or Israel) is to be a light to the nations, so that he (or the people) will take salvation to the ends of the earth (Isa. 49.6).

13.43b-49). What outraged the Jews (or many of them, since some did believe) was Paul's teaching that with the arrival of the Messiah, Jesus, the time had come for the word of God, the communication between God and people that had hitherto been the exclusive privilege of Israel, to be given to all the nations. Their response in Antioch, as also in Thessalonica (13.44a, cf. 17.5 AT), was to be filled with zeal to defend their heritage and to attack Paul for daring to say that it was for the Gentiles too. What specifically disturbs the Thessalonian Jews, then, is that they hear that 'the word of God', highlighted in the Bezan phrase (see *Critical Apparatus*), had been proclaimed in yet another city, as it had already in Thessalonica, and, moreover, that Gentiles had accepted it. The reference is not to the gospel, for which Codex Bezae uses the phrase 'the word of the Lord' (see *Excursus* 1), but to communication between God and people in a more general sense. The Bezan wording here also underlines the response of the Jews in travelling to Beroea – they did, once they were aware of what was happening, pursue Paul to Beroea.

[a'] 17.13b *They Stir Up the Crowds*

17.13b Once there, they use the same tactics as in Antioch of Pisidia (13.50), Iconium (14.2, 5), Lystra (14.19) and Thessalonica (17.5) of creating a disturbance among the local people, usually referred to as 'the crowds'. The words Luke chooses to describe their stirring up trouble in Beroea are precisely two terms found (in the reverse order) in the account of the opposition of the Gentiles to Paul and Silas in Philippi (16.19-39): ταράσσω ('throw into confusion', 16.20) was used of the preaching activity of Paul and Silas, and σαλεύω (lit. 'shake', 16.26) of the earthquake that was a sign of God's intervention to save them from imprisonment. The first term is found in Psalm 2, which was seen to be a possible paradigm underlying the episode in Philippi, where it is used of the Gentiles who will be punished by YHWH for their combined attack on him (see *Excursus* 10); the two terms are found again in Psalm 48 (47 LXX), again in the context of punishment of the nations that converge against God's people.[71] The irony is powerful: what God had promised to do to the nations because of their attack on 'the Lord and his anointed (his 'Messiah')', Luke portrays the Jews from Thessalonica as doing to the Gentile city of Beroea – as doing so because it was a means to attack Paul and Silas, the representatives of the Messiah. This is not how it was meant to be. The situation demonstrates just how unsuccessful is Paul's plan of trying to win over the Jews in order to to prepare the way for the entry of the Gentiles into Israel, and that his strategy is essentially flawed.

---

71. Cf. Ps. 47.6 LXX: οἱ βασιλεῖς συνέχθησαν ... ἐπὶ τὸ αὐτὸ ... ἐταράχθησαν, ἐσαλεύθησαν.

[C'] 17.14-34 *Greece I: Athens*

Overview

The sequence that presents Paul in Athens is particularly important because it shows his handling of a situation in which his interlocutors are all Gentiles who are capable of discussing with him on his own intellectual level. This is the first time that such a situation has arisen. Only once previously has Paul been portrayed addressing a wholly Gentile audience – that was in Lystra (14.8-18) when he was seen to have considerable difficulty in making himself understood as he struggled to address the local people in language and with concepts that were comprehensible to them (see *Commentary*, 14.11). In this second speech addressed to Gentiles, certain points will be taken up again (notably, the theme of a living God who intervenes in the affairs of the world) and this time, despite a small number of people among the Athenians who show interest or even believe in what Paul is saying, the overall result of his ministry there will be only a limited success. In consequence, he leaves Athens immediately after his speech, for a more congenial place where he will once more find Jews with whom to associate (18.1 D05).

Structure and Themes

A first episode serves as a transition passage, linking the new sequence to the previous one [D'], and providing a degree of overlap between the two sequences. There follow a second and third episode that correspond to each other, as Paul speaks first in an informal setting, and secondly in a more formal one.

[C'-A] 17.14-15 Journey to Athens
  [a] 17.14a   The brethren send Paul away
  [b] 17.14b   Silas remains in Beroea with Timothy
  [c] 17.15a   Men accompany Paul to Athens
  [d] 17.15b   They are forbidden to speak in Thessaly
  [e] 17.15c   Those accompanying Paul go away
[C'-B] 17.16-18 Paul in the synagogue and in the Agora
  [a] 17.16   Paul in a city full of idols
  [b] 17.17   Paul in the synagogue and in the Agora
  [c] 17.18a   Epicurean and Stoic philosophers
  [b'] 17.18b   The Epicureans' opinion of Paul
  [a'] 17.18c   The Stoics' opinion of Paul
[C'-B'] 17.19-34 Paul's Areopagus speech
  [a] 17.19-20 The philosophers take him to the Areopagus
  [b] 17.21   Information about the philosophers
  [c] 17.22-31 Paul's speech
  [c'] 17.32   Contrasting reactions
  [b'] 17.33   Paul leaves them
  [a'] 17.34   Certain people believe

Translation

Codex Bezae D05	Codex Vaticanus B03
[Aa]	**17.14a** So Paul, the brethren sent him off to go away to the sea.	**17.14a** Immediately, the brethren then sent Paul off to continue his journey to the sea.

[b]	**14b** (Silas stayed behind there, however, and Timothy, too.)	**14b** (Silas and Timothy stayed behind there, however.)
[c]	**15a** The people appointed to escort Paul took him as far as Athens.	**15a** The people appointed to escort Paul took him as far as Athens,
[d]	**15b** (He passed round Thessaly, since he was prevented from preaching the word to them.)	
[e]	**15c** Then, having received an order from Paul for Silas and Timothy, that they should come to him quickly, they went away.	**15b** and having received an order for Silas and for Timothy, that they should come to him as quickly as possible, they went away.
[Ba]	**16** While he, Paul, was waiting in Athens, his spirit was exasperated within him because he saw the city was full of idols.	**16** While Paul was waiting for them in Athens, his spirit was exasperated within him as he saw the city full of idols.
[b]	**17** So he debated in the synagogue with the Jews and the God-fearers, and also with the people in the market place, day in and day out, talking to those who chanced to be there.	**17** So he debated in the synagogue with the Jews and the God-fearers, and also in the market place, day in and day out, talking to whoever was passing by.
[c]	**18a** Some, even, of the Epicurean and the Stoic philosophers argued with him;	**18a** Even some of the Epicurean and Stoic philosophers used to argue with him;
[b']	**18b** some said, 'Whatever is this babbler trying to say?';	**18b** some said, 'Whatever is this babbler trying to say?';
[a']	**18c** others said, 'He seems to be a herald of foreign deities'.	**18c** others said, 'He seems to be a herald of foreign deities' (because he was announcing the good news about Jesus and about the resurrection).
[B'a]	**19** After some days, they took him and presented him to the Areopagus, enquiring and saying, 'May we know what is this new teaching proclaimed by you? **20** – for you bring some strange words to our ears;' and, 'We want to know, then, what these words might mean'.	**19** They took him and presented him to the Areopagus, saying, 'May we know what is this new teaching spoken by you? **20** – for you introduce some strange things to our ears;' and, 'We want to know, then, what these things mean'.
[b]	**21** (Now all Athenians, and those foreigners residing among them had no time for anything other than speaking about or listening to the latest novelty.)	**21** (Now all Athenians and the foreigners residing there had no time for anything other than speaking about the latest novelty or listening to it.)
[c]	**22** Paul stood in the middle of the Areopagus and said,	**22** Paul stood in the middle of the Areopagus and said,
[αα]	'Men of Athens, I see how very religious you are in every way,	'Men of Athens, I see how very religious you are in every way,
[αβ]	**23a** for as I was passing along and carefully examining your objects of worship I found among them an altar with the inscription "To an Unknown God".	**23a** for as I was passing along and observing your objects of worship I found among them an altar on which had been written "To an Unknown God".

[αα′] **23b** Well, what you worship in ignorance, this I proclaim to you.

[βα] **24** The God who made the world and everything in it, this God, since he is the Lord of heaven and earth, does not dwell in temples made with hands **25a** nor is he served by human hands as if he had need of anything,

[ββ] **25b** because this God, who gave to all things life and breath and everything, **26** made out of one blood every human nation, to dwell on the face of the earth where he allotted in advance fixed seasons according to the boundaries of their territory; **27** but above all, to seek the divine being – 'if possibly they might grope for it or find it' – though it is not far from any one of us.

[ββ′] **28** For 'In her we live and move and have our being, day by day' – just as some of your own poets have indeed said – 'Of this one, we are the race'.

[βα′] **29** Well, that we are the race of God, we ought not to accept, nor that the divine being is like gold or silver or stone, a sculpted work of human art or human thinking.

[α′α] **30** Now, given that God has turned his eyes away from the times of this ignorance, he now gives the order to men that everyone everywhere to repent

[α′β] **31a** because he has fixed a day to judge the entire world in righteousness by a man, Jesus,

[α′γ] **31b** whom he appointed to bring about faith for everyone, having raised him from the dead.'

[c′] **32** When they heard about a resurrection of the dead, some people started jeering; others, however, said, 'We should like to hear you on this man again'.

[b′] **33** Thereupon Paul left them.

[a′] **34** Some men, however, who joined with him believed, among whom were Dionysius, a certain Areopagite of good standing, and others with them.

23b Well, what you worship in ignorance, this I proclaim to you.

24 The God who made the world and everything in it, this God, seeing as he is the Lord of heaven and earth, does not dwell in temples made with hands **25a** nor is he served by human hands as if he had need of anything

25b since he himself gives to all things life and breath and everything. **26** He made out of one person the whole human race, to dwell on the face of the earth where he allotted fixed epochs and boundaries of their territory; **27** to seek the divine being, – 'if by chance they might grope for him or find him' – and, indeed, he is not far from any one of us.

28 For 'In him we live and move and have our being – just as some of your own poets have indeed said – 'Of this one, we are the offspring'.

29 So, being the offspring of God, we ought not to suppose that the divine being is like gold or silver or stone, a sculpted work of human art and thinking.

30 Now, given that God has looked beyond the times of ignorance, he now declares to men that everyone everywhere should repent

31 because he has fixed a day when he will judge the entire world in righteousness, by a man

whom he appointed, providing proof to all by raising him from the dead.'

32 When they heard about a resurrection of the dead, some people started jeering; others, however, said, 'We should like to hear you again on this man'.

33 Thereupon Paul left them.

34 Some men, however, who had joined with him believed, among whom were Dionysius an Areopagite, and a woman called Damaris and others with them.

Critical Apparatus

The proportion of variant readings in 17.14-15 continues to be high (cf. 17.12-13), with an equal amount of additional and alternative material (see the comparative charts in Read-Heimerdinger, *The Bezan Text*, pp. 11–16).

17.14 Εὐθέως δὲ τότε τὸν Παῦλον ἐξαπέστειλαν οἱ ἀδελφοὶ πορεύεσθαι B 𝔓⁷⁴ ℵ *rell* ‖ Τὸν μὲν οὖν Π. οἱ ἀδ. ἐξ. ἀπελθεῖν D (*statimque Paulum fratres dismiserunt abire* d syᵖ).— ἕως (ἐπὶ τὴν θάλασσαν) B 𝔓⁴⁵ᵛⁱᵈ·⁷⁴ ℵ A E 33. 81. 104. 181. 323. 945. 1175. 1739. 1891 *al* ar e l vg sa boᵐˢˢ ‖ ὡς H L P Ψ 056. 0142. 614 𝔐 syʰ; Chr ‖ *om.* D d 049. 88. 431. 440. 618. 915. 919. 1243. 1518. 2344 *pc* gig syᵖ saᵐˢˢ boᵐˢˢ aeth.

In both texts, Paul becomes the new topic as his name is placed before the verb. B03 underlines the speed with which the brethren reacted to the arrival of the Thessalonian Jews in Beroea (Εὐθέως ... τότε), and marks the new development with the conjunction δέ. D05, in contrast, presents the action of the brethren as the first of two outcomes (μὲν οὖν) resulting from the action of the Thessalonian Jews, which went on for some time (cf. 17.13b), in Beroea; the second will follow in 17.15 (δέ) after a parenthetical statement contrasting Silas and Timothy with Paul. The relationship between the brethren and Paul is indicated in D05 by the juxtaposition of his name and the noun οἱ ἀδελφοί, the latter thus being fronted as the subject of the verb.

The difference in the infinitive reflects a difference in the intention of the brethren in each text: in the AT, they send Paul to continue his journey (πορεύεσθαι, pres.) as far as the sea, ἕως ἐπὶ τὴν θάλασσαν, whereas in the D05 they send him to go away (ἀπελθεῖν, aor.) to the sea (*ad mare versus* d). In both cases, the goal of the journey is the sea; however, with the adverbial modifier ἕως, B03 seems to insinuate that Paul will not actually travel on the sea but, once at the coast, will rather turn south and travel overland to Athens (cf. Ropes, *Text*, p. 164). D05, in contrast, makes no such insinuation and thereby anticipates a journey by sea.

ὑπέμειναν τε B 𝔓⁴⁵·⁷⁴ ℵ 81. 1270*. 2344 (ἐπ- 69. 88. 104. 1837 ǀ ἀπ- E 33. 2344) ǀ ὑπ- δέ 547. 945. 1739. 1891 ǀ ὑπέμενον δέ H L P 056. 1. 226. 330. 440. 618. 927. 1243. 1245. 1646. 1828. 2492 ‖ ὑπέμεινεν δέ D, *substinuit autem* d (τε A 614. 1505. 1611. 2147. 2412. 2495 ǀ -μενεν δέ 049. 323. 1854).— ὅ τε (Σιλᾶς) B 𝔓⁴⁵ ℵ *rell* ‖ ὁ D 𝔓⁷⁴ 6. 326. 1837 *pc*.

The surprising third person singular of D05 indicates that it was Silas who was principally responsible for the decision to stay in Beroea. He nevertheless is not portrayed as forming a united team with Timothy (both names are articular; see Heimerdinger and Levinsohn, 'The Use of the Article', p. 29). In the AT, the verb is plural and, at the same time, the togetherness of Silas and Timothy are indicated by the use of τε ... καί.

The phonetic confusion between τε and δέ has given rise to a number of *vll* in the conjunction linking this clause to the previous one.

17.15 (οἱ δὲ) καθιστάνοντες B 𝔓⁷⁴ A 104 ǀ καθιστῶντες ℵ² (-σπάντες ℵ*) Dᴴ E H L P Ψ 049. 056. 33ᵛⁱᵈ. 1739 𝔐 ‖ καταστανόντες D* 𝔓⁴⁵.

The variation in the verbal form reflects a difference in tense of the verb καθιστάνω (late form of -ίστημι, Zerwick, *Biblical Greek*, §493). B03 has the present participle, and D05 the future (derived from the contract form καταστανῶ, cf. ἀποκαταστανεῖς, future, Acts 1.6 D05; ἀποκαταστανεῖ, future, Mk 9.12 D05). The meaning is 'appoint', 'put in charge' (B-A-G, 2; 'Ceux à qui l'on confiait la charge de Paul l'amenèrent jusqu'à Athènes', Delebecque, *Les deux Actes,* p. 107).

The participle has the force of a purpose clause (cf. Zerwick, *Biblical Greek,* §284: 'The question may be raised, whether the present participle may not at times stand for the future one indicating the end in view'). Cf. 15.27 where the present participle is also used in B03 in place of a future to express purpose.

The Majority text does have a different verb, καθιστάω, with a similar meaning, ('hinstellen, vorführen', Mayser I, III, p. 223.8-11).

παρῆλθεν δὲ τὴν Θεσσαλίαν· ἐκωλύθη γὰρ εἰς αὐτοὺς κηρύξαι τὸν λόγον D, *transiit vero Thessaliam: vetatus est enim super eos praedicare sermonem* d; (ˢEphr) ‖ *om.* B 𝔓⁴⁵·⁷⁴ ℵ *rell.*

The reading of D05 is by no means impossible (*pace* Boismard and Lamouille, II, p. 121): for a third time, Paul is prevented (by God, divine passive) from preaching the word in Thessaly and so by-passes the region without stopping there, going to Athens instead round the coast by boat: 'Le préverbe implique un itinéraire qui longe la côte, apparemment par mer' (Delebecque, *Les deux Actes,* p. 340).

καὶ λαβόντες ἐντολήν B 𝔓⁷⁴ ℵ *rell* Ι κ. λαβ. ἐπιστολὴν παρ' αὐτοῦ E ‖ λαβ. δὲ ἐντολὴν παρὰ Παύλου D, *ut accepissent mandatum a Paulo* d.

The subject of the new clause continues uninterrupted in B03, which therefore links it with καί to the previous one. In D05, however, there has been an intervening parenthetical clause and so this new sentence begins a new development with δέ. D05 further makes it clear that the order the people from Beroea receive comes from Paul.

τὸν (Τιμόθεον) B 𝔓⁴⁵ ℵ E 33. 81. 1243. 1270. 2344 ‖ *om.* D 𝔓⁷⁴ A H L P Ψ 049. 056. 614. 1739 𝔐.

B03 continues to view Silas and Timothy as separate individuals. D05 at this point sees them from Paul's point of view, as a pair of co-workers who are ordered to undertake an action together.

ἵνα ὡς τάχιστα (ἔλθωσιν) B 𝔓⁷⁴ ℵ *rell, ut quam celeriter* d ‖ ὅπως ἐν τάχει D (gig).

The B03 construction of ἐντολή ... ἵνα + subjunctive, instead of the more usual infinitive in Hellenistic Greek, is also found at Jn 13.34; 15.12; 1 Jn 3.23 ℵ01; 4.21; 2 Jn 6. It has the force of an imperative here (Zerwick, *Biblical Greek,* §415). The construction of ὅπως + subjunctive in D05 underlines the purpose of Paul's instructions.

The B03 reading ὡς τάχιστα is unique in the New Testament. Luke often uses, on the other hand, the D05 reading of ἐν τάχει: Lk. 18.8; Acts 10.33 D05; 12.7; 22.18; 25.4.

17.16 (ἐκδεχομένου) αὐτοὺς τοῦ Παύλου B 𝔓⁷⁴ ℵ² A Dᶜ *rell* ‖ αὐτοῦ τ. Παύ. D*, (*[expectante]eo Paulum* d!) syᴾ ‖ αὐτοῦ ℵ*.

τοῦ Παύλου in D05 stands in apposition to the pronoun αὐτοῦ of the genitive absolute; ℵ01* omits the apposition; B03 corrects αὐτοῦ to αὐτούς, causing τοῦ Παύλου to be the subject of the genitive absolute, in an awkward position.

τὸ (πνεῦμα) B 𝔓⁴⁵·⁷⁴ ℵ Dᴰ/ᶜ *rell* ‖ *om.* D*.

The omission of the article in D05* is due to homoioteleuton: ΠΑΡΩΞΥΝΕ-ΤΟΤΟ.

(αὐτῷ) θεωροῦντος B ℵ A E 33. 81. 104. 323. (614). 927. 945. 1175. 1270. 1739. 1828. 1891 *al* ‖ -ντι D H L P Ψ 049. 056 𝔐.

The genitive θεωροῦντος in B03 agrees with τοῦ Παύλου, which was taken as the subject of the initial genitive absolute; D05 takes the participle as in apposition to ἐν αὐτῷ.

17.17 τοῖς (ἐν τῇ ἀγορᾷ) D, *his (qui in foro)* d 383. 614. 1799. 2147. 2412 syʰᵐᵍ sa ‖ *om.* B 𝔓⁴⁵ᵛⁱᵈ·⁷⁴ ℵ *rell.*— (πρὸς τοὺς) παρατυγχάνοντας B 𝔓⁴⁵·⁷⁴ ℵ Dᶜ *rell* ‖ -τυχόντας D* (*et his qui forte aderant* d).

With the dative articular pronoun, D05 first identifies a third group of people Paul used to debate with as those in the Agora; they are then identified more closely, as those who happened to be there, with the preposition πρός marking the more personal connection as the narrator becomes more specific (Read-Heimerdinger, *The Bezan Text*, pp. 176–82), and moves away from the synagogue to concentrate on Paul's debates in the market-place.

According to B03, Paul used to debate with those passing by (παρατυγ-χάνοντας, pres. part.); according to D05, it is those who happened to have come there (παρατυχόντας, aor. part.), a more permanent group.

17.18 τῶν (Στοϊκῶν) D H P L 049. 056. 614. 1739ᶜ 𝔐 ‖ *om.* B 𝔓⁷⁴ ℵ E Ψ 33. 81. 104. 440. 945. 1175. 1270. 1505. 1611. 1739*. 1891. 2147. 2344. 2495.

With the repetition of the article, D05 takes care to distinguish between the two groups of philosophers, in anticipation of the distinct opinions belonging to each that are about to be cited.

συνέβαλλον (αὐτῷ) B 𝔓⁷⁴ ℵ Dᴬ *rell* ‖ -βαλον Dᶜʲ· (-ΛΑΒΟΝ D*) L 36. 69. 181. 226ᶜ. 330. 431. 453. 547. 614. 913. 1245. 1505. 1518. 1611. 1739. 1799. 1891. 1898. 2138. 2401. 2412. 2492*. 2495; Chr Theoph Aug.

The imperfect of B03 implies that apart from the passers-by (cf. 17.17), some of the philosophers used to argue with him as well, on repeated occasions. The original hand of D05 inverted the consonants в and ʌ by metathesis, which D^A corrected but at the same time changed the aorist to the imperfect, following the AT reading. The aorist refers to people among those who happened to be in the Agora, and who had arguments with Paul.

(τί ἄν) θέλοι B 𝔓⁷⁴ ℵ *rell* $D^{H?}$ ‖ θέλῃ D* | θέλει 33. 2412.

B03 has the optative of θέλω (*optativus potentialis*, see B-D-R, §385.1 and cf. 17.20 D05, below), where D05 has the subjunctive.

(εἶναι), ὅτι τὸν Ἰησοῦν καὶ τὴν Ἀνάστασιν εὐηγγελίζετο B ℵ* E L P Ψ 049. 056. 6. 36. 226. 330. 440. 453. 547. 618. 1175. 1241. 1243. 1646ᶜ *al* syʰ sa (+ αὐτοῖς 𝔓⁷⁴ ℵ² A E 33. 1739 𝔐 vg syᵖ bo) ‖ *om.* D d gig; Aug.

The B03 clause (a gloss probably derived from 17.31) implies perhaps that Paul's audience (in particular the Stoics) have interpreted Ἀνάστασις as a feminine deity parallel to Jesus (Metzger, *Commentary*, p. 455; but see the objections to this idea in Barrett, II, p. 831). According to Boismard and Lamouille (II, p. 122), 'l'addition s'inspire peut-être de 4,2'. D05 omits this gloss.

17.19 Ἐπιλαβόμενοι δὲ (αὐτοῦ) B Ψ 33. 36. 81. 453. 1241. 1837. 2344 *al* | ἐπιλαβόμενοί τε ℵ A E H L P 049. 056. 1739 𝔐 ‖ Μετὰ δὲ ἡμέρας τινὰς ἐπιλ. D (*Post dies aliquos adpraehensumque eum* d) 257. 383. 1799. 2147 (+ τε 614. 2412) syʰ**.— ἐπὶ τὸν Ἄρειον πάγου ἤγαγον B 𝔓⁷⁴ ℵ *rell* ‖ ἤγ. αὐτὸν ἐπὶ (+ τὸν D^B) Ἄρ. πάγ. D*, *adduxerunt ad Arium Pagum* d (1518) gig; Chr.— πυνθανόμενοι καὶ (λέγοντες) D, *cogitantes et* d ‖ *om.* B 𝔓⁷⁴ ℵ *rell*.

The time detail in D05 is typical of the introduction to a new episode, here marking the beginning of the episode [C'-B] within the wider sequence [C'] concerning Paul in Athens. It presents Paul's stay in Athens as continuing over a certain length of time.

The word order of B03 accords importance to the location of the Areopagus, which is at the same time treated, by the retention of the article, as a known or expected place. The single object pronoun αὐτοῦ for two verbs which govern different cases (genitive and accusative) is unusual in Luke's writing, but comparable instances are found when the first verb is one involving the idea of arrest (see Read-Heimerdinger, 'The Tracking of Participants', pp. 444–46).

D05 focuses more on the action of the philosophers with respect to Paul, repeating the object pronoun as a means to underline their seizing of him and their taking him away; furthermore, it presents the Areopagus as of some significance, drawing attention to the seriousness with which the philosophers viewed Paul. The additional participle πυνθανόμενοι enables the words of the two schools to continue to be distinguished (cf. 17.18b, 18c).

αὕτη (ὑπὸ σοῦ) B D 1243. 1799 *pc* ‖ αὕτη ἡ 𝔓⁷⁴ ℵ *rell*.— λαλουμένη (διδαχή) B 𝔓⁷⁴ ℵ A H L P Ψ 049. 056. 33. 1739 𝔐 ‖ λεγομ- E 81 vg ‖ καταγγελλομ- D, *narratio* d syᵖ.

The omission of the article ἡ after αὕτη by both B03 and D05 could be due to haplography. On the other hand, it is superfluous, except in so far as the phrase it introduces, ἡ ὑπὸ σοῦ λαλουμένη/καταγγελλομένη, is considered to be in apposition to ἡ καινὴ αὕτη ... διδαχή.

The verb καταγγέλλω of which D05 reads the participle has the force of 'proclaim', missing from the weaker verb λαλέω.

17.20 (τινὰ) εἰσφέρεις (-ρει ℵ* *pc* ‖ φέρεις Ψ 522. 917) B 𝔓⁷⁴ ℵ² *rell* ‖ φέρεις ῥήματα D (*adferens interlocutiones* d) sa bo ‖ ῥήματα εἰσφέρεις E.

The prefix εἰς- of the compound verb in B03 anticipates the preposition before the noun τὰς ἀκοάς. With the neuter noun ῥήματα as the direct object of the verb in D05, in addition to the neuter adjective ξενίζοντα, the force of the prefix is unnecessary.

τίνα θέλει (ταῦτα) B 𝔓⁷⁴ ℵ A Ψ (33). 36. 81. 945. 1175. 1739 *al* ‖ τί ἂν θέλοι D, *quid nunc sibi vellint* d E H L P 049. 056 𝔐.

The neuter plural τίνα in B03 is the subject of the verb θέλει (B-D-R, §299, n. 1), where the indicative expresses the potential sense (B-D-R, §385, n. 1). In D05, the neuter singular τι corresponds to the predicate (B-D-R, §299,1), and the optative (ἂν θέλοι) expresses the indirect rhetorical question (B-D-R, §385, n. 2); cf. τί ἂν θέλοι, 17.18 B03.

17.21 (ἐπιδημοῦντες) εἰς αὐτούς D ‖ *om.* B 𝔓⁷⁴ ℵ *rell* d.

The prepositional phrase in D05 has the function of clearly distinguishing between the Athenians (the Epicureans) and the foreigners among them (the Stoics).

τι (καινότερον) B 𝔓⁷⁴ ℵ A Ψ 104 *pc* sy ‖ *om.* D d E H L P 049. 056. 33. 1739 𝔐 (gig); Aug.

The repetition of τι in B03 enhances the distinction between the two activities: speaking (corresponding to the Epicureans) and listening (corresponding to the Stoics; see *Commentary*).

17.22 ὁ Παῦλος D 𝔓⁷⁴ E H L P Ψ 049. 056. 33. 1739 𝔐 ‖ Παῦλος B ℵ A 326. 1245. 1837 *pc*; Theoph.— ἔφη B D 𝔓⁷⁴ A *rell* ‖ εἶπεν ℵ E.

The article before the name of Paul in D05 is expected since he has always been in focus throughout this scene. B03 typically omits the article before major speeches (Read-Heimerdinger, *The Bezan Text*, p. 135).

The imperfect ἔφη is used to introduce a speech elsewhere in Acts (7.2, Stephen; 10.28, Peter; 10.30, Cornelius; 11.28 D05, Agabus; 19.25 D05, Demetrius). The justification for the imperfect is clear in most instances (Stephen begins a long and complex speech; Peter and Cornelius find themselves in a difficult situation where they express themselves hesitantly; Demetrius carefully seeks for a way to persuade his fellow craftsmen of the problem posed by Paul). Here before the Areopagus, where Paul addresses a large Gentile audience whom he has never addressed successfully before, the imperfect expresses aptly his lack of assurance.

17.23 ἀναθεωρῶν (τὰ σεβάσματα) B 𝔓⁷⁴ ℵ Dᴱ *rell, perspiciens* d ‖ διϊστορῶν D*; (ἱστορῶν Cl)ᵖᵗ.

The verb διϊστορέω in D05 is a *hapax legomenon* of the New Testament, expressing not only a close examination, as ἀναθεωρέω of B03, but also a quest for information (Delebecque, *Les deux Actes*, p. 108: 'cherchant à me renseigner sur').

(ἐν ᾧ) ἐπεγέγραπτο B 𝔓⁷⁴ ℵ *rell* ‖ ἦν (Dᴮ) γεγραμμένον D, *scriptum erat* d.

The periphrastic perfect of D05 reflects better the permanence of the inscription than does the pluperfect of B03.

ὃ ... τοῦτο B D 𝔓⁷⁴ ℵ* A* (81). 1175 *pc* lat; Or ‖ ὃν ... τοῦτον ℵ² A² E Ψ 33. 1739 𝔐 sy; Cl Aug.

The reading of B03/D05 anticipates the neuter τὸ θεῖον of 17.27 D05, 29.

17.24 (γῆς) ὑπάρχων κύριος B 𝔓⁷⁴ ℵ A E 33. 69. 81. 88. 181. 242. 323. 431. 467ᶜ. 522. 614. 915. 927. 945. 1175. 1270. 1739. 1891. 1898. 2298. 2344, 2412 *al* gig vg; Theoph ‖ κ. ὑπ. D, *dominus qui est* d H L P 049. 056. 33. 1739 𝔐; Irˡᵃᵗ Cl.

The position of κύριος following the participle in B03 presents the notion of the lordship of God as new information; its position preceding the participle in D05 stresses rather the causal nature of Paul's argument, which depends on his audience's prior acceptance of the lordship of God ('*since* he is Lord').

17.25 ὡς (προσδεόμενος) ℵ* 104. 1829. 1838, *tamquam* d e gig; Irˡᵃᵗ ‖ *om.* B D 𝔓⁷⁴ ℵ² A E H L P Ψ 049. 056. 33. 1739 𝔐.— (προσδεόμενός) τινος B 𝔓⁷⁴ ℵ (τι Dᴴ) *rell* ‖ *om.* D* d 1646 *pc*.

The presence of ὡς in ℵ01 and d5 makes clear the force of the participle προσδεόμενος.

The omission of τινός in D05 could be due to homoioteleuton. The line is exceptionally short in both D05 and the Latin page d5.

αὐτὸς διδοὺς (πᾶσιν) B 𝔓⁷⁴ Dᴮ *rell* ‖ ὅτι (– Dˢ·ᵐ·) οὗτος ὁ δούς D* (*quod ipse dederit* d).

B03 views the participial clause as qualifying the previous one in a relationship of reason. The clause refers to the subject (God) with the emphatic pronoun αὐτός and uses the present participle διδούς, in apposition to προσδεόμενος, to refer to his ongoing activity of creating and sustaining life. D05 views the participial clause as subordinate to a new clause, which is linked with ὅτι to the previous one and has the finite verb ἐποίησεν (see next variant).

17.26 (ἐποίησέν) τε B 𝔓⁷⁴ ℵ *rell* ‖ *om.* D d E vg^OS sa bo.

B03 begins a new clause with the verb ἐποίησεν, linking it with τε to the previous clause; in D05, the verb ἐποίησεν is the finite verb of the clause introduced with ὅτι (see previous variant).

ἐξ ἑνός B 𝔓⁷⁴ ℵ A 33. 81. 181. 323. 536. 1175. 1739. 1891. 1898 c dem p ph ro w vg sa^mss bo (aeth); Cl ‖ ἐξ ἑνὸς αἵματος D, *ex uno sanguine* d E H L P 049. 056. 614 𝔐 ar e gig vg^D sy^p.h; Ir^lat Chr Ephr Thret Beda^gr mss aac. to ‖ ἐξ ἑνὸς στόματος Ψ.— (πᾶν ἔθνος) ἀνθρώπων B 𝔓⁷⁴ ℵ *rell, hominum* d ‖ -ου D.

B03 leaves the referent of ἑνός undefined; it probably means 'one person' (masc. gen.), rather than one nation (neut. gen.). D05, with a wide range of support, specifies the referent as 'blood', making it clear that a person rather than a nation is intended. The phrase πᾶν ἔθνος ἀνθρώπων in B03 could be taken to mean 'the whole human race', in line with Stoic teaching (Zerwick and Grosvenor, *Analysis,* p. 410). The singular ἀνθρώπου in D05 tallies with αἵματος in the previous phrase, and concords with the biblical idea of God creating every separate nation.

προστεταγμένους (καιρούς) B 𝔓⁷⁴ ℵ Dᴬ *rell, imperata* d ‖ προτετ- D* 323. 629. 1022. 1270. 1799. 1898 *pc* bo; (Ir^lat).— καὶ τὰς ὁροθεσίας B 𝔓⁷⁴ ℵ Dᴱ *rell, et determinationes* d ‖ κατὰ ὁροθεσίαν D*; Ir^lat.

The prefix προ- in D05 expresses the notion 'in advance'. B03 has God fixing the seasons, or epochs, and the boundaries of human habitation on the earth. D05 connects the two, saying that God fixed the seasons depending on the boundaries, that is, according to where people live.

17.27 ζητεῖν τὸν θεόν B 𝔓⁷⁴ ℵ A H L Ψ 049. 056. (33^illeg·). 36. 81. 88. 181. 307. 453. 610. 614. 945. 1175. (1505). 1678. 1739. 1891. 2147. 2344. (2495) ar^(2) c dem p ph ro^(2) (w) vg^(mss) (sy^p.h) sa bo; Chr ‖ ζητ. τ. κύριον E P 𝔐 e ‖ μάλιστα ζητ. τὸ θεῖόν ἐστιν D (*quaerere quod divinum est* d gig; Ir^lat Cl Ambr).

Between ζητεῖν and τὸ θεῖόν ἐστιν a word has been omitted in D05 through haplography, either τί (Zahn, p. 616, n. 74) or ὅ (Delebecque, *Les deux Actes,* p. 108). Metzger (*Commentary,* p. 405) refers to two suggestions for changing τό to ὅ, or eliminating ἐστίν. The explanation that τὸ θεῖον was written under the influence of its occurrence in 17.29b is unsatisfactory, for it is in fact part of a wider unit of variation, to which belongs also the neuter pronoun αὐτό in the following conditional clause, and the neuter participle ὄν in the final concessive clause of the verse. Furthermore, the term ὁ θεός is used at 17.29a between this occurrence of τὸ θεῖον and the next one. It is more likely that τὸ θεῖον was altered to τὸν θεον because τὸ θεῖον was felt to be too vague as a reference to the one true God.

(εἰ ἄρα) ψηλαφήσειαν (-ειεν ℵ E 049ᶜ. 104. 2492 | -αιεν 1739)... εὕροιεν B 𝔓⁷⁴ ℵ *rell*; Cl ‖ ψηλαφήσαισαν ... εὕροισαν (-ιεν Dˢ·ᵐ·) D*.— αὐτόν B 𝔓⁷⁴ ℵ *rell* ‖ αὐτό D, *illud* d (gig); Irˡᵃᵗ.— καὶ (εὕροιεν) B ℵ E H L P 049. 056. 33 𝔐 ‖ ἢ (εὕροισαν D*) D 𝔓⁷⁴ A Ψ 36. 323. 431. 453. 945. 1175. 1739. 1891. 1898. 2298 *pc* lat saᵐˢˢ; Irˡᵃᵗ Cl.

For the optative third plural ending -σαν, see Mayser, I, II, pp. 88.18-22, 28, 34, 44; 89.3-4. B03 conjoins the two verbs with καί, whereas D05 presents them as alternatives with ἤ.

αὐτό in D05 agrees with τὸ θεῖον (see above).

καί γε B Dˢ·ᵐ· H L P Ψ 049. 056. 33 𝔐 | καίτοιγε ℵ 242. 323. 522. 945. 1270. 1739. 1891. 2298 *al*; Irˡᵃᵗ Oecumˡᵃᵗ ‖ καίτοι Dᶜʲ· (ΚΑΙΤΕ D*) 𝔓⁷⁴ A E 1891 *pc* bo; Cl.— οὐ μακρὰν ἀπὸ (ἀφ’ E 1739 *al*) ἑνὸς ἑκάστου ἡμῶν (ὑμῶν A* L 69. 1505. 2344) ὑπάρχοντα (-ος E 1828; Cl | ἀπέχοντα 945. 1739. 1891) B 𝔓⁷⁴ ℵ A E H L P 049. 056. 33ᵛⁱᵈ. 1739 𝔐; Cl | οὐκ ἀπὸ μακρὰν ἑνὸς ἐκ. ὑμῶν ὑπ. Ψ ‖ οὐ μακρὰν ὂν ἀφ’ ἑνὸς ἐκ. ἡμῶν (+ ὑπάρχων Dᴱ) D* (*non longe ab unoquoque nostrorum* d); Irˡᵃᵗ ᵛⁱᵈ.

B03 reinforces the possibility of seeking and finding God with an emphatic affirmation that he is not far from people; D05 qualifies the possibility with a clause of concession, this being Paul's own reflexion on the words he has just cited from a Greek author (see *Commentary* for this suggestion).

The present participle ὂν in D05 agrees with τὸ θεῖον (see above). B03 reads the accusative masculine participle ἀπέχοντα in its place, agreeing with τὸν θεόν.

17.28 (’Εν) αὐτῷ B 𝔓⁷⁴ ℵ Dᶜ⁇ *rell* ‖ αὐτῇ D*.— (ἐσμὲν) τὸ καθ’ ἡμέραν D, *diurnum* d gig aeth; Irˡᵃᵗ Ambst Pac Ambr Pel Aug ‖ *om.* B 𝔓⁷⁴ ℵ *rell* lat sy co; Cl Or Iosip Chr Hier.

The feminine αὐτῇ of D05* refers to a feminine divinity and is used in a citation from a Greek writer (in his own words, Paul uses the neuter τὸ θεῖον, cf. v. 29). This quotation goes from ’Εν αὐτῇ γάρ to τὸ καθ’ ἡμέραν.

ὡς καί τινες τῶν καθ’ ἡμᾶς ποιητῶν (εἰρήκασιν) B 𝔓⁷⁴ 049. 326. 614. 1646ᶜ. 1837. 2412. (2344) *pc*; Did? / ... ὑμᾶς... ℵ A E H L P Ψ 056. 1739 𝔐 lat syᵖ·ʰ sa bo; Cl Or Iosip Chr Hier | κ. ὡς τινὲς τῶν καθ’ ὑμᾶς Irˡᵃᵗ ‖ ὥσπερ καὶ τῶν καθ’ ὑμᾶς τινες D, *sicut qui secundum vos sunt quidam* d gig aeth; Irˡᵃᵗ Ambst Pac Ambr Pel Aug.

The word order variation arises because of the presence (B03) or absence (D05) of the noun ποιητῶν. The first person pronoun ἡμᾶς has probably arisen through itacism.

Τοῦ (γάρ) B 𝔓⁷⁴ ℵ Dˢ·ᵐ· *rell*; Cl ‖ τούτου D*, *huius* d 88. 618 *al* (τοῦτο 614. 2344).

The quotation in B03 is presented as separate from the previous one: Τοῦ γὰρ καὶ γένος ἐσμέν, where the articular pronoun is used as a demonstrative (Zerwick and Grosvenor, *Analysis*, p. 411, 'τοῦ *of him*; ὁ as demonstrative prn archaic'). The quotation is a literal quotation from a hexameter by the Stoic poet Aratus (c. 270 BCE) dedicated to Zeus, *Phainomena*, 5: Πάντη δὲ Διὸς κεχρήμεθα πάντες· τοῦ γὰρ καὶ γένος ἐσμέν. In contrast, according to D05, the pronoun τούτου refers to τὸ θεῖον and serves to introduce a second quotation, probably from Cleantes (332–31 BCE; *Hymn to Zeus*, 4: ἐκ σοῦ γὰρ γένος ἐσμέν, ἑνὸς μίμημα λαχόντες μοῦνον, ὅσα ζώει τε καὶ ἕρπει θνήτ' ἐπὶ γαῖαν).

17.29 χρυσῷ B D^s.m. H L P Ψ 049. 056. 614. 1739 𝔐 | χρυσίῳ ℵ 𝔓^41.74 A E 104. 326. 1270. 1837. 2344 *pc* ‖ οὔτε χρυσῷ D*, *neque auro* d.— (ἢ) ἀργύρῳ B D ℵ H L P Ψ 049. 056. 614. 1739 𝔐 ‖ -ίῳ 𝔓^41.74 A E 33^vid. 36. 104. 453. 1270. 2344 *pc*.

By means of the correlating particles οὐκ ... οὔτε D05 presents Paul as distancing himself from the first notion (γένος οὖν ὑπάρχοντες τοῦ θεοῦ οὐκ ὀφείλομεν νομίζειν) as much as from the second (οὔτε χρυσῷ ἢ ... ἢ ... τὸ θεῖον εἶναι ὅμοιον). The omission of οὔτε in B03 causes Paul to agree with the sentence attributed to Aratus (γένος οὖν ὑπάρχοντες τοῦ θεοῦ) and the negative clause, οὐκ ὀφείλομεν νομίζειν, prepares for the series of alternatives: χρυσῷ ἢ ... ἢ ... τὸ θεῖον εἶναι ὅμοιον.

καὶ ἐνθυμήσεως ἀνθρώπου B ℵ A E H L P Ψ 049. 056. 33^vid. 614. 1739 𝔐, *et cupiditatis humanae* d ‖ ἢ ἐνθ. ἀνθ. D bo; Ir^lat Chr | *om.* 𝔓^74.

D05 makes a point of distinguishing between an engraved work of art and human thought, so giving salience to the activity of the philosophers.

17.30 (τῆς ἀγνοίας) ταύτης D* *huius* d (τὰ τῆς 1646. 1891) vg ‖ *om.* B 𝔓^74 D^s.m. ℵ *rell.*— ὑπεριδὼν B 𝔓^74 ℵ D^D *rell* ‖ παρ- D*, *despiciens* d vg.

The demonstrative in D05 makes it clear that Paul is referring specifically to the wrong thinking and practices he has been talking about in his speech so far.

The prefix ὑπερ- in B03 conveys the idea of God looking beyond the times of ignorance to the time when he would order people to repent; the prefix in D05 expresses rather the notion of God turning his eyes away from the times of ignorance. Delebecque (*Les deux Actes*, pp. 108–109) suggests the translation 'passant le regard au-delà' for B03 and 'détournant les yeux' for D05.

(τὰ νῦν) ἀπαγγέλλει B ℵ* 915 ar, *adnuntiat* d e gig ph vg bo^?; Ath^pt ‖ παραγγέλλει D 𝔓^41.74 ℵ^2 A E L P Ψ 049. 056. 614. 1739 𝔐 m sy^p.h sa; Ir^lat Ath^pt Cyr | παραγγελεῖ H 330. 1646. 1891. 2344.— (τοῖς ἀνθρώποις) πάντας B 𝔓^41.74 ℵ D^D A E 1175. 2344 | πᾶσιν H L P Ψ 049. 056. 614. 1739 𝔐 ‖ ἵνα πάντες D*, *ut omnes* d gig vg.

The verb ἀπαγγέλλω in B03 does not have the imperative force of the D05 verb παραγγέλλω.

πάντας in B03 is the subject of the infinitive μετανοεῖν ; D05 has ἵνα followed by the infinitive instead of the more usual subjunctive: 'wie nahe in solchen Begerungssätzen der Infinitiv und ὅπως (ἵνα) mit Konjunktiv berühren, begegnet in anakolutischer Weise nach ὅπως (ἵνα) der Infinitiv' (Mayser, II, 1, p. 257).

17.31 (ἡμέραν) ἐν ᾗ μέλλει B 𝔓⁴¹·⁷⁴ ℵ *rell* ‖ *om.* D d, sa bo^mss; Ir^lat Aug Spec.—
κρίνειν B 𝔓⁴¹·⁷⁴ ℵ *rell* ‖ κρῖναι D, *iudicare* d 522 *pc* gig; Meth.

The present infinitive in B03 completes the auxiliary verb μέλλει; in D05, however, the aorist infinitive expresses purpose (cf. Lk. 9.16; 10.40; Delebecque, *Les deux Actes*, p. 196).

(ἐν δικαιοσύνῃ), ἐν ἀνδρί B 𝔓⁴¹·⁷⁴ ℵ *rell*, lat sy^p.h sa bo aeth; Or^lat Athan Chr Cyr Proc Nest Thret Ambr Aug ‖ ἀνδρί, Ἰησοῦ D ar (*in viro Iesu* d vg^D); Ir^lat.—
(πίστιν) παρασχών B 𝔓⁷⁴ ℵ *rell* ‖ παρασχεῖν (-ΕΣ- D*) D, *exhibere* d gig.

According to B03, the first clause ἐν ἀνδρὶ ᾧ ὥρισεν is the equivalent of ἐν ἀνδρὶ ὃν ὥρισεν, where the dative pronoun is used by attraction to the antecedent. The same explanation for the dative pronoun is valid for D05, but the construction there is rather: ἀνδρί, Ἰησοῦ, ὃν ὥρισεν, where 'Jesus' stands in apposition to 'a man' and is the subject of the aorist infinitive παρασχεῖν (an action which it is his purpose to accomplish, just as with the infinitive κρῖναι; see Delebecque, *Les deux Actes*, p. 268).

17.32 περὶ τούτου καὶ πάλιν B 𝔓⁷⁴ ℵ A 33. 945. 1175. 1739. 1891. 2344 ‖ π. τ. πάλιν D, *de hoc iterum* d E gig vg | πάλιν π. τ. H L P Ψ 049. 056. 614 𝔐.

D05 lacks the emphatic adverb καί.

17.34 κολληθέντες (αὐτῷ) B 𝔓⁷⁴ ℵ D^D *rell, cum <ha>esitassent* d vg ‖ ἐκολλήθησαν D* gig.— Ἀρεοπαγίτης B ‖ τις Ἀρ. D, *quis Areopagita* d h vg^C | ὁ Ἀρ. 𝔓^74vid ℵ A E H L P Ψ 049. 056. 33^vid. 1739 𝔐.— καὶ γυνὴ (+ τίμια E) ὀνόματι Δάμαρις B 𝔓⁷⁴ ℵ A E *rell* ‖ εὐσχήμων D, *conplacens* d e.

cum haesitassent in d5 translates κολληθέντες, taking the verb *haesito* in the literal sense of '*stick fast, remain fixed* in a place'. Although it is possible to understand the two finite verbs as being linked asyndetically in D05* – ἐκολλήθησαν αὐτῷ, ἐπίστευσαν – it could also be that the original copyist accidentally omitted a relative pronoun <οἳ> before ἐκολλήθησαν. On this reading, in D05 as in B03, the men who joined with Paul and believed are among those Stoics who had asked to hear him again.

Both B03 and D05 consider Dionysius to be a member of the Areopagus council, but with τις D05 accords him the role of being a representative. ℵ01 and the rest of the MSS go further by portraying him, with the article, as a supreme example of an Areopagite. While D05 qualifies him as being of good standing, εὐσχήμων, B03 adds the name of a woman, Damaris.

Commentary

[C'-A] 17.14-15 *Journey to Athens*

The structure of this introductory episode is linear, the successive steps of the transition from Beroea to Athens following the progress of Paul's journey.

[a] 17.14a *The Brethren Send Paul Away*

17.14a In order to avoid a crisis such as was provoked in Thessalonica, the brethren get Paul away this time before the Jews have opportunity to take them to the city authorities. The Alexandrian text in particular underlines the haste with which they acted. The escape route they have in mind is by sea, perhaps with the idea that it would be harder for would-be pursuers to catch him if he were not on land. The sea, as often in Luke's work, contains the notion of a personal exodus, whereby Paul on this occasion would be moving away from his strategy of concentrating his proclamation of the gospel in Jewish circles, which had entrapped him and was preventing him from reaching the Gentiles. In view of the positive connotations of the sea, the intention of the brethren in Beroea is to be interpreted as being to get Paul back on the *Via Egnatia*, which he had left by coming to Beroea when he had had to flee from Thessalonica (cf. 16.10). If he crossed the sea from the closest point to Beroea, he could have headed north-eastwards to pick up the road close to Thessalonica once more, and from there continue the journey he had started towards Rome (see *Commentary*, 16.6-10).

[b] 17.14b *Silas Remains in Beroea with Timothy*

17.14b At the point when Paul leaves Beroea, a tension between Paul and his fellow travellers is felt, not for the first time. A hint had been given in the Bezan text already at the beginning of the previous episode, when the brethren sent Paul and Silas to Beroea: until that moment, Paul and Silas had always been mentioned jointly, as forming a united pair, but then were identified separately (see *Critical Apparatus*, 17.10). In the Alexandrian text, the decision to stay behind in Beroea is taken by Silas and Timothy together, whereas in Codex Bezae the decision is imputed to Silas alone, and Timothy follows suit. The result in any case is that Paul will now be entirely on his own, which is not what the Holy Spirit intended at the start of the mission from Antioch (cf. 13.2, 4), nor what Paul himself had intended when he left Antioch for a second time (cf. 15.40). His isolation will prove to be a dangerous thing for, as will be seen straightaway, Paul will turn away from the road to Rome to head in the opposite direction.

[c] 17.15a *Men Accompany Paul to Athens*

17.15a People from Beroea accompany Paul on his journey. These men may have perhaps been chosen to accompany him to make sure that he gets well away from the places where he has caused trouble and where problems could be started up again by the Jews opposed to his teaching and his activities among the Gentiles. However, if the plan of the church in Beroea had been for Paul to go back towards the road to Rome, his escorts are not successful in keeping him to the plan since he is next seen going southwards.[72] Although stopping in Athens means that he will be confronting a Gentile environment, which will be a positive step, on the other hand, all of this sequence in Athens, and then the next sequence in Corinth (18.1-23), will be holding him back from continuing his journey to Rome.

Athens was a relatively prosperous, cosmopolitan city in the part of Greece referred to as Achaia, holding on to its reputation as a centre of learning and a place where philosophical ideas and religious practices proliferated and were explored in a thriving atmosphere of enquiry and debate.

[d] 17.15b *They Are Forbidden to Speak in Thessaly*
17.15b A narrative aside is included only in the Bezan text, to the effect that Paul was not allowed to preach in Thessaly, the region immediately south of Beroea. By these few words, Paul's plan becomes clear: once he had reached the sea to where the brethren in Beroea had sent him, he wanted to turn south, by land, away from the *Via Egnatia*. However, his plan was thwarted because he was not allowed to preach the word in Thessaly – this should have prompted him to head north as he was supposed to, but instead he boards a boat going south and by this means goes round the coast of Thessaly[73] to Athens. The men from Beroea looking after Paul go with him and thus end up in Athens (ἕως ᾿Αθηνῶν) with him.

Quite what form the obstacle placed in his way took is not specified, but the intention is clear: Paul is prevented from going back on to dry land. The comment echoes two previous ones, made during the journey of Paul and Silas westwards from Galatic Phrygia (16.6, the Holy Spirit; 16.7, the Spirit of Jesus) where it was observed that the divine interventions prevented Paul from moving away from the route heading towards Rome, which is where he was meant to be going (see *Commentary, ad loc.*).

[e] 17.15c *Those Accompanying Paul Go Away*
17.15c The imperfect of the verb suggests a hesitation, on the part of those accompanying Paul, to leave him.[74] They are forced to do so, however, since they have an order to transmit to Silas and Timothy.

---

72. The preposition ἕως before Athens, in place of the more expected εἰς, expresses the idea of a destination that was not intended. In point of fact, Paul did not plan to spend any length of time there but was only expecting to stay as long as it took for Silas and Timothy to reach him (cf. 17.15c).

73. The verb παρέρχομαι has the sense of 'going along' the coast (cf. 16.8 AT): 'Le préverbe παρα- implique un itinéraire qui longe la côte, apparemment par mer' (Delebecque, *Les deux Actes*, p. 340). See also Hemer, *Hellenistic History*, p. 116.

74. The verb ἔξειμι that Luke uses here is exclusive to Luke in the New Testament: cf. Acts 13.42; 17.15; 20.4 D05, 7; 21,17 D05^vid; 27.43. None of these departures is straightforward, as if the notion of reluctance is attached (by the context) to the departure.

Paul is thus left alone in Athens, as a city of refuge but where any missionary purpose is unclear: the brethren in Beroea sent him away, Silas and Timothy stayed behind there, and the people who had accompanied him to Athens have also gone away. He has ended up there because he had been forced to leave Macedonia by the attacks of the Jews who were provoked by his preaching in the synagogues. He has been prevented from repeating the same mistake in Thessaly, where he had attempted to go according to Codex Bezae, and has continued his journey south by sea to Athens. He has thus not directly opposed the will of God, but nor has he embraced it whole-heartedly.

[C'-B] 17.16-18 *Paul in the Synagogue and in the Agora*

The second episode sets the scene for the major speech of Paul in the Areopagus that will take up the bulk of the third and final episode [C'-B']. It is set in the city of Athens, moving from the synagogue to the Agora, a public area in the lower part of the city that was used as a market-place and, consequently, as a convenient location for public speaking. The centre of the episode [c] brings into the narrative the two schools of philosophers who will be the addressees of Paul's speech in 17.22-31 at the same time as providing a framework around which the speech is built.

A striking duality may be observed throughout the preparation for Paul's speech as well as in the speech itself. The parallel features relating simultaneously to the Epicureans and the Stoics in the preparation for the speech are 305
identified in the following analysis by different formats (italic type for the Epicureans and bold for the Stoics):

> **17.18** τινὲς δὲ καὶ *τῶν Ἐπικουρείων (Epicureans)* καὶ **τῶν Στοϊκῶν (Stoics)** φιλοσόφων συνέβαλον αὐτῷ,
> καί τινες ἔλεγον *(Ep.)·* *Τί ἂν θέλοι ὁ σπερμολόγος οὗτος λέγειν;*
> οἱ δέ **(St.)·** **Ξένων δαιμονίων** δοκεῖ καταγγελεὺς εἶναι.
>
> **19** Μετὰ δὲ ἡμέρας τινὰς ἐπιλαβόμενοι αὐτοῦ ἤγαγον αὐτὸν ἐπὶ Ἄρειον Πάγον πυνθανόμενοι **(St.)** καὶ λέγοντες *(Ep.)·*
>
> **(St.:)** Δυνάμεθα γνῶναι τίς ἡ καινὴ αὕτη ἡ ὑπὸ σοῦ καταγγελλομένη διδαχή; **20 ξενίζοντα** γάρ τινα φέρεις ῥήματα εἰς **τὰς ἀκοὰς ἡμῶν·**
> *(Ep.:) Βουλόμεθα οὖν γνῶναι τί ἂν θέλοι ταῦτα εἶναι.*
>
> **21** *Ἀθηναῖοι δὲ πάντες (Ep.)* καὶ **οἱ ἐπιδημοῦντες εἰς αὐτοὺς ξένοι (St.)** εἰς οὐδὲν ἕτερον ηὐκαίρουν ἢ *λέγειν τι (Ep.)* ἢ **ἀκούειν καινότερον (St.).**

[a] 17.16 *Paul in a City Full of Idols*

17.16 After the departure of the brethren back to Beroea (cf. 17.15c), Paul is left on his own in a foreign city, waiting for Silas and Timothy to join him and horrified by what he observes in the city. Luke uses the expression 'his spirit within him' to express the depth of his feelings of exasperation.[75] The wording of the Bezan text contrasts the two occupations of Paul: he is there in Athens, waiting for his companions to arrive, and while he is waiting, he looks around him and observes the state of the city.

[b] 17.17 *Paul in the Synagogue and in the Agora*

17.17 Because he was waiting for Silas and Timothy with no activity to occupy him in Athens, and because he was so deeply affected by what he saw there, he took the opportunity to debate with people,[76] taking up his lecturing style that he had initiated in Beroea (cf. on 17.2 above). He thus goes to the synagogue, yet again, where he talks as in previous cities with the Jews and the Gentile sympathizers, the God-fearers. It was observed, with reference to Beroea, that this approach is different from that of the preaching and announcing of the gospel, consisting of questions and answers, an exchange of views leading to debate rather than a direct proclamation of facts. In fact, Paul does not only go to the synagogue but also to the Agora, the public area in the city where people congregated for trading as well as for participating in public speaking.[77] In Codex Bezae, the people in the Agora are presented as a third group, parallel to the two in the synagogue, with whom Paul engaged in debate (see *Critical Apparatus*). These people are portrayed in the Alexandrian text as people passing by, hardly a group at all but rather individuals on their way to other business. In the Bezan text, the group is not a fixed one either, but is made up of people who happened to have come to the Agora. It is noticeable how Paul observes a hierarchy: first the Jews, then the God-fearers, and finally the Gentiles with no connection with Judaism. The attention of the narrative will now turn to focus on these people, as Paul debates with them day after day, unlike in the synagogue where he presumably chiefly went on the Sabbath. In neither place is any kind of reaction described, suggesting that nothing of note occurred[78] – until, that is, some people in the market place took a particular interest in debating with Paul.

---

75. The verb παροξύνω, 'exasperate', is used only here and at 1 Cor. 13.5; the cognate noun παροξυσμός is found at Acts 15.39 to describe the height of the conflict between Paul and Barnabas (see *Commentary, ad loc.*), and in a positive sense at Heb. 10.24. Luke expresses elsewhere the notion of a person's innermost being with τὸ πνεῦμα: Lk. 1.47, Mary; 8.55, Jairus' daughter; 23.46, Jesus; Acts 7.59, Stephen; 17.16; 19.21; 20.22, Paul; 18.25, Apollonius (Apollo, AT).

76. The connective μὲν οὖν, with which Paul's response to his situation is introduced, anticipates a second event arising from Paul's enforced stay and his lecturing in Athens. This occurs in v. 18 (introduced with δέ), being the participation of the philosophers in the debate which will then lead on to Paul's speech.

77. The practice of public discussion in the Agora is particularly associated with Socrates, the Athenian philosopher of the fifth century BCE.

78. So far, Luke has always indicated the reaction to Paul, whether it was negative or positive, except at Salamina (13.5) where his purpose in mentioning the visit to the synagogue of the Jews was to contrast this strategy with the presence of John-Mark as a 'keeper' of the gospel (see *Commentary, ad loc.*).

[c] 17.18a *Epicurean and Stoic Philosophers*

17.18a Among the people in the Agora, a place where public speaking and discussions were commonly carried out, were some philosophers. Just as the people in the synagogue belonged to one of two groups, so also among the philosophers there are two particular groups: the Epicureans and the Stoics. Both represent schools of thinking that had their origin in Athens towards the end of the fourth century BCE and continued to be active in the first century CE. The former held that the goal of life was to achieve a state of perfect tranquility, by means of freedom from fear and a true perception of the world. This was a state enjoyed by the gods, whose existence the Epicureans did not deny but they believed that they were far removed from the world of human beings and that they had no interest in or influence on the life of people. Since everything, including the soul and the divine, was believed to be made up of atoms, nothing persisted after death. Tranquility was reached through a correct understanding of such things, enhanced by an ascetic lifestyle. Thus the pleasure, or happiness, that accompanied this state was obtained through a balancing of the greater and lesser pain. Far from being a purely self-seeking way of life, friendship was a highly valued component. Epicureans appear to have been admired for their simplicity and their rejection of superstitious practices that arose from fear of the gods.[79] They were not numerous nor a particularly powerful group in the first century CE. They did, on the other hand, have their equivalents in Judaism, who were referred to as the 'Apikurim', those heretics who challenged the Law, did not believe that God took care of the world, and did not accept the resurrection or any ideas of life after death.[80]

The Stoics were by far the dominant philosophers by the time of the Roman Empire, though their founder, Zeno, had originated in Cyprus (c. 340–265), which may account for the term 'foreign' being consistently associated with them in these verses that prepare for Paul's speech (see *Overview*). Their attitude to the world was that everything, from the universe to the individual, was controlled by destiny, and that the greatest happiness, or 'virtue', lay in accepting what was ordained, and living in harmony with what had been decreed. The existence of a governing force was acknowledged, but it was thought of as a creative power, rather than as a 'god', which pervaded the universe and was present in humans as the soul. True knowledge of reality, and therefore living in harmony with it, was achieved through a correct application of reason, λόγος, to the perception of the senses. Since passions interfered with this procedure, an important goal was to become free from anything that might disturb the ability to live conformably with what providence had decreed. Nevertheless, despite the high ideals, it seems that by the first century Sto-

---

79. For further details on the Epicureans, the following works may be consulted for a summary of beliefs and practices: E. Asmis, 'Epicureanism', *ABD*, II, pp. 559–61; F.W. Beare, 'Epicureans', *Interpreter's Dictionary*, II, pp. 122–23.

80. Josephus (*Ant.* X, 7) has the first recorded reference to the Apikurim. See G. Deutsch, 'Apikoros', *Jew. Enc.* I, pp. 656–66.

icism had been degraded, having adopted various myths and superstitious practices including astrology and divination.[81]

Unlike the synagogue audience, concerning whom Luke records no reaction, the philosophers have plenty to say to Paul, and Paul in turn will respond to their comments. Though they are presented together, the Bezan text distinguishes between them (with the repeated article, see *Critical Apparatus*) as two separate schools, which indeed they were. Thus distinguished, it is easier to see how the following remarks that Luke attributes to them relate to each of the schools in turn. The distinction will be maintained in their questions that they later put to him in the Areopagus (see *Excursus* 12).

[b'] 17.18b *The Epicureans' Opinion of Paul*
17.18b The response of the Epicureans is somewhat mocking and disparaging. They treat Paul as a 'seed gatherer' (σπερμολόγος), someone who collects other people's ideas at random without any original contribution of his own.

[a'] 17.18c *The Stoics' Opinion of Paul*
17.18c The response of the Stoics is positive in comparison with that of the first group, and may even seek to answer the jeering question of the Epicureans. They interpret Paul as introducing new, or foreign, deities, a 'herald' in the sense of one who announces news of events to the city.

The Alexandrian text gives an explanation of the Stoics' interpretation, spelling out the content of the news that Paul was announcing as 'Jesus and the resurrection', as if in a narrative aside that looks like an editorial gloss. The use of the verb εὐαγγελίζομαι here is out of place, for Paul will not use it at all in his speech (unlike that to the synagogue in Antioch of Pisidia, 13.32), nor will Luke use it of him.[82] Moreover, according to the Alexandrian text, Paul never mentions the name of Jesus in his speech to the Athenians (but cf. 17.31 D05); and when he does mention the 'resurrection from the dead' it provokes an outcry (cf. 17.32). The explanation may well have been added to clarify that the charge against Paul as a herald of 'foreign deities' was in no way true but was based on an uninformed misinterpretation.

[C'-B'] 17.19-34 *Paul's Areopagus Speech*

The main points are that, contrary to the Athenian thought concerning the gods and their worship of them, the true God has no need of a dwelling place or service provided by human hands; secondly, God cannot be represented by human artefacts. In conclusion, God is presented as a merciful judge who,

81. On the philosophy of Stoicism, see F.W. Beare, 'Stoics', *Interpreter's Dictionary*, IV, pp. 443–45; T. Schmeller, 'Stoics, Stoicism', *ABD*, VI, pp. 210–14.

82. From the time of the exorcism of the slave-girl in Philippi (cf. 16.17 D05), Luke does not use the verb εὐαγγελίζομαι of Paul, but rather uses καταγγέλλω (17.3, 13, 19 D05; 23; 26.23) or διαλέγομαι (17.2, 17; 18.4, 19, 28 D05; 19.8, 9; 20.7, 9; 24.12, 25).

being the creator of the world, far from condemning people for their ignorance, has intervened in the world to provide them with a means to avoid the consequences of it by repenting and believing in Jesus, whose resurrection is evidence of God's intervention in and care for the world (see *Excursus* 12 for a structural analysis of the speech, bringing out the three main clauses).

Paul takes up both philosophical and popular concepts familiar to his Athenian audience, apparently accepting them though he himself would have put a different interpretation on them. This is particularly true of the Bezan text where, at the end of his exposition, he does in fact openly refuse to accept the pantheistic view of people being of the same race as God.

The speech is brought abruptly to an end when the Epicureans interrupt him as he introduces the theme of the resurrection. The same parallelism of response is seen at the end of the speech as was observed in the preparation for it (see introductory remarks to the previous episode [C'-B], 17.16-18, above).

[a] 17.19-20 *The Philosophers Take Him to the Areopagus*

17.19a The Bezan text portrays these discussions going on more or less peacefully over some days. However, in the end, the philosophers take Paul to the Areopagus. The 'Areopagus' was the council of Athens, presided over by men from the aristocracy and which met, originally if not still in the first century,[83] on the hill near the Parthenon overlooking the Agora, known as the 'hill of Ares', the Greek god of war. It had authority especially in moral and religious affairs at this time. The philosophers took Paul to the court not necessarily by force[84] but with the intention of making sure that an official evaluation was made by the council members about what he was saying.[85]

17.19b-20 Once at the Areopagus, each of the two groups summarizes what it is they want to know. As Luke moves from narrative to direct speech, the two verbs in the Bezan text make it clear that the two requests correspond to the separate philosophical schools as they 'enquire' and 'say'. Their distinct identity is established by the repetition of key terms (see *Excursus* 12). The Stoics are the first to speak: they have already been identified in their initial response to Paul with the theme of 'foreign' or 'strange' (Greek root ξεν-; cf. ξένων, 17.18c); a second characteristic idea that is introduced at this point is that of 'hearing' (Greek root ἀκο-). Their 'enquiry' (πυνθανόμενοι) is formulated as a question to Paul, expressing their desire to know just what it is that

---

83. There is some debate as to whether the council met on the hill from which it took its name, or, instead, in a place within the Agora; see Hemer, *Hellenistic History*, p. 117.

84. ἐπιλαμβάνομαι is a term Luke uses frequently (Lk × 5; Acts × 7), unlike the other evangelists (Mt. × 1; Mk × 1). It can denote violence (cf. Lk. 23.26; Acts 18.17; 21.30, 33) but, as in classical Greek, it can also be used in a favourable sense (cf. Acts 9.27, where Barnabas takes Saul and presents him [ἐπιλαβόμενος αὐτὸν ἤγαγεν] to the apostles). Luke may well have intended the ambiguity here.

85. The mention at 17.34 of 'Dionysius, a certain Areopagite of good standing' (D05; 'Dionysius an Areopagite', AT), and 'others with them' indicates that members of the council were present, and confirms that taking Paul to the Areopagus was for a formal hearing.

Paul has been proclaiming (talking about, AT), since they have not heard of such things before. The use in the Bezan text of the phrase 'strange words' (ξηνίζοντα … ῥήματα) is striking, for the term 'words' is the same as that used of the words addressed by Paul to the magistrates in Philippi but, as was remarked concerning that occurrence (see *Commentary*, 16.38), it is not the usual one Luke uses to refer to the preaching of the word of the gospel (λόγος). The implication here, as in the Philippi scene, is that Paul's words do not have the power of the gospel but are other kinds of words (see *Excursus* 1). This conclusion is consistent with the use in the Bezan text of the verb καταγγέλλω instead of εὐαγγελλίζομαι, since the former is also a negative term compared with the latter, without the connotations of preaching the good news (cf. the Stoics use of καταγγελεύς, 'herald', 17.18c). The Alexandrian text in contrast, by not including the term ῥήματα here, and by the choice of the verb λαλέω instead of καταγγέλλω, does not convey this negative evaluation of Paul's activity.

As for the Epicureans, they were previously identified in their initial response as somewhat cynical; they are characterized by the phrase τί ἄν θέλοι (θέλῃ D05), 'what might this mean', and by the verb 'say' (Greek root λεγ-; cf. 17.18b). It is to them that the participle 'saying' (λέγοντες) applies in introducing the separate comments of the two groups of philosophers. The expression 'what might this mean' is repeated now as they demand to know what Paul's words (D05; or simply 'things', AT, see *Critical Apparatus*) mean. The Epicureans are portrayed as arrogant and self-sufficient, challenging Paul rather than being open to hear answers to their questions. In comparison, the Stoics are more open and display a courteous attitude and a willingness to learn from Paul.

[b] 17.21 *Information about the Philosophers*
17.21 In a narrative aside, Luke makes a comment on the philosophers, relating their desire to know more from Paul to well-known characteristics of people in Athens – both the native Athenians themselves, and also foreigners who had come to live among them. Luke thus maintains the parallelism between the Epicureans and the Stoics. The former are identified once more with speaking (λέγειν), and the latter with the term 'foreign' (ξένοι) and with 'hearing' (ἀκούειν). Both groups are obsessed with all things new, a feature that was recognized by several ancient writers.

[c] 17.22-31 *Paul's Speech*
On the structure of the speech itself, and the interplay of themes and terms, see *Excursus* 12. Paul begins with a brief *Introduction* [α] (17.22b-23) designed to make a point of contact with his audience. He then moves on to set out his essential teaching in the *Exposition* [β] (17.24-29). He begins an exhortation or *Parenesis* [α′] (17.30-31) but this is almost immediately interrupted so he is not able to develop it to its conclusion.

Throughout the speech, Paul deals with the notions of God as creator and God as Lord, notions that were familiar to both Stoics and Epicureans either because they upheld them or denied them. They were topics, however, that were popular subjects of debate, and that could have been of interest to people in Athens who did not adhere to one or other of these two philosophies. His treatment of them tends to be more favourable to the Stoics though, in fact, some of his statements are ambiguous in that they can be interpreted as expressing a biblical point of view that would not be in conformity with that of the Stoics.

17.22a Paul stands to speak to the council, a normal position in a Greek or Roman court, recalling Peter as he addressed the people in Ierousalem (2.14) or Stephen as he stood in the middle of the Sanhedrin Council (6.15 D05), or Paul himself again during the shipwreck (27.21). The description 'in the middle' suggests that he was surrounded by people attentive to what he was about to say; it corresponds to the account of his leaving the council when his speech is interrupted (cf. 17.33, ἐκ μέσου αὐτῶν, lit. 'out from the middle of them').

[α] 17.22b-23 *Introduction*
17.22b Paul begins his answer to the questioning of the Epicureans and the Stoics by addressing the Areopagus council as 'Men of Athens' – this conventional style of address establishes that it is a speech for Greek people, expecting no prior familiarity with Judaism. Only on one previous occasion has Paul spoken to such an audience, in Lystra where it was noted that he, together with Barnabas, failed to communicate with the local people (14.15-17, see *Commentary, ad loc.*).

[αα] 17.22c *His Observation*
17.22c He addresses his audience in Athens on the basis of what he has observed about their religious practices and attitudes referring, not without a touch of irony,[86] to what he has seen in the city as demonstrating to him how very 'religious' the people were. The term, expressing as it does a range of religious sentiment from respect for the gods to superstitious fear and servility, could be understood as one of approval[87] but it is difficult to see how the Epicureans, at least, would have taken it in a positive sense since their goal was to eliminate any kind of religious fear and consequently practices arising from it. Paul would no doubt be aware of how his words would be perceived differently by the different groups of philosophers, and this is but one instance of ambiguity among others that will be noted in his speech.

[αβ] 17.23a *An Altar to An Unknown God*
17.23a He mentions the many objects of worship (that is, idol worship from his point of view, though he refrains from overt criticism) that had struck him

---

86. Luke puts into Paul's mouth the same verb θεωρέω as he used as the narrator to describe Paul's irritation at seeing the city full of idols when he first arrived there (cf. 17.16).

87. Barrett, II, pp. 835–56, gives many examples from ancient literature of the word δεισιδαίμων in both positive and negative senses.

as he walked through the city, in particular an altar he came across with the words 'To an Unknown God' written on it. Such a concept, without expressing directly either the Epicurean or the Stoic view of the gods, corresponds, on the one hand, to the Epicurean teaching that the gods existed but were far removed from the world, without any possibility of relationship with them; it was they who had said to Paul that they wanted to 'know' what his words meant (17.19b). On the other hand, the concept of an 'unknown god' tallies with the Stoic notion that, although the ideal for humankind was to live in harmony with the governing force of the universe, this force was not a personal god and could only be known if reason was correctly applied to perception by the senses; it was they who had asked to 'know' the new and strange teaching they had heard Paul proclaiming (17.19c).

[αα'] 17.23b *His Intention*
17.23b Paul makes use of his discovery to provide a basis for the explanation he has been asked to give about his own ideas, convinced that only the God he has experienced can provide any kind of knowledge to fill the void implied by the words 'unknown god'. He will give them precise knowledge about the deity they revere. The neuter pronouns 'what' (ὅ) and 'this' (τοῦτο), rather than masculine ones, deliberately avoid any suggestion that the object of worship through the altar to the 'unknown god' can be identified with the one true God about whom Paul will speak; furthermore, it anticipates the neuter term 'the divine being' (τὸ θεῖον) with which Paul will refer to the notion of divinity later in his speech (17.27 D05, 29).

[β] 17.24-29 *Exposition*
Having prepared the ground by putting forward something with which the Athenians were familiar, Paul now goes on to set out his argument. The flow of the argument will be followed in the text of Codex Bezae (see *Excursus* 12) since it differs in several places from that of the Alexandrian text. The logical steps of the speech and the connections between them in the Alexandrian text can be followed in the *Translation* and in the *Critical Apparatus*.

[βα] 17.24-25a *Two Principal Themes*
Paul begins by stating the two themes, which concern features of the God he will proclaim.
    17.24a Following the introduction of 'God' as the subject, he first presents two participial clauses that express positively fundamental statements on the two themes: *A* God is the creator of everything, and *B* he is Lord of heaven and earth. While both the Epicureans and the Stoics would assign to the gods the role of creator, the Epicureans would deny that they had any involvement in the world or human affairs as ruler. The Stoics, in contrast, would acknowledge the role of the gods not only as the source of life but also as providence, controlling the world as a force for good.

17.24b-25a Two negative statements follow as parallel main clauses deriving from the above basic tenets: *A* Since he is the creator, God does not live in temples made by hand – the kind of things Paul had seen around the city of Athens – and *B* since he is the Lord, he is not served by human hand. While the Epicureans would agree with this, refusing any notion that the gods should be served or placated, the Stoics with their syncretistic blend of religious practices would be prepared to build places to worship the gods and to carry out rituals as a means to appease them.

[ββ] 17.25b-27 *Explanation*
The next sentence in the Bezan text is a subordinate clause of reason, containing within it two dependent infinitives expressing purpose.

17.25b-26 Paul develops the idea of a creator God, explaining why he has said that he is not confined to hand-made shrines nor has need of anything people can offer him: it is because he himself is the one who made people. Paul's words at this point can be taken in two ways: God is portrayed as creating, from a first man (made explicit in Codex Bezae with the term 'blood'), either the whole human race or each and every nation. The former interpretation, which is probably that adopted by the Alexandrian text (see *Critical Apparatus*), accords with Stoic teaching on the unity of the human race whereas the latter, with its focus on the many nations, reflects the biblical idea of the God of Israel being responsible for each of the nations, and for subsequently controlling the scope and place of each one on earth (see 17.26b).[88] It is this latter idea that seems to be the dominant one in Codex Bezae, though it is possible that ambiguity is present in both texts. Paul may be well aware that the concepts he understands in a Jewish way will be interpreted differently by his audience, but they give him a point of contact from which to pursue his argument.

God's purpose in creating humankind, whether understood as the human race or all the nations, is defined as twofold. The first aspect was for people to inhabit the whole of the earth, God having determined the 'times' (καιρούς) and the boundaries for them. Again, there is ambiguity as to which Paul may have intended: the 'times' may refer to the seasons (cf. 14.17) that varied according to the territory that God allocated to the different nations, a biblical tradition (cf. Deut. 32.8) that is more probably being alluded to in the Bezan text; alternatively, the 'times' may be a reference to historical epochs and the boundaries as the limits of the habitable earth.[89] In any case, Paul underlines the role of God in intervening actively in the history of the world, of determining limits and order in a variety of ways that the Epicureans would deny but the Stoics accept.

17.27 Paul then states God's second purpose in creating people, which the Bezan text highlights as the principal one: it is to seek (ζητεῖν) the divine

---

88. Zerwick (*Biblical Greek*, §§190–91) discusses these two possibilities, which depend on whether πᾶς without the article is taken in its classical or Hellenistic sense.

89. These alternatives are proposed by Zerwick and Grosvenor, *Analysis*, pp. 410–11.

being (τὸ θεῖον), or God (τὸν θέον) as the Alexandrian text has it. According to the reading of Codex Bezae, Paul is speaking more about a quest for the divine principal in general terms, rather than God himself who, in Jewish terms, can only be known through revelation. What Paul means, however, by 'seek' (the biblical sense of living in obedience to and reliance on God's laws and will), and what the Greek audience may have understood by it (more a search through intellectual reasoning and philosophical speculation,[90] as the Stoics advocated) is a further illustration of the potential ambiguity in the speech. However, in this case, Paul takes up the Stoic sense by presenting evidence that has all the signs of being a quotation from some Greek writer: it is introduced by a series of three particles that are found nowhere else in the New Testament (εἰ ἄρα γε), followed by two rare optatives (ψηλαφήσαισαν ... εὔροισαν, with a highly unusual personal ending in the Bezan text, see *Critical Apparatus*).

The quotation shows that seeking the divine was indeed a philosophical concern but that, from the point of view of the Greek audience, there was considerable doubt as to the success of the search. Paul will go on to contradict this doubt by indicating in a subordinate clause of concession that according to what he knows and has experienced of God, the divine is, in fact, accessible and can be known. It is not until the parenesis that he will explain how this is so.

[ββ'] 17.28 *Justification*
In a subordinate clause of justification, Paul adduces evidence from Greek writings to back up his previous statement and give authority to it from the point of view of his audience. The elements [ββ] and [ββ'] thus mirror each other.

17.28 That the divine was regarded as accessible among the Greeks is justified by two citations Paul puts forward without, however, accepting the truth of them, as will be clear in the Bezan text of the following main clause. He makes clear that he is quoting from Greek writers (the AT specifies that they are poets) with a parenthetical reference to them, which he places after the first quotation and before the second. They are both pantheistic in outlook: that everything we do and are is 'in her', a reference to a feminine deity in Codex Bezae though the exact source of the quotation has not been identified in either text;[91] and that we are God's 'race' (lit., γένος), attributed with more certainty to Aratus, a Hellenistic poet who studied in the Stoic school in Athens in the late fourth to early third centuries BCE. The familiar English translation of 'offspring' replaces the usual one of 'race', 'species' or 'family', because in the Alexandrian text, the text usually followed, Paul will go on to affirm the truth

---

90. See B. Gärtner, *The Areopagus Speech and Natural Revelation* (Lund: C.W.K. Gleerup, 1955), p. 156. Gärtner argues that it is the alternative biblical sense Paul intended here, but while this may indeed be the meaning he would accept, it is the philosophical sense Paul takes up as he develops his argument.

91. Various suggestions for the author of the sentiments expressed have been put forward (see Barrett, II, pp. 347–48; Bruce, *Acts*, p. 359;), though the inclusion in D05 of 'day by day' has not been accounted for.

of this statement, and so a word must be found that does not conflict with the biblical teaching that clearly distinguishes between the nature of God as creator and the nature of humankind as creation. In point of fact, the concept is entirely pantheistic, expressing the thought that humans and the gods share in the same divine nature.[92] Paul in the Bezan text, however, denies that we are the γένος of God.

[βα'] 17.29 *Refutation*

In the final element of his exposition, Paul returns to the theme of religious shrines and objects made by people to revere or otherwise serve the gods (cf. 17.24-25a). The correspondence between the two elements [βα] and [βα'] is reinforced by their position at the beginning and the end of the exposition respectively.

17.29 According to the Alexandrian text, Paul continues with a subordinate clause of consequence (οὖν) deriving from the second of the two quotations, where he accepts the truth that 'we are God's offspring' (making explicit that 'God' is viewed as the point of origin). For Paul to agree with this statement involves him attaching quite a different meaning to the expression than the pantheistic sense that was intended by the author of the quotation. On the basis of its truth, he goes on to challenge the attempts he has seen all around him in Athens to represent the divine in material objects fashioned by human skill and imagination. Admiration of artistic works, including those that were created to venerate the gods, was a particular characteristic of the Epicureans. The Stoics, on the other hand, with their conception of the gods as an abstract force and not personal beings, would be happier to concur with the criticism of the shrines and artistic representations of the divine. Paul's point in the Alexandrian text would seem to be that the divine cannot be reproduced by any creative attempt on the part of the 'offspring', since it is the divine that comes first and therefore cannot be created by what has come from it.

A supplementary negative particle in the Bezan text (giving the parallel negative construction οὐκ ... οὔτε) alters the point being made by Paul with respect to the second quotation. Looking at his line of argument again, this time following the Bezan text, he starts by rephrasing the quotation, making explicit God as the point of origin in place of the undefined 'this'. Furthermore, as he resumes his argument (οὖν), he now uses the stronger verb ὑπάρχω to express the state of existence in a more emphatic sense than the alternative εἶναι verb used in the quotation. Paul refuses to allow that it should be accepted. His refusal is expressed tentatively,[93] in line with the way he has been putting forward ambiguous statements throughout his speech that reflect Greek thinking in one sense (and so he appears to be in sympathy with his audience) but that he interprets in a different way according to his own

92. The point is well made by R. Faber, 'The Apostle and the Poet: Paul and Aratus', *Clarion* 42 (1993), pp. 291–305.

93. The reiteration of the quotation is done with the present participle ὑπάρχοντες, functioning as a verbal noun.

Jewish tradition, without overtly making clear the difference. His aim is to refute the Greek philosophies but without ridiculing them and antagonizing his audience.[94] Here in Codex Bezae, he begins as if he were supporting the tenet that we are the descendants of God, then goes on to deny it, just as he then also denies, as a separate though related issue, the use of either human art or human thinking to represent the divine – the two aspects are distinguished, giving greater salience to the philosophical attempts to represent the divine than in the Alexandrian text where art and thinking are grouped together.

[α'] 17.30-31 *Parenesis*

Having stated his case against the idolatry of the Athenians, using concepts and writings familiar to his audience to argue his points, Paul is now ready to draw lessons from his demonstration a) that God is the Creator of people who have a separate nature as created beings, and b) that God rules and controls the world. He introduces at this point the idea that the false understanding of God and the idolatry he has exposed merit punishment, presenting God as a judge with consequences for people after death. The Epicureans in particular could be expected to have problems with the tenets of Paul's final exhortation, for the themes of God as judge in relation to life after death are particular notions that were denied by the Epicureans.[95] It is they who will interrupt Paul's exhortation before he is able to bring it to a conclusion (17.32).

Paul's exhortation, as far as he gets with it, consists of a single sentence that moves through three stages, expressed as a main clause [α'α] with a subordinate clause of reason dependent on it [α'β], and a further relative clause dependent in turn on the clause of reason [α'γ].

[α'α] 17.30 *Repentance*

17.30 Paul begins the new stage in his speech with the connective μὲν οὖν to introduce a first point and anticipating a second (normally signalled with δέ), which he does not have opportunity to move on to before he is interrupted.

He begins by addressing a call to repentance to the Athenians, continuing nevertheless to be careful not to appear hostile to his audience. He thus reassures them that their false beliefs and attitudes, 'the times of this ignorance' as Codex Bezae puts it or, more generally according to the Alexandrian text, 'the times of ignorance', have not been held against them by the God whom he has been proclaiming to them. The ignorance which has led them into error has been 'overlooked', in the sense of 'turning a blind eye' (Codex Bezae), or in the sense of God looking ahead beyond the times of ignorance to the time of repentance (AT). Paul had expressed a similar idea in talking to the people in Lystra (14.16). Here, he takes up the word 'ignorance' from the inscription he

---

94. See Faber, 'The Apostle and the Poet'.

95. The importance of the theme of theodicy for Paul's Epicurean audience has been examined in J.H. Neyrey, 'Acts 17, Epicureans and Theodicy: A Study in Stereotypes', in D. Balch and W. Meeks (eds), *Greeks, Romans and Christians* (Minneapolis: Fortress Press, 1990), pp. 118–34.

had used as a springboard for his speech (cf. 17.23) and, putting it to one side, explains to them what the situation is now, in the present time: God has intervened in the affairs of the world in anticipation of the judgement he will execute, giving an order (or simply an announcement, AT) to people all over the world to repent. With the emphatic 'everyone everywhere', Paul makes sure that his Athenian audience understand that he is not talking about something just for Jews, or restricted to any particular country – this is not some 'foreign' god as the Stoics had initially understood him to be proclaiming (cf. 17.18c), but one who is concerned with the whole of humanity.

[α'β] 17. 31a *Judgement*

17. 31a In a subordinate clause of reason, Paul gets to the heart of the matter: God has fixed a time when he is going to judge the world, with the term again conveying the idea that it is the whole world that will be affected – Paul is speaking not about localized beliefs but about universal truths.

He then qualifies the judgement by adding two modifiers. First, the judgement will be made in righteousness, a notion fundamental to teaching in the Jewish Scriptures where the same words as Paul uses, 'judge the world in righteousness', occur three times in the Septuagint version of the Psalms.[96] The judgement, then, will be just and true.

The second piece of information Paul gives concerning the judgement is that it will be made by a man. The Bezan text names the man as Jesus.

[α'γ] 17.31b *Resurrection*

17.31b With a relative clause, Paul expands on the mention of the man. The Alexandrian text says of the man that God 'appointed' him as the judge, before going on to adduce the proof that, strange as it may seem, a man would effect the judgement on the world – God has provided the proof of this by raising him from the dead. The word used for 'proof' (πίστις) is the one that elsewhere in the New Testament always means 'faith', but that meaning in the Alexandrian text is difficult to sustain.

The Bezan constructs the sentence differently, saying that God had appointed Jesus himself to provide πίστις, which can mean 'faith' here, and he is able to do this because God has raised him from the dead.

This is the third time that Paul uses the verb ὁρίζω or the related noun (ὁροθεσία, cf. 17.26b), expressing the idea of 'fixing' or 'ordaining' and illustrating how he sees God as intervening in the world: as he announced in his opening statement, God is 'Lord of heaven and earth' (17.24a) because he rules over it and decides how things will happen.

Paul uses the same expression as Peter in the house of Cornelius in Caesarea (cf. 10.42) to explain that Jesus had been appointed as judge. In the case of Peter, he was interrupted by the Holy Spirit before he could begin to exhort

---

96. Cf. Ps. 9.9; 95.13; 97.9 LXX: κρινεῖ τὴν οἰκουμένην ἐν δικαιοσύνῃ.

his audience to take any action (cf. 10.44),[97] whereas Paul is interrupted by members of the Areopagus council. The insistence on judgement, intended to prompt people to repent by the implicit threat of punishment, does not produce the reaction Paul hoped for.

[c'] 17.32 *Contrasting Reactions*
17.32 Just as in the preparation for Paul's speech in Athens the reactions and questions of the two philosophical schools, the Epicureans and the Stoics, were distinguished (cf. 17.18-20), so the account of the response to the speech demonstrates two parallel reactions. Paul is interrupted by the scoffing reaction to the mention of the resurrection, a response that echoes the mocking scorn that characterized the initial reaction of the Epicureans to Paul (17.18b, cf. 20b). The Stoics, in contrast, are sufficiently interested to ask to hear him on another occasion speaking about the same subject – the demonstrative 'this' (τούτου) may be indefinite but it may equally well refer to 'this man', Jesus, about whom Paul has begun to speak. The verb 'hear' (ἀκουσόμεθα) was associated with the Stoics in the preparatory verses (cf. 17.20a, 21; see also the introductory remarks to the episode [C'-B], 17.16-18).

[b'] 17.33 *Paul Leaves Them*
17.33 It was the philosophers who had taken Paul to the Areopagus to hear further explanation of his teaching (17.19) but he now leaves of his own accord. The brevity of the statement that he 'left them' is striking, underlining the fact that his speech has not led to conversions among the Athenians. The terms Luke uses echo those with which he presented Paul in the Areopagus at the outset of his speech: 'Paul stood in the middle of the Areopagus (ἐν μέσῳ τοῦ Ἀρείου πάγου)' (17.22), for here he says (lit.): 'He went out from the middle of them (ἐκ μέσου αὐτῶν)'.

He has experienced yet again a rejection of his message, even though it is attenuated, as before also, by an expression of interest. So far, this interest has not led any further but the final element in the sequence will add some more information.

[a'] 17.34 *Certain People Believe*
17.34 Although so far it has seemed that Paul has experienced total failure in Athens, Luke closes the scene with an indication of some positive results. According to the version presented by the Alexandrian text, after Paul had left, some of the men who joined up with him – the Stoics of 17.32b – believed.[98] Two of them are mentioned by name, Dionysius who was a member of the Areopagus council, and a woman called Damaris. The reference to

---

97. See *The Message of Acts*, II, pp. 275–77 for the interpretation that Peter was interrupted by the Holy Spirit because of his insistence on judgement.

98. The action of the aorist participle κολληθέντες is closely associated with that of the aorist finite verb, ἐπίστευσαν.

'others with them' is somewhat superfluous, given that it has already been stated that these two named characters are part of the group that joined Paul and believed.

The Bezan text paints a slightly different picture: only Dionysius is named but he is presented as a character who is a representative of the members of the Areopagite,[99] leaving room for the conclusion that other Areopagites took a similar step at some point. Dionysius stands out because he is a man of good standing, like those Gentiles who had accepted Paul's teaching in Thessalonica and Beroea. Since no name is given of anyone other than Dionysius, the final mention of 'others with them' is not superfluous but refers to yet others who followed the Stoics as they joined Paul and believed.

At the end of Paul's stay in Athens, a number of inferences may be made from the Bezan text in particular:

1. Silas and Timothy, despite the order to go as quickly as possible from Beroea to Athens (cf. 17.15) had not arrived;
2. of the Jews and the God-fearers with whom he had debated in the synagogue (cf. 17.17), no mention is made of any conversions, even though he had gone to them first;
3. the Stoics' positive response indicates that their way of thinking was closer to that of Paul than was that of the Epicureans. Unlike the latter who consistently mocked him, they had reacted favourably to his initial discussions in the Agora (17.18c), and expressed curiosity to know more in the Areopagus (17.19b-20a); after the Epicureans had interrupted his talk of Jesus and the resurrection, they again wanted to hear more (17.32b) and later, some of them became believers (17.34b). Paul includes at least two quotations from their poets (17.28-29), and even though he distances himself from the intended meaning, he does it with respect and tact;
4. the conversion of Dionysius, a distinguished personality, is another illustration of Paul's success among people of the higher classes;
5. the inclusion of some other Athenians, in addition to the Stoics who joined up with Paul and became believers, is a sign that Paul's proclamation had some effect among the citizens in general, not just the philosophers;
6. the fact that Paul does not stay in Athens but leaves, with some degree of urgency according to Codex Bezae (18.1 D05), is evidence that he was not comfortable in Athens and had not achieved his goal – in particular, the absence of any mention of success among the Jews will have gone contrary to his hopes and expectations.

99. His function as a representative of the Athenian council is comparable to that of Joseph of Arimathea, also a council member, though in his case the Jewish Sanhedrin (cf. Lk. 23.50).

Excursus 12

Paul's Speech in the Areopagus of Athens

In the following analysis of the speech, the logical (semantic) relations between the various propositions are indicated by setting out each clause on a separate line and specifying at the end of the line the nature of its relationship to the previous clause. The clauses on the left stand as main clauses with finite verbs, and the subordinate clauses are shifted to the right of the one on which they are dependent.

The three parts of the speech itself are titled *Introduction, Exposition* and *Parenesis*, the latter of which is cut short. It is striking how, all the way through the exposition, there is a series of two propositions in parallel (numbered 1 and 2 on the diagram). The pattern is the same as the one evident in the narrative that prepares for the speech and follows it, but whereas in the preparatory narrative the parallel elements correspond to the two philosophical schools, in the speech itself these do not seem to be the governing factors.

Introduction:

[α]			
[αα]	**22**	Ἄνδρες Ἀθηναῖοι, κατὰ πάντα ὡς δεισιδαιμονεστέρους ὑμᾶς θεωρῶ·	MAIN
[αβ]	**23a**	διερχόμενος γὰρ καὶ διϊστορῶν τὰ σεβάσματα ὑμῶν εὗρον καὶ βωμὸν ἐν ᾧ ἦν γεγραμμένον· Ἀγνώστῳ θεῷ.	EXPANSION 1
[αα']	**23b**	ὃ οὖν ἀγνοοῦντες εὐσεβεῖτε, τοῦτο ἐγὼ καταγγέλλω ὑμῖν.	EXPANSION 2

Exposition:

[β]			
[βα]	**24**	ὁ θεὸς	
		ὁ ποιήσας τὸν κόσμον καὶ πάντα τὰ ἐν αὐτῷ,	
		οὗτος οὐρανοῦ καὶ γῆς κύριος ὑπάρχων,	
		οὐκ ἐν χειροποιήτοις ναοῖς κατοικεῖ	MAIN 1
	25a	οὐδὲ ὑπὸ χειρῶν ἀνθρωπίνων θεραπεύεται προσδεόμενος,	MAIN 2
			CIRCUMSTANCE
[ββ]	**25b**	ὅτι οὗτος	
		ὁ δοὺς πᾶσι ζωὴν καὶ πνοὴν καὶ τὰ πάντα	REASON 1
	26	ἐποίησεν ἐξ ἑνὸς αἵματος πᾶν ἔθνος ἀνθρώπου	EXPANSION
		κατοικεῖν ἐπὶ παντὸς προσώπου τῆς γῆς,	REASON 2
		ὁρίσας προτεταγμένους καιροὺς κατὰ ὁροθεσίαν τῆς κατοικίας αὐτῶν	PURPOSE 1
	27	μάλιστα ζητεῖν τὸ θεῖόν ἐστιν,	CIRCUMSTANCE
		εἰ ἄρα γε ψηλαφήσαισαν αὐτὸ	PURPOSE 2
		ἢ εὕροισαν,	CONDITIONAL 1
		καίτοι οὐ μακρὰν ὂν ἀφ' ἑνὸς ἑκάστου ἡμῶν·	CONDITIONAL 2
			CONCESSION
[ββ']	**28**	Ἐν αὐτῇ γὰρ ζῶμεν	JUSTIFICATION 1
		καὶ κινούμεθα	
		καὶ ἐσμὲν τὸ καθ' ἡμέραν	
		– ὥσπερ καί τῶν καθ' ὑμᾶς τινες εἰρήκασιν –	NARRATIVE ASIDE
		Τούτου γὰρ καὶ γένος ἐσμέν.	JUSTIFICATION 2

[βα']	**29**	γένος οὖν ὑπάρχοντες τοῦ θεοῦ
		οὐκ ὀφείλομεν νομίζειν
		οὔτε χρυσῷ ἢ ἀργύρῳ ἢ λίθῳ,
		χαράγματι τέχνης
		ἢ ἐνθυμήσεως ἀνθρώπου,
		τὸ θεῖον εἶναι ὅμοιον.

NEGATIVE CONTENT 1
MAIN
NEGATIVE CONTENT 2
EXPANSION 1
EXPANSION 2

Parenesis:

[α']		
[α'α]	**30**	τοὺς μὲν οὖν χρόνους τῆς ἀγνοίας ταύτης παριδὼν
		ὁ θεὸς τὰ νῦν παραγγέλλει τοῖς ἀνθρώποις
		ἵνα πάντες πανταχοῦ μετανοεῖν,
[α'β]	**31a**	καθότι ἔστησεν ἡμέραν κρῖναι τὴν οἰκουμένην
		ἐν δικαιοσύνῃ
		ἀνδρὶ, Ἰησοῦ,
		ᾧ ὥρισεν
[α'γ]	**31b**	πίστιν παρασχεῖν πᾶσιν
		ἀναστήσας αὐτὸν ἐκ νεκρῶν...

CIRCUMSTANCE
MAIN
CONTENT
REASON
MANNER
MEANS
EXPANSION
PURPOSE
CIRCUMSTANCE

	32	ἀκούσαντες δὲ ...

(interruption)

[B′] 18.1-17 *Greece II: Corinth*

Overview

After his unsatisfactory experience of attempting to talk with Gentiles on their own terms in Athens (17.16-34), Paul leaves the city to move further south to the next Greek city of importance, Corinth. He is still alone, but will be joined by Silas and Timothy who had been instructed to join him (18.5; cf. 17.15b). He will revert here to his tactic of trying to reach the Jews, by going to the synagogue and lecturing to them. Luke continues to be critical of this approach, highlighting the negative response of the Jews who attempt yet again to have him silenced. Nevertheless, in Corinth, he will take further steps in his contact with the Gentiles whom, for once, the Jews are not able to enlist for their cause – quite the opposite, since the Greeks end up attacking the Jews for their opposition to Paul.

Structure and Themes

The sequence is relatively brief, and is made up of two episodes. The theme of the relations between Jews and Gentiles as they react to Paul's teaching, seen throughout the mission as early as in Paphos (cf. Bar-Iesoua and Sergius Paulus, 13.6-12), takes on a new turn here as he has an increasingly positive impact on the Gentiles. Just as in previous sequences, Paul is seen in the first episode in the synagogue of the city, and in the second in the wider context of the city itself:

[B′-A]	18.1-11	In the synagogue
[a]	18.1	Paul's departure to Corinth
[b]	18.2	Meeting with Aquila and Priscilla
[c]	18.3	His stay in their house
[d]	18.4a	Debate in the synagogue
[e]	18.4b	Paul persuades Jews and Greeks
[f]	18.5a	The Arrival of Silas and Timothy
[g]	18.5b	Paul devotes himself to the word
[f′]	18.6	Opposition from the Jews
[e′]	18.7	Paul's move to the house of Justus
[d′]	18.8a	Conversion of Crispus, the synagogue leader
[c′]	18.8b	Conversion of many Corinthians
[b′]	18.9-10	Paul's vision
[a′]	18.11	Paul's stay in Corinth
[B′-A′]	18.12-17	Before the proconsul Gallio
[a]	18.12a	The Jews attack Paul
[b]	18.12b-13	They take him into court
[c]	18.14-15	Gallio's response
[b′]	18.16	He dismisses the Jews
[a′]	18.17	The Greeks beat Sosthenes before the court

The first episode [A] begins with Paul's arrival in Corinth [a] and concludes with his extended stay there [a′]. A summary statement concerning Paul's dedication to witnessing to the Jews is at the centre of the structure [g], with the preceding elements preparing for it [b-f], and the elements that follow describing the events resulting from it [f′-b′]. The structure in the Bezan text is different at several places from that of the Alexandrian text, principally because of variation in sentence connectives.

In the second episode [A′], Paul is no longer in focus as the theme switches temporarily to the Jews. At the two mentions of his name, he is referred to only obliquely as the object of the Jews' attack (18.12) or as being about to defend himself but not doing so (18.14). The centre of the structure [c] is Gallio's response to the Jewish accusations against Paul.

Translation

Codex Bezae D05		Codex Vaticanus B03
[Aa]	**18.1** Taking refuge from Athens, he went to Corinth,	**18.1** After that, having left Athens he went to Corinth,
[b]	**2** and finding a certain Jew called Aquila – a man of Pontus by race who had recently come from Italy and Priscilla his wife, too, because Claudius had issued an order for all Jews to leave Rome and so they had come to live in Achaia – Paul approached him;	**2** and finding a certain Jew called Aquila – a man of Pontus by race who had recently come from Italy and Priscilla his wife, too, because of the issuing of an edict for all Jews to leave Rome – he approached them;
[c]	**3** and, since he shared the same trade, he stayed in their house and began working.	**3** and, because he was of the same trade, he stayed with them and they began working (for they were tent makers by trade).
[d]	**4a** Going into the synagogue every Sabbath, he lectured there.	**4a** He would lecture in the synagogue every Sabbath,
[e]	**4b** And by introducing the name of the Lord, Jesus, he tried to persuade not only Jews but even Greeks.	**4b** and he tried to persuade Jews and Greeks.
[f]	**5a** Silas and Timothy arrived then from Macedonia.	**5a** When Silas and Timothy came down from Macedonia.
[g]	**5b** Paul began to devote himself to the word, witnessing to the Jews that the Messiah was the Lord, Jesus.	**5b** Paul began to devote himself to the word, witnessing to the Jews that the Messiah was Jesus.
[f′]	**6** However, while, on the one hand, much talking was going on and the Scriptures were being interpreted and, on the other, they were resisting and blaspheming, Paul shook out his clothes and said to them, 'Your blood be on your own heads; I am clean from you! Now I am going to the Gentiles.'	**6** However, since they were contradicting and blaspheming, he shook out his clothes and said to them, 'Your blood be on your own heads; I am clean. From now on, I will go to the Gentiles.'
[e′]	**7** Moving away from Aquila's, what he did was to go to the household of a certain God-fearer by the name of Justus, whose house was next door to the synagogue.	**7** And moving away from there, he went into the house of a certain God-fearer by the name of Titius Justus, whose house was next door to the synagogue.
[d′]	**8a** The leader of the synagogue, Crispus, came to believe in the Lord with the whole of his household.	**8a** Crispus, the synagogue leader, believed in the Lord with the whole of his household.

[c′]	**8b** And many of the Corinthians who heard began believing one by one, and were baptized as they believed in God through the name of our Lord Jesus Christ.	**8b** And many of the Corinthians who heard began believing one by one and were baptized.
[b′]	**9** The Lord said through a vision to Paul in the night, 'Stop being afraid, but carry on speaking and do not become silent, **10** because I myself am with you and no one shall attack causing you to be harmed, because I have a large people in this city'.	**9** The Lord said in the night through a vision to Paul, 'Stop being afraid, but carry on speaking and do not become silent **10** because I myself am with you and no one shall attack you to harm you, because I have a large people in this city'.
[a′]	**11** And he remained in Corinth for a year and six months, teaching them the word of God.	**11** He remained a year and six months, teaching the word of God among them.
[A′a]	**18.12a** When Gallio was proconsul of Achaia, the Jews in unison rose up against Paul, having spoken together about him.	**18.12a** When Gallio was proconsul of Achaia, the Jews rose up in unison,
[b]	**12b** Laying hands on him, they took him into the court **13** shouting out and saying, 'This man is inciting people to worship God contrary to the law'.	**12b** and they took him into the court **13** saying, 'This man is inciting people to worship God contrary to the law'.
[c]	**14** As Paul was about to open his mouth, Gallio said to the Jews, 'If there had been some crime or fraudulent wrong-doing, I would be right to accept the complaint from you, Jewish men; **15** but if you have a controversy about doctrines and titles and this law of yours, you must see to it yourselves. I do not wish to act as a judge of these matters.'	**14** As Paul was about to open his mouth, Gallio said to the Jews, 'If there had been some crime or fraudulent wrong-doing, I would be right to accept the complaint from you Jews; **15** but if it is a matter of questions about doctrines and titles and this law of yours, you must see to them yourselves. I have no desire to act as a judge of these matters.'
[b′]	**16** And he sent them away from the court.	**16** And he drove them out from the court.
[a′]	**17** However, all the Greeks took aside Sosthenes, the leader of the synagogue but, while they were beating him in front of the court, Gallio pretended not to see.	**17** They all took hold of Sosthenes, the leader of the synagogue, and began beating him in front of the court, and Gallio took no notice of any of it.

Critical Apparatus

In chapter 18, there is the highest amount of additional material compared with the AT in the whole of Bezan Acts. It is concentrated in the first sequence, 18.1-11, and in 18.24-28, which is the start of the next and final part of Acts. Thereafter, throughout the remaining extant Bezan chapters (19.1–22.29), the proportion of additional to alternative material will be inverted as the trends follow a steady path in opposite directions (Read-Heimerdinger, *The Bezan Text*, pp. 7–16).

18.1 Μετὰ (+ δὲ 𝔓⁴¹) ταῦτα χωρισθεὶς ἐκ (τῶν ᾿Αθηνῶν) B 𝔓⁽⁴¹⁾·⁷⁴ ℵ 33. 2344 *pc* gig vg sa bo; Aug Ι Μετὰ (+ δὲ E Ψ 𝔐 syʰ) τ. χωρ. ὁ Παῦλος ἐκ A E H L P

Ψ 049. 056. 1739 𝔐 e h sy^(p) bo^ms aeth; Or^lat (Chr) Cassian ‖ Ἀναχωρήσας δὲ ἀπό D, *Regressus vero ab* d h.

The verb χωρίζω in B03, meaning 'depart', is followed by the preposition ἐκ, in place of the more usual ἀπό (cf. next verse, 18.2). ἐκ conveys the idea that there had been considerable prior involvement in the place left, which is the case for Paul with respect to Athens (Read-Heimerdinger, *The Bezan Text*, pp. 191–92). The absence of connective at the start of this new sequence in B03 causes the new episode to be viewed as quite separate from the previous incident in Athens. This is the only instance in Acts where μετὰ ταῦτα is used to introduce a new development in the story without some other connecting word (Levinsohn, *Textual Connections*, p. 154).

D05, in contrast, connects the new incident to the previous one, not only with the conjunction δέ but also by means of the verb ἀναχωρέω with ἀπό, which at every occurrence in the LXX and the New Testament has the meaning of 'take refuge from peril' (B-A-G).

18.2 (διὰ τὸ) διατετάχεναι Κλαύδιον (– Κλ. B) 𝔓^74 א^2 A H Ψ (-χθ- 049. 614) 1739 𝔐 ǀ προσ- Κλ. 056 1 ‖ τεταχ. Κλ. (Κλ-ος D*) D^A א* E L P 33^vid. 69. 88. 104. 323. 927. (-χθ- 1175). 1241. 1270. 1646. 1837. 2147. 2344 *pm.*— (πάντας) τοὺς Ἰουδαίους B 𝔓^74 א *rell* ‖ Ἰουδ. D.

The compound verb διατάσσω in B03 has a stronger force than the simple τάσσω of D05, though both refer to the imperial edict. The omission of the reference to Claudius in B03 may reflect uncertainty, even in the early centuries, as to the date of the edict. While there is some consensus today that it was issued by Claudius, the evidence is sometimes confusing (Hemer, *Hellenistic History*, pp. 167–68; cf. Barrett, II, pp. 860–61; Witherington, *Acts*, pp. 539–44). The nominative Κλαύδιος in the first hand of D05 is a grammatical error.

With the article before Ἰουδαίους, B03 refers to the Jews as a category of people living in Rome; the absence of the article in D05 causes the reference to be a general one, to Jews of all kinds whether Jesus-believers or not (as at Acts 26.4 B03; cf. B-D-R, §275.1, cf. 2).

(Ῥώμης), οἳ καὶ κατῴκησαν εἰς τὴν Ἀχαίαν D, *qui et demorati sunt in Achaiam* d h sy^hmg ‖ *om.* B 𝔓^74 א *rell.*— (προσῆλθεν) αὐτοῖς B 𝔓^74 א D^B *rell* (*ad eos Paulus* d) ‖ αὐτῷ ὁ Παῦλος D*.

The reading of the manuscript D05 is OIKEKATΩKHΣEN, on which two comments are needed. First, KE stands for καί and has arisen through itacism (see also at Lk. 3.5 [E > AI]; Acts 4.15 [ΚΑΙΛΕΥΣΑΝΤΕΣ > ΚΕΛΕΥΣΑΝΤΕΣ]; 20.16 [ΚΑΙΚΡΙΚΙ > ΚΕΚΡΙΚΕΙ]; Scrivener [p. xlvi] cites it as a harsh itacism but finds on the whole that there are fewer itacisms in D05 than א01). Secondly, the singular verb κατῴκησεν is probably an error for κατῴκησαν, especially in view of the plural pronoun οἳ; it could possibly be viewed as referring to the couple as a single unit, in the same way that a singular verb is also used with Paul and Barnabas (13.46 D05; cf. 14.3b D05 [αὐτοῦ > αὐτῶν]).

The relative clause in D05 makes explicit that Aquila and Priscilla had come to live in Greece. The force of καί before the finite verb is adverbial, drawing attention to the coming of the couple to Achaia (cf. the adverbial force of καί between a participle and a main verb in D05; see Read-Heimerdinger, *The Bezan Text*, pp. 208–210).

The singular pronoun following the main verb προσῆλθεν refers to Aquila, who was the object of the verb at the beginning of the sentence before the long parenthesis (ending with εἰς τὴν ᾿Αχαίαν). The use of the name of Paul is not necessary for the sense, but it makes clear that he is still the theme of the episode despite the introduction of other characters (cf. 18.6 below); it also avoids any ambiguity as to who is the subject of the verb after the long parenthesis (cf. Delebecque, *Les deux Actes*, p. 324).

18.3 (ὁμότεχνον) εἶναι B 𝔓⁷⁴ ℵ *rell* ‖ *om.* D d.— (ἔμενεν) παρ᾽ αὐτοῖς B 𝔓⁷⁴ ℵ *rell* ‖ πρὸς αὐτούς D, *apud eos* d 36. 431. 453 *pc.*— (καὶ) ἠργάζοντο B ℵ* saᵐˢˢ bo aeth ‖ -ζετο D, *operabatur* d 𝔓⁷⁴ ℵ² A E H L P Ψ 049. 056. 33. 1739 𝔐 lat syᵖ·ʰ saᵐˢˢ; Chr (Aug Spec).— ἦσαν γὰρ σκηνοποιοὶ τῇ τέχνῃ B 𝔓⁷⁴ ℵ *rell* ‖ *om.* D d gig.

The infinitive εἶναι in B03 completes the parenthetical clause, though it is not essential. The preposition πρός in D05 expresses more precisely than παρά the intimacy of being in the house of the couple.

The plural verb ἠργάζοντο in B03 corresponds to the final explanatory clause, which could well be a gloss rather than an accidental omission in D05, similar to that of 17.18 (see *Critical Apparatus*, *ad loc.*). D05, with the singular verb, continues to view Paul as the thematic character.

18.4 διελέγετο δὲ ἐν τῇ συναγωγῇ κατὰ πᾶν (πάντα 33 ‖ μίαν H) σάββατον B 𝔓⁷⁴ ℵ *rell* ‖ εἰσπορευόμενος δὲ εἰς τὴν συναγωγὴν κ. πᾶν σ. διελέγετο D, *ingressus autem in synagogam per omne sabbatum disputabat* d h vgᵀ.— καὶ ἐντιθεὶς τὸ ὄνομα τοῦ κυρίου ᾿Ιησοῦ D, *et interponens nomen Domini Iesu* d c dem gig h q w vgᶿᵂ tpl syʰᵐᵍ ‖ *om.* B 𝔓⁷⁴ ℵ *rell*.

The wording of D05 underlines Paul's action in going into the synagogue, a particular concern of Luke's in that text (see *Commentary*). The content of his lecturing is also a matter of interest that Luke draws attention to for the sake of bringing out Paul's intentions in going to the synagogue: he 'introduced' the name of the Lord Jesus, where the idea (especially in view of 18.5 D05 below) could well be that it was into his exegesis of the Scriptures that he inserted the name of Jesus, as the Lord about whom they spoke (cf. Epp, *The Theological Tendency*, p. 86). It should be noted that the full title of Jesus is not read (despite the popular misconception that D05 regularly includes the complete title), for Paul's purpose is to demonstrate precisely the identity of Jesus as κύριος, the Lord with whom the synagogue audience was familiar (cf. 18.5 below).

ἔπειθέν τε Ἰουδαίους καὶ Ἕλληνας B 𝔓⁷⁴ ℵ *rell* ‖ καὶ (– Dˢ·ᵐ·) ἔπ. δὲ οὐ μόνον Ἰ. ἀλλὰ καὶ Ἕλ. D*, *et persuadebat non solos Iudaeos sed et Graecos* d h vgᵀ.

Paul's concern with the Greeks as well as Jews is highlighted in D05 where the narrator maintains, throughout all the narrative relating to Paul's mission, a consistent interest in his teaching among Gentiles.

18.5 ὡς δὲ κατῆλθον B 𝔓⁷⁴ ℵ *rell* ‖ παρεγένοντο δέ D (*ut vero advenerunt* d h).— ὅ τε Σιλᾶς καὶ ὁ Τιμόθεος B 𝔓⁷⁴ ℵ *rell* (d) ‖ τότε (ὅ τε Dˢ·ᵐ· Ψ 88) Σ. καὶ Τιμ. D* (Ψ 88), *tunc* h.— ὁ (Παῦλος) B 𝔓⁷⁴ ℵ *rell* ‖ *om.* D 88. 242. 915. 919 *pc*.

B03 relates the departure of Silas and Timothy from Macedonia in a subordinate clause of time, the main verb being συνείχετο in the next clause. The two disciples are viewed as separate individuals, with the repeated article (cf. the double article at the previous mention, 17.15).

The wording of D05 focuses on the arrival of the disciples (in Athens) with the finite aorist verb παρεγένοντο. τότε could be viewed as an adverb (as in Old Latin h), though a corrector has altered it to reflect the B03 reading. From a discourse point of view, the absence of the article before Silas and Timothy is justified by the fact that they have been absent from the narrative since 17.15; furthermore, they are contrasted with Paul, who is similarly anarthrous in D05. It is typical of D05 to distinguish Paul from other characters in this way (see Read-Heimerdinger, *The Bezan Text*, p. 131).

(Χριστὸν) κύριον D, *dominum* d ‖ *om.* B 𝔓⁷⁴ ℵ *rell*.

The concern seen in D05 to identify the topic of Paul's teaching as the Lord (cf. 18.4 above) is maintained here. It is omitted by B03, as it was at 18.4.

18.6 πολλοῦ δὲ λόγου γινομένου καὶ γραφῶν διερμηνευομένων D (*multoque verbo facto et Scripturis disputantibus* d) h (syʰᵐᵍ) ‖ *om.* B 𝔓⁷⁴ ℵ *rell*.

D05 reads two genitive absolutes, followed by two more, all the actions taking place at the same time (present participles), but the two sets presented in opposition to each other: δέ ... καί (Paul's lecturing) ‖ δέ ... καί (the Jewish opposition). B03 retains only the second set, and so omits further evidence of the content of Paul's teaching (cf. 18.4 above).

τὰ ἱμάτια B 𝔓⁷⁴ ℵ *rell* ‖ ὁ Παῦλος τ. ἱμ. αὐτοῦ D, *Paulus vestimenta sua* d (h vgᵐˢˢ) ‖ αὐ. τ. ἱμ. 36. 323. 945. 1175. 1739 *al* gig vgᶜˡ.

The focus on Paul is maintained in D05 with not only the mention of his name but also the possessive pronoun to refer to his clothes. The effect is to create a dramatic portrayal of Paul in opposition to the Jews.

(καθαρὸς) ἐγώ· ἀπὸ τοῦ νῦν B 𝔓⁷⁴ ℵ Dᴮ *rell* ‖ ἐγὼ ἀφ' ὑμῶν. νῦν D*ᵛⁱᵈ, *ego a vobis. nunc* d (h).— (εἰς τὰ ἔθνη) πορεύσομαι B 𝔓⁷⁴ ℵ Dᴮ ‖ πορεύομαι D*, *vado* d H L.

The reconstruction of D05* from the Latin page is near certain: καθαρός ἐγὼ ἀφ' ὑμῶν are found in the same line, while the following one begins with νῦν. A similar construction is found in Acts 20.26: καθαρός εἰμι ἀπὸ τοῦ αἵματος πάντων (cf. also Mt. 27.24). Epp (*The Theological Tendency*, p. 87) rejects this punctuation on the grounds that 'it is impossible in [Old Latin] h', where *ab vobis* is placed oddly at the end of the sentence ('h place ἀφ' ὑμῶν de façon aberrante', Boismard and Lamouille, II, p. 126); Delebecque (*Les deux Actes*, p. 366) likewise starts a new sentence with ἀφ' ὑμῶν, understanding a contrast between 'from you' and 'to the Gentiles'.

The future πορεύσομαι of B03 tallies with ἀπὸ τοῦ νῦν; the present of D05*, with νῦν. It would appear to be the change in sentence division that has caused the change in tense.

18.7 καὶ μεταβὰς ἐκεῖθεν B 𝔓⁷⁴ ℵ Dᴮ || μετ. ἀπὸ τοῦ 'Ακύλα D*ᵛⁱᵈ (*et cum recessisset ab Acyla* d h) | μετ. ἐκεῖθεν ἀπὸ τοῦ (– 2147) 'Ακ. 614. 2147. 2412.— ἦλθεν εἰς οἰκίαν B Dᴮ E H L P Ψ 049. 056. 614. 2147. 2412 𝔐 | εἰσῆλθεν εἰς οἰκίαν 𝔓⁷⁴ ℵ A (33). 104. 323. 945. 1175. 1270. 1739. 1837. 1891. (2344), *introivit in domum* d lat syᵖˑʰᵐᵍ || καὶ ἦλθεν εἰς τὸν οἶκον D*ᵛⁱᵈ.

The B03 text speaks of a move by Paul away from the synagogue where he had been lecturing (ἐκεῖθεν, 'from there'), whereas D05 specifies Aquila with whom he had been staying until then (cf. 18.2-3). The place that he goes to, according to B03, is a house (οἰκίαν, cf. discussion of the parallel terms with reference to οἶκος/οικία in 16.15, 32, 34), belonging to a certain Titus Justus. D05, in contrast, has him going into the household (οἶκον) or family of a certain Justus (see next variant).

The manuscript of D05 is partially illegible from μεταβὰς to ἦλθεν but the evidence for the reconstruction given here is good (cf. Epp, *The Theological Tendency*, pp. 91–92, though he takes this line to be spoken by Paul because of καί before the finite verb). The sentence is linked asyndetically to the previous words spoken by Paul (18.6), throwing Paul's action of moving to the household (οἶκος) of a Gentile into sharp relief; the article before Aquila is to be expected, the reference being anaphoric (cf. 18.2); and καί between a participle and a main verb is a feature of the Bezan text (cf. on 18.2 above).

In principle, the text could also be reconstructed as μεταβὰς δὲ ἀπὸ 'Ακύλα (N-A²⁷; cf. d5) where δέ marks the new development following Paul's declaration, and the absence of the article before Aquila establishes the contrast between him and Justus in the following line.

(τινὸς) ὀνόματι Τιτίου 'Ιούστου B* 𝔓⁷⁴ᵛⁱᵈ Dᴮ syʰ | ὀν. Τίτου 'Ιού. ℵ E P 36. 242. 453. 945. 1175. 1311. 1739. 1891. 2298 *pc* lat syᵖ bo; Theoph | ὀν. 'Ιού. B² H L Ψ 049. 056. 33. 614 𝔐, *nomine Iusti* d h p aeth; Chr || ΟΝΟΜΑΤ.ΣΙΟΥΣΤΟΥ D* | ὀν. Τίτου syᵖ sa boᵐˢ.

D05* seems to have read ὀνόματος 'Ιούστου, which is difficult to make sense of unless the name is taken in apposition to τινὸς ... σεβομένου. The inclusion of the name Titius, as in B03, may be due to dittography: ΟΝΟΜΑΤΙΤΙΤΙΟΥ.

ℵ01 has the name of the Greek companion of Paul (cf. 2 Cor. 7.6-7, 13-15; cf. 2.13; Gal. 2.1-3), who is never mentioned in Acts. The inclusion of Titius makes this the only place in Luke–Acts where a character is introduced with ὀνόματι and two names; if the second is some kind of given name, Luke would normally indicate it as such with a term like καλούμενος (see *Excursus* 2).

18.8 Κρίσπος δὲ ὁ ἀρχισυνάγωγος B 𝔓⁷⁴ ℵ *rell* ‖ ὁ δὲ ἀρχ. Κρ. D, *vero archisynagogus Crispus* d (h).

The B03 word order is the more usual one, where the interest lies in the person himself. With the order function – name, D05 displays a greater interest in the function of Crispus as the leader of the synagogue than as a person in his own right. This focus is in keeping with the attention paid by the D05 text throughout this episode to Paul's synagogue activity (cf. 18.4, 6). The term ὁ ἀρχισυνάγωγος follows directly from the mention of the synagogue in the previous clause, the contiguity of the two terms reflecting the link between them.

(ἐπίστευσεν) τῷ κυρίῳ B 𝔓⁷⁴ ℵ *rell* ‖ εἰς τὸν κύριον D, *in domino* d h vg°.

The B03 construction with the dative is found at 8.12; 16.34; 26.27; that with εἰς + accusative, at 14.23. These are the only places in Acts where a preposition is used with the verb πιστεύω. Here, where the subject is a Jew, it is not a question of putting his trust in the Lord or of believing in his existence, but rather of believing that Jesus was the Lord whom he already knew as YHWH, the God of Israel.

(ἐπίστευον) καὶ ἐβαπτίζοντο B 𝔓⁷⁴ ℵ *rell* lat (syᵖ) sa bo aeth ‖ κ. ἐβαπτ. πιστεύοντες τῷ θεῷ διὰ τοῦ ὀνόματος τοῦ κυρίου ἡμῶν Ἰησοῦ Χριστοῦ D, *et baptizabantur credentes in deo per nomen domini nostri Iesu Christi* d (h) | (ἐπίστευσαν) διὰ τοῦ ὀν. τ. κυ. (+ ἡμῶν 2147) Ἰ. Χρ. κ. ἐβαπτίζοντο 614. 1799. 2147. 2412 syʰ**.

The account in D05 of the conversion of people from Corinth has God as the object of their belief, in line with the consistent practice of this text (Read-Heimerdinger, *The Bezan Text*, p. 286). The association of the full title of Jesus with baptism and belief is typical of formal speech acts in D05 (*The Bezan Text*, p. 271). Cf. 20.21 D05, where Paul declares that he has given testimony to faith, διὰ τοῦ κυρίου ἡμῶν Ἰησοῦ Χριστοῦ. The repetition of the verb πιστεύω with the paronomastic present participle is not redundant; Delebecque (*Les deux Actes*, p. 187) describes it as good Greek style (cf. the same phenomenon at 13.45).

18.9 ὁ (κύριος) B 𝔓⁷⁴ ℵ *rell* ‖ *om.* D.

When κύριος introduces the speaker of divine speech, the article is regularly omitted in D05 (cf. 2.17 D05, 34; 7.49; 15.17; see Read-Heimerdinger, *The Bezan Text*, p. 295). Omitting the article before the name is a way of drawing attention to the speaker when the speech is of particular importance. The same pattern of omitting the article before κύριος as speaker can also be observed in the LXX – though to conclude that inarticular κύριος in the New Testament is always a reference to YHWH is unwarranted (cf. J.D.G. Dunn, 'ΚΥΡΙΟΣ in Acts', in *Christ and the Spirit*. I. *Christology*, pp. 241–53; G.D. Kilpatrick, *The Principles and Practice of New Testament Textual Criticism*, pp. 216–22; C.K. Rowe, *Early Narrative Christology: The Lord in the Gospel of Luke*, *Appendix* 2). Here, the speaker is to be understood as Jesus in view of the two references to him as κύριος in the previous verse (18.8a, 8b); prefacing his speech with a phrase that is evocative of the Jewish Scriptures is part of the process of identifying him with YHWH.

ἐν νυκτὶ δι' ὁράματος τῷ Παύλῳ B 𝔓⁷⁴ ℵ 33. 69. 945. 1175. 1739. 1837. 1891. 2344 I δι' ὁρ. ἐν νυκ. τ. Παύ. (A) E L (τῆς νυκτός H) P Ψ 049. 056. 614 𝔐 I ἐν ὁρ. ἐν νυκ. τ. Παύ. 1241. 1518. 2495 I ἐν ὁράματι τ. Παύ. A (h) syᵖ; Chr II δι' ὁράματος τ. Π. ἐν νυκ. D, *per visum Paulo per noctem* d gig; Theoph.

B03 highlights the time of the Lord's speaking by placing the adverbial phrase of time before the manner of speaking and Paul as the indirect object; D05 highlights, in contrast, the vision, in keeping with the preface to the speech (see above), which recalls the Lord speaking to his messengers in the Scriptures. The same order 'in a vision … at night' is found at 16.9 D05.

18.10 (ἐπιθήσεταί) σοι B 𝔓⁷⁴ ℵ *rell, te* d II *om.* D E e gig h vgᶜᵀ.

The omission of the pronoun in D05 after ἐπιθήσεταί arises because the verb is being used in that text in an absolute sense. As Delebecque comments (*Les deux Actes*, p. 219): 'La promesse de Dieu est plus directe: "Personne ne s'efforcera de t'opprimer".'

18.11 ἐκάθισεν δέ B 𝔓⁷⁴ ℵ A Ψ 33. 69. 614. 945. 1175. 1505. 1611. 1739. 1837. 1891. 2147. 2344. 2412. 2495 I ἐκάθισέν τε E H L P 049. 056 𝔐 II καὶ ἐκ. ἐν Κορίνθῳ D, *et consedit in Corintho* d h (syᵖ·ʰ**).— (ἐνιαυτὸν) ἕνα (ΚΕΝΑ ℵ*) ℵ² II *om.* B D 𝔓⁷⁴ *rell*.

δέ in B03 treats the statement about Paul's continued residence in Corinth as a new development following the vision of encouragement in 18.9-10. καί, in contrast, treats the vision and Paul's response as one unit, all of it in effect preparing for the new sequence beginning at 18.12. Stating the name of the city also serves to re-establish the setting as part of the preparation, as well as reinforcing the correspondence between this element [a'] and the opening one of the sequence [a]. It tallies with the description of Paul's teaching as 'the word of God', this being the term reserved by Luke in this part of Acts, according to D05, for preaching to the Gentiles (see *Excursus* 1).

ℵ01 makes explicit the number of years.

(διδάσκων) ἐν αὐτοῖς B 𝔓⁷⁴ *rell, penes ipsos* d ‖ αὐτούς D 056 syᴾ aeth; Oecumˡᵃᵗ.

The direct correspondence between a place and the inhabitants, seen here in the direct object of D05, was also noted in a similar context at 16.10b B03. See also Mk 1.21 D05: εἰσελθὼν εἰς τὴν συναγωγὴν ἐδίδασκεν αὐτούς. The B03 reading presents Paul's teaching in Corinth as less personal and less purposeful.

18.12 (Γαλλίωνος) δέ B 𝔓⁷⁴ ℵ *rell* ‖ τε D, *-que* d.— οἱ 'Ιουδαῖοι ὁμοθυμαδόν B 330. 1505. 1828. 2495 ‖ ὁμ. οἱ 'Ιουδ. D, *unanimiter Iudaei* d 𝔓⁷⁴ ℵ A E H L P Ψ 049. 056. 33. 1739ᶜ 𝔐 (h).— τῷ Παύλῳ B 𝔓⁷⁴ ℵ *rell* ‖ συλλαλήσαντες μεθ' ἑαυτῶν ἐπὶ τὸν Παῦλον D, *conloquentes inter semet ipsos de Paulo* d h.— (καὶ) ἐπιθέντες τὰς χεῖρας D, (*imponentes manum* d h syʰ** sa) ‖ *om.* B 𝔓⁷⁴ ℵ *rell.*

τε read by D05 is assumed to have arisen through phonetic confusion with δέ, since the fronting of Gallio clearly signals a new episode, which Luke always connects with δέ to the previous one (Levinsohn, *Discourse Features*, pp. 17–18).

The place of ὁμοθυμαδόν before the subject in D05 makes it clear that it refers to the first verb and not the second (omitted by B03).

From a grammatical point of view, D05 has two examples in this verse of a series of two verbs that have the same object, specified only once despite the two verbs requiring different cases. Thus, D05 spells out four actions on the part of the Jews: they launched a united attack on Paul after conferring among themselves, and having seized him they took him off to the court. B03 omits the second and the third of these actions. The hostility of the Jews is accentuated in D05 compared with B03; a similar comparison could be made with Paul's letters where the denunciation of the Jewish opposition to himself is even stronger than in D05 of Acts. Such observations tell against the author of D05 writing from a Gentile point of view or adding his anti-Judaic sentiments as a later revision of the original.

(ἤγαγον) ἐπὶ τὸ βῆμα B D, *ad tribunal* d 𝔓⁷⁴ *rell* ‖ παρὰ τ. β. ℵ.

With παρά in ℵ01, βῆμα would be the platform in the Agora from where justice was administered and to which Paul was taken. In the other MSS that read the preposition ἐπί, βῆμα refers to the court overall, by way of metonymy.

18.13 καταβοῶντες καὶ (λέγοντες) D, *clamantes et* d h ‖ *om.* B 𝔓⁷⁴ ℵ *rell.*— ἀναπείθει οὗτος B 𝔓⁷⁴ ℵ A 33. 927. 945. 1270. 1739. 1837. 1891. 2344 ‖ οὗτος ἀν. D E (H) L P Ψ 049. 056. 614 𝔐 e gig vg.

καταβοάω in D05 is a New Testament hapax; the insistence on the noise made by those opposing Paul is typical of Codex Bezae (cf. 16.22 D05, 39b D05; 17.6).

οὗτος in pre-verb position in D05 brings Paul into an emphatic position and also aligns him more closely with the charge that he is acting παρὰ τὸν νόμον.

18.14 ἄνδρες (᾿Ιουδαῖοι) D, *viri* d h vg ‖ *om.* B 𝔓⁷⁴ ℵ *rell.*

The form of address in D05 is found in other speeches in Acts (1.11; 2.14, 22; 3.12; 5.35; 13.16, 26; 15.7, 13; 17.22). The presence of ἄνδρες here tempers any annoyance in Gallio's response (a similar reading is found in Peter's speech to the Jews at 3.17 D05); it also highlights their identity as Jews (B-A-G, ἀνήρ, 4).

ἀνεσχόμην (ὑμῶν) B 𝔓⁷⁴ ℵ A (33). 1837. 2344 ‖ ἠν- D ℵ² E H L P Ψ 049. 056. 614.1739 𝔐.

The two verb forms are different forms of the second aorist middle of ἀνέχω; that of B03 is rare.

18.15 (εἰ δὲ) ζητήματά ἐστιν B ℵ A E 33. 88. 104. 323. 614. 945. 1175. (1270). 1505. 1611. 1646. 1739. 1891. 2147. 2412. 2495 *al* lat sy co | ζήτημά ἐστιν 𝔓⁷⁴ H L P Ψ 049. 056 𝔐, *quaestio est* d e ‖ ζήτημα (-ατα Dᴰ) ἔχετε D* gig.

B03 reads the plural noun with the singular verb, as permitted with a neuter plural, where ζητήματα has the sense of 'questions, issues'. With the singular ζήτημα and the verb ἔχετε, D05 expresses more forcefully that the 'debate' or 'controversy' is an internal Jewish one that was going on amongst the Jews themselves.

(οὐ) βούλομαι B 𝔓⁷⁴ ℵ *rell* ‖ θέλω D, *nolo* d.

In so far as there is any difference between these two verbs, the former conveys more specifically the idea of a deliberated decision (B-A-G, βούλομαι 2; B-D-R, §101). The D05 thus expresses with less vigour Gallio's refusal to intervene.

18.16 (καὶ) ἀπήλασεν B 𝔓⁷⁴ ℵ Dᴰ *rell, abiecit* d ‖ ἀπέλυσεν D* h.

B03 has the aorist of ἀπελαύνω, 'drive out' (Bailly, 'pousser hors de, chasser'); D05 has the aorist of ἀπολύω, 'send away' (Bailly, 'congédier, renvoyer'). This is the third variant (see 18.14, 15 above) that causes Gallio's annoyance to be less strong in D05 compared with B03.

18.17 ἐπιλαβόμενοι δέ B 𝔓⁷⁴ ℵ Dᴰ *rell, adpraehendentes* d, *comprehenderunt* h ‖ ἀπο- D*.— (πάντες) οἱ ῞Ελληνες D, *Graeci* d E H L P Ψ 33. 1739 𝔐 ar e gig (h) vgᴰ syᵖ·ʰ sa aeth; Chrᵖᵗ (Aug) Bedaᵍʳ ᵐˢ ᵃᶜᶜ· ᵗᵒ | οἱ ᾿Ιουδαῖοι 36. 307. 431. 453. 610. 1678 *pc* | οἱ πεπιστευκότες ῞Ελληνες Ephrᶜ ‖ *om.* B 𝔓⁷⁴ ℵ A 323. 629 c dem p ph ro w vg bo.

B03 uses the middle voice of ἐπιλαμβάνω, meaning 'seize' (Bailly, 'mettre la main sur, d'où se saisir de, s'emparer de'); D05 has ἀπολαμβάνω, also in the middle, with the meaning 'take to one side' (Bailly, 'prendre à part, en particulier').

The subject of the participle, and the main verb following (ἔτυπτον) is πάντες, which D05, with an extensive range of support, qualifies as 'the Greeks'.

ὅταν (Σωσθένην) D^{cj.}, *cum* d ‖ *om.* B 𝔓^{74} ℵ D^{s.m.} *rell.*— καὶ οὐδὲν τούτων τῷ Γαλλίωνι ἔμελεν B 𝔓^{74} A D^D 440 ‖ κ. οὐδ. τ. Γαλ. ἔμελεν τούτων Ψ ‖ κ. οὐδ. τούτων τ. Γαλ. ἔμελεν ℵ E H L P 049. 056. 614 𝔐 ‖ κ. οὐδ. τούτων ἔμελλε τ. Γαλ. 945. 1739. 1891 ‖ τότε τούτων οὐδ. τῷ Γαλ. ἔμελεν D^{cj.} (*tunc Gallio fingebat eum non videre* d h; Ephr).

There is a gap equivalent to four letters and a space in D05 at the beginning of the line before Σωσθένην. According to the conjecture of Ussher (see Scrivener, p. 445), ὅταν would have been read, in anticipation of τότε in the next line of the original D05*.

This next line in D05 is partially erased and has been completed by a later corrector (Parker, *Codex Bezae*, p. 152). From the few letters of the first hand that are said to be visible, T.............ΠΓΑΛΛΙΩΝ...........ΕΝ, the original reading of D05 has to be reconstructed. About 14 to 15 letters seem to have been erased from between the initial T and Ω. The conjectured reading of Kipling is cited by Scrivener, who accepts it in preference to the reading of Wetstein: '*Quae restant p. m. scripta (a Kiplingio post Wetst. perperam lecta* τοτε γαλλιων) *dedimus*' (p. 445). On this reading, τότε corresponds to ὅταν supplied at the beginning of the previous line; ΕΝ at the end of the line could be the ending of ἔμελεν (as read by B03), where the imperfect is appropriate because of the construction ὅταν ... τότε.

The erased letters in the manuscript are, however, extremely difficult to read and Kilpling's conjecture can be questioned in view of the reading of d5 *tunc Gallio fingebat eum non videre*, supported as it is by both h12 and Ephraem, which suggests an equivalent reading in Greek for D05*. Taking Kipling's reading of the manuscript first, three possible wordings may be conjectured, which respect the space and the original letters that he claimed to read (shown here in capitals):

Τότε προσεποιεῖτο Ο ΓΑΛΛΙΩΝ αὐτὸν μὴ ἰδεῖΝ
Τότε προσεποιεῖτο Ο ΓΑΛΛΙΩΝ ὅτι αὐτὸν οὐκ εἶδΕΝ
Τοτε προσεποιήθη ΤΩΓΑΛΛΙΩνι αυτον μη ιδειΝ

Alternatively, taking Wetstein's reading (ΤΟΤΕ ΓΑΛΛΙΩΝ), the original could have been (cf. Clark, *Acts*, p. 118):

τότε Γαλλίων προσεποιεῖτο αὐτὸν μὴ ἰδεῖν

Commentary

[B′-A] 18.1-11 *In the Synagogue*

As Paul moves to Corinth, a number of secondary characters are introduced into the narrative, either ones already encountered or others that are completely new. In the Bezan text, the spotlight nevertheless remains clearly directed upon Paul, maintaining him more strongly in focus than in the Alexandrian text. Silas and Timothy are brought back into the story as they come from Macedonia to join Paul (cf. 17.15b-16), but they no sooner arrive than they disappear again from the story, this time for good. Aquila and Priscilla are brought in for the first time and will remain to be part of the bridge between this part of Acts and the next and final part (18.24–28.31). By their association with Rome, the city is named for the first time in Acts; this is not without significance as it is the place to where Paul is meant to be heading (cf. 19.21). For the time being, since he has been avoiding travelling directly to his final destination (see *Commentary*, 16.6-10), Paul is brought into indirect contact with Jews who have recently had to flee from the city.

[a] 18.1 *Paul's Departure to Corinth*

18.1 The new sequence opens with Paul's departure from Athens and his arrival in Corinth. His decision to get away from Athens seems to have been his own choice, and one very likely taken because of the disappointing lack of success in the city. From among the Jews and God-fearers of the synagogue, no response was recorded (cf. 17.17); the Greek philosophers were at worst negative (the Epicureans, cf. 17.32a), and at best merely interested in talking again some time (the Stoics, cf. 17.32b). The narrator does, nonetheless, provide some positive information about conversions among the Stoics and others from the city but it is almost parenthetical (17.34); Paul is not seen in any way being involved with them, nor is he detained by them. It is conversions among his own people that he has been so much hoping for.[100]

He leaves Athens without waiting for Silas and Timothy to arrive from Macedonia, suggesting that his departure was precipitated by the unenthusiastic response in Athens, for his original intention had been to wait for them there (cf. 17.15b, 16). The verb used by the Bezan text to describe his departure expresses more specifically than that of the Alexandrian text the idea of going away towards a place of safety or refuge (see *Critical Apparatus*). The Alexandrian text does not make a strong link at all between the events in Athens and Paul's departure to Corinth, saying simply 'After that'. The journey from Athens to Corinth would have been made by land, a distance of some 50 miles along the coast road south-west of Athens, so continuing to move Paul away from Macedonia as he crossed on to the southern peninsula of the Peloponnese (cf. *Commentary*, 17.15).

Corinth was a city of some reputation, a large commercial centre, having enjoyed the status of a Roman colony for 100 years or so when Paul visited it and having superseded Athens as the capital. It had ports providing access to Italy in the east and to Asia in the west, the latter of which, Cenchrea, will be mentioned as Paul's port of departure for Syria at the end of the sequence (18.18). It was thus a thriving and prosperous city, with a mixed population from a wide range of ethnic and social backgrounds, amongst whom was a strong

---

100. In almost every city Paul had visited during the two phases of his mission there were reports of Jews or God-fearers who became believers: in Antioch of Pisidia (13.43); Iconium (14.1); Lystra (cf. 16.1, Timothy's mother was Jewish); Philippi (16.15); Thessalonica (17.4); Beroea (17.11-12). The same will be true of Corinth in the sequence.

Jewish contingent. Paul's own letters to the Corinthians provide interesting background information about the people and the situations he encountered there, especially that known as 1 Corinthians.[101]

[b] 18.2 *Meeting with Aquila and Priscilla*

18.2 Once in Corinth, Paul lost no time in seeking out fellow Jews.[102] The couple he found, Aquila and Priscilla, had come to Corinth from Rome which they had been forced to flee because of an imperial edict affecting all Jews, without distinction between those who were believers in Jesus and those who were not.[103] They were originally from Pontus, the area associated with Bithynia where the Spirit of Jesus had not allowed Paul and Silas to go as they were heading westwards from Galatic Phrygia (16.7). Now, Paul has a chance to meet with Jews from precisely that area, recalling a similar opportunity he took in Philippi to talk and spend time with a Jewish sympathizer, Lydia, from Asia where he had also been prevented from speaking at the earlier stage of his journey (16.6, cf. 16.14).

Their coming to Corinth is underlined in the Bezan text, with the mention of the southern part of Greece by its geographical name of Achaia. The introduction of the name at this point anticipates the importance of the role that will be played by the proconsul of the province in the second part of the sequence. Meanwhile, it has here the more immediate function of underlining the ironic coincidence in Paul's being able to meet, there in Corinth, people from an area from which he had earlier been diverted as he was being steered by divine intervention towards Rome (see *Commentary*, 16.6-10). Rome is, of course, the very place Aquila and Priscilla had just left so that there is a double irony: Paul has been resisting going to Rome, most recently since he started to head south as he escaped from Thessalonica, and now in Corinth as he meets Jews who had first-hand experience of that city.

Aquila is presented first and foremost as a Jew, though his knowledge of the teaching of Jesus (cf. 18.26) without any mention being made of his conversion could suggest that he and his wife were already Jesus-believers when Paul met them. This would imply, in turn, that there was already a community of believers in Rome by this time, in the early 50s. Luke presents Aquila, in fact, as a representative of a community with his key word 'a certain';[104] at the

---

101. For further detailed presentation on Corinth in the first century, see B. Witherington, *Conflict and Community in Corinth* (Grand Rapids: Eerdmans, 1995), pp. 5–35.

102. The verb εὑρών may be taken in the sense of 'come across by chance', but since Paul was in the habit of making contact with Jews as soon as he arrived in a new place, there is every reason to take it in the sense of 'he sought out' (cf. 13.6, in Paphos).

103. The edict probably dates from 49 CE; for a thorough discussion, see Witherington, *Acts*, pp. 539–44. It is unlikely that literally 'all the Jews' (AT) had to leave, but it does seem that if the edict applied to 'all Jews' (D05) then it affected those who believed in Jesus as well as those who did not.

104. τις is commonly used by Luke to introduce a representative of a type (cf. 3.2; 5.1, 34; 8.9; 9.10, 33, 36, 43; 10.1, 5, 6; 13.6; 14.8; 16.1, 9, 14, 16).

same time, he is a real person in his own right as indicated by his name and
the presence of his wife. He will play an important role in the opening
sequence of the final part (Part Four) of Acts (18.24-28). Because of the
importance of Aquila and Priscilla to the narrative, and apparently to Paul, it
is strange that so little is specified concerning their belief in Jesus, or their
relationship with Paul (cf. on 18.18, 19 below).

Codex Bezae maintains the focus on Aquila in particular as Paul approaches
him ('them', AT).

[c] 18.3 *His Stay at their House*

18.3 Having met up with Aquila, Paul arranged to stay with him, with the
wording of Codex Bezae expressing a closer relationship than that of the
Alexandrian text.[105] The arrangement was appropriate because Paul exercised
the same trade as Aquila (and possibly Priscilla). The Bezan text omits the
explanation in the Alexandrian text that this was tent-making – it is possible
that this is an error but the omission of other background information
concerning Paul in the Bezan text (cf. the description of Tarsus at 21.39)
should also be noted. Codex Bezae tends not to provide background details for
their own sake, but only when they serve as figurative cues to theological
meaning. It is more likely that the explanation is a gloss in the Alexandrian
text, derived from διὰ τὸ ὁμότεχνον, which could explain the plural verb
ἠργάζοντο in the Alexandrian text.

In Codex Bezae, the comment about working refers to Paul only, not the
whole group. It is in his activity that the narrator is interested. It can be seen
from his subsequent correspondence with the Corinthians that it was a matter
of the greatest importance to Paul that he did not demand or expect to live at
the expense of those he was teaching (cf. 1 Cor. 4.12; 9.3-18; 2 Cor. 11.9; 1
Thess. 2.9; 2 Thess. 3.8; Acts 20.34), and Luke's narrative here accurately
reflects that attitude. The fact that Paul works when he first arrives in Corinth
implies that he had no other source of money, a situation that appears to be
altered by the arrival of Silas and Timothy (see on 18.5a, 5b below).

[d] 18.4a *Debate in the Synagogue*

18.4a Paul's work means that he is not free to lecture in the market place as he
had in Athens (cf. 17.17) but is limited to spending time only on the Sabbath
to go to lecture in the synagogue. The Bezan text displays a particular interest
in his visits to the synagogue, as it has on previous occasions where it has
become clear that the narrator does not approve of Paul's strategy of seeking
out Jews or God-fearers with the aim of persuading them about the truth of
Jesus, because it is a tactic that prevents him from fulfilling the order he received
from Jesus to go to the Gentiles (cf. 22.18-21, esp. D05). His efforts with regard
to the Gentiles have been so far limited and his two recorded speeches to
Gentiles have barely produced fruit (cf. 14.15-18; 17.22-31).

---

105. On the prepositions, see Winer, *Grammar*, p. 504, esp. n. 4.

Since Paul's visit to the synagogue in Beroea, where it was first recorded that he went on successive Sabbaths (17.2) as he does now in Corinth, Luke has used the verb διαλέγομαι to describe his activity of 'lecturing' or 'debating' in the synagogues (cf. 17.2, 17). The content of his lectures was most fully summarized on the first occasion in Beroea: he talked to them about the Messiah as he was foretold in the Scriptures, from which he demonstrated that his suffering and also his resurrection were part of the divine plan, and that furthermore the Messiah was Jesus. In Corinth, likewise, he 'introduced the name of the Lord, Jesus', according to the Bezan text. This is not some pious clarification but a comment that illustrates what precisely was Paul's aim as he lectured in the synagogue: he sought to identify the Lord, the κύριος, or YHWH whose name the synagogue participants had hitherto refrained even from mentioning, as Jesus. He gave the Lord a name, and that name was Jesus.

[e] 18.4b *Paul Persuades Jews and Greeks*
18.4b Paul's intention in lecturing in the synagogue and introducing the name of the Lord was to persuade the Jews and also, perhaps more surprisingly, the Greeks. This fact is presented emphatically in Codex Bezae,[106] underlining the attention paid by Paul to Gentiles among the synagogue audience who, since they are not referred to as 'God-fearers', may be assumed to be local people who attended the synagogue without participating as fully as God-fearers. In the synagogues of previous cities, God-fearers have been mentioned alongside the Jews (Antioch of Pisidia, 13.16, 26; Athens, 17.17; cf. Lydia on her own as a God-fearer in Philippi, 16.15) but elsewhere Greeks have also been mentioned in the context of the synagogue (Iconium, 14.1, 'Jews and Greeks'; Thessalonica, 17.4 D05, 'many of the God-fearers and a great number of Greeks'; Beroea, 17.12 D05, 'some ... from among the Greeks').[107]

[f] 18.5a *The Arrival of Silas and Timothy*
18.5a Silas and Timothy were last seen in Beroea, from where Paul was taken by local brethren to Athens (17.14). The people who accompanied him to Athens were sent back to Beroea with the message that Silas and Timothy were to join him as soon as possible (17.15c). There is no mention of them

---

106. The two parallel sentences of 18.4a and 4b in D05 are striking, each with a participle followed by a finite verb: εἰσπορευόμενος δὲ ... διελέγετο ‖ καὶ ἐντιθεὶς ... καὶ ἔπειθεν δέ. The second finite verb is underlined with adverbial καί and is further reinforced with δέ. The use of καί ... δέ is found elsewhere in Luke (cf. Lk. 1.76; 2.35 D05; Acts 5.32 D^C H P Ψ; 6.15) to insist on the importance of the verb as the second in a series (Bailly, δέ, B VII, '*pour marquer une progression, au sens de* bien plus, et même, *particul. après* καί').

107. Paul's practice in directing his teaching in the synagogue to Gentiles was unlikely to have been innovative, for there is evidence that the Jews in the Diaspora in the first century CE, even if not aggressively engaged in proselytizing, at the very least advocated a positive openness of the synagogue to the Gentiles; see Philo, *Spec. Leg.* I, 320–23; *Leg. Gai.*, 31.211. For an evaluation of the evidence for and against aggressive proselytism, see J.C. Paget, 'Jewish Proselytism at the Time of Christian Origins: Chimera or Reality?', *JSNT* 62 (1996), pp. 65–103.

going to Athens; on the contrary, Paul was on his own there but is now joined by the two disciples in Corinth,[108] with the verb of the Bezan text expressing the idea of 'arriving into the presence of someone', rather than simply 'come down' in a geographical sense as in the Alexandrian text. The result is that in the Bezan text Silas and Timothy are seen in relation to Paul in particular; they are also presented there as a united pair, rather than as distinct individuals (see *Critical Apparatus*). Though Luke does not spell out the significance of their arrival, it is apparent from the following clause that it enabled Paul to devote himself entirely at that point to 'the word', that is, his teaching activity (see 18.5b below). From one of his letters later written to the believers of Corinth (2 Cor. 11.9; cf. Phil. 4.15), it is known that 'the brethren who came from Macedonia' brought money for Paul when he was there. It is typical of Luke to make no mention of money, for he is remarkably silent throughout the whole of Acts about any collections of money from the churches Paul established and the information has to be deduced from the context and confirmed, where appropriate, from Paul's letters.

This will be the last mention of Silas and Timothy in Acts, probably a signal that they were not in harmony with Paul, as earlier clues already suggested with respect to Silas at least (see *Commentary* on 17.14b).

[g] 18.5b *Paul Devotes Himself to the Word*

18.5b The Alexandrian text presents the journey of Silas and Timothy from Macedonia in a time clause that provides a time frame for the next clause describing Paul's teaching activity. In Codex Bezae, the two clauses are placed side by side without making explicit the connection between them; the asyndeton that connects this sentence to the previous one is striking, underlining the close dependence of the second sentence on the first at the same time as drawing attention to Paul's witness to the Jews.[109] Furthermore, the absence of the article before the names of Silas and Timothy on the one hand, and of Paul on the other, suggests a relationship of contrast whereby the disciples' arrival sets Paul's activity in relief. The Alexandrian text makes the time connection more overtly with the use of the subordinating conjunction ὡς, 'when', but also leaves unexplained the logical connection between the departure (in the case of the AT) of Silas and Timothy from Macedonia and Paul's intense preoccupation with the word. It was at that point, however, that he began to devote himself[110] to the word. The money they would have

---

108. Paul's references to Timothy in 1 Thess. 3.1-2, 6, where he speaks of sending Timothy to Thessalonica while he remained alone in Athens, do not mean that Timothy was with Paul in Athens at any point. He had been left in Beroea with Silas, and Paul (according to the account of Acts) would have instructed Timothy to go from there to give help to the brethren in Thessalonica, rather than coming immediately with Silas to join him in Athens. That would account for the delay in their travelling south and explain why they did not meet up with Paul until he was in Corinth.

109. The sequence of tenses, where the aorist παρεγένοντο is followed by the imperfect συνείχετο, indicates a time connection between the two sentences.

110. The imperfect tense has an inceptive force here.

brought with them enabled him to give himself more fully to teaching instead of having to earn his money with tent-making.

The content of Paul's teaching is stated for a second time, according to Codex Bezae, but for the first time according to the Alexandrian text. As at the previous Bezan reference, the focus is on Jesus, again as the Lord in the Bezan text, and now referred to as the Messiah. His point is to identify the Messiah as Jesus, and also as 'the Lord' in Codex Bezae. Here, as elsewhere, the Alexandrian text avoids identifying Jesus as YHWH of the Jewish Scriptures.[111] The context of Paul's 'word', to which he now gave himself entirely, continues to be Jewish with no mention of any preaching in terms that would be comprehensible to people who had no prior contact with the synagogue; indeed, his audience are now 'the Jews' alone.

[f'] 18.6 *Opposition from the Jews*

18.6 The reaction of Paul's audience makes itself felt as they resist him and blaspheme. The term 'blaspheme' was also used to describe the hostile response of the Jews in Antioch of Pisidia (cf. 13.45), where it was concluded that the blasphemy consisted in opposing a message given by God. Codex Bezae fills in the context of their opposition: it happened as there was much talk going on and as the Scriptures were being interpreted, both referring to Paul's activities.[112] The two parallel sets of actions (much talk and the interpretation of the Scriptures ‖ resisting and blaspheming) are clearly set against each other in contrast.

Paul's response is to make a formal break from his fellow Jews, by shaking out his clothes to show, in this symbolic gesture, that he was loosening himself completely from them,[113] with the Bezan text underlining his attitude by means of a dual reference to Paul (name and possessive pronoun, see *Critical Apparatus*). His protestation of innocence with regard to the fate that awaits them for their rejection of the gospel is then made in a formal statement in which he declares that the blood of the Jews is 'on their own head', thus removing any guilt on his part, as he confirms in saying, 'I am clean (from you, D05)'. Echoing the words of the prophet Ezekiel regarding the innocence of the prophet who delivered the message of warning to the people and his corresponding guilt if he failed to do so (cf. Ezek. 33.4-6), Paul makes plain that he regards himself as having fulfilled his prophetic responsibility in

---

111. Cf., e.g., 2.17; 7.30; 13.47; 15.18; 20.28. On the avoidance in the AT of assimilating Jesus with YHWH, see Read-Heimerdinger, *The Bezan Text*, pp. 292–93.

112. The same expression πολὺς λόγος is found at 13.44 with specific reference to Paul's preaching.

113. Shaking out (ἐκτινάσσω) one's garments occurs in the book of Nehemiah, where it is a sign that the Jews are to be 'shaken out of their houses' because they have not been faithful to their promise (Neh. 5.13). More appropriate for this context is the use of the symbol in an early Egyptian papyrus, where the gesture of shaking out one's garments seems to signify that the person is taking absolutely nothing with them (U. Wilcken [ed.], *Urkunden der Ptolmäerzeit* [2 vols.; Berlin: De Gruyter, 1927–57], I, p. 647, Seite 128).

giving the message concerning Jesus to the Jews; since they have refused to accept it, they are the guilty ones, but he is 'clean', there is no blood on his head (cf. Pilate with regard to Jesus, Mt. 27.24-25).

Just as he warned the Jews in Antioch of Pisidia that if they rejected the Messiah and the possibility of repentance, they would be overrun with Gentiles (13.40-41; cf. Hab. 1.5), so now also a crisis point has been reached, at which Paul acknowledges that the response of his own people testifies to their rejection of the Messiah and that he must go to the Gentiles. In the Alexandrian text, this is a decision for the future ('from now on ... I will go') whereas in the Bezan text the rupture with the Jews is more forceful as he decisively withdraws from them 'now', to go immediately to the Gentiles.

This is the second time that he has made this declaration. The first time was in Antioch of Pisidia, together with Barnabas (13.46), but it was quickly seen that, in fact, Paul did not modify the strategy he had been adopting, of going to the synagogue to try to persuade the Jews of the message concerning the Messiah, since in the next town of Iconium he did exactly the same thing (cf. 14.1). A repetition of this going back on his decision will be soon evident, as he makes his way to the synagogue in the next town of Ephesus (cf. 18.18). It will not be until the third time Paul states his decision to leave the Jews and go to the Gentiles, when he is in Rome, that he will finally act in accordance with his decision (cf. 28.25-28), at which point Luke will bring his book to an end.

[e'] 18.7 *Paul's Move to the House of Justus*

18.7 Following his announcement that he is going to the Gentiles, Paul moves to a different house. The account of the Alexandrian text is straightforward, describing his move 'from there', that is the synagogue where he had been speaking, to the house of Titius Justus, who was a certain God-fearer and whose house was next door to the synagogue. The text of Codex Bezae includes several significant details: first, that he moved away from Aquila, that is, he left the Jewish community that Aquila represented (cf. on 18.2 above) and where he had been staying in Corinth until then; secondly, expressed emphatically, that he went to the household, the family, of a certain God-fearer called Justus, who is set in contrast to Aquila by the omission of the article before both names (see *Critical Apparatus*) – just as Aquila represented a Jewish community, so Justus represents a community of God-fearers; finally, as in the Alexandrian text, he had a house (referring now to the building) next to the synagogue. What Paul has done, in other words, after declaring that he is going 'now' (D05, v. 6) to the Gentiles, is to have left the house of the Jewish community to go to that of the God-fearers. The move takes him to Gentiles, but scarcely alters the religious sphere of his living and teaching since he is still within the confines of a society that has close contact with Judaism. The physical proximity of Justus' house to the synagogue is emblematic of this close contact. The break with the Jews that he has just proclaimed is hardly radical, and he will not take long to go back to the synagogue (in Cenchrea,

18.18 D05; cf. Ephesus, 18.19). Nevertheless, he has taken a step in the right direction and following this move his work does indeed bear fruit among Gentiles as well as Jews (cf. 18.8b).

[d']18.8a *Conversion of Crispus, the Synagogue Leader*

18.8a An important event set in the context of Paul's move to the house next to the synagogue is that the leader 'believed in the Lord'. The word order of the Bezan text presents his function as the more important piece of information, whereas the Alexandrian text is more interested in his name. Within the framework of his Jewish beliefs, that 'he believed in the Lord' means that he believed in Jesus as the Lord, since his faith in YHWH as Lord was already something that defined him as a Jew. The wording of the Bezan text distinguishes this step of belief from that of believing for the first time (see *Critical Apparatus*). Moreover, like Cornelius in Antioch, Lydia in Philippi and the jailor there, too, the whole of his household joined him in his new belief.

[c'] 18.8b *Conversion of Many Corinthians*

18.8b Further impact of Paul's teaching on the people of Corinth is recorded. These are Greeks who may be presumed to have not been previously associated with the synagogue. They believe, too, and make public testimony of their faith by baptism. Codex Bezae carefully specifies the content of their belief: unlike Crispus who believed 'in the Lord', the object of their faith is God, always an essential step for Gentiles who are viewed as knowing neither God nor the Lord until they become Jesus-believers.[114] However, the explanation continues with the information that their belief was 'through the name of our Lord Jesus Christ'. This account of the Gentiles' faith authenticates it and shows the basis on which Paul accepts their joining the community of Jesus-believers – that is, without circumcision or following the Law, but on the grounds of their full belief in every aspect of the teaching of Paul concerning Jesus. The insistence expressed by Codex Bezae suggests that some were contesting the faith of the Gentiles and their inclusion among the Jesus-believing community. The use of the full title for Jesus, ὁ κύριος ἡμῶν Ἰησοῦς Χριστός, is rare (it is only found elsewhere in Acts at 15.26; 20.21 D05) but it is interesting to note that Paul uses it five times in the opening chapter of his first letter to the Corinthians (cf. 1 Cor. 1.1-13).

[b'] 18.9-10 *Paul's Vision*

18.9 It is at this point, when a whole section of the Jewish community has accepted Paul's teaching about Jesus, and many of the Gentiles in the city, too, that he appears particularly vulnerable. His state of mind is apparent from the appearance to him of the Lord, who addresses him with words of reassurance and encouragement. The vision recalls the one that he had seen in Troas,

---

114. In Codex Bezae, Gentiles always put their faith in God first, cf. Sergius Paulus, 13.12 D05.

when he was exhorted to cross over to help the people of Macedonia (cf. 16.9-10). Now in Corinth, when he has had to face strong opposition from his own people but has nevertheless also encountered positive results among some of them and among the Gentiles as well, Jesus tells him to stop being afraid, and encourages him to continue speaking as he has been doing. It can be deduced from these words that Paul had been on the point of giving up in Corinth, made fearful by the hostility and uncertain as to the feasibility of staying on there.

18.10 The positive aspect of Jesus' words justifies the commands he gives Paul. First, he promises that he is with him, using an expression that has been used with other people chosen by God,[115] and he therefore assures him that he will not be harmed when he is attacked (cf. Lk. 10.19). The truth of this promise will be seen in the second episode [B'-A'], when the assault on him by the Jews comes to nothing. Secondly, Jesus reveals to Paul that he has 'a large people' in the city of Corinth.[116]. The word 'people', λαός, is a technical term in Luke's writings when it has the article, meaning 'the people of Israel'. Here, without the article, a radical shift in perspective is indicated, as it comes to mean 'people' of all races, not just the Jews. The idea that there is in Corinth a people for Jesus, regardless of ethnic origin or religion, contradicts the tradition expressed by James at the Jerusalem meeting (cf. 15.14, *Commentary, ad loc.*), namely that God had chosen a people (Israel) for his name from among the nations (λαὸς ἐξ ἐθνῶν), with whom the Gentiles would be assimilated at the time of the Messiah. The 'people' whom Jesus has in Corinth belong to him directly, without any reference to Israel.

[a'] 18.11 *Paul's Stay in Corinth*

18.11 The sequence closes with a summary of Paul's stay in Corinth, specifying the time as 18 months and his activity as teaching the word of God. Small differences between the two texts give this final statement a different orientation. The Alexandrian text introduces it as a development following on from the vision (δέ), not mentioning the name of the city but saying that he taught 'among them', that is the local inhabitants. The Bezan text presents both the vision and his extended stay (καί) as preparatory for the next sequence (δέ, 18.12); the mention of the name of the city is unnecessary, but by its inclusion it draws together the beginning of this sequence and the end of it (cf. 18.1); finally, Paul addresses his teaching directly to the Gentile Corinthians, which tallies with the description of its contents as the 'word of God', quite distinct from his teaching in the synagogue (cf. 18.4a D05, 6 D05; see *Excursus* 1 on the phrase 'the word of God').

---

115. Cf. Lk. 1.66, John the Baptist; 2.40, the child Jesus; Acts 7.9, Joseph, son of Jacob; 10.38, Jesus, the anointed.

116. The reference to a 'large people', underlined by the word order in the Greek text (λαός ἐστί μοι πολύς), may well be a deliberate allusion to the prophecies concerning the invasion of Israel by a 'large and powerful people' on the day of the Lord (Joel 2.2, 5, λαὸς πολὺς καὶ ἰσχυρός ; cf. Zach. 2.11 [15 LXX]). Cf. the prophecy of Hab. 1.5 cited by Paul as a warning to the Jews in Antioch of Pisidia (Acts 13.40-41, see *Commentary, ad loc.*).

The 18 months seem to be viewed as additional to any time Paul had spent so far in Corinth, going up to, and beyond, his appearance before Gallio (18.12, cf. 18.18). The verb here is καθίζομαι, literally meaning 'sit', so implying that he settled there for an extended stay, not thinking of moving on at any moment.[117] He is seen, in consequence, obeying Jesus' order to continue speaking in Corinth (cf. 18.9). So far, the longest stay of Paul in a place was in Antioch of Syria where he and Barnabas were teaching for a year (11.26). In Ephesus, he will stay for two years at the school of Tyrannus, or three years in total (19.9-10; cf. 20.31). The progression may be deliberate, as each time the extended period of teaching produces fruit. The theme of Paul's teaching is particularly strong in the Bezan text.[118]

[B'-A'] 18.12-17 *Before the Proconsul Gallio*

This second episode brings the events in Corinth to a close. There is a climactic attack on Paul before the Roman proconsul, but it becomes, in fact, an anti-climax as it leads to nothing. The result of the attack is in accordance with the promise of Jesus that Paul would not be harmed in Corinth (18.9-10), a promise that is fulfilled as he obeys the command not to be afraid but to speak.

[a] 18.12a *The Jews Attack Paul*
18.12a The mention of the Roman proconsul Gallio by name and by the district of which he was in charge provides information that anchors the narrative to a particular date, for historical records allow the period when Gallio held office to be calculated as between 51 and 52 CE.[119] This date fits with the departure of Aquila and Priscilla from Rome in 49 CE (cf. on 18.2 above), since it means that Paul would have been in Corinth from some time in 50 CE. The introduction to this new episode, 'When Gallio was proconsul of Achaia', could even be taken as meaning that he took on the role while Paul was there in Corinth and that the incident in the court took place once he had taken up his position. As procurator, Gallio stands for the Roman authorities, in the same way as did the three-tiered hierarchy of rulers in Philippi (cf. 16.19b). Unlike those of Philippi, however, he will not be seen opposing Paul but rather manifesting a certain indifference.

The Jews are now the main protagonists as they work out a way to attack Paul. The reason for their attack is to be found in his teaching the word of God to the Gentiles. It was in Antioch of Pisidia that this term was first noted as provoking the anger of the Jews, because it involved a whole area of contention between Paul and the Jews, expressing his understanding that the time

---

117. Cf. the use of καθίζομαι with reference to the apostles' stay in Hierosoluma (ἐν τῇ πόλει) at Lk. 24.49.

118. Apart from a more frequent association in D05 of the ideas of word – hearing – Paul (e.g. 13.44-45), there are additional mentions of Peter or Paul engaged in teaching (11.2; 14.7, 19; 17.4).

119. See Bruce, *Text*, p. 346; Hemer, *Hellenistic History*, pp. 252–56.

had come for the word of God, previously the exclusive possession of Israel, to be given also to the Gentiles (cf. 13.45-50, esp. D05; see *Commentary, ad loc.* and *Excursus* 6). Following the incident in Antioch of Pisidia, the term 'word of God' is a kind of shorthand to refer to this teaching of Paul's.

Here, the Bezan text presents the Jews as first getting together to talk about him, obviously still bothered by his continued presence in the town after their earlier attempts to silence him (cf. 18.6). Their unanimity in taking action against Paul is expressed by the word ὁμοθυμαδόν, emphasized by Codex Bezae.

[b] 18.12b-13 *They Take Him into the Court*
18.12b-13 The Jews seize Paul and take him to the court, βῆμα – the word may refer to the raised platform in the market place, which still stands in Corinth, or more probably the court over which Gallio would have presided. As elsewhere in the Bezan text, his opponents are presented as particularly noisy (see *Critical Apparatus*). Their accusation is that Paul, somewhat jeeringly referred to as 'this man', was encouraging people to worship in a way that was against the law. The phrase 'contrary to the law' is placed at the front of the sentence, drawing attention to the crux of the complaint – an ambiguous phrase since the Jews would expect Gallio to understand that they are talking about the Roman law whereas their own concern would be the Jewish Law. The choice of the vague term 'people' (τοὺς ἀνθρώπους) further allows for an entirely general interpretation. Their need to meet first to work out how they would formulate a charge against Paul is obvious (cf. 18.11 D05)!

[c] 18.14-15 *Gallio's Response*
18.14-15 Just as he was about to defend himself, Paul was interrupted.[120] Gallio speaks instead and weighs up the accusation the Jews have made. Addressing the Jewish accusers formally as 'Jews' (AT) or, perhaps less harshly, as 'Jewish men' (D05), he presents them with two possibilities. The first is expressed as a potential situation that, as far as he is concerned, has not been realized:[121] if they were bringing a charge concerning some deliberate crime (ἀδίκημα) or fraud of some kind (ῥᾳδιούργημα), it would be his role to act as judge in the matter. The situation, however, is quite different in his view, for their complaint in fact[122] pertains to matters of their own Law in which Gallio has no reason to interfere. The wording of the Bezan text is even more restrictive than that of the Alexandrian text, whereby Gallio makes it plain that he views the accusation of the Jews against Paul as a purely internal quarrel. From what is known of the Roman system of government and jurisdiction in the colonies, Gallio's refusal to act as judge (again more harshly expressed in the AT) was entirely appropriate.[123]

---

120. The graphic expression ἀνοίγειν τὸ στόμα αὐτοῦ serves to underline the action of speaking; cf. Mt. 5.2; 13.35; Lk. 1.64; Acts 8.32, 35; 10.34.

121. εἰ + imperfect indicative followed by ἄν + aorist indicative.

122. Gallio's second conditional sentence expresses a real fact: εἰ + present indicative.

123. See Witherington, *Acts*, pp. 553–54.

[b′] 18.16 *He Dismisses the Jews*

18.16 The outcome, then, of the Jewish attack on Paul was that the case was simply dismissed, and the harm intended came to nothing because the proconsul refused to get involved in what he perceived to be a purely internal matter. Although there are no indications at all that Gallio was aware of protecting Paul or siding with him, his total lack of interest in the complaint brought to him was the critical factor in ensuring that no harm came to Paul, so causing the promise of Jesus to him to be fulfilled (cf. 18.9-10).

In accordance with his response, Gallio sent away the Jewish opponents and, presumably, Paul as well. The Alexandrian text, for a third time, is more antagonistic in its account of Gallio as he is said to have 'driven them out' from the court; the Bezan text is more neutral in saying simply that 'he sent them away'. Overall, the portrayal of Gallio in Codex Bezae is of a Roman official who is more respectful in his attitude towards the Jewish provocations.[124]

[a′] 18.17a *The Greeks Beat Sosthenes before the Court*

18.17 The final scene in the episode is almost burlesque, though what exactly happens next varies according to the text and is open to interpretation in both cases. In broad terms, 'all' took the leader of the synagogue, Sosthenes, who may have replaced Crispus when he became a Jesus-believer or, equally possible, ruled alongside him (cf. 18.10a),[125] and beat him in front of the court, but Gallio for his part ignored them. According to the Alexandrian text, the people who were responsible for beating Sosthenes are not defined: they could be the Jews (just referred to in the previous sentence as the direct object of the verb [αὐτούς]), who all turned against their leader because they were angry with him for not obtaining a satisfactory outcome with regard to Paul. Alternatively, the people could be the Greek citizens of Corinth, bystanders at the court, who attacked the representative of the Jews, though their reasons for doing so are not at all obvious.[126]

Codex Bezae, on the other hand, is clear that the people who took Sosthenes were Greeks. The Greeks have already been mentioned in the context of those who became believers by means of Paul's teaching (18.8b, cf. v. 4b), in the context of his teaching in the synagogue (18.8a, cf. v. 7). However, the use of the hyperbolic 'all' (πάντες) signals that the narrator moves into a register that is other than a purely narrative one at this point, as he has done else-

---

124. It is interesting that the proconsul Gallio had a reputation for being a pleasant and agreeable person, to judge from the remarks of his brother, the younger Seneca: *Solebam tibi dicere Gallionem si, fratrem meum, quem nemo non parum amat, etiam qui amare plus non potest, alia uitia non nosse, hoc eum odisse* (*Nat. Quaest.* 4.11).

125. On the existence of more than one synagogue ruler, cf. on 13.15.

126. See, e.g., Bruce, *Acts*, 375; Witherington, *Acts*, pp. 555–56; however, no explanation is given that satisfactorily accounts for the attack on Sosthenes.

where.[127] 'All the Greeks' refers, on a theological level as opposed to the level of the story, to the Gentiles as distinct from the Jews; their mistreatment of the leader of the synagogue expresses their discontent with the Jews for attacking Paul and attempting to have him silenced. They thus claim their right to hear what Paul has been teaching them in Corinth. In this sense, their behaviour is comparable to that of the slave girl with the spirit of divination in Philippi when she declared, on behalf of the Gentiles in general, that the 'we'-group was proclaiming to them the gospel of salvation. In so far as Paul has been entrusted with the gospel to the Gentiles (cf. 22.14-21, esp. 22.21 D05) and that Jesus has promised him that he has 'a large people' in Corinth, the Greeks defend what belongs to them as they take revenge on the Jews for threatening Paul's growing confidence and openness towards Gentiles.

This action of 'all the Greeks' serves as a lesson to Paul, showing him the consequences of his determination to persuade the Jews of the truth of the gospel, for it has led to an attempt to get him silenced by the Roman author-ities. This is the third such lesson – the first was in Philippi when the owners of the slave girl succeeded in getting him imprisoned by the city magistrates, because he drove out the spirit that let the Gentiles know who was proclaim-ing the gospel to them (16.20-21); the second was in Thessalonica when the Jews tried to get him arrested by the politarchs for teaching them about Jesus (17.5-7). Paul, for his part, is still far from clearly recognizing the specific and exclusive goal of his mission to the Gentiles.

Meanwhile, Gallio ignores the action of the Greeks, with the Bezan text making quite explicit that he turned a blind eye to their attack on Sosthenes. It was one thing for him to tell the Jews to see to their own internal disagree-ments, but it is another for him to ignore a conflict between Greeks and Jews. In 'pretending not to see', he is implicitly party to an attack that he knows to be wrong but that he allows to happen – he, too, is a Gentile who needs to hear the gospel Paul has been entrusted with.

[A'] 18.18-23 *Epilogue*

Overview

Events in the closing sequence of the third part of Acts unfold at a rapid pace, with successive series of participles separated by καί, or not as is the case of the Alexandrian text at several places. The actions are closely connected and it is not always possible to determine independent steps.

The identification of 18.23 as the end of the last sequence in Section III (16.1–18.23), and in the third part of Acts (13.1–18.23) depends on a number of factors, already discussed above (*General Overview*, Section III). 18.23 is the end of a unit of development, the beginning of which is marked with δέ at

---

127. Cf. the indiscriminate use of the label οἱ ᾽Ιουδαῖοι at 13.45 to refer to the Jews in general, and the insistence on the adjective ὅλος at 13.43b-44 D05 to refer to the Gentiles, again in general (cf. 13.46b, 48a); see *Commentary, ad loc.* See also, e.g., 1.19; 2.14, 17, 47; 3.9, 11; 4.10, 16.

18.19b, that brings Paul back to the starting point of Antioch from where he was first sent out with Barnabas at the beginning of this third part of Acts (cf. 13.1-3). On this third occasion, however, he does not stay for any length of time in Antioch but moves, without a pause, as it were, into the third phase of his mission as he returns for the third time to the region of Galatia and Phrygia. At the end of this sequence, he is again seen strengthening the brethren, just as he was seen strengthening the churches in Syria and Cilicia at the end of the previous one (cf. 15.41).

Thus, the content of 18.23 already prepares for the fourth and final part of the book of Acts, which will see Paul developing the third phase of his mission (cf. 19.1). As has been observed elsewhere (cf. notably 6.1), the separations between the ends and beginnings of sections or sequences do not represent clean breaks, but rather they form overlaps that connect in a kind of spiral as the narrative of the new division returns after a few verses to the theme of the end of the previous one. This is what happens here, between the end of Part Three of Acts and the beginning of Part Four, for Paul is seen again in Phrygia at 19.1, following an episode concerning other characters when Paul himself is out of the picture.

Structure and Themes

The story switches back to focus on Paul as the main theme of the narrative after the Jews have been temporarily the theme in the last episode [B'-A']. The first part of the new sequence builds up to Paul's lecturing in the synagogue of Ephesus, which had been a main topic throughout all of this part of Acts (seen as early as 13.5). The second part unfolds from a corresponding promise to return to the Jews at a later date, which leads on to a rapid succession of visits, eventually bringing Paul back to the doorstep of Asia once more. The close of this sequence thus creates anticipation as to the next stage of the narrative:

[a]	18.18	Paul's departure to Syria
[b]	18.19a	Paul leaves Priscilla and Aquila in Ephesus
[c]	18.19b	He lectures in the synagogue
[c']	18.20-21	He promises to return
[b']	18.22	His visits to Caesarea, Jerusalem and Antioch
[a']	18.23	His visit to Galatia and Phrygia

Translation

Codex Bezae D05

[a] **18.18** Paul, after staying on for a considerable number of days more, bade farewell to the brethren and set sail for Syria, and with him Priscilla and Aquila, after cutting his hair in Cenchrea (for it had a synagogue).

[b] **19a** Having gone down to Ephesus, on the very next Sabbath, he left them there.

Codex Vaticanus B03

18.18 Paul, after staying on for a considerable number of days more, bade farewell to the brethren and was intending to sail off to Syria, and with him Priscilla and Aquila, after cutting in Cenchrea his hair (for he had a vow).

19a They went down to Ephesus and he left them there.

[c]   **19b** He, for his part, entered the synagogue and began lecturing to the Jews.

[c']   **20** When they asked him to stay with them
for longer, he did not accept **21** but after
bidding them farewell and saying, 'I must
at all costs celebrate the coming feast day
in Hierosoluma; I will return to you when
God wills', he set sail from Ephesus.

[b']   **22** After travelling down to Caesarea, and
going up and greeting the church, he came
down to Antioch.

[a']   **23** Having spent some time there, he went
away, travelling through place after place
in the territory of Galatia and Phrygia and
strengthening all the disciples.

19b He, for his part, entered the synagogue and lectured to the Jews.

20 When they asked him to stay for
longer, he did not accept **21** but after
bidding them farewell and saying, 'I
will come back to you again, God
willing', he set sail from Ephesus.

22 After travelling down to Caesarea,
going up and greeting the church, he
came down to Antioch.

23 Having spent some time there, he
went away, travelling through place
after place in the territory of Galatia and
Phrygia, strengthening all the disciples.

Critical Apparatus

18.18 (ἀποταξάμενος) ἐξέπλει Β $\mathfrak{P}^{74}$ ℵ *rell* ‖ ἔπλευσεν D, *navigavit* d E².

B03 reads the imperfect of the compound verb ἐκπλέω, while D05 has the aorist of the simple verb, focusing more on the destination than the point of departure (cf. 15.39).

(κειράμενος) ἐν Κεγχρεαῖς τὴν κεφαλήν Β $\mathfrak{P}^{74}$ ℵ A 33. 69. 945. 1175. 1739. 1891 ‖ τ. κεφ. ἐν Κεγ. D, (*tonso*) *capite in Cenchris* d E H L P Ψ 049. 056. 614 $\mathfrak{M}$ e.— (εἶχεν γὰρ) εὐχήν Β $\mathfrak{P}^{74}$ ℵ D^H *rell* ‖ προσευχήν D, *orationem* d.

The B03 word order gives prominence to the place, Cenchrea, by its position between the verb and the direct object, highlighting it against Syria, which is the final destination. D05 maintains the usual order, which confers a natural salience on Cenchrea by its position at the end of the sentence; it also facilitates taking the place as the subject of the following sentence.

In B03, Paul is the subject of the imperfect verb εἶχεν and the clause explains that the reason for Paul cutting his hair was that he had a vow. The reading of προσευχήν in D05 can mean 'prayer', but it is also the word used to designate a synagogue (cf. 16.13, 16). When taken in the second sense, the subject of the verb is not Paul but the place, Cenchrea.

18.19 κατήντησαν (δέ) Β ℵ A E 33. 181. 927. 1311. 1898. 2344 (*devenerunt* d) c e vg^mss sy^p sa aeth^pt ‖ -σεν $\mathfrak{P}^{74}$ H P Ψ 049. 056. 614 $\mathfrak{M}$ ar dem gig p ph ro w vg sy^h bo; Chr ‖ καταντήσας D h aeth^pt.

The plural verb in B03 refers to Paul with Priscilla and Aquila (cf. 18.18). The singular aorist participle καταντήσας in D05 (like the singular finite verb κατήντησεν) refers to Paul alone and maintains him in the spotlight as the linguistic theme of this episode.

κἀκείνους Β $\mathfrak{P}^{74}$ ℵ *rell* ‖ καὶ τῷ ἐπιόντι σαββάτῳ ἐκείνους D, *et sequenti sabbato illos* d 257. 383. 1799. 2401^c (^s καὶ 614. 2147. 2412 h sy^h**) sa.— αὐτοῦ Β

Ψ H P L 049. 056. 0120. 614. 1739 𝔐 bo; Chr Theoph ‖ ἐκεῖ 𝔓⁷⁴ᵛⁱᵈ ℵ D A E 33. 104. 326. 1241. 1837 *al*.

B03 continues from the finite verb κατήντησαν with the connective καί joined with ἐκείνους; καί in D05 is adverbial, coming as it does between the participle καταντήσας and the finite verb κατέλιπεν; there is furthermore a time detail, with a reference to the following Sabbath.

αὐτοῦ at the end of the sentence in B03 is locative, and is replaced in D05 by the adverb ἐκεῖ.

διελέξατο (τοῖς Ἰουδαίοις) B 𝔓⁷⁴ ℵ A 33. 945. 1175. 1739. 1891 *pc* ǀ -λέχθη E H L P Ψ 049. 056. 614 𝔐 ‖ -λέγετο D, *disputabat* d 937. 1270 *pc* bo.

B03 reads the aorist of διαλέγομαι, while D05 has the imperfect, conveying the idea that this was Paul's habitual practice.

18.20 ἐρωτώντων δὲ αὐτῶν B 𝔓⁷⁴ ℵ Dᴴ E H P Ψ 049. 33 𝔐 ǀ ἐρ. δὲ αὐτόν Dᴴ L 056. 69. 440. 927. 1175. 1739. 1828. 2495 ‖ ἐρ. τε αὐτῶν D*, *rogabantibusque eis* d.

There is phonetic confusion in D05* between τε and δέ since the new sentence stands in contrast to the previous one.

μεῖναι B 𝔓⁷⁴ ℵ* A Ψ 33. 36. 181. 255. 431. 453. 522. 945. 1108. 1175. 1506. 1518. 1611. 1739. 1891. 1898. 2138. 2495 *al* vg sa ǀ ἐπι- ℵ² ‖ μεῖναι παρ' αὐτοῖς D E H P L 049. 056. 226ᶜ. 614 𝔐 w sy saᵐˢ bo aeth; Ephr ǀ παρ' αὐ. μεῖναι 226* ǀ παραμ- αὐ. 104.

D05 makes it clear that the Jews wanted him to stay with them.

18.21 (ἀποταξάμενος) καὶ εἰπών· Δεῖ με (Dᴴ ǀ δὲ D*) πάντως τὴν ἑορτὴν ἡμέραν ἐρχομένην ποιῆσαι εἰς Ἱεροσόλυμα D, *oportet me solemnem diem advenientem facere Hierosolymis* d ǀ (ἀπετάξατο αὐτοῖς) εἰπών· Δεῖ με πάν. τ. ἑορ. τὴν ἐρχ. ποι. εἰς Ἱερ. H L P Ψ 049. 056. 614. 1739 𝔐 a b ar dem gig ph w vg^DΘMW tpl syᵖ·ʰ; Chr ‖ (ἀποταξάμενος [+ αὐτοῖς E 945. 1739. 1891]) καὶ εἰπών B 𝔓⁷⁴ ℵ A E 33. 36. 242. 307. 453. 522. 536. 610. 945. 1409. 1678. 1739. 1891. 2344 c e p ro vg sa bo aeth.— Πάλιν ἀνακάμψω B 𝔓⁷⁴ ℵ A E 33. 36. 945. 1175. 1505. 1739. 1891. 2495 *al* vg ǀ πάλιν δὲ ἀνακ. H L P Ψ 049. 056. 614 𝔐 gig sy ǀ ἀν. sa boᵖᵗ ‖ ἀναστρέψω Dᶜʲ· (*et reverti* d).

The correction of με for δέ is attributed by Scrivener to Corrector H (p. 445), but cf. Parker, *Codex Bezae*, p. 297, 'not H'. Since B03 does not include Paul's declaration of D05 that it is the divine will that he celebrate the forthcoming feast (probably Passover) in Hierosoluma, Paul's words begin Πάλιν ἀνακάμψω, 'I will come back' (cf. Lk. 10.16). The original reading of D05 has been erased between ANA and Ω, and the letters KAMΨ written in, *laxe*, 'spaciously' (Scrivener, p. 445), since there is room for more. Probably the letters effaced were ΣΤΡΕΨ, and the verb originally was ἀναστρέψω with its sense of 'return from a place' (cf. Acts 5.22; 15.16 B03), tallying with Paul's mention of Hierosoluma.

ἀνήχθη B D, *redi<it>* d 𝔓⁷⁴ ℵ² A 945. 1175. 1739. 1891 (ἀπ- 33) ar vg syᵖ sa bo ‖ ἀν. δέ ℵ* ‖ καὶ ἀν. E H L P Ψ 049. 056. 0120. 614 𝔐 e gig.— τῆς ('Εφέσου) B 𝔓⁷⁴ ℵ Dᴴ *rell* ‖ τοῦ D*.

Both B03 and D05 continue from the participles ἀποταξάμενος καὶ εἰπών with a finite verb ἀνήχθη, which is linked by ἀλλά to the previous main verb ἐπένευσεν. While ℵ01 reads δέ, many other witnesses read an adverbial καί, which is not at all usual practice in the MSS other than D05.

The masculine article in D05 in place of the feminine seems to indicate that Ἔφεσος was referred to by both genders, as was Κόρινθος (Bailly, L-S-J). At 18.26 D05; 19.17; 20.16, the article is feminine.

18.22 καὶ (ἀναβάς) D, *et* d 1831 gig syᵖ·ʰ ‖ *om.* B 𝔓⁷⁴ ℵ *rell.*

D05 has a connective between each of the three aorist participles (κατελθὼν καὶ ἀναβὰς καὶ ἀσπασάμενος), but B03 omits the first one.

18.23 στηρίζων B 𝔓⁷⁴ ℵ A 33. 1891 *pc* ‖ καὶ ἐπιστηρ. D ‖ ἐπιστηρ. E H L P Ψ 049. 056. 0120. 614. 1739 𝔐.

D05 again connects participles with καί, διερχόμενος καὶ ... ἐπιστηρίζων. The compound verb in D05 echoes the use of the same verb with reference to Peter (11.2b D05), Paul with Barnabas (14.22), Paul and Silas (15.41).

Commentary

[a] 18.18 *Paul's Departure to Syria*

18.18 Following his experience in the court of Corinth, where he was first accused by the Jews then avenged by the Greeks according to Codex Bezae, Paul stayed on for some days, apparently taking advantage of his escape from the punishment the Jews had hoped for to continue his missionary activity. Gallio, unwittingly, has prevented the Jews from forcing him to leave the city before he had finished his work there. Finally, however, he takes his leave of the community of believers in the city, and goes away from Corinth.

The circumstantial information that the narrator gives concerning Paul's departure from Corinth packs together a number of significant details. First, when he went away from Corinth, he was heading for Syria, that is Antioch, his own church base. The second phase of his mission is drawing to a close.

Secondly, Priscilla and Aquila (in that order) went with him. Following the aorist participle, ἀποταξάμενος, to refer to his taking leave of the brethren, the Alexandrian text uses the imperfect finite verb, ἐξέπλει, expressing his wish or intention of sailing away, so that the mention of Priscilla and Aquila accompanying him sounds as if it were the decision of the community that they should go with him.[128] In the Bezan text, the two verbs are in the aorist, so that the presence of Priscilla and Aquila is not realized until he actually sets sail; moreover, the simple verb 'sail' is used in place of 'sail off', so that it does not convey the same sense of departing from the community, but focuses instead on the destination.[129] It will be recalled that Paul had left Aquila (made explicit in the Bezan text) when he went to the house of Justus next door to the synagogue (18.7, esp. D05). Now, however, the couple go with him, and the mention of the name of Priscilla first here may well indicate that it was at her insistence, that she led in this case. Quite why they went, however, is a question that is not explicitly answered. They have been close to Paul in that he had stayed in their house and worked with them (cf. 18.2) – that is, at least until he was able to devote himself entirely to preaching once he received money from Macedonia (18.5), and until he was forced to move out of their house when trouble erupted with the Jews in the synagogue (18.6-7). Was their travelling with him a gesture of solidarity? Or was it to keep an eye on him, in the same way as Silas (cf. 15.34, see *Commentary, ad loc.*)? Their role will be examined in more detail with reference to 18.24-28.

Finally, before Paul set off on his journey by sea, he cut his hair in Cenchrea.[130] This town was the port that served Corinth on the eastern side of the isthmus, from where ships would sail to the coast of Asia on the other side of the Aegean Sea. According to the Alexandrian text he cut his hair because 'he had a vow' (εὐχή). What exactly this vow might represent has been much debated. The association of the vow with the cutting of hair suggests that it was a Nazirite vow (as recorded in Num. 6.1-21), which involved setting aside a period of time (a minimum of 30 days according to later Rabbinic prescriptions) during which certain activities (consumption of alcohol, cutting of hair and coming into contact with a corpse) were scrupulously avoided, as a mark of consecration, like a priest, to God; the end of the period was marked by a complex set of rituals, including the cutting of the hair and offering it as part of a sacrifice in the Temple. Thus Paul's cutting his hair in Cenchrea would coincide with the end of his vow period. While the available evidence principally indicates that the hair must be cut in Ierousalem since it was to be offered in sacrifice at the Temple, Rabbinic discussion does show that it was also allowed to be done elsewhere (cf. *Naz.* 6.8).[131] That Paul was heading for

128. The succession of the aorist participle and the imperfect finite verb places the two actions in close connection with one another.

129. Delebecque, *Les deux Actes*, p. 284: 'le préverbe insiste sur le point de depart'.

130. Although it is grammatically possible that the cutting of the hair refers to Aquila, it is not in accordance with the discourse focus on Paul in this sentence where he is the subject (highlighted by its position at the beginning of the sentence) of the two preceding participles προσμείνας and ἀποταξάμενος, and the preceding finite verb ἔπλευσεν/ἐξέπλει, as well as, in D05, of the singular participle καταντήσας following the mention of the vow.

131. For an evaluation of Paul's vow as a Nazirite vow, see B. Koet, 'Why Did Paul Shave his Hair? Nazirite and Temple in the Book of Acts', in M. Poorthuis and C. Safrai (eds), *The Centrality of Jerusalem: Historical Perspectives* (Kampen: Kok Pharos, 1996), pp. 128–42. The

Jerusalem is made clear in his explanation to the synagogue, according to the Bezan text, of why he could not stay longer in Ephesus (18.21 D05, though he calls it Hierosoluma), and is implied by the rapid summary of his journey in the following verse (cf. 18.22). If his visit to Jerusalem did have anything to do with a Nazirite vow, it can be assumed that he stayed there at least for the regulation 30 days.[132]

Whatever the particular reason for Paul taking a Nazirite vow in Corinth, the effect of it would have been to show to everyone that he was Law-abiding – the importance of such a demonstration is obvious given the accusations made against him (18.13, cf. 18.6). It may be recalled that Paul had been about to offer a defence before Gallio, but that he was not given the opportunity to do so (18.14). Taking a Nazirite vow after the charges had been formally made against him before the court in Corinth would be an ostensible means to prove that he had not abandoned the Law;[133] it would be not unlike the gesture James invites him to make on a later occasion in Jerusalem (cf. 21.23-24).

In any case, the taking of vows was commonplace in Jewish life and should not be seen as so exceptional as to be unthinkable for someone like Paul.[134] It does reveal a certain contradiction with some passages in his letters where he declares the Law to be of no value (cf., e.g., Rom. 3.20; Gal. 2.16), although in demonstrating his regard for the Law in Corinth he makes no statement about its value for salvation. On the other hand, Paul's ambivalence to the Law and his own changing attitude is precisely an aspect of the development of his faith that Luke is at pains to bring out in the Bezan text.

The presence of Priscilla and Aquila seem to have some role in relation to Paul's cutting of his hair in Cenchrea, since they are re-introduced into the narrative immediately before mention is made of his action. As representatives of the Jewish community in Corinth (cf. on 18.2 above) who, even as Jesus-believers, will be seen to be attached to the synagogue (18.26, cf. on 18.19b below), they may perhaps have been particularly concerned to witness Paul's demonstration of his faithfulness to the Law.

What has been said here about Paul's vow in the Alexandrian text may also be valid for the Bezan text, where the word in the explanatory clause is προσευχή instead of the word εὐχή. This word means 'a prayer', but also 'a

case made by R. Tomes ('Why Did Paul Get his Hair Cut? [Acts 18.18; 21.23-24]', in C.M. Tuckett [ed.], *Luke's Literary Achievement: Collected Essays* [JSNTSup. 116; Sheffield: Sheffield Academic Press, 1995], pp. 188–97) that the vow is to be understood in the context of pagan sacrifices is unconvincing in so far as it does not take account of the provision for completing the Nazirite vow away from Israel nor, on a broader scale, of Luke's portrait of Paul as a Jew anxious to prove his Jewish credentials.

132. Koet, 'Why Did Paul Shave his Hair?', p. 140.

133. Koet ('Why Did Paul Shave his Hair?', p. 140, n. 47) rightly points out that the mention of the period of a 'considerable number of days' during which Paul remained in Corinth after the court appearance may indeed be precisely a reference to the length of time needed to perform his vow, at the end of which he 'cut his hair'.

134. See the discussion by M. McNamara, *Palestinian Judaism and the New Testament* (Good News Studies 4; Wilmington, Delaware: Michael Glazier, 1983), pp. 197–99.

place of prayer', and as such is a common term for the 'synagogue' (as in Philippi, cf. 16.13, 16). Given this reading, and since it makes little sense to say
that Paul cut his hair because 'he had a prayer', it appears that the subject of
the verb 'had' (εἶχεν) is the town of Cenchrea and not Paul at all.[135] Con-
struing the sentence in this way is natural because of the word order of the
sentence immediately preceding the explanatory gloss in the Bezan text,
where the name of Cenchrea and not the word 'head' is placed last in the
phrase (see *Critical Apparatus*). Consequently, the explanation for Paul cutting
his hair in the port before he set off for Syria is that there was a synagogue
there.[136]

Since no mention is made of a vow in Codex Bezae, an alternative explanation for Paul's act of cutting his hair may be offered, which has no association with a vow as such but rather is to be interpreted as a gesture expressing
grief or mourning. The choice of verb to refer to the cutting of hair tends to
point to this interpretation, for the verb used in the context of the Nazirite vow
is ξυράω ('shave', cf. Num. 6.9, 18; Acts 21.24) whereas here in Acts 18.18 it
is κείρω ('cut'). When κείρω is used of people in the Greek Scriptures, it is in
the context of repentance or lamentation.[137] The cause of Paul's grief would
be precisely the obstinate refusal by his own people to accept Jesus as the
Messiah. Since he had broken off relations with the synagogue in Corinth
(18.6), it would have been impossible for him to go there to carry out the public ritual, but the opportunity would present itself in Cenchrea since, as the
narrator explains, there was a synagogue in the port. Again, the witness of
Aquila and Priscilla, who had seen what had happened among the Jews in
Corinth over the time Paul had spent there, would be important.

The absence of detailed explanation for Paul's action in Cenchrea – the
significance of the cutting of his hair, the reason for it and the connection with
a synagogue (Codex Bezae) or a vow (AT) – suggests that the matter would be
clear to Luke's addressee and that any difficulties for the present-day reader are
more to do with the current state of knowledge than with Luke's text as such.[138]

[b] 18.19a *Paul Leaves Priscilla and Aquila in Ephesus*

18.19a The narrative in the Bezan text continues with Paul as the singular
protagonist, although the Alexandrian text begins with a plural verb referring
to all three characters who had left Corinth together (cf. on 18.18 above). The
sea journey from Cenchrea would have ended at Ephesus, the principal city of

135. For other examples in the New Testament of the verb ἔχω predicated of a place or a city,
see Acts 27.39; Heb. 9.4; 11.10; Rev. 21.12, 14.

136. If this interpretation of προσευχή at 18.18 D05 is correct, further historical study of the
two parallel terms, συναγωγή and προσευχή, as terms denoting the synagogue would be useful.

137. Cf. Job 1.20; Jer. 7.29.

138. A further point of note is that in his first letter to the church in Corinth, Paul deals at
some length with the question of cutting hair, using both ξυράω and κείρω (1 Cor. 11.1-16), and
arising in the context of traditions that he had delivered to them on his previous visit (11.2).

the Roman province of Asia, and a large port on the route between Rome and the east.

For the first time in Acts, the city of Ephesus is named – there has been indirect allusion to the place earlier in Acts (cf. 16.6b) but no precise mention. It will be a place of considerable significance to Paul where he will eventually spend three years. For the time being, however, he will allow himself to be only briefly detained there.

No sooner has the group arrived in Ephesus than the narrator of the Bezan text zooms straight in on the first Sabbath day when Paul leaves Aquila and Priscilla; the Greek presents with some emphasis this fact (see *Critical Apparatus*). The reason for this is not immediately apparent, though that there is a connection between the two is obvious. In the Alexandrian text, where no mention is made of the Sabbath day, it is possible to think that 'he left them there' refers to the wider picture of Paul's journey between Corinth and Syria, and that the following sentence in 18.19b has the status of a parenthesis.

[d] 18.19b *He Lectures in the Synagogue*

18.19b Paul's intention in leaving Priscilla and Aquila, if not his motive, becomes clearer in this next sentence, which presents him as going to the synagogue. His pattern of behaviour is now so familiar that it no longer occasions any particular comment from the narrator. What has been brought out, especially in the Bezan text, is that Paul has distanced himself from Aquila and Priscilla in Ephesus. They are there in the background, possibly even in the synagogue but no longer with Paul (cf. 18.18). It is as if for some reason he wished to be independent of them as he went to the synagogue. Was it that they disagreed with him in some way? This is another question to add to the others concerning Aquila and Priscilla that have already been noted (cf. 18.2, 18).

Paul 'lectured' in the synagogue as he had done in each synagogue he visited from Thessalonica onwards (17.2). By his consistent repetition of the verb διαλέγομαι, Luke insinuates that on each occasion the same teaching was given – that is, the demonstration from the Scriptures that the death and resurrection of the Messiah were part of the plan of God, and that Jesus was the Messiah (cf. 17.2-3; 18.2 D05).

[c′] 18.20-21 *He Promises to Return*

18.20 In Ephesus, Paul arouses the interest of the Jews in the synagogue, who ask him to stay on. The Bezan text makes explicit that it is with them, the Jews, that they want Paul to stay, but he declines the invitation.

18.21 His refusal is not due to any idea of going to the Gentiles instead; on the contrary, he promises to return, though he does make it conditional on the will of God (τοῦ θεοῦ θέλοντος, 'God willing', lit.), a reminder of the obstacle placed in his way by the Holy Spirit on his outward journey (cf. 16.6). In the Alexandrian text, the phrase is an absolute condition, the equivalent of 'if God wills', and the sentence reads oddly, even with the adverbial 'again' (πάλιν). The reason for his haste to leave Ephesus is spelt out in Codex Bezae: he is under pressure to continue his journey, because he believes it to be the divine plan (δεῖ) for him to spend the next feast day in Hierosoluma. The feast in question is almost certainly Passover,[139] which he intends to celebrate with the Jesus-believing church in Hierosoluma (cf. the last mention at 16.4) as distinct from the Jewish institution in Ierousalem (see *General Introduction*, §VII). The reason for the imperative is not explained, though the haste can be accounted for by the fact that the crossing by sea would have become possible only shortly before the date of Passover.[140] It was not normally binding on Jews in the Diaspora to go to Jerusalem for the Passover festival, even though it is clear that a great number did go (cf. 2.5-11). This visit to Hierosoluma, and Paul's understanding that it is God's plan for him to undertake it, anticipates his later visit to Hierosoluma, when it will be made clear over and over again (especially in Codex Bezae) that it was most definitely not the divine plan. Even at this point, although no further obstacles will be put in Paul's way before he reaches Jerusalem, it is questionable how accurate Paul's understanding was, given that there have been repeated attempts throughout this phase of his mission to keep him heading towards Rome.

In view of the allusion to the divine will in his explanation regarding his imminent departure from Ephesus to Hierosoluma, the condition Paul makes for his return visit can be understood as more of a time condition, 'when God wills'. Meanwhile, he leaves Ephesus without waiting any longer, embarking on a ship bound for the port of Caesarea.

[b'] 18.22 *His Visits to Caesarea, Jerusalem and Antioch*

18.22 The itinerary followed by Paul once he arrived in Caesarea, and the quick succession of visits to the three places mentioned, is summarized in a series of participial phrases. Starting from Caesarea, he 'goes up and greets' the church. The choice of the verb, ἀναβαίνω, tells against this church being that of Caesarea (although there was a community of disciples there led by Philip, cf. 8.40; 21.8), since it always denotes travel to Jerusalem and, in fact, the Jewish religious centre of Ierousalem. From the Bezan text, it is known that it was Paul's intention to go to Jerusalem to celebrate Passover, but he had specified Hierosoluma (cf. 18.21 D05). He did, indeed, 'greet the church' there, but it is possible that there was rather more to his visit and that he was concealing his intention of contacting Jews who were not believers and who were therefore associated with Ierousalem – the same thing will be apparent in his later visit, which was ostensibly to Hierosoluma but which turned out in the end to be to Ierousalem (Hierosoluma: 19.1 D05; 20.16 D05, 22 D05, 23 D05; 21.4. Cf. Ierousalem: 21.11, 12, 13).[141]

---

139. The word used, ἡ ἑορτή, unqualified and with the article, always refers to Passover in the New Testament: Mt. 26.5; 27.15; Mk 14.2; 15.6.

140. For estimates of dates, see Bruce, *Acts*, p. 378; Hemer, *Hellenistic History*, pp. 257–58.

141. For a fuller analysis and discussion of the pattern of spellings with regard to Paul's last journey to Jerusalem, see Read-Heimerdinger, *The Bezan Text*, pp. 333–42.

Paul's purpose in going to Ierousalem can be assumed to have been to try, as he has so often done in the synagogues throughout his mission, to persuade the Jews to accept his message about Jesus. The authorities there will not have been strangers to him; on the contrary, he is likely to have known a number of people with whom he would want to talk.

The next stage of his journey is 'down' to Antioch, for which Luke uses the verb καταβαίνω (cf. Lk. 10.30, 31; Acts 8.26) corresponding to 'go up' (to Ierousalem), so confirming the previous deduction that Paul had gone to the Jewish religious institution as well as to the church.

[a'] 18.23 *His Visit to Galatia and Phrygia*

18.23 In Antioch, Paul would be with his own church (cf. 13.1) from where he had initially been sent out with Barnabas on his mission. He spends some time, but apparently not very long, before setting off again to the districts visited with Barnabas on the first phase of his mission (14.1-25), referred to now as Galatia and Phrygia.[142] The second phase of his mission is thus brought to a conclusion, with a series of corresponding elements between the two opening sequences of the section, [A] 16.1-4 and [B] 16.5-10, and the closing one [A'] 18.18-23, that give a coherence and unity to this section, Section III, overall.[143]

---

142. The difficulties with the terminology, and the conflict with the differing references to a similar area at 16.6, have been noted (see Bruce, *Acts*, p. 380, esp. n. 46; Hemer, *Hellenistic History*, p. 120; cf. 205–206).

143. The corresponding elements in the first two sequences, [A] and [B], and the last one [A'] may be noted as follows: κατήντησεν εἰς Δέρβην (16.1) // κατήντησαν (AT) / καταντήσας (D05) εἰς Ἔφεσον (18.19); ἐν Ἰεροσολύμοις (16.4) // εἰς Ἰεροσόλυμα (18.21 D05); αἱ μὲν οὖν ἐκκλησίαι (16.5) // τὴν ἐκκλησίαν (18.22); ἐστερεοῦντο (16.5) // (ἐπι)στηρίζων (18.23b); διῆλθον δὲ τὴν Φρυγίαν καὶ Γαλακτικὴν χώραν (16.6) // διερχόμενος καθεξῆς τὴν Γαλακτικὴν χώραν καὶ Φρυγίαν (18.23a); κωλυθέντες ... οὐκ εἴασεν (16.6-7) // οὐκ ἐπένευσεν ... δεῖ με πάντως (18.20, 21 D05); ἤθελαν (16.7 D05) // τοῦ θεοῦ θέλοντος (18.21); κατέβησαν (AT) / κατήντησαν (D05) εἰς Τρῳάδα (16.8) // κατέβη εἰς Ἀντιόχειαν (18.22); ἐξελθεῖν (16.10 AT) // ἐξῆλθεν (18.23).

BIBLIOGRAPHY

I. *Works of Reference and Frequently Cited Works*

The following works are referred to either by an abbreviation or, in the case of commentaries on Acts, by the name of the author.

Abécassis, A. and G. Nataf, *Encyclopédie de la mystique juive* (Paris: Berg, 1977).

Aland, B. and K., *et al.* (eds), *Novum Testamentum Graece* (Stuttgart: Deutsche Bibelgesellschaft, 27th edn, 1993).

— *The Greek New Testament* (Stuttgart: Deutsche Bibelgesellschaft/United Bible Societies, 4th edn, 1993).

The American and British Committees of the International Greek New Testament Project (eds), *The Gospel According to St. Luke.* Part I, Chapters 1–12; Part II, Chapters 13–28 (Oxford: Clarendon Press, 1984, 1987).

Bailly, A., *Dictionnaire grec-français* (Paris: Hachette, 16th edn, 1950).

Balz, H. and G. Schneider (eds), *Exegetisches Wörterbuch zum Neuen Testament* (3 vols; Stuttgart: Verlag W. Kohlhammer GmbH, 1980–83).

Barrett, C.K., *A Critical and Exegetical Commentary on the Acts of the Apostles* (2 vols; Edinburgh: T&T Clark, 1994, 1998).

Bauer, W., *A Greek English Lexicon of the New Testament and Other Early Christian Literature* (ed. and trans. W.F. Arndt and F.W. Gingrich; Chicago: Chicago University Press, 1957).

Berlin, A. and M.Z. Brettler (eds), *The Jewish Study Bible* (Jewish Publication Society; TANAKH Translation; Oxford: Oxford University Press, 2004).

Blass, F., A. Debrunner and F. Rehkopf, *Grammatik des neutestamentlichen Griechisch* (Göttingen: Vandenhoeck & Ruprecht, 15th edn, 1979).

Boismard, M.-É. and A. Lamouille, *Le texte occidental des Actes des Apôtres: Reconstitution et réhabilitation.* I. *Introduction et textes*; II. *Apparat critique* (Paris: Éditions Recherche sur les Civilisations, 1984).

Brown, F., S. Driver and C. Briggs, *Hebrew and English Lexicon* (Peabody, MA: Hendrickson Publishers Inc., repr. 2003).

Bruce, F.F., *The Acts of the Apostles. The Greek Text with Introduction and Commentary* (London: The Tyndale Press, 1951).

— *Commentary on the Book of Acts. The English Text with Introduction, Exposition and Notes* (London: Marshall, Morgan and Scott, 1954).

Buttrick, G.A. (ed.), *The Interpreter's Dictionary of the Bible: An Illustrated Encyclopaedia* (4 vols; New York: Abingdon Press, 1962).

Charles, R.H., *et al* (eds), *The Apocrypha and Pseudepigrapha of the Old Testament in English* (2 vols; Oxford: Clarendon Press, 1963 repr.), I, *Apocrypha*.

Clark, A.C., *The Acts of the Apostles* (Oxford: Clarendon Press, 1933; repr. 1970).

Conzelmann, H., *Acts of the Apostles* (trans. J. Limburg, A.T. Kraabel and D.H. Juel; ed. E.J. Epp; Philadelphia: Fortress Press, 1987).

Delebecque, É., *Les Actes des Apôtres* (Paris: Belles Lettres, 1982).

— *Les deux Actes des Apôtres* (ÉBib, NS, 6; Paris: J. Gabalda, 1986).

Dennison, J.D., *The Greek Particles* (2nd edn; rev. K.J. Dover; London: Bristol Classical Press, 2002).

Dunn, J.D.G., *The Acts of the Apostles* (Peterborough: Epworth Press, 1996).

Epp, E.J., *The Theological Tendency of Codex Bezae Cantabrigiensis in Acts* (Cambridge: Cambridge University Press, 1966).

Foakes Jackson, F.J. and K. Lake (eds), *The Beginnings of Christianity.* I. *The Acts of the Apostles* (5 vols; London: Macmillan, 1920–33).

Frankel, E. and B.P. Teutsch (eds), *The Encyclopaedia of Jewish Symbols* (Northvale, N.J.: Jason Aronson Inc., 1995).

Freedman, D.N. (ed.), *Anchor Bible Dictionary* (6 vols; New York: Doubleday, 1992).

Ginzberg, L., *The Legends of the Jews* (7 vols; Philadelphia: The Jewish Publication Society of America, 11th edn, 1892).

Goodenough, E.R., *Jewish Symbols in the Greco-Roman Period* (13 vols; New York: Pantheon Books, 1953–65).

Gryson, R. (dir. Vetus Latina Institut, Beuron), *Vetus Latina Database* (Brepols: Turnhout, 2002).

Haenchen, E., *The Acts of the Apostles: A Commentary* (trans. B. Noble, G. Shinn and R. McL. Wilson; Oxford: Blackwells, 1981).

Harl, M. (ed.), *La Bible d'Alexandrie* (12 vols; Paris: Éditions du Cerf, 1986–2005).

Hatch, E. and H.A. Redpath, *A Concordance to the Septuagint and Other Greek Versions of the Old Testament* (2 vols; Graz: Akademische Druck- und Verlagsanstalt, 1954).

Heimerdinger, J. and S.H. Levinsohn, 'The Use of the Definite Article before Names of People in the Greek Text of Acts with Particular Reference to Codex Bezae', *FN* 5 (1992), pp. 15–44.

Johnson, L.T., *The Acts of the Apostles* (Sacra Pagina, 5; Collegeville, MN: The Liturgical Press, 1992).

Lake, K. and H.J. Cadbury, *English Translation and Commentary,* in Foakes Jackson and Lake (eds), *The Beginnings of Christianity*, IV (1933).

Levinsohn, S.H., *Textual Connections in Acts* (Atlanta: Scholars Press, 1987).

— *Discourse Features of New Testament Greek* (Dallas: Summer Institute of Linguistics, 1992).

Liddell, H.G., R.J. Scott and H.S. Jones, *A Greek-English Lexicon: A New Edition* (Oxford: Clarendon Press, 1940).

Louw, J.P. and E.A. Nida, *Greek-English Lexicon of the New Testament Based on Semantic Domains* (2 vols; New York: United Bible Societies, 2nd edn, 1989).

Marshall, I.H., *The Acts of the Apostles* (Tyndale New Testament Commentaries; Leicester: IVP, 1980).

Mayser, E., *Grammatik der Griechischen Papyri aus Ptolemäerzeit* (2 vols; Berlin: Walter de Gruyter, 2nd edn, 1970).

Metzger, B.M., *A Textual Commentary on the Greek New Testament* (Stuttgart: Deutsche Bibelge-sellschaft, 1st edn, 1975; 2nd edn, 1994).

Moule, C.F.D., *An Idiom-Book of New Testament Greek* (Cambridge: Cambridge University Press, 2nd edn, 1959).

Moulton, J.H., *A Grammar of New Testament Greek*. I. *Prolegomena* (Edinburgh: T&T Clark, 1908).

Moulton, J.H. and W.F. Howard, *A Grammar of New Testament Greek*. II. *Accidence and Word-Formation* (Edinburgh: T&T Clark, 1929).

Nestle, E., *Novi Testamenti Graeci: Supplementum editionibus de Gebhardt Tischendorfianis; Codex Cantabrigiensis Collatio* (Leipzig: Tauchnitz, 1896).

Neusner, J. and W.S. Green (eds), *Dictionary of Judaism in the Biblical Period 450 BCE to 600 CE* (New York: Macmillan Reference Library, 1996).

Parker, D.C., *Codex Bezae. An Early Christian Manuscript and its Text* (Cambridge: Cambridge University Press, 1994).

Parsons, M.M. and M.M. Culy, *Acts: A Handbook on the Greek Text* (Waco, TX: Baylor University Press, 2003).

Porter, S.E., *Idioms of New Testament Greek* (Biblical Languages: Greek, 2; Sheffield: JSOT Press, 1992).

Pritchard, J. (ed.), *Atlas of the Bible* (London: HarperCollins, 2nd edn, 1989).

Rahlfs, A. (ed.), *Septuaginta* (Stuttgart: Deutsche Bibelstiftung, 1985).

Read-Heimerdinger, J., *The Bezan Text of Acts. A Contribution of Discourse Analysis to Textual Criticism* (JSNTSup, 236; Sheffield: Sheffield Academic Press, 2002).

Resch, A., *Agrapha. Aussercanonische Schriftfragmente* (Darmstadt: Wissenschaftliche Buchge-sellschaft; 2nd edn, 1967).

Rius-Camps, J., *Comentari als Fets dels Apòstols* (4 vols; Barcelona: Facultat de Teologia de Catalunya-Herder, 1991–2000).

Rius-Camps, J. and J. Read-Heimerdinger, *The Message of Acts in Codex Bezae: A Comparison with the Alexandrian Tradition*. I. *Acts 1.1–5.42: Jerusalem* (JSNTSup, 257; London: T&T Clark, 2004); II. *Acts 6.1–12.25: From Judaea and Samaria to the Church in Antioch* (LNTS, 302; London: T&T Clark, 2006).

Robertson, A.T., *A Grammar of the Greek New Testament in the Light of Historical Research* (Nashville, TN: Broadman, 4th edn, 1934).

Ropes, J.H., *The Text of Acts*, in Foakes Jackson and Lake (eds), *The Beginnings of Christianity*, III (1926).

Roth, C. (ed.), *Encyclopaedia Judaica* (16 vols; Jerusalem: Ketev Publishing House, 3rd edn, 1974).

Safrai, S. and M. Stern (eds), *The Jewish People in the First Century* (2 vols; I, Philadelphia: Fortress Press, 1974; II, Assen: Van Gorcum, 1976).

Schneider, G., *Die Apostelgeschichte* (2 vols; Herders Theologische Kommentar zum Neuen Testament; Freiburg: Herder, 1980, 1982).

Schürer, E., *The History of the Jewish People in the Age of Jesus Christ* (3 vols; rev. and ed. G. Vermes, F. Millar and M. Black; Edinburgh: T&T Clark, 1973).

Scrivener, F.H., *Bezae Codex Cantabrigiensis* (repr.; Pittsburgh, PA: Pickwick Press, 1978).

Singer, I. (ed.), *The Jewish Encyclopaedia* (12 vols; New York: KTAV Publishing House, 1901).

Spencer, F.S., *Acts* (Readings: A New Biblical Commentary; Sheffield: Sheffield Academic Press, 1997).

Strack, H.L. and P. Billerbeck, *Kommentar zum Neuen Testament aus Talmud und Midrasch* (6 vols; München: C.H. Beck, 6th edn, 1974–75).

Swanson, R., *New Testament Greek Manuscripts: Variant Readings Arranged in Horizontal Lines against Codex Vaticanus. The Acts of the Apostles* (Sheffield: Sheffield Academic Press, 1998).

Turner, N., *A Grammar of New Testament Greek*. III. *Syntax*; IV. *Style* (Edinburgh: T&T Clark, 1963, 1976).

Wallace, D.B., *Greek Grammar beyond the Basics* (Grand Rapids: Zondervan Publishing House, 1996).

Winer, G.B., *A Treatise on the Grammar of New Testament Greek* (trans. W.F. Moulton; Edinburgh: T&T Clark, 1882).

Witherington, B., *The Acts of the Apostles: A Socio-Rhetorical Commentary* (Grand Rapids: Eerdmans/Carlisle: Paternoster, 1998).

Zahn, Th., *Die Apostelgeschichte des Lukas* (2 vols; Leipzig: A. Diechertsche Verlagsbuchhandlung Werner Scholl, 1919–21).

Zerwick, M., *Biblical Greek* (trans., rev. and ed. J. Smith; Rome: Biblical Institute Press, 1963).

Zerwick, M. and M. Grosvenor, *A Grammatical Analysis of the Greek New Testament* (Rome: Biblical Institute Press, 1981).

Zorell, F., *Lexicon Graecum Novi Testamenti* (Paris: P. Letheilleux, 1961).

II. *Other Works Referred to*

Asmis, E., 'Epicureanism', *ABD*, II, pp. 559–61.

Balch, D. and W. Meeks (eds), *Greeks, Romans and Christians* (Minneapolis: Fortress Press, 1990).

Barc, B., *Les arpenteurs du temps: Essai sur l'histoire religieuse de la Judée à la période héllenistique* (Lausanne: Éditions du Zèbre, 2000).

Bar-Efrat, S., *Narrative Art in the Bible* (Sheffield: Sheffield Academic Press, 1989; repr. T&T Clark, 2004).

Barker, M., *The Great Angel: A Study of Israel's Second God* (London: SPCK, 1992).

— *The Great High Priest: The Temple Roots of Christian Liturgy* (London: T&T Clark, 2003).

Bauckham, R., *James* (London: Routledge, 1999).

Beare, F.W., 'Epicureans', in Buttrick (ed.), *Interpreter's Dictionary,* II, pp. 122–23.

—'Stoics', *Interpreter's Dictionary*, IV, pp. 443-45.

Beattie, D.R.G. and M.J. McNamara (eds), *The Aramaic Bible: Targums in their Historical Context* (JSOTSup, 166; Sheffield: Sheffield Academic Press, 1994).

Black, M. (ed.), *Rituale Melchitarum* (Stuttgart: Kohlhammer, 1938).

Bolen, T., www.bibleplaces.com/pantioch.htm (accessed 12/01/07), n.p.

— www.bibleplaces.com/derbelystra.htm (accessed 12/01/07), n.p.

Borgen, P., *Early Christianity and Hellenistic Judaism* (Edinburgh: T&T Clark, 1996).

Bowers, W.P., 'Paul's Route through Mysia: A Note on Acts 16.8', *JTS* 30 (1979), pp. 507–11.

Bowker, J.W., 'Speeches in Acts: A Study in Proem and Yelammedenu Form', *NTS* 14 (1967–68), pp. 96–111.

Bruce, F.F., 'Phrygia', *ABD*, V, pp. 366–67.

Büchler, A., 'Archon (Archontes or Archonteia)', *Jew. Enc.,* II, pp. 86–87.

Cadbury, H.J., 'Dust and Garments', in Foakes Jackson and Lake, *The Beginnings of Christianity,* V, pp. 269–77.

— *The Making of Luke-Acts* (London: SPCK, 1968).

Campbell, D.A., 'Paul in Pamphylia (Acts 13.13-14a; 14.24b-26): A Critical Note', *NTS* 46 (2000), pp. 595–602.

— 'Possible Inscriptional Attestation to Sergius Paul(l)us (Acts 13.6-12), and the Implications for Pauline Chronology', *JThS* 56 (2005), pp. 1–29.

Cerfaux, L. and J. Dupont, *Les Actes des Apôtres* (Paris: Éditions du Cerf, 1953).

Chilton, B., *The Glory of Israel: The Theology and Provenience of the Isaiah Targum* (JSOT Sup, 23; Sheffield: JSOT Press, 1982).

— 'Aramaic and Targumic Antecedents of Pauline Justification', in Beattie and McNamara (eds), *The Aramaic Bible*, pp. 379–97.

— *Rabbi Paul. An Intellectual Biography* (New York: Doubleday, 2004).

Chilton, B.D. and J. Neusner, *The Brother of Jesus: James the Just and his Mission* (Louisville: Westminster John Knox, 2001).

Clarke, E.G. (ed.), *Targum Pseudo-Jonathan: Deuteronomy* (*The Aramaic Bible*, Vb; Edinburgh: T&T Clark, 1998).

Deutsch, G., 'Apikoros', *Jew. Enc.* I, pp. 656–66.

Doeve, J.V., *Jewish Hermeneutics in the Synoptic Gospels and Acts* (Assen: Van Gorcum, 1953).

Dogniez, C. and M. Harl, *Le Deutéronome*, in Harl (ed.), *La Bible d'Alexandrie*, V (1992).

Dunn, J.D.G., *Christ and the Spirit* (2 vols; Edinburgh: T. & T. Clark, 1998).

— 'ΚΥΡΙΟΣ in Acts', in *Christ and the Spirit*, I. *Christology*, pp. 241–53.

Dupont, J., 'ΤΑ 'ΟΣΙΑ ΤΑ ΠΙΣΤΑ (Actes 13,34 = Isaïe 55,3)', in *Études sur les Actes des Apôtres* (Lectio Divina, 45; Paris: Éditions du Cerf, 1967), pp. 337–59.

Eisenman, R.H., *James, the Brother of Jesus. Recovering the True History of Early Christianity* (London: Faber and Faber, 1997).

Ellul, D., 'Antioche de Pisidie: Une prédication … trois credos? (Actes 13,13-43)', *Fil Neo* 5 (1992), pp. 3–14.

Enns, P., *Exodus Retold: Ancient Exegesis of the Departure from Egypt in Wis 10:15-21 and 19:1-9* (Harvard Semitic Museum Monographs, 57; Atlanta: Scholars Press, 1997).

Faber, R., 'The Apostle and the Poet: Paul and Aratus', *Clarion* 42 (1993), pp. 291–305.

Gärtner, B., *The Areopagus Speech and Natural Revelation* (Lund: C.W.K. Gleerup, 1955).

Goodman, M., *Rome and Jerusalem: The Clash of Ancient Civilisations* (London: Allen Lane, 2007).

Gordon, R.P., 'Targumic Parallels to Acts XIII 18 and Didache XIV 3', *Nov. Test.* 16 (1974), pp. 285–89).

— 'The Targumists as Eschatologists', in *Göttingen Congress Volume* (SVT 29; Leiden: Brill, 1978), pp. 113–30.

Grant, M., *The Jews in the Roman World* (London: Weidenfeld and Nicolson, 1973).

Green, J.B. and M. Turner (eds), *Jesus of Nazareth: Lord and Christ* (Grand Rapids: Eerdmans, 2002).

Hemer, C.J., *The Book of Acts in the Setting of Hellenistic History* (ed. C.H. Gempf; Tübingen: J.C.B. Mohr, 1989).

Hengel, M., 'Proseuche und Synagoge', in Jeremias, Kuhn and Stegemann (eds), *Tradition und Glaube*, pp. 157–84.

— *The 'Hellenization' of Judaea in the First Century after Christ* (London: SCM, 1989).

Hills, J. (ed.), *Common Life in the Early Church* (Harrisburg, Pennsylvania: Trinity Press International, 1998).

Holmes, B.H., 'Luke's Description of John Mark', *JBL* 54 (1935), pp. 63–72.

Ilan, T., *A Lexicon of Jewish Names*. I. *Palestine 330 BCE–200 CE* (Tübingen: Mohr-Siebeck, 2003).

Jeanmaire, H., 'Le substantif HOSIA et sa signification comme terme technique dans le vocabulaire religieux', *REG* 58 (1945), pp. 66–89.

Jeremias, G., H.-W. Kuhn and H. Stegemann (eds), *Tradition und Glaube. Das frühe Christentum in seiner Umwelt* (Göttingen: Vandenhoeck und Ruprecht, 1971).

Kilgallen, J., 'Acts 13,38-39: Culmination of Paul's Speech in Pisidia', *Bib.* 69 (1988), pp. 480–506.

— 'Hostility to Paul in Pisidian Antioch', *Bib.* 84 (2003), pp. 1–15.

Kilpatrick, G.D., *The Principles and Practice of New Testament Textual Criticism* (ed J.K. Elliott.; Leuven: Leuven University Press, 1990).

Klawans, J., 'Concepts of Purity in the Bible', *Jewish Study Bible*, pp. 2041–47.

Koet, B.J., *Five Studies on Interpretation of Scriptures in Luke-Acts* (SNTA, 14; Leuven: University Press, 1989).

— 'Why Did Paul Shave his Hair? Nazirite and Temple in the Book of Acts', in Poorthuis and Safrai (eds), *The Centrality of Jerusalem*, pp. 128–42.

Lagrand, J., 'Luke's Portrait of Simeon (Luke 2.25-35)', in Hills (ed.), *Common Life in the Early Church*, pp. 175–85.

Lambertz, M., 'Zur Ausbreitung des Supernomen oder Signum im römischen Reiche', I, *Glotta* 4 (1912), pp. 78–143; II, *Glotta* 5 (1913), pp. 99–170.

Leary, T.J., 'Paul's Improper Name', *NTS* 38 (1992), pp. 467–69.

Le Déaut, R., *A Rabbinic Anthology* (ed. C.G. Montefiore and H. Loewe, London: Greenwich Editions, 1940).

— 'Targumic Literature and New Testament Interpretation', *Biblical Theology Bulletin* 4 (1974), pp. 243–89.

Levinskaya, I., *The Book of Acts in its Diaspora Setting*, in Winter (series ed.), *The Book of Acts in its First Century Setting*, V (1996).

Lieu, J., *Neither Jew Nor Greek: Constructing Early Christianity* (London: T&T Clark, 2007).

McNamara, M., *Palestinian Judaism and the New Testament* (Good News Studies 4; Wilmington, Delaware: Michael Glazier, 1983).

— (ed.), *Targum Neofiti* 1: *Deuteronomy* (*The Aramaic Bible*, Va; Edinburgh: T&T Clark, 1997).

Mann, J., *The Bible as Read and Preached in the Old Synagogue*, I (New York: KTAV, 1940; 2nd edn, 1971); II (ed. I. Sonne; Ohio: Hebrew Union College, 1966).

Mateos, J., *Los "Doce" y otros seguidores de Jesús en el Evangelio de Marcos* (Madrid: Cristiandad, 1982).

Michael, J. Hugh, 'The Original Position of Acts 14.3', *ET* 40 (1928–29), pp. 514–16.

Mitchell, S., 'Galatia', in *ABD*, II, pp. 870–72.

Montefiore, C.G. and H. Loewe (eds), *A Rabbinic Anthology* (London: Greenwich Editions, 1940).

Mulder, O., *Simon the High Priest in Sirach 50. An Exegetical Study of the Significance of Simon the High Priest as Climax to the Praise of the Fathers in Ben Sira's Concept of the History of Israel* (Leiden: Brill, 2003).

Muraoka, T. and J.F. Elwode (eds), *Sirach, Scrolls and Sages* (Leiden: Brill, 1977).

Neusner, J., *Judaism When Christianity Began: A Survey of Belief and Practice* (Louisville: Westminster John Knox Press, 2002).

Neyrey, J.H., 'Acts 17, Epicureans and Theodicy: A Study in Stereotypes', in Balch and Meeks (eds), *Greeks, Romans and Christians*, pp. 118–34.

— 'Luke's Social Location of Paul: Cultural Anthropology and the Status of Paul in Acts', in Witherington (ed.), *History, Literature and Society in the Book of Acts*, pp. 251–79.

Nicklas, T. and M. Tilly (eds), *Apostelgeschichte als Kirchengeschichte. Text, Traditionen und antike Auslegungen* (BZNW, 122; Berlin-New York: Walter de Gruyter, 2003).

Nolland, J., 'A Fresh Look at Acts 15.10', *NTS* 27 (1980), pp. 105–115.

Paget, J.C., 'Jewish Proselytism at the Time of Christian Origins: Chimera or Reality', *JSNT* 62 (1996), pp. 65–103.

Perrot, C., *La lecture de la Bible* (Hildesheim: Verlag Dr. H.A. Gerstenberg, 1973).

Pierri, R. (ed.), *Grammatica Intellectio Scripturae: Saggi filologici di Greco biblico in onore di padre Lino Cignelli, OFM* (Studium Biblicum Franciscanun Analecta 68; Jerusalem: Franciscan Printing Press, 2006).

Poorthuis, M. and C. Safrai (eds), *The Centrality of Jerusalem: Historical Perspectives* (Kampen: Kok Pharos, 1996).

Pope, R. (ed.), *Honouring the Past and Shaping the Future: Religious and Biblical Studies in Wales* (Leominster: Gracewing, 2003).

Read-Heimerdinger, J., 'Barnabas in Acts: A Study of his Role in the Text of Codex Bezae', *JSNT* 72 (1998), pp. 23–66.

— 'Luke's Use of ὡς and ὡσεί: Comparison and Correspondence as a Means to Convey his Message', in Pierri (ed.), *Grammatica Intellectio Scripturae*, pp. 251–74.

— 'The Tracking of Participants with the Third Person Pronoun: A Study of the Text of Acts', *RCatT* 31 (2006), pp. 439–55.

— 'The Distinction between ἅπας and πᾶς in the Work of Luke' (forthcoming).

Read-Heimerdinger, J. and J. Rius-Camps, 'Emmaous or Oulammaous? Luke's Use of the Jewish Scriptures in the Text of Luke in Codex Bezae', *RCatT* 27 (2002), pp. 23–42.

Riesner, R., 'James' Speech (Acts 15.13-21), Simeon's Hymn (Luke 2.29-32), and Luke's Sources', in Green and Turner (eds), *Jesus of Nazareth*, pp. 263–78.

Rius-Camps, J., 'Qui és Joan, l'anomenat "Marc"?', *RCatT* 5 (1980), pp. 297–329.

— *El camino de Pablo a la misión de los paganos. Comentario lingüístico y exegético a Hch 13–28* (Madrid: Cristiandad, 1984).

— *De Jerusalén a Antioquía: Génesis de la iglesia cristiana. Comentario lingüístico y exegético a Hch 1–12* (Córdoba: El Almendro, 1989).

— 'The Gradual Awakening of Paul's Awareness of his Mission to the Gentiles', in Nicklas and Tilly (eds), *Apostelgeschichte als Kirchengeschichte*, pp. 281–96.

— '"Nazareno" y "Nazoreo", con especial atención al Códice Bezae', in Pierri (ed.), *Grammatica Intellectio Scripturae*, pp. 183–204.

Rius-Camps, J. and J. Read-Heimerdinger, 'After the Death of Judas: A Reconsideration of the Status of the Twelve Apostles', *RCatT* 29 (2004), pp. 305–34.

Rosenfield, L.W., 'A Practical Celebration of Epidexis' (www.natcom.org/convention/2002/keynote%20materials/rosenfield.htm; accessed 10/4/2007).

Rowe, C.K., *Early Narrative Christology: The Lord in the Gospel of Luke* (BZNW, 139: Berlin: Walter de Gruyter, 2006).

Schmeller, T., 'Stoics, Stoicism', *ABD*, VI, pp. 210–14.

Simon, M., 'The Apostolic Decree and its Setting in the Ancient Church', *Bulletin of the John Rylands Library* (52), 1970, pp. 437–60.

Smallwood, E.M., *The Jews under Roman Rule: From Pompey to Diocletian* (Leiden: E.J. Brill, 1976).

Smith, M.S., 'Grammatically Speaking: The Participle as a Main Verb of Clauses (Predicative Participle) in Direct Discourse and Narrative in Pre-Mishnaic Hebrew', in Muraoka and Elwode (eds), *Sirach, Scrolls and Sages*, pp. 278–332.

Stanton, G.N. and G.G. Stroumsa (eds), *Tolerance and Intolerance in Early Judaism and Christianity* (Cambridge: Cambridge University Press, 1998).

Steyn, G.J., *Septuagint Quotations in the Context of the Petrine and Pauline Speeches of the Acta Apostolorum* (Kampen: Kok Pharos, 1995).

Strelan, R., 'Who Was Bar Jesus (Acts 13.6-12)?', *Bib.* 85 (2004), pp. 65–81.

Taylor, J., 'Why Did Paul Persecute the Church?', in Stanton and Stroumsa (eds), *Tolerance and Intolerance in Early Judaism and Christianity*, pp. 99–120.

— *Les Actes des Deux Apôtres.* V. *Commentaire historique* (Act 9.1–18.22) (ÉBib, NS, 23; Paris: J. Gabalda, 1998).

Thrall, M.E., 'Paul of Tarsus: a Hellenistic Jew', in Pope (ed.), *Honouring the Past and Shaping the Future*, pp. 97–111.

Tomes, R., 'Why Did Paul Get his Hair Cut? (Acts 18.18; 21.23-24)', in Tucket (ed.), *Luke's Literary Achievement: Collected Essays*, pp. 188–97.

Trompf, G.W., *The Idea of Historical Recurrence in Western Thought: From Antiquity to Reformation* (Berkeley: University of California Press, 1979).

Tuckett, C.M. (ed.), *Luke's Literary Achievement: Collected Essays* (JSNTSup, 116; Sheffield: Sheffield Academic Press, 1995).

— 'How Early is the "Western" Text of Acts?', in Nicklas and Tilly (eds), *Apostelgeschichte als Kirchengeschichte*, pp. 69–86.

Urbán, Á., 'Bezae Codex Cantabrigiensis (D): intercambios vocálicos en los textos griegos de Lucas y Hechos', *Collectanea Christiana Orientalia* 3 (2006), pp. 269–316.

Wall, R.W., *Acts of the Apostles* (New Interpreter's Bible, 10; ed. L.E. Keck; Nashville, TN: Abingdon Press, 2002).

Welch, J.W., *Chiasmus in Antiquity* (Hildesheim: Gerstenberg, 1981).

Wilcken, U. (ed.), *Urkunden der Ptolmäerzeit* (2 vols; Berlin: De Gruyter, 1927–57).

Wilcox, M., *The Semitisms of Acts* (Oxford: Clarendon Press, 1965).

— 'The Promise of the "Seed" in the New Testament and the Targumim', *JSNT* 5 (1979), pp. 275–93.

Winter, B. (series ed.), *The Book of Acts in its First Century Setting* (6 vols; Grand Rapids: Eerdmans, 1994–98).

Witherington, B., *Conflict and Community in Corinth* (Grand Rapids: Eerdmans, 1995).

— (ed.), *History, Literature and Society in the Book of Acts* (Cambridge: Cambridge University Press, 1996).

Wright, N.T., *What Saint Paul Really Said: Was Paul of Tarsus the Real Founder of Christianity?* (Oxford: Lion, 1997).

Young, R.A., *Intermediate New Testament Greek* (Nashville, TN: Broadman & Holman, 1994).